Now in 4-Color!

Your Students' passport to the real world of criminal justice, in a brief, affordable text!

Now George Cole and Christopher Smith have made their brief, affordable, and best-selling text even better than ever. ***Criminal Justice in America***, Second Edition is an accessible paperback that's just the right length (just over 400 pages) and priced for your introductory students without skimping on coverage of all the important elements. Now with a greater emphasis on careers in the criminal justice field, this lively Second Edition features more of what your students want:

- More depth with greater accessibility. Solid coverage of police, courts, and corrections written in a clear, concise style.
- More real-world career direction, including new "Workperspectives" boxes with revealing testimonials from numerous criminal justice professionals.
- Solid pedagogy including new "Checkpoints" summaries at the end of major sections.
- Original, part-ending essays: "A Journey Inside the Criminal Justice System and Beyond," a compelling, autobiographical account of the system from a former convict's perspective.
- A brand new design featuring a bold and dynamic new four-color interior filled with late-breaking news photographs and examples.
- Part III, Courts, now reorganized to be more logical.

Plus the ultimate selection of supplemental teaching and learning tools featuring the best of high-quality video, online resources, cutting-edge technology, and more!

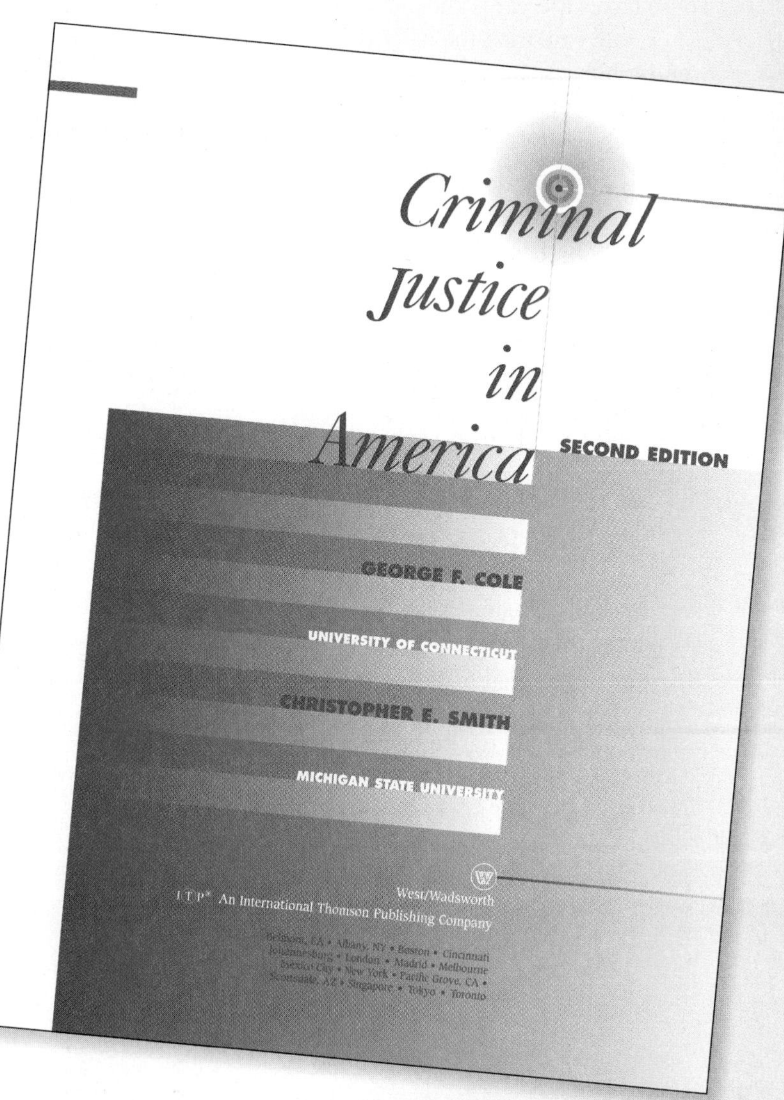

Perspective

The Real World of Criminal Justice Careers...at Your Students' Fingertips!

Found throughout the book, new "Workperspectives" boxes are fascinating first-person accounts from professionals in various areas of criminal justice. These boxes are your students' key to exploring the dailytrials and tribulations of police officers, counselors, investigators, attorneys, judges, and many others!

them according to their goals and values, as discussed by Police Commander John L. Buchanan in the Workperspective.

WORK *Perspective*

I began my policing career upon graduation from college in 1973. After the academy, I was assigned as a patrol officer and later as a narcotics investigator in the Scottsdale Police Department. To take advantage of the opportunities of a larger department I transferred to the Phoenix Police Department in 1977 and was promoted to sergeant in 1982 after nine years of patrol and investigative experience. In 1984 I attended the FBI National Academy and was promoted to lieutenant in 1987.

In the Phoenix Police Department sergeants generally supervise a squad of six to ten officers or detectives. Lieutenants are responsible for an entire shift in one precinct, usually about sixty officers, or a specialized investigative unit dealing with, for example, gangs, homicide, or sex crimes. In 1989 I was assigned to the Internal Affairs Unit for six months and then was assigned to coordinate a new multijurisdictional drug demand reduction program known as "Do Drugs, Do Time."

In 1990 I was promoted to commander and assigned as duty officer, responsible for

John L. Buchanan
Police Commander
Phoenix Police Department

The Powerful Inside Story of a Former Offender, Told in the First Person!

New at the end of each part in the book, "A Journey Inside the Criminal Justice System and Beyond" are grippingly personal essays by Chuck Terry, an ex-inmate who reveals the details of his experiences in every avenue of the criminal justice system from arrest to court to hard time in prison.

INSIDE THE CRIMINAL JUSTICE SYSTEM AND BEYOND: ONE MAN'S JOURNEY

Written by Chuck Terry

My Affair with Heroin

Seldom do we have the opportunity to view the criminal justice system through the eyes of a person who has experienced it. Chuck Terry is most unusual in that, after more than twenty years of heroin addiction, twelve of them incarcerated, he has "beaten the habit" and is now pursuing a Ph.D. The vivid chronicles of his journey, which conclude each part of this book, provide rare insights into the workings of "the system." His reflections should be thoughtfully considered by all students of criminal justice.

Tight handcuffs. Loud cellblocks. Racial tension. No women, kids, or pets. Violence. Road dogs (close friends). Iron bars. Concrete beds. Hate. Guard towers. Getting booked. Count times. Food lines. Parole boards. Judges. Degradation. District attorneys. Death. Cops. A.M.'s and P.M.'s—year in and year out. Monotony. Withdrawals. Preliminary hearings. The need to show no pain—ever. Release dates. Parole officers. Alienation. Hopelessness. Determinate sentencing. A guard on the way out of prison: "See you when you get back, Terry. Guys like you are job security for guys like me." A lot to deal with for a white, California-raised kid from middle-class suburbia. A lot for anybody.

From my first arrest in 1970 to my last discharge from parole in 1992, I became intimately familiar with all the components of the criminal justice system. Over the course of this twenty-plus-year "career," which included spending over twelve years inside state (prisons) and county (jails) "correctional" facilities for drug-related crimes, I experienced almost everything the system has to offer—except the death penalty or a sentence of life without possibility of parole.

These experiences have taught me that the way "criminals" are dealt with in America is anything but "fair" or "just." Rather, their fate is determined by who they are and how they are seen by system actors such as judges and prosecutors and by the general public. It is important to note that this "seeing" varies dramatically and is relative to an ever-changing social, economic, political, and historical context.

Crime today is politicized and a main focus of media attention. The "threat" posed by "criminals" is used to generate fear and legitimate spending millions on more police, more prisons, and more mechanisms of social control. The reasons for this are complex and controversial. But it hasn't always been like this.

I was a kid in the 1960s, when the civil rights movement, protests against the Vietnam war, and an anti-establishment-oriented "counterculture" were in full swing. Instead of bombarding the public with visions of low-level street crime, the nightly news sent us images from the war, urban riots, and people getting beaten by police for participating in nonviolent sit-ins. Governmental policies and social inequality rather than addicts and "juvenile predators" were seen as "criminal" by a significant portion of the population. Rules and rule enforcers (like racial segregation policies, drug laws, government officials) were the targets of attention. In defiance of "the way things were," we grew our hair, spoke out against social norms, and got high.

My own drug use began in 1967 and escalated over time. Initially, I used whatever was available: alcohol, marijuana, reds, yellows, whites, LSD. In 1969 I used heroin for the first time.

Now, how could any sane person try heroin? Doesn't everyone know it's a "bad" thing to do? Though it was scary, I rationalized it as being okay. After all, I knew several people who used it. They seemed to be fine. Everything I had been told about all the other drugs I used had proved to be a lie; we were told that if we smoked pot we'd lie down on train tracks, and if we took LSD we'd jump out of tall buildings and lose our minds. So one night at a party I gave it a shot. Or, I should say, I stuck my arm out and a friend gave me a shot.

Turning points. Crossroads. Where do we go from here? The first thing I

69

Journey

C H E C K P O I N T

1. Is crime a dramatic, new problem for the United States?
2. How does the crime problem in the United States compare to crime problems in other countries?

(Answers are at the end of the chapter.)

C H E C K P O I N T

3. What are the five main types of crime?
4. What is the function of organized crime?
5. Who commits "visible" or "street" crimes?
6. What is meant by the term "crimes without victims"?
7. What are political crimes?

Help students remember more critical concepts with new "Checkpoints."

Placed at the end of major sections, these new elements are designed to reinforce key chapter concepts and encourage critical thinking.

C H E C K P O I N T

3. What issues concerning plea bargaining has the Supreme Court examined?
4. What are justifications for plea bargaining?
5. What are criticisms of plea bargaining?

Supplements

Instructor's Supplements

Build your own incredible teaching package!

A complete line of state-of-the-art teaching and learning materials helps you bring more of the real world of criminal justice into your classroom.

Instructor's Resource Manual and Thomson World-Class Testing Tools

This full-fledged manual developed by the authors features detailed chapter outlines, highlights major themes, and offers lecture suggestions. Homework exercises are also included.

The comprehensive test bank includes multiple-choice, true/false, and essay questions. Available for Windows or Macintosh.

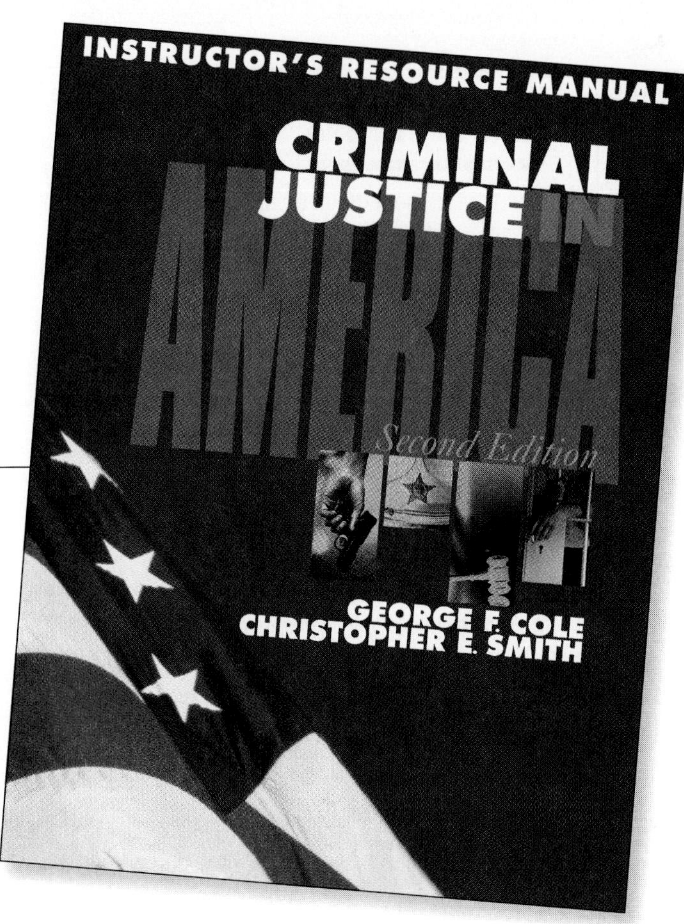

Call-In Testing

Adopters of this title are eligible for our call-in testing service. Requests received before 12:00 P.M. EST will be processed within 72 hours. For more information on this service, please contact Tammi Potter, Call-In Testing Administrator, at 1-800-423-0563 ext. 5403 or tpotter@kdc.com.

PowerPoint Presentation Tool for Windows and Macintosh

Prepare for your class in half the time with these exciting, colorful, and powerful PowerPoint lecture slides. Over 450 slides featuring main concepts and lecture ideas.

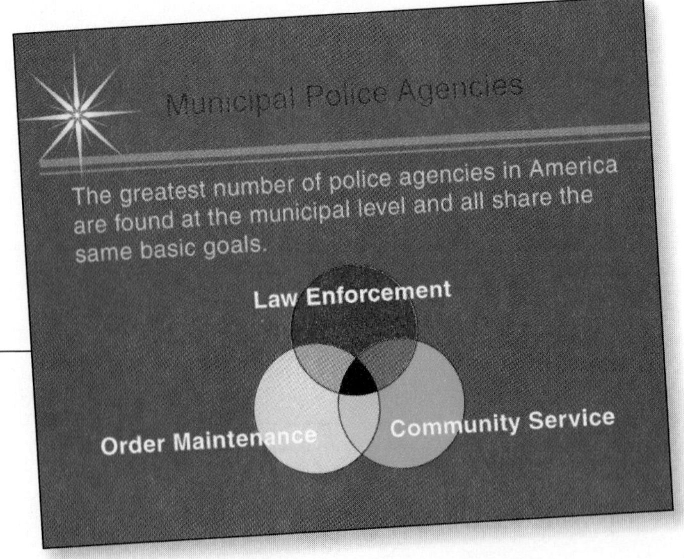

Supplements

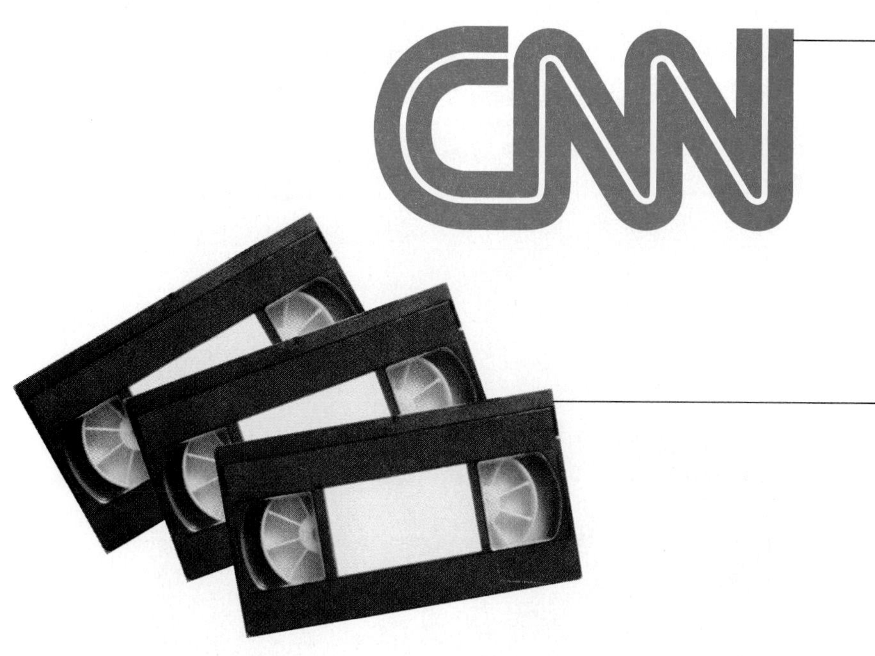

NEW! CNN Criminal Justice in the News Video

This compelling video features current news footage from CNN's comprehensive archives. Stories are organized in 3- to 5-minute segments for easy integration into classroom discussions.

NEW! Films for the Humanities Customized Video

Featuring 12 short (5- to 15-minute) segments on current crime topics, this video lets you build interest and classroom discussion without losing an entire class to watching a video. Follows the organization of the text.

Wadsworth Criminal Justice Video Library

Our extensive collection of criminal justice videos include selections from the following:

NEW! Court TV Videos

Spotlighting provocative court cases such as *California v. Powell* (the "Rodney King Beating" trial), *Florida v. Smith* in which William Kennedy Smith is tried for rape, and many others, this selection of one-hour videos helps you bring the realities of court into your classroom.

A&E American Justice Series

Qualified adopters may choose from our intriguing and current selection of A&E documentaries and exposés, including "Cruel and Unusual," "LAPD," "Why O. J. Simpson Won," and many others.

ABC News and MPI Home Video

Selections for qualified adopters include "A Question of Evidence: The O. J. Simpson Hearing" (MPI Home Video), "Guns: A Frightening Exposé on Firearms in America" (ABC News), and "Men, Sex, and Rape" (ABC News).

National Institute of Justice Crime File Videos

Qualified adopters may choose from "Biology and Crime," "Crime and Public Housing," "Drinking and Crime," "Heroin," and dozens more.

Supplements

Student's Supplements

Build a Complete Learning Environment for Your Students!

This superior selection of student learning tools includes everything you need to provide a richer and more applicable learning experience.

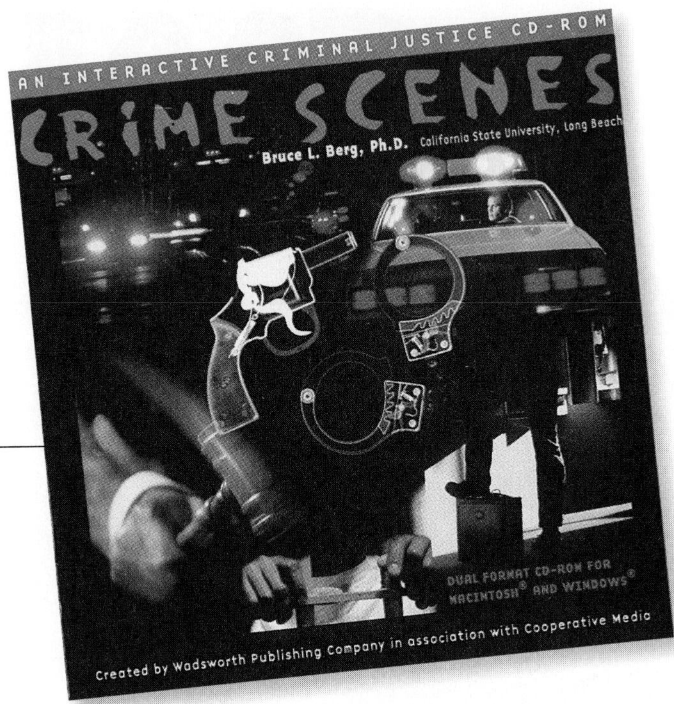

NEW! Crime Scenes: An Interactive Criminal Justice Cross-Platform CD-ROM for Windows and Macintosh

The first introductory criminal justice CD-ROM available, this interactive multimedia environment places your students in various roles as they explore all aspects of the criminal justice system, including policing and investigations, courts, sentencing, and corrections.

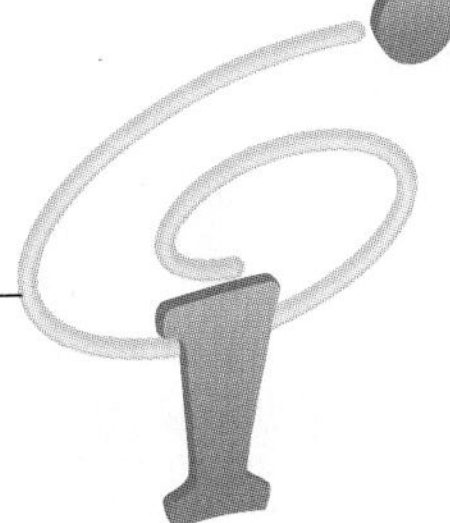

NEW! InfoTrac College Edition

The online university library that puts access to over 600 publications at students' fingertips! They get 24-hour access to full-length articles from scholarly and popular periodicals such as *U.S. News and World Report, Corrections Today, Prison Journal, American Criminal Law Review*, and many others. Students can print complete articles or use the cut/paste and e-mail features to save and share them with others. Available exclusively through Information Access Company and Wadsworth Publishing.

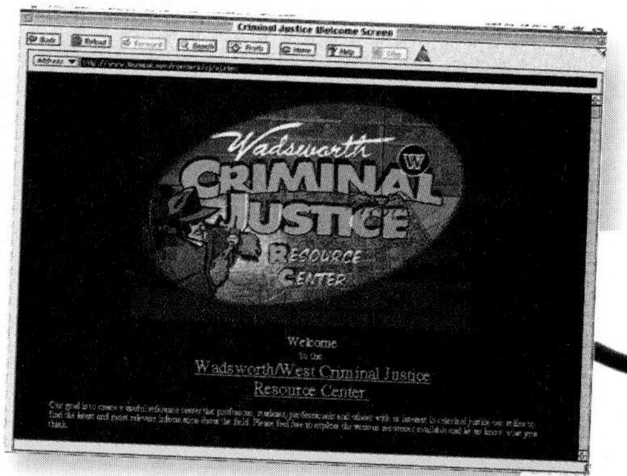

NEW! The Virtual Classroom

An amazing Web supplement to the text! Dozens of helpful links are arranged by chapter. Also features electronic homework, quizzes, Internet projects, self-testing activities for each chapter, and a scavenger hunt activity with 50 clues to help students test their knowledge. Students can also communicate and collaborate with other students and faculty across the country using the Mailing List feature.

Supplements

Mind of a Killer CD-ROM

(Kozel Multimedia)

This interactive CD-ROM provides a chilling look into the realm of serial murderers. Featuring more than 80 minutes of video, 3D simulations, an extensive mapping system and library, and graphic crime scene photos. Available only as a bundle and in Windows.

NEW! Internet Investigator II

An indispensable brochure listing the most popular criminal justice Internet sites by topic.

NEW! Internet Guide for Criminal Justice

by Daniel J. Kurland & Christina Polsenberg

Intended for the novice Internet user, this handy reference offers background information on the Internet and how to use it, plus dozens of search tips, criminal justice–related Web sites, and Internet project ideas.

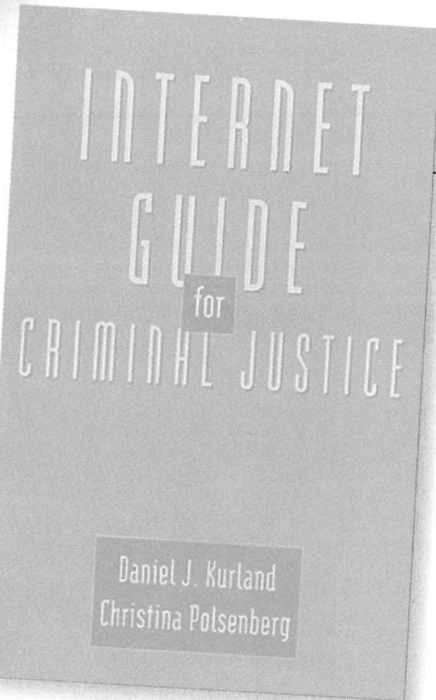

Supplements

Student's Supplements

NEW!

Seeking Employment in Criminal Justice and Related Fields

Second Edition

by J. Scott Harr and Karen M. Hess

A valuable and complete reference packed with excellent job search strategies, including sample résumés and cover letter, interview techniques, self-tests, practice questions, and career advice.

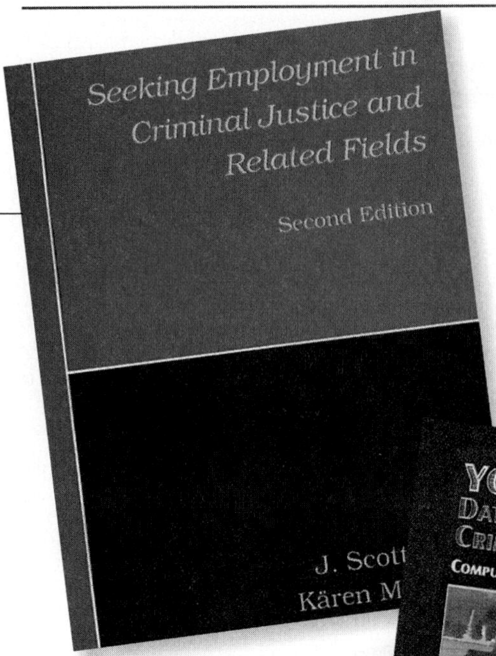

Your Research: Data Analysis for Criminal Justice and Criminology

Second Edition

A powerful yet easy-to-use data analysis and graphics program with an accompanying workbook replete with examples of criminological research projects. Available only in DOS.

Study Guide

An extensive study guide featuring a variety of pedagogical aids that cater to your students' various learning styles and needs. Each chapter is outlined, major terms are defined, summaries are given, and sample tests are provided. Also included are worksheets that help students to confront hypothetical criminal justice situations where decisions must be made.

Lecture Notes

1.1 Why does the United States have a more serious crime problem than do other industrialized countries? The differences in crime rates that are evident between various countries strongly indicate that differences in histories, traditions, conditions, compositions, and values of various societies affect the extent to which they experience various kinds of crimes. Although it is difficult to develop a concise answer to this question, there are many ways in which the United States differs from other countries, and these differences can affect the nature and extent of crime.

For example, the United States has a tradition of individualism in which people learn to act in their own best interests in order to gain economic advantages. In some other countries, people possess a much greater sense that they should be concerned about whether their actions are good or bad for their societies.

The United States is a more heterogenous society than most other societies. The United States contains a mix of ethnic groups and these groups each have a history of conflict with other groups as they endured discrimination in the course of becoming, to a greater or lesser extent, assimilated into American society. Members of some groups have had fewer economic opportunities, have been herded into ghettoes through employment and housing discrimination, and have thereby become participants in the close association between crime, poverty, and deteriorating urban locations. This was true to some extent for many Irish immigrants a century ago, for many African Americans who migrated to northern cities during the twentieth century, and for many immigrants from Asia, Latin America, and elsewhere late in the twentieth century.

The United States provides less of a social safety net than those provided in most other industrialized countries. Poor people in the United States receive less generous unemployment and welfare benefits, health care services, and housing allowances. Thus, there are more distinct and significant gaps involving resources and quality of life between socioeconomic classes in the United States than those in other industrialized countries.

The United States has a historical tradition of violence, from the frontier attacks on Native Americans to slavery to the Civil War to race riots and other civil disturbances. Moreover, as a society that developed from the expansion of a western frontier, the American tradition of widespread private ownership of firearms has contributed to violent crime patterns that are unknown in industrialized societies that restrict access to firearms.

None of these examples of differences between the United States and other countries explain why crime rates in the United States are so different, but they all provide plausible factors that could contribute to crime patterns in the United States.

1.2 If the United States eliminated illegal drugs, would it thereby eliminate violent crimes in urban areas? The elimination of illegal drugs would reduce incentives for violent battles between drug dealers and thefts and muggings by drug addicts. In the absence of illegal drugs, however, criminal organizations that currently rely on drug dealing might simply shift their focus to other profitable illegal activities, such as prostitution or gambling. People prone to abuse mind-altering substances might switch to alcohol. Although alcohol is sufficiently inexpensive that abusers would not need to maintain cocaine-addiction crime levels in order to "get high," people under the influence of alcohol can also make impulsive or otherwise misguided decisions that result in robberies and other forms of crime. Changes in social conditions will change the nature and extent of crime, but it is unrealistic to think about any single reform producing the elimination of a complex problem such as crime.

1.3 What is the association between moral values and the definition of crimes? There is no consistent association between morality and criminal law. For some acts, such as forcibly taking someone else's money, there is a societal consensus about the "wrongness" of such actions and the need to provide punishment for such actions. For other acts, such as telling lies, there is probably a societal consensus about the wrongness of such actions, yet only certain categories of lies, such as fraud and perjury, are proscribed. For some other acts, such as driving a car at a speed of 60 miles per hour, there is no moral dimension. This act is illegal, however, in areas with posted speeds of 55 miles per hour or less because of policy choices about the need to protect public safety through slower speeds on certain roadways.

1.4 What are the risks and consequences of overcriminalization? If too many activities are defined as criminal, there is a risk that the criminal justice system will be overburdened with the responsibility for processing and punishing many offenders whose offense caused no demonstrable harm to society. Moreover, the limitations of law enforcement resources may make it impossible to enforce all laws and therefore police will have to prioritize. If it becomes publicly known that certain laws will not be enforced, does that potentially diminish the public's respect for law in general? In addition, extra laws give police officers additional tools for using their discretion to make arrests. Expansion of police authority creates risks to individual liberty since police may use these powers in a discriminatory fashion or to harass selected individuals.

1.5 Why do gambling laws take the form that they do? Gambling is arguably a "victimless" crime in that consenting adults voluntarily exchange their money for the risk-laden opportunity to make even more money. Despite the voluntary nature of the activity, most forms of gambling are illegal.

For many years in inner-city communities, the police chased and arrested "numbers runners" who worked for private lottery operations in which poor people wagered small amounts of money. However, in the 1970s, when many states realized how much money they could make from starting their own lotteries, suddenly government officials actively spent public funds to encourage people to wager — but only in the official state lottery; other lotteries remained illegal. The differential criminalization of the same act — betting on a lottery — reflected the political interests of those who controlled the legislatures empowered to write the criminal laws.

Is investing in the stock market different than other forms of gambling? People place their money in a company with the hope that the company will be profitable and thereby give them additional funds. There is also the attendant risk that they, like other gamblers, will lose their money. However, this form of "gambling," namely investing in stocks, is considered an essential component of the American free enterprise economy as the means for companies to raise needed capital. It is not illegal because it serves the interests and policy preferences of those who possess political power.

1.6 If the United States eliminated poverty, would it thereby eliminate crime? Although certain categories of crimes are more prevalent among poor people, especially in urban areas, the elimination of poverty would change but not solve the crime problem. Even if the United States had full employment and every family had adequate housing, health care, education, and other services, there would still be crime. Crime has complex causes. In any society, some people, even those who are wealthy, may choose to violate criminal laws by stealing or by physically harming spouses and acquaintances with whom they have conflict.

1.7 Why have victims traditionally been ignored by the criminal justice system? The primary purposes of the criminal justice system are to control and prevent crime. Thus the system's focus is on the apprehension, processing, and punishment of offenders. Because criminal law punishes offenders for violating society's rules rather than for hurting an individual, the system operates by having the government proceed against the offender rather than having the victim as the focal point of attention. Theoretically, victims can take legal action through civil tort suits in order to seek compensation from those who harm them. Realistically, however, many offenders are poor and have little or nothing to recover in a civil suit. Thus an outlet has always existed for victims to use the legal system against criminal offenders, but the outlet has seldom been a productive focus for victims' energy and attention.

While criminal laws focus on offenders' transgressions against society, criminal procedure focuses on the rights of criminal defendants rather than on the rights of victims. Constitutional rights were developed to protect citizens from excessive governmental actions in the criminal justice process. No rights were established for victims and only in recent years have legislatures begun to give more attention, resources, and protection to crime victims.

1.8 What are possible explanations for the differences in crime rates for men and women? The possible influences or sources of difference are as varied as the range of positivist theories about the causes of crime. From a biological perspective, for example, there may be basic differences in men and women, such as difference in hormones or chromosomes, that make men more aggressive and violent. From a psychological perspective, women may naturally have different personality traits, such as being nurturing or being better able to listen to antagonists in conflict situations, that lead them to behave differently than men. These personality differences may stem from differences in the experiences of men and women as children. From a sociological perspective, women may have been denied opportunities to engage in various crimes because they automatically assumed the twenty-four-hour-per-day job of raising children, cooking, cleaning, and regularly experiencing the physically limiting effects of pregnancy. Moreover, the rigid definition of women's roles meant that only men developed as criminal role models for male children who learned and emulated such roles.

1.9 Could we get rid of racial discrimination in the justice system by getting rid of discretion? For example, if we made death sentences mandatory for first-degree murder, wouldn't we get rid of racial discrimination in capital sentencing? One of the overriding realities of the criminal justice system is that discretion cannot be eliminated. Efforts to "eliminate" discretion, such as the creation of mandatory sentences, simply serve to shift discretion to other stages in the system. For example, mandatory death sentences would not eliminate discrimination because the death penalty decision is the product of a cumulative series of discretionary acts. Prosecutors use discretion to decide which cases to pursue as death penalty cases. Mandatory sentences would not change that fact. It is even more difficult to imagine how to control the discretion of police officers. They cannot be closely supervised and monitored, yet their decisions determine who enters the system by being arrested.

1.10 Why can't the United States solve its crime problem? The government is frequently the vehicle through which Americans attempt to solve or reduce social problems. The government is the source of society's pooled resources through the taxes paid by citizens, and government is vested with the authority to take action by making and enforcing rules. Crime is an especially difficult problem to address through public policy initiatives because there is no consensus among Americans about what measures will control crime.

This lack of consensus reflects differing value-laden assessments about the causes of crime and the most effective strategies for deterring crime. Some people believe that crime stems from social problems, such as poverty, so that solutions should address the broad causes of crime. Other people believe that lawbreakers make choices about whether or not to commit crimes, so that solutions involve merely identifying and punishing the individuals who choose to violate society's rules. In reality, because the causes of crime are complex and not easily reduced to a single source, it is difficult to think about "solving" crime, a problem that has always been present in society. Instead, it is more realistic to think about how to reduce crime.

At a Glance

Chapter One

Chapter Outline	Instructional Ideas	Supplement Sources
Crime in America	Lecture Suggestions 1.1–1.2	True-False 1.1–1.2 Multiple Choice 1.1
Defining Crime Sources	Lecture Suggestions 1.3–1.5 Class Discussion Exercise 1.1 PowerPoint 2.1–2.3 FFH Video White Collar Crime	Multiple Choice 1.2 Study Guide Worksheet 1.1 Crime Scenes CD-ROM Inside Job
Types of Crime *Occupational Crime* *Organized Crime* *Visible Crime* *Crimes Without Victims* *Political Crime*	CNN Video #1: Legalization of Prostitution	Multiple Choice 1.3–1.10 True-False 1.3–1.6
How Much Crime Is There? *Uniform Crime Report* *National Crime Victimization Survey* *Trends in Crime*	Lecture Suggestion 1.6 PowerPoint 2.4–2.10 PowerPoint 2.14–2.15	Multiple Choice 1.11–1.13 True-False 1.7–1.8
Crime Victimization *Who Is Victimized?* *The Impact of Crime* *The Experience of Victims in the Criminal Justice Experience*	Lecture Suggestion 1.7 PowerPoint 2.11–2.13 PowerPoint 3.16	Multiple Choice 1.14–1.16 True-False 1.9–1.11 Essay Question 1.1 Study Guide Worksheet 1.2
Women and Crime	Lecture Suggestion 1.8 CNN Video #8: Rape Prosecution	Multiple Choice 1.17–1.18
Crime and Justice in a Multicultural Society	Lecture Suggestion 1.9 Court TV Video: *New York v. Nelson* CNN Videos: #1, DARE, and #2, Legalization of Prostitution	Multiple Choice 1.19–1.20
Crime and Justice as Public Policy Issues	Lecture Suggestion 1.10	True-False 1.12–1.14 Essay Question 1.2

INTERNET RESOURCES: Virtual Classroom Web Site and InfoTrac College Edition

Lecture Notes

2.1 Why doesn't the United States have a unified system of justice instead of a fragmented, patchwork system of competing and overlapping organizations? The design of the American system evolved from the country's history rather than from any carefully planned and rational design. At the formation of the country during the end of the eighteenth century, the various states were wary of surrendering any of their power to a national government. Although the eventual development of the U.S. Constitution created and empowered a national government, the document's authors had to permit states to retain significant authority over their own affairs in order to ensure that the citizens of the various states would agree to ratify the new Constitution. Thus the American system of federalism under the Constitution was born and endures to this day.

Because the states retained control over many of their own affairs, including the definition and enforcement of criminal laws, they also developed their own criminal justice institutions. Traditionally, these institutions were a source of political patronage as police officers, bailiffs, and justices of the peace were selected as a reward for supporting specific political parties or candidates. Although police officers have generally become civil service professionals, political patronage remains an important component of personnel selection for many positions within courthouses (e.g., bailiffs, clerks, etc.). Because the fragmentation within the system serves certain political interests, there is always resistance to reform efforts that may unify organizations within the justice system. Moreover, the fragmentation within the system permits local values and policy preferences to be expressed in the decisions and processes of the criminal justice system. This local control is another element that impedes any proposals to unify the organization of the criminal justice system within states.

2.2 How much control does the U.S. Supreme Court have over the criminal justice system? The U.S. Supreme Court is a powerful institution as it stands as the symbolic and literal pinnacle of the American judicial system. Despite its position and potential power, the Supreme Court has relatively little direct control over the vast majority of criminal cases. Supreme Court decisions have defined the rules that criminal justice actors must follow in order to protect the rights of criminal defendants. For example, the Sixth Amendment—right of indigent defendants to be represented by counsel in cases when they face incarceration—stemmed from a Supreme Court decision. Thus the Supreme Court has helped to shape some of the boundaries in which discretionary decisions, negotiations, and exchange relationships determine case outcomes.

With respect to specific cases, there are many reasons why the Supreme Court does not directly affect many case outcomes. The vast majority of case dispositions are determined by plea bargains. Because plea bargains are voluntary admissions of guilt by defendants, very few of them raise appealable issues that the Supreme Court is likely to review. In addition, the Supreme Court only gives full review to fewer than 100 cases each year out of the nearly 7,000 cases presented to them. Only a portion of these 100 (or fewer) cases are criminal cases, and they represent only a minute fraction of the hundreds of thousands of criminal cases processed by the courts throughout the country. In the 1995–96 U.S. Supreme Court term, for example, only 22 out of 75 full opinion decisions concerned criminal justice issues. The cases selected for hearing by the Supreme Court are determined by the discretionary decisions of the justices who happen to be serving at a given moment in history. When a majority of justices on the Supreme Court are either hostile to the rights of criminal defendants or interested in other kinds of legal issues, there is little reason to expect the Supreme Court to play an active role in influencing the outcomes produced by the criminal justice process.

2.3 What are the consequences of discretionary decisions and the other characteristics of the criminal justice system? As indicated by the textbook, discretion and the other system characteristics permit the efficient processing of criminal cases in an environment of scarce resources. However, because individual human beings are applying their discretion in filtering decisions and exchange relationships, there will inevitably be various forms of discrimination present in case outcomes. Human beings inevitably apply their values, policy preferences, and biases in making decisions. Thus, similarly situated defendants may receive very different outcomes. Depending on the values and biases of the decision makers, the discriminatory results may fit systematic patterns by, for example, increasing the likelihood that someone who is poor or African American or young will be processed through the system and punished rather than diverted away through filtering. On the other hand, discrimination may be individualistic as specific defendants simply have the "bad luck" of having their cases handled by the toughest prosecutor or most punitive judge.

At a Glance

Chapter Two

Chapter Outline	Instructional Ideas	Supplement Sources
The Goals of Criminal Justice *Doing Justice* *Controlling Crime* *Preventing Crime*		Multiple Choice 2.1–2.2 True-False 2.1–2.3
Criminal Justice in a Federal System *Two Justice Systems* *Expansion of Federal Involvement*	Lecture Suggestions 2.1–2.22 PowerPoint 1.4–1.6	Multiple Choice 2.3–2.6 True-False 2.4–2.5
Criminal Justice as a System *The System Perspective*		True-False 2.6–2.7 Multiple Choice 2.7
Characteristics of the Criminal Justice System *National Crime*	Class Discussion Exercise 2.1 Lecture Suggestion 2.3 PowerPoint 1.13	Study Guide Worksheet 2.1 Essay Question 2.1 Multiple Choice 2.8–2.10 True-False 2.8–2.12
Operations of the Criminal Justice System *Police* *Courts* *Corrections*	PowerPoint 1.7–1.12	Multiple Choice 2.11–2.13
The Flow of Decision Making in the Criminal Justice System *Steps in the Decision-Making Process* *The Criminal Justice Wedding Cake* *Crime Control versus Due Process*	PowerPoint 1.14–1.16	Multiple Choice 2.14–2.21 True-False 2.13–2.14 Essay Question 2.2 Study Guide Worksheet 2.2 Crime Scenes CD-ROM Behind Bars

INTERNET RESOURCES: Virtual Classroom Web Site and InfoTrac College Edition

3.1 Why should the defendant's insanity provide a defense to a criminal charge? The insanity defense is controversial because the public perceives that people who commit harmful criminal acts are somehow absolved of responsibility by pleading insanity. Some people argue that if these people are dangerous or incapable of following society's rules, then they should be dealt with by the criminal justice system whether or not they understood what they were doing. In other words, the protection of society and its laws should take precedence over the protection of harmful troubled people.

The insanity defense reflects the longstanding principle that criminal acts require some level of intention (*mens rea*) and that some people lack the capacity to form the necessary intent. Thus the application of punishment by the state will not have its desired effect if the person does not understand what is happening. Moreover, because the criminal law punishes and stigmatizes defendants, modern society has maintained the idea that people who are "ill" should be treated rather than punished. As indicated by the states that have implemented "guilty but mentally ill" verdicts, the traditional consensus about *mens rea* and about the need to treat rather than punish the mentally ill has begun to break down. Because legislatures control the definitions of crimes and defenses, they may react to pressure from the public and interest groups (e.g., prosecutors, police, etc.) to reform the insanity defense further.

3.2 Why do criminal defendants have rights? People often wonder why criminal defendants do not forfeit their rights upon being accused of violating society's rules. No forfeiture occurs because the U.S. Constitution clearly indicates that criminal defendants have specific procedural rights designed to ensure that their fates are determined by fair proceedings. The authors of the Bill of Rights recognized that anyone could be a criminal defendant. Their own experiences with British authorities prior to the Revolution taught them that the preservation of individuals' liberties was a primary mechanism for ensuring that government officials would not go too far in the exercise of power. The existence of constitutional rights creates limitations on the exercise of power by government officials. Because arrestees include both the innocent and guilty, the Constitution seeks to preserve some essential rights for defendants in order to diminish the possibility that zealous police and prosecutors might use their powers to imprison innocent people either intentionally or inadvertently.

3.3 What were the consequences of the Supreme Court's decisions incorporating provisions of the Bill of Rights and applying them against the states? The Supreme Court's decisions effectively nationalized the Bill of Rights so that people throughout the country would possess a common set of rights that would limit the potential for abusive actions by all levels of government, state and local as well as federal. Many state constitutions provide extra protections for people within those states, so the Warren Court decisions on criminal procedure merely ensured that a baseline set of protections existed throughout the country. In some states, however, these baseline protections represented a gigantic step forward for the protection of individuals' rights.

A concrete and controversial aspect of the incorporation decisions was to thrust the Supreme Court directly into the role of defining many law enforcement policies and procedures for police officers throughout the country. The decisions reduced local law enforcement agencies' ability to develop their own practices and procedures because they had to follow the judicially established rules about search and arrest procedures. Many critics believed that these judicial decisions improperly infringed on the ability of the legislative and executive branches of government to develop criminal justice policies.

3.4 Should improperly obtained evidence be excluded so that prosecutors cannot use the evidence against lawbreakers? The exclusionary rule has been the focus of great debates. The Supreme Court applied the rule to all law enforcement officers in 1961 because the justices had concluded that there was no other effective mechanism available to deter police misconduct during searches and police interrogations. If there is nothing to deter police misconduct, then innocent people as well as guilty people may find themselves at the mercy of random police searches.

Critics claimed that the rule harmed society by permitting guilty defendants to go free. Studies have shown, however, that exclusionary rule issues arise only in a small minority of cases and that defendants frequently lose their exclusionary rule claims. A small percentage of drug and weapons cases tend to be lost by prosecutors because those cases may rely exclusively on the admissibility of physical evidence in the form of items seized during a search. Critics also claimed that the rule punished the prosecutor rather than the police and that other mechanisms were available to prevent police misconduct, such as internal disciplinary procedures and civil lawsuits.

Ultimately the exclusionary rule was not altered because of a consensus about the rule's policy consequences. Instead, events within the political system, namely the election of conservative presidents and the appointment of new justices, led to a reshaping of the rule. The various exceptions to the exclusionary rule created by the Supreme Court in the 1980s (i.e., good faith exception, inevitable discovery rule, public safety exception) have given law enforcement officials much more flexibility to conduct searches and interrogations. Although the exclusionary rule continues to exist, libertarian critics of the Supreme Court claim that the rule has primarily symbolic value because of the broad applicability of exceptions.

At a Glance

Chapter Three

Chapter Outline	Instructional Ideas	Supplement Sources
Foundations of Criminal Law *Criminal versus Civil Law* *Substantive and Procedural Criminal Law*		Multiple Choice 3.1–3.3 True-False 3.1–3.3
Criminal Justice in a Federal System *Seven Principles of Criminal Law* *Elements of a Crime* *Statutory Definitions of Crimes* *Responsibility for Criminal Acts* *CLOSE-UP: Jeffrey Dahmer: The Insanity Plea That Didn't Work*	Lecture Suggestions 3.1 Class Discussion Exercise 3.1 PowerPoint 3.11–3.20 Court TV Video: *Cabey v. Goetz, Florida v. Smith* and *Vermont v. Grace*	Multiple Choice 3.4–3.13 True-False 3.4–3.12 Essay Question 3.1–3.12 Study Guide Worksheet 3.1–3.2 Crime Scenes CD-ROM Arresting Force and Reason to Search
Procedural Criminal Law *The Principles of Procedural Criminal Law* *The Bill of Rights and the History of Defendants' Rights* *The Fourteenth Amendment and Due Process Revolution* *The Fourth Amendment* *The Fifth Amendment* *The Sixth Amendment* *The Eighth Amendment*	Lecture Suggestions 3.2–3.4 PowerPoint 3.24–3.30	Multiple Choice 3.14–3.29 True-False 3.13–3.18 Crime Scenes CD-ROM Reason to Search
Constitutional Rights and Criminal Justice Professionals		Essay Question 3.3

INTERNET RESOURCES: Virtual Classroom Web Site and InfoTrac College Edition

4.1 What are the intended and unintended consequences of police reform? The police have a very difficult role in American society. The public has specific expectations about what the police should accomplish, including impossible tasks such as controlling crime. In addition, the police must adjust their resources and methods to address changing social circumstances. Such social processes as urbanization, immigration, unemployment, and technological development affect the ways in which people interact with each other and create new opportunities for conflict and victimization.

When planning the goals, methods, and organization of police to meet society's needs, reformers inevitably identify specific problems that need to be addressed. The identification of problems involves value judgments and may ignore or underestimate the extent of other societal needs. The professional movement, for example, raised internal and external expectations about police crime-fighting capabilities that the police have never been able to fulfill. In addition, the reforms led to criticisms that the police were increasingly isolated from the communities that they were to serve. Although these unintended consequences led to later reform efforts to initiate community policing, the professionalization movement succeeded in achieving other goals.

Most police departments developed civil service personnel procedures that distanced them from the political patronage that had previously shaped the composition and behavior of cities' police forces. Professionalization spurred the introduction of training and the development of rules and procedures to help standardize police practices and give guidance to some aspects of discretionary decision making. The professional model's advocates also encouraged the adoption of technological innovations, such as patrol cars and radios, that have benefits for service and order maintenance functions as well as for their intended crime-fighting purposes.

Community policing reforms are intended to get the police back into direct contact with citizens and to reduce disorder and the fear of crime through concentrated order maintenance activities. While these reforms are aimed at specific problems, such as the fear and criminality that may grow in disorderly and deteriorating neighborhoods, attempts to redress these problems create new situations for police to apply their discretion. Will police activities to prevent disorderly conduct that is not illegal create new tensions between concerns for crime prevention and concerns about protecting civil liberties? Should the police have the authority, for example, to tell teenagers that they cannot congregate and play their "boom boxes" in a public park? Whenever value choices are made about desirable police goals and methods, there will be consequences for a variety of other types of police decisions and contacts with the public.

4.2 If the police are not able to control crime effectively, why does the public (including new police recruits) continue to view the police primarily as crime fighters? Crime is an issue of great concern to the public. Because of widespread fear of crime, the public wants to identify a source of authority and power that can address this difficult issue. Police executives can use the public's fears and concerns as a means to gain resources. The public and elected officials may not be willing to earmark more taxpayer money for general service professionals, but their concerns about the crime issue may make them more willing to increase the resources available to the crime-fighting agency. Thus, public expectations and the opportunity to gain and maintain resources encourage police to perpetuate their image as crime fighters even though that may be the least prevalent and least effective function that they serve.

4.3 If police responses to domestic violence are apparently improved by requiring police to arrest abusive husbands and boyfriends, why not simply remove police discretion in other situations through the development of clear rules that will diminish the risks of bias and discrimination? Although police departments can attempt to reduce police discretion and the attendant risks of discrimination by the creation of clear rules for specific situations, there are many practical barriers to the reduction of police discretion. First, many kinds of situations, such as barroom disputes, are much more ambiguous than domestic violence situations in which a rule can be tied to a specific investigatory question: Did one spouse strike the other spouse? Police in a barroom disturbance may be dealing with many more people and a broader range of actions (e.g., threats, pushing, claims of self-defense, etc.) within a single event and context. Dealing with a crowd in a bar is not the same as dealing with two individuals inside a home. Thus, in the barroom situation and in other kinds of situations it is much more difficult to clearly define rules for police action.

Efforts to limit police discretion will also tax police resources. Mandatory arrests in specific situations may increase the number of arrests, contribute to jail overcrowding, involve police officers in more time filling out paperwork and appearing in court, and otherwise limit other kinds of resource allocation choices for the police department. Moreover, the department has a limited ability to monitor police officers' compliance with detailed rules. Officers on the street may be overlooking many situations which, unlike domestic violence, do not have a specific complainant requesting police action against a specific suspect.

At a Glance
Chapter Four

Chapter Outline	Instructional Ideas	Supplement Sources
The Development of Police in the United States *The English Roots of American Policing* *Policing in the United States*	Lecture Suggestions 4.1 PowerPoint 5.1–5.11, 6.14	Multiple Choice 4.1–4.12 True-False 4.1–4.9 Essay Question 4.1
Organization of the Police *Federal Agencies* *State Agencies* *County Agencies* *Municipal Agencies*	PowerPoint 5.12–5.19	Multiple Choice 4.13–4.15 True-False 4.10–4.12 Study Guide Worksheet 4.1
Police Policy		Multiple Choice 4.16–4.17 True-False 4.13 Study Guide Worksheet 4.2
Police Functions *Order Maintenance* *Law Enforcement* *Service* *Implementing the Mandate*	Lecture Suggestions 4.2 PowerPoint 6.5 CNN Video #6: Police and Technology	Multiple Choice 4.18–4.19 True-False 4.14–4.15 Essay Question 4.2
Police Actions *Encounters between Police and Citizens* *Police Discretion* *Domestic Violence*	Class Discussion Exercise 4.1 Lecture Suggestion 4.3 PowerPoint 6.11–6.12 FFH Video: Domestic Violence	Multiple Choice 4.20–4.24 True-False 4.16–4.18

INTERNET RESOURCES: Virtual Classroom Web Site and InfoTrac College Edition

5.1 Why do the sizes of police departments in large cities vary so greatly and why are the various sizes so disconnected from the population and crime rate statistics for the cities? Although it might seem logical to presume that cities would naturally have larger police forces in locations with larger populations and higher crime rates, in fact, the size of a police department is shaped by a variety of other factors. Increases in the size of a police force may depend on the public's perception of crime within the city and the willingness of voters to make a larger police force a primary political issue. Specific politicians may be able to push this issue in order to advance their political self-interest, but in many cities other kinds of issues may be more important during specific election campaigns. In addition, taxpayers in some cities may be less willing to spend money on personnel increases, especially if there is any public awareness that personnel increases do not necessarily affect the crime rate. In other cities, in which police officers' unions cooperate with and provide political support for specific politicians, these elected officials may be happy to support measures that increase the size and strength of their union allies. As with other issues affecting the criminal justice system, the size and organization of police departments will be shaped by political processes and social conditions within each locality.

5.2 How many different exchange relationships affect police officers' actions and decisions? Police have significant discretion to make decisions that will affect people's lives by entering them into the criminal justice system. These decisions are influenced by the need for the police to maintain relationships with various constituencies. First, the police need to attempt to maintain a positive relationship with the public. Public cooperation is essential for reporting and investigating crimes. Thus police may overlook certain crimes, such as run-of-the-mill traffic offenses, in order to avoid antagonizing the citizenry through zealous enforcement.

Police also need to maintain positive relationships with neighboring law enforcement agencies or with state and federal police officials. The success of future investigations may depend on maintaining cooperative relationships. Toward that end, police may overlook traffic violations by other law enforcement officials or otherwise bend rules to assist their nearby counterparts. In Ohio, for example, police officers' family members, friends, and supporters carry Fraternal Order of Police (FOP) issued "courtesy cards" or have FOP decals on their cars so that police will recognize allies and use their discretion to overlook traffic offenses.

Police need to maintain cooperative relationships with prosecutors and judges in order to maintain smooth processing of criminal justice cases. Police do not want to see the system free the suspects that they have arrested, so the police have an incentive to cooperate with and assist the other professionals within the criminal justice system.

Police also need to maintain good relationships with elected officials in state legislatures and city councils in order to ensure that such officials continue to provide resources in the annual police department budget. Thus police may be responsive to the enforcement preferences of such officials (e.g., a highly publicized drug or prostitution crackdown in an official's ward or district). Police may also provide extra security for these officials at public gatherings, overlook traffic and other violations, and otherwise endear themselves to the people who control resources.

5.3 How do social and political processes affect the definition of rights for criminal defendants? Judicial officers, especially justices on the U.S. Supreme Court, are the key decision makers who have formally defined the rights under the U.S. Constitution, including the Fourth, Fifth, and Sixth Amendment rights that affect police and the judicial process. These decision makers are selected through political processes that reflect, in a rough manner, contemporary social values. For example, as society changed in a more liberal direction with respect to support for civil rights and opposition to the death penalty during the 1960s, liberal presidents (John Kennedy and Lyndon Johnson) appointed Supreme Court justices who were supportive of broad constitutional rights. Richard Nixon managed to tap the public's increasing fear of crime in 1968 and 1972 and thereby capitalize on conservatizing trends affecting other issues, such as busing for school desegregation. By electing a more conservative president, American voters placed the judicial appointment power in the hands of a President who put four new justices on the Supreme Court. These new justices were much less supportive of broad rights for criminal defendants. Similarly, conservative voter behavior in elections during the presidential elections of the 1980s permitted Presidents Ronald Reagan and George Bush to appoint additional justices who narrowed the scope of many constitutional rights for criminal defendants.

Although the Supreme Court declares what the Constitution means and thereby tells police officers how they must treat criminal suspects, these judicial declarations do not necessarily control police behavior. Research on the *Miranda* decision, for example, found that officers in smaller, less professionalized police departments had less access to information about Supreme Court mandates and were therefore less likely to follow new judicial rules for police conduct. Thus, the social context of police departments can affect whether or not decisions about constitutional rights are implemented. If a department does not have continuous training for its officers or does not closely follow legal rulings, the police will not obey Supreme Court decisions as they should.

In addition, many judicial rulings are somewhat ambiguous. It is not always clear whether a particular decision applies to a broad or narrow range of situations. Thus police and prosecutors have the opportunity to test the limits of new judicial rulings by using their discretion to interpret those rulings narrowly. There is always a risk that a criminal defendant will appeal and thereby cause a court to examine police behavior in a specific case. However, because most defendants plead guilty after plea bargain negotiations, the defendants themselves often determine their own fate by admitting their guilt and thereby diminish or preclude their own opportunities and bases for appeal.

At a Glance
Chapter Five

Chapter Outline	Instructional Ideas	Supplement Sources
Organization of the Police	Lecture Suggestions 5.1–5.2 PowerPoint 6.1	Multiple Choice 5.1–5.2 True-False 5.1
Police Response and Action *Organizational Response* *Productivity*	PowerPoint 6.3, 6.21	Multiple Choice 5.3–5.10 True-False 5.2–5.4
Delivery of Police Services *Patrol Functions* *Issues in Patrolling* *The Future of Patrol* *Investigation* *Special Operations*	Class Discussion Exercise 5.1 PowerPoint 6.4–6.13; 6.15–6.19; 1.32, 1.34 FFH Video: Forensics Court TV Video: *Georgia v. Redding*	Multiple Choice 5.11–5.21 True-False 5.5–5.18 Study Guide Worksheet 5.1–5.2 Essay Question 5.1 Crime Scenes CD-ROM Instrument of Death
Police Actions and the Rule of Law *Search and Seizure* *Arrest* *Interrogation*	Lecture Suggestion 5.3 PowerPoint 8.2–8.11; 8.15–8.23 Court TV Video: *California v. Chance and Powell*	Multiple Choice 5.22–5.26 True-False 5.19–5.22 Essay Question 5.2 Crime Scenes CD-ROM Instrument of Death, Arresting Force, and Reason to Search

INTERNET RESOURCES: Virtual Classroom Web Site and InfoTrac College Edition

Lecture Notes

6.1 Why would a woman want to become a police officer? Since the 1970s, many people in American society have been setting aside old stereotypes about the types of occupations best suited to men and women. The consequence of those stereotypes had always been to limit the opportunities available to women and force them into "pink-collar" occupations as secretaries, teachers, and nurses — the few professional occupations regarded by society as suitable for women. Women were denied access to other jobs and seldom had opportunities to gain the money, power, and status available to men in a variety of professions.

The women's movement helped to challenge existing stereotypes. Political and legal actions by women seeking equality not only opened doors to new kinds of jobs for women, they also inspired many young women in the next generations to be open-minded and ambitious about career options. Thus women began to seek careers as police officers, an occupation that had traditionally been closed to women.

In essence, women want to become police officers for the same reasons that men want to become police officers. Women are attracted to a job that serves the public, provides job security and good retirement benefits, involves a variety of tasks every day, and has the potential to provide moments of excitement.

6.2 Why is racial prejudice such a significant problem among police officers? Problems of racial polarization and prejudice are evident throughout American society. Because police officers are drawn from American society, it is no surprise that they bring to their jobs the attitudes and biases generated by their socialization and experiences as Americans.

Police officers' biases may be exacerbated by several elements of their experience as police officers. First, their contacts with citizens in minority communities are likely to be in moments of stress and conflict. When police are intervening in a disturbance, making an arrest, or issuing a traffic citation, they are likely to face hostility from the citizens involved as well as bystanders. This hostility may be compounded if the police officers are insensitive to the values, concerns, customs, and language of people in minority neighborhoods. If people from minority groups believe that police treat them more harshly than others in American society, the hostility and uncooperative attitudes that they direct toward the police may build or reinforce negative attitudes by the police.

Second, because many urban minority neighborhoods are predominantly lower class, police officers may associate people in those neighborhoods, or even people who merely look like they may be from those neighborhoods, with the types of criminality associated with lower socioeconomic groups. Thus, police may treat entire categories of people harshly and suspiciously because of their skin color, accents, or other characteristics.

Third, white officers in many departments may believe that their promotion opportunities have been unfairly curtailed by affirmative action programs designed to create new opportunities for people from groups that were traditionally victimized by employment discrimination. Thus, if white officers are angry about their perception that African-American and other officers receive preferential treatment, this resentment may become focused more widely at minority group members in general. Although conflicts about affirmative action have occurred throughout American society, many police departments have been especially affected because they are public agencies targeted for reform that often engaged in overt discrimination in the not-too-distant past.

The problem of police bias is especially problematic because all members of the public need to be able to rely on the police for assistance and the police need the assistance of the public in order to perform their functions effectively.

6.3 Why is it considered corruption if police receive free coffee or meals from a business? While there may be nothing inherently wrong with a single act of generosity or gratitude directed toward the police, there are risks that such actions will produce preferential treatment toward people who give benefits to the police. Will the police vigorously enforce traffic and other laws against people who have given them gifts? Will the police treat these people in the same manner that they treat other people who have not given gifts? Human experience indicates that people tend to favor others who are kind or generous to them. In fact, an expectation may develop among police officers that they are "owed" special favors by businesses or that they "owe" preferential treatment to their benefactors. Such expectations could be the basis for exploitation, either of the public by police seeking favors or of the police by others seeking favoritism. Moreover, whether or not the police ever favor their benefactors, there is an appearance of impropriety and a perception of potential favoritism in the eyes of the public. Thus, the only way to ensure that acts of kindness will not produce undesirable consequences is to enforce a clear, absolute rule that police officers are not to accept gifts from anyone.

6.4 What problems are presented by the use of civil litigation to hold police officers accountable? Traditionally, under the doctrine of "sovereign immunity," people were not permitted to file tort lawsuits against the government. Over time, however, legislatures created various statutes to permit lawsuits for personal injuries, civil rights violations, and other injuries caused by police and government officials.

If police misconduct leads to a lawsuit that results in a significant financial judgment against the police, the money is actually paid by the city or by the city's insurance company. Thus, it is not the police who must pay compensatory and punitive damages, it is usually the citizens and taxpayers of the city who pay the cost through direct financial obligations or increased insurance premiums. Civil liability may be an effective accountability mechanism because it threatens the police and thereby encourages them to conform to proper professional standards. On the other hand, misconduct by a particular police officer may have a significant impact on the ability of a municipality to provide police and other services if resources must be used to pay a claim. Moreover, litigation can be a very expensive means of processing claims against the police and cities may find themselves expending significant legal resources defending against claims that have little merit and a slim chance of success for the claimants.

At a Glance

Chapter Six

Chapter Outline	Instructional Ideas	Supplement Sources
Who Are the Police? *Recruitment* *Training* *The Changing Profile of Police*	Lecture Suggestions 6.1 PowerPoint 7.7–7.10 CNN Video #5: Women in Policing	Multiple Choice 6.1–6.4 True-False 6.1–6.4
The Police Subculture *The Working Personality* *Police Isolation* *Job Stress*	Lecture Suggestion 6.2 PowerPoint 7.1–7.2, 7.4, 7.18–7.20 FFH Video: Suicide and the Police Officer	Multiple Choice 6.5–6.10 True-False 6.5–6.6 Study Guide Worksheet 6.1
Police and the Community *Policing in a Multicultural Society* *Community Crime Prevention*	Court TV Video: *New York v. Nelson* CNN Video #1: DARE Program	Multiple Choice 6.11–6.14 True-False 6.7–6.8 Essay Question 6.1
Police Abuse of Power *Use of Force* *Corruption*	Lecture Suggestion 6.3 PowerPoint 7.13–7.16, 7.21–7.26 Court TV Video: *California v. Powell* and *California v. Chance and Powell* CNN Video #4: Police Abuse of Power	Multiple Choice 6.15–6.20 True-False 6.9–6.12 Crime Scenes CD-ROM Arresting Force
Civic Accountability *Internal Affairs Units* *Civilian Review Boards* *Standards and Accreditation* *Civil Liability Suits*	Class Discussion Exercise 6.1 Lecture Suggestion 6.4	Multiple Choice 6.21–6.22 True-False 6.13–6.14 Essay Question 6.2 Study Guide Worksheet 6.2
Private Policing *Functions of Private Police* *Private Employment of Public Police* *The Public-Private Interface* *Recruitment and Training*	PowerPoint 5.22	Multiple Choice 6.23–6.25 True-False 6.15–6.17 Essay Question 6.3 Study Guide Worksheet 6.3

INTERNET RESOURCES: Virtual Classroom Web Site and InfoTrac College Edition

Lecture Notes

7.1 Why doesn't each state simply impose the elements of court reform and administrative centralization on courts throughout the state? There are two primary impediments to court reform. First, powerful political interests benefit from fragmented courts. Judges have more power over their own courthouses when the administration of courts is not determined by a central authority. Moreover, political parties benefit from fragmented courts because they can use patronage positions within local courthouses as a means to reward party loyalists. Thus, these interests (judges and political parties) may use their influence to persuade legislators to leave the fragmented system in place.

Second, even if reforms are imposed, it does not mean that they will accomplish their intended goals. Judges still have significant discretionary authority, courtroom workgroups can still determine outcomes in cases, and local legal culture will still shape the timing and nature of case dispositions. Formal court reforms may not be worthwhile if they do not take into account the interests and behavior of actors within the court system and the influences that shape decision making and procedures.

7.2 Since many judges are elected officials who need to impress the voters, why don't judges insist that every defendant go to trial in order to show the public that the judge is "tough on crime" and will not let criminals off lightly through plea bargaining? Trials are difficult and time consuming. Trials place judges in the position of making difficult and immediate rulings on evidentiary motions. Judges must also supervise the selection of the jury and instruct the jury on how to decide the case. There are many opportunities for judges to make errors during trials that might lead to reversal on appeal. In sum, trials are difficult and fraught with risk. By contrast, because it is in the defendants' self-interest to plead guilty in exchange for a lighter sentence or reduced charges, it is easier for judges to record the certain conviction than risk the errors and acquittals that will inevitably occur after some trials. In addition, the plea bargaining process usually relieves the judge of sole responsibility for determining the sentence in a particular case. Many judges find sentencing to be their most difficult responsibility, but by supervising and participating in negotiated plea agreements, judges are spared their most difficult decision and can help to shape a sentence produced by the interactions of several actors. Judges may also be sensitive to caseload pressures, so there is little incentive to encourage trials when convictions and sentences can be produced more easily through the plea bargaining process.

7.3 What kinds of discretionary considerations can affect a judge's decision about bail? Judges normally weigh the seriousness of the crime and the defendant's characteristics, such as prior criminal record. In addition, however, there may be a variety of other considerations. For example, a judge may want to try to rehabilitate a young offender by initially setting a high bail and then lowering the bail after a day or two so that the young person can learn a lesson from a having a brief "taste" of jail. Judges could also use bail to speed processing for minor cases. A poor defendant can be faced with the choice of pleading innocent and then sitting in jail by being unable to make bail or pleading guilty and receiving probation, which means that he or she can go home. Thus, bail can be used coercively to elicit quick guilty pleas. State judges, in particular, may also be concerned about public reactions to bail decisions. Because many state judges are elected, they may be inclined to set high bail for people accused of highly publicized crimes in order to show the public that they are tough on crime. Elected judges may also lean toward high bail for fear that they will be blamed, and thereby suffer adverse consequences at the next election, if someone released on bail disappears or commits another crime.

7.4 How does the bail-setting process illustrate the dominant characteristics of the criminal justice system? The bail process illustrates the importance of discretion within the system. Prosecutors have significant discretion about what bail amount to recommend to the judge. Judges have significant discretion about what bail amount to set for each defendant. Bail bondsmen have significant discretion to decide which clients to accept. The bail process also illustrates resource scarcity in the system, especially because overcrowding in jails can affect the ability of judges and prosecutors to seek to have a defendant detained. With respect to exchange relations, judges and prosecutors cooperate to achieve their goals of spreading responsibility for bail decisions and, as elected officials, avoiding the risk of being blamed if someone released on bail commits another crime. The bail bondsmen use police officers and other court personnel as brokers who will steer business to the bondsmen in exchange for bondsmen's cooperation in turning down defendants whom the police wish to see kept in jail. The prosecutor may cooperate with the police in recommending a high bail in such cases in order to maintain good relations because the prosecutor relies on the police for investigative resources and for feeding solid cases into the system.

7.5 If the local legal culture determines how cases are processed, how does a new attorney know how to act as a prosecutor or defense attorney? New attorneys may enter the courts with idealistic notions about how the criminal justice system ought to work, but they quickly become socialized into local practices. New attorneys will quickly see what kinds of decisions and relationships produce smooth case processing. They will also begin to see how the local "going rate" of punishment for specific crimes is not intended or regarded as providing a benefit for criminals, but instead is an effort to achieve a just punishment based on shared values within the local court. If new attorneys resist the practices of the local legal culture, they will be less effective in their jobs. Therefore, there are significant incentives for newcomers to learn how cases are processed in their local courthouse.

At a Glance

Chapter Seven

Chapter Outline	Instructional Ideas	Supplement Sources
The Structure of American Courts	PowerPoint 9.1–9.2, 9.4–9.5, 9.7–9.14	Multiple Choice 7.1–7.4 True-False 7.1–7.4
Effective Management of State Courts	Lecture Suggestion 7.1 PowerPoint 9.6, 9.15–9.17 CNN Video #7: Courtroom of the Future	Multiple Choice 7.5–7.8 True-False 7.5–7.7 Essay Question 7.1
To Be a Judge *Who Becomes a Judge?* *Functions of the Judge* *How to Become a Judge*	Lecture Suggestion 7.2 Class Discussion Exercise 7.1 PowerPoint 9.18–9.20 FFH Video: The Court Process—The Judge	Multiple Choice 7.9–7.15 True-False 7.8–7.15 Study Guide Worksheet 7.1
From Arrest to Trial or Plea	PowerPoint 11.1–11.5	Multiple Choice 7.16–7.20 True-False 7.16–7.17
Bail: Pretrial Release *The Reality of the Bail System* *The Bail Bondsman* *Setting Bail* *Reforming the Bail System*	Lecture Suggestion 7.3 Lecture Suggestion 7.4 PowerPoint 11.6–11.11	Multiple Choice 7.21–7.30 True-False 7.18–7.23 Essay Question 7.2–7.3 Study Guide Worksheet 7.2
Pretrial Detention	PowerPoint 11.12–11.13 FFH Video: Pretrial Process	Multiple Choice 7.31–7.32
The Courtroom: How It Functions *The Courtroom Workgroup* *The Impact of Courtroom Workgroups*	Lecture Suggestion 7.5	Multiple Choice 7.33–7.37 True-False 7.24–7.32 Essay Question 7.4

INTERNET RESOURCES: Virtual Classroom Web Site and InfoTrac College Edition

Lecture Notes

8.1 Why would a prosecutor expend significant time and money on an unsuccessful prosecution, such as the O. J. Simpson case? Prosecutors do not seek to waste resources. However, because their decisions are guided by a variety of factors and judgments, they cannot always predict when a case is not going to produce a conviction that justifies the level of public expenditures. In a preschool child abuse case, the prosecutor may perceive public pressure to pursue a case even if the quality of the evidence is uncertain. This is especially true for elected prosecutors. Moreover, if a particular crime has captured nationwide public attention, an ambitious prosecutor can gain name recognition and political stature by aggressively prosecuting such allegations. Prosecutors cannot always predict how a judge or jury will react to witness testimony. Prosecu-tions may be based on prosecutors' perceptions that a witness will provide strong, believable testimony, yet an effective defense attorney may poke holes in the testimony during cross-examination or the jury may, for a variety of reasons, view the testimony less favorably than the prosecutor expected.

8.2 Why aren't prosecutors' offices placed under centralized control in order to achieve consistent decisions and smoother cooperation among criminal justice agencies? The organization of prosecution reflects the American tradition of local political control over many facets of public policy and administration. Local control permits local values to shape policy decisions. The United States has a system of federalism in which states rather than the federal government have significant control over various public policy issues, including the administration of justice. Each state may, in turn, decide for itself how much local control will exist within each county or city. Moreover, because political parties gain benefits from decentralization through the use of local prosecutors' offices as springboards to higher office and as sources of political patronage job appointments for loyalists, there is significant political resistance to most reform efforts.

8.3 Shouldn't someone supervise prosecutors' decisions so that they do not make mistakes or show favoritism in deciding not to prosecute specific cases? If prosecutors are to be supervised, who would be the supervisor? Judges cannot act as supervisors over all aspects of prosecution, because judges must maintain a posture of impartiality over cases. Thus, a judge's decision to overrule the dropping of charges would give the appearance that the judge had already decided on the likelihood of a defendant's guilt. Although the few states with centralized prosecution (e.g., Connecticut) create the possibility of supervision, such state-level supervision clashes with the tradition of local control over public policy and administration. The prosecutorial system generally depends on the most basic form of democratic accountability, namely voters having the opportunity to select new prosecutors periodically if they are unhappy with the actions of incumbents. This is an ineffective mechanism of control, in that the public is not going to supervise individual decisions. It is, however, a mechanism of *accountability* in a general sense because prosecutors who become too out of touch with local opinion and values will find themselves targeted by political opponents during the next election.

8.4 Why can't prosecutors make principled decisions without being influenced by exchange relations and organizational factors? Prosecutors cannot make simple decisions about cases because they work in a complex system in which they do not have adequate resources under their control. Because prosecutors depend on the police for investigations and arrests, they cannot ignore the concerns and interests of police in making prosecutorial decisions. Similarly, because prosecutors depend on judges to ensure that convicted offenders receive appropriate punishments, prosecutors' goals would be thwarted if they could not maintain cooperative relationships with judges. Prosecutors need the cooperation of defense attorneys in order to make the plea bargaining process function smoothly. Prosecutors must rely upon and consider the interests of other actors (e.g., the public, the news media, corrections agencies) in order to be effective in their jobs. Prosecutors are the central and most influential figures in the criminal justice process. However, they do not control the process and they do not control their own resources, so they must develop cooperative, exchange relations with other actors.

8.5 Why couldn't a defense attorney vigorously defend each client if he or she wanted to? A defense attorney can vigorously defend each client. There is nothing that prohibits a defense attorney from doing so. However, the nature of the criminal justice process creates influences and incentives that encourage defense attorneys to cooperate. The financial incentives for assigned counsel push them toward disposing of cases quickly through plea bargaining. The reality that lawyers must keep working with the same prosecutors and judges in future cases pushes defense attorneys to cooperate in negotiating plea bargains, both for their own sake and for the sake of their clients (and future clients). The defense attorney's reliance on prosecutors and police for access to information creates an incentive to have a workable, cooperative relationship rather than risking that valuable time will be spent in fighting over access to reports and witness lists. Thus, it is the nature and structure of case processing and criminal defense that operate to lead defense attorneys to adopt a cooperative rather than an adversarial stance.

8.6 Would indigent defendants be more cooperative if they were allowed to select their own defense attorneys? There might be an increase in cooperation and in acceptance of the results of judicial process if indigent defendants could select their own attorneys. There is no escaping the fact, however, that the nature of the criminal justice process would still encourage these attorneys to negotiate, cooperate, and compromise in developing plea negotiations for their clients. The caseload pressures and scarce resources would still dictate the actions of public defenders, and financial considerations and exchange relations would still affect the strategies of assigned counsel. Although public defenders are currently viewed as "traitors" by many indigent criminal defendants, a choice system might simply make assigned counsel share the public defender's scapegoat role for embodying the gap between actual criminal justice processes and the ideal of adversary justice that many defendants share with the rest of the public.

8.7 Why doesn't the government hire, train, and pay attractive salaries to top-notch attorneys to represent indigent criminal defendants? The criminal justice system has scarce resources. How much is the public willing to pay to carry the costs of increased competence and adversarialness in criminal defense work? This is not a high priority for the public. It certainly is not a priority for politicians in legislatures, who would not gain any credit with the voters for advocating increased expenditures to benefit criminal defendants. The public usually prefers to see extra money spent on police protection or more prisons: programs that the taxpaying public sees as benefiting the deserving, law-abiding citizens. Many members of the public share the view that criminal defendants have too many rights and that too many defendants escape punishment due to legal technicalities. The quality of representation for criminal defendants is not a high priority for policy makers.

8.8 What would an attorney actually have to do to be found to have provided ineffective assistance of counsel? It is obvious from the standards discussed by the Supreme Court in the *Cronic* and *Strickland* cases that courts do not want to second-guess lawyers' courtroom strategies. If an attorney declines to cross-examine a witness for strategic reasons, should they run the risk that the failure to cross-examine will result in a claim against the attorney? Judges, as lawyers themselves, are very wary of making judgments about their fellow professionals who represent criminal defendants. Moreover, the Supreme Court clearly is not interested in encouraging prisoners to file ineffective assistance of counsel claims. Without a difficult standard for finding ineffective assistance, many more prisoners would have nothing to lose by seeking to have a judge second-guess their trial attorneys' actions. Thus, it is very difficult to say what would constitute ineffective assistance. If an attorney was intoxicated in court and that intoxication affected his or her behavior, a reviewing court would not want to endorse such behavior. If an attorney merely made strategic errors, however, judges want to act very cautiously before declaring that any errors were so unreasonable or outrageous that they would justify a new trial. New trials would create additional burdens on the court system and encourage more prisoners to seek judicial review of convictions.

At a Glance

Chapter Eight

Chapter Outline	Instructional Ideas	Supplement Sources
The Prosecutorial System *Politics and Prosecution* *The Prosecutor's Influence* *The Prosecutor's Roles* *Discretion of the Prosecutor* *Key Relationships of the Prosecutor* *Decision-Making Policies* *Implementing Prosecution Policy*	Lecture Suggestion 8.1–8.4 PowerPoint 10.1–10.6, 10.21 FFH Video: The Court Process—The Prosecutor CNN Video #8: Rape Prosecution	Multiple Choice 8.1–8.17 True-False 8.1–8.14 Essay Question 8.1–8.2 Study Guide Worksheet 8.1
The Defense Attorney: *Image and Reality* *The Role of the Defense Attorney* *Realities of the Defense Attorney's Job* *Private Counsel: An Endangered Species?* *The Environment of Criminal Practice* *Counsel for Indigents* *Methods of Providing Indigents with Counsel* *Private versus Public Defense* *Defense Counsel in the System* *Attorney Competence*	Lecture Suggestion 8.5–8.8 PowerPoint 10.7–10.19 FFH Video: The Court Process—The Public Defender	Multiple Choice 8.18–8.32 True-False 8.15–8.25 Essay Question 8.3–8.4

INTERNET RESOURCES: Virtual Classroom Web Site and InfoTrac College Edition

Lecture Notes

9.1 Why would someone plead guilty in an implicit plea bargain without an actual promise of consideration in sentencing? Administrative systems can run on expectations that are informal and based on past practices. Even if a prosecutor were to abolish plea bargaining, defense attorneys would still expect prosecutors to appreciate and therefore reward guilty pleas which save the prosecutor and the court system the time and trouble of trial. If the prosecutors did not reward plea bargains, even those that were not formally negotiated, by reducing charges or recommending lighter sentences, there would be little incentive for defendants to plead guilty and the prosecutors would risk increasing their workload at a time when their resources are already severely stretched.

9.2 Why would someone plead guilty to a crime that they did not commit? There are several reasons that plea bargaining runs the risk of encouraging innocent people to plead guilty. First, the bail system may affect poor people in a way that they can keep their jobs and go home immediately by pleading guilty and taking probation as a punishment rather than pleading not guilty and staying in jail pending trial. Second, people who lack faith in the judicial system may believe that they will be convicted no matter what they do and therefore they are better off pleading guilty to a lesser offense rather than risking a more severe penalty. Many poor people feel fatalistic and unable to control their own lives. Unlike middle-class and affluent people who have enjoyed some success in life and therefore possess a degree of optimism and confidence, poor people may believe that things always go wrong and are out of their control. Thus they may opt to accept criminal punishment to avoid the risk of maximum penalties.

9.3 Why can't states effectively ban plea bargaining? Because bargaining advances the interests of all actors, plea bargaining cannot be abolished. Like other forms of discretion within the criminal justice system, it simply assumes new forms and moves to new points in the process. Without plea bargaining, many prosecutors and defense attorneys will engage in charge bargaining — bargaining about charges rather than about sentences. If prosecutors cannot engage in plea bargaining, judges may step into the process and take a more active role in discussing sentence agreements with defense attorneys. When California banned plea bargaining in Superior Court, bargaining simply moved to the preliminary proceedings in the Municipal Court. The movement of bargaining to an earlier stage in the proceeding was not necessarily beneficial because all parties were then engaged in bargaining at an early moment before the crime was completely investigated. By waiting until a later point, all parties involved could have had more complete and accurate information about the case in order to make a bargain that served all relevant interests, including the system's.

9.4 Are jurors sufficiently capable of comprehending what occurs at trial? A major debate among scholars concerns the capability of jurors to understand such things as expert testimony and judges' jury instructions. Clearly, many jurors base their decisions on improper considerations such as whether they like a certain witness, or whether they feel sorry for the defendant. In the American system, however, we have decided that we are willing to assume the risk of some "bad" jury decisions in order to use the jury as the mechanism to prevent abusive prosecutions and to have the voice of the community decide significant criminal justice cases. The potential deficiencies in individual jurors' capabilities are presumably balanced in many cases by the presence of jurors who possess a better grasp of the relevant evidence and issues.

9.5 What reforms might make juries better at performing their functions? A continuing criticism of juries is that they do not represent a cross-section of the community. Reforms might be aimed at expanding the juror pool beyond registered voters by including lists of licensed drivers, welfare recipients, and utilities customers. Because many poor people suffer greater burdens in serving on juries, greater consideration might be given to paying jurors a competitive wage for the time that they lose from work. Moreover, if a county made a real commitment to facilitating jury service, perhaps it could offer transportation and child care for jurors and thereby solve two problems that lead some people to avoid jury service.

With respect to the jury's participation in a trial, two innovations are emerging which are intended to help the jury have more complete information. Some judges permit jurors to take notes during the trial. Traditionally, jurors have been barred from taking notes for fear that they would miss some important testimony while they were busy writing and because anything written down inaccurately will seem to be correct, despite protestations to the contrary by other jurors, simply because it is on paper. By permitting jurors to take notes, judges hope to improve their memory and understanding of key facts. A second innovation is to permit jurors to ask questions of witnesses. Judges may permit jurors to submit written questions which, after being shown to the prosecutor and defense attorney, will be asked by the judge if approved. This permits jurors to have pertinent questions answered and, because the questioning is controlled by the judge, it avoids the presentation of any irrelevant or improper questions.

9.6 Why should prisoners be allowed to file appeals at all if they were represented by an attorney during the trial that resulted in their convictions? Representation by an attorney does not guarantee that a trial was fair or that a defendant's constitutional rights were respected. The appellate process provides a mechanism for reviewing whether mistakes were made by the actors who made critical decisions affecting a defendant's case. Moreover, the existence of the appellate process adds to the image of justice by conveying to observers, including defendants, the idea that the system will take care to ensure that proceedings were fair and relatively error-free. During the 1980s and 1990s, more than a dozen people were released from death row because it turned out that they were not guilty of the murders of which they were convicted. If there were no appellate process, innocent people might have been wrongly executed. The appellate process also provides a mechanism for encouraging relatively uniform and equitable outcomes among trial courts within an appellate court's jurisdiction. If one trial judge is notably harsh or lenient, the appeals process can push the deviant judge back into line with the other trial judges. Most importantly, the appeals process provides the mechanism for upholding individuals' constitutional rights. The rights asserted by criminal defendants, such as the right to be free from unreasonable searches and seizures, protect the innocent citizen as well as the guilty citizen, so there needs to be a mechanism for examining and vindicating the fundamental rights that protect everyone in the United States.

At a Glance

Chapter Nine

Chapter Outline	Instructional Ideas	Supplement Sources
Plea Bargaining *Exchange Relationships in Plea Bargaining* *Legal Issues in Plea Bargaining* *Justifications for Plea Bargaining* *Reforming Plea Bargaining*	Lecture Suggestion 9.1–9.3 Class Discussion Exercise 9.1 PowerPoint 11.18–11.26 FFH Video: Plea Bargaining	Multiple Choice 9.1–9.5 True-False 9.1–9.6 Essay Question 9.1 Study Guide Worksheet 9.1 Crime Scenes CD-ROM Fatal Trick and Inside Job
Trial: The Exceptional Case *Jury Trial* *The Trial Process* *Evaluating the Jury System*	Lecture Suggestion 9.4–9.5 Class Discussion Exercise 9.2 PowerPoint 12.1–12.2, 12.4, 12.14–12.30	Multiple Choice 9.6–9.24 True-False 9.7–9.18 Essay Question 9.2 Study Guide Worksheet 9.2 Crime Scenes CD-ROM Fatal Trick
Appeals *Basis for Appeals* *Habeas Corpus* *Evaluating the Appellate Process*	Lecture Suggestion 9.6 PowerPoint 12.34	Multiple Choice 9.25–9.26 True-False 9.19

INTERNET RESOURCES: Virtual Classroom Web Site and InfoTrac College Edition

Lecture Notes

10.1 If it is expensive to maintain prisons, why don't we just kill all convicts or send them to a deserted island? American approaches to sentencing are complicated by several factors. First, the prevailing philosophy of punishment at a given moment in history may keep society from disposing of criminal offenders. Rehabilitation theories, for example, are premised on the idea that deviants can be cured or otherwise redeemed. Retribution theories are based on the idea that crimes deserve measured punishments equal in severity to the harm caused by the crime. Second, the requirements of the U.S. Constitution limit the scope of punishments. The Eighth Amendment explicitly forbids "cruel and unusual punishments," and this requirement has been interpreted by the Supreme Court to include a prohibition on punishments that are disproportionate to a crime. Third, because of the fact that innocent people are sometimes wrongly convicted, there may be a reluctance to treat all offenders in an extreme manner that may make it difficult or impossible to reverse mistakes made in the judicial process.

10.2 Why do some critics consider the rehabilitation approach to be inhumane? Although rehabilitation theories are infused with humanitarian ideals about the possibility of "saving" deviants through appropriate treatment, rehabilitation-based punishments tend to seem unfair. For example, a murderer who was quickly regarded as rehabilitated could walk out of prison while a shoplifter with a bad attitude would remain behind, serving a longer sentence for a lesser crime. Such sentencing practices also create extreme uncertainty for prisoners who are left with no idea about how long they will have to serve for a specific crime. Indeterminate sentences may ultimately be counterproductive if they are destructive to the prisoners' morale and incentives for good behavior.

10.3 Which theory of punishment provides the most coherent justification for capital punishment? Deterrence is asserted to be a primary justification for capital punishment, but the evidence is mixed concerning the deterrence benefits of the death penalty. Deterrence presumes rationality, but many intentional homicides, especially those during the course of robberies or emotion-laden interpersonal conflicts, are impulsive rather than carefully calculated. And, of course, people seldom believe that they will be caught. Moreover, many criminal acts are committed during irrational states of being under the influence of alcohol, drugs, or emotional upset. Capital punishment does not have value for rehabilitation, except possibly if someone possesses religious beliefs about an afterlife or reincarnation. Capital punishment achieves incapacitation, but incapacitation would not seem to provide a specific justification for execution since life imprisonment achieves the same purpose just as effectively without the risk of irreversible error if an innocent person is wrongly convicted. Thus, arguably the most coherent justification for capital punishment is retribution. If one believes as a philosophical matter that "an eye for an eye" is an appropriate response to murder, then capital punishment is consistent with that philosophy for murderers. However, many people do not agree with this underlying philosophical assumption.

10.4 Why can't American society get tough on crime through the use of mandatory sentences enacted by legislatures? Because of the system characteristics of the criminal process, police, prosecutors, and defense attorneys can undercut mandatory sentencing in the charging and plea bargaining processes. If police or prosecutors believe that the legislature's mandatory sentence would be too severe in a particular case, they can charge the person with a lesser offense to avoid the mandated punishment. In addition, mandatory sentences may put extra pressure on the resources of corrections institutions.

10.5 Why can't we eliminate appeals for people sentenced to death in order to speed up the process of executions? Because people have a right to "due process" under the U.S. Constitution, we are not simply concerned with punishing wrongdoers. We also want to make sure that their trials were fair and accurate. Thus in the most serious cases that represent the top of the "Wedding Cake," there is extra activity by lawyers to ensure that proper procedures were followed. Several innocent people have recently been freed from death row who would have been wrongly executed if no appeals process existed. Some justices on the Supreme Court have argued that the appeals process can be limited because governors will use their commutation and pardon powers to handle any cases in which someone was wrongly convicted. However, because governors do not want to alienate a voting public that is angry about crime, such elected officials may be reluctant to commute sentences in some cases for fear that the voters do not recognize that an injustice is about to be done. Because most inmates on death row are poor and many are from minority groups, these people lack the resources and social standing to generate public sympathy and support, even when there are strong indications that they were wrongly convicted.

10.6 Is it desirable to permit judges to use their discretion in determining the appropriate sentence for convicted offenders? The application of judicial discretion permits judges to individualize punishments. Judges can consider whether a particular defendant shows promise of rehabilitation or whether the defendant is more culpable for showing no remorse. Discretion also permits judges to consider the individual circumstances of each crime and each criminal. On the other hand, however, discretion always produces discrimination. Offenders who have been convicted of the same offense will receive different sentences because a judge may be more sympathetic to one defendant. Similarly, defendants sentenced by different judges may receive differing sentences because the values and attitudes of each judge are different rather than the seriousness of the offenses being different. In sum, the question is answerable only in terms of the observer's sense about how the criminal justice system ought to operate and what sentencing priorities ought to be.

At a Glance
Chapter Ten

Chapter Outline	Instructional Ideas	Supplement Sources
The Goals of Punishment *Retribution—Deserved Punishment* *Deterrence* *Incapacitation* *Rehabilitation*	Lecture Suggestion 10.1–10.3 PowerPoint 13.2–13.4	Multiple Choice 10.1–10.5 True-False 10.1–10.8 Study Guide Worksheet 10.1 Essay Question 10.1–10.2 Crime Scenes: CD-ROM Behind Bars
Forms of the Criminal Sanction *Incarceration* *Intermediate Sanctions* *Probation* *Death*	Lecture Suggestion 10.4–10.5 PowerPoint 13.1, 13.6–13.11, 13.14–13.15, 13.17–13.21 CNN Video #9: Death Penalty	Multiple Choice 10.6–10.18 True-False 10.9–10.15 Essay Question 10.3 Crime Scenes CD-ROM Instrument of Death
The Sentencing Process *The Administrative Context of Courts* *Attitudes and Values of Judges* *Presentence Report* *Sentencing Guidelines* *Who Gets the Harshest Punishment?*	Lecture Suggestion 10.6 Class Discussion Exercise 10.1 PowerPoint 12.41, 13.12–13.13, 13.16	Multiple Choice 10.19–10.23 True-False 10.16–10.20 Essay Question 10.4 Study Guide Worksheet 10.2 Crime Scenes CD-ROM Instrument of Death

INTERNET RESOURCES: Virtual Classroom Web Site and InfoTrac College Edition

Lecture Notes

11.1 Does imprisonment work? The history of the penitentiary indicates that at various stages in time people have had differing expectations about how imprisonment ought to affect crime and criminal offenders. Much of the history of imprisonment reflects efforts to reform individuals so that they will no longer commit crimes. Recent usage of imprisonment has focused on retribution and incapacitation with little regard for or confidence in notions of rehabilitation. The effectiveness of imprisonment can only be assessed when one specifies which goals are being pursued. If the effectiveness of imprisonment is judged according to whether or not it reduces the crime rate, then history seems to indicate that imprisonment has questionable impact. Crime in the 1980s remained at fairly high levels even as prison populations soared. High imprisonment rates may have prevented crime rates from moving higher, but it seems quite clear that American society contains plenty of people who, under current social conditions, will commit crimes no matter how imprisonment is used within boundaries of constitutional law. If imprisonment is for the purpose of punishment rather than for crime prevention, then it "works" in the sense that it imposes hardships on offenders who must suffer the "pains of imprisonment."

11.2 If half of the people in jails had not yet been convicted of any crime and therefore are presumed innocent, shouldn't jail facilities and conditions be better than those in prison so that these people are not "punished" until after they are convicted? Ideally, people who have not yet been convicted of any crime should be merely held and not "punished" like convicted offenders. However, because local governments are responsible for jails and have few incentives for investing scarce resources in the comfort of people drawn into the criminal justice system, jail conditions are frequently much worse than those in prisons. It is regarded as too expensive to build separate holding facilities for the unconvicted detainees and the convicted misdemeanants. Moreover, because jails have "revolving doors" with respect to people released on bail or those who have charges dropped, there is little incentive to give sustained attention to the experiences of detainees who will likely be inside for only a short period of time. In addition, because most of the unconvicted detainees in jails are poor (i.e., they could not make bail), they and their families have no political clout with which to pressure legislatures to reform jail conditions.

11.3 Should jails have fire escapes? Because many people in jails have never been convicted of criminal offenses—and even those who have been convicted are generally serving only brief sentences for minor offenses, it seems especially unjust to imagine that these people might die if there was a fire at a jail. However, because corrections-type facilities are built to keep people in and prevent escapes, many jails, especially older ones, have no mechanisms for preventing deaths in the event of a fire. Some courts have ordered local jails to improve conditions, but local officials frequently have little money to spend on jails—and they do not wish to use resources in a way that their political opponents might label as "coddling criminals." Thus, even needed improvements in jail facilities are hampered by politics, tradition, and scarce resources.

At a Glance

Chapter Eleven

Chapter Outline	Instructional Ideas	Supplement Sources
Development of Corrections *Invention of the Penitentiary* *Reform in the United States* *Reformatory Movement* *Improving Prison Conditions for Women* *Reforms of the Progressives* *Rehabilitation Model* *Community Model* *Crime Control Model*	Lecture Suggestion 11.1 Class Discussion Exercise 11.1 FFH Video: The History of Corrections CNN Video #10: Tough Prison Alternative CNN Video #12: Women in Prison	Multiple Choice 11.1–11.13 True-False 11.1–11.8 Essay Question 11.1 Study Guide Worksheet 11.1
Organization of Corrections in the United States *Federal Corrections System* *State Corrections System* *Jails: Local Correctional Facilities*	Lecture Suggestion 11.2–11.3	Multiple Choice 11.16–11.21 True-False 11.9–11.13 Essay Question 11.2
Issues in Corrections *Incarceration Trends* *Who Is in Prison?*		Multiple Choice 11.22–11.26 True-False 11.14 Essay Question 11.3 Study Guide Worksheet 11.2
What of the Future?		

INTERNET RESOURCES: Virtual Classroom Web Site and InfoTrac College Edition

Lecture Notes

12.1 If probationers have already been given due process rights when they were convicted of crimes, why should they have additional due process rights when they violate the terms of their probation? The Supreme Court's requirement of providing hearings for probation revocation represents a recognition that the Bill of Rights is intended to protect against arbitrary and abusive exercises of governmental power. If there were no hearing requirement, probation revocation might occur instantly at the discretion of a probation officer. Thus there would be no official procedure to check whether an actual violation had indeed occurred or whether a vindictive probation officer was unfairly seeking to have a probationer incarcerated without an appropriate reason. The loss of liberty that is represented by incarceration is a serious matter under American democratic and legal traditions, so the Court has simply required that this serious matter be given the attention that it deserves in order to protect the individual from the risk of arbitrary government action.

12.2 If the technical aspects of electric monitoring devices can be perfected, why wouldn't home detention be an excellent — and inexpensive — alternative to incarceration? If the monitoring devices had no problems, home detention would indeed be a less expensive alternative to incarceration. Significant problems would still remain with respect to its usage. Home monitoring still requires personnel for supervision and enforcement of violations. In addition, there are questions about whether home monitoring is sufficient "punishment" for crimes. If offenders are sitting at home in their livingrooms watching television every night with their friends and families, little may have been accomplished by the criminal justice system except for limiting the movement of offenders. Moreover, the offenders' continued contacts with friends in the neighborhood environment may not have any effect on disrupting ongoing criminal enterprises in which the offender has participated.

12.3 If some prisoners choose prison instead of intensive probation supervision (IPS), why don't we just force them into IPS rather than giving them a choice? Probationers need self-motivation in order to fulfill the conditions of IPS. If they would rather go to prison, it is not worthwhile to place them in IPS since they will simply violate the terms of the probation and force authorities to place them into prison anyway.

At a Glance

Chapter Twelve

Chapter Outline	Instructional Ideas	Supplement Sources
Community Corrections: Assumptions		Multiple Choice 12.1–12.3 True-False 12.1 Essay 12.1
Probation: Correction Without Incarceration *Origins and Evolution of Probation* *Organization of Probation* *Probation Services* *Revocation of Probation* *Assessing Probation*	Lecture Suggestion 12.1	Multiple Choice 12.4–12.12 True-False 12.2–12.4 Essay Question 12.2 Study Guide Worksheet 12.1
Intermediate Sanctions in The Community *Intermediate Sanctions Administered Primarily by the Judiciary* *Intermediate Sanctions Administered in the Community* *Intermediate Sanctions Administered in Institutions and the Community* *Implementing Intermediate Sanctions*	Lecture Suggestion 12.2–12.3	Multiple Choice 12.13–12.22 True-False 12.5–12.12 Essay Question 12.3
Community Corrections: Approaching the Twenty-First Century	Class Discussion Exercise 12.1	True-False 12.13 Study Guide Worksheet 12.2

INTERNET RESOURCES: Virtual Classroom Web Site and InfoTrac College Edition

Lecture Notes

13.1 Why don't prisons hire more guards or assert more control over prisoners so that there is no risk of correctional officers' co-optation from dependence on exchange relations? First, it is expensive to hire additional personnel, especially if one considered how many more officers would have to be hired to even begin reducing the ratio of prisoners per officer. Second, officers are often dealing with "clients" who feel that they have little, if nothing, to lose by misbehaving. When prisoners are serving long terms, relatively few sanctions and rewards are meaningful. Moreover, the necessity of creating rewards automatically generates a situation in which cooperative human interactions may produce the risk of co-optation. Finally, judicial decisions and institutional policies limit the kinds of actions that officers can take in order to sanction prisoners. These limitations stem, in part, from a historical recognition that unlimited power on the part of government officials may produce abusive behavior. In the prison context, such abusive behavior led to torture, beatings, and other inhumane actions directed at prisoners in earlier generations.

13.2 Why can't correctional officials stamp out the prisoner economy since it can increase the risk of conflicts, thefts, and exploitation of prisoners by other prisoners? Correctional institutions rely heavily on prisoners to perform many of the tasks needed to keep the institution functioning. Prisoners work in the kitchen, laundry, furniture repair shop, and many other locations within the prison. These jobs give the prisoners opportunities to obtain goods and provide the fuel for the economy. It would be very expensive to replace prisoners with full-time state employees in these positions. Moreover, these positions provide the opportunities for prisoners to earn money for their accounts, gain skills, and occupy their time in a useful manner. Thus the prisoner economy is a natural by-product of the everyday functions of the institution. Many economists would claim that human beings will naturally engage in exchanges in order to satisfy their needs for goods and services. Any actions to eliminate the prisoner economy would probably just force the economy to adapt, adjust, and assume a new form.

13.3 Would there be any possible benefits from having "coed" correctional institutions that have men and women serving time in the same institutions? Penal institutions (e.g., local jails) initially housed every demographic group together. Early corrections reformers sought the creation of separate facilities for men and women. While some people may believe that the presence of women may soften some of the tougher aspects of male prisons, there are also risks that women may be victimized or may become the focus of conflicts between male prisoners. Some observers are also concerned that only selected prisoners can be trusted to behave appropriately in a mixed setting. Co-corrections facilities exist in the U.S. and provide a means to give women access to the same programs available to men. The nature of these institutions can vary. Some simply house both sexes under one roof, but others mix men and women together for programs and other daily activities. Such institutions may require special restrictions and supervision. As prison crowding increases, however, correctional administrators may be forced to find ways to use co-corrections as the most effective method of allocating scarce resources.

13.4 What kinds of tangible steps can a prison administrator take to reduce the risk of violence? Administrators must think in terms of motivations for and opportunities for violence. Inmates' psychological frustrations may, for example, be reduced if they believe that the institution listens to their concerns, including concerns about alleged mistreatment by correctional officers. Thus the creation of a credible grievance process may help to alleviate some anger that may develop within the institution. In addition, institutions can create mechanisms so that prisoners who are fearful of victimization can come forward and seek assistance from staff. Opportunities for violence can be reduced by redesigning facilities to prevent the existence of "blind spots" that cannot be observed by staff. Administrators can also increase conflict resolution training for staff and perhaps develop other kinds of training that will enable them to control prisoners without generating violent conflicts.

13.5 Why should prisoners have rights? Haven't they forfeited their rights by breaking society's rules? Under a "social contract" philosophy, people who break society's rules will lose the protections and benefits of being members of society. The U.S. Constitution, however, is not based on a social contract philosophy. It does not say anything about the forfeiture of rights. Instead, it is based on "natural rights" ideas that everyone automatically possesses specific rights. Thus the Eighth Amendment's prohibition against "cruel and unusual punishments" may be ambiguous, but it clearly dictates *some kind of limitation* on what the government can do to people who violate criminal laws. By its words and intentions, the Constitution clearly does not contemplate a complete forfeiture of rights.

13.6 Why do judges have the authority to tell correctional officials how to manage prisons? This power exercised by judges is subject to dispute. Normally we expect legislatures to create laws which are administered by officials in the executive branch of government. Corrections officials are executive branch officers who normally use their expertise and discretion to decide how best to run government institutions. However, because judges have the responsibility for determining whether or not prisoners' constitutional rights have been violated, judges inevitably find themselves "second guessing" decisions and actions taken by corrections officials which may violate the Constitution. In this process of overseeing corrections policies and decisions, judges find themselves telling corrections officials what they can and cannot do. Many judges do everything possible to avoid telling corrections officials that they must take specific actions. Instead, they tell the officials which conditions need to be corrected and then leave it to the officials to decide how best to achieve the conditions and practices necessary to uphold constitutional standards. When the corrections officials do not cooperate or lack the resources to comply with judges' orders, judges often involve themselves in day-to-day operations of correctional institutions in order to ensure that a prison's policies and practices do not violate constitutional standards.

At a Glance

Chapter Thirteen

Chapter Outline	Instructional Ideas	Supplement Sources
The Modern Prison: Legacy of the Past		Multiple Choice 13.1–13.3 True-False 13.1–13.2
Goals of Incarceration		Multiple Choice 13.4 True-False 13.3 Study Guide Worksheet 13.1 Crime Scenes CD-ROM Behind Bars
Prison Organization *Three Lines of Command* *The Importance of Management*		Multiple Choice 13.5–13.7 True-False 13.4–13.5 Crime Scenes CD-ROM Behind Bars
Governing a Society of Captives *The Limits of Total Power* *Rewards and Punishments* *Gaining Cooperation: Exchange Relationships* *Inmate Leadership* *The Challenge of Governing Prisons*	Lecture Suggestion 13.1	Multiple Choice 13.8–13.10 True-False 13.6–13.7
Correctional Officers: The Linchpin of Management *The Officer's Role* *Recruitment of Officers*		Multiple Choice 13.11–13.12 True–False 13.8–13.10 Essay Question 13.1
The Convict World *Adaptive Roles* *The Prison Economy*	Lecture Suggestion 13.2 FFH Video: Prison Society	Multiple Choice 13.13–13.19 True-False 13.11–13.12
Women in Prison *Social Relationships* *Male and Female Subcultures Compared* *Programs and the Female Role* *Medical Services* *Mothers and Their Children*	Lecture Suggestion 13.3 CNN Video #11: Prison Medical Services CNN Video #12: Women in Prison	Multiple Choice 13.20–13.25 True-False 13.13–13.16 Essay Question 13.2
Prison Programs *Classification of Prisoners* *Educational Programs* *Vocational Education* *Prison Industries* *Rehabilitative Programs*		Multiple Choice 13.26–13.30 Study Guide Worksheet 13.2
Violence in Prisons *Assaultive Behavior and Inmate Characteristics* *Prison–Prisoner Violence* *Prison–Officer Violence* *Officer–Prisoner Violence* *Decreasing Prison Violence*	Lecture Suggestion 13.4 Class Discussion Exercise 13.1	Multiple Choice 13.31–13.33 True-False 13.17–13.19 Study Guide Worksheet 13.3 Essay Question 13.3
Prisoner's Rights *First Amendment* *Fourth Amendment* *Eighth Amendment* *Fourteenth Amendment* *Redress of Grievances* *A Change of Judicial Direction?* *Impact of the Prisoner's Rights Movement*	Lecture Suggestion 13.5–13.6 Class Discussion Exercise 13.2	Multiple Choice 13.34–13.41 True-False 13.20–13.22 Study Guide Worksheet 13.4 Essay Question 13.4

INTERNET RESOURCES: Virtual Classroom Web Site and InfoTrac College Edition

Lecture Notes

14.1 In order to avoid the risk of discrimination by parole boards, couldn't set criteria for release be established and applied without creating a system in which everyone automatically was released on parole? In mandatory release systems, the risk of discrimination is avoided by applying such parole guidelines and determinate sentences. However, this creates the potential for making nearly any prisoner eligible for parole if they exhibit acceptable behavior. This alternative is not attractive in many states because of some policy makers' concerns that certain prisoners should *not* be released and because of a recognition that set criteria might not adequately distinguish between risky and less-risky potential parolees. For example, if one requirement for release was participation in education, counseling, or other prison programs, how does one know what the *quality* of the prisoner's participation has been? How can any criteria adequately judge the prisoner's attitude? How does one account for the heinous nature of varying acts by different prisoners which might all have resulted in convictions on the same charge of "aggravated assault"? Parole boards are very imperfect mechanisms for making consistent, equitable decisions. However, such boards provide a basis for preventing releases when there are questions about qualitative factors that underlie the criteria for release. Parole boards also provide reassurance to the public that *someone* has examined the prisoner's situation before deciding on release, and such boards also provide a focal point for public dissatisfaction if a parolee commits a serious crime. Thus, discretion and attendant discrimination are an understandable part of the process in many states.

14.2 Shouldn't parole boards always be composed of corrections professionals rather than citizens who happen to have some political connections? Corrections professionals might make different decisions than citizens would make. However, no one can accurately predict the future behavior of criminal offenders. Moreover, even corrections professionals would be guided by values and subjective judgments in determining which offenders qualify as good risks who are deserving of early release. In some respects, a citizen parole board helps to deflect pressure away from corrections professionals who might otherwise receive more "blame" and perhaps even threats to their job security if a parolee commits crimes soon after release.

14.3 Shouldn't parole officers be instructed to have "zero tolerance" for any violations by people who have already proven in the past that they cannot live by society's rules? Parole officers can be instructed to have "zero tolerance," but that never means that they will act on that basis. Even tough parole officers may be flexible concerning what they view as inadvertent violations, such as, for example, a curfew violation when the parolee's mother's car breaks down while bringing the parolee back to a halfway house after a Sunday family dinner. Moreover, the administrative pressures on parole officers with high caseloads may lead them to let "small" violations slip rather than go through revocation procedures when their time is better spent monitoring other, more serious offenders.

At a Glance
Chapter Fourteen

Chapter Outline	Instructional Ideas	Supplement Sources
Parole: Reentry into Society *The Origins of Parole* *The Development of Parole in the United States*		Multiple Choice 14.1–14.4 True-False 14.1–1.4
Release Mechanisms *Discretionary Release* *Mandatory Release* *Unconditional Release* *The Organization of Releasing Authorities* *The Decision to Release*	Lecture Suggestion 14.1–14.2 Class Discussion Exercise 14.1	Multiple Choice 14.5–14.11 True-False 14.5–14.11 Study Guide Worksheet 14.1
Supervision in the Community *Community Programs Following Release* *Parole Officer: Cop or Social Worker?* *Adjustment to Life Outside Prison* *Revocation of Parole*	Lecture Suggestion 14.3 CNN Video #3: Sex Offender Registration Laws	Multiple Choice 14.12–14.16 True-False 14.12–14.18 Essay Question 14.3 Study Guide Worksheet 14.2 Crime Scenes CD-ROM Behind Bars
Pardon		Multiple Choice 14.17 True-False 14.19
The Civil Disabilities of Ex-Felons		Multiple Choice 14.18 True-False 14.20

INTERNET RESOURCES: Virtual Classroom Web Site and InfoTrac College Edition

Lecture Notes

15.1 If juveniles commit terrible crimes, why shouldn't society treat them as adults no matter how old they are? One fundamental question in our legal system in how old someone must be in order to be held fully responsible for their actions. With respect to children, how old must a child be to understand the nature and consequences of their actions? If a four-year-old child finds a gun in a drawer and shoots a playmate, does that child have sufficient understanding of the wrongfulness of the action? The determination of age of responsibility may vary by the individual child, but it is not necessarily easy for a judge to make the determination. Moreover, because of the rehabilitation orientation of juvenile justice during the twentieth century, the system's processes have automatically been premised on the idea that juveniles are amenable to treatment and should not be punished in the same manner as adults.

15.2 Why can't we develop a system that does not place so much discretion in the hands of justice system officials? For example, the tremendous discretion exercised by police creates the risk of discrimination. The tremendous discretion exercised by intake officials in the juvenile system is enhanced by the rehabilitation philosophy that has served as the foundation of twentieth century juvenile justice. Someone must make determinations about which youngsters will be amenable to which forms of treatment and education. However, even if the system was changed to a retribution orientation in which every juvenile would receive the same punishment for the same crime, there would still be discretion in the system. Mandatory sentences in the juvenile system cannot prevent police officers from making initial discretionary decisions about which juveniles to arrest, which to release to their parents, and which to make subject to the pursuit of formal charges.

15.3 How might critics of the juvenile system seek to reform the system? Critics who believe that juveniles do not receive adequate punishment would like to see more juveniles treated in the same manner as adults, i.e., through the application of retribution rather than rehabilitation. Critics who believe that the system sweeps in too many young people would like to see neglect and dependency cases moved outside of a system that focuses on treating and punishing misbehavior. Moreover, critics seek to prevent serious punishments against juveniles for actions that would not be crimes if committed by adults. In addition, critics argue that juveniles, who risk being detained until the age of majority, should not be held for longer periods than adult offenders.

At a Glance

Chapter Fifteen

Chapter Outline	Instructional Ideas	Supplement Sources
Youth Crime in the United States	Class Discussion Exercise 15.1 CNN Video #1: DARE Program	Multiple Choice 15.1–15.3 True-False 15.1
The Development of Juvenile Justice *The Refuge Period* *The Juvenile Court Period* *The Juvenile Rights Period* *The Crime Control Period*	Lecture Suggestion 15.1	Multiple Choice 15.4–15.11 True-False 15.2–15.7 Essay Question 15.1 Study Guide Worksheet 15.1
The Juvenile Justice System *Age of Clients* *Categories of Cases Under Juvenile Court Jurisdiction*	FFH Video: Juvenile Justice Court TV Video: *Washington v Drake*	Multiple Choice 15.2–15.3 Multiple Choice 15.8–15.10
Juvenile Justice Operations *Police Interface* *Intake* *Diversion* *Transfer to Adult Court* *Detention* *Adjudication* *Corrections*	Lecture Suggestion 15.2 CNN Video #14: Teenage Killer CNN Video #15: Youth Bootcamp	Multiple Choice 15.14–15.21 True-False 15.11–15.19 Essay Question 15.2 Crime Scenes CD-ROM Instrument of Death
Problems and Perspectives	Lecture Suggestion 15.3	Multiple Choice 15.22–15.23 True-False 15.20 Study Guide Worksheet 15.2

INTERNET RESOURCES: Virtual Classroom Web Site and InfoTrac College Edition

Criminal Justice in America

About the Authors

GEORGE F. COLE (below right) is Professor of Political Science at the University of Connecticut. A specialist in the administration of criminal justice, he has published extensively on such topics as prosecution, courts, and corrections. George Cole is also co-author with Christopher Smith of *The American System of Criminal Justice*, co-author with Todd Clear of *American Corrections*, and co-editor with Marc Gertz of *Criminal Justice System: Politics and Policies.* He developed and directed the graduate corrections program at the University of Connecticut and was a Fellow at the National Institute of Justice (1988). Among his other accomplishments, he has been granted two awards under the Fulbright-Hays Program to conduct criminal justice research in England and the former Yugoslavia. In 1955 he was named a Fellow of the Academy of Criminal Justice Sciences for distinguished teaching and research.

Christopher E. Smith (below left) is Associate Professor of Criminal Justice at Michigan State University. Trained as a lawyer and social scientist, he is the author of thirteen books and more than sixty scholarly articles on law, courts, and criminal justice policy. His most recent books include *Courts, Politics, and the Judicial Process*, 2nd Ed. (1997) and *The Rehnquist Court and Criminal Punishment* (1997). He is also the co-author, with George F. Cole, of *The American System of Criminal Justice* (1998).

Criminal Justice in America

SECOND EDITION

GEORGE F. COLE

UNIVERSITY OF CONNECTICUT

CHRISTOPHER E. SMITH

MICHIGAN STATE UNIVERSITY

West/Wadsworth

I(T)P® An International Thomson Publishing Company

Belmont, CA • Albany, NY • Boston • Cincinnati
Johannesburg • London • Madrid • Melbourne
Mexico City • New York • Pacific Grove, CA
Scottsdale, AZ • Singapore • Tokyo • Toronto

Criminal Justice Editor SABRA HORNE
Development Editor DAN ALPERT
Project Development Editor CLAIRE MASSON
Editorial Assistant CHERIE HACKELBERG
Marketing Manager MIKE DEW
Project Manager DEBBY KRAMER
Production GREG HUBIT BOOKWORKS
Print Buyer KAREN HUNT
Permissions Editor SUSAN WALTERS
Text and Cover Design NORMAN BAUGHER
Copy Editor FRAN HASELSTEINER
Photo Research ROBERTA SPIECKERMAN ASSOCIATES
Cover Imaages FLAG: CORBIS/WESTLIGHT, RON WATTS; GUN: A. RAMEY/WOODFIN CAMP & ASSOCAITES; BADGE: MIKE JENSEN/FROZEN IMAGES, INC.; GAVEL: S. FIELD/H. ARMSTRONG ROBERTS; JAIL: PHOTODISK
Compositor and Illustrator ROSA+WESLEY DESIGN ASSOCIATES
Prepress H&S GRAPHICS
Text and Cover Printer VON HOFFMANN PRESS

FOR MORE INFORMATION, CONTACT WASDWORTH PUBLISHING COMPANY, 10 DAVIS DRIVE, BELMONT, CA 94002 OR ELECTRONICALLY AT HTTP://WWW.THOMSON.COM/WADSWORTH.HTML

International Thomson Publishing Europe
Berkshire House 168-173
High Holborn
London WC1V 7AA, England

Thomas Nelson Australia
102 Dodds Streest
South Melbourne 3205
Victoria, Australia

Nelson Canada
1120 Birchmount Road
Scarborough, Ontario
Canada M1K 5G4

International Thomson Editores
Campos Eliseos 383, Piso 7
Col. Polanco
11560 México D.F. México

International Thomson Publishing Asia
60 Albert Street
#15-01 Albert Complex
Singapore 189969

International Thomson Publishing Japan
Hirakawacho Kyowa Building, 3F
2-2-1 Hirakawacho
Chiyoda-ku, Tokyo 102, Japan

International Thomson Publishing
Southern Africa
Building 18, Constania Park
240 Old Pretoria Road
Halfway House, 1685 South Africa

Printed in the United States of America
1 2 3 4 5 6 7 8 9 10

Library of Congress Cataloging-in-Publication Data
Cole, George F.
Criminal justice in America / George F. Cole, Christopher E. Smith—2nd ed.
p. cm.
Includes bibliographical references and index.
ISBN 0-534-54666-8
1. Criminal justice, Administration of—United States. I. Smith, Christopher E. II. Title.
KF9223.C648 1999
364.973—dc20

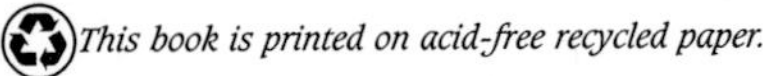
This book is printed on acid-free recycled paper.

BRIEF Contents

Preface xi

PART I *The Criminal Justice Process*

CHAPTER 1 Crime and Justice in America 2
CHAPTER 2 The Criminal Justice System 25
CHAPTER 3 Criminal Justice and the Rule of Law 46

PART II *Police*

CHAPTER 4 Police 72
CHAPTER 5 Police Operations 93
CHAPTER 6 Policing: Issues and Trends 122

PART III *Courts*

CHAPTER 7 Courts and Pretrial Processes 150
CHAPTER 8 Prosecution and Defense 176
CHAPTER 9 Determination of Guilt: Plea Bargaining and Trials 202
CHAPTER 10 Punishment and Sentencing 224

PART IV *Corrections*

CHAPTER 11 Corrections 254
CHAPTER 12 Community Corrections: Probation and Intermediate Sanctions 275
CHAPTER 13 Incarceration and Prison Society 295
CHAPTER 14 Release and Supervision in the Community 326

PART V *The Juvenile Justice System*

CHAPTER 15 Juvenile Justice 352

APPENDIX A *Constitution of the United States: Criminal Justice Amendments 377*

APPENDIX B *Careers in Criminal Justice 378*

References 383
Glossary 392
Name Index 397
Subject Index 401
Credits 406

Contents

Preface xi

PART I *The Criminal Justice Process*

CHAPTER 1
Crime and Justice in America 2

Crime in America 3

Defining Crime 4

Types of Crime 4

Occupational Crime 5

Organized Crime 5

Visible Crime 6

Crimes without Victims 6

Political Crime 7

How Much Crime Is There? 7

The Uniform Crime Reports 8

The National Crime Victimization Surveys 9

Trends in Crime 10

Crime Victimization 12

Who Is Victimized? 12

The Impact of Crime 15

The Experience of Victims within the Criminal Justice System 16

The Role of Victims in Crime 17

Women and Crime 17

Crime and Justice in a Multicultural Society 18

Explanation 1: Minorities Commit More Crimes 19

Explanation 2: The Criminal Justice System Is Racist 20

Explanation 3: America Is a Racist society 21

Crime and Justice as Public Policy Issues 21

CHAPTER 2
The Criminal Justice System 25

The Goals of Criminal Justice 26

Doing Justice 26

Controlling Crime 27

Preventing Crime 27

Criminal Justice in a Federal System 28

Two Justice Systems 28

Expansion of Federal Involvement 29

Criminal Justice as a Social System 30

The System Perspective 31

Characteristics of the Criminal Justice System 31

Operations of Criminal Justice Agencies 34

Police 35

Courts 35

Corrections 36

The Flow of Decision Making in the Criminal Justice System 37

Steps in the Decision-Making Process 38

THE CRIMINAL JUSTICE WEDDING CAKE 41

CRIME CONTROL VERSUS DUE PROCESS 43

CHAPTER 3
Criminal Justice and the Rule of Law 46

Foundations of Criminal Law 47

SUBSTANTIVE LAW AND PROCEDURAL LAW 48

Substantive Criminal Law 48

SEVEN PRINCIPLES OF CRIMINAL LAW 49

ELEMENTS OF A CRIME 51

STATUTORY DEFINITIONS OF CRIMES 51

RESPONSIBILITY FOR CRIMINAL ACTS 52

Procedural Criminal Law 58

THE BILL OF RIGHTS 58

THE FOURTEENTH AMENDMENT AND DUE PROCESS 59

THE DUE PROCESS REVOLUTION 59

THE FOURTH AMENDMENT: PROTECTION AGAINST UNREASONABLE SEARCHES AND SEIZURES 60

THE FIFTH AMENDMENT: PROTECTION AGAINST SELF-INCRIMINATION AND DOUBLE JEOPARDY 62

THE SIXTH AMENDMENT: THE RIGHT TO COUNSEL AND A FAIR TRIAL 64

THE EIGHTH AMENDMENT: PROTECTION AGAINST EXCESSIVE BAIL, EXCESSIVE FINES, AND CRUEL AND UNUSUAL PUNISHMENT 65

Constitutional Rights and Criminal Justice Professionals 66

A Journey Inside the Criminal Justice System and Beyond: One Man's Journey
My Affair with Heroin 69

PART II *Police*

CHAPTER 4
Police 72

The Development of Police in the United States 73

THE ENGLISH ROOTS OF THE AMERICAN POLICE 73

POLICING IN THE UNITED STATES 75

Organization of the Police 80

FEDERAL AGENCIES 80

STATE AGENCIES 81

COUNTY AGENCIES 81

MUNICIPAL AGENCIES 82

Police Policy 82

Police Functions 85

ORDER MAINTENANCE 86

LAW ENFORCEMENT 87

SERVICE 87

IMPLEMENTING THE MANDATE 88

Police Actions 88

ENCOUNTERS BETWEEN POLICE AND CITIZENS 88

POLICE DISCRETION 89

DOMESTIC VIOLENCE 89

CHAPTER 5
Police Operations 93

Organization of the Police 94

Police Response and Action 96

ORGANIZATIONAL RESPONSE 96

PRODUCTIVITY 98

Delivery of Police Services 98

PATROL FUNCTIONS 99

ISSUES IN PATROLLING 100

THE FUTURE OF PATROL 109

INVESTIGATION 109

SPECIAL OPERATIONS 114

Police Actions and the Rule of Law 115

SEARCH AND SEIZURE 116

ARREST 118

INTERROGATION 118

CHAPTER 6
Policing: Issues and Trends 122

Who Are the Police? 123

Recruitment 123

Training 123

The Changing Profile of the Police 124

The Police Subculture 126

The Working Personality 127

Police Isolation 128

Job Stress 129

Police and the Community 130

Policing in a Multicultural Society 131

Community Crime Prevention 133

Police Abuse of Power 134

Use of Force 134

Corruption 136

Civic Accountability 138

Internal Affairs Units 138

Civilian Review Boards 138

Standards and Accreditation 139

Civil Liability Suits 140

Private Policing 141

Functions of Private Police 141

Private Employment of Public Police 143

The Public-Private Interface 144

Recruitment and Training 145

A Journey Inside the Criminal Justice System and Beyond: One Man's Journey
Stepping into a New World: Arrested, Booked, Charged, Jailed, and Investigated 147

PART III Courts

CHAPTER 7
Courts and Pretrial Processes 150

The Structure of American Courts 151

Effective Management of the State Courts 153

To Be a Judge 153

Who Becomes a Judge? 154

Functions of the Judge 154

How to Become a Judge 156

From Arrest to Trial or Plea 159

Bail: Pretrial Release 161

The Reality of the Bail System 162

Bail Bondsmen 162

Setting Bail 163

Reforming the Bail System 166

Pretrial Detention 169

The Courtroom: How It Functions 170

The Courtroom Workgroup 171

The Impact of Courtroom Workgroups 172

CHAPTER 8
Prosecution and Defense 176

The Prosecutorial System 177

Politics and Prosecution 178

The Prosecutor's Influence 178

The Prosecutor's Roles 179

Discretion of the Prosecutor 180

Key Relationships of the Prosecutor 181

Decision-Making Policies 183

The Defense Attorney: Image and Reality 187

The Role of the Defense Attorney 188

Realities of the Defense Attorney's Job 188

Private Counsel: An Endangered Species? 191

The Environment of Criminal Practice 192

Counsel for Indigents 193

Private versus Public Defense 197

CHAPTER 9
Determination of Guilt: Plea Bargaining and Trials 202

Plea Bargaining 203
Exchange Relationships in Plea Bargaining 204
Legal Issues in Plea Bargaining 206
Justifications for Plea Bargaining 207
Criticisms of Plea Bargaining 207
Reforming Plea Bargaining 208

Trial: The Exceptional Case 209
Jury Trial 210
The Trial Process 212
Evaluating the Jury System 218

Appeals 219
Basis for Appeals 219
Habeas Corpus 220
Evaluating the Appellate Process 221

CHAPTER 10
Punishment and Sentencing 224

The Goals of Punishment 225
Retribution—Deserved Punishment 225
Deterrence 226
Incapacitation 227
Rehabilitation 228

Forms of the Criminal Sanction 230
Incarceration 230
Intermediate Sanctions 234
Probation 234
Death 235

The Sentencing Process 239
The Administrative Context of the Courts 240
Attitudes and Values of Judges 242
Presentence Report 244
Sentencing Guidelines 246
Who Gets the Harshest Punishment? 248

A Journey Inside the Criminal Justice System and Beyond: One Man's Journey
Prosecution, Adjudication, and Sentencing 250

PART IV *Corrections*

CHAPTER 11
Corrections 254

Development of Corrections 255
The Invention of the Penitentiary 255
Reform in the United States 256
The Reformatory Movement 258
Improving Prison Conditions for Women 259
The Reforms of the Progressives 260
The Rehabilitation Model 260
The Community Model 261
The Crime Control Model 262

Organization of Corrections in the United States 262
Federal Corrections System 262
State Corrections Systems 263
Jails: Local Correctional Facilities 266

Issues in Corrections 267
Incarceration Trends 267
Who Is in Prison? 271

CHAPTER 12
Community Corrections: Probation and Intermediate Sanctions 275

Community Corrections: Assumptions 276

Probation: Correction without Incarceration 277
Origins and Evolution of Probation 278

Organization of Probation 279

Probation Services 279

Revocation of Probation 282

Assessing Probation 283

Intermediate Sanctions in the Community 283

Intermediate Sanctions Administered Primarily by the Judiciary 284

Intermediate Sanctions Administered in the Community 286

Intermediate Sanctions Administered in Institutions and the Community 289

Implementing Intermediate Sanctions 290

Community Corrections: Approaching the Twenty-First Century 292

CHAPTER 13

Incarceration and Prison Society 295

The Modern Prison: Legacy of the Past 296

Goals of Incarceration 297

Prison Organization 298

Three Lines of Command 298

The Importance of Management 301

Governing a Society of Captives 301

The Limits of Total Power 302

Rewards and Punishments 302

Gaining Cooperation: Exchange Relationships 302

Inmate Leadership 303

The Challenge of Governing Prisons 303

Correctional Officers: The Linchpin of Management 304

The Officer's Role 304

Recruitment of Officers 304

The Convict World 306

Adaptive Roles 309

The Prison Economy 309

Women in Prison 311

Social Relationships 311

Male and Female Subcultures Compared 312

Programs and the Female Role 313

Medical Services 313

Mothers and Their Children 313

Prison Programs 314

Classification of Prisoners 315

Educational Programs 315

Vocational Education 315

Prison Industries 316

Rehabilitative Programs 316

Violence in Prison 317

Assaultive Behavior and Inmate Characteristics 317

Prisoner-Prisoner Violence 318

Prisoner-Officer Violence 319

Officer-Prisoner Violence 319

Decreasing Prison Violence 319

Prisoners' Rights 320

First Amendment 321

Fourth Amendment 321

Eighth Amendment 322

Fourteenth Amendment 322

Impact of the Prisoners' Rights Movement 323

CHAPTER 14

Release and Supervision in the Community 326

Parole: Reentry into Society 327

The Origins of Parole 328

The Development of Parole in the United States 329

Release Mechanisms 329

Discretionary Release 329

Mandatory Release 330

Unconditional Release 330

The Organization of Releasing Authorities 330

The Decision to Release 331

Supervision in the Community 335

Community Programs Following Release 337

Parole Officer: Cop or Social worker? 340

Adjustment to Life Outside Prison 342

Revocation of Parole 344

The Future of Parole 345

A Journey Inside the Criminal Justice System and Beyond: One Man's Journey
Prison 347

PART V *The Juvenile Justice System*

CHAPTER 15
Juvenile Justice 352

Youth Crime in the United States 353

The Development of Juvenile Justice 354

The Refuge Period (1824–1899) 355

The Juvenile Court Period (1899–1960) 356

The Juvenile Rights Period (1960–1980) 357

The Crime Control Period (1980–Present) 358

The Juvenile Justice system 358

Age of Clients 359

Categories of Cases under Juvenile Court Jurisdiction 359

Juvenile Justice Operations 360

Police Interface 362

Intake 364

Diversion 364

Transfer to Adult Court 364

Detention 366

Adjudication 367

Corrections 369

Problems and Perspectives 371

A Journey Inside the Criminal Justice System and Beyond: One Man's Journey
Reflections 374

APPENDIX A:
Constitution of the United States: Criminal Justice Amendments 377

APPENDIX B:
Careers in Criminal Justice 378

References 383

Glossary 392

Name Index 397

Subject Index 401

Credits 406

Preface

CRIMINAL JUSTICE IN AMERICA, Second Edition, is designed to serve those instructors who want a textbook that introduces students to the dynamics of the American system of criminal justice without overwhelming them. This need was brought to our attention by faculty who reviewed the proposal, those who participated in a focus group at meetings of the Academy of Criminal Justice Sciences, and the enthusiastic comments of those who used the first edition. Faculty told us that they wanted a briefer introductory book than was currently available. Instructors told us that they were unable to cover all of the material presented in the major texts, that they wanted to be able to supplement a core text with other readings, and that they wanted a book that was user friendly to them and to their students.

Criminal Justice in America is an offspring of *The American System of Criminal Justice*, now in its eighth edition. However, it has not been created by merely dropping chapters, combining others, and limiting the graphic elements in order to reduce the page count. *Criminal Justice in America* relies on the research and conceptual framework of the larger text, but the material has been rewritten in a style that is descriptive and informative but not overly theoretical. Additional study and review aids have been incorporated to address the needs of students. Throughout the book examples from today's headlines are used to link the concepts and information to real-life criminal justice situations. Our goal has been to make this edition more current, vital, cohesive, and appealing to students and instructors alike.

THE APPROACH OF THIS TEXT: TWIN THEMES

Two key assumptions about the nature of criminal justice as a discipline and the way the introductory course should be taught run throughout the book:

- *Criminal justice involves public policies* that are developed within the political framework of the democratic process.
- *The concept of social system is an essential tool* for explaining and analyzing the way criminal justice is administered and practiced.

This book's approach might be characterized as the dominant paradigm in criminal justice education. Criminal justice is interdisciplinary, with criminology, sociology, law, history, psychology, and political science contributing to the field. The twin themes of public policy and social system help to place the research contributions of these disciplines in a context that allows students to better understand the dynamics of criminal justice. The themes are introduced in Chapters 1 and 2 and reiterated in the chapters that follow.

The *role of public policy* in criminal justice is developed through examples and explicit discussions throughout the text. For example, we examine policies such as "three strikes and you're out," assistance to crime victims, community policing, and the death penalty for both their content and their potential impact on the system. Throughout the book students are reminded that the definition of behaviors as criminal, the funding of criminal justice operations, and the election of judges and prosecutors result from decisions that are politically influenced.

The *system perspective* is also carried through the book as a concept that is useful in analyzing criminal justice operations. It is reinforced graphically with illustrations that remind students of exchange relationships, the flow of decision making, and the way the criminal justice system is itself embedded in a larger governmental and societal context.

HIGHLIGHTS OF THE SECOND EDITION

This edition has been revised in both content and presentation. Users of the first edition will find significant changes in the order of several chapters and further streamlining of the entire book. The organization of each chapter has also been reexamined and improved.

In addition to these structural changes, the content, research sources, examples, and emphasis have been updated in every chapter. The text has been rewritten to make descriptions succinct and clear and chapters and sections cohesive. The text's special features help the student see the significance of important issues and the context in which they occur. The book is also now more accessible to students at all levels. The use of full color clarifies and enhances the many graphs, photos, and illustrations, bringing to life the discussion of the rapidly changing aspects of criminal justice today. We hope that these changes make this second edition even more usable and "teachable" than its predecessor. Let's look more closely at the book's principal features and the ways they promote content mastery and thoughtful learning.

Content Mastery: Coverage, Organization, and Study Aids

Although current users will find the basic plan of the text familiar, this edition embodies several important changes. First, we have augmented and updated our coverage of the following topics:

Crime and Justice in a Multicultural Society

Disparities in the treatment of African Americans, Hispanic Americans, and other minorities are pervasive in the criminal justice system. This issue is addressed in Chapter 1 and reexamined in succeeding chapters in discussions of what minority-group members experience when they come in contact with the police, the courts, and corrections. The complex issue of attributing criminality to race is carefully examined.

Crime Control Policy

Recent years have seen a major shift to a greater emphasis on crime control. Legislatures have toughened sentences, enacted "three strikes" provisions, increased the number of police officers, and reduced funding for rehabilitative programs. We examine this shift in light of the decrease in crime rates now being documented. These policy issues are presented so as to encourage students to consider the policy the United States should adopt.

Improved Coverage of Policing

Major changes are occurring in American policing as the law enforcement–crime fighter emphasis of past years is supplemented by a focus on community policing and problem solving. Part Two (Chapters 4, 5, and 6) has been reoriented to illustrate this shift in police operations, and the most up-to-date research has been incorporated into the text. Problems affecting the police—stress, excessive use of force, and corruption—are explored more deeply than in the first edition.

Study and Review Aids

To help students identify and master core concepts, the text provides several study and review aids:

- *Chapter Outlines* preview the structure of each chapter.
- *Opening Vignettes* introduce the chapter topic with a high-interest, real-life episode.
- *Questions for Inquiry* highlight the chapter's key topics and themes.
- *Checkpoints* throughout each chapter allow students to test themselves on content.
- *Chapter Summaries* and *Questions for Review* reinforce key concepts and provide further checks on learning.
- *Key Terms* are defined throughout the text in the margins of each chapter and can also be located in the Glossary.
- *Key Cases* explain major issues decided by the courts.

Enhanced Graphics

For this edition, outstanding graphic art and photo research have helped to develop an impressive array of full-color illustrations that add interest and convey information. Quantitative data are illuminated by conversion into bar graphs, pie charts, and other graphic forms; written summaries guide comprehension of the graphic presentations. Special care has been taken to place photographs and their captions so that the images are linked to the message of the text.

Promoting Critical Understanding

Aided by the features just described, a diligent student can master the essential content of the introductory course. While such mastery is no small achievement, most of us aim higher: we want our students, whether future criminal justice professionals or simply citizens, to complete this course able to take a more thoughtful and critical approach to issues of crime and justice than they did at the start of the course. The second edition provides several features that help students learn *how to think* about the field.

Close-ups and Other Real-Life Examples

Understanding criminal justice in a purely theoretical way is not enough. Helping students gain a balanced understanding, the wealth of examples in this book shows how theory plays out in practice and what the human implications of policies and procedures are. In addition to the many examples in the text, the *Close-up* features in each chapter draw from newspapers, court decisions, first-person accounts, and other current sources.

A Question of Ethics

Criminal justice requires that decisions be made within the framework of law but also that they are consistent with the ethical norms of American society. In each chapter *A Question of Ethics* scenario places students in the role of decision makers faced with a realistic ethical dilemma.

Ideas in Practice

Through the real-life examples provided in *Ideas in Practice* students apply important ideas discussed in the chapter to actual criminal justice practice. By thinking about and discussing the issues presented, students gain a greater appreciation of the challenges that criminal justice professionals face.

A Journey Inside the Criminal Justice System and Beyond

Many students of criminal justice have limited first-hand knowledge of what it is like to be "processed" by the criminal justice system. We are pleased to introduce a new feature in this edition, a serialized essay by Chuck Terry titled "A Journey Inside the Criminal Justice System and Beyond: One Man's Journey." Each part of the book concludes with a segment of Terry's moving story, providing a rare "insider's" look at the steps of the criminal justice process.

Careers in Criminal Justice

One of our goals for this edition is to help students of criminal justice make informed career decisions. We have strengthened our coverage of careers in two ways:

- Workperspectives, written by fourteen criminal justice professionals, give students an insider's view of careers and work experiences.
- An appendix on careers in criminal justice describes the mission, agencies, and entry requirements for a range of criminal justice positions.

SUPPLEMENTS

The most extensive package of supplemental aids for a criminal justice text accompanies this edition. The following items have been developed to enhance the course and to assist instructors and students.

Instructor's Edition

New to this book is an instructor's edition featuring Chapter-at a-Glance and Lecture Notes. This feature will assist instructors in organizing their classroom presentations and reinforcing the themes of the course. Each chapter ties all of the supplements and instructor's notes directly to the topics in the text.

Instructor's Resource Manual and Computerized Test Bank

A full-fledged *Instructor's Resource Manual* has been developed by Christopher Smith. The manual includes resource lists, lecture outlines, and testing suggestions that will help time-pressed teachers more effectively communicate with their students and also strengthen coverage of course material. Each chapter has multiple-choice and true/false test items, as well as sample essay questions. The *Instructor's Resource Manual* is backed up by a computerized test bank available in Windows and Macintosh formats.

Call-In Testing

Adopters of this book are eligible for our call-in testing service. Requests received before 12:00 P.M. EST will be processed within 72 business hours. For more information on this service, please contact Tammi Potter, Call-In Testing Administrator, at 1-800-423-0563, ext. 5403 or tpotter@kdc.com.

PowerPoint Presentation Tool '99

This tool is especially designed to work with the PowerPoint Presentation '99 program. PowerPoint slides are provided for each chapter of the text for faculty to use in their lecture discussions.

Videos

We offer an extensive library of video resources:

- Films for the Humanities customized video is composed of 10- to 15-minute segments covering major criminal justice topics. Instructors may draw on a particular segment to further illustrate a lecture topic or to stimulate class discussion.
- CNN Customized Video is composed of 2- to 5-minute current news stories covering major criminal justice topics. Particular segments can be used to amplify lectures and generate discussion.
- Court-TV programs expose students to real-life courtroom situations. Choose from any of eight 1-hour programs.
- Wadsworth Criminal Justice Video Library offers an extensive selection of criminal justice videos covering contemporary topics from A&E American Justice Series, ABC News and MPI Home Video Series, and National Institute of Crime File Videos.

Crime Scenes: An Interactive Criminal Justice CD-ROM

The first introductory criminal justice CD-ROM available. This interactive presentation allows students to walk through a variety of criminal cases and play the roles of various criminal justice practitioners, such as police officers, prosecutors, jurors, and parole board members. Six original, high-interest scenarios expose students to all major aspects of the criminal justice system. Available for both Windows and Macintosh platforms.

InfoTrac College Edition

This online research tool provides students with access to current articles from over 600 scholarly and popular publications, including magazines, journals, encyclopedias, and newsletters. Student subscribers receive personalized "account ID numbers" that give them unlimited access to InfoTrac College Edition for four full months at any hour of the day.

The Virtual Criminal Justice Classroom

Designed by the foremost criminal justice Internet expert, Professor Cecil Greek of the School of Criminology of Florida State University, the Virtual Criminal Justice Classroom is the best book-specific Web site on the Internet. Students can use this site as a launching point for research, meet other students in cyberspace to discuss criminal justice topics, and improve test scores by taking online quizzes.

The Virtual Criminal Justice Classroom includes the following features:

- Hundreds of links to other criminal justice sites. For ease of use, these links are keyed to each chapter of this text.
- A scavenger hunt to help students learn to navigate the information superhighway for criminal justice–related research. The "Hunt" contains fifty clues. All answers can be found through the links of the Virtual Classroom. The student can have fun exploring the Internet, but the hunt is not easy!
- A mailing list for students and instructors to post comments, homework suggestions, exemplary student papers, and so forth. By posting questions and answers on the Internet students can learn from one another.
- Online quizzes specific to each chapter allow students to prepare for upcoming exams.
- Online homework exercises drawn from the text allow students to submit answers to professors electronically.

Transparencies

Based on the *American System of Criminal Justice*, Eighth Edition, fifty full-color transparency masters for overhead projection bring the graphic portions of the text to the classroom. The transparencies help instructors fully discuss concepts and research findings with students.

Study Guide

An extensive student guide has been developed for this edition by Christopher Smith. Because students learn in different ways, a variety of pedagogical aids is included in the guide to help them. Each chapter is outlined, major terms are defined, summaries and sample tests are provided.

Employment in Criminal Justice

Written by J. Scott Harr and Kären Hess of Normandale Community College, this practical book, now in its second edition, helps students develop a search strategy to find employment in criminal justice and related fields. Each chapter includes "insiders' views" written by individuals in the field and addressing such issues as promotions and career planning.

Criminal Justice Internet Investigator II

This handy brochure lists the most useful criminal justice links on the World Wide Web. It includes the most popular criminal justice sites organized by major topics, such as policing, investigations, juveniles, courts, and corrections.

Internet Guide for Criminal Justice

Developed by Daniel Kurland and Christina Polsenberg, this easy reference text helps newcomers as well as experienced Web surfers use the Internet for criminal justice research.

Mind of a Killer CD-ROM

Based on Eric Hickey's book *Serial Murderers and Their Victims*, this award-winning CD-ROM offers viewers a look at the terrifying psyches of the world's notorious killers. The student can view confessions of and interviews with serial killers and examine famous cases through original video documentaries and news footage. Included are 3-D profiling simulations, extensive mapping systems that seek to find out what motivates these killers.

Your Research: Data Analysis for Criminal Justice and Criminology

Written by criminal justice experts Michael Blankenship and Gennaro Vito, this book, in its second edition, is an easy-to-use data analysis and graphics program with an accompanying workbook replete with examples of criminological research projects. Software available for DOS.

A GROUP EFFORT

It is not possible to be expert about every aspect of the criminal justice system. Authors need help in covering new developments and ensuring that research findings are correctly interpreted. This revision has greatly benefited from the advice of three sets of scholars. One group of almost 2,500 participated in a national survey designed to reveal to us more about the way the introductory course is taught and the type of text that instructors and students want. A second group of criminal justice scholars was asked to comment on the entire manuscript, especially its organization and pedagogical usefulness. These reviewers were chosen from the wide range of colleges and universities throughout the country that have used previous editions, so their comments concerning presentation, levels of student abilities, and the requirements of introductory courses at their institutions were especially useful. Reviewers in the third group we consulted are nationally recognized experts in the field; they focused their attention on the areas in which they specialize. Their many comments helped us avoid errors and drew our attention to points in the literature that had been neglected.

The many criminal justice students and instructors who used the first edition also contributed abundantly to this edition. Several hundred readers returned the questionnaire included in that edition. Their comments provided crucial practical feedback. Others gave us their comments personally when we lectured in criminal justice classes around the country.

We have also been assisted in writing this edition by a diverse group of associates. Chief among them was our editor, Sabra Horne, who was supportive of our efforts and kept us on our course. The help of developmental editor Dan Alpert was extremely valuable as we revised the book. The project has benefited much from the attention of Deborah Kramer, project manager. Our talented designer, Norman Baugher, designed the interior of the book. Claire Masson was invaluable in helping us develop the supplemental aids. Ultimately, however, the full responsibility for the book is ours alone.

George F. Cole
gcole@uconnvm.uconn.edu
Christopher E. Smith
smithc28@pilot.msu.edu

Acknowledgments

We wish to thank the following reviewers for their valuable guidance throughout the revision process of *Criminal Justice in America*:

Allan R. Barnes, University of Alaska-Anchorage; Paula M. Broussard, University of Southwestern Louisiana; Avon Burns, Charles S. Mott Community College; Larry Farnsworth, Unity College; Pamela Hart, Iowa Western Community College; Mark Jones, East Carolina University; William E. Kelly, Auburn University; Walter Lewis, St. Louis Community College at Meramac; Lee Libby, Shoreline Community College; William McCarney, Western Illinois University; James Madden, Lake Superior State University; Dale T. Mooso, San Antonio College; Frank Morgan, Richard Bland College; and Richard Ramos, Contra Costa College.

We also appreciate the constructive comments of the reviewers of the first edition of *Criminal Justice in America*: Jerry Armor, Calhoun Community College; W. H. Copley, College of Denver; John Dempsey, Suffolk Community College; Daniel Doyle, University of Montana: Robert M. Hurley, Sacramento State University; Tim Jones, Athens State College; Thomas D. McDonald, North Dakota State University; Nicholas Mejer, Kalamazoo Valley Community College; Patrick Patterson, Mohawk Valley Community College; Patricia Payne, Middlesex County College; Tim Perry, Shoreline Community College; Rudy K. Prine, Valdosta State University; Walter F. Ruger, Nassau Community College; Angelo Triniti, Passaic County Community College; Melvin Wallace, McHenry County College; Bob Walsh, University of Houston, Downtown; and Vincent J. Webb, University of Nebraska, Omaha.

What is the sequence of events in the criminal justice system?

This flowchart provides an overview of the criminal justice system as it will be described in this book. It is important to recognize that the system portrayed here is a social system. Each event depicted represents a complex interaction of people, politics, and procedures.

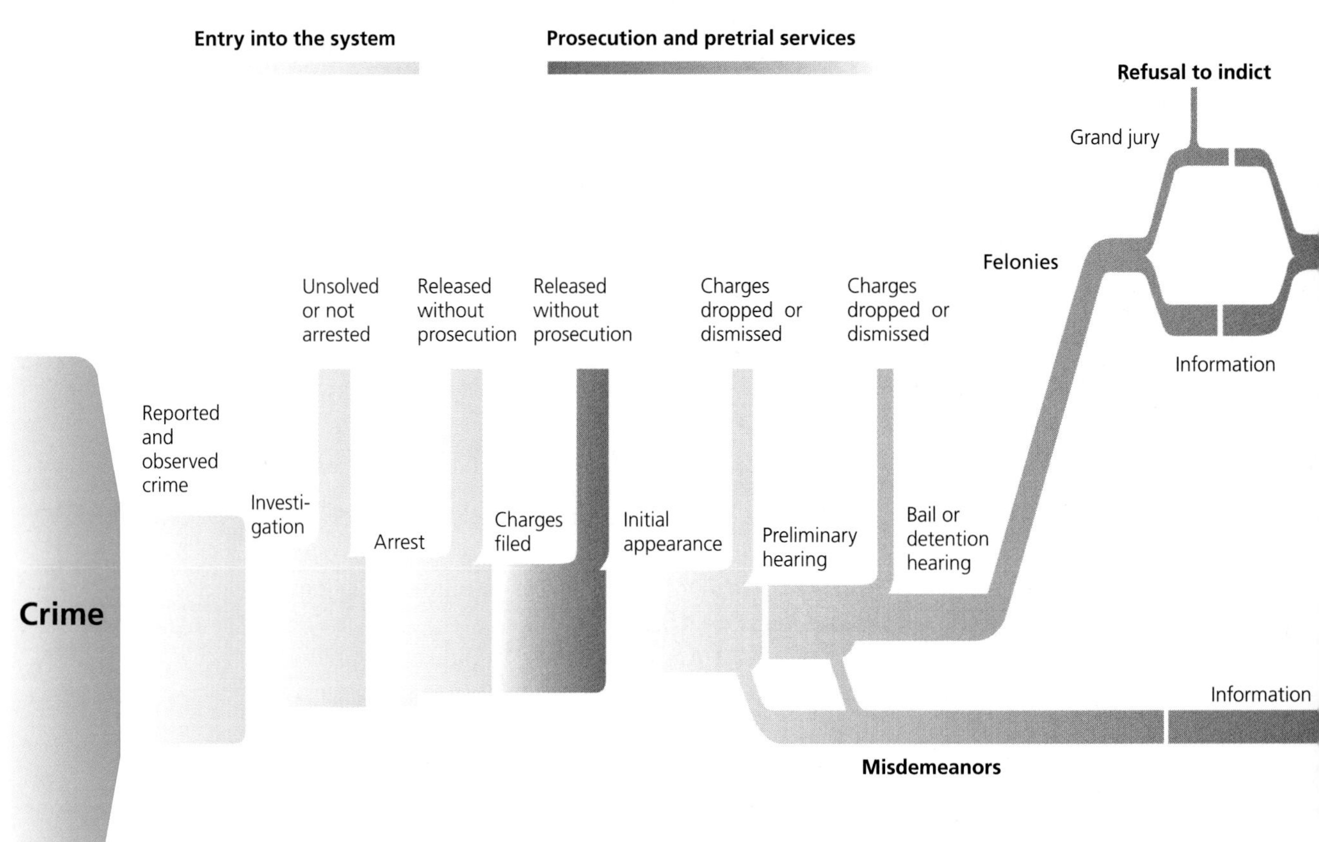

Originally published by the President's Commission on Law Enforcement and Administration of Justice in 1967, the flowchart was revised in 1997 by the Bureau of Justice Statistics.

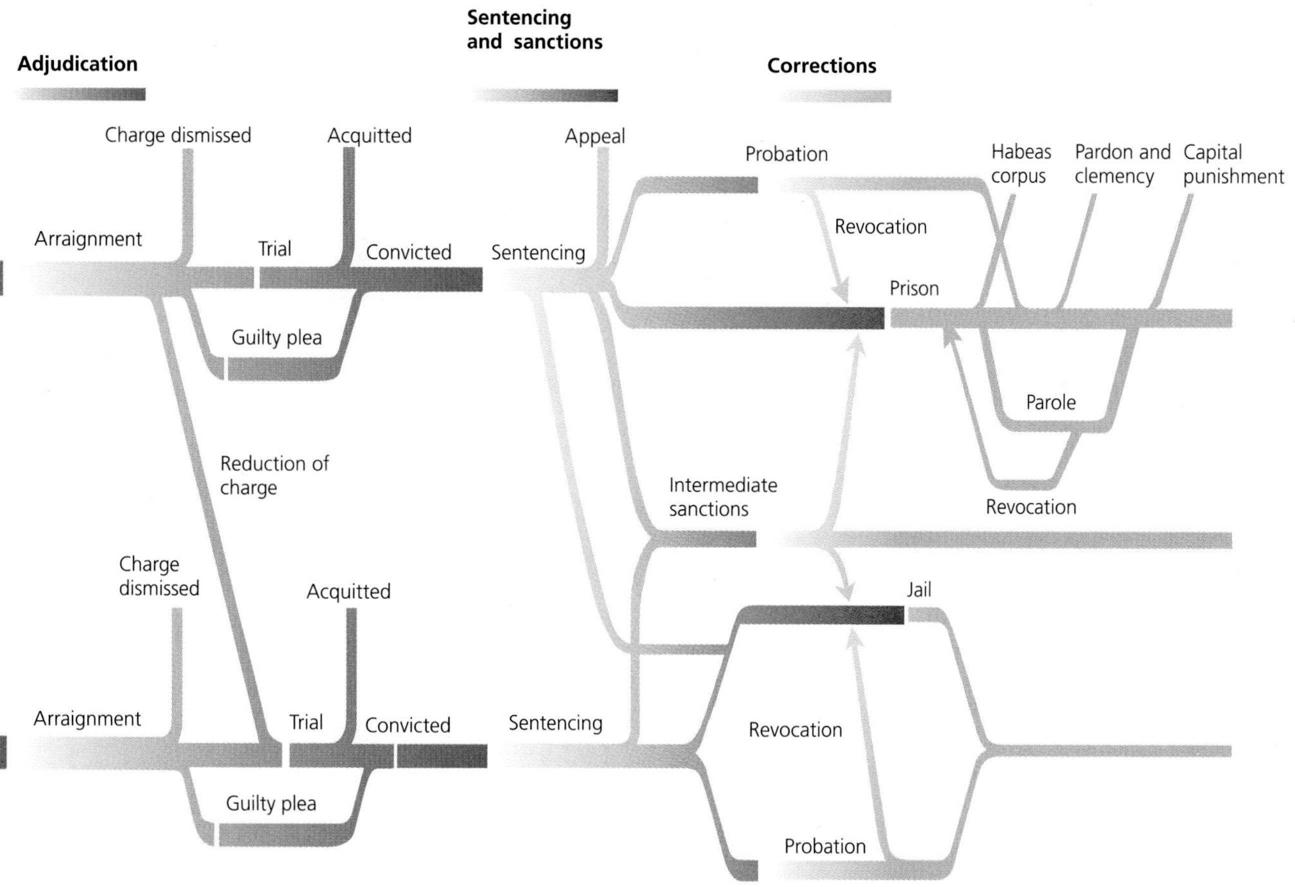
Adjudication
Sentencing and sanctions
Corrections
Charge dismissed
Acquitted
Appeal
Probation
Habeas corpus
Pardon and clemency
Capital punishment
Arraignment
Trial
Convicted
Sentencing
Revocation
Prison
Guilty plea
Parole
Reduction of charge
Intermediate sanctions
Revocation
Charge dismissed
Acquitted
Jail
Arraignment
Trial
Convicted
Sentencing
Revocation
Guilty plea
Probation

Criminal Justice in America

Part 1

The Criminal Justice Process

1 CRIME AND JUSTICE IN AMERICA

2 THE CRIMINAL JUSTICE SYSTEM

3 CRIMINAL LAW AND PROCEDURE

THE American system of criminal justice is a response to a problem that has required the attention of all societies from the beginning of time: crime. To understand how the system works and why crime persists in spite of our efforts to control it, we need to examine both the nature of criminal behavior and the functioning of the justice system itself. As we will see, the reality of crime and justice involves much more than "cops and robbers," the details of legal codes, and the penalties for breaking laws. From defining what behavior counts as criminal to deciding the fate of offenders who are caught, the process of criminal justice is a social process that is subject to many influences other than written law.

In introducing the study of this process, Part One provides a broad framework for analyzing how our society tries to deal with the age-old problem of crime.

Chapter 1

Crime and Justice in America

Crime in America

Defining Crime

Types of Crime

- *Occupational Crime*
- *Organized Crime*
- *Visible Crime*
- *Crimes without Victims*
- *Political Crime*

How Much Crime Is There?

- *The Uniform Crime Reports*
- *The National Crime Victimization Surveys*

Trends in Crime

Crime Victimization

- *Who Is Victimized?*
- *The Impact of Crime*
- *The Experience of Victims within the Criminal Justice System*
- *The Role of Victims in Crime*

Women and Crime

Crime and Justice in a Multicultural Society

- *Explanation 1: Minorities Commit More Crimes*
- *Explanation 2: The Criminal Justice System Is Racist*
- *Explanation 3: America Is a Racist Society*

Crime and Justice as Public Policy Issues

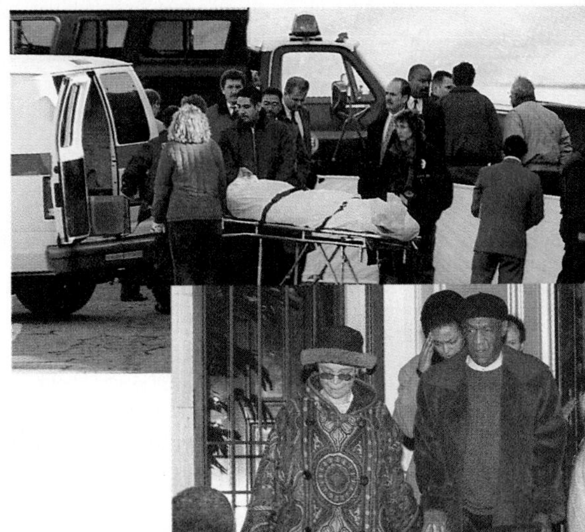

IN THE EARLY MORNING hours of January 23, 1997, a man tried to fix the flat tire on his luxury car along the side of a Los Angeles road. Another car stopped. Minutes later, the man lay dead, shot to death in an apparent robbery attempt.

In some respects, this was just another terrible crime devastating yet another family. In other ways, this killing was particularly stunning to people throughout the country, because the murder victim was Ennis Cosby, son of the beloved actor and comedian, Bill Cosby. Ennis Cosby was a likeable college graduate who was pursuing a career as a teacher of children with learning disabilities. Unfortunately, he had a flat tire at the wrong place and the wrong time. Crime can touch anyone, rich or poor, famous or anonymous. Everyone faces the risk of crime.

The tragic killing of Ennis Cosby and the news media coverage that followed it helped to reinforce the public's idea that crime is everywhere and we are constantly in danger. News broadcasts are filled with reports about murders, robberies, and rapes.

Responding to the public's fear, politicians have tried to outdo one another in being "tough on crime." This toughness has led to shifts in public policies: adding thousands more police officers, building more prisons, extending the death penalty to cover sixty federal offenses, mandating longer sentences, and requiring parolees to register with the police. Many of these policies, such as building prisons, cost large sums of money.

Meanwhile public opinion polls indicate people remain very fearful of crime, without realizing that serious crime has declined since the record-setting years of the early 1980s. Serious crime fell 4 percent in 1997, its sixth annual decline. Violent crimes declined 5 percent, and the number of murders was down 9 percent. Rapes were down 1 percent, reaching their lowest level since 1989. In addition, property crime has dropped sharply since 1980 (*New York Times*, May 18, 1998, p. A15.) In reality, everyone is at risk from crime, but the actual risk for most people is quite small. Yet despite this good news Americans "are afraid of and obsessed with crime" (Donziger, 1996:1).

Are Americans' fears about crimes justified? Should the government spend more and more money on prisons and law enforcement? In fact, however, there is no national crime wave. The news that crime is not rampant may surprise most Americans, but FBI data support this view.

In this chapter, we will examine the complex issue of crime. We will look at how crime is defined and measured. Next we will examine crime victimization. We will also see how crime is an important public policy issue for the United States.

Questions for Inquiry

What are the major types of crimes in the United States?

How much crime is there, and how is crime measured?

Who are the victims of crime?

What is the role of women and minority group members in crime and criminal justice?

CRIME IN AMERICA

Public opinion polls show that Americans rank **crime** among the nation's greatest problems. Crimes are behaviors that violate specific societal rules and that the government uses its power to punish. Many people believe that the crime rate is rising, even though it has declined. Is crime still at record levels? Is the United States the most crime-ridden nation of the world's industrial democracies? How do we measure the amount of crime? What are the current and future trends? By trying to answer these questions, we can gain a better understanding of the crime problem itself and the public's beliefs about it.

crime

A specific act of commission or omission in violation of the law for which a punishment is prescribed.

There has always been too much crime, and ever since the nation's founding people have felt threatened by it. There were outbreaks of violence after the Civil War, after World War I, during Prohibition, and during the Great Depression (Friedman, 1993). Organized crime was rampant during the 1930s. The murder rate, which reached a high in 1933 and a low during the 1950s, rose to a new high in 1980 and has been falling since 1993 (Figure 1.1). Thus, ours is neither the best nor the worst of times.

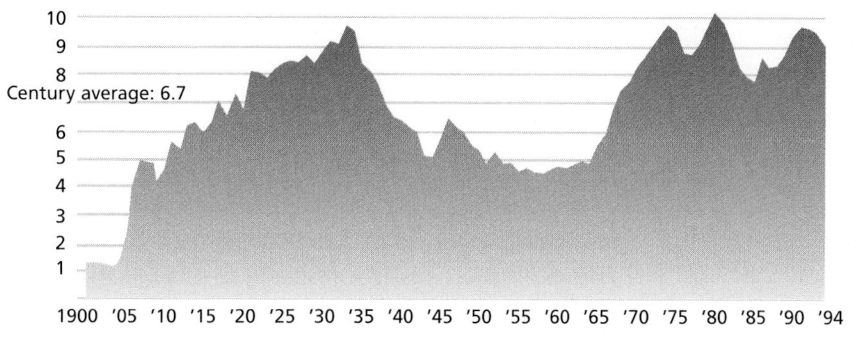

Figure 1.1
A Century of Murder

The murder rate per 100,000 people in the United States has risen, fallen, and since 1960 risen again. Data from the last few years show a decline from the peak in 1980. What causes these trends?

SOURCE: Data from Census Bureau and Federal Bureau of Investigation; *New York Times*, January 28, 1996, p. E5.

How does the amount of crime in the United States compare to the amount in other countries? James Lynch compared crime rates in the United States and in Australia, Canada, England and Wales, West Germany, France, the Netherlands, Sweden, and Switzerland (Lynch,1995:11). Both police and victim data showed that the homicide rate in the United States was more than twice that in Canada, the next highest country, and many times that in the other countries. The same was generally true for robbery. However, the victim surveys showed that for other violent crimes, such as assault and robbery, rates of victimization were lower for Americans than for Canadians, Australians, and Spaniards (Donziger, 1996:10). Data for burglary and motor vehicle theft show a 40 percent higher rate in Australia than in the United States, a 12 percent higher rate in Canada, and a 30 percent higher rate in England and Wales. In sum, the risk of lethal violence is much higher in the United States than in other industrial democracies. But the risk of minor violence is not greater than in other common law countries. In contrast, the United States has lower rates of serious property crime than many countries and even lower rates than many countries that are thought to be safer (Lynch, 1995:17).

CHECKPOINT

1. Is crime a dramatic, new problem for the United States?
2. How does the crime problem in the United States compare to crime problems in other countries?

(Answers are at the end of the chapter.)

DEFINING CRIME

Why does the law label some types of behavior as criminal and not others? For example, why is it a crime to use marijuana when it is legal to drink alcohol, a substance that also has serious intoxicating, addictive, and harmful health impacts?

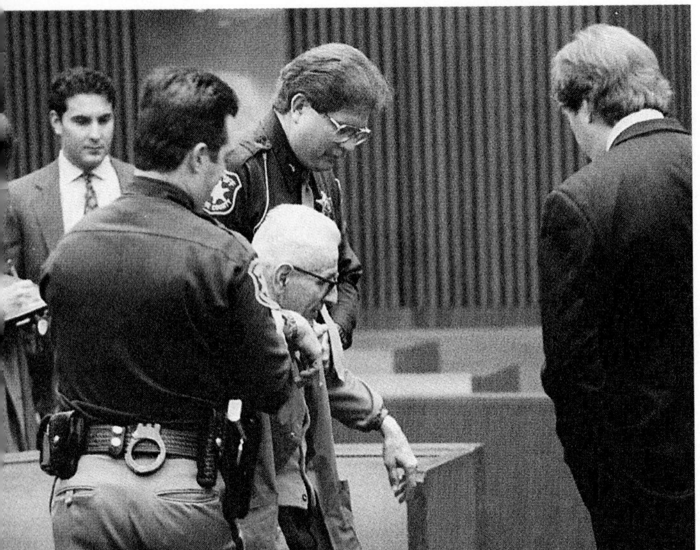

Dr. Jack Kevorkian goes limp in The Detroit's Recorders Court after Judge Thomas Jackson ordered his bond increased in the assisted suicide cases against him. To what extent has Kevorkian's crusade changed public thinking about assisted suicide?

Elected representatives in state legislatures and Congress make choices about the behaviors that the government will punish. Some of these choices reflect broad agreement in society that certain actions, such as rape and murder, are so harmful that they must be punished. For other criminal laws, legislatures make decisions even though there may be disagreement in society about the harmfulness of certain acts. Everyone does not agree, for example, that gambling, prostitution, and drug use should be punished. Some people view these behaviors as free choices that adults should be able to make for themselves.

Evidence from a national survey helps show the extent to which Americans agree about the behaviors that should be defined as crimes (Bureau of Justice Statistics [BJS], 1988. *Report to the Nation on Crime and Justice*:16). In this study, respondents were asked to rank the seriousness of 204 illegal events. The results (see Table 1.1) showed wide agreement on the severity of certain crimes. However, crime victims scored those acts higher than did nonvictims. The ratings assigned by minority-group members tended to be lower than those assigned by whites. Thus there is disagreement about which behaviors to punish as crimes.

TYPES OF CRIME

Crimes can be classified in a number of ways. For example, crimes can be classified as either **felonies** or **misdemeanors**. Felonies are crimes punishable by one year or more of imprisonment or by death. Misdemeanors are crimes punishable by one year or less of imprisonment and by community punishments such as probation, fines, and community service.

felonies

Serious crimes usually carrying a penalty of death or incarceration for more than one year.

Another approach classifies crimes by the nature of the act and the kind of person most likely to commit it. This approach produces five types of crime:

Severity Score	Ten Most Serious Offenses
72.1	Planting a bomb in a public building. The bomb explodes and twenty people are killed.
52.8	A man forcibly rapes a woman. As a result of physical injuries, she dies.
43.2	Robbing a victim at gunpoint. The victim struggles and is shot to death.
39.2	A man stabs his wife. As a result, she dies.
35.7	Stabbing a victim to death.
35.6	Intentionally injuring a victim. As a result, the victim dies.
33.8	Running a narcotics ring.
27.9	A woman stabs her husband. As a result, he dies.
26.3	An armed person skyjacks an airplane and demands to be flown to another country.
25.8	A man forcibly rapes a woman. No other physical injury occurs.

Severity Score	Ten Least Serious Offenses
1.3	Two persons willingly engage in a homosexual act.
1.1	Disturbing the neighborhood with loud, noisy behavior.
1.1	Taking bets on the numbers.
1.1	A group continues to hang around a corner after being told by a police officer to break up.
.9	A youngster under 16 runs away from home.
.8	Being drunk in public.
.7	A youngster under 16 breaks a curfew law by being on the street after the hour permitted by law.
.6	Trespassing in the backyard of a private home.
.3	A person is vagrant. That is, he has no home and no visible means of support.
.2	A youngster under 16 is truant from school.

Table 1.1
How do people rank the severity of a crime?

Respondents to a survey were asked to rank 204 illegal events ranging from school truancy to planting a deadly bomb. A severity score of 40 indicates that people believe the crime is twice as bad as a severity score of 20.

SOURCE: U.S. Department of Justice, Bureau of Justice Statistics, *Report to the Nation on Crime and Justice*, 2d ed. (Washington, D.C.: Government Printing Office, 1988), 16.

occupational crime, organized crime, visible crime, victimless crime, and political crime. Each type has its own level of risk and reward, each arouses varying degrees of public disapproval, and each is committed by a certain kind of offender.

Occupational Crimes

Occupational crimes are committed in the context of a legal business or profession. Sometimes viewed as shrewd business practices rather than as illegal acts, they are crimes that, if "done right" are never discovered. They are often committed by respectable, well-to-do people taking advantage of opportunities arising from their business dealings. These crimes include price fixing, embezzlement, fraud, employee theft, and tax evasion. Such crimes cost businesses, governments, and society billions of dollars each year. Although they are highly profitable, most types of occupational crime do not come to public attention. In general, Americans have not realized the huge costs that these crimes impose on society.

Former Arizona Governor Fife Symington grimaces after being sentenced to two-and-a-half years in prison, to pay a fine, and serve five years on probation for providing false statements to lenders to win loans to shore up his failing real estate empire.

Organized Crime

Organized crime refers to a *framework* within which criminal acts are committed, rather than referring to the acts themselves. A crime organization is a tightly knit group of associates engaged in criminal activity, which can range from a neighborhood gang to an international syndicate. Organized criminals provide goods and services that are in high demand but are illegal to millions of people. They will engage in any activity that provides a minimum of risk and a maximum of profit. Thus organized crime involves a network of activities, usually cutting across state and national borders, that range from legitimate businesses to shady deals with labor unions, to providing illegal goods and services such as drugs, sex, and pornography. In recent years organized crime has been involved in new services such as commercial arson, illegal disposal of toxic wastes, and money laundering (Szasz, 1986).

Although the public often associates organized crime with Italian Americans, other ethnic groups have been dominant at various times. The Irish were the first group to organize criminal activity on a large scale in the United States. They were followed by Jews who dominated gambling and labor rackets at the turn of the century. The Italians came next, but they did not climb very far up the ladder until the late 1930s (Ianni, 1973:1-2). Over the last few decades, the Mafia has been greatly weakened by law enforcement efforts (Jacobs, 1994). Today African Americans, Hispanics, Russians, and Asians have formed organized crime groups in some cities (Chin, 1990). Drug dealing has brought Colombian and Mexican crime groups to U.S. shores, and Vietnamese-, Chinese-, and Japanese-led groups have been formed in California (California, Attorney General, 1986). These new groups do not fit the Mafia pattern, and law enforcement agencies have had to find new ways to deal with them (Kleinknecht, 1996).

misdemeanors

Offenses less serious than felonies and usually punishable by incarceration of no more than a year, probation, or an intermediate sanction.

occupational crime

Criminal offenses committed through opportunities created in a legal business or occupation.

organized crime

A framework for the perpetration of criminal acts—usually in fields such as gambling, drugs, and prostitution—providing illegal services that are in great demand.

Visible Crime

Visible crime, often referred to as "street crime" or "ordinary crime," ranges from shoplifting to homicide. For offenders, these crimes are the least profitable and, because they are visible, the most vulnerable to apprehension. There is broad agreement among the public that these acts are criminal. Most law enforcement resources focus on these acts, which include violent crimes such as homicide and rape, as well as property crimes like theft, larceny, and burglary. Visible crimes also include public order offenses such as public drunkenness, aggressive panhandling, street prostitution, vandalism, and disorderly conduct. Although the police tend to treat these behaviors as minor offenses, according to increasing evidence this type of disorderly behavior instills fear in citizens, leads to more serious crimes, and hastens urban decay (Kelling and Coles, 1996).

Those who commit visible crimes tend to be young, low-income males. In some places, minority-group males are overrepresented among those involved. Some argue that this is due to the class bias of a society that has singled out visible crimes rather than occupational crimes for priority enforcement.

Skinhead Nathan Thill confessed to the hate-murder of Oumar Dia, a West African immigrant. "In a war, anybody wearing the enemy's uniform. . . should be taken out, "Thill said, adding that he shot Dia "because he was black."

Crimes without Victims

Crimes without victims involve a willing and private exchange of goods or services that are in strong demand but are illegal—in other words, offenses against morality. Examples include prostitution, gambling, and drug sales and use. These are called "victimless" crimes because those involved do not feel that they are being harmed. Prosecution for these offenses is justified on the grounds that society as a whole is harmed because the moral fabric of the community is threatened. However, using the law to enforce moral standards is costly. The system is swamped by these cases, which often require the use of police informers and thus open the door for "payoffs" and other kinds of corruption.

Can any crime be truly victimless? Some may argue that adults should be left free to harm their bodies with drug use or to gamble away their money. Others believe that this point of view ignores the impacts of such crimes on family members and others.

visible crimes

Offenses against persons and property committed primarily by members of the lower class. Often referred to as "street crimes" or "ordinary crimes," these are the offenses most upsetting to the public.

Political Crime

Political crime refers to criminal acts by the government itself or against the government that are carried out for ideological purposes (Hagan, 1997:2). Political criminals believe they are following a morality that is above the law. In pardoning government officials involved in the Iran-Contra conspiracy to sell weapons illegally to Iran, President George Bush said that they were acting on what they believed was in the national interest (Hagan, 1997:81).

In some authoritarian states, merely making statements that are critical of the government is a crime that may lead to prosecution and imprisonment. In Western democracies today there are few political crimes other than treason, sedition (rebellion), and espionage, all of which are rare. Many illegal acts, such as the World Trade Center and Oklahoma City bombings, can be traced to political motives. But they have been prosecuted as visible crimes under laws against bombing, arson, and murder.

crimes without victims

Offenses involving a willing and private exchange of illegal goods or services that are in strong demand. Participants do not feel they are being harmed, but these crimes are prosecuted on the grounds that society as a whole is being injured.

Which of the five main types of crime is of greatest concern to you? If you are like most people, it is visible crime. Thus, as a nation, we devote most of our criminal justice resources to dealing with such crimes. To develop policies to address these crimes, we need to know more about the amount of crime and types of crimes that occur in the United States.

political crimes

Acts that constitute a threat against the state (such as treason, sedition, or espionage).

CHECKPOINT

3. What are the five main types of crime?
4. What is the function of organized crime?
5. Who commits "visible" or "street" crimes?
6. What is meant by the term "crimes without victims"?
7. What are political crimes?

HOW MUCH CRIME IS THERE?

We do not know exactly how many crimes are committed each year. Our knowledge depends on the reports of victims and witnesses, yet many people do not report crimes to the police. This may seem odd, but there are many reasons people do not report crimes, even though they often know who victimized them. For example, if a drug-addicted relative steals their money, they may not want the relative to go to prison. If they are victims of rape or assault, they may be too embarrassed by public disclosure or fear re-living the experience by testifying in court. The large amount of crime that extends beyond those acts reported to the police is referred to as the **dark figure of crime**. We know that many crimes are not reported to police or counted in crime statistics.

dark figure of crime

A metaphor that emphasizes the dangerous dimension of crime that is never reported to the police.

As indicated in Figure 1.2, there are differences in the reporting rates for various crimes. Certain crimes are almost always reported, such as homicide when a person is missing or a body is found. Auto theft is reported regularly because people need a police report to get insurance money. Other crimes are not reported as consistently.

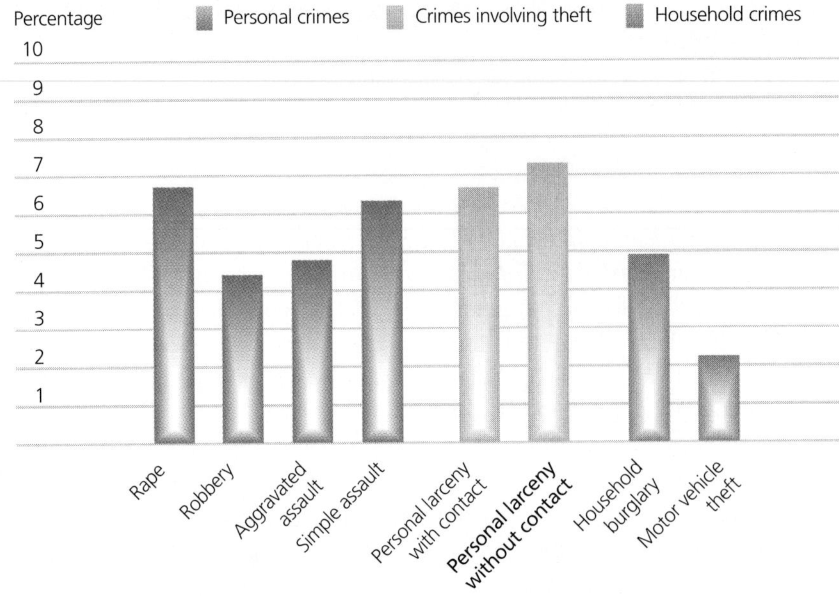

Figure 1.2
Percentage of victimizations not reported to the police

Why do some people not report crimes to the police? What can be done to encourage reporting?

Source: U.S. Department of Justice, Bureau of Justice Statistics, *Bulletin* (April 1996), 1.

The *Uniform* Crime Reports

Issued each year by the FBI, the ***Uniform Crime Reports*** is a statistical summary of crimes reported to the police. At the urging of the International Association of Chiefs of Police, Congress authorized this system for compiling crime data in 1930 (Rosen, 1995). The *UCR* comes from a voluntary national network of some 16,000 local, state, and federal law enforcement agencies providing police services to 95 percent of the U.S. population.

The *UCR* uses standard definitions to ensure uniform data on the 29 types of crimes listed in Table 1.2. For 8 major crimes—Part I or "index offenses"—the data show factors such as age, race, and number of reported crimes solved. For the other 21 crimes, the data are less complete.

The *UCR* provides a useful, but incomplete, picture of crime levels. Because it covers only reported crimes, it does not include crimes for which people failed to call the police. Also, the *UCR* does not measure all reported crimes, only the 29 covered offenses. Since reporting is voluntary, police departments may not take the time to make complete and careful reports (Biderman and Lynch, 1991).

In response to criticisms of the *UCR*, the FBI has made some changes in the program that are now being implemented nationwide and are to be fully implemented

Table 1.2
***Uniform Crime Reports* Offenses**

The *UCR* presents data on 8 index offenses and 21 other crimes for which less information is available. A limitation of the *UCR* is that it tabulates only those crimes reported to the police.

Source: U.S. Department of Justice, Federal Bureau of Investigation, *Crime in the United States—1996* (Washington, D.C.: Government Printing Office, 1997).

Part I (Index Offenses)

1. Criminal homicide
2. Forcible rape
3. Robbery
4. Aggravated assault
5. Burglary
6. Larceny-theft
7. Auto theft
8. Arson

Part II (Other Offenses)

9. Simple assaults
10. Forgery and counterfeiting
11. Fraud
12. Embezzlement
13. Buying, receiving, or possessing stolen property
14. Vandalism
15. Weapons (carrying, possession, etc.)
16. Prostitution and commercialized vice
17. Sex offenses
18. Violation of narcotic drug laws
19. Gambling
20. Offenses against the family and children
21. Driving under the influence
22. Violation of liquor laws
23. Drunkenness
24. Disorderly conduct
25. Vagrancy
26. All other offenses (excluding traffic)
27. Suspicion
28. Curfew and loitering (juvenile)
29. Runaway (juvenile)

by 1999. Some offenses have been redefined, and police agencies are being asked to report more details about crime events. Using the **National Incident-Based Reporting System** (NIBRS), police agencies are to report all crimes committed during an incident, not just the most serious one, as well as data on offenders, victims and the places where they interact. While the *UCR* now counts incidents and arrests for the 8 index offenses and counts arrests for other crimes, NIBRS provides detailed incident data on 46 offenses in 22 crime categories. The NIBRS, unlike the *UCR*, will distinguish between attempted and completed crimes (BJS, *Bulletin,* October 1993).

Uniform Crime Reports (UCR)

An annually published statistical summary of crimes reported to the police, based on voluntary reports to the FBI by local, state, and federal law enforcement agencies.

The National Crime Victimization Surveys

National Incident-Based Reporting System (NIBRS)

A reporting system in which the police describe each offense in a crime incident, together with data describing the offender, victim, and property.

A second source of crime data is the **National Crime Victimization Surveys** (NCVS). Since 1972, the Census Bureau has done surveys to find out about the extent and nature of crime victimization, gathering data on unreported as well as reported crimes. Interviews are conducted with a national probability sample of about 100,000 people in 50,000 households. The same people are interviewed twice a year for three years and asked if they have been victimized in the last six months.

Each person is asked a set of "screening" questions (for example, did anyone beat you up, attack you, or hit you with something like a rock or bottle?) to determine whether he or she has been victimized. The person is then asked about specific details concerning the event, the offender, and any financial losses or physical disabilities caused by the crime.

National Crime Victimization Surveys (NCVS)

Interviews of samples of the U.S. population conducted by the Bureau of Justice Statistics to determine the number and types of criminal victimizations and thus the extent of unreported as well as reported crime.

In addition to the household interviews, surveys are carried out in the nation's twenty-six largest cities; separate studies are done to find out about victimization of businesses. These data allow us to estimate how many crimes have occurred, learn more about the offenders, and note demographic patterns (BJS, 1994. *National Crime Victimization Survey*, October). The results for 1995 show that for the crimes measured (rape, robbery, assault, burglary, theft) there were 38.5 million victimizations including property crimes affecting 27 percent of the country's 102 million households (BJS, 1997. *National Crime Victimization Survey,* April)

Although this level is much higher than that indicated by the number of crimes reported to the police, both the NCVS and the *UCR* indicate that crime has decreased in the 1990s (BJS, 1997. *National Crime Victimization Survey,* April).

The NCVS provides a more complete picture of the nature and extent of crime, but it too has flaws. Because the survey is done by government employees, the people interviewed are unlikely to report crimes in which they or members of their family took part. They also may not want to admit that a family member engages in crime, or they may be too embarrassed to admit that they have allowed themselves to be victimized more than once.

The NCVS is also imperfect because it depends on the victim's *perception* of an event. The theft of lunch money by a bully at school may be reported as a crime by one parent but not mentioned by another child's parent. People's memories of dates may fade, and they may misreport the year in which a crime occurred even though they clearly remember the event itself. In 1993 the Bureau of Justice Statistics made some changes in the NCVS to improve its accuracy and detail (Ibid.)

The next time you hear or read about rising crime rates, take into account the source of the data and its possible limitations. Table 1.3 compares the *Uniform Crime Reports* and the National Crime Victimization Surveys.

	Uniform Crime Reports	National Crime Victimization Surveys
Offenses measured	Homicide	
	Rape	Rape
	Robbery (personal and commercial)	Robbery (personal)
	Assault (aggravated)	Assault (aggravated and simple)
	Burglary (commercial and household)	Household burglary
	Larceny (commercial and household)	Larceny (personal and household)
	Motor vehicle theft	Motor vehicle theft
	Arson	
Scope	Crimes reported to the police in most jurisdictions; considerable flexibility in developing small-area data	Crimes both reported and not reported to the police; all data are for the nation as a whole; some data are available for a few large geographic areas
Collection method	Police department reports to FBI	Survey interviews: periodically measures the total number of crimes committed by asking a national sample of 49,000 households representing 101,000 people over the age of 12 about their experiences as victims of crime during a specific period
Kinds of information	In addition to offense counts, provides information on crime clearances, persons arrested, persons charged, law enforcement officers killed and assaulted, and characteristics of homicide victims	Provides details about victims (such as age, race, sex, education, income, and whether the victim and offender were related) and about crimes (such as time and place of occurrence, whether or not reported to the police, use of weapons, occurrence of injury, and economic consequences)
Sponsor	Department of Justice's Federal Bureau of Investigation	Department of Justice's Bureau of Justice Statistics

Table 1.3
The UCR *and the NCVS*

Compare the data sources. Remember that the *UCR* tabulates only crimes reported to the police, while the NCVS is based on interviews with victims.

TRENDS IN CRIME

Contrary to public opinion and the claims of politicians, crime rates have not been steadily rising. In fact, the rates for many crimes have dropped since the early 1980s.

The National Crime Victimization Surveys show that the victimization rate peaked in 1981 and has declined since then. The greatest declines are in property crimes, but crimes of violence have also dropped, especially since 1990. The *Uniform Crime Reports* show similar results. They reveal a rapid rise in crime rates beginning in 1964 and continuing until 1980, when the rates began to level off or decline. The overall crime rate has declined each year since 1991.

The most surprising trend has been the decline in violent crimes since 1993. As shown in Figure 1.3, both the NCVS and the *UCR* show downward trends for violent crime. From 1994 to 1995 the *UCR* showed a decline in all violent crimes,

Figure 1.3
Trends in violent crime

Data from both the *UCR* and the NCVS show that violent crime has declined in recent years. What might account for the decline?

SOURCE: U.S. Department of Justice, Bureau of Justice Statistics, *Bulletin* (April,1997), updated November 7, 1997.

NOTE: The violent crimes included are rape, robbery, aggravated assault, and homicide. The vertical line at 1992 indicates that because of changes made to the victimization survey, data prior to 1992 are adjusted to make them comparable to data collected under the redesigned methodology.

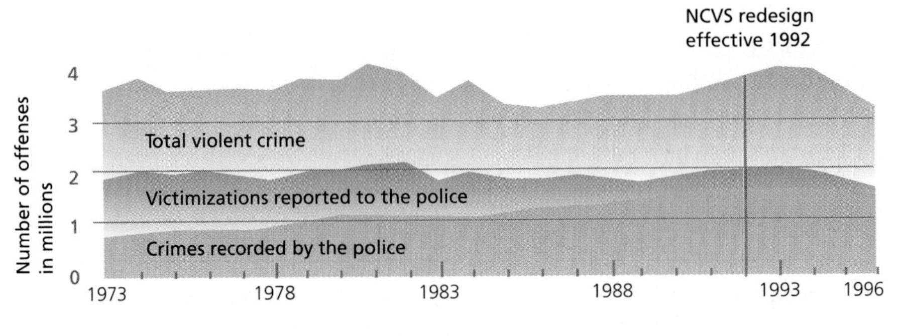

led by an 8 percent drop in homicides. This was confirmed by the NCVS data, which showed a 9 percent drop in violent crime, including an 18 percent decrease in rapes, a 14 percent decrease in robberies, and a 19 percent decrease in aggravated assaults (murders are not included in NCVS statistics).

The NCVS and *UCR* show different trends becuse they are based on diffderent sources and different populations. Remember, the *UCR* is based on crimes reported to the police, while the NCVS records crimes experienced by victims. Over time the gap between the *UCR* and NCVS data has narrowed, indicating greater willingness to report crimes. The introduction of 911 emergency phone numbers, the increased presence of police in many communities, and the spread of neighborhood watch programs have all played a role in this change (Fisher,1993). Also, the rise in violent crime from 1973 to 1992 as reported by the *UCR* may have been the result of increased police efficiency in recording crime incidents, not of more crime (O'Brien, 1996:204).

Changes in the age makeup of the population are a key factor in the analysis of crime trends. For example, it has long been known that males aged 16 to 24 are the most crime-prone group. In 1996, the *UCR* disclosed that 30.2 percent of those arrested for serious crimes were under 18. Almost half (45.7 percent) of those arrested for violent crimes and 58.4 percent of those arrested for property crimes were under 25 (Federal Bureau of Investigation [FBI], 1997).

The rise in crime in the 1970s has been blamed on the post–World War II baby boom. By the 1970s the "boomers" had entered the high-risk crime group of 16- 24-year-olds. They made up a much larger portion of the U.S. population than had been true in the past. Between 40 and 50 percent of the total arrests during that decade could have been expected as a result of the growth in the total population and in the size of the crime-prone age group. Likewise, the decline in most crime rates that began during the 1980s has been attributed to the maturing of the post–World War II generation.

At present the 16- to 24-year cohort (group) is smaller than it has been at any time since the early 1960s, but as Figure 1.4 shows, those numbers are beginning to climb. John DiIulio notes, "By the year 2000 there will be about 500,000 more 14- to 17-year-old males in the population than there are today" (DiIulio, 1995). In short, a large number of young people are about to enter the crime-prone years.

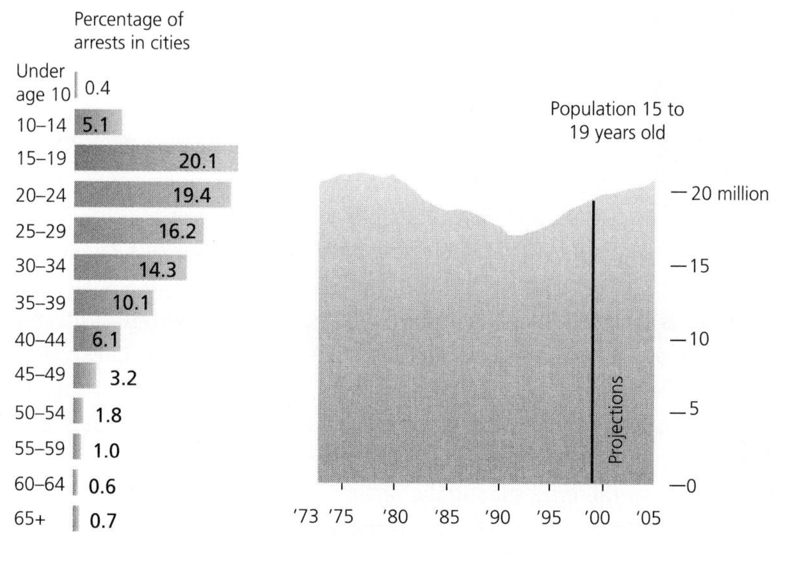

Figure 1.4
Young toughs: teenagers and the crime rate

Although the number of young males is low right now, that cohort will grow in the next decade.

SOURCE: *New York Times*, November 13, 1994, sec. 4, p. 4.

In the words of James Fox, "To prevent a blood bath in the year 2005, when we will have a flood of 15-year olds, we have to do something today with the 5-year olds) (*New York Times*, November 13, 1994:4).

With respect to youth crime, it is interesting to note that the violent crime rates for youths actually dropped in the years following Professor Fox's prediction about the effect of the growing "crime-prone" youth group. Violent crimes by teenagers dropped by 2.9 percent in 1995 and by an additional 9.4 percent in 1996. In 1996, arrests of teenagers for murders dropped 10.7 percent from the prior year, the third straight annual decline (*Lansing (Mich.) State Journal*, October 3, 1997:1A). A variety of forces may be reducing the predicted impact of the growing youth cohort. For example, cities' efforts to implement community policing programs may be producing beneficial effects. Alternatively, the positive economic climate of the 1990s may have created more job opportunities for youths. There are other possible explanations, too, such as changes in punishment policies and community corrections programs. In any case, the size of the "crime-prone" group may not be the sole cause of changes in the crime rate.

CHECKPOINT

8. What are the two main sources of crime data?
9. What is a key factor in crime trends?

victimology

A field of criminology that examines the role the victim plays in precipitating a criminal incident.

CRIME VICTIMIZATION

Until the past few decades, researchers paid little attention to crime victims. The field of **victimology**, which emerged in the 1950s, focuses attention on four questions: (1) Who is victimized? (2) What is the impact of crime? (3) What happens to victims in the criminal justice system? (4) What role do victims play in causing the crimes they suffer? We discuss research on these questions in the next section.

Fashion designer Gianni Versace was murdered outside his Miami Beach home by serial-killer Andrew Cunanan, who had been on the FBI's Most Wanted list. Four other deaths were blamed on Cunanan, who later committed suicide with a .40-caliber semiautomatic weapon.

Who Is Victimized?

Everyone does not have an equal chance of being a crime victim. Research shows that certain groups are more likely to be victimized than others. As Andrew Karmen notes, "Vulnerability to crime is always a matter of degree."Victimologists have puzzled over this fact and come up with several answers (Karmen, 1996).

One answer is that demographic factors (age, gender, income) affect lifestyle—people's routine activities, such as work, home life, and recreation. Lifestyles, in turn, affect people's exposure to dangerous places, times, and people. Thus, differences in lifestyles lead to varying degrees of exposure to risks (Meier and Miethe, 1993:466).

Figure 1.5 shows the links among the factors used in the lifestyle-exposure model of personal victimization. Using this model, think of a person whose lifestyle includes going to night clubs in a "shady" part of town. Such a person runs the risk

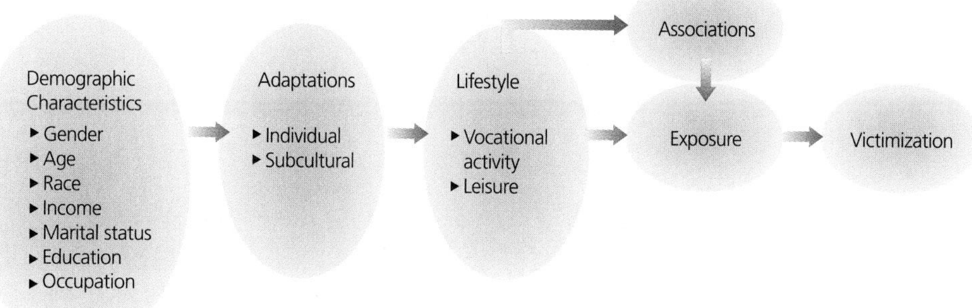

Figure 1.5
Lifestyle-exposure model of victimization

Demographic and subcultural factors determine personal lifestyles, which in turn influence exposure to victimization.

SOURCE: Adapted from Robert F. Meier and Terance D. Miethe, "Understanding Theories of Criminal Victimization," *Crime and Justice: A Review of Research*, ed. Michael Tonry (Chicago: University of Chicago Press, 1993), 467.

of being robbed if she walks alone through a dark high-crime area at two in the morning to her luxury car. By contrast, an older person who watches television at night in her small-town home has a very low chance of being robbed. But these cases do not tell the entire story. What other factors make victims more vulnerable than nonvictims?

Males, Youths, Nonwhites

The lifestyle-exposure model and survey data shed light on the links between personal characteristics and the chance that one will become a victim. Figure 1.6 shows the influence of gender, age, and race on the risk that an individual will be victimized by a violent crime, such as rape, robbery, or assault.

If we apply these findings to the lifestyle-exposure model, we might suggest that teenage African-American males are the most likely to be victimized because of where many live (urban, high-crime areas), how many spend their leisure time (on the streets late at night), and the other people found in these settings (other violence-prone youths). Lifestyle factors may also explain why elderly white females are least likely to be victimized by a violent crime. Perhaps it is because they are less likely to go out at night, don't associate with people who are prone to crime, carry few valuables, and take precautions such as locking their doors. Thus, lifestyle choices have a direct effect on the chances of victimization.

Race is a key factor in exposure to crime. African Americans and other minorities are more likely than whites to be raped, robbed, and assaulted. White Americans are fearful of being victimized by African-American strangers (Skogan,1995:59). However, most violent crime is *intraracial*: three of every four victims are of the same race as the attacker. The same is true of property crimes: most victims and offenders are of the same race and social class. Probably this is related to the fact that many people come into contact primarily with others of the same race in modern America.

Low-Income City Dwellers

Income is also closely linked to exposure to crime. Economic factors largely determine where people live, work, and seek recreation. For low-income people these choices are limited. Some may have to live in crime-prone areas, may lack security devices to protect their homes, cannot avoid contact with people who are prone to crime, or cannot spend their leisure time in safe areas. Poor people and minorities have a greater risk of being victimized than other segments of the population

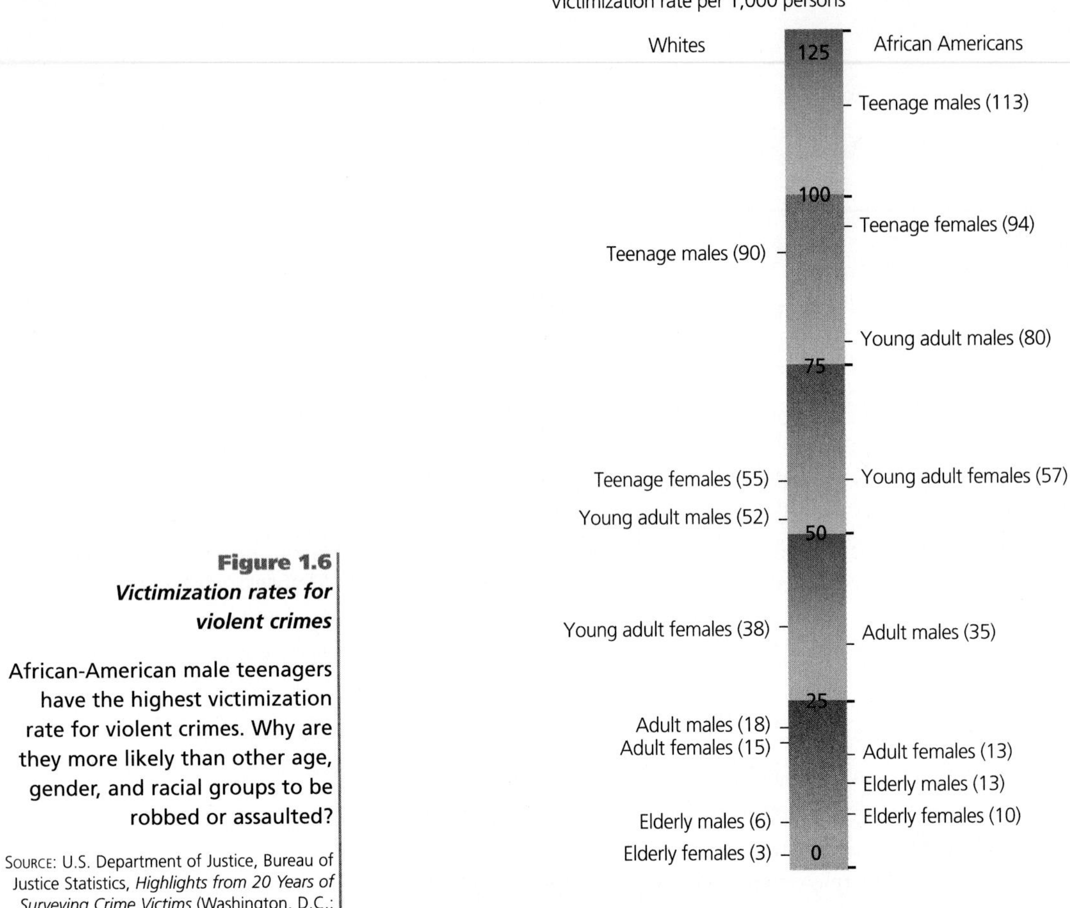

Figure 1.6
Victimization rates for violent crimes

African-American male teenagers have the highest victimization rate for violent crimes. Why are they more likely than other age, gender, and racial groups to be robbed or assaulted?

SOURCE: U.S. Department of Justice, Bureau of Justice Statistics, *Highlights from 20 Years of Surveying Crime Victims* (Washington, D.C.: Government Printing Office, 1993), 20.

because they are likely to live in inner-city zones with high rates of street crime. People with higher incomes have more lifestyle-exposure choices open to them and can avoid risky situations (Meier and Miethe, 1993:468).

Living in a city is, in fact, a key factor in victimization. Violent crime occurs mainly in large cities. Of the 1.8 million violent offenses known to the police in 1995, more than 1.7 million occurred in cities. Studies have shown that crime rates are higher in areas closer to the center of an urban area (FBI, 1996:59).

We cannot conclude, however, that crime rates will be high in any poor urban area. There is more crime in some poor areas than in others. The crime rate in an area may be affected by other factors, such as the physical condition of the neighborhood, the residents' attitudes toward society and law, the extent of opportunities for crime, and social control by families and government (Stark, 1987).

CHECKPOINT

10. What are the main elements of the lifestyle-exposure model?
11. What are the characteristics of the group that is most victimized by violent crime? Of the least victimized group?

The Impact of Crime

Crime affects not only the victim but all members of society. We all pay for crime through higher taxes, higher prices, and fear. However, it is hard to estimate the precise impact of crime.

Costs of Crime

Crime has many kinds of costs. First, there are the economic costs—lost property, lower productivity, and the cost of medical care. Second, there are psychological and emotional costs—pain, trauma, and lost quality of life. Third, there are the costs of operating the criminal justice system.

A recent study estimates the total annual cost of tangible losses from crime (medical expenses, damaged or lost property, work time) at $105 billion. The intangible costs (pain, trauma, lost quality of life) to victims are estimated at $450 billion. Operating the criminal justice system costs taxpayers more than $70 billion a year. These figures do not include the costs of occupational and organized crime to consumers. In addition, there are the costs to citizens who install locks and alarms or employ guards and security patrols (National Institute of Justice [NIJ], 1996. *Victim Costs and Consequences: A New Look*).

Fear of Crime

One impact of crime is fear. Fear limits freedom. Because they are fearful, many people limit their activities to "safe" areas at "safe" times. Fear also creates anxieties that affect physiological and psychological well-being. And the very persons who have the least chance of being victimized, such as women and the elderly, are often the most fearful (Miethe, 1995:14).

Since 1965, public opinion polls have asked Americans whether they "feel more uneasy" or "fear to walk the streets at night." Over time more than 40 percent of respondents say that fear of crime limits their freedom. In large cities more than 60 percent of residents say that they are afraid to walk through their neighborhoods at night, while in small towns and rural areas fewer than 30 percent express this concern. High levels of fear are found among nonwhites and people with low incomes, the groups that are most likely to be victimized. However, women, the elderly, and upper-income suburban dwellers—groups with low rates of victimization—are also more fearful than the average citizen (Warr, 1993:25).

Crime rates are down, yet Americans seem to be as fearful as ever. People do not have a clear picture of the actual risk of crime in their lives. Their views about crime seem to be shaped by what they see on television, by talk at their workplace, and by what politicians are saying.

Most people do not experience crime directly but instead learn about it indirectly (Skogan and Maxfield, 1981:157). The media have a major impact on attitudes about crime (Surette, 1992; Kurz, 1997). Although fewer than 8 percent of victimizations are due to violent crime, such crimes are the ones most frequently reported by the media (Alderman, 1994:26). The amount of news coverage of crime, compared to coverage of the economy or government, can be startling (Chermak, 1995:48). In addition, tabloid shows like "Hard Copy" and "A Current Affair" present reports of heinous crimes almost daily (Kappeler et al., 1996:47). Crime stories sell newspapers and build viewership and appeal to certain types of audiences (Graber, 1980; Warr, 1994). Researchers believe that conversations with friends also tend to magnify the amount of local violence. Stories about defenseless victims create a feeling that violent crime lurks everywhere.

There is evidence of a link between fear of crime and disorderly conditions in neighborhoods and communities (Wilson and Kelling, 1982; Skogan, 1990). As discussed by George Kelling and Catherine Coles, in urban areas, disorderly behavior—public drunkenness, urination, aggressive panhandling, and menacing behavior—offends citizens and instills fear. Unregulated disorderly behavior is a signal to citizens that an area is unsafe. Because of this fear they "will stay off the streets, avoid certain areas, and curtail their normal activities and associations" (Kelling and Coles, 1996:20). Avoidance by residents of "unsafe" business areas may lead to store closings, declines in real estate values, and flight to more orderly neighborhoods.

The Experience of Victims within the Criminal Justice System

After a crime has occurred, the victim is often forgotten. Victims may have suffered physical, psychological, and economic losses, yet the criminal justice system focuses on finding and prosecuting the offender.

Too often the system is not sensitive to the needs of victims. For example, defense attorneys may ask them hostile questions and attempt to paint them, rather than the defendant, as guilty. Likewise, while victims are a key source of evidence, the police may question them closely—and in a hostile fashion—to find out if they are telling the truth. Often the victim never hears the outcome of a case.

Victims may be forced to miss work and lose pay in order to appear at judicial proceedings. They may be summoned to court again and again, only to learn that the arraignment or trial has been postponed. Any recovered property may be held by the court for months until the case is concluded. In short, after cases have been completed, victims may feel that they have been victimized twice, once by the offender and once by the criminal justice system.

During the past two decades, justice agencies have become more sensitive to the interests of crime victims. This has happened partly because victims often are the only witnesses to the crime and their help is needed.

Proposals for a federal "Crime Victims' Bill of Rights" would grant victims the right to be informed about plea bargains, to obtain restitution for losses, and to bar offenders from earning income from books and films about their crimes. At least twenty states have amended their constitutions to achieve these objectives.

Programs that give information, support, and compensation to victims have been started in many states. In some states the investigating officer gives the victim a booklet listing the steps that will be taken and telephone numbers that can be called should questions arise.

Support is most important when the victim faces medical, emotional, or financial problems as a result of a crime. Such support is offered by rape crisis centers, victim assistance programs, and family shelters. In most states compensation programs help victims of violent crime by paying the medical expenses of those who cannot afford them. When property has been stolen or destroyed, compensation programs encourage judges to order restitution by the offender.

CHECKPOINT

12. What are some of the impacts of crime?
13. Why is fear of crime high among some groups?
14. What are the costs of crime?

The Role of Victims in Crime

Victimologists study the role that victims play in some crimes. Researchers have found that many victims behave in ways that invite the acts committed against them. This is not to say that it is the victim's fault that the crime occurred. It is merely to recognize that the victim's behavior may have led to the crime through consent, provocation, enticement, risk taking, or carelessness with property.

What do studies tell us about these situations? First, some people do not take proper precautions to protect themselves. For example, they may leave keys in their cars or enter unsafe areas.

Using common sense may be part of the price of living in modern society. Second, some victims may provoke crime by engaging in an argument or participating in some other type of conflict. Third, victims of crimes by relatives or acquaintances may not be willing to help with the investigation and prosecution. These behaviors do not excuse criminal acts, but they do force us to recognize the role of victims in commission of many crimes.

CHECKPOINT

15. What behaviors of victims can invite crime?

WOMEN AND CRIME

Only in the past few decades has research focused on women and crime. Except in the case of so-called female crimes such as prostitution and shoplifting, before the 1970s little research was done on the female offenders, who account for fewer than 10 percent of arrests. It was assumed that most women, because of their nurturant and dependent nature, were unable to commit serious crimes. Those who did commit crimes were deemed to be "bad" women. Unlike male criminals, female criminals were viewed as moral offenders—"fallen women." Today criminologists are looking more closely at female offenders (Daly and Chesney-Lind, 1988:497).

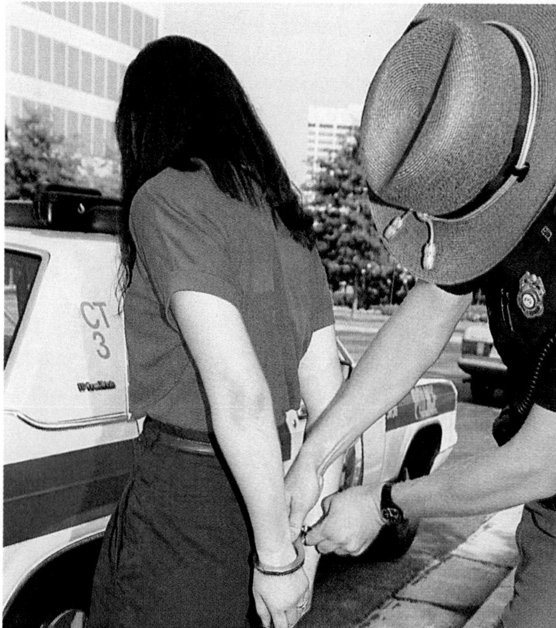

Women most often commit property and drug offenses; however, in recent years an increasing number have been arrested for crimes of violence. This California woman was arrested for assault.

Two books published in 1975, Freda Adler's *Sisters in Crime: The Rise of the New Female Criminal* and Rita Simon's *Women and Crime*, led to a new view of gender and crime (Adler, 1975; Simon, 1975). Both books looked at increases in female crimes, but they reached different conclusions.

Adler stresses the impact of the women's movement. She believed that as the roles of women changes, their criminality will be more like that of men. As she noted, "When we did not permit women to swim at the beaches, the female drowning rate was quite low. When women were not permitted to work as bank tellers or presidents, the female embezzlement rate was low" (Adler, 1975: 31). In other words, as women and men become more equal, gender differences will decrease.

According to Simon, because of recent changes, women now have greater freedom, are less likely to be victimized and oppressed by men, and are less likely to be dependent on them. Simon placed less emphasis than Adler on the women's movement and more on changes in the job market. She argued that with new opportunities for women, the number of business-related and property crimes committed by women is likely to rise (Simon, 1975:19).

But has there really been a change in female criminality? Some scholars believe that arrest data do not suggest major shifts in the types of crimes committed by women (Steffensmeier, 1983:1010). However, the number of women committing crimes appears to be growing faster than the number of male offenders. Over the last twenty-five years, the amount of reported crime committed by males rose by 80 percent while the amount committed by women rose by 160 percent. The data show an increase of 150 percent in the number of women arrested for property offenses and an increase of more than 270 percent in arrests of women for drug dealing and use. Even with these increases, though, the amount of crime committed by women is small compared to that committed by men. Women make up fewer than 16 percent of arrestees for all types of crime except larceny-theft.

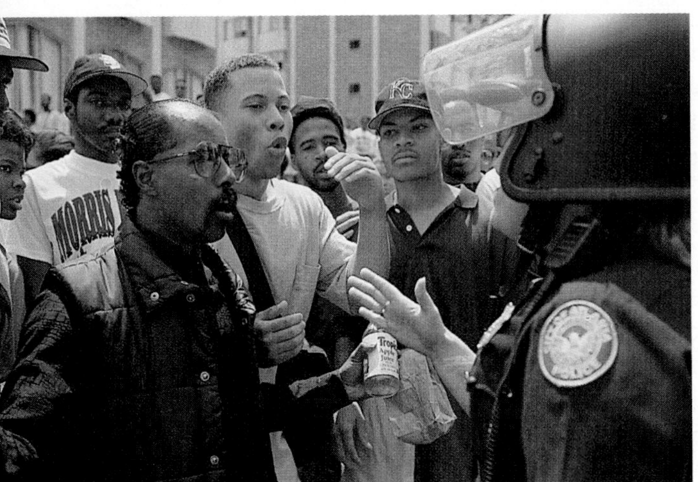

The police often become targets for tensions arising in a multicultural society, such as this riot in Atlanta. How should the officers react in such situations?

As the status of women changes and as more women pursue careers in business and industry, some scholars believe that women will commit more economic and occupational crimes, such as embezzlement and fraud. However, research continues to show that arrested women, like male offenders, tend to come from poor families in which physical and substance abuse are present (Rosenbaum, 1989:31). Other researchers believe that the higher crime rates among women are due in part to greater willingness of police and prosecutors to treat them like men. Thus far, the findings of research on gender differences in crime are not conclusive (Decker et al., 1993:142).

CHECKPOINT

16. What have Freda Adler and Rita Simon contributed to theories of female criminality?

CRIME AND JUSTICE IN A MULTICULTURAL SOCIETY

African Americans, Hispanic Americans, and other minorities are subjected to the criminal justice system at much higher rates than the white majority (Hagan and Peterson,1995:14). For example:

- African Americans account for one-third of all arrests and one-half of all incarcerations in the United States.
- Since 1980 the proportion of Hispanic Americans among all inmates in U.S. prisons has risen from 7.7 percent to 14.3 percent.

- About one-fifth of all 16- to 34-year-old African-American males are under criminal justice supervision.
- The rate of unfounded arrests of Hispanics in California is double that of whites.
- Among 100,000 black males aged 15-19, 68 will die as the result of a homicide involving a gun, compared to about 6 among 100,000 white males in the same age group.
- The crime victimization rate is 260 per 1,000 Hispanic households versus 144 per 1,000 non-Hispanic households.

A central question is whether racial and ethnic **disparities** like those just listed are the result of discrimination (Mann, 1993:vii-xiv; Wilbanks, 1987). However, scholars have studied this question only recently (Free, 1996). One reason for this neglect is the lack of good data for minorities other than African Americans (Flowers, 1988:57). Much of our discussion therefore will focus on African Americans.

disparities

The inequality of treatment of one group by the criminal justice system, compared to the treatment accorded other groups.

Racial disparities in criminal justice are often explained in one of three ways: (1) African Americans and Hispanics commit more crimes, (2) the criminal justice system is racist, with the result that people of color are treated more harshly, or (3) the criminal justice system expresses the racism found in society as a whole. We consider each of these views in turn.

Explanation 1: Minorities Commit More Crimes

Nobody denies that the proportion of minorities arrested and placed under correctional supervision (probation, jail, prison, parole) is greater than their proportion of the general population. However, people disagree over whether bias is responsible for the disparity.

Disparities in arrests and sentences may be due to legitimate factors. For example, prosecutors and judges are supposed to take into account differences between serious and petty offenses, and between repeat and first-time offenders. It follows that more people of color will end up in the courts and prisons if they are more likely to commit more serious crimes and have more serious prior records than do whites (Walker, Spohn, and DeLone, 1996:15-16).

But why do minorities commit more crimes? The most extreme answer is that they are more predisposed to criminality. This assumes that people of color are a "criminal class." There is little evidence to support this view. For example, self-report studies, in which people are asked to report on their own criminal behavior, have shown that nearly everyone has committed a crime, although most are never caught. Studies of illicit drug use find that whites are slightly *more* likely than African Americans to admit to using illegal substances (Kopstein and Roth, 1990:13). Moreover, recent research challenges the notion that African Americans are socialized into a subculture of violence (Cao, Adams, and Jensen, 1997).

The link between crime and economic disadvantage is significant. Minority groups suffer greatly from poverty. Nearly half (46 percent) of African-American children and 39 percent of Hispanic-American children are poor, compared to only 16 percent of white children (Sherman, 1994). Unemployment rates are highest among people of color, and family income is lowest. Thus, it would be natural to expect Hispanic Americans and African Americans to engage in more crimes.

One way to explain racial disparities in the criminal justice system, then, is to point out that African Americans and Hispanic Americans are arrested more often and for more serious offenses than whites. Some analysts argue that the most effective crime control policies would be those that reduce the social problems contributing to higher crime rates among the poor (Tonry, 1995).

Explanation 2: The Criminal Justice System Is Racist

Racial disparities may result if people who commit similar offenses are treated differently by the criminal justice system because of their race or ethnicity. In this view, the fact that people of color are arrested more often than whites does not mean that they are more crime-prone. For example, although African Americans are arrested for drug offenses more often than whites, they do not engage in drug use more often (Blumstein, 1993). One study found that the police make *unfounded* arrests of African Americans four times as often as of whites (Donziger, 1996:109).

The disparity between crime rates and rates of incarceration is a key factor in the claim by some that the criminal justice system is biased against minority groups. Indeed, the rate of incarceration of poor and minority citizens is greater than even their higher offense rates would justify. For example, 29 percent of rape victims report that their assailant was African American, but 43 percent of persons arrested for rape are African American. Similarly, 22.6 percent of assault victims say the offender was African American, but 34 percent of those arrested for assault are African Americans. In sum, the odds of arrest are higher for African-American offenders than for white offenders.

Some point to the fact that 51 percent of the prison population is African American as further evidence of a racist system. One study found that differences in incarceration rates of African Americans and whites reflected "significant disparities that could not be attributed to arrest charges [or] prior criminal charges" (New York, Office of Justice Systems Analysis, 1991:1).

Criminal justice officials need not act in racist ways to cause disparities in arrest and incarceration rates. At each stage of the process, the system operates in ways that may put minority-group members at a disadvantage. For example, while African Americans constitute 13 percent of monthly drug users, they represent 35 percent of arrests for drug possession, 55 percent of convictions, and 74 percent of prison sentences (Butterfield,1995). The number of minority arrests may be greater because police patrols are more heavily concentrated in areas where nonwhites live, where drug use is more open, and where users are more likely to be observed by police.

Further, a study of 150,000 cases in Connecticut found that on average, an African-American or Hispanic-American man must pay *double* the bail that would be paid by a white man for the same offense (Donziger, 1996:111). Most pretrial release practices take into account factors such as employment status, living arrangement, and prior criminal record. Poor offenders are less likely to be able to make bail and hire their own lawyer. Prosecutors may be less likely to dismiss charges against a poor, unemployed African-American or Hispanic offender. These offender characteristics may further skew sentencing.

Is the criminal justice system racist? The result of the system's decisions cannot be disputed—African-American and Hispanic-American males end up in prison and jails in higher proportions than can be explained by their crime and arrest rates. In a recent review of thirty-eight studies more than two-thirds of the studies had uncovered biases in the system that were disadvantageous to African Americans.

The authors concluded that "race is a consistent and frequently significant disadvantage when [imprisonment] decisions are considered . . . [but] race is much less of a disadvantage when it comes to sentence length" (Chiricos and Crawford, 1995).

Explanation 3: America Is a Racist Society

Some people claim that the criminal justice system is racist because it is embedded in a racist society. In fact, some accuse the system of being a tool of a racist society.

There is evidence of racism in the way society asks the criminal justice system to operate. For example, federal sentencing guidelines punish users of crack cocaine about one hundred times more harshly than users of powder cocaine, even though the drugs are almost identical (BJS, 1988. *Report to the Nation on Crime and Justice*:16). The only difference is that whites tend to use cocaine in its powder form, while people of color in the inner cities tend to use crack cocaine.

In addition, sentencing studies find a stronger link between unemployment rates and rates of imprisonment than between crime rates and rates of imprisonment. This suggests that prisons are used to confine people who cannot find jobs—and many of the unemployed are African-American males (Chiricos and Bales, 1991).

Other evidence of racism in American society may be seen in the stereotyping of offenders. As Coramae Richey Mann points out, such stereotyping varies among racial and ethnic groups, depending on the crime and the section of the country. She suggests that white Americans view the rapist as a "black man," the opium user as a "yellow man," the knife wielder as a "brown man," the drunken Indian as a "red man," and people of color as the cause of the "crime problem"(Mann, 1993:vii).

That racist stereotyping affects police actions can be seen in cases of African-American and Hispanic-American professionals who have been falsely arrested when the police were looking for a person of color and these individuals happened to be "out of place." Judge Claude Coleman was handcuffed and dragged through crowds of shoppers in Short Hills, New Jersey, while protesting his innocence; Harvard philosopher Cornel West was stopped on false cocaine charges while traveling to Williams College; and law student Brian Roberts was pulled over by the police as he drove in an affluent St. Louis neighborhood on his way to interview a judge for a class project (Tonry, 1995:51).

If people of color are overrepresented in the justice system because the larger society is racist, the solution may seem a bit daunting. Nobody knows how to quickly rid a society of racist policies, practices, and attitudes.

CHECKPOINT

17. What is meant by racial or ethnic disparities in criminal justice?
18. What three explanations may account for such disparities?

CRIME AND JUSTICE AS PUBLIC POLICY ISSUES

Crime and justice are crucial public policy issues. In a democracy we struggle to strike a balance between maintaining public order and protecting individual

President Clinton has tried to make the crime issue his own, with public appearances including an address at the National Peace Officers Memorial Service at the Capitol. Prior to the service, he announced new Federal grants that will let states, cities, and towns hire nearly 9,000 more officers under the Violent Crime Control and Law Enforcement Act.

freedom. In addition, we must be concerned about fairness and equality, especially in applying the laws to women and minority-group members. We could impose policies that make us feel safe from crime, such as placing a police officer on every street corner and executing suspected criminals. Such severe practices have been used elsewhere in the world. While they may reduce crime, they also fly in the face of democratic values. If we gave law enforcement officers a free hand, we would be giving up individual freedom, due process, and our conception of justice.

Conservatives believe that the answer lies in stricter enforcement of the law through the expansion of police forces and the enactment of laws that require swift and certain punishment of criminals (Logan and DiIulio, 1993:486). Advocates of such policies have been politically dominant since the early 1980s. They argue that we must strengthen crime control, which they claim has been hindered by certain decisions of the U.S. Supreme Court and by programs that substitute government assistance for individual responsibility.

In contrast, liberals argue that stronger crime control measures endanger the values of due process and justice (Walker, 1993:504). They claim that strict measures are ineffective because the answer lies in reshaping the lives of offenders and changing the social and economic conditions from which criminal behavior springs.

Note that the competing policy approaches relate to the theories about the causes of crime. The conservative view sees crime as the result of rational decisions and free will. The liberal view is most closely related to sociological ideas about the causes of crime. Can we expect either approach, by itself, to "solve" the crime problem? Not unless we truly believe that all crimes have the same cause. In reality, we know that some people, such as white collar embezzlers, make rational decisions about criminal acts, while young street toughs may reflect elements of the sociological approach, such as poverty and lack of opportunity. No single approach to crime can easily address all these factors while also protecting other important values, such as the rights of individuals.

Americans agree that criminal justice policies should control crime by enforcing the law *and* should protect the rights of individuals. But these goals are difficult to achieve. They involve questions such as the amount of power police should have to search persons without a warrant, the rules judges must follow in deciding if certain types of evidence may be used, and the power of prison wardens to punish inmates. These questions are answered differently in a democracy and an authoritarian state.

The administration of justice in a democracy differs from that in an authoritarian state. A democracy provides protections for an accused person as guilt is determined and punishment is imposed. The police, prosecutors, judges, and correctional officials are expected to act according to democratic values—especially respect for the rule of law and the maintenance of civil rights and liberties.

Our laws begin with the premise that all people—the guilty as well as the innocent—have rights. Moreover, unlike laws in some other countries, our laws reflect the desire not to unnecessarily deprive people of liberty, either by permitting the police to arrest people at will or by punishing a person for a crime that he or she did not commit.

Although all Americans prize freedom and individual rights, they often disagree about policies to deal with crime. Our greatest challenge as we move toward the twenty-first century may be to find ways to remain true to the principles of fairness and justice while operating a system that can effectively protect, investigate, and punish. This may be especially difficult because the American public's fear of crime exceeds the actual risk and extent of crime. Politicians can use those fears to develop policies intended to show their "toughness" on crime rather than to address crime problems in a realistic fashion. Tragic murders, such as the death of Ennis Cosby described at the beginning of the chapter, add fuel to the fire of public fears when they receive sustained attention in the national news media.

CHECKPOINT

19. What criminal justice policies are advocated by conservatives?
20. What criminal justice policies are advocated by liberals?
21. What are the two criminal justice goals that Americans agree on?

Summary

- Today's crime problem is not unique. Throughout the history of the United States, there have been times when crime has reached high levels.
- Violent crime is the only type that occurs at a higher rate in the United States than in similar countries.
- There are five broad categories of crime: occupational crime, organized crime, visible crime, crimes without victims, and political crime.
- Each type has its own level of risk and profitability, each arouses varying degrees of public disapproval, and each has its own group of offenders with differing characteristics.
- The amount of crime is difficult to measure. The *Uniform Crime Reports* and the National Crime Victimization Surveys are the best sources of crime data.
- Only in recent decades have researchers directed their attention to the victims of crime. Research has focused on who is victimized, the impact of crime, the experiences of victims in the criminal justice system, and victim precipitation of crime.
- The criminality of women has only recently been studied. It is argued that, as women become more equal with men in society, crimes committed by females will increase in number.
- Racial disparities in criminal justice are explained in one of three ways: minorities commit more crimes; the criminal justice system is racist; the criminal justice system expresses the racism of society.
- Crime and justice are high on the agenda of national priorities.
- Crime and justice are public policy issues.
- In a democracy there is a struggle to strike a balance between maintaining public order and protecting individual freedom.

Questions for Review

1. What are the five types of crimes?
2. What are the positive and negative attributes of the two major sources of crime data?
3. What are the four types of victimization studies?
4. What are the proposed explanations for the involvement of women and racial minority group members in crime?

ANSWERS TO CHECKPOINTS

1. Crime has been a serious problem throughout American history.
2. The United States has more serious rates of violent crimes, but other countries have higher rates of property crime.
3. Occupational crime, organized crime, visible crime, crime without victims, political crime.
4. To provide goods and services that are in high demand but are illegal.
5. Young, low-income males tend to commit a disproportionate share of visible crimes.
6. These are crimes against morality in which the people involved do not believe they are being harmed.
7. Crimes such as treason and espionage committed for a political purpose.
8. *Uniform Crime Reports*, National Crime Victimization Surveys
9. The number of young men in their crime-prone years at any given moment in history.
10. Demographic characteristics, adaptations, lifestyle, associations, exposure.
11. Most victimized: young African-American males. Least victimized: elderly white females.
12. Fear, financial costs, emotional costs, lifestyle restrictions.
13. Because they learn about crime through the media and conversations that emphasize the most shocking crimes.
14. Financial costs (lost property, medical care); psychological and emotional costs; costs of the criminal justice system
15. Failing to take precautions; taking actions that may provoke or entice; not assisting police with investigations.
16. The idea that women commit more crimes as they become more liberated and gain equality as participants in all aspects of society.
17. That racial and ethnic minorities are subjected to the criminal justice system at much higher rates than the white majority.
18. Minorities commit more crime; the criminal justice system is racist; America is a racist society.
19. Stricter enforcement of the law through the expansion of police forces and the enactment of laws that require swift and certain punishment of offenders.
20. Stronger crime measures may endanger the values of due process and justice so the focus should be on improving social conditions, such as combating poverty.
21. That criminal justice policies should control crime by enforcing the law and should protect the rights of individuals.

Chapter 2

The Criminal Justice System

The Goals of Criminal Justice

- *Doing Justice*
- *Controlling Crime*
- *Preventing Crime*

Criminal Justice in a Federal System

- *Two Justice Systems*
- *Expansion of Federal Involvement*

Criminal Justice as a Social System

- *The System Perspective*
- *Characteristics of the Criminal Justice System*

Operations of Criminal Justice Agencies

- *Police*
- *Courts*
- *Corrections*

The Flow of Decision Making in the Criminal Justice System

- *Steps in the Decision-Making Process*
- *The Criminal Justice Wedding Cake*
- *Crime Control versus Due Process*

IN AUGUST 1992, U.S. marshals went to Ruby Ridge in rural Idaho to arrest white separatist Randy Weaver on weapons charges. Gunfire was exchanged when Weaver reacted against the federal agents whom he saw intruding on the isolated mountain hideaway where he had moved his family to get away from society. U.S. Marshal William Degen was killed. The FBI, U.S. marshals, and other federal authorities mobilized personnel and weaponry to bring in Weaver and his friend Kevin Harris who were holed up in the mountain cabin, now surrounded by heavily armed federal officers. During the standoff, FBI sharpshooter Lon Horiuchi fired through the door at a figure visible in the cabin. His shot killed Weaver's wife, rather than one of the two men sought by the law enforcement officials.

Eventually, Weaver surrendered. He was not convicted for killing Degen, but he served a brief prison sentence for weapons charges.

Critics of the federal government believed that the FBI acted too aggressively in the actions that led to Mrs. Weaver's death. Moreover, there were indications that high-level FBI officials may have sought to cover up evidence of who issued the "shoot-to-kill" order. After a two-year investigation by the U.S. Justice Department, it was concluded that sharpshooter Hariuchi had committed no federal crime and that there was not enough evidence to charge upper-level FBI officials with any crimes associated with the alleged cover-up.

In August 1997, however, Boundary County Prosecutor Denise Woodbury filed manslaughter charges against Agent Horiuchi for the shooting of Mrs. Weaver. Suddenly, an FBI agent, who claimed to be following orders by firing during a standoff with armed criminal suspects, faced the prospect of imprisonment under Idaho law.

How could this be? Didn't the U.S. Justice Department investigate the case and conclude that Agent Horiuchi did not commit any crime? Isn't the Idaho prosecutor on the same side as the FBI in seeking to stop crime and apprehend criminal suspects? What does this case show us about the nature of the American criminal justice system?

The Ruby Ridge incident and the later prosecution of Agent Horiuchi show that the criminal justice system is complex. There is no single authority to control and coordinate the actions of law enforcement officials and agencies throughout the nation. Many decision makers at various levels of government must work together if criminal justice processes are to run smoothly. This does not always happen, however.

In this chapter, we will examine how the criminal justice system really works. In many important respects, the manner in which the system operates is different from the idealistic image of law and justice that we learned in eighth-grade civics classes. Criminal justice is a system with certain important characteristics. These characteristics shape the processing of cases and determine the fates of individual defendants. Throughout this process, formal rules of law have less impact on case outcomes than many people believe.

Questions for Inquiry

What are the goals of the criminal justice system?

How is criminal justice pursued in a federal system of government?

What are the major features of criminal justice as a social system?

What are the main agencies of criminal justice, and how do they interrelate?

What is the flow of decision making from arrest to correction and release?

THE GOALS OF CRIMINAL JUSTICE

To begin our study of the criminal justice system, we must ask this question: What goals does the system serve? Although these goals may seem straightforward as ideas, it can be hard to say exactly what they mean in practice.

In 1967 the President's Commission on Law Enforcement and Administration of Justice described the criminal justice system as the means that society uses to "enforce the standards of conduct necessary to protect individuals and the community (President's Commission, 1967:7).

This statement is the basis of our discussion of the goals of the system. Although there is much debate about the purposes of criminal justice, most people agree that the system has three goals: (1) doing justice, (2) controlling crime, and (3) preventing crime.

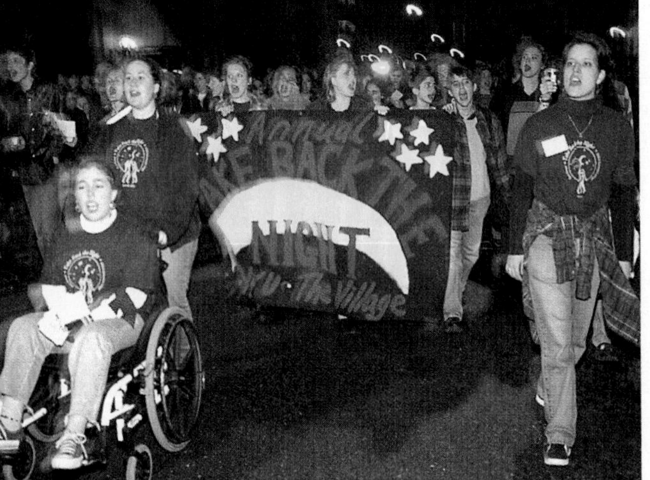

The goals of criminal justice cannot be accomplished solely by the police, courts, and corrections. All citizens should take an interest such as this "Take Back the Night" demonstration against rape and sexual violence.

Doing Justice

Doing justice is the basis for the rules, procedures, and institutions of the criminal justice system. Without the principle of justice, there would be little difference between criminal justice in the United States and in authoritarian countries. Fairness is essential. We want to have fair laws. We want to investigate, judge, and punish fairly. Doing justice also requires upholding the rights of individuals and punishing those who violate the law. Thus, the goal of doing justice embodies three principles: (1) offenders will be held fully accountable for their actions, (2) the rights of persons who have contact with the system will be protected, and (3) like offenses will be treated alike and officials will take into account relevant differences among offenders and offenses (DiIulio, 1993:10).

Successfully doing justice is a tall order, and it is easy to identify situations in which criminal justice agencies and processes fall short of this ideal. In authoritarian political systems, criminal justice clearly serves the interests of those in power. In such countries, the people are powerless to stop officials from arresting and prosecuting anyone without providing a fair trial. By making justice a key goal, a democratic society encourages the public to cooperate with and adhere to the law. As a result it is viewed as legitimate and thus is able to pursue the secondary goals of controlling and preventing crime.

Controlling Crime

The criminal justice system is designed to control crime by arresting, prosecuting, convicting, and punishing those who disobey the law. A major constraint on the system is that efforts to control crime must be carried out within the framework of law. The criminal law not only defines what is illegal but also outlines the rights of citizens and the procedures officials must use to achieve the system's goals.

In any city or town we can see the goal of crime control being actively pursued: police officers walking a beat, patrol cars racing down dark streets, lawyers speaking before a judge, probation officers visiting clients, or the wire fences of a prison stretching along a highway. Taking action against wrongdoers helps to control crime, but the system must also attempt to prevent crimes from happening.

Preventing Crime

Crime can be prevented in various ways. Perhaps most important is the deterrent effect of the actions of police, courts, and corrections. These actions not only punish those who violate the law, but also provide examples that are likely to keep others from committing wrongful acts. For example, a racing patrol car is responding to a crime situation but is also serving as a warning that law enforcement is present in the community.

Crime prevention depends on the actions of criminal justice officials and citizens. Unfortunately, many people do not take the often simple steps necessary to protect themselves and their property. For example, they leave their homes and cars unlocked, do not use alarm systems, or walk in dangerous areas.

Citizens do not have the authority to enforce the law; society has assigned that responsibility to the criminal justice system. Thus, citizens must rely on the police to stop criminals; they cannot take the law into their own hands. If citizens attempt to handle such matters themselves, there are risks of social disorder as well as injuries to suspects, crime victims, and bystanders. (See A Question of Ethics)

The ways in which American institutions have developed to achieve the goals of doing justice, controlling crime, and preventing crime lead to a series of choices. Decisions must be made that reflect legal, political, social, and moral values. As we study the system, we must be aware of the possible conflicts among these values and the implications of choosing one value over another. The tasks assigned to the

A Question of ETHICS

After his jewelry store had been burglarized for the third time in less than six months, Tom Henderson was frustrated. The police were of little help, merely telling him that a patrol officer would keep watch during nightly rounds. Henderson had added new locks and an electronic security system. When he unlocked his shop one morning, he saw that he had been cleaned out again. He looked around the store to see how the thief had entered, because the door was locked and the security alarm evidently had not sounded. Suddenly, he noticed that the glass in a skylight was broken.

"Damn, I'll fix him this time," Henderson cursed.

That evening, after replacing the glass, he stripped the insulation from an electric cord and strung it around and across the frame of the skylight. He plugged the cord into the socket, locked the store, and went home.

Two weeks later, when he entered the store and flipped the light switch, nothing happened. He walked toward the fuse box. It was then that he noticed the burned body lying on the floor below the skylight.

To what extent can someone freely choose the methods to "protect his castle"? If the police are unable to solve a crime problem, is it ethical for individuals to take matters into their own hands?

criminal justice system could be much easier to perform if they were clearly defined so that citizens and officials could act with precise knowledge of their duties.

CHECKPOINT

1. What are the three goals of the criminal justice system?
2. What is meant by "doing justice"?

CRIMINAL JUSTICE IN A FEDERAL SYSTEM

federalism

A system of government in which power is divided between a central (national) government and regional (state) governments.

Criminal justice, like other aspects of American government, is based on the concept of **federalism**—that is, power is divided between a central (national) government and regional (state) governments. States have a great deal of authority over their own affairs, but the federal government handles matters of national concern. Because of federalism, no single level of government is solely responsible for the administration of criminal justice. For this reason the U.S. Department of Justice could determine that Agent Horiuchi violated no federal laws at Ruby Ridge, but it could not control whether an Idaho prosecutor would believe that state criminal laws were violated.

The American governmental structure was created in 1789 with the ratification of the U.S. Constitution. The Constitution gives the national government certain powers—to raise an army, to coin money, to make treaties with foreign countries—but all other powers, including police power, were retained by the states. No national police force with broad powers may be established in the United States.

The Constitution does not include criminal justice among the federal government's powers. However, this national government is involved in criminal justice in many ways. The Federal Bureau of Investigation (FBI), is a national law enforcement agency. Federal criminal cases are tried in U.S. district courts, which are federal courts, and there are federal prisons throughout the nation. Most criminal justice activity, however, occurs at the state rather than the national level.

Two Justice Systems

Both the national and state systems of criminal justice enforce laws, try criminal cases, and punish offenders, but their activities differ in scope and purpose. The vast majority of criminal laws are written by state legislatures and enforced by state agencies. In addition, a variety of national criminal laws have been enacted by Congress and are enforced by the FBI, the Drug Enforcement Administration, the Secret Service, and other federal agencies.

Except in the case of federal drug offenses, relatively few offenders break federal criminal laws compared to the large numbers who break state criminal laws. For example, only small numbers of people violate the federal law against counterfeiting and espionage, while far more violate state laws against assault, larceny, and drunk driving. Even in the case of drug offenses, which during the 1980s and 1990s swept large numbers of offenders into federal prisons, many violators end up in state corrections systems because such crimes violate both state and federal laws.

The role of criminal justice agencies after the assassination of President John F. Kennedy in November 1963 illustrates the division of jurisdiction between federal and state agencies. Because Congress had not made killing the president a federal offense, the suspect, Lee Harvey Oswald, would have been charged under Texas laws had he lived (Oswald was shot to death by Jack Ruby shortly after his arrest). The U.S. Secret Service had the job of protecting the president, but apprehending the killer was the formal responsibility of the Dallas police and other Texas law enforcement agencies.

Expansion of Federal Involvement

Federal involvement in the criminal justice system has slowly expanded over time, especially regarding crimes spanning state borders. For example, crime syndicates and gangs deal with drugs, pornography, and gambling on an interstate basis. As a result, Congress has expanded the powers of the FBI and other federal agencies to pursue criminal activities that formerly were the responsibility of the states.

Congress has also passed laws designed to allow the FBI to investigate situations in which local police forces are likely to be less effective. Under the National Stolen Property Act, for example, the FBI may investigate thefts of more than $5,000 in value when the stolen property is likely to have been transported across state lines. As a national agency, the FBI is better able than any state agency to pursue criminal investigations across state borders.

Disputes over jurisdiction may occur when an offense violates both state and federal laws. If the FBI and local agencies do not cooperate, they may each seek to catch the same criminals. This can have major implications if the court to which the case is brought is determined by the agency that makes the arrest. Usually, however, law enforcement officials at all levels of government seek to cooperate and to coordinate their efforts.

Because of the existence of both state and federal systems, criminal justice in the United States is highly decentralized. As Figure 2.1 shows, two-thirds of all criminal justice employees work for local government. The majority of workers in all of

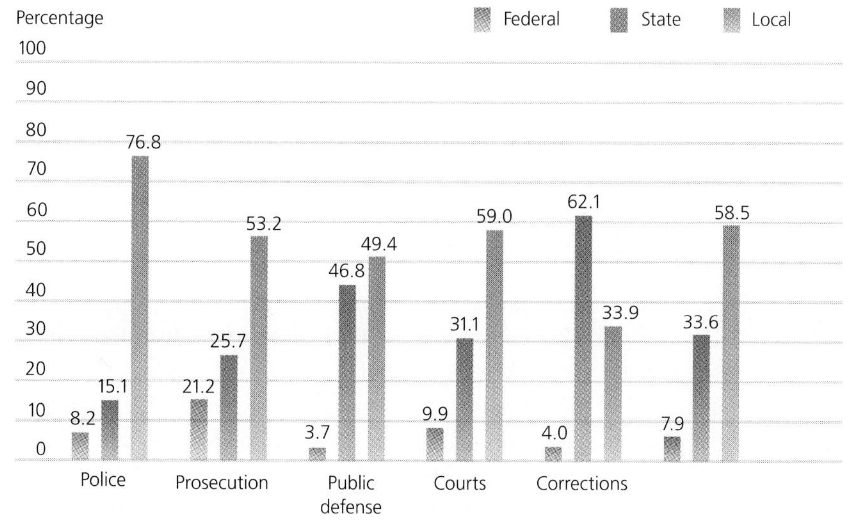

Figure 2.1
Percentage (rounded) of criminal justice employees at each level of government

The administration of criminal justice in the United States is very much a local affair, as these employment figures show. It is only in corrections that states employ a greater percentage of workers than do municipalities.

SOURCE: U.S. Department of Justice, Bureau of Justice Statistics, *Bulletin* (September 1993).

the subunits of the system—except corrections—are tied to local government. Likewise, the costs of criminal justice are distributed among the federal, state, and local governments, as shown in Figure 2.2.

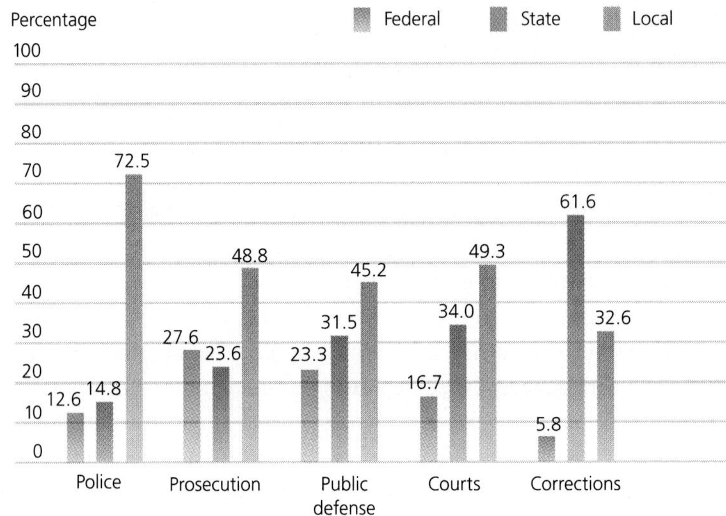

Figure 2.2
Who pays for criminal justice services?

State and local governments bear the brunt of the costs.

SOURCE: U.S. Department of Justice, Bureau of Justice Statistics, *Bulletin* (September 1993).

Because laws are enforced and offenders are brought to justice mainly in the states, counties, and cities, the way criminal justice agencies operate is shaped by local traditions, values, and practices. Local leaders, whether members of the city council or influential citizens, can help set law enforcement priorities by putting pressure on the police. Will the city's police officers crack down on illegal gambling? Will juvenile offenders be turned over to their parents with stern warnings, or will they be sent to state institutions? The answers to these and other important questions vary from city to city.

CHECKPOINT

3. What is the key feature of federalism?
4. What powers does the national government have in the area of criminal justice?
5. What factor has caused federal involvement in criminal justice to expand?

CRIMINAL JUSTICE AS A SOCIAL SYSTEM

system

A complex whole consisting of interdependent parts whose operations are directed toward goals and are influenced by the environment within which it functions.

To achieve the goals of criminal justice, many kinds of organizations—police, prosecution, courts, corrections—have been formed. Each has its own functions and personnel. On the surface, we might assume that criminal justice is an orderly process in which a variety of professionals act on each case on behalf of society. To know how the **system** really works, however, we must look beyond its formal organizational chart and examine the system itself. A system can be defined as a complex whole made up of interdependent parts whose actions are directed toward goals and influenced by the environment in which it functions.

The System Perspective

Criminal justice is a system made up of a number of parts or subsystems. The subsystems—police, courts, corrections—have their own goals and needs but are also interdependent. When one unit changes its policies, practices, or resources, other units will be affected. An increase in the number of people arrested by the police, for example, will affect not only the judicial subsystem, but also the probation and correctional subsystems. For criminal justice to achieve its goals, each part must make its own unique contribution; each must also have at least minimal contact with at least one other part of the system.

Exchange relationships influence decision making throughout the criminal justice system. Here, Attorney Terry Gilbert, center, and Chief Assistant Cuyahoga County Prosecutor Carmen Marino, right, talk with Judge Ronald Suster. Suster is hearing a motion to have Dr. Sam Sheppard, who was convicted of murdering his wife, in 1954, declared innocent and wrongly imprisoned, as indicated by DNA tests.

Understanding the nature of the entire criminal justice system and its subsystems is important, but we must also see how each individual in the system, or actor, plays his or her role. The criminal justice system is made up of a great many persons doing specific jobs. Some, such as police officers and judges, are well known to the public. Others, such as bail bondsmen and probation officers, are less well known. Each has goals that he or she cannot perform alone, and all perform their roles through **exchange**, the mutual transfer of resources. Each needs to gain the cooperation and assistance of other individuals by helping them achieve their own goals.

There are many kinds of exchange relationships in the criminal justice system, some more visible than others. Probably the most obvious example is **plea bargaining**, in which the defense attorney and the prosecutor reach an agreement: the defendant agrees to plead guilty in exchange for a reduction of charges or a lighter sentence. As a result of this exchange, the prosecutor gains a quick, sure conviction, the defense achieves a shorter sentence, and the defense attorney can move on to the next case. Thus, the cooperation underlying the exchange promotes the goals of each participant.

exchange

A mutual transfer of resources; balance of benefits and deficits that flow from behavior based on decisions about the values and costs of alternatives.

The concept of exchange reminds us that decisions are the products of interactions among individuals. In the example above, the case's outcome is based on the interactions of individuals who have considerd the benefits and costs of different courses of action. In this way the subsystems of the criminal justice system are tied together by the actions of individual decision makers. Figure 2.3 presents selected exchange relationships between a prosecutor and other individuals and agencies involved in the criminal justice process.

The concepts of system and exchange are closely linked, and they are useful tools for the analysis of criminal justice. In this book, these concepts serve as an organizing framework to describe individual subsystems and actors and help us see how the justice process really works. However, several other characteristics of the system shape the decisions that determine the fates of defendants.

plea bargain

A defendant's plea of guilty to a criminal charge with the reasonable expectation of receiving some consideration from the state for doing so, usually a reduction of the charge. The defendant's ultimate goal is a penalty lighter than the one formally warranted by the charged offense.

Characteristics of the Criminal Justice System

The workings of the criminal justice system have four major characteristics: (1) discretion, (2) resource dependence, (3) sequential tasks, and (4) filtering.

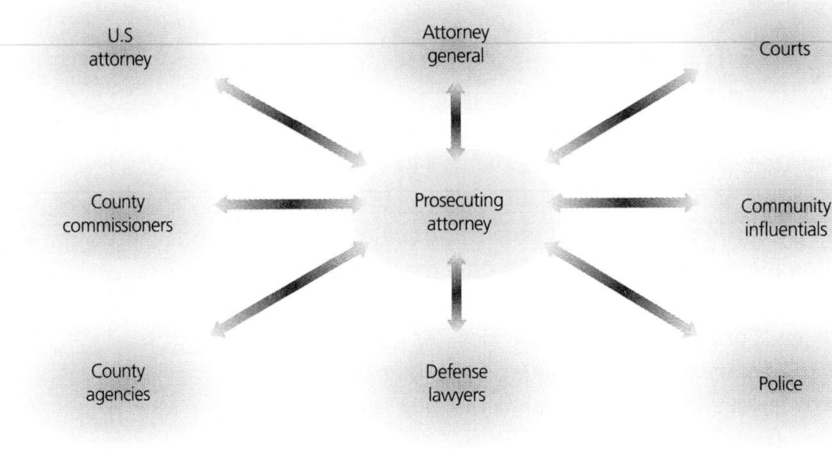

Figure 2.3
Exchange relationships between prosecutors and others

The prosecutor's decisions are influenced by relationships with other agencies and members of the community.

Discretion

At all levels of the justice process, there is a high degree of **discretion**. This term refers to officials' freedom to act according to their own judgment and conscience (see Table 2.1). For example, police officers decide how to handle a crime situation, prosecutors decide what charges to file, judges decide how long a sentence will be, and parole boards decide when an offender may be released from prison.

discretion

The authority to make decisions without reference to specific rules or facts, using instead one's own judgment; allows for individualization and informality in the administration of justice.

The extent of such discretion may seem odd, given that the United States is ruled by law and has created procedures to ensure that decisions are made in accordance with law. However, instead of a mechanistic system in which decisions are automatically and consistently determined by the letter of the law, criminal justice is a system in which actors may take many factors into account and exercise many options as they dispose of a case.

Two arguments are often used to justify discretion in the criminal justice system. First, discretion is needed because the system lacks the resources to treat every case

Table 2.1
Who exercises discretion?

Discretion is exercised by various actors throughout the criminal justice system.

These Criminal Justice Officials . . .	. . . Must Often Decide Whether, or How, to:
Police	Enforce specific laws Investigate specific crimes Search people, vicinities, buildings Arrest or detain people
Prosecutors	File charges or petitions for adjudication Seek indictments Drop cases Reduce charges
Judges or magistrates	Set bail or conditions for release Accept pleas Determine delinquency Dismiss charges Impose sentence Revoke probation
Correctional officials	Assign to type of correctional facility Award privileges Punish for infractions of rules Determine date and conditions of parole Revoke parole

SOURCE: U.S. Department of Justice, Bureau of Justice Statistics, *Report to the Nation on Crime and Justice*, 2d ed. (Washington, D.C.: Government Printing Office, 1988), 59.

the same way. If every violation of the law were pursued through trial, the costs would be immense. Second, many officials believe that discretion permits them to achieve greater justice than rigid rules would produce.

Resource Dependence

Criminal justice agencies do not generate their own resources but depend on other agencies for funding. Therefore, actors in the system must cultivate and maintain good relations with those who allocate resources—that is, political decision makers, such as legislators, mayors, and city council members. Some police departments gain revenue through traffic fines and property forfeitures, but these sources are not enough to sustain their budgets.

Because budget decisions are made by elected officials who seek to please the public, criminal justice officials must also maintain a positive image and good relations with voters. If the police have strong public support, for example, the mayor will be reluctant to reduce the law enforcement budget. Criminal justice officials also seek positive coverage from the news media. Because the media often provide a crucial link between government agencies and the public, criminal justice officials may announce notable achievements while trying to limit publicity about controversial cases and decisions.

Sequential Tasks

Decisions in the criminal justice system are made in a specific sequence. The police must arrest a person before the case is passed to the prosecutor to determine if charges should be brought. Defendant is passed along to the prosecutor. This decision influences the nature of the court's workload. Officials cannot achieve their goals by acting out of sequence. For example, prosecutors and judges cannot bypass the police by making arrests, and corrections officials cannot punish anyone who has not passed through the earlier stages of the process.

The sequential nature of the system is a key element in the exchange relationships among the justice system's decision makers who depend on one another to achieve their goals. Thus, the system is highly interdependent.

Filtering

The criminal justice system may be viewed as a **filtering process**. At each stage some defendants are sent on to the next stage, while others are either released or processed under changed conditions. As shown in Figure 2.4, persons who have been arrested may be filtered out of the system at various points. Note that relatively few suspects who are arrested are then prosecuted, tried, and convicted. Some go free because the police decide that a crime has not been committed or that the evidence is not sound. The prosecutor may decide that justice would be better served by sending the suspect to a substance abuse clinic. Many defendants will plead guilty, the judge may dismiss charges against others, and the jury may acquit a few defendants. Most of the offenders who are actually tried, however, will be convicted. Thus, the criminal justice system is often described as a funnel—many cases enter it, but only a few result in conviction and punishment.

filtering process

A screening operation; a process by which criminal justice officials screen out some cases while advancing others to the next level of decision making.

To summarize, the criminal justice system is composed of a set of interdependent parts (subsystems). This system has four key attributes: (1) discretion, (2) resource dependence, (3) sequential tasks, and (4) filtering. Using this framework, we look next at the operations of criminal justice agencies and then examine the flow of cases through the system.

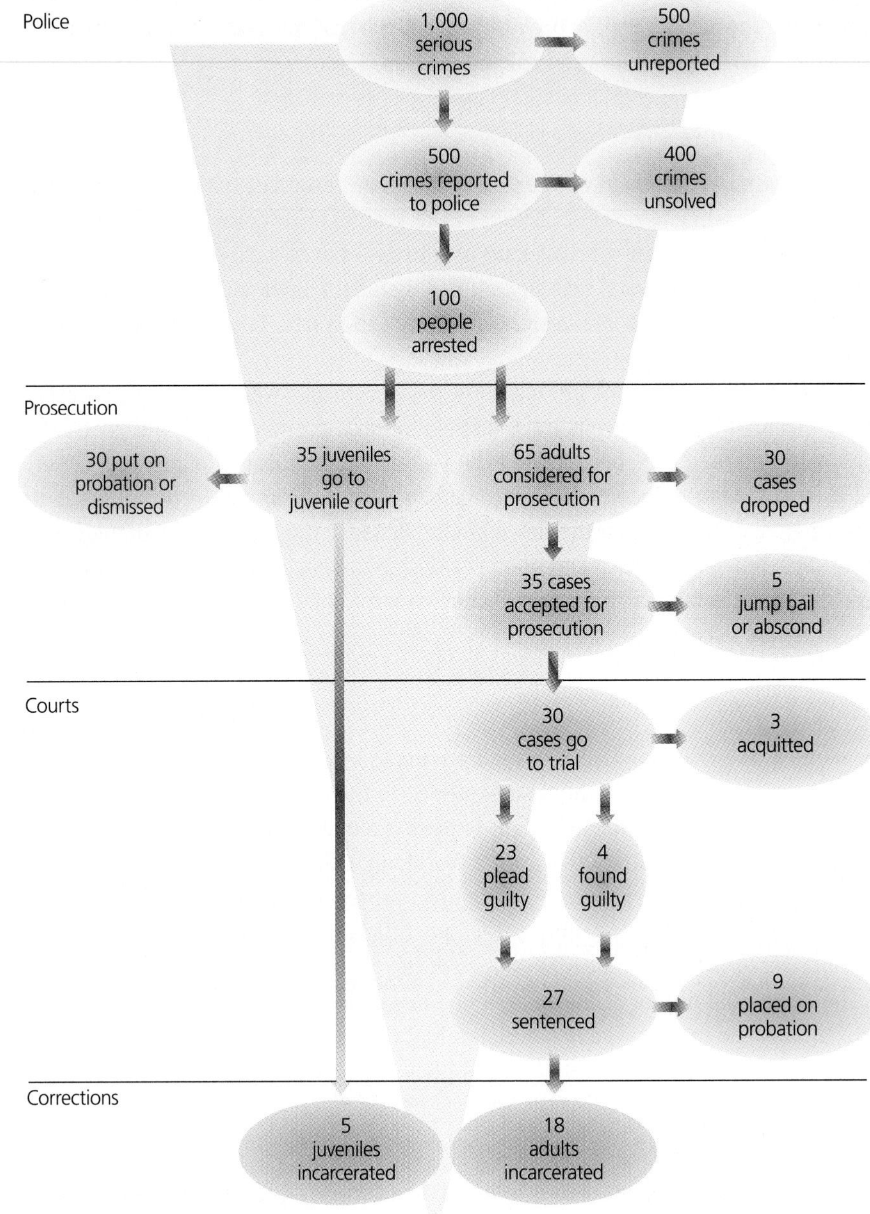

Figure 2.4
Criminal justice as a filtering process

Decisions at each point in the system result in some cases being dropped while others are passed to the next point. Are you surprised by the small portion of cases that remain?

SOURCE: Data from this figure have been drawn from many sources, including U.S. Department of Justice, *Sourcebook of Criminal Justice Statistics*, 1992 (Washington, D.C.: Government Printing Office, 1993) and Bureau of Justice Statistics, *Bulletin* (January 1988, February 1989).

CHECKPOINT

6. Define a system.
7. Give an example of an exchange relationship.
8. What are the major characteristics of the criminal justice system?

OPERATIONS OF CRIMINAL JUSTICE AGENCIES

The criminal justice system has been formed to deal with persons who are accused of violating the criminal law. Its subsystems consist of more than 60,000 public and private agencies with an annual budget of more than $94 billion and almost 1.8 million employees (BJS, 1997. *Sourcebook*:2,18). Here we review the main parts of the criminal justice system and their functions.

Police

We usually think of the police as being on the "front line" in controlling crime. When we use the term *police*, however, we are referring not to a single agency or type of agency, but to many agencies at each level of government. The complexity of the criminal justice system can be seen in the large number of organizations engaged in law enforcement. Of the 17,000 law enforcement agencies in the United States, only 50 are federal and another 49 are state agencies (Hawaii has no state police). The remaining 16,901 agencies are found in counties, cities, and towns, reflecting the fact that the police function is dominated by local governments. At the state and local levels, these agencies have more than 840,000 employees and a total annual budget that exceeds $41 billion (BJS, 1993. *Bulletin*. July).

In emotionally charged situations, such as this protest sparked by an accident in which a Hasidic motorist struck and killed a black child in the Crown Heights section of New York City, the police must take stock of the circumstances before they act.

Police agencies have four major duties:

1. **Keeping the Peace** This broad and important mandate involves the protection of rights and persons in situations ranging from street-corner brawls to domestic quarrels.
2. **Apprehending Violators and Combating Crime** This is the task that the public most often associates with police work, although it accounts for only a small proportion of police time and resources.
3. **Preventing Crime** By educating the public about the threat of crime and by reducing the number of situations in which crimes are likely to be committed, the police can lower the rate of crime.
4. **Providing Social Services** Police officers recover stolen property, direct traffic, give emergency medical aid, help people who have locked themselves out of their homes, and provide other social services.

Courts

The United States has a **dual court system** that consists of a separate judicial system for each state in addition to a national system. Each system has its own series of courts; the U.S. Supreme Court is responsible for correcting certain errors made in all other court systems. Although the Supreme Court can review cases from both the state and federal courts, it will hear only cases involving federal law or constitutional rights.

dual court system

A system consisting of a separate judicial structure for each state in addition to a national structure. Each case is tried in a court of the same jurisdiction as that of the law or laws broken.

With a dual court system, the law may be interpreted differently in various states. Although the wording of laws may be similar, state courts do not necessarily interpret the words in the same way. To some extent, these variations reflect different social and political conditions. The dominant values of citizens and judges may differ from one region to another. Differences in interpretation may also be due to attempts by state courts to solve similar problems by different means. For example, before the U.S. Supreme Court ruled that evidence the police obtained in illegal ways should be excluded from use at trials, some states had already established rules barring the use of such evidence.

adjudication

The process of determining the guilt or innocence of a defendant.

Courts are responsible for **adjudication**. In the case of criminal justice, the term refers to the process of determining if a defendant is guilty. In so doing, courts must use fair procedures that will produce just, reliable decisions. Courts must also impose sentences that are appropriate to the behavior being punished.

Corrections

On any given day, more than 5 million American adults are under the supervision of state and federal corrections systems. There is no "typical" corrections agency or official system. Instead, a variety of agencies and programs are provided by private and public organizations—including federal, state, and local governments—and carried out in many different community and closed settings.

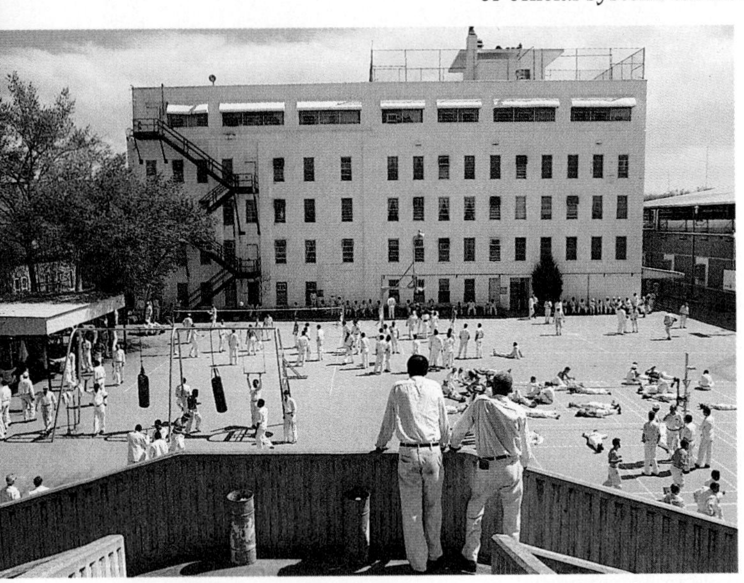

The public often equates corrections with prisons, yet only about one-third of convicted offenders are incarcerated. Two-thirds of offenders in the community are on probation or parole.

While the average citizen may equate corrections with prisons, only about one-third of convicted offenders are in prisons and jails; the rest are being supervised in the community. Probation and parole have long been important aspects of corrections, as have community-based halfway houses, work release programs, and supervised activities.

The federal government, all the states, most counties, and all but the smallest cities engage in corrections. Nonprofit private organizations such as the YMCA have also contracted with governments to perform correctional services. In recent years, for-profit businesses have also entered into contracts with governments to build and operate correctional institutions.

The police, courts, and corrections are the main agencies of criminal justice. Each is a part, or subsystem, of the criminal justice system. Each is linked to the other two subsystems, and the actions of each affect the others. These effects can be seen as we examine the flow of decision making within the criminal justice system.

CHECKPOINT

9. What are the four main duties of police?
10. What is a dual court system?
11. What are the major types of state and local correctional facilities and programs? What type of organizations operate them?

THE FLOW OF DECISION MAKING IN THE CRIMINAL JUSTICE SYSTEM

The processing of cases in the criminal justice system involves a series of decisions by police officers, prosecutors, judges, probation officers, wardens, and parole board members. At each stage in the process, they decide whether a case will move on to the next stage or be dropped from the system. Although the flowchart shown in Figure 2.5 appears streamlined, with cases entering at the top and moving swiftly toward the bottom, the actual route taken may be quite long and may involve many

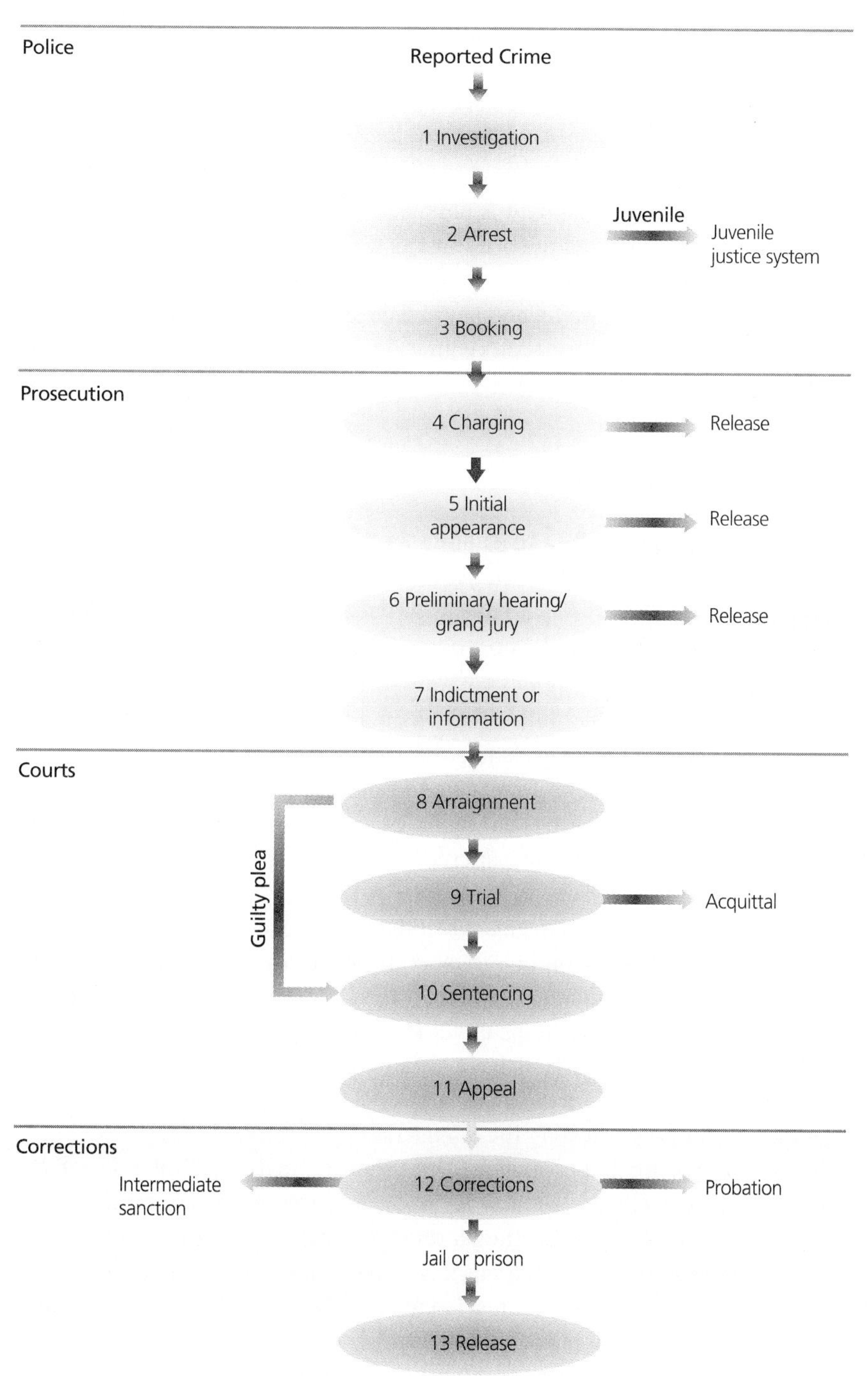

Figure 2.5
The flow of decision making in the criminal justice system

Each agency is responsible for a part of the decision-making process. Thus the police, prosecution, courts, and corrections are bound together through a series of exchange relationships.

detours. At each step, officials have the discretion to decide what happens next. Many cases are filtered out of the system, others are sent to the next decision maker, and still others are dealt with by informal means.

Moreover, the flowchart does not show the influences of social relations or the political environment. For example, in 1997 reports surfaced indicating that the late Michael Kennedy, then a thirty-nine-year-old lawyer and nephew of the late President John F. Kennedy, had carried on an affair with his children's baby sitter beginning when the baby sitter was only 14 years old. If true, Kennedy would automatically have been guilty of statutory rape, since it is a serious felony to have sexual relations with an underage girl, even if she willingly participates. Amid reports that Kennedy's lawyers were negotiating a quiet financial settlement with the girl and her family, the local prosecutor announced that no criminal charges would be filed because the girl—now a college student—refused to provide any evidence against Kennedy.

In other cases, prosecutors and judges may pressure witnesses to testify, sometimes even jailing reluctant witnesses for contempt of court. Did the prosecutor decline to press charges because Kennedy was a member of a politically powerful family? We cannot know for sure; it is possible that political factors or behind-the-scenes negotiations influenced the prosecutor's discretionary decision. Such factors may influence decisions in ways that are not reflected in a simple description of decision-making steps. As we follow the thirteen steps of the criminal justice process, bear in mind that the formal procedures do not hold in every case. Discretion, political pressure, and other factors may alter the outcome for different individuals.

Steps in the Decision-Making Process

The criminal justice system consists of thirteen steps that cover the stages of law enforcement, adjudication, and corrections. The system looks like an assembly line where decisions are made about **defendants**—persons charged with crimes. As these steps are described, recall the concepts discussed earlier: system, discretion, sequential tasks, filtering, and exchange. Be aware that the terms used for different stages in the process may differ from state to state and that the sequence of the steps differs in some parts of the country. In general, however, but the flow of decision making generally follows this pattern.

defendant

A person charged with a crime.

1. Investigation. The process begins when the police believe that a crime has been committed. At this point an investigation is begun. The police normally depend on a member of the community to report the offense. Except for traffic and public order offenses, it is unusual for the police to observe illegal behavior themselves. Since most crimes have already been committed and offenders have left the scene before the police arrive, the police are at a disadvantage in quickly finding and arresting the offenders.
2. Arrest. If the police find enough evidence showing that a particular person has committed a crime, an arrest may be made. An **arrest** involves physically taking a person into custody pending a court proceeding. This action not only restricts the suspect's freedom, but it is also the first step toward prosecution.

   Under some conditions, arrests may be made on the basis of a **warrant**—a court order issued by a judge authorizing police officers to take certain actions, such as arresting suspects or searching premises. In practice, most arrests are

arrest

The physical taking of a person into custody on the grounds that there is reason to believe that he or she has committed a criminal offense. Police may use only reasonable physical force in making an arrest. The purpose of the arrest is to hold the accused for a court proceeding.

made without warrants. In some states, police officers may issue a summons or citation that orders a person to appear in court on a certain date. This avoids the need to hold the suspect physically until decisions are made about the case.

warrant

A court order authorizing police officials to take certain actions, for example, to arrest suspects or to search premises.

3. Booking. After an arrest the suspect is usually transported to a police station for booking, in which a record is made of the arrest. When booked, the suspect may be fingerprinted, photographed, questioned, and placed in a lineup to be identified by the victim or witnesses. All suspects must also be warned that they have the right to counsel, that they may remain silent, and that any statement they make may be used against them later. Bail may be set so that the suspect learns what amount of money must be paid or what other conditions must be met to gain release from custody until the case is processed.
4. Charging. Prosecuting attorneys are the key link between the police and the courts. They must consider the facts of the case and decide whether there is reasonable cause to believe that an offense was committed and that the suspect committed the offense. The decision to charge is crucial because it sets in motion the adjudication of the case.
5. Initial appearance. Within a reasonable time after arrest, the suspect must be brought before a judge. At this point, suspects are given formal notice of the charge(s) for which they are being held, advised of their rights, and, if approved by the judge, given a chance to post bail. At this stage, the judge decides whether there is enough evidence to hold the suspect for further criminal processing. If enough evidence has not been produced, the judge will dismiss the case.

   The purpose of bail is to permit the accused to be released while awaiting trial and to ensure that he or she will show up in court at the appointed time. Bail requires the accused to provide or arrange a surety (or pledge), usually in the form of money or a bond. The amount of bail is based mainly on the judge's view of the seriousness of the crime and the defendant's prior criminal record. Suspects may also be released on their own recognizance—a promise to appear in court at a later date without the posting of bail. In a few cases bail may be denied and the accused held because he or she is viewed as a threat to the community.
6. Preliminary hearing/grand jury. After suspects have been arrested, booked, and brought to court to be informed of the charges against them and advised of their rights, a decision must be made as to whether there is enough evidence to proceed. The preliminary hearing, used in about half the states, allows a judge to decide whether there is probable cause to believe that a crime has been committed and that the accused person committed it. If the judge does not find probable cause, the case is dismissed. If there is enough evidence, the accused is bound over for arraignment on an **information**—a document charging a person with a specific crime.

   In the federal system and in some states, the prosecutor appears before a grand jury, which decides whether there is enough evidence to file an **indictment** or "true bill" charging the suspect with a specific crime. The preliminary hearing and grand jury are designed to prevent hasty and malicious prosecutions, to protect persons from mistakenly being humiliated in public, and to decide whether there are grounds for prosecution.
7. Indictment/information. If the preliminary hearing leads to information or the grand jury vote leads to an indictment, the prosecutor prepares the formal charging document and presents it to the court.
8. Arraignment. The accused person appears in court to hear the indictment or information read by a judge and to enter a plea. Accused persons may plead

information

A document charging an individual with a specific crime. It is prepared by a prosecuting attorney and presented to a court at a preliminary hearing.

indictment

A document returned by a grand jury as a "true bill" charging an individual with a specific crime on the basis of a determination of probable cause as presented by a prosecuting attorney.

guilty or not guilty, or in some states, stand mute. If the accused pleads guilty, the judge must decide whether the plea is made voluntarily and whether the person has full knowledge of the consequences. When a guilty plea is accepted as "knowing" and voluntary, there is no need for a trial and the judge imposes a sentence.

Plea bargaining may take place at any time in the criminal justice process, but it is likely to be completed before or after arraignment. Very few criminal cases proceed to trial. Most move from the entry of the guilty plea to the sentencing phase.

9. Trial. For the small percentage of defendants who plead not guilty, the right to a trial by an impartial jury is guaranteed by the Sixth Amendment if the charges are serious enough to warrant a prison sentence of more than six months. In many jurisdictions, lesser charges do not entail a right to a jury trial. Most trials are summary or bench trials—that is, they are conducted without a jury. Because the defendant pleads guilty in most criminal cases, only about 10 to 15 percent of cases go to trial and only about 5 percent are heard by juries. Whether a criminal trial is held before a judge alone or before a judge and jury, the procedures are similar and are set out by state law and Supreme Court rulings. A defendant may be found guilty only if the evidence proves beyond a reasonable doubt that he or she committed the offense.
10. Sentencing. Judges are responsible for imposing sentences. The intent is to make the sentence suitable to the offender and the offense within the limits set by the law. Although criminal codes place limits on sentences, the judge still has leeway. Among the judge's options are a suspended sentence, probation, imprisonment, or other sanctions such as fines and community service.
11. Appeal. Defendants who are found guilty may appeal convictions to a higher court. An appeal may be based on the claim that the trial court failed to follow the proper procedures or that constitutional rights were violated by the actions of police, prosecutors, defense attorneys, or judges. The number of appeals is small compared with the total number of convictions, and in about 80 percent of appeals, trial judges and other officials are ruled to have acted properly. Even defendants who win appeals do not go free right away. Normally the defendant is given a second trial, which may result in an acquittal, a second conviction, or a plea bargain to lesser charges.
12. Corrections. The court's sentence is carried out by the correctional subsystem. Probation, intermediate sanctions such as fines and community service, and incarceration are the sanctions most often imposed. Probation allows offenders to serve their sentences in the community under supervision. Youthful offenders, first offenders, and those convicted of minor violations are most likely to be sentenced to probation rather than incarceration. The conditions of probation may require offenders to observe certain rules—to be employed, maintain an orderly life, or attend school—and to report to their supervising officer from time to time. If these requirements are not met, the judge may revoke the probation and impose a prison sentence.

    Many new types of sanctions have been used in recent years. These intermediate sanctions are more restrictive than probation but less restrictive than incarceration. They include fines, intensive supervision probation, boot camp, home confinement, and community service.

    Whatever the reasons used to justify them, prisons exist mainly to separate criminals from the rest of society. Those convicted of misdemeanors usually serve their time in city or county jails, while felons serve time in state prisons. Isolation from the community is one of the most painful aspects of incarceration. Not only are letters and visits restricted, but supervision and censorship are ever present. In order to maintain security, prison officials make unannounced searches of inmates and subject them to strict discipline.

13. Release. Release may occur when the offender has served the full sentence imposed by the court, but most offenders are returned to the community under the supervision of a parole officer. Parole continues for the duration of the sentence or for a period specified by law. Parole may be revoked and the offender returned to prison if the conditions of parole are not met or if the parolee commits another crime.

CHECKPOINT

12. List the steps of the criminal justice process.

The Criminal Justice Wedding Cake

Although the flowchart shown in Figure 2.5 is helpful, we must note that not all cases are treated equally (Friedman and Percival, 1981). The process applied to a given case, as well as its outcome, is shaped by the importance of the case to decision makers, the seriousness of the charge, and the defendant's resources.

Some cases are highly visible either because of the notoriety of the defendant or victim or because of the shocking nature of the crime. At the other extreme are "run-of-the-mill cases" involving unknown persons charged with minor crimes.

As shown in Figure 2.6, the criminal justice process can be compared to a wedding cake. This model shows clearly how different cases receive different kinds of treatment in the justice process.

Layer 1 of the "cake" consists of "celebrated" cases that are highly unusual, get great public attention, result in a jury trial, and often drag on through many appeals. These cases embody the ideal of an adversary system of justice in which each side actively fights against the other, either because the defendant faces a stiff sentence or because the defendant has the financial resources to pay for a strong defense. The cases of Oklahoma City bombing defendants Timothy McVeigh and Terry Nichols and, of course, the celebrated trial of O. J. Simpson on double murder charges are of this type. Not all cases in Layer 1 receive national attention. From time to time, local crimes, especially cases of murder and rape, are treated in this way.

The trial of Terry Nichols attracted much public attention. Nichols was convicted of conspiracy and involuntary manslaughter, but not of murder in connection with the Oklahoma City Federal Building bombing. Highly visible cases like this do not give an accurate picture of the criminal justice system.

These cases are like morality plays. The carefully crafted arguments of the prosecution and defense are seen as expressing key issues in our society or tragic flaws in individuals. Too often, however, the public concludes that all criminal cases follow this model.

Layer 2 consists of **felonies** that are considered serious by officials: violent crimes committed by persons with long criminal records against victims unknown to them. Police and the prosecutors speak of these as "heavy" cases that should result in "tough" sentences. In such cases the defendant has little reason to plead guilty and the defense attorney must prepare for trial.

Layer 3 also consists of felonies, but the crimes and the offenders are seen as less important than those in Layer 2. The offenses may be the same as in Layer 2, but the offender may have no record, and the victim may have had a prior relationship with the accused. The main goal of criminal justice officials is to dispose of such cases quickly. For this reason, many are filtered out of the system, often through plea bargaining.

felonies

Serious crimes usually carrying a penalty of death or incarceration for more than one year.

Layer 4 is made up of **misdemeanors**. About 90 percent of all cases fall into this category. They concern such offenses as public drunkenness, shoplifting, prostitution, disturbing the peace, and traffic violations. Looked upon as the "garbage" of the system, these cases are handled by the lower courts, where speed is essential. Prosecutors use their discretion to reduce charges or recommend probation as a way to encourage defendants to plead guilty quickly. Trials are rare, processes are informal, and fines, probation, or short jail sentences result.

misdemeanors

Offenses less serious than felonies and usually punishable by incarceration of no more than a year, probation, or intermediate sanction.

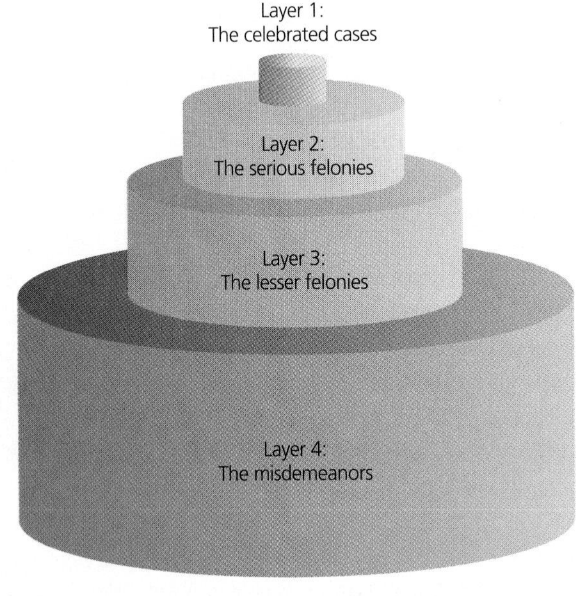

Figure 2.6
The criminal justice wedding cake

This figure shows that different cases are treated in different ways. Only a very few cases are played out as "high drama"; most are handled through plea bargaining and dismissals.

SOURCE: Drawn from Samuel Walker, *Sense and Nonsense about Crime and Drugs*, 3d ed. (Belmont, Calif.: Wadsworth Publishing Co., 1994), 30-32.

The wedding cake model is a useful way of viewing the criminal justice system. Cases are not treated equally; some are seen as very important, others as merely part of a large caseload that must be processed. When one knows the nature of a case, one can predict fairly well how it will be handled and what its outcome will be.

CHECKPOINT

13. What is the purpose of the "wedding cake model"?
14. Describe the types of cases found on each layer.

Crime Control versus Due Process

Keep the "wedding cake" model in mind as we consider other models that give us a more complete and accurate picture of how the criminal justice system really operates. Scholars often use models to organize their thinking about a subject and to guide their research. Models are representations of something that cannot be visualized, permitting generalized statements to be made about it and evaluations of its strengths and weaknesses.

In one of the most important contributions to systematic thought about the administration of justice, Herbert Packer (1968) described two competing models of the administration of criminal justice: the **crime control model** and the **due process model**. These are opposing ways of looking at the goals and procedures of the criminal justice system. The crime control model is much like an assembly line, while the due process model is like an obstacle course.

In reality, of course, no one official or agency functions according to one model or the other. Elements of both models are found throughout the system. However, the two models reveal key tensions within the criminal justice process, as well as the gap between how we describe the system and the way most cases are actually processed. Table 2.1 presents the major elements of each model.

crime control model

A model of the criminal justice system that assumes freedom is so important that every effort must be made to repress crime; it emphasizes efficiency, speed, finality, and the capacity to apprehend, try, convict, and dispose of a high proportion of offenders.

due process model

A model of the criminal justice system that assumes freedom is so important that every effort must be made to ensure that criminal justice decisions are based on reliable information; itemphasizes the adversarial process, the rights of defendants, and formal decision-making procedures.

Crime Control: Order as a Value

The crime control model assumes that every effort must be made to repress crime. It emphasizes efficiency and the capacity to catch, try, convict, and punish a high proportion of offenders; it also stresses speed and finality. This model places the goal of controlling crime uppermost, putting less emphasis on protecting individual rights. As Packer points out, in order to achieve liberty for all citizens, the crime control model calls for efficiency in screening suspects, determining guilt, and applying sanctions to the convicted. Because of high rates of crime and the limited resources of law enforcement, speed and finality are necessary. All these elements depend on informality, uniformity, and few challenges by defense attorneys or defendants.

In this model, police and prosecutors decide early on how likely the suspect is to be found guilty. If a case is unlikely to end in conviction, the prosecutor may drop the charges. At each stage, from arrest to preliminary hearing, arraignment, and trial, established procedures are used to determine whether the accused should be passed on to the next stage. Rather than stressing the combative aspects of the courtroom, this model promotes bargaining between the state and the accused. Nearly all cases are disposed of through such bargaining, and they typically end with the defendant pleading guilty. Packer's description of this model as an assembly-line process conveys the idea of quick, efficient decisions by actors at fixed stations that turn out the intended product—guilty pleas and closed cases.

Due Process: Law as a Value

If the crime control model looks like an assembly line, the due process model looks more like an obstacle course. This model assumes that freedom is so important that every effort must be made to ensure that criminal justice decisions are based on reliable information. It stresses the adversarial process, the rights of defendants, and formal decision-making procedures. For example, it assumes that police and prosecutors may be wrong in presuming a defendant to be guilty because people are poor observers of disturbing events. Thus, the accused should be labeled as criminal only on the basis of conclusive evidence. To reduce error, the government must be forced to prove beyond a reasonable doubt that the defendant is guilty of the crime. Therefore, the process must give the defense every opportunity to show that the evidence is not conclusive, and the outcome must be decided by an impartial judge and jury. According to Packer, the assumption that the defendant is innocent until proved guilty has a far-reaching impact on the criminal justice system.

	Goal	Value	Process	Major Decision Point	Basis of Decision Making
Due process model	Preserve individual liberties	Reliability	Adversarial	Courtroom	Law
Crime control model	Repress crime	Efficiency	Administrative	Police, pretrial processes	Discretion

Table 2.2
Due process model and crime control model compared

What other comparisons can be made between the two models?

In the due process model, the state must prove that the person is guilty of the crime as charged. Prosecutors must prove their cases while obeying rules dealing with such matters as the admissibility of evidence and respect for defendants' constitutional rights. Forcing the state to prove its case in a trial protects citizens from wrongful convictions. Thus, the due process model emphasizes particular aspects of the goal of doing justice. It protects the rights of individuals and reserves punishment for those who unquestionably deserve it. These values are stressed even though some guilty defendants may go free because the evidence against them is not conclusive enough. By contrast, the crime control model values efficient case processing and punishment over the possibility that innocent people might be swept up in the process.

CHECKPOINT

15. What are the main features of the crime control model?
16. What are the main features of the due process model?

Summary

- The three goals of the criminal justice system are: doing justice, controlling crime, and preventing crime.
- Both the national and state systems of criminal justice enforce laws, try cases, and punish offenders.
- Criminal justice is a system made up of a number of parts or subsystems—police, courts, corrections.
- Exchange is a key concept for the analysis of criminal justice processes.
- Four major characteristics of the criminal justice system are discretion, resource dependence, sequential tasks, and filtering.
- The processing of cases in the criminal justice system involves a series of decisions by police officers, prosecutors, judges, probation officers, wardens, and parole board members.

- The criminal justice system consists of thirteen steps that cover the stages of law enforcement, adjudication, and corrections.
- The four-layered criminal justice wedding cake model makes us realize that not all cases are treated equally.
- The crime control model and the due process model are two ways of looking at the goals and procedures of the criminal justice system.

ANSWERS TO CHECKPOINTS

1. Doing justice, controlling crime, preventing crime.
2. Offenders are held fully accountable for their actions; the rights of persons who have contact with the system will be protected; and like offenses will be treated alike and officials will take into account relevant differences among offenders and offenses.
3. A division of power between a central (national) government and regional (state) governments.
4. Enforcement of federal criminal laws.
5. The expansion of criminal activities across state borders.
6. A complex whole made up of interdependent parts whose actions are directed toward goals and influenced by the environment within which it functions.
7. Plea bargaining.
8. Discretion, resource dependence, sequential tasks, filtering.
9. Keeping the peace, apprehending violators and combating crime, preventing crime, providing social services.
10. A separate judicial system for each state in addition to a national system.
11. Prisons, jails, probation, parole, intermediate sanctions. Public, nonprofit, and for-profit agencies carry out these programs.
12. (1) Investigation, (2) Arrest, (3) Booking, (4)Charging, (5)Initial appearance, (6) Preliminary hearing/grand jury, (7)Indictment/information, (8) Arraignment, (9) Trial, (10) Sentencing, (11) Appeal, (12) Corrections, (13) Release.
13. To show that not all cases are treated equally.
14. Layer l: celebrated cases in which the adversarial system is played out in full. Layer 2: serious felonies committed by persons with long criminal records against victims unknown to them. Layer 3: felonies in which the crimes and the offenders are viewed as less serious than in Layer 2. Layer 4: misdemeanors.
15. Every effort must be made to repress crime through efficiency, speed, and finality.
16. Every effort must be made to ensure that criminal justice decisions are based on reliable information. It stresses the adversarial process, the rights of defendants, and formal decision-making procedures.

Questions for Review

1. What are the goals of the criminal justice system?
2. What is meant by the concept of system? How is the administration of criminal justice a system?
3. Why is it suggested that the criminal justice wedding cake is a better depiction of reality than a linear model of the system?
4. What are the major elements of Packer's due process model and crime control model?

Chapter 3

Criminal Justice and the Rule of Law

Foundations of Criminal Law

- *Substantive Law and Procedural Law*

Substantive Criminal Law

- *Seven Principles of Criminal Law*
- *Elements of a Crime*
- *Statutory Definitions of Crimes*
- *Responsibility for Criminal Acts*

Procedural Criminal Law

- *The Bill of Rights*
- *The Fourteenth Amendment and Due Process*
- *The Due Process Revolution*
- *The Fourth Amendment: Protection against Unreasonable Searches and Seizures*
- *The Fifth Amendment: Protection against Self-Incrimination and Double Jeopardy*
- *The Sixth Amendment: The Right to Counsel and a Fair Trial*
- *The Eighth Amendment: Protection against Excessive Bail, Excessive Fines, and Cruel and Unusual Punishment*

Constitutional Rights and Criminal Justice Professionals

LEROY HENDRICKS was convicted of six sexual offenses against children over a thirty-year period and had spent much of his adult life in prison. Every time he finished serving a prison sentence or gained parole release, he eventually victimized more children and returned to prison. After serving nearly ten years in prison for his most recent crime—molesting two teenage boys—he was scheduled to move to a halfway house in the community as the first step toward release in 1994.

As Hendricks neared the end of his prison sentence, the Kansas legislature passed a new law, permitting the state to hold sex offenders in mental hospitals *after* they served their prison sentences. As a result of Kansas's new Sexually Violent Predator Act, Hendricks was transferred from a prison to a mental hospital at the end of his sentence.

Hendricks had paid his debt to society by serving the prison sentence imposed for his crime. Yet, after serving his full sentence, he did not gain his freedom. The new law permitted Kansas to keep him locked up forever.

Is it fair to serve a full prison sentence for a crime and still remain behind bars? Hendricks believed that the Kansas law was unfair. He took his case to court claiming that the law was punishing him a second time for his crime. If that was true, the Kansas law could be violating the right against "double jeopardy"—being tried or punished twice for the same offense. Hendricks also argued that the law improperly imposed a new punishment on him after he committed his crime and served his sentence. Thus he claimed that the Sexual Predator Act was an *"ex post facto law,"* the kind of law prohibited by the U.S. Constitution because it applies new rules and punishments that did not exist at the time an offender violated previously existing laws.

Should Hendricks be entitled to release? Is it fair to create new rules which keep people locked up after they serve their full prison sentences? Was Hendricks being punished twice for his crimes? These are important questions because, like other difficult questions concerning crime and justice, they determine whether a person will lose his or her freedom. The answers to these questions will be decided by law, the legal rules that govern society.

On the one side, an individual claims that he is unfairly deprived of his freedom. On the other side, the State of Kansas seeks to protect society from sex offenders who seem unable to control themselves. In the middle of this dispute is the U.S. Supreme Court, the group of nine judges—called "justices"—who must decide how the nation's highest law, expressed in the U.S. Constitution, answers the difficult questions.

In 1997, the Supreme Court tackled the issues raised by Hendricks. Ultimately, Hendricks remained locked up. Only four of the nine justices believed that Kansas unfairly created new rules after the fact when it kept Hendricks in custody. The majority of the Supreme Court—five justices—decided that this was not a second or after-the-fact punishment because Kansas sought to use the law to provide "treatment" rather than to impose "punishment" *(Kansas v. Hendricks)*.

The Hendricks case shows us important aspects of law in American criminal justice. We use law to decide who will be punished, who will lose their freedom, and, in death penalty cases, who will lose their lives. The rules of law also determine what kinds of actions governments may take. Sometimes our legal rights prevent government officials, including police officers and prosecutors, from searching, questioning, and punishing suspected criminals. Frequently, the rules of law are not crystal clear. There may be significant questions about whether certain actions are really crimes under the law or whether people possess certain legally protected rights. For answers to these difficult questions, we look to judges, whose jobs include the important responsibility of interpreting the law and informing society of the law's meaning.

In this chapter, we will examine the origins and essential elements of laws affecting criminal justice. Criminal laws tell us which forbidden actions are "crimes." In addition, various provisions of the U.S. Constitution spell out rights for criminal defendants and rules for criminal justice officials. All of these aspects of law are important for criminal justice.

Questions for Inquiry

What are the bases and sources of American criminal law?

How does substantive criminal law define a crime and the legal responsibility of the accused?

How does procedural criminal law define the rights of the accused and the processes for dealing with a case?

How has the United States Supreme Court interpreted the criminal justice amendments to the Constitution?

FOUNDATIONS OF CRIMINAL LAW

Laws tell citizens what they can and cannot do. Laws also tell government officials when they can seek to punish citizens for violations and how they must go about it. Government officials may not do whatever they want. Presidents, governors, senators, judges, and all other American officials must follow the law. Thus, in a democracy laws are a major tool to prevent government officials from seizing too much power or using power improperly.

Substantive Law and Procedural Law

The Draconian Code, promulgated in classical Greece in the seventh century, B.C., is one of the earliest foundations of Western law.

Criminal law is only one category of law. People's lives and actions are also affected by **civil law**, which governs business transactions, contracts, real estate, and the like. For example, if you damage other people's property or harm them in an accident, they may sue you to pay for the damage or harm. By contrast, the key feature of criminal law is the government's power to punish people for damage they have done to society.

Criminal law is divided into two categories, substantive and procedural. **Substantive criminal law** defines actions that may be punished by the government. It also defines the punishments for such offenses. Often called the "penal code," substantive law answers the question "*What* is illegal?" Elected officials in Congress, state legislatures, and city councils write the substantive criminal laws. They decide which kinds of behaviors are so harmful that they deserve to be punished. They also decide whether each violation should be punished by imprisonment, a fine, probation, or another kind of penalty.

Procedural criminal law defines the rules that govern *how* the laws will be enforced. It protects the constitutional rights of defendants and provides the rules that officials must follow in all areas of the criminal justice system. The U.S. Supreme Court and state supreme courts play key roles in defining procedural criminal law. These courts define the meaning of constitutional rights in the U.S. Constitution and in state constitutions. Their interpretations of constitutional provisions create rules on such issues as when and how police officers can question suspects and when defendants can receive advice from their attorneys.

civil law

Law regulating the relationships between or among individuals, usually involving property, contract, or business disputes.

substantive criminal law

Law defining the acts that are subject to punishment, and specifying the punishments for such offenses.

procedural criminal law

Law defining the procedures that criminal justice officials must follow in enforcement, adjudication, and correction.

CHECKPOINT

1. What is contained in a state's penal code?
2. What is the purpose of procedural criminal law?

SUBSTANTIVE CRIMINAL LAW

Substantive criminal law is based on the doctrine that no one may be convicted of or punished for an offense unless the offense has been defined by the law. In short, people must know in advance what is required of them. Thus, no act can be regarded as illegal until it has been defined as punishable under the criminal law. While this sounds like a simple notion, the language of law is often confusing and ambiguous. As a result, judges must become involved in interpreting the law so that the meaning intended by the legislature can be understood.

Seven Principles of Criminal Law

The major principles of Western criminal law were summarized in a single statement by the legal scholar Jerome Hall (1947). In order to convict a defendant of a crime, prosecutors must prove that all seven principles have been fulfilled (see Figure 3.1).

A crime is	
1 legally proscribed	(legality)
2 human conduct	*(actus reus)*
3 causative	(causation)
4 of a given harm	(harm)
5 which conduct coincides	(concurrence)
6 with a blameworthy frame of mind	*(mens rea)*
7 and is subject to punishment	(punishment)

Figure 3.1
The Seven Principles of Criminal Law

These principles of Western law are the basis for defining acts as criminal and the conditions required for successful prosecution.

1. Legality. There must be a law that defines the specific action as a crime. Offensive and harmful behavior is not illegal unless it has been prohibited by law before it was committed. The U.S. Constitution forbids *ex post facto* laws, or laws written and applied after the fact. Thus, when the legislature defines a new crime, people can be prosecuted only for violations that occur after the new law has been passed.
2. *Actus reus.* Criminal laws are aimed at people's actions as well as some acts that a person failed to undertake. The U.S. Supreme Court has ruled that people may not be convicted of a crime simply because of their status, thoughts, or condition. Under this *actus reus* requirement, for a crime to occur there must be a guilty act of either commission or omission by the accused. In *Robinson v. California* (1962), for example, the Supreme Court struck down a California law that made it a crime to be addicted to drugs. States can prosecute people for using, possessing, selling, or transporting drugs when they catch them performing these acts, but states cannot prosecute them for the mere status of being addicted to drugs.
3. Causation. For a crime to have been committed, there must be a cause-and-effect relationship between an act and the harm suffered. In Ohio, for example, a prosecutor tried to convict a burglary suspect on a manslaughter charge when a victim, asleep in his house, was killed by a stray police bullet as officers fired at the unarmed, fleeing suspect. The burglar was acquitted on the homicide charge because his actions in committing the burglary and running away from the police were not the direct cause of the victim's death (*Akron Beacon Journal*, December 3, 1991: B6).
4. Harm. To be a crime, an act must cause harm to some legally protected value. The harm can be to a person, property, or some other object that a legislature deems valuable enough to deserve protection through the government's power to punish. This principle is often questioned by those who feel that they are not committing a crime because they may be causing harm only to themselves.

Laws that require motorcyclists to wear helmets have been challenged on this ground. Such laws, however, have been written because legislatures believe enough harm exists to require protective laws. These forms of harm include injuries to helmetless riders, tragedy and loss for families of injured cyclists, and the medical costs imposed on society for head injuries that could have been prevented.

An act can be deemed criminal if it could do harm that the law seeks to prevent. Thus, the criminal law includes conspiracies and attempts, even when the lawbreaker does not complete the intended crime. The potential for grave harm from such acts justifies the application of the government's power to punish, even before the final act is completed. Such crimes are called **inchoate offenses**.

inchoate offense

Conduct that is criminal even though the harm that the law seeks to prevent has not been done but merely planned or attempted.

5. Concurrence. For an act to be considered a crime, the intent and the act must be present at the same time (Hall, 1947:85). For example, let's imagine that Joe is planning to murder his arch-enemy, Bill. He plans to abduct Bill and carry out the murder. While driving home from work one day, Joe accidentally hits and kills a jogger who suddenly—and foolishly—ran across the busy street without looking. The jogger turns out to be Bill. Although Joe had planned to kill Bill, he is not guilty of murder because the accidental killing was not connected to Joe's intent to carry out a killing.
6. *Mens rea*. The commission of an act is not a crime unless it is accompanied by a guilty state of mind. This concept is related to intent. It seeks to distinguish between harm-causing *accidents*, which generally are not subject to criminal punishment, and harm-causing *crimes*, in which some level of intent is present. Certain crimes require a specific level of intent. Examples include first-degree murder, which is normally a planned, intentional killing, and larceny, which involves the intent to permanently and unlawfully deprive an owner of his or her property. Later in this chapter we will examine several defenses, such as necessity and insanity, that can be used to assert that a person did not have a ***mens rea***—"guilty mind" or blameworthy state of mind—and hence should not be held responsible for a criminal offense.

   Exceptions to the concept of *mens rea* are **strict liability** offenses involving health and safety, in which it is not necessary to show intent. Legislatures have criminalized certain kinds of offenses in order to protect the public. For example, a business owner may be held responsible for violations of a toxic waste law whether or not the owner actually knew that his employees were dumping polluting substances into a river. The purpose of such laws is to put pressure on business owners to make sure that their employees obey regulations designed to protect the health and safety of the public.
7. Punishment. There must be a provision in the law calling for punishment of those found guilty of violating the law. The punishment is enforced by the government and may carry with it loss of freedom, social stigma, a criminal record, and loss of rights.

mens rea

"Guilty mind" or blameworthy state of mind, necessary for legal responsibility for a criminal offense; criminal intent, as distinguished from innocent intent.

strict liability

An obligation or duty that when broken is an offense that can be judged criminal without a showing of *mens rea*, or criminal intent; usually applied to regulatory offenses involving health and safety.

The seven principles of substantive criminal law allow authorities to define certain acts as being against the law and provide the accused with a basis for mounting a defense against the charges. During a criminal trial, defense attorneys will often try to show that one of the seven elements either is unproven or can be explained in a way that is acceptable under the law.

CHECKPOINT

3. What are the seven principles of criminal law?

Elements of a Crime

Legislatures define certain acts as crimes when they fulfill the seven principles just outlined and they occur under certain "attendant circumstances" while the offender is in a certain state of mind. These three factors—the act (*actus reus*), the attendant circumstances, and the state of mind (*mens rea*)—are together called the elements of a crime. They can be seen in the following section from a state penal code:

> **Section 3502. Burglary**
> 1 *Offense defined*: A person is guilty of burglary if he enters a building or occupied structure, or separately secured or occupied portion thereof, with intent to commit a crime therein, unless the premises are at the time open to the public or the actor is licensed or privileged to enter.

The elements of burglary are, therefore, entering a building or occupied structure (*actus reus*) with the intent to commit a crime therein (*mens rea*) at a time when the premises are not open to the public and the actor is not invited or otherwise entitled to enter (attendant circumstances). For an act to be a burglary, all three elements must be present. All three elements must also be proven by the prosecution.

Statutory Definitions of Crimes

Federal and state penal codes often define criminal acts somewhat differently. To find out how a state defines an offense, one must read its penal code; which will give a general idea of which acts are illegal. To understand the court's interpretations of the code, one must analyze the judicial opinions that have sought to clarify the law.

The classification of criminal acts becomes complicated when statutes divide related acts, such as the taking of another person's life, into different offenses. For example, the definition of "criminal homicide" has been subdivided into degrees of murder and voluntary and involuntary manslaughter. In addition, some states have created new categories, such as reckless homicide, negligent homicide, and vehicular homicide. Each of these definitions involves slight variations in the *actus reus* and the *mens rea*. Table 3.1 defines the eight index crimes of the *Uniform Crime Reports*, including the various forms of homicide.

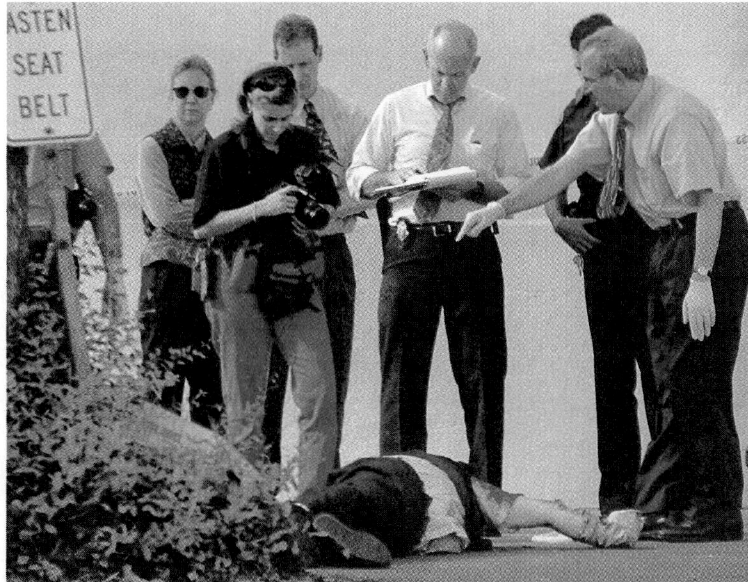

Homicide investigators examine the body of a postal worker in Miami Beach. Police and prosecutors must convince a jury that the crime fits the definition of criminal homicide as outlined in the penal code.

1 Criminal homicide:
a. Murder and nonnegligent manslaughter; the willful (nonnegligent) killing of one human being by another. Deaths caused by negligence, attempts to kill, assaults to kill, suicides, accidental deaths, and justifiable homicides are excluded. Justifiable homicides are limited to:
(1) the killing of a felon by a law enforcement officer in the line of duty; and
(2) the killing of a felon by a private citizen.
b. Manslaughter by negligence: the killing of another person through gross negligence. Excludes traffic fatalities. While manslaughter by negligence is a Part I crime, it is not included in the Crime Index.

2 Forcible rape:
The carnal knowledge of a person forcibly and against his or her will. Included are rapes by force and attempts or assaults to rape. Statutory offenses (no force used—victim under age of consent) are excluded.

3 Robbery:
The taking or attempting to take anything of value from the care, custody, or control of a person or persons by force or threat of force of violence and/or by putting the victim in fear.

4 Aggravated assault:
An unlawful attack by one person upon another for the purpose of inflicting severe or aggravated bodily injury. This type of assault usually is accompanied by the use of a weapon or by means likely to produce death or great bodily harm. Simple assaults are excluded.

5 Burglary—breaking or entering:
The unlawful entry of a structure to commit a felony or a theft. Attempted forcible entry is included.

6 Larceny-theft (except motor vehicle theft):
The unlawful taking, carrying, leading, or riding away of property from the possession or constructive possession of another. Examples are thefts of bicycles or automobile accessories, shoplifting, pocket-picking, or the stealing of any property or article that is not taken by force and violence or by fraud. Attempted larcenies are included. Embezzlement, "con" games, forgery, worthless checks, and so on, are excluded.

7 Motor vehicle theft:
The theft or attempted theft of a motor vehicle. A motor vehicle is self-propelled and runs on the surface and not on rails. Specifically excluded from this category are motorboats, construction equipment, airplanes, and farming equipment.

8 Arson:
Any willful or malicious burning or attempt to burn, with or without intent to defraud, a dwelling house, public building, motor vehicle or aircraft, personal property of another, and so on.

Table 3.1
Definitions of offenses in the Uniform Crime Reports (Part 1)

The exact descriptions of offenses differ from one state to another, but these *UCR* definitions provide a national standard that helps us distinguish among criminal acts.

SOURCE: U.S. Department of Justice, Federal Bureau of Investigation, *Uniform Crime Reports, 1996* (Washington, D.C.: Government Printing Office, 1997).

In legal language, the phrase *malice aforethought* is used to distinguish murder from manslaughter. This phrase indicates that the crime of murder is a deliberate, premeditated, and willful killing of another human being. Most states extend the definition of murder to these two circumstances: (1) defendants knew their behavior had a strong chance of causing death, showed indifference to life, and thus recklessly engaged in conduct that caused death, or (2) defendants' behavior caused death while they were committing a felony. Mitigating circumstances, such as "the heat of passion" or extreme provocation, would reduce the offense to manslaughter because the requirement of malice aforethought would be absent or reduced. Manslaughter might also include a death resulting from recklessness or negligence.

CHECKPOINT

4. What are the elements of a crime and how do they apply to homicide offenses?

Responsibility for Criminal Acts

Thus far we have studied the elements that constitute a crime and the legal definition of offenses; we now need to look at the question of responsibility. Of the seven principles of criminal law, *mens rea* is crucial in establishing responsibility for the act. To obtain a conviction, the prosecution must show that the offender not only committed the illegal act but also did so in a state of mind that makes it appropriate to hold him or her responsible for the act. The analysis of *mens rea* is difficult because the court must inquire into the defendant's mental state at the time the offense was committed.

Although many defendants admit that they committed the harmful act, they may still plead not guilty. They—or their attorneys—may believe that *mens rea* was not present. Accidents are the clearest examples of such situations: the defendant argues that the gun went off accidentally and the neighbor was killed, or that the pedestrian suddenly crossed into the path of the car.

When an event is not an accident, there are eight defenses that can be used to claim a defendant lacked the necessary intent to commit the crime: entrapment, self-defense, necessity, duress, immaturity, mistake of fact, intoxication, and insanity. These defenses may be used to avoid conviction or to reduce the severity of a charge if, for example, a person lacked the highest levels of intent in committing an act. The person's action may have been merely negligent or reckless instead of deliberate.

Entrapment

Entrapment is a defense that may be used to show lack of intent. The law excuses a defendant when it is shown that government agents have induced the person to commit the offense. Police can use undercover agents to set a trap for criminals but the entrapment defense may be used when the police have acted so as to *encourage* the criminal act. Entrapment raises tough questions for judges who must decide whether the police went too far toward making a crime occur and that the crime otherwise would not have happened (Camp, 1993).

The key question is the predisposition of the defendant. In 1992 the Supreme Court stressed that the prosecutor must show beyond a reasonable doubt that a defendant was predisposed to break the law before he or she was approached by government agents. The case involved Keith Jacobson, a Nebraska farmer who ordered magazines containing photographs of nude boys from a California bookstore. The U.S. Postal Service and the Customs Service set up phony organizations that sent letters to Jacobson and others who were on the bookstore's mailing list. The letters urged Jacobson to order items that "we believe you will find to be both interesting and stimulating" (*New York Times*, April 7, 1992: A25). Jacobson ordered the material and was arrested by federal agents. No other pornographic material was found in his home.

In the majority opinion, Justice Byron White wrote that government officials may not "originate a criminal design, implant in an innocent person's mind the disposition to commit a criminal act, and then induce commission of the crime so that the government may prosecute" (*Jacobson v. United States*,1992). Jacobson's conviction on child pornography charges was overturned.

Self-Defense

A person who feels that he or she is in immediate danger of being harmed by another person may ward off the attack in *self-defense*. The laws of most states also recognize the right to defend others from attack, to protect property, and to prevent a crime.

The level of force used in self-defense cannot exceed the person's reasonable perception of the threat. Thus, a person may be justified in shooting a robber who is

IDEAS IN PRACTICE

The New York Penal Code provides that a person is guilty of murder when, "under circumstances evincing a depraved indifference to human life, [he or she] recklessly engages in conduct that creates a grave risk of death to another person, and thereby causes the death of that person."

You are counsel for Richard Kane, who is charged with murder. Kane spent a cold, winter evening drinking in a tavern with George Telling. The bartender told the police that Telling was in an intoxicated condition and was flashing a wad of hundred-dollar bills when he left the bar in Kane's company at approximately 9:00 P.M.

Your client admits that he drove Telling out of town, robbed him, took his trousers, shirt, and glasses, and left him on a rural dirt road. The temperature was near zero, and visibility was obscured by blowing snow.

At about 10:00 P.M. Michael Brose was traveling in his pickup truck down the road at approximately 50 miles per hour. As he drove over a rise, he spotted a naked man standing in the middle of the road but "didn't have time to react" before his vehicle struck Telling. The medical examiner ruled that Telling died of massive head injuries and that his blood alcohol level was proof of a high degree of intoxication.

What will be your defense to the murder charge?

entrapment

The defense that the individual was induced by the police to commit the criminal act.

holding a gun to her head and threatening to kill her, but homeowners generally are not justified in shooting an unarmed burglar who has left the house and is running across the lawn.

Necessity

Unlike self-defense, in which a defendant feels that he or she must harm an aggressor to ward off an attack, the *necessity* defense is used when people break the law in order to save themselves or prevent some greater harm. A person who speeds through a red light to get an injured child to the hospital or breaks into a building to seek refuge from a hurricane could claim to be violating the law out of necessity.

The English case *The Queen v. Dudley and Stephens* (1884) is a famous example of necessity. After their ship sank, four sailors were adrift in the ocean without food or water. Twenty days later, two of the sailors, Thomas Dudley and Edwin Stephens, killed the youngest sailor, the cabin boy, and ate his flesh. Four days later they were rescued by a passing ship. When they returned to England, they were tried and convicted for murder because the court did not accept their necessity defense. However, the Crown later reduced their sentences from the death penalty to six months in prison.

Duress (Coercion)

The defense of *duress* arises when someone commits a crime because he or she is coerced by another person. During a bank robbery, for instance, if an armed robber forces one of the bank's customers at gunpoint to drive the getaway car, the customer would be able to claim duress. However, courts generally are not willing to accept this defense if people do not try to escape from the situation.

Immaturity

Anglo-American law excuses criminal acts by children under age seven on the grounds of their *immaturity* and lack of responsibility for their actions—*mens rea* is not present.

Common law has presumed that children aged 7 to 14 are not liable for their criminal acts; however, prosecutors have been able to present evidence of a child's mental capacity to form *mens rea*. Juries can assume the presence of a guilty mind if it can be shown, for example, that the child hid evidence or tried to bribe a witness. As a child grows older, the assumption of immaturity weakens. Since the development of juvenile courts in the 1890s, children above age 7 have not been tried by the same rules as adults. In some situations, however, children may be tried as adults—if, for example, they are repeat offenders or are charged with a particularly heinous crime. A key issue in the debate over the death penalty is the justification for executing youths who have committed murder.

Mistake

The courts have generally upheld the view that ignorance of the law is no excuse for committing an illegal act. But what if there is a *mistake* of fact? If an accused person has made a mistake on some crucial fact, that may serve as a defense (Christopher, 1994). For example, suppose some teenagers ask your permission to grow sunflowers in a vacant lot behind your home. You help them weed the garden and water the plants. Then it turns out that they are growing marijuana. You were not aware of this because you have no idea what a marijuana plant looks like. Should you be convicted for growing an illegal drug on your property? The answer depends on the specific degree of knowledge and intent that the prosecution must prove for that offense. The success of such a defense may also depend on the extent to which jurors understand and sympathize with your mistake.

Intoxication

The law does not relieve an individual of responsibility for acts performed while voluntarily intoxicated. There are, however, cases in which intoxication can be used as a defense, as when a person has been tricked into consuming a substance without knowing that it may cause intoxication. More complex are cases in which the defendant must be shown to have had a specific, rather than a general, intent to commit a crime. For example, someone may claim that they were too drunk to realize that they had left a restaurant without paying the bill. Drunkenness can also be used as a mitigating factor to reduce the seriousness of a charge. Nevertheless, in 1996 the U.S. Supreme Court narrowly approved a Montana law that barred the use of evidence of intoxication as a defense. Defendants could not claim that their intoxicated condition prevented them from forming the specific intent necessary to be guilty of a crime (*Montana v. Egelhoff*). Thus states may enact laws that prevent the use of an intoxication defense.

CLOSE-UP

Jeffrey Dahmer: The Insanity Plea That Didn't Work

The veteran Milwaukee police officers were understandably shocked when, in August 1991, they entered Jeffrey Dahmer's apartment and found two human heads in a refrigerator, two in a freezer, and seven others boiled clean. In the basement, they found an acid-filled barrel of body parts. Investigators soon learned the full extent of Dahmer's crimes. The 31-year-old laborer confessed to the police that he lured young men and boys from gay bars to his apartment, drugged and killed them, had sex with their corpses, and dissected and cannibalized the bodies.

Jeffrey Dahmer was charged with killing and dismembering fifteen young men and boys. Dahmer thus joined that small fraternity of notorious serial killers such as Charles Manson, "Son of Sam" David Berkowitz, and John Wayne Gacy. Given the horrific aspects of their crimes, the defendants' legal responsibility for their actions became an issue. Were they sane when they committed their crimes? Were their rights protected as they proceeded from arrest to trial? What is an appropriate punishment for such individuals?

After it was established that Dahmer had committed the gruesome acts, a jury faced a difficult issue in the penalty phase of Dahmer's trial. Judge Lawrence Gram, Jr., asked the jury to decide whether "as a result of mental disease or defect, [Jeffrey Dahmer] lacked substantial capacity to appreciate the wrongfulness of his conduct to conform his conduct to the requirements of the law."

Most people would agree that Dahmer was insane when he committed the crimes. As journalist Richard Moran noted before the trial, "All the defense really has to do is describe the contents of his refrigerator and freezer. Normal murderers do not mutilate their victims, nor do they display their heads or hearts. Cannibalism is not an alternative lifestyle, nor is necrophilia just some odd sexual preference." Nevertheless, public concerns were raised as early as the pretrial phase that Dahmer would be "let off" and released to the community. This alarm stemmed in part from that part of Wisconsin law that gives insanity acquitees the right to petition the court every six months for conditional release. People seemed not to notice that a right to file a petition did not mean that Dahmer would ever be released.

It was perhaps this concern that led the Wisconsin jury not to accept Dahmer's insanity defense. Judge Gram gave him the maximum sentence, fifteen consecutive life terms. Ultimately, Dahmer's stay in prison was relatively short because he was murdered by a fellow inmate in December 1994.

SOURCES: Adapted from Richard Moran, "His Insanity Plea Can't Free Jeffrey Dahmer," *The Boston Globe*, 2 February 1992, p. 60, and Tom Mathews, "Secrets of a Serial Killer," *Newsweek*, 3 February 1992, pp. 44–49.

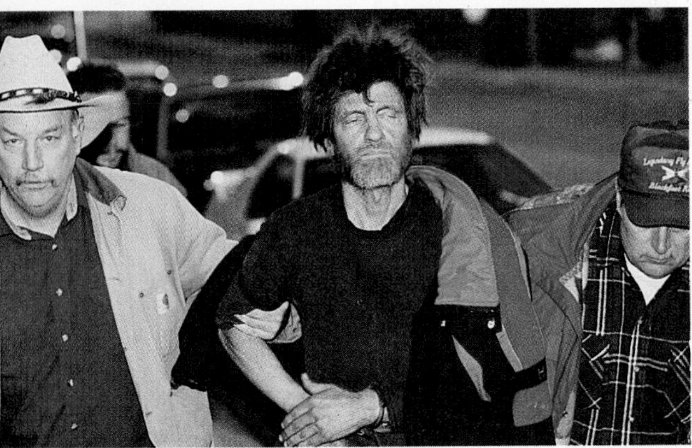

Theodore Kaczynski's attorneys believed his best hope of escaping a death sentence was to plead mental illness. The Unabomer refused and tried to fire his counsel. The case raised fundamental questions about a defendant's right to participate in his own defense and the role of psychiatry in the courtroom.

Insanity

The defense of *insanity* has been a subject of heated debate. The public believes that many criminals "escape" punishment through the skillful use of psychiatric testimony. Yet only about 1 percent of incarcerated offenders are held in mental hospitals because they had been found "not guilty by reason of insanity" (NIJ, n.d. *Crime File* "Insanity Defense,"). The insanity defense is rare and is generally used only in serious cases or where there is no other valid defense.

Over time American courts have used five tests of criminal responsibility involving insanity: the M'Naghten Rule, the Irresistible Impulse Test, the Durham Rule, the *Model Penal Code's* Substantial Capacity Test, and the test defined in the federal Comprehensive Crime Control Act of 1984. These tests are summarized in Table 3.2.

M'Naghten Rule More than a dozen American states use this rule, which was developed in England in 1843. Daniel M'Naghten killed a man who he mistakenly thought was the prime minister of Great Britain. M'Naghten was acquitted because he claimed that he was delusional at the time of the killing. In developing the M'Naghten Rule, the British court established a standard for determining criminal responsibility known as the "right-from-wrong test." It asks whether "at the time of the committing of the act, the party accused was laboring under such a defect of reason, from disease or the mind, as not to know the nature and quality of the act he was doing, or if he did know it that he did not know he was doing what was wrong." (*Queen v. M'Naghten*, 1843).

Test	Legal Standard Because of Mental Illness	Final Burden of Proof	Who Bears Burden of Proof
M'Naghten (1843)	"didn't know what he was doing or didn't know it was wrong"	Varies from proof by a balance of probabilities on the defense to proof beyond a reasonsble doubt on the prosecutor	
Irresistible Impulse (1897)	"could not control his conduct"		
Durham (1954)	"the criminal act was caused by his mental illness"	Beyond a reasonable doubt	Prosecutor
Model Penal Code (1972)	"lacks substantial capacity to appreciate the wrongfulness of his conduct or to control it"	Beyond a reasonable doubt	Prosecutor
Present federal law	"lacks capacity to appreciate the wrongfulness of his conduct"	Clear and convincing evidence	Defense

Table 3.2
Insanity defense standards

The standards for the insanity defense have evolved over time.

SOURCE: U.S. Department of Justice, National Institute of Justice, *Crime File*, "Insanity Defense," a film prepared by Norval Morris (Washington, D.C.: Government Printing Office, n.d.).

Irresistible Impulse Test Four states have supplemented the M'Naghten Rule with the Irresistible Impulse Test. Because psychiatrists argue that some people can feel compelled by their mental illness to commit criminal actions even though they recognize the wrongfulness of their conduct, the Irresistible Impulse Test is designed to bring the M'Naghten Rule in line with modern psychiatry. Thus, the Irresistible Impulse Test permits defendants to avoid criminal culpability when a mental disease controlled their behavior, even if they knew that what they were doing was wrong.

The Durham Rule New Hampshire developed and still applies the rule that took its name from a federal court case (*Durham v. United States*, 1954). Under this rule, an accused is not criminally responsible if his or her actions were "the product of mental disease or defect".

***Model Penal Code's* Substantial Capacity Test** Because the Durham Rule lacks precise definition, half of the states have adopted the Substantial Capacity Test from the *Model Penal Code*. This rule states that a defendant cannot be held culpable "if at the time of such conduct as a result of mental disease or defect he lacks the substantial capacity either to appreciate the criminality of his conduct or to conform his conduct to the requirements of the law." This test essentially combines and broadens the M'Naghten Rule and the Irresistible Impulse Test. By stressing "substantial capacity," the test does not require that a defendant be unable to distinguish right from wrong.

Comprehensive Crime Control Act of 1984 The Comprehensive Crime Control Act of 1984 changed the federal rules on the insanity defense by limiting it to those who are unable to understand the nature or the wrongfulness of their acts as a result of severe mental disease or defect. This change means that the Irresistible Impulse Test cannot be used in the federal courts. It also shifts the burden of proof from the prosecutor, who in some federal courts had to prove beyond a reasonable doubt that the defendant was not insane, to the defendant, who has to prove his or her insanity. The act also creates a new procedure whereby a person who is found not guilty only by reason of insanity must be committed to a mental hospital until he or she no longer poses a danger to society. These rules apply only to federal courts, but they are spreading to a number of states.

Defendants' Mental Capacity: Recent Developments The 1984 changes in federal law came about, in part, because of John Hinckley's attempt to assassinate President Ronald Reagan in 1981. Television news footage showed that Hinckley had shot the president. Yet, with the help of psychiatrists, Hinckley's lawyers were able to counteract the prosecution's efforts to persuade the jury that Hinckley was sane. When Hinckley was acquitted the public was outraged, and several states acted to limit or abolish the insanity defense. Twelve states introduced the defense of "guilty but mentally ill" (Klofas and Yandrasits, 1989). This defense allows a jury to find the accused guilty but requires that he or she be given psychiatric treatment while in prison (Callahan et al., 1992).

In 1997 a Pennsylvania jury found multimillionaire John duPont guilty of third-degree murder but mentally ill in the shooting of Olympic wrestler David Schultz. Under Pennsylvania law, a verdict of guilty but mentally ill means the defendant was sane enough to understand right from wrong. Third-degree murder is defined as killing without premeditation. Psychiatrists had testified that duPont was a paranoid schizophrenic and that this mental illness contributed to the murder. The verdict means that duPont will first go to a mental institution and then, if medical authorities say he is well enough, to prison to serve his sentence (*USA Today*, February 26, 1997: 1).

The movement away from the insanity defense reduces the importance of *mens rea*. Many reform efforts have aimed at punishing crimes without regard for the knowledge and intentions of the offender.

In practice, the outcomes of the various insanity tests frequently depend on jurors' reactions to the opinions of psychiatrists presented as expert witnesses by the prosecution and defense. For example, the prosecution's psychiatrist will testify that the defendant does not meet the standard for insanity, while the defendant's psychiatrist will testify that the defendant does meet that standard. The psychiatrists themselves do not decide whether the defendant is responsible for the crime. Instead the jurors decide, based on the psychiatrists' testimony and other factors. They may take into account the seriousness of the crime and their own beliefs about the insanity defense. The rules for proving insanity thus clearly favor wealthy defendants who can afford to hire psychiatrists as expert witnesses.

Even when defendants are acquitted by reason of insanity, they are nearly always committed to a mental hospital (Robinson, 1993). Although the criminal justice system does not consider hospitalization to be "punishment," commitment to a psychiatric ward results in loss of liberty and often a longer period of confinement than if the person had been sentenced to prison. A robber may have faced only ten years in prison, yet an acquittal by reason of insanity may lead to a lifetime of hospital confinement if the psychiatrists never find that he has recovered enough to be released. Thus the notion that those acquitted by reason of insanity have somehow "beaten the rap" may not reflect reality.

CHECKPOINT

5. What kind of offense has no *mens rea* requirement?
6. What are the defenses in substantive criminal law?
7. What are the tests of criminal responsibility used for the insanity defense?

PROCEDURAL CRIMINAL LAW

procedural due process

The constitutional requirement that all persons be treated fairly and justly by government officials. An accused person can be arrested, prosecuted, tried, and punished only in accordance with procedures prescribed by law.

Procedural law defines how the state must process cases. According to **procedural due process**, accused persons must be tried in accordance with legal procedures. Some procedural rules, such as the right to a jury trial, may advance the truth-seeking goals of the criminal justice process. Others, such as the prohibition of unreasonable searches and seizures, are designed to protect individuals, including guilty people, from heavy-handed actions by government officials. American history contains many examples of police officers and prosecutors harassing and victimizing those who lack political power, including poor people, racial and ethnic minorities, and unpopular religious groups. Procedural due process is designed to insure that officials follow the law as they carry out their duties.

Bill of Rights

The first ten amendments added to the U.S. Constitution to protect individuals' rights against infringement by government.

Because it has the authority to review cases from state supreme courts as well as from federal courts, the U.S. Supreme Court has played a major role in defining procedural criminal law. The Supreme Court's influence stems from its power to define the meaning of the U.S. Constitution, especially the **Bill of Rights**—the first ten amendments to the Constitution, which list legal protections against actions of the government.

The Bill of Rights

The U.S. Constitution contained few references to criminal justice when it was ratified in 1789. Because many people were concerned that the document did not set forth the rights of individuals in enough detail, ten amendments were added in 1791. Four of those amendments focus on criminal justice issues. The Fourth Amendment bars unreasonable searches and seizures. The Fifth Amendment outlines basic due process rights in criminal cases. For example, protection against **self-incrimination** means that persons cannot be forced to respond to questions whose answers may reveal that they have committed a crime. The protection against **double jeopardy** means that a person may be subjected to only one prosecution or punishment for a single offense within the same jurisdiction. The Sixth Amendment provides for the right to a speedy, fair, and public trial by an impartial jury, as well as the right to counsel. The Eighth Amendment bars excessive bail, excessive fines, and cruel and unusual punishment.

For most of American history the Bill of Rights did not apply to most criminal cases because it was designed to protect people from abusive actions by the *federal* government. It did not seek to protect people from the actions of state and local officials, who handled nearly all criminal cases. This view was upheld by the U.S. Supreme Court in the 1833 case of ***Barron v. Baltimore***. However, as we will see shortly, this view gradually changed in the late nineteenth and early twentieth centuries.

self-incrimination

The act of exposing oneself to prosecution by being forced to respond to questions whose answers may reveal that one has committed a crime. The Fifth Amendment protects defendants against self-incrimination. In any criminal proceeding the prosecution must prove the charges by means of evidence other than the testimony of the accused.

double jeopardy

The subjecting of a person to prosecution more than once in the same jurisdiction for the same offense; prohibited by the Fifth Amendment.

The Fourteenth Amendment and Due Process

After the Civil War, three amendments were added to the Constitution. These amendments were designed to protect individuals' rights against infringement by state and local government officials. The Fourteenth Amendment, ratified in 1868, barred states from violating people's right to due process of law. It states that "no State shall . . . deprive any person of life, liberty, or property without due process of law; nor deny to any person within its jurisdiction the equal protection of the laws." These rights to due process and equal protection served as a basis for protecting individuals from abusive actions by local criminal justice officials. However, the terms *due process* and *equal protection* are so vague that it was left to the U.S. Supreme Court to decide if and how these new rights applied to the criminal justice process.

For example, in ***Powell v. Alabama*** (1932), the Supreme Court ruled that the due process clause required courts to provide attorneys for poor defendants facing the death penalty. This decision stemmed from a notorious case in Alabama in which nine African-American men, known as the "Scottsboro boys," were quickly convicted and condemned to death for allegedly raping two white women, even though one of the alleged victims later admitted that she had lied about the rape.

In early cases, the justices had not developed clear rules for deciding which specific rights applied to the state and local officials as components of the due process clause of the Fourteenth Amendment. At that point they indicated that procedures must meet a basic standard of **fundamental fairness**. In essence, the justices simply reacted against unfair or brutal situations that shocked their consciences. In doing so, they showed the importance of procedural criminal law in protecting individuals from abusive and unjust actions by government officials.

***Barron v. Baltimore* (1833)**

The protections of the Bill of Rights apply only to actions of the federal government.

***Powell v. Alabama* (1932)**

An attorney must be provided to a defendant facing the death penalty.

fundamental fairness

A legal doctrine supporting the idea that so long as a state's conduct maintains basic standards of fairness, the Constitution has not been violated.

The Due Process Revolution

From the 1930s to the 1960s, a majority of the Supreme Court justices supported the fundamental fairness doctrine. It was applied on a case-by-case basis, not always in a consistent way. After Earl Warren became Chief Justice in 1953, he led

rule established in *Mapp v. Ohio*, the drugs should have been excluded because the search warrant was defective. However, because the police had tried to follow proper procedures, and a judge, not the police, had made the error in issuing the improper warrant, the Supreme Court ruled that the evidence could be used against the defendant.

The Burger and Rehnquist Courts did not abolish the exclusionary rule, but they limited its applicability, giving police greater flexibility in investigating criminal cases. For example, the Rehnquist Court made it much easier for police to conduct warrantless searches of cars and closed containers found inside cars (*California v. Acevedo*, 1991). As can be seen in the Question of Ethics example, when the courts give police more flexibility in search and seizure actions, there are risks that innocent citizens will feel that their rights have been infringed (Robin, 1993; Janikowski and Giacopassi, 1993).

CHECKPOINT

11. What controversial principle was applied against the states in *Mapp v. Ohio*?

A Question of ETHICS

The short, muscular African-American man strode through the Los Angeles International Airport carrying an attaché case and a small piece of luggage. He abruptly set down the bag and walked to a row of pay phones. His conversation was interrupted by two Drug Enforcement Administration (DEA) agents, who grabbed the phone and started asking him questions. When the suspected "drug smuggler" did not respond, he fell or was thrown to the floor and was handcuffed and led away for questioning. Only after he protested that they had stopped the wrong person was Joe Morgan—a television broadcaster, former Cincinnati Reds second baseman, and National Baseball Hall of Fame member—released.

Los Angeles narcotics detective Clayton Searle and DEA agent Bill Woessner claimed that they had done nothing wrong; they merely responded to a DEA-developed profile of persons likely to be drug couriers. The fact that race is a key element of this profile has been justified as conforming to reality. African and Hispanic Americans, it is argued, are more likely than whites to act as couriers in the drug trade. Others have claimed that the DEA profile is an expression of institutional racism—the darker your skin, the more likely it is that you will be stopped for questioning.

Is it ethical to base law enforcement actions on physical characteristics? Or should government agents stop and question only those whose behavior indicates that they are committing or about to commit a crime?

The Fifth Amendment: Protection against Self-Incrimination and Double Jeopardy

No person shall be held to answer for a capital, or otherwise infamous crime, unless on a presentment or indictment of a Grand Jury, except in cases arising in the land or naval forces, or in the Militia, when in actual service in time of war or public danger; nor shall any person be subject for the same offense to be twice put in jeopardy of life or limb; nor shall be compelled in any criminal case to be a witness against himself, nor be deprived of life, liberty, or property, without due process of law; nor shall private property be taken for public use, without just compensation.

The Fifth Amendment clearly states some key rights related to the investigation and prosecution of criminal suspects. Here we explore two of them: the protections against compelled self-incrimination and against double jeopardy.

Self-Incrimination

One of the most important due process rights is the protection against compelled self-incrimination—that is, people cannot be pressured to act as witnesses against themselves (Gardner, 1993). This right is consistent with the assumption that the state must prove the defendant's guilt. It is connected to other protections, especially the Sixth Amendment right to counsel, because representation by a defense attorney is seen as a means of preventing self-incrimination during questioning by police or prosecutors (Richardson, 1993).

In the past the validity of confessions hinged on their being voluntary, because, by their very nature, a confession involves self-incrimination. Under the doctrine of fundamental fairness, which was applied before the 1960s, the Supreme Court was unwilling to allow confessions that were beaten out of suspects, that emerged after extended questioning, or that resulted from the use of other physical tactics. In the cases of ***Escobedo v. Illinois*** (1964) and ***Miranda v. Arizona*** (1966), the Warren Court outraged politicians, law enforcement officials, and members of the public by placing limits on the ability of police to question suspects without an attorney present. The justices ruled that, prior to questioning, the police must inform suspects of their right to remain silent and their right to have an attorney present. In response, many police officers argued that they depended on interrogations and confessions as a major means of solving crimes. Nearly three decades later, however, many suspects continue to confess for a number of reasons, such as feelings of guilt, inability to understand their rights, and the desire to gain a favorable plea bargain (Leo, 1996).

Escobedo v. Illinois (1964)

An attorney must be provided to suspects when they are taken into police custody.

Miranda v. Arizona (1966)

Confessions made by suspects who were not notified of their due process rights cannot be admitted as evidence.

The justices were not seeking to limit police officers' ability to investigate crimes when they required them to read the "Miranda warnings" to suspects. They were trying to satisfy the Fifth Amendment prohibition of compelled self-incrimination. They also knew that confessions can be unreliable, especially if no limits are set on questioning by the police. The justices knew that law enforcement officials often "solve" crimes when they are allowed to badger, intimidate, or coerce suspects into confessing. This may mean that the crime is "solved," but whether the person who confessed is actually the one who committed the crime is not always clear.

The Warren Court made the exclusionary rule applicable to violations of Fifth Amendment as well as Fourth Amendment rights. If police questioned suspects without giving them proper warnings and access to an attorney, incriminating statements and confessions by those suspects could not be used against them. However, just as the Burger Court created the "good-faith" exception in a Fourth Amendment case, other exceptions to the exclusionary rule were created in the Fifth Amendment context. For example, the Court ruled that evidence obtained from improper questioning could be used if the situation posed an immediate threat to public safety, such as seeking information from a suspect about a gun that the police believed to be hidden somewhere nearby (*New York v. Quarles*, 1984).

By creating the exceptions to the exclusionary rule for the Fifth Amendment, the Burger and Rehnquist Courts weakened the clarity and impact of the *Miranda* precedent, although they never overturned *Miranda*.

Double Jeopardy

Because of the limit imposed by the Fifth Amendment, a person charged with a criminal act may be subjected to only one prosecution or punishment for that offense in the same jurisdiction. As interpreted by the Supreme Court, however, the right against double jeopardy does not prevent a person from facing two trials or receiving two sanctions from the government (Hickey, 1995; Lear, 1995; Henning, 1993). Because a single criminal act may violate both state and federal laws, for example, a person may be tried in both courts. Thus, after Los Angeles police officers were acquitted of assault charges in a state court after they had been videotaped beating motorist Rodney King, they were convicted in a federal court for violating King's civil rights.

The Sixth Amendment: The Right to Counsel and a Fair Trial

> In all criminal prosecutions, the accused shall enjoy the right to a speedy and public trial, by an impartial jury of the State and district wherein the crime shall have been committed, which district shall have been previously ascertained by law, and to be informed of the nature and cause of the accusation; to be confronted with the witnesses against him; to have compulsory process for obtaining witnesses in his favor, and to have the assistance of counsel for his defense.

The Sixth Amendment includes a number of provisions dealing with fairness in a criminal prosecution. These include the right to counsel, to a speedy and public trial, and to an impartial jury.

The Right to Counsel

Gideon v. Wainwright (1963)

Defendants have a right to counsel in felony cases. States must provide defense counsel in felony cases for those who cannot pay for it themselves.

Although the right to counsel in a criminal case had prevailed in federal courts since 1938, not until the Supreme Court's landmark decision in ***Gideon v. Wainwright*** (1963) was this requirement made binding on the states. Many states already provided attorneys, but the Court forced all of the states to meet Sixth Amendment standards. Although the *Gideon* ruling directly affected only those states that did not already provide poor defendants with attorneys, it set in motion a series of cases that affected all the states by deciding how the right to counsel would be applied in various situations. Beginning in 1963, the Court extended the right to counsel to preliminary hearings, initial appeals, post-indictment identification lineups, and children in juvenile court proceedings. (*Coleman v. Alabama*, 1970); *Douglas v. California,* 1963); *United States v. Wade*, 1967); *In re Gault*, 1967). Later, however, the Burger Court declared that attorneys need not be provided for discretionary appeals or for trials in which the only punishment is a fine (*Ross v. Moffitt*, 1974); *Scott v. Illinois*, 1979).

The Right to an Impartial Jury

Juries allow citizens to play a role in courts' decision making and to prevent prosecutions in cases in which there is not enough evidence. Several Supreme Court decisions have dealt with the composition of juries. For example, it has held that the amendment requires selection procedures that create a jury pool made up of a cross section of the community. Most scholars believe that an impartial jury can best be achieved by drawing jurors at random from the broadest possible base (Hans and Vidmar, 1986; Levine, 1992). The jury is expected to represent the community, and the extent to which it does so is a central concern of jury administration (Smith, 1994). Prospective jurors are usually summoned randomly from voter registration lists or drivers' license records. After the jury pool has been formed, attorneys for each side may ask potential jurors questions and seek to exclude specific jurors (Smith and Ochoa, 1996). Thus the final group of jurors may not, in fact, reflect the diversity of a particular city or county's residents (King, 1994).

Criminal juries may have fewer than the traditional twelve members (*Williams v. Florida*, 1970). In addition, the Constitution does not require that juries reach unanimous verdicts (*Apodaca v. Oregon*, 1972). Thus state legislatures pass statutes to define the size of juries and whether unanimous verdicts are required.

The Supreme Court has also declared that there is no right to a jury trial when facing charges for "petty offenses," those with punishments of six months or less, even if there are multiple petty charges that might lead to a long prison term from serving back-to-back consecutive sentences (*Lewis v. United States*, 1996).

The Eighth Amendment: Protection against Excessive Bail, Excessive Fines, and Cruel and Unusual Punishment

> Excessive bail shall not be required, nor excessive fines imposed, nor cruel and unusual punishment inflicted.

Although it is the briefest of the amendments, the Eighth Amendment deals with the rights of defendants during the pretrial (bail) and corrections (fines, punishment) phases of the criminal justice system.

Release on Bail

The purpose of bail is to allow for the release of the accused while he or she is awaiting trial. The Eighth Amendment does not require that all defendants be released on bail, only that the amount of bail not be excessive. Despite these provisions, many states do not allow bail for those charged with some offenses, such as murder, and there seem to be few limits on the amounts that can be required. In 1987 the Supreme Court, in *United States v. Salerno and Cafero*, upheld provisions of the Bail Reform Act of 1984 that allow federal judges to detain without bail suspects who are considered dangerous to the public.

Cruel and Unusual Punishment

The Warren Court set the standard for judging issues of cruel and unusual punishment in a case dealing with a former soldier who was deprived of U.S. citizenship for deserting his post during World War II (*Trop v. Dulles*, 1958). Chief Justice Earl Warren declared that judges must use the values of contemporary society to determine whether a specific punishment is cruel and unusual. This test has been used in death penalty cases, but the justices have strongly disagreed over the values of American society on this issue. For example, only three justices, William Brennan, Thurgood Marshall, and Harry Blackmun—all of whom retired in the early 1990s—believed that the death penalty always violates the Eighth Amendment's ban on cruel and unusual punishments.

In 1972, a majority of justices decided that the death penalty was being used in an arbitrary and discriminatory way (*Furman v. Georgia*, 1972). After many state legislatures passed new laws that required more careful decision-making procedures in death penalty cases, a majority of justices in ***Gregg v. Georgia*** (1976) allowed the states to reactivate the death penalty. The new procedures require a trial to determine the defendant's guilt and a separate hearing to consider whether he or she deserves the death penalty. In the sentencing hearing, the jury or judge must examine any factors that make the offender especially deserving of the most severe punishment—for example, "aggravating factors" such as an especially gruesome

***Gregg v. Georgia* (1976)**

Capital punishment statutes are permissible if they provide careful procedures to guide decision making by judges and juries.

killing. They must also examine any "mitigating factors" that make the offender less deserving of the death penalty, such as youth or mental retardation (Acker and Lanier, 1995; Acker and Lanier, 1994).

In the 1980s, lawyers brought new cases to the Supreme Court in an unsuccessful effort to persuade the justices to declare the death penalty a cruel and unusual punishment. *McCleskey v. Kemp* (1987) presented the Court with statistics showing that the process in Georgia to decide who will receive the death penalty discriminated against African Americans. African-American defendants charged with killing white victims are much more likely to be sentenced to death than white killers of African Americans (Baldus, Woodworth and Pulaski, 1994; Keil and Vito, 1992). A narrow majority of the justices rejected the use of statistics to prove such discrimination and stated that defendants must show clear evidence of racial bias in specific cases—not in the Georgia criminal justice system generally—in order to challenge a conviction.

Since 1976 about 250 offenders each year have been added to death rows around the country. The pace of executions has gradually increased from an average of 18 each year in the late 1980s to 74 in 1997 (Butterfield, 1998).

CHECKPOINT

12. What are the main criminal justice rights set forth in the Fifth Amendment?
13. What are the main criminal justice rights set forth in the Sixth Amendment?
14. What are the main criminal justice rights set forth in the Eighth Amendment?

CONSTITUTIONAL RIGHTS AND CRIMINAL JUSTICE PROFESSIONALS

As a result of the Supreme Court's decisions, people in all states now enjoy the same minimum protections against illegal searches, improper police interrogations, and other violations of constitutional rights.

In response to these decisions, police, prosecution, and corrections officers have had to develop policies and guidelines to inform criminal justice professionals about what they are and are not permitted to do while investigating, prosecuting, and punishing criminal offenders.

If you were a police officer, prosecutor, or correctional officer, how would you feel about the Supreme Court's decisions defining rights that benefit criminal defendants? While you would recognize the desirability of upholding constitutional rights in order to maintain democratic freedoms, you might also feel frustrated when court decisions excluded relevant evidence. Thus the Supreme Court's rules could lead to the release of a guilty offender in some cases. In addition, you would be concerned about whether the Supreme Court's decisions give you clear guidance about what to do. You would not want to make an unintentional error that prevents an offender from being properly convicted of a crime.

Many people question whether the Supreme Court has struck the proper balance between the protection of constitutional rights and the ability of criminal justice officials to punish offenders. Some people believe that the Supreme Court favors law enforcement at the expense of constitutional rights. Others argue that criminal defendants' rights are too broad. These debates are likely to continue even though the Supreme Court has moved consistently in one direction during the past two decades. In cases affecting criminal justice, the contemporary Supreme Court endorses the actions of police officers and prosecutors in more than two-thirds of cases (Smith, 1996). This has been especially true since William Rehnquist became Chief Justice in 1986 (Hensley, Smith, and Baugh, 1997).

Summary

- Criminal law focuses on the state's prosecution and punishment of people who violate specific laws enacted by legislatures, while civil law concerns disputes between private citizens or businesses.
- Criminal law is divided into two parts: substantive law that defines offenses and penalties, and procedural law that defines individuals' rights and the processes that criminal justice officials must follow in handling cases.
- Substantive criminal law involves seven important elements that must exist and be demonstrated by the prosecution in order to obtain a conviction: legality, *actus reus*, causation, harm, concurrence, *mens rea*, punishment.
- The *mens rea* element, concerning intent or state of mind, can vary with different offenses, such as various degrees of murder. The element may also be disregarded for strict liability offenses that punish actions without considering intent.
- Criminal law provides opportunities to present several defenses based on lack of criminal intent: entrapment, self-defense, necessity, duress (coercion), immaturity, mistake, intoxication, and insanity.
- Standards for the insanity defense vary by jurisdiction with various state and federal courts using several different tests: M'Naghten Rule, Irresistible Impulse Test, Durham Rule, Comprehensive Crime Control Act Rule, the *Model Penal Code* rule.
- The provisions of the Bill of Rights were not originally applicable to state and local officials. The Supreme Court incorporated most of the Bill of Rights' specific provisions into the due process clause of the Fourteenth Amendment and thereby applied them to state and local officials during the twentieth century.
- The Fourth Amendment prohibition on unreasonable searches and seizures has produced many cases questioning the application of the exclusionary rule. Decisions by the Burger and Rehnquist Courts during the 1970s, 1980s, and 1990s have created several exceptions to the exclusionary rule and given greater flexibility to law enforcement officials.
- The Fifth Amendment provides protections against compelled self-incrimination and double jeopardy. As part of the right against compelled self-incrimination, the Supreme Court created *Miranda* warnings that must be given to suspects before they are questioned.
- The Sixth Amendment includes the right to counsel and the right to an impartial jury.
- The Eighth Amendment includes protections against excessive bail, excessive fines, and cruel and unusual punishments. Many of the Supreme Court's most well-known Eighth Amendment cases concern the death penalty, which the Court has endorsed, provided that states employ careful decision-making procedures that consider aggravating and mitigating factors.

Questions for Review

1. What are the two major divisions of the criminal law?
2. List the seven principles of criminal law theory.
3. What is meant by *mens rea*? Give examples of defenses that may be used by defendants in which they deny that *mens rea* existed when the crime was committed.
4. What is meant by the "incorporation" of the Fourteenth Amendment to the U.S. Constitution?

ANSWERS TO CHECKPOINTS

1. Penal codes contain substantive criminal law that defines crimes and also punishments for those crimes.
2. Procedural criminal law specifies the defendants' rights and tells justice system officials how they can investigate and process cases.
3. Legality, *actus reus*, causation, harm, concurrence, *mens rea*, punishment.
4. Three factors—the act (*actus reus*), the attendant circumstances, and the state of mind (*mens rea*)—are together called the elements of a crime. In homicide cases, the state of mind (intent) will determine which category of murder or manslaughter is charged in a particular case.
5. Strict liability offenses.
6. Entrapment, self-defense, necessity, duress (coercion), immaturity, mistake, intoxication, insanity.
7. M'Naghten Rule (right-from-wrong test), Irresistible Impulse Test, Durham Rule, *Model Penal Code*, federal (Crime Control Act).
8. Taking a right from the Bill of Rights and applying it against state and local officials by making it a component of the due process clause of the Fourteenth Amendment.
9. Fundamental fairness.
10. Warren Court.
11. Exclusionary rule.
12. The right against compelled self-incrimination and against double jeopardy (also due process).
13. The right to counsel, to a speedy and fair trial, to a jury trial (also confrontation and compulsory process).
14. The right to protection against excessive bail, excessive fines, and cruel and unusual punishments.

INSIDE THE CRIMINAL JUSTICE SYSTEM AND BEYOND: ONE MAN'S JOURNEY

Written by Chuck Terry

My Affair with Heroin

Seldom do we have the opportunity to view the criminal justice system through the eyes of a person who has experienced it. Chuck Terry is most unusual in that, after more than twenty years of heroin addiction, twelve of them incarcerated, he has "beaten the habit" and is now pursuing a Ph.D. The vivid chronicles of his journey, which conclude each part of this book, provide rare insights into the workings of "the system." His reflections should be thoughtfully considered by all students of criminal justice.

Tight handcuffs. Loud cellblocks. Racial tension. No women, kids, or pets. Violence. Road dogs (close friends). Iron bars. Concrete beds. Hate. Guard towers. Getting booked. Count times. Food lines. Parole boards. Judges. Degradation. District attorneys. Death. Cops. A.M.'s and P.M.'s—year in and year out. Monotony. Withdrawals. Preliminary hearings. The need to show no pain—ever. Release dates. Parole officers. Alienation. Hopelessness. Determinate sentencing. A guard on the way out of prison: "See you when you get back, Terry. Guys like you are job security for guys like me." A lot to deal with for a white, California-raised kid from middle-class suburbia. A lot for anybody.

From my first arrest in 1970 to my last discharge from parole in 1992, I became intimately familiar with all the components of the criminal justice system. Over the course of this twenty-plus-year "career," which included spending over twelve years inside state (prisons) and county (jails) "correctional" facilities for drug-related crimes, I experienced almost everything the system has to offer—except the death penalty or a sentence of life without possibility of parole.

These experiences have taught me that the way "criminals" are dealt with in America is anything but "fair" or "just." Rather, their fate is determined by who they are and how they are seen by system actors such as judges and prosecutors and by the general public. It is important to note that this "seeing" varies dramatically and is relative to an ever-changing social, economic, political, and historical context.

Crime today is politicized and a main focus of media attention. The "threat" posed by "criminals" is used to generate fear and legitimate spending millions on more police, more prisons, and more mechanisms of social control. The reasons for this are complex and controversial. But it hasn't always been like this.

I was a kid in the 1960s, when the civil rights movement, protests against the Vietnam war, and an anti-establishment-oriented "counterculture" were in full swing. Instead of bombarding the public with visions of low-level street crime, the nightly news sent us images from the war, urban riots, and people getting beaten by police for participating in nonviolent sit-ins. Governmental policies and social inequality rather than addicts and "juvenile predators" were seen as "criminal" by a significant portion of the population. Rules and rule enforcers (like racial segregation policies, drug laws, government officials) were the targets of attention. In defiance of "the way things were," we grew our hair, spoke out against social norms, and got high.

My own drug use began in 1967 and escalated over time. Initially, I used whatever was available: alcohol, marijuana, reds, yellows, whites, LSD. In 1969 I used heroin for the first time.

Now, how could any sane person try heroin? Doesn't everyone know it's a "bad" thing to do? Though it was scary, I rationalized it as being okay. After all, I knew several people who used it. They seemed to be fine. Everything I had been told about all the other drugs I used had proved to be a lie; we were told that if we smoked pot we'd lie down on train tracks, and if we took LSD we'd jump out of tall buildings and lose our minds. So one night at a party I gave it a shot. Or, I should say, I stuck my arm out and a friend gave me a shot.

Turning points. Crossroads. Where do we go from here? The first thing I

ONE MAN'S JOURNEY (CONTINUED)

thought when I felt the effects of heroin was, "I can't believe I've been doing anything in life other than trying to use this stuff all the time." For the next twenty-plus years I did just that. Heroin made me feel "normal," like I fit, belonged, was not out of place. It is a powerfully enticing drug: many first-time users instantly fall in love with it. I was one of those people. It provided me with a clear purpose in life and, though I didn't know it at first, a future that would involve spending a lot of time inside the various worlds of the criminal justice system.

Once I began using illegal drugs, I started seeing anyone affiliated with any type of legal authority as a potential enemy—especially police, whose job (in my mind) was to "catch" or "arrest" me. This distrustful outlook became magnified once I began using heroin. After all, heroin users are seen as "real" criminals.

The people in my life changed as my heroin habit took hold. Where I used to have friends who were about my age and white, now I frequently hung out with older people who were often a different color, brown or black. Their images remain. A 40-year-old hooker fixing (injecting narcotics), sores all over her body, pushing scabs on her arms out of the way with the needle in a desperate attempt to find a vein. A 65-year-old, jaundiced-eyed black man welcoming me into his home to share the joys of addiction. Trips into ethnic neighborhoods to buy dope where few, if any, white people were seen. Nodding. Throwing up. People getting arrested, disappearing, overdosing, dying. As my social circle changed, so did the way I saw the world and myself. Without realizing it I was "becoming" what society calls "criminal."

My love of heroin took me down a road that included many unplanned pit stops. I was investigated, arrested, booked more times than I care to recall. I appeared more than once at a preliminary hearing, still going through withdrawal—looking sickly and feeling weak as I interacted with bailiffs, public defenders, judges, and other prisoners. The road took me through cramped cellblocks, courtroom holding tanks, and jailhouse chow halls—to places where I witnessed alcoholics suffering from the DT's, epileptics and diabetics going into convulsions from a lack of medication, people jammed into cells with bullets still in their bodies, and more. From four different prison commitments came years behind walls, isolated from the world. My love of heroin took me down a path where I was either on the run, locked up, or on probation or parole for more than twenty years. The pieces that conclude each part of this book are scenes from that journey.

Part II

Police

4 POLICE

5 POLICE OPERATION

6 POLICING ISSUES AND TRENDS

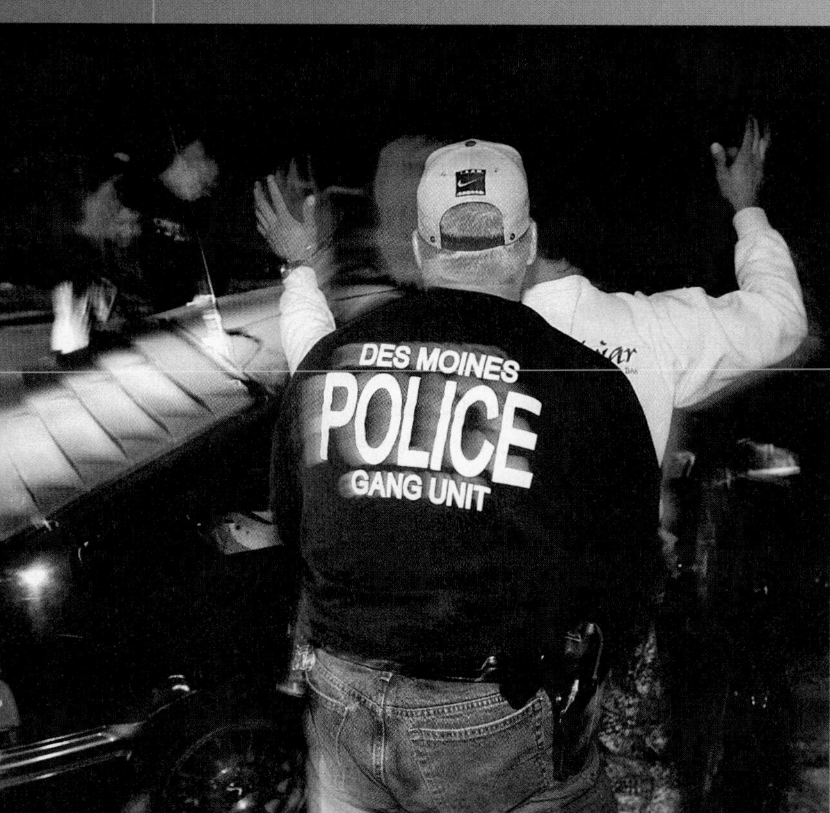

MOST OF US have an image of the police that we get from movies and television, but the reality differs greatly from the dramatic exploits of the cops in *The Fugitive* or on *NYPD Blue*. Although the police are the most visible agents of the criminal justice system, our images of them come mainly from fiction.

In Part Two we deal with the police as the key unit of the criminal justice system—the one that confronts crime in the community. Chapter 4 traces the history of policing and looks at its function and organization. Chapter 5 explores the daily operations of the police, and Chapter 6 analyzes current issues and trends in policing. As we will see, police work is often done in a hostile environment in which life and death, honor and dishonor may be at stake. Police officers are given discretion to deal with many situations; how they use it has an important effect on the way society views policing.

Chapter 4 Police

The Development of Police in the United States

- *The English Roots of the American Police*
- *Policing in the United States*

Organization of the Police

- *Federal Agencies*
- *State Agencies*
- *County Agencies*
- *Municipal Agencies*

Police Policy

Police Functions

- *Order Maintenance*
- *Law Enforcement*
- *Service*
- *Implementing the Mandate*

Police Actions

- *Encounters between Police and Citizens*
- *Police Discretion*
- *Domestic Violence*

AT 9:02 A.M. on April 19, 1995, a bomb blast ripped through the Alfred P. Murrah Federal Building in Oklahoma City, collapsing nine floors and piling debris on almost two hundred of the five hundred people in the building. When the dust and smoke had cleared 168 bodies, 19 of them children, were found at the site. This was the deadliest act of terrorism in the history of the United States.

While public safety agencies rushed to the bomb site, Timothy McVeigh was 60 miles north of Oklahoma City, tooling along I-35 in his yellow 1977 Mercury Marquis. He was pulled over by a state trooper who noticed that the car didn't have license tags. McVeigh was arrested on a firearms charge after the traffic stop and held pending bail. On April 21, as he was about to make bail, federal authorities arrested McVeigh because he resembled the bombing suspect labeled "John Doe No.1." This arrest, and the investigation and trial that followed led to McVeigh's death sentence by a Denver jury in June, 1997.

The events at Oklahoma City gave Americans a lesson in the complex nature of law enforcement in the United States. Within hours of the blast units from the Federal Bureau of Investigation; Drug Enforcement Administration; Bureau of Alcohol, Tobacco and Firearms; Department of Defense, Oklahoma National Guard, Oklahoma Department of Public Safety, and the Oklahoma City Police were on the scene to rescue survivors, remove the dead, and track down the people responsible for the bombing.

Before the destruction of the Murrah Building few Americans had ever heard of the Bureau of Alcohol, Tobacco, and Firearms of the U.S. Treasury Department—or had known that it might act in such circumstances. The fact that so many different law enforcement agencies were involved was further evidence of the network of relationships among national, state, and local police forces. This complexity may have surprised and confused those who think only of their local police when they think of law enforcement.

The men and women in blue are the most visible presence of government in our society. Whether they are members of the local or state police, sheriff's departments, or federal agencies, the more than 800,000 sworn officers in the country play key roles in American society. Citizens look to them to perform a wide range of functions: crime prevention, law enforcement, order maintenance, and community services. However, the public's expectations of the police are not always clear. Citizens also form judgments about the police, and those judgments have a strong impact on the way the police function.

In a free society the police are required to maintain order. In performing this task, police officers are given a great deal of authority. Using their powers to arrest, search, detain, and use force, they can interfere with the freedom of any citizen. If they are excessive in the use of such powers, they can threaten the basic values of a stable, democratic society.

In this chapter we examine several aspects of policing. A brief history of the police is followed by discussions of how police officers carry out their duties and how law enforcement decisions are made.

Questions for Inquiry

How has policing evolved in the United States?

What are the main types of police agencies, and how are they organized ?

What influences police policy and styles of policing?

What are the functions of the police?

How do police officers balance action, decision making, and discretion?

THE DEVELOPMENT OF POLICE IN THE UNITED STATES

Law and order is not a new concept; it has been a subject of debate since the first police force was formed in London in 1829. Looking back even further, the Magna Carta signed by England's King John in 1215 placed limits on constables and bailiffs. We can read between the lines of that historic document to surmise that the problems of police abuse, maintenance of order, and the rule of law in thirteenth-century England were similar to those faced by modern societies. The same remedies—recruiting better-qualified police, stiffening the penalties for official misconduct, creating a civilian board of control—were suggested even then to ensure that order was kept in accordance with the rule of law.

The English Roots of the American Police

The roots of American policing lie in the English legal tradition. Three major aspects of American policing evolved from that tradition: (1) limited authority, (2) local control, and (3) fragmented organization. Like the English police, but unlike police in continental Europe, the police in the United States have limited authority; their powers and duties are specifically defined by law. England, like the United States, has no national police force; each unit is under local control. However, in contemporary England there are closer links between the central government and the local constabularies than is the case in the United States (Bayley, 1992:509) In the United States policing is fragmented: there are many types of agencies—constable, county sheriff, city police, FBI—each with its own special **jurisdiction** and responsibilities.

jurisdiction

The geographic territory or legal boundaries within which control may be exercised; the range of authority.

History tells us that systems for protecting citizens and property existed before the thirteenth century. The **frankpledge** system required that groups of ten families, called "tithings", agree to uphold the law, keep order, and bring violators to a court. By custom, every male above the age of 12 was part of the system. When a man became aware that a crime had occurred, he was obliged to raise a "hue and cry" and to join others in his tithing to track down the offender. The tithing was fined if members did not perform its duties.

frankpledge

A system in old English law in which members of a tithing, a group of ten families, pledged to be responsible for keeping order and bringing violators of the law to court.

Over time England developed a system in which individuals were chosen within each community to take charge of catching criminals. The Statute of Winchester, enacted in 1285, set up a parish constable-watch system. Members of the community were still required to pursue criminals, just as they had been under the frankpledge system, but now a constable supervised those efforts. The constable was a man chosen from the parish to serve without pay as its law enforcement officer for one year. The constable had the power to call the entire community into action if a serious disturbance arose. Watchmen, who were appointed to help the constable, spent most of their time patrolling the town at night to ensure that "all's well" and enforcing the criminal law. They were also responsible for lighting street lamps and putting out fires.

Not until the eighteenth century did an organized police force evolve in England. With the growth of commerce and industry, cities expanded while farming declined as the main source of employment and the focus of community life. In the larger cities these changes produced social disorder.

In the mid-eighteenth century, the novelist Henry Fielding and his brother, Sir John Fielding, led efforts to improve law enforcement in London. They wrote newspaper articles to inform the public about crime and published flyers describing known offenders. After Henry Fielding became a magistrate in 1748, he organized a small group of "thief-takers" to pursue and arrest lawbreakers. The government was so impressed with Fielding's Bow Street Amateur Volunteer Force (known as the "Bow Street Runners") that it paid the volunteers and attempted to form similar groups in other parts of London.

After Henry Fielding's death in 1754, these efforts declined. As time went by, it became clear to many that the government needed to assert itself in enforcing laws and maintaining order. London, with its unruly mobs, had become an especially dangerous place.

In the early 1800s there were several attempts to create a centralized police force for London. While people saw the need for social order, some feared that a police force would threaten the freedom of citizens and lead to tyranny. Finally, in 1829, Sir Robert Peel, Home Secretary in the British Cabinet, pushed Parliament to pass the Metropolitan Police Act, which created the London police force.

This agency was organized like a military unit, with a 1,000-man force commanded by two magistrates, later called "commissioners." The officers were called "bobbies" after Sir Robert Peel. Under Peel's direction the police had a four-part mandate:

1. To prevent crime without using repressive force and to avoid having to call upon the military to control riots and other disturbances.
2. To maintain public order by nonviolent means, using force to obtain compliance only as a last resort.
3. To reduce conflict between the police and the public.
4. To show efficiency through the absence of crime and disorder rather than through visible police actions. (Manning, 1977:82)

In effect, this meant keeping a low profile while maintaining order. Because of fears that a national force would threaten civil liberties, political leaders made every effort to focus police activities at the local level. These concerns were transported to the United States.

CHECKPOINT

1. What are the three main features of American policing that were inherited from England?
2. What was the frankpledge and how did it work?
3. What did the Statute of Winchester (1285) establish?
4. What did the Metropolitan Police Act (1829) establish?
5. What were the four mandates of the English police in the nineteenth century?

(Answers are at the end of the chapter.)

Policing in the United States

Before the Revolution, Americans shared the English belief that members of a community had a duty to help maintain order; therefore they adopted the offices of English constable, sheriff, and night watchman. The watch system was the main means of keeping order and catching criminals. Each citizen was required to be a member of the watch, but paid watchmen could be hired as replacements. Over time cities began to hire paid, uniformed watchmen to deal with crime.

After the formation of the federal government in 1789, police power remained with the states, again in response to fear of centralized law enforcement. However, the American police developed under conditions that were different from those in England. Unlike the British, police in the United States had to deal with ethnic diversity, local political control, regional differences, the exploration and settling of the West, and a generally more violent society.

American policing is often described in terms of three historical periods: the political era (1840-1920), the professional model era (1920-1970), and the community model era (1970-present) (Kelling and Moore, 1988). This description has been criticized because it applies only to the urban areas of the Northeast and does not take into account the very different development of the police in rural areas of the South and West. Still, it is useful as a framework for exploring the organization of the police, the focus of police work, and the strategies employed by police (Williams and Murphy, 1990).

The Political Era: 1840–1920

The period from 1840 to 1920 is called the political era because of the close ties that were formed between the police and local political leaders. In many cities the police seemed to work for the mayor's political party rather than for the citizens. This relationship served both groups in that the political "machines" recruited and maintained the police while the police helped the machine leaders get out the vote for favored candidates. Ranks in the police force were often for sale to the highest bidder, and many officers were "on the take" (Johnson, 1981:61).

During the Political Era the officer on a neighborhood beat dealt with crime and disorder as it arose. Police also performed various social services, such as caring for derelicts.

In the United States as in England, the growth of cities led to pressures to modernize law enforcement. Social relations in cities were quite different from those in the towns and countryside. In fact, from 1830 to 1870 there was much civil disorder in the large cities. Ethnic conflict, hostility toward nonslave blacks and abolitionists, mob actions against banks during economic declines, and violence in settling questions of morality, such as the use of alcohol—all these factors contributed to fears that a stable democracy would not survive.

Around 1840 the large cities began to create police forces. In 1845 New York City established the first full-time, paid police force. Boston and Philadelphia were the first to add a daytime police force to supplement the night watchmen; other cities—Chicago, New Orleans, Cincinnati—quickly followed.

By 1850 most major cities had created police departments organized on the English model. Departments were headed by a chief appointed by the major and council. The city was divided into precincts, and full-time, paid patrolmen were assigned to each. Early police forces sought to prevent crimes and keep order through the use of foot patrols. The officer on the beat dealt with crime, disorder, and other problems as they arose. The Close-up by Edward H. Savage, a fifteen year veteran of the Boston Police Department, summarizes the role of the urban police officer during this period.

In addition to foot patrols, the police performed a number of service functions, such as caring for derelicts, operating soup kitchens, regulating public health, and handling medical and social emergencies. In cities across the country, the police provided beds and food for homeless people. In station houses, overnight "lodgers" might sleep on the floor or sometimes in clean bunkrooms (Monkkonen, 1981:127). Because they were the only governmental agency that had close contact with life on the streets of the city, the police became general public servants as well as crime control officers. Their close links with the community and the service they provided fostered the support of citizens (Monkkonen, 1992:554).

Police developed differently in the South because of the existence of slavery and the agrarian nature of that region. Historians note that the first organized police agencies with full-time officers developed in cities with large numbers of slaves (Charleston, New Orleans, Savannah, and Richmond), where white owners feared slave uprisings (Rousey, 1984:41). The owners created "slave patrols" to deal with runaways. The patrols had full power to break into the homes of slaves who were suspected of keeping arms, to physically punish those who did not obey their orders, and to arrest runaways and return them to their masters.

Westward expansion in the United States produced conditions quite different from those in either the urban East or the agricultural South. The frontier was settled before order could be established. Thus, those who wanted to maintain law and order often had to take matters into their own hands by forming vigilante groups.

One of the first official positions created in rural areas was that of sheriff. Although the sheriff had duties similar to those of the "shire reeves" of seventeenth-century England, the American sheriff was elected and had broad powers to enforce the law. As elected officers, sheriffs had close ties to local politics. They also depended on the men of the community for assistance. This is how the *posse comitatus* (Latin for "power of the county"), borrowed from fifteenth-century Europe, came into being. Local men above the age of fifteen were required to respond to the sheriff's call for assistance, forming a body known as a posse.

After the Civil War the federal government appointed U.S. marshals to help enforce the law in the western territories. Some of the best-known folk heroes of American policing were U.S. Marshals Wyatt Earp, Bat Masterson, and Wild Bill Hickok, who tried to bring law and order to the "Wild West" (Calhoun, 1990). While some marshals did extensive law enforcement work, most had mainly judicial duties, such as keeping order in the courtroom and holding prisoners for trial.

During the twentieth century all parts of the country became increasingly urban. This change blurred some of the regional differences that had helped define policing

CLOSE-UP

Advice to a Young Policeman

MY FRIEND: You have recently been appointed, and are about to assume the responsibilities of an office the duties of which are much more varied and difficult, and the trust of which is of much more importance to the public and to yourself, than is generally admitted.

Do not forget that in this business your character is your capital. Deal honorably with all persons, and hold your word sacred. . . . Make it your business to know what is doing on every part of [your beat]; let no person or circumstance escape your notice. Learn the people residing or doing business on your beat; protect their property; make yourself useful, and aid them in all their lawful pursuits, and by an upright and straightforward course, and a close attention to duty, endeavor to merit the good will of all good citizens. You know not how soon you may need their aid, and their favor will add much to your power and influence to do good. But in the pursuance of your duties, as much as possible avoid laying yourself under special obligations to any one; let your services rather place others under an obligation to you.

Lend a willing ear to all complaints made to you in your official capacity; the most unworthy have a right to be heard, and a word of comfort to the afflicted, or advice to the erring, costs you nothing, and may do much good.

Remember that in your official duties, you are continually and eminently exposed to the ten thousand snares and temptations in city life. Treat all persons kindly; avoid discussion in politics; . . . I might say more, but should I, you would still have to go out and learn your duty.

SOURCE: Edward H. Savage, *A Chronological History of the Boston Watch and Police from 1631 to 1865*, 2nd ed. (Boston: J. E. Farwell, 1865), p. 127.

in the past. In addition, growing criticism of the influence of politics on the police led to efforts to reform the nature and organization of the police. Reformers sought to make police more professional and to reduce their ties to local politics.

The Professional Model Era: 1920–1970

American policing was greatly influenced by the Progressive movement. These reformers had two goals: more efficient government and more governmental services to assist the less fortunate. A related goal was to reduce the influence of party politics and patronage (favoritism in handing out jobs) on government. The Progressives saw a need for professional law enforcement officials who would use modern technology to benefit society as a whole, not just local politicans.

The key to the Progressives' concept of professional law enforcement is found in their slogan, "The police have to get out of politics, and politics has to get out of the police." August Vollmer, chief of police of Berkeley, California, from 1909 to 1932, was one of the leading advocates of professional policing. He initiated the use of motorcycle units, handwriting analysis, and fingerprinting. With other police reformers, such as Leonhard Fuld, Raymond Fosdic, Bruce Smith, and O. W. Wilson, he urged that the police be made into a professional force, a nonpartisan agency of government committed to public service. This model of professional policing has six elements:

1. The force should stay out of politics.
2. Members should be well trained, well disciplined, and tightly organized.
3. Laws should be enforced equally.
4. The force should use new technology.
5. Personnel procedures should be based on merit.
6. The main task of the police should be fighting crime.

Refocusing attention on crime control and away from maintaining order probably did more than anything else to change the nature of American policing. But the narrow focus on crime fighting broke many of the ties that the police had formed with the communities they served. By the end of World War I, police departments had greatly reduced their involvement in social services. Instead, for the most part, cops became crime fighters (Monkkonen, 1981:127).

O. W. Wilson, a student of Vollmer, was a leading advocate of professionalism. He promoted the use of motorized patrols, efficient radio communication, and rapid response. He believed that one-officer patrols were the best way to use personnel and that the two-way radio, which allowed for supervision by commanders, made officers more efficient (Reiss, 1992:51). He rotated assignments so that officers on patrol would not become too familiar with people in the community (and thus prone to corruption).

Advocates of professionalism urged that the police be made aware of the need to act lawfully and to protect the rights of all citizens, including those suspected of crimes. They sought to instill a strong—some would even say rigid ("Just the facts, ma'am")—commitment to the law and to equal treatment (Goldstein, 1990:7).

By the 1930s, the police were using new technologies and methods to combat serious crimes. They became more effective against crimes like murder, rape, and robbery—an important factor in gaining citizen support. By contrast, efforts to control victimless offenses and to strictly maintain order often aroused citizen opposition. As Mark Moore and George Kelling have noted, "The clean, bureaucratic model of policing put forth by the reformers could be sustained only if the scope of police responsibility was narrowed to 'crime fighting'" (Moore and Kelling, 1983:55).

In the 1960s the civil rights and antiwar movements, urban riots, and rising crime rates challenged many of the assumptions of the professional model. In their attempts to maintain order during public demonstrations, the police in many cities seemed to be concerned mainly with maintaining the status quo. Police officers found themselves enforcing laws that tended to discriminate against African Americans and the poor. With America's growing numbers of low-income racial minorities living in the inner cities, the professional style isolated the police from the communities they served. In the eyes of many inner-city residents, the police were an occupying army keeping them at the bottom of society, rather than public servants helping all citizens.

Although the police continued to portray themselves as crime fighters, citizens became aware that the police often were not effective in this role. Crime rates rose for many offenses, and the police were unable to change the perception that the quality of urban life was declining.

The Community Policing Model Era: 1970–Present

Beginning in the 1970s, there were calls for a move away from the crime-fighting focus and toward greater emphasis on keeping order and providing services to the community. Research studies revealed the complex nature of police work and the extent to which day-to-day practices deviated from the professional ideal. The research also questioned the effectiveness of the police in catching and deterring criminals.

Three findings of this research are especially noteworthy:

1. Increasing the number of patrol officers in a neighborhood was found to have little effect on the crime rate.
2. Rapid response to calls for service did not greatly increase the arrest rate.
3. It is difficult to improve the percentage of crimes solved.

Such findings undermined acceptance of the professional crime-fighter model (Moore, 1992:99). Critics argued that the professional style isolated the police from the community and reduced their knowledge about the neighborhoods they served, especially when police patrolled in cars. Use of the patrol car prevented personal contacts with citizens. Instead, it was argued, police should get out of their cars and spend more time meeting and helping residents. This would permit the police to help people with a range of problems and in some cases to prevent problems from arising or growing worse.

In a provocative article titled "Broken Windows: The Police and Neighborhood Safety," James Q. Wilson and George L. Kelling argued that policing should work more on "little problems" such as maintaining order, providing services to those in need, and adopting strategies to reduce the fear of crime (Wilson and Kelling, 1982:29). They based their approach on three assumptions:

1. Neighborhood disorder creates fear. Areas with street people, youth gangs, prostitution, and drunks are high-crime areas.
2. Just as broken windows are a signal that nobody cares and can lead to more serious vandalism, untended disorderly behavior is a signal that the community does not care. This also leads to more serious disorder and crime.
3. If the police are to deal with disorder and thus reduce fear and crime, they must rely on citizens for assistance.

Advocates of the community policing approach urge greater use of foot patrols so that officers will become known to citizens, who in turn will cooperate with the police. They believe that through attention to little problems, the police may not only reduce disorder and fear but also improve public attitudes toward policing. When citizens respond positively to police efforts, the police will have improved bases of community and political support.

A problem-oriented approach to policing means that officers must be prepared to handle a range of problems. In dealing with noisy teenagers, battered spouses, accident victims, and other problems, police should try to address the underlying causes of these problems. In so doing they could reduce disorder and fear of crime (Goldstein, 1979:236).

In *Fixing Broken Windows*, George Kelling and Catherine Coles call for strategies to restore order and reduce crime in public spaces in U.S. communities (1996). In Baltimore, New York, San Francisco, and Seattle, police are paying greater attention to "quality-of-life crimes"—by arresting subway fare-beaters, rousting loiterers and panhandlers from parks, and aggressively dealing with those obstructing sidewalks, harassing, and soliciting. By handling these "little crimes," the police not only help restore order but often prevent more serious crimes. In New York, for example, searching fare-beaters often yielded weapons, questioning a street vendor selling hot merchandise led to a fence specializing in stolen weapons, and arresting a person for urinating in a park resulted in discovery of a cache of weapons.

Although reformers argue for a greater focus on order maintenance and service, they do not call for an end to the crime-fighting role. Instead, they want a shift of emphasis. The police should pay more attention to community needs and seek to understand the problems underlying crime, disorder, and incivility. These proposals have been adopted by police executives in many cities and by influential organizations like the Police Foundation and the Police Executive Research Forum.

Can—and should—community policing be implemented throughout the nation? The populations of some cities, especially in the West, are too dispersed to permit a switch to foot patrols. In many cities foot patrols and community police stations have been set up in public housing projects. Time will tell if this new approach will become as widespread as the focus on professionalism was in the first half of this century.

Whichever approach the police take—professional, crime fighting, or community policing—it must be carried out through a bureaucratic structure. We therefore turn to a discussion of police organization in the United States.

CHECKPOINT

6. What are the three historical periods of American policing?
7. What was the main feature of the political era?
8. What were the major recommendations of the Progressive reformers?
9. What are the main criticisms of the professional era?
10. What is community policing?

ORGANIZATION OF THE POLICE

As we saw in Chapter 2, the United States has a federal system of government with separate national and state structures, each with authority over certain functions. Most of the 17,500 police agencies at the national, state, county, and municipal levels are responsible for carrying out three functions: (1) law enforcement, (2) order maintenance, and (3) service to the community. They employ a total of more than 800,000 people, sworn and unsworn. The agencies include the following:

- 12,502 municipal police departments
- 3,086 sheriffs' departments
- 1,721 special police agencies (jurisdictions limited to transit systems, parks, schools, and so on)
- 49 state police departments (all states except Hawaii)
- 50 federal law enforcement agencies (FBI, 1997. *Crime in the United States—1996*:278).

This list shows both the fragmentation and the local orientation of American police. Also indicating that law enforcement is primarily local in nature, the national government spends only 12 percent of all funds for police work and state governments only 15 percent. Municipal and county governments spend the other 73 percent. Each level of the system has different responsibilities, either for different kinds of crimes, such as the federal authority over counterfeiting, or for different geographic areas, such as state police authority over major highways. The broadest authority tends to lie with local units.

Federal Agencies

Federal law enforcement agencies are part of the executive branch of the national government. They investigate a specific set of crimes defined by Congress. Recent federal efforts against drug trafficking, organized crime, insider stock trading, and environmental pollution have attracted attention to these agencies even though they employ few agents and handle relatively few crimes.

The Federal Bureau of Investigation (FBI) is an investigative agency within the U.S. Justice Department with the power to investigate all federal crimes not placed under the jurisdiction of other agencies. Established as the Bureau of Investigation in 1908, it came to national prominence under J. Edgar Hoover, its director from 1924 until his death in 1972. Hoover made major changes in the Bureau (renamed the Federal Bureau of Investigation in 1935) in order to increase its professionalism. He sought to remove political factors from the selection of agents, established the national fingerprint filing system, and oversaw the development of the Uniform Crime Reporting System. Although Hoover has been criticized for many aspects of his career, such as FBI spying on civil rights and antiwar activists during the 1960s, his role in improving police work and the FBI's effectiveness is widely recognized.

Solving the bombing of Oklahoma City's Alfred P. Murrah Building involved law enforcement agencies from many levels of government.

Specialization in Federal Law Enforcement

Other federal agencies are concerned with specific kinds of crimes. Within the FBI is the semiautonomous Drug Enforcement Administration (DEA). As part of the Treasury Department, the Internal Revenue Service (IRS) pursues violations of tax laws; the Bureau of Alcohol, Tobacco, and Firearms deals with alcohol, tobacco, and gun control; and the Customs Service enforces customs regulations. Other federal law enforcement agencies include the Secret Service Division of the Treasury Department (counterfeiting, forgery, and protection of the president), the Bureau of Postal Inspection of the Postal Service (mail offenses), and the Border Patrol of the Department of Justice's Immigration and Naturalization Service (INS). Some other departments of the executive branch, such as the U.S. Coast Guard and the National Parks Service, have police powers related to their specific duties.

State Agencies

Every state except Hawaii has its own police force with statewide jurisdiction. Most of these agencies are small and do not handle the bulk of the police work. The American reluctance to centralize police power has generally kept state police forces from replacing local ones. The Pennsylvania State Constabulary, formed in 1905, was the first such force. By 1925 almost all of the states had police forces.

All state forces regulate traffic on main highways, and two-thirds of the states have also given them general police powers. In only about a dozen populous states are these forces able to perform law enforcement tasks outside the cities. Where the state police are well established—as in Pennsylvania, New York, New Jersey, Massachusetts, and Michigan—they also provide services in rural areas. For the most part, however, they operate only in areas where no other form of police protection exists or where local officers ask for their help. In many states, for example, the crime lab is run by the state police as a means of assisting local law enforcement agencies.

County Agencies

Sheriffs are found in almost every one of the 3,100 counties in the United States. They are responsible for policing rural areas, but over time, especially in the

Northeast, the state and lcoal police have assumed many of their criminal justice functions. In parts of the South and West, the sheriff's department is a well-organized force. In thirty-three states sheriffs are elected and hold the position of chief law enforcement officer in the county. Even when the sheriff's office is well organized, however, it may lack jurisdiction over cities and towns. In these situations, the sheriff and his or her deputies patrol unincorporated parts of the county or small towns that do not have police forces of their own.

In addition to performing law enforcement tasks, the sheriff is often an officer of the court; sheriffs may operate jails, serve court orders, and provide the bailiffs who maintain order in courtrooms. In many counties, politics mixes with law enforcement: sheriffs may be able to appoint their political supporters as deputies and bailiffs. In other places, such as Los Angeles County and Oregon's Multnomah County, the sheriff's department is staffed by professionals.

Municipal Agencies

The police departments of cities and towns have general law enforcement authority. City police forces range in size from more than 35,000 employees in the New York City Police Department to only one sworn officer in 1,602 small towns. Nearly 90 percent of local police agencies serve populations of 25,000 or less, but half of all sworn officers are employed in cities of at least 100,000 (*New York Times*, April 17,1995:9)

In a metropolitan area consisting of a central city and suburbs, policing is usually divided among agencies at all levels of government, giving rise to conflicts between jurisdictions that may interfere with the efficient use of police resources. The city and each suburb buys its own equipment and deploys its officers without coordinating with those of nearby jurisdictions. In some areas with large populations, agreements have been made to enhance cooperation among jurisdictions.

In essence, the United States is a nation of small police forces, each of which is authorized, funded, and operated within the limits of its own jurisdiction. Because of the fragmentation of police agencies in the United States, each jurisdiction develops its own enforcement goals and policies. Each agency must make choices about how to organize itself and use its resources to achieve its goals.

CHECKPOINT

11. What is the jurisdiction of federal law enforcement agencies?
12. What are the functions of most state police agencies?
13. Besides law enforcement, what functions do sheriffs perform?
14. What are the main features of the organization of the police in the United States?

POLICE POLICY

The police cannot enforce every law and catch every lawbreaker. Legal rules limit the ways officers can investigate and pursue lawbreakers. For example, the constitutional ban on unreasonable searches and seizures prevents police from investigating many crimes without a search warrant.

Because the police have limited resources, they cannot have officers on every street at all times of the day and night. This means that they must make choices about how to deploy their resources. They must decide which offenses will receive the most attention and which tactics will be used. Police chiefs must decide, for example, whether to have officers patrol neighborhoods in cars or on foot. Changes in policy—such as increasing the size of the night patrol or tolerating prostitution and other vice crimes—affect the amount of crime that gets official attention and the system's ability to deal with offenders.

As we have seen, for most of the past half-century the police have emphasized their role as crime fighters. As a result, police in most communities focus on the crimes covered by the FBI's *Uniform Crime Reports*. These are the crimes that make headlines and that politicians point to when they call for increases in the police budget. They are also the crimes that tend to be committed by the poor. White-collar crimes like forgery, embezzlement, or tax fraud are viewed as less threatening by the public and thus get less attention from the police. Voters pressure politicians and the police to enforce laws that help them feel safe and secure in their daily lives.

Decisions about how police resources will be used affect the types of people who are arrested and passed through the criminal justice system. Think of the hard choices you would have to make if you were a police chief. Should more officers be sent into high-crime areas? Should more officers be assigned to the central business district during shopping hours? What should be the mix between traffic control and crime fighting? These questions have no easy answers. Police officials must answer them according to their goals and values, as discussed by Police Commander John L. Buchanan in the Workperspective.

WORK*Perspective*

John L. Buchanan
Police Commander

Phoenix Police Department

I began my policing career upon graduation from college in 1973. After the academy, I was assigned as a patrol officer and later as a narcotics investigator in the Scottsdale Police Department. To take advantage of the opportunities of a larger department I transferred to the Phoenix Police Department in 1977 and was promoted to sergeant in 1982 after nine years of patrol and investigative experience. In 1984 I attended the FBI National Academy and was promoted to lieutenant in 1987.

In the Phoenix Police Department sergeants generally supervise a squad of six to ten officers or detectives. Lieutenants are responsible for an entire shift in one precinct, usually about sixty officers, or a specialized investigative unit dealing with, for example, gangs, homicide, or sex crimes. In 1989 I was assigned to the Internal Affairs Unit for six months and then was assigned to coordinate a new multijurisdictional drug demand reduction program known as "Do Drugs, Do Time."

In 1990 I was promoted to commander and assigned as duty officer, responsible for

How did the police gain such broad responsibilities? In many places the police are the only public agency that is available seven days a week and twenty-four hours a day to respond to calls for help. They are also best able to investigate many kinds of problems. Moreover, the power to use force when necessary allows them to intervene in problem situations.

The functions of the police can be classified into three groups: (1) order maintenance, (2) law enforcement, and (3) service. Police agencies divide their resources among these groups on the basis of community need, citizen requests, and department policy.

Figure 4.1
Police Functions

The police are given a wide range of responsibilities, from directing traffic to solving homicides, but the work can be divided into three categories: order maintenance, law enforcement, and service. Departments will emphasize one or more of these functions according to the community's government structure and socioeconomic characteristics.

Order Maintenance

Preventing behavior that disturbs or threatens to disturb the peace. In these situations the police exercise discretion to determine if the law has been broken.

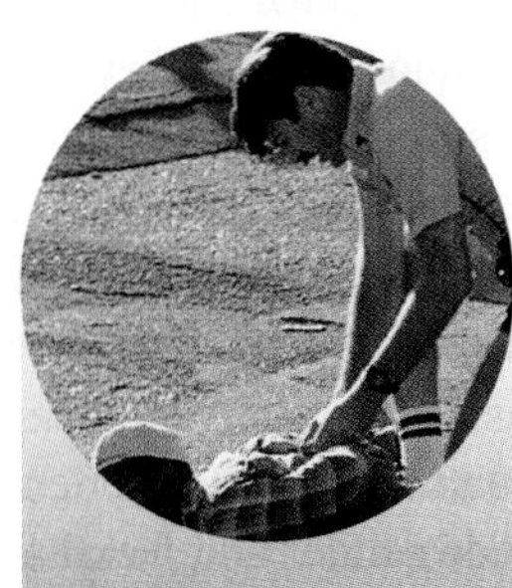

Law Enforcement

Controlling crime by intervening in situations where the law has been broken and the identity of the guilty person must be established.

Service

Providing help to the public, ranging from checking door locks to providing medical assistance to finding missing persons.

Order Maintenance

order maintenance

The police function of preventing behavior that disturbs or threatens to disturb the public peace or that involves face-to-face conflict among two or more persons. In such situations the police exercise discretion in deciding whether a law has been broken.

The **order maintenance** function is a broad mandate to prevent behavior that disturbs or threatens to disturb the peace or involves face-to-face conflict among two or more persons. A domestic quarrel, a noisy drunk, loud music in the night, a beggar on the street, a tavern brawl—all are forms of disorder that may require action by the police.

Unlike most laws that define specific acts as illegal, laws regulating disorderly conduct deal with ambiguous situations that may be viewed in different ways by different police officers. For many crimes, it is easy to see when the law has been broken. But order maintenance requires officers to decide not only whether a law has been broken, but also whether any action should be taken, and if so, who should be blamed. In a bar fight, for example, the officer must decide who started the fight, whether an arrest should be made for assault, and whether to arrest other people besides those who started the conflict.

Patrol officers deal mainly with behavior that either disturbs or threatens to disturb the peace. They confront the public in ambiguous situations and have wide discretion in matters that affect people's lives. If an officer decides to arrest someone for disorderly conduct, that person may spend time in jail and could lose his or her job even without being convicted of the crime.

Officers often must make judgments in order maintenance situations. They may be required to help persons in trouble, manage crowds, supervise various kinds of

Because the police have limited resources, they cannot have officers on every street at all times of the day and night. This means that they must make choices about how to deploy their resources. They must decide which offenses will receive the most attention and which tactics will be used. Police chiefs must decide, for example, whether to have officers patrol neighborhoods in cars or on foot. Changes in policy—such as increasing the size of the night patrol or tolerating prostitution and other vice crimes—affect the amount of crime that gets official attention and the system's ability to deal with offenders.

As we have seen, for most of the past half-century the police have emphasized their role as crime fighters. As a result, police in most communities focus on the crimes covered by the FBI's *Uniform Crime Reports*. These are the crimes that make headlines and that politicians point to when they call for increases in the police budget. They are also the crimes that tend to be committed by the poor. White-collar crimes like forgery, embezzlement, or tax fraud are viewed as less threatening by the public and thus get less attention from the police. Voters pressure politicians and the police to enforce laws that help them feel safe and secure in their daily lives.

Decisions about how police resources will be used affect the types of people who are arrested and passed through the criminal justice system. Think of the hard choices you would have to make if you were a police chief. Should more officers be sent into high-crime areas? Should more officers be assigned to the central business district during shopping hours? What should be the mix between traffic control and crime fighting? These questions have no easy answers. Police officials must answer them according to their goals and values, as discussed by Police Commander John L. Buchanan in the Workperspective.

WORK*Perspective*

John L. Buchanan
Police Commander

Phoenix Police Department

I began my policing career upon graduation from college in 1973. After the academy, I was assigned as a patrol officer and later as a narcotics investigator in the Scottsdale Police Department. To take advantage of the opportunities of a larger department I transferred to the Phoenix Police Department in 1977 and was promoted to sergeant in 1982 after nine years of patrol and investigative experience. In 1984 I attended the FBI National Academy and was promoted to lieutenant in 1987.

In the Phoenix Police Department sergeants generally supervise a squad of six to ten officers or detectives. Lieutenants are responsible for an entire shift in one precinct, usually about sixty officers, or a specialized investigative unit dealing with, for example, gangs, homicide, or sex crimes. In 1989 I was assigned to the Internal Affairs Unit for six months and then was assigned to coordinate a new multijurisdictional drug demand reduction program known as "Do Drugs, Do Time."

In 1990 I was promoted to commander and assigned as duty officer, responsible for departmental operations after normal business hours. Fifteen months later I was transferred to command a precinct consisting of 220 personnel and providing patrol services to the city's west side (50 square miles and 180,000 inhabitants). After three years as a precinct commander (one of the best jobs I've ever had), I was appointed commander of the Planning and Research Bureau, a position I occupied for two years, until I was asked to lead a small team to redesign the department's planning process.

Planning for future operations is essential in all large organizations. Crime is a major concern for our community, and we confront gang, drug, and violence problems daily. With well over 3,000 personnel and an annual budget of $240 million, the department serves 1.2 million Phoenix residents who live over a 470-square-mile area. In the past the department had used three- and five-year plans aimed at improving quality of service, but most of these efforts tended to be budget driven and thus did not always have satisfactory results.

The Strategic Planning Team was charged with developing a system to address this challenge in a way that would take advantage of the department's progressive history without burdening already-overworked personnel.

Planning is essential if police departments are to effectively serve the community. However, there are problems that must be recognized if a plan is to succeed. At the street level police work often requires a short-term, problem-centered outlook. Such a focus involves responding to crime scenes and improvising solutions before going on to the next crisis. Increasingly, though, a longer view is necessary at both the line and administrative levels. This is not only good management but it is also a major component of the community policing approach, which emphasizes problem solving through community-police partnerships.

While short-term efforts can sometimes be effective, the crush of day-to-day activity makes it difficult to step back and determine how, or if, the different parts of the total policing effort fit together. Planning is a continuous process of learning, reviewing, and redesigning to establish priorities and a unified direction. It is a process that is essential to achieve an effective policing organization.

During fifteen of my twenty-four years in policing, I have been either a line officer or supervisor in patrol or investigations. Each of my promotions was made based on competitive examinations. For sergeant and lieutenant these exams consisted of both written and oral sections. Those competing often spend more than six months in preparation. Candidates are ranked on a two-year promotional list by score, and it is not uncommon for one or two points to separate several candidates. The test for captain (changed to commander in 1994, when the ranks of captain and major were eliminated) was a two-day assessment.

Although I have held many assignments, the most enjoyable for me have been those that involve working on the streets in uniform. That is where the most interesting and important work is done and where a person can, once in a while, overcome the frustration for which police work is known and feel the satisfaction of making a significant contribution. Often that involves seeing to it that a "bad guy" is held to answer for a serious crime. But sometimes it may mean just offering some comforting words to a person in need.

WORK*Perspective*

American cities differ in governmental, economic, and racial and ethnic characteristics as well as in their degree of urbanization. These factors can affect the style of policing expected by the community. In a classic study, James Q. Wilson found that citizen expectations regarding police behavior are brought to bear through the political process in the choice of the top police executive. Chiefs who run their departments in ways that antagonize the community are not likely to stay in office very long. (See Ideas in Practice.) Wilson's key finding was that a city's political culture, which reflects its socioeconomic characteristics and its governmental organization, had a major impact on the style of policing found there. Wilson described three different styles of policing—the watchman, legalistic, and service styles (Wilson, 1968).

Departments with a *watchman* style stress order maintenance. Patrol officers may ignore minor violations of the law, especially those involving traffic and juveniles, as long as there is order. The police exercise discretion and deal with many infractions in an informal way. Officers make arrests only for flagrant violations and when order cannot be maintained. One problem, however is that the broad discretion exercised by officers can produce discrimination when officers do not treat members of different racial and ethnic groups in the same way. The beating of Rodney King by Los Angeles police officers is an example of an abuse resulting from the watchman style.

In departments with a *legalistic* style, police work is marked by professionalism and emphasis on law enforcement. Officers are expected to detain a high proportion of juvenile offenders, act vigorously against illicit enterprises, issue traffic tickets, and make a large number of misdemeanor arrests. They act as if there is a single standard of community conduct—that prescribed by the law—rather than different standards for juveniles, minorities, drunks, and other groups. Thus, while officers may not discriminate in making arrests and issuing citations, the strict enforcement of laws, including traffic laws, can seem overly harsh to some groups in the community.

Suburban middle-class communities often experience a *service* style. Residents expect the police to provide service and feel that they deserve individual treatment. Burglaries and assaults are taken seriously, while minor infractions tend to be dealt with by informal means such as stern warnings. The police are expected to deal with the misdeeds of local residents in a personal, nonpublic way so as to avoid embarrassment.

Regardless of the style of policing being used, even before officers investigate crimes or make arrests, each police chief decides on policies that will govern the level and type of enforcement in the community. Because the police are the entry point to the criminal justice system, all segments of the system are affected by the decisions made by police officials. Just as community expectations shape decisions about enforcement goals and the allocation of police resources, they also shape the cases that will be handled by prosecutors and corrections officials.

CHECKPOINT

16. What are the characteristics of the watchman style of policing?
17. What is the key feature of the legalistic style of policing?
18. Where are you likely to find the service style of policing?

POLICE FUNCTIONS

The police are expected to maintain order, prevent crime, and serve the community. However, they perform other tasks as well, many of them having little to do with crime and justice. They direct traffic, handle accidents and illnesses, stop noisy parties, find missing persons, enforce licensing regulations, provide ambulance services, take disturbed people into protective custody, and so on. The list is long and varies from place to place. Some researchers have suggested that the police have more in common with social service agencies than with the criminal justice system.

IDEAS IN PRACTICE

Soon after his appointment as chief of the Ledgecrest Police Department, Hal Lewis learned that he could not use the same tactics as when he was a captain in the Millbridge Police Department. In Millbridge, an industrial town of 150,000, youths arrested for stealing cars were taken to the station, booked, and usually given a night in jail.

Warned by Ledgecrest's assistant chief John Manning that in this upper-income suburban community the residents expected their delinquent sons and daughters to be brought home, not to the stationhouse, by the arresting officer, Lewis exploded, saying, "I'm no babysitter, I'm going to enforce the law, and that may mean that some of these snobby kids will learn what it's like to break the law!"

After 17-year-old Chip Lawson told his parents that he had been mistreated while awaiting their arrival at the stationhouse to post bond, the *Ledgecrest Ledger* editorialized that perhaps the "heavy-handed policies" of the new chief were not for the community. The editorial commented, "Perhaps that style worked in Millbridge, which has a crime problem, but in Ledgecrest we expect more from our police department."

If you were in Chief Lewis's position, what style of policing would you adopt for the Ledgecrest department?

How did the police gain such broad responsibilities? In many places the police are the only public agency that is available seven days a week and twenty-four hours a day to respond to calls for help. They are also best able to investigate many kinds of problems. Moreover, the power to use force when necessary allows them to intervene in problem situations.

The functions of the police can be classified into three groups: (1) order maintenance, (2) law enforcement, and (3) service. Police agencies divide their resources among these groups on the basis of community need, citizen requests, and department policy.

Figure 4.1
Police Functions

The police are given a wide range of responsibilities, from directing traffic to solving homicides, but the work can be divided into three categories: order maintenance, law enforcement, and service. Departments will emphasize one or more of these functions according to the community's government structure and socioeconomic characteristics.

Order Maintenance

Preventing behavior that disturbs or threatens to disturb the peace. In these situations the police exercise discretion to determine if the law has been broken.

Law Enforcement

Controlling crime by intervening in situations where the law has been broken and the identity of the guilty person must be established.

Service

Providing help to the public, ranging from checking door locks to providing medical assistance to finding missing persons.

Order Maintenance

order maintenance

The police function of preventing behavior that disturbs or threatens to disturb the public peace or that involves face-to-face conflict among two or more persons. In such situations the police exercise discretion in deciding whether a law has been broken.

The **order maintenance** function is a broad mandate to prevent behavior that disturbs or threatens to disturb the peace or involves face-to-face conflict among two or more persons. A domestic quarrel, a noisy drunk, loud music in the night, a beggar on the street, a tavern brawl—all are forms of disorder that may require action by the police.

Unlike most laws that define specific acts as illegal, laws regulating disorderly conduct deal with ambiguous situations that may be viewed in different ways by different police officers. For many crimes, it is easy to see when the law has been broken. But order maintenance requires officers to decide not only whether a law has been broken, but also whether any action should be taken, and if so, who should be blamed. In a bar fight, for example, the officer must decide who started the fight, whether an arrest should be made for assault, and whether to arrest other people besides those who started the conflict.

Patrol officers deal mainly with behavior that either disturbs or threatens to disturb the peace. They confront the public in ambiguous situations and have wide discretion in matters that affect people's lives. If an officer decides to arrest someone for disorderly conduct, that person may spend time in jail and could lose his or her job even without being convicted of the crime.

Officers often must make judgments in order maintenance situations. They may be required to help persons in trouble, manage crowds, supervise various kinds of services, and help people who are not fully accountable for what they do. The officers have a high degree of discretion and control over how such situations will develop. Patrol officers are not subject on the scene to direct control by their superiors. They have the power to arrest, but they may also decide not to make an arrest. The order maintenance function is complex, given all the possibilities that can arise. In an emotionally charged atmosphere the patrol officer is normally expected to "handle" a situation rather than to enforce the law. In controlling a crowd outside a rock concert, for example, the arrest of an unruly person may restore order by removing a troublemaker and also serving as a warning to others that they could be arrested if they do not cooperate. On the other hand, an arrest may cause the crowd to become hostile toward the officers, making things worse. It can be very difficult for officers to predict precisely how their discretionary decisions may promote or hinder order maintenance.

Law Enforcement

The **law enforcement** function applies to situations in which the law has been violated, the offender needs to be identified or located, and the suspect must be apprehended. Police officers who focus on law enforcement are in specialized branches such as the vice squad and the burglary detail. Although the patrol officer may be the first officer on the scene of a crime, in serious cases a detective usually prepares the case for prosecution by bringing together all the evidence for the prosecuting attorney. When the offender is identified but not located, the detective conducts the search. If the offender is not identified, the detective must analyze clues to find out who committed the crime.

law enforcement

The police function of controlling crime by intervening in situations in which the law has clearly been violated and the police need to identify and apprehend the guilty person.

Although the police often portray themselves as enforcers of the law, one can ask how effective they are in this function. For example, when a property crime is committed, the perpetrator usually has a time advantage over the police. This limits the ability of the police to identify, locate, and arrest the suspect. Burglaries, for instance, usually occur when people are away from home. The crime may not be discovered until hours or days later. The effectiveness of the police is also reduced when assault or robbery victims are unable to identify the offender. Victims often delay in calling the police, reducing the chances that a suspect will be apprehended.

Service

Police perform a broad range of services, especially for lower-income citizens, that are not related to crime. This **service** function—providing first aid, rescuing animals, helping the disoriented, and so on—has become a major police function, especially at night and on weekends. An analysis of more than 26,000 calls to twenty-one police departments found that about 80 percent of requests for police assistance do not involve crimes; in fact, the largest percentage of calls, 21 percent, were requests for information (Scott, 1981). Because the police are available twenty-four hours a day, this is the agency people turn to in times of trouble. Many departments provide information, operate ambulance services, locate missing persons, check locks on vacationers' homes, and intervene in suicide attempts.

service

The police function of providing assistance to the public, usually in matters unrelated to crime.

It may appear that valuable resources are being diverted from law enforcement to services. However, performing service functions can help police control crime. Through the service function, officers gain knowledge about the community, and citizens come to trust the police. Checking the security of buildings clearly helps prevent crime, but other activities—dealing with runaways, drunks, and public quarrels—may help solve problems before they lead to criminal behavior.

Implementing the Mandate

While the public may depend most heavily on the order maintenance and service functions of the police, many believe that law enforcement—the catching of law-breakers—is the most important function. According to public opinion polls, the crime-fighter image of the police is firmly rooted in citizens' minds. Crime fighting is also the main reason given by recruits for joining the force.

But do the police prevent crime? David Bayley claims that they do not. He says that "the experts know it, the police know it, but the public does not know it" (Bayley, 1994:3). He bases this claim on two facts. First, that no link has been found between the number of police officers and crime rates. Second, the main strategies used by modern police have little or no effect on crime. Those strategies are street patrolling by uniformed officers, rapid response to emergency calls, and expert investigation of crime by detectives. Bayley says that these are the strategies the police believe are essential to protect public safety, yet there is no evidence that they achieve this goal (Bayley, 1994:5).

CHECKPOINT

18. Define the order maintenance function. What are officers expected to do to maintain order in these situations?
19. Compare law enforcement situations with order maintenance situations.

POLICE ACTIONS

Police officers often must deal with citizens in emotionally charged situations, in matters of utmost importance (life and death, honor and dishonor), and in an environment that is apprehensive and perhaps hostile.

We have seen how the police are organized and how the three functions of policing—law enforcement, order maintenance, and service—operate. Now let us look at the everyday actions of the police as they deal with citizens in often highly discretionary ways. We will then discuss domestic violence as an example of the way police respond to one of many serious problems.

Encounters between Police and Citizens

Police depend on the public to help them identify crime and carry out investigations. Although most people are willing to help the police, fear, self-interest, and other factors keep some from cooperating. Many people fail to call the police because they think it is not worth the effort and cost. They do not want to spend time filling out forms at the station, appearing as a witness, or confronting a neighbor or relative in court. In some low-income neighborhoods, citizens are reluctant to assist the police because their past experience has shown that contact with law enforcement "only brings trouble." Without information about a crime, the police may decide not to pursue an investigation. Clearly, then, citizens have some control over the work of the police through their decisions to call or not to call them.

Police Discretion

As mentioned earlier, the judgments of police officers determine which crimes will be targeted and which suspects will be arrested. Patrol officers—the most numerous, the lowest-ranking, the newest to police work—have the most discretion. This is necessary because they are out on the streets dealing with ambiguous situations. If they chase a young thief into an alley, they can decide, outside of the view of the public, whether to make an arrest or just recover the stolen goods and give the offender a stern warning.

Patrol officers' main task is to maintain order and enforce ambiguous laws like those dealing with disorderly conduct, public drunkenness, breach of the peace, and other situations in which it is unclear if a law has been broken, who committed the offense, and whether an arrest should be made.

In the final analysis, it is the officer on the scene who must define the situation, decide how to handle it, and determine whether and how the law should be applied. Four factors are especially important:

1. The nature of the crime. The less serious a crime is to the public, the more freedom officers have to ignore it.
2. The relationship between the alleged criminal and the victim. The closer the personal relationship, the more variable the use of discretion. Family squabbles may not be as grave as they appear, and police are wary of making arrests, because a spouse may later decide not to press charges.
3. The relationship between the police and the criminal or victim. A polite complainant will be taken more seriously than a hostile one. Likewise, a suspect who shows respect to an officer is less likely to be arrested.
4. Department policy. The policies of the police chief and city officials will promote more or less discretion (Jacob, 1973:27).

In encounters between citizens and police, fairness is often affected by department policy. When should the patrol officer frisk a suspect? When should a deal be made with the addict-informer? Which disputes should be mediated on the spot and which left to more formal procedures? Surprisingly, these conflicts between the demands of fairness and policy are seldom decided by heads of departments but are left largely to the discretion of the officer on the scene. In fact, in many areas the department has little control over police actions.

Although some people call for detailed guidelines for police officers, such guidelines would probably be useless. No matter how detailed they were, the officer would still have to make judgments about how to apply them in each situation. At best, police administrators can develop guidelines and training that, one hopes, will give officers shared values and make their judgments more consistent.

Domestic Violence

Looking at how the police deal with domestic violence can show us the links between police-citizen encounters, the exercise of discretion, and actions taken

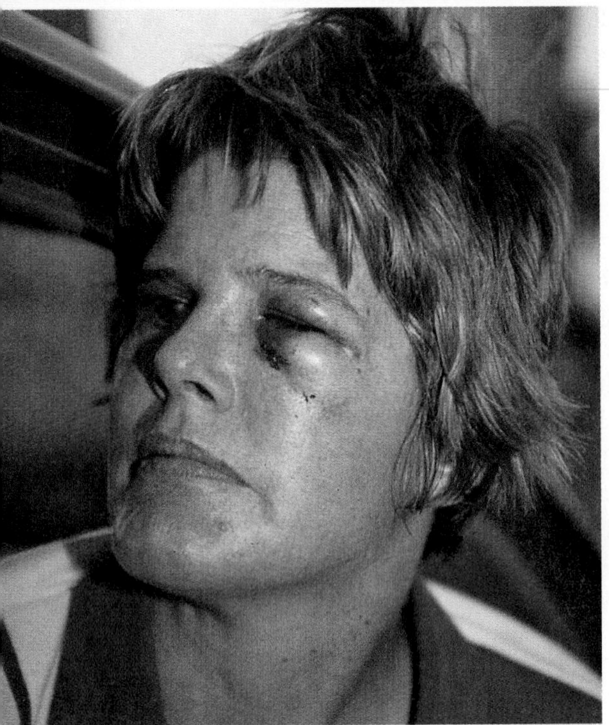

Until the 1970s most citizens and criminal justice agencies viewed domestic violence as a "private" affair best settled within the family. Today the largest number of calls to the police involve family disturbances.

(or not taken) by officers. Domestic violence, also called "battering" and "spousal abuse," has been defined as assaultive behavior involving adults who are married or who have a prior or an ongoing intimate relationship. In most cases it is carried out by a man against a woman of the same race or ethnic group. African-American and white women and Hispanic and non-Hispanic women sustain about the same amount of violence by an intimate (husband, ex-husband, boyfriend, or ex-boyfriend). Women aged 19 to 29 and women in families with incomes below $10,000 are more likely than other women to sustain violence by an intimate. In fact, a National Crime Victimization Survey estimated that during any one year 1.5 million women aged 12 or older had been victims of violence by an intimate. The survey also found that 28 percent of all female murder victims were killed by an intimate (BJS, 1995. *Special Report*:4).

Despite (or perhaps because of) the high level of domestic violence in American society, in the past not much was done about it. Before 1970 most citizens and criminal justice agencies viewed domestic violence as a "private" affair best settled within the family. It was thought that police involvement might make the situation worse for the victim because she faced the possibility of reprisal (Buzawa and Buzawa, 1990). Yet today the largest number of calls to the police involve family disturbances (Elliott, 1989:427).

From the viewpoint of most police departments, domestic violence was thought to be a "no-win" situation in which officers responding to calls for help were often set upon by one or both disputants. (See Ideas in Practice.) If an arrest was made, the police found that the victim often refused to cooperate with the prosecution. In addition, entering a home to deal with an emotion-laden incident was thought to be more dangerous than investigating "real" crimes. Many officers believed that trying to deal with family disputes was a leading cause of officer deaths and injury (Hirschel et al., 1992:247). However, this belief has been challenged by researchers who have found that domestic violence cases are no more dangerous to officers than other incidents (Garner and Clemmer, 1986; Stanford and Mowry, 1990:244-249).

Police response to domestic violence is a highly charged, uncertain, and possibly dangerous encounter with citizens in which officers must exercise discretion. In such a situation, how does an officer maintain order and enforce the law in accordance with the criminal law, department policies, and the needs of the victim?

CHECKPOINT

20. Why do patrol officers have so much discretion?
21. Why have police in the past failed to arrest in domestic violence situations?

In the past, most police departments advised officers to try to calm the parties and refer them to social service agencies rather than arrest the attacker. They began to rethink this policy when research in Minneapolis and other cities found that abusive spouses who are arrested and jailed briefly are much less likely to commit acts of domestic violence again (Sherman and Berk, 1984:261). Although the studies did not produce identical results, the research led some departments to order officers to make an arrest in every case in which there was evidence of an assault (Sherman et al., 1991:821). Police officers may have supported the arrest policy because it gave them a clear directive as to what to do (Friday, Metzger, and Walters, 1991:198-213). But officers in Minneapolis told researchers they preferred to retain the discretion to do what was necessary (Steinman, 1988:1-5).

If arrest will stem domestic violence in some cases, it has been suggested that arrest followed by prosecution will have a greater impact. However, a study of prosecutorial discretion in domestic violence cases in Milwaukee showed that factors such as the victim's injuries and the defendant's arrest record influenced the decision to charge, not just the fact of spouse abuse (Schmidt and Steury, 1989:487).

In many states policies have been changed as a result of lawsuits by injured women who claimed that the police ignored evidence of assaults and in effect allowed the spouse to inflict serious injuries. In addition, there is a growing sense that domestic violence can no longer be left to the discretion of individual patrol officers. In some states the law now requires the arrest of suspects in violent incidents without a warrant, even if the officer did not witness the crime but has probable cause to believe that the suspect committed one. Most large departments and police academies have programs to educate officers about the problem. However, as Sherman cautions, arrest may not "work best in every community, or for all kinds of people" (Sherman, 1992:2).

Even though we can point to a number of policy changes on dealing with domestic violence, the fact remains that it is the officer in the field who must handle these situations. As with most law enforcement situations, laws, guidelines, and training can help; but, as is often true in police work, in the end the discretion of the officer inevitably determines what actions will be taken.

IDEAS IN PRACTICE

Once more, the police were called to the Trembley apartment. At the door, a distraught Janet Trembley met Officers Kendall and Park. She was crying, and there was a red swelling on her face. The two Trembley children, also crying, clutched at their mother's legs.

"This time I want him arrested," she told the officers.

"Are you sure? The last time this happened you were at the station the next morning pleading for his release," responded Officer Kendall.

"I know. But this time, I mean it. We can't go on like this," said Janet.

"Are you going to let him back into this apartment when he is released?" queried Officer Park.

"I'm going to have to face that when the time comes. I have nowhere to go, and we need his earnings. But he can't continue to act like that."

"All right. Do you know where we can find him?"

"Yes, he's probably at the Tip Top Bar, down the street."

What should Officers Kendall and Park do? Can arrest and prosecution solve this problem?

Summary

- Developments in policing in England in the early nineteenth century formed the foundation of policing in the United States.
- Like their English counterparts, the American police have limited authority, are under local control, and are organizationally fragmented.
- Three eras of American policing are: the political era (1840-1920), the professional era (1920-1970), and the community policing era (1970-present).
- In our federal system of government, police agencies are found at the national, state, county, and municipal levels.
- Police executives develop policies on how they will allocate their resources according to one of three styles: the watchman, legalistic, or service styles.
- The functions of the police are order maintenance, law enforcement, and service.
- Discretion is a major factor in police actions and decisions. Patrol officers exercise the greatest amount of discretion.
- The problem of domestic violence illustrates the links between police encounters with citizens, their exercise of discretion, and the actions they take.

Questions for Review

1. What principles borrowed from England still underlie policing in the United States?
2. What are the three eras of policing in the United States and what are the characteristics of each?
3. What are the functions of the police?
4. How do communities influence police policy and police styles?
5. How does the problem of domestic violence illustrate basic elements of police action?

ANSWERS TO CHECKPOINTS

1. Limited authority, local control, fragmented organization.
2. Required groups of ten families to uphold the law and maintain order.
3. Established a parish constable-watch system. Citizens were required to pursue criminals but under supervision of a constable.
4. Established the first organized police force in London.
5. To prevent crime without the use of repressive force, to manage public order nonviolently, to reduce conflict between citizens and the police, and to demonstrate efficiency through the absence of crime.
6. Political era, professional era, community policing era.
7. Close ties between the police and local politicans, leading to corruption.
8. The police should be removed from politics, police should be well trained, the law should be enforced equally, technology should be used, merit should be the basis of personnel procedures, the crime-fighting role should be prominent.
9. The professional, crime-fighting role isolated the police from the community. The police should try to solve the problems underlying crime.
10. The police should be close to the community, should provide services, and should deal with the "little problems."
11. To enforce the laws of the federal government.
12. All state police agencies have traffic law enforcement responsibilities and in two-thirds of the states they have general police powers.
13. In addition to law enforcement functions, sheriffs operate jails, serve court orders and provide court bailiffs.
14. Local control, fragmentation.
15. Emphasis on order maintenance, extensive use of discretion, and differential treatment of racial and ethnic groups.
16. Professionalism and using a single standard of law enforcement throughout the community.
17. Suburban middle-class communities.
18. Police have a broad mandate to prevent behavior that disturbs or threatens to disturb the peace or involves face-to-face conflict among two or more people. Officers are expected to "handle" the situation.
19. The police in order maintenance situations must first determine if a law has been broken, but in law enforcement situations that fact is already known. Thus officers must only find and apprehend the offender.
20. They deal with citizens, often in private, and are charged with maintaining order and enforcing laws. Many of these laws are ambiguous and deal with situations in which the participants' conduct is in dispute.
21. Officers are often set upon by both parties, the victim is often uncooperative, and intervention is thought to be dangerous.

Chapter 5

Police Operations

Organization of the Police

Police Response and Action

- *Organizational Response*
- *Productivity*

Delivery of Police Services

- *Patrol Functions*
- *Issues in Patrolling*
- *The Future of Patrol*
- *Investigation*
- *Special Operations*

Police Actions and the Rule of Law

- *Search and Seizure*
- *Arrest*
- *Interrogation*

"OFFICER DOWN!" burst over the radios of patrol cars in Bristol, Connecticut, a city of 60,000, on a Saturday evening in May 1996. As police sped to 10 Addison Street, 26-year-old Officer John Reilly lay sprawled on a driveway, bleeding from eight gunshot wounds to his arm, shoulder, abdomen, and legs.

Earlier that day Reilly had responded to a domestic disturbance call at the Addison Street address, where he found that the male suspect had already left. He returned that evening to arrest the suspect when he came home. Reilly was sitting in his patrol car across from the house when a car drove into the driveway. Assuming that he had found his man, Reilly pulled his car behind the one in the driveway. As he approached, the driver ran behind a garage. Reilly followed, but as he turned the corner the suspect fired, hitting him twice. The suspect then made a full circle around the garage, approached Reilly, and shot him six more times. Even as he lay on the ground, Reilly was able to return fire and radio for help as the suspect fled.

Four hours later the suspect, Brent McCall, was spotted limping on his wounded leg as he tried to make his way to his sister's house. When McCall saw the police, he started shooting again. He was finally subdued by the officers' bullets. But McCall, wanted for a series of armed robberies, was not the suspect that Reilly had been seeking.

The shoot-out on Addison Street is the type of incident that gets attention. But in much of America, law enforcement agencies often face tough situations as they deal with crime, violence, racial tensions, and drugs. Handling such situations, usually without warning or with incomplete information, is a tall order for patrol officers—especially because they must try to do so within the limits of the law.

In this chapter we focus on the actual work of the police as they pursue suspects and prevent crimes. The police must be organized so that patrol efforts can be coordinated, investigations carried out, arrests made, evidence gathered, crimes solved, and violators prosecuted.

ORGANIZATION OF THE POLICE

Questions for Inquiry

How are the police organized?

What is the nature of the police response to crime?

What are the main functions of police patrol, investigation, and special operations units?

What legal mandates guide police actions?

Most police agencies are organized in a military manner. A structure of ranks—patrol officer, sergeant, lieutenant, captain, and on up to chief—makes clear the powers and duties of officers at each level. Relationships between superiors and subordinates emphasize discipline, control, and accountability. These values are important in efficiently mobilizing police resources and ensuring that civil liberties are protected. If police officers are accountable to their superiors, they are less likely to abuse their authority by needlessly interfering with the freedom and rights of citizens.

Large police departments divide the city into districts or precincts. This allows them to allocate resources and supervise personnel, taking into account the needs and problems of each district. Although specialized units are often located at headquarters, patrol and traffic units may be located in district stations.

Urban police departments assign officers to special units that focus on specific functions: patrol, investigation, traffic, vice, and juvenile (Figure 5.1). These units perform the basic tasks of crime prevention and control. The patrol and investigation units are the core of the modern department. The patrol unit handles a wide range of functions, including preventing crime, catching suspects, mediating quarrels, helping the ill, and giving aid at accidents. The investigation, or detective, unit identifies, apprehends, and collects evidence against lawbreakers who commit serious crimes. The separation of patrol and investigation can cause problems because of their overlapping responsibilities. While the investigation unit usually focuses on murder, rape, and major robberies, the patrol unit has joint responsibility for investigating those crimes and is also responsible for investigation of the more numerous lesser crimes.

The extent to which departments create specialized units may depend on the size of the city and its police force. While many departments have traffic units, only those in mid-sized to large cities also have vice and juvenile units. As a result of the war on drugs, some cities have special units working only on this problem.

Large departments usually have an internal affairs section to investigate charges of corruption against officers and other problems associated with the staff and officers. The juvenile unit works with young people, focusing mainly on crime prevention. All special units depend on the patrol officers for information and assistance.

The police play an important role as a bureaucracy within the broader criminal justice system. Three issues arise in the organizational context within which the police operate. *First*, the police are the gateway through which information and individuals enter the justice system to be processed. Police have the discretion to determine which suspects will be arrested and moved into the system. Cases that are sent to the prosecutor for charging and then to the courts for adjudication begin with an officer's decision that there is probable cause for an arrest. The care taken by the officer in making the arrest and collecting evidence has a major impact on the ultimate success of the prosecution. The outcome of the case, whether through plea bargaining by lawyers or through a trial with a judge and jury, hinges on the officer's judgment and evidence-gathering activities.

Second, the police operate in an environment in which the outcome of a case is largely in the hands of others. The police bring suspects into the criminal justice process, but they cannot control the decisions of prosecutors and judges. In some cases, police officers may feel that their efforts have been wasted if the prosecutor agrees to a plea bargain that does not, in the eyes of the officer, adequately punish the offender. The potential for conflict in the system is increased by the difference in social status between lawyers and judges, who have graduate degrees, and police officers, many of whom do not have college degrees.

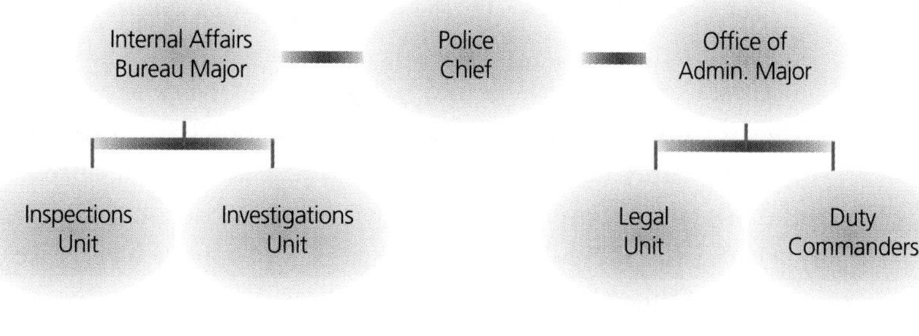

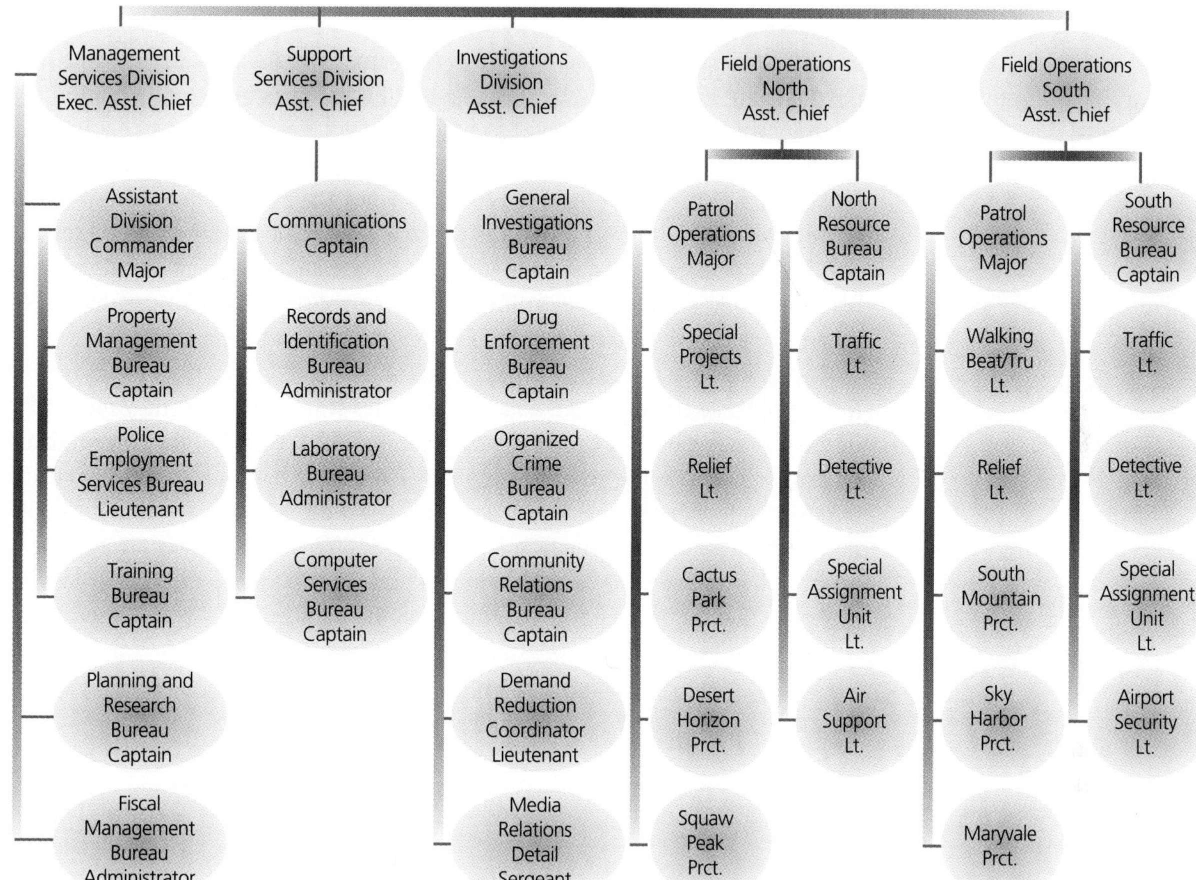

Figure 5.1
Organization of the Phoenix, Arizona, Police Department

This is a typical structure. Note the major divisions of management and support services, investigations, field operations (patrol), and special operations. The internal affairs bureau reports directly to the chief.

SOURCE: City of Phoenix, Arizona, Police Department, *Annual Report*, 1990.

Third, as part of a bureaucracy, police officers are expected to observe rules and follow the orders of superiors while making independent, discretionary judgments. They must stay within the chain of command, yet they also make choices in response to events that occur on the streets. To understand the impact of these factors on the behavior of the police, let us examine two aspects of their daily work—organizational response and productivity.

CHECKPOINT

1. What are the five main divisions of a large urban department?

(Answers are at the end of the chapter.)

POLICE RESPONSE AND ACTION

reactive

Occurring in response, such as police activity in response to notification that a crime has been committed.

proactive

Acting in anticipation, such as an active search for offenders initiated by the police without waiting for a crime to be reported. Arrests for crimes without victims are usually proactive.

In a free society people do not want police on every street corner asking them what they are doing. Thus, the police are mainly **reactive** (responding to citizen calls for service) rather than **proactive** (initiating actions in the absence of citizen requests). Studies of police work show that 81 percent of actions result from citizen telephone calls, 5 percent are initiated by citizens who approach an officer, and only 14 percent are initiated in the field by an officer. These facts affect the way departments are organized and the way the police respond to a case.

Because they are mainly reactive, the police usually can arrive at the scene only after the crime has been committed and the perpetrator has fled. This means that the police are hampered by the time lapse and sometimes by inaccurate information given by witnesses. For example, a mugging may happen so quickly that victims and witnesses cannot accurately describe what happened. In about a third of cases in which police are called, no one is present when the police arrive on the scene. Citizens have come to expect that the police will respond quickly to *every* call, whether it requires immediate attention or can be handled in a more routine manner. The result is what is called "incident-driven policing." To a large extent, then, reports by victims and observers define the boundaries of policing.

The police do use proactive strategies such as surveillance and undercover work to combat some crimes. When addressing crimes without victims, they must rely on informers, stakeouts, wiretapping, stings, and raids. Because of the current focus on drug offenses, police resources in many cities have been assigned to proactive efforts to apprehend people who use or sell illegal drugs. Because victims usually do not report these crimes, crime statistics on such offenses are nearly always rates of arrest rather than rates of known criminal acts. The result is a direct link between the crime rate for these proactive efforts and the number of police assigned.

Organizational Response

Aggressive take-back-the-streets tactics have made a big dent in urban crime. But in some cities a tough question is being raised: does that style of policing come at an unacceptable price?

How the police respond to citizens' calls is influenced by how the police bureaucracy is organized. Factors that affect the response process include the separation of police into various functional groups (patrol, vice, investigation, and so on), the quasi-military command system, and the techniques used to induce patrol officers to respond in desired ways.

Police departments are being reshaped by new communications technology, which has tended to centralize decision making. The core of the department is the communications center, where commands are given to send officers into action. Patrol officers are expected to be in constant touch with headquarters and must report each of their actions. Two-way radio is the primary means by which administrators monitor the decisions of officers in the field. In the past, patrol officers might have administered on-the-spot justice to a mischievous juvenile, but now they must file a report, take the youth into custody, and start formal proceedings. Because officers must call headquarters with reports about each incident, headquarters is better able to guide officers and ensure that they comply with department policies.

In most cities, citizens can call 911 to report a crime or obtain help or information. The 911 system has brought a flood of calls to police departments—many not directly related to police responsibilities. In Baltimore a "311 system" has been implemented to help reduce the number of nonemergency calls, estimated to be 40 percent of total calls. Residents have been urged to call 311 when they need assistance that does not require the immediate dispatch of an officer. A 1997 study found that this innovation reduced calls to 911 by almost 25 percent and resulted in extremely high public support (*New York Times*, October 10, 1997, p. A12). The Close-up shows how emotionally draining the work of a 911 operator is.

To improve efficiency, some police departments use a **differential response** system that assigns priorities to calls for service. This system assumes that rushing a patrol car to the scene when a call is received is not always necessary. The appropriate response depends on several factors—such as whether the incident is in

differential response

A patrol strategy that assigns priorities to calls for service and chooses the appropriate response.

CLOSE-UP

Holding the 911 Line

It's a new day. I walk down to the basement of the public-safety building, pass through a secured entrance, and walk slowly down a long, quiet corridor. My stomach tightens a bit as I approach a final locked door. I'm in the Phoenix Police Communications Center, known as "911."

It's 0800 hours. I take a deep breath, say a little prayer, and hope that I don't make any mistakes that might get me on the 6 o'clock news. This will be my not-so-happy home for the next 10 hours.

"911, what is your emergency?" It's my first call of the day. The woman is crying but calm. She has tried to wake her elderly husband. With the push of a button I connect her to the fire department. They ask if she wants to attempt CPR, but she says, "No, he's cold and blue ... I'm sure he's dead." I leave the sobbing widow in the hands of the fire dispatcher. I'm feeling sad, but I just move on. I have more incoming calls to take. It's busy this morning. The orange lights in each corner of the room are shining brightly, a constant reminder that nonemergency calls have been holding more than 90 seconds. My phone console appears to be glowing, covered with blinking red lights. It's almost hypnotic, like when you sit in the dark and stare at a lit Christmas tree or gaze into a flickering fireplace. But then I remember that each light represents a person—a person with a problem, someone in crisis.

A loud bell is ringing. It means an emergency call is trying to get through but the lines are jammed. All operators are already on a call. I quickly put my caller on hold. He's just reporting a burglary that occurred over the weekend. ...

"911, what is your emergency?" This one's serious. A bad traffic accident, head-on collision. "Yes, sir, we'll get right out there." I get officers started and advise the fire department. Now everyone in the vicinity of the accident is calling. "Yes, ma'am, we're on the way." "We'll be out shortly, sir, thanks for calling." My supervisor comes out of his office to advise us of something. He always looks serious, but this time it's different. He looks worried and upset. He tells us that two of our detectives were involved in the collision. He doesn't know who they are or how badly they're injured. My heart stops momentarily because my husband is a detective. I quickly call the office and confirm that he is safe. I'm relieved but still stunned. ... But there's not much time for sentiment. There are more calls to take, more decisions to make, and more pressures needing attention. ...

"911, what is your emergency?" It's just a boy on a phone getting his kicks by calling me vulgar names. He hangs up before I have a chance to educate him on correct 911 usage. We get a lot of trivial calls, pranksters, hang-ups, citizens complaining to us about a noncrime situation, something they should handle themselves. People call us because they don't know where to turn. Everyone must be treated fairly and with respect. It's a difficult balance to maintain.

My supervisor again comes out to advise us. His face shows a sadness I've never seen in him. "The officers were killed in the accident." A quietness descends over the room. I suppose the bells are still ringing and the lights flashing, but I don't hear or see them. The typing stops; talking ceases. I just want to get out of here and cry, but I have to stay and do my job. I have to keep going. I can break down on my long drive home tonight; for now I have phones to answer, people to help.

SOURCE: Tracy Lorenzano, "Holding the 911 Line," *Newsweek*, June 20, 1994, p. 10.

progress, has just occurred, or occurred some time ago; and whether anyone is or could be hurt. A dispatcher receives the calls and asks for certain facts. The dispatcher may send someone to the scene right away, give the call a lower rank so that the response is delayed, send someone other than a sworn officer, or refer the caller to another agency.

Some experts are critical of centralized communications and decision making. For instance, many advocates of community policing believe that certain technologies tend to isolate the police from citizens. As we saw in Chapter 4, widespread use of motorized patrols has meant that residents get only a glimpse of officers as they cruise through their neighborhoods. Community-oriented policing attempts to overcome some of the negative aspects of centralized response.

Productivity

clearance rate

The percentage of crimes known to the police that they believe they have solved through an arrest; a statistic used to measure a police department's productivity.

Measuring the quantity and quality of police work is difficult, partly because of the wide range of duties and day-to-day tasks of officers. In the past, the crime rate and the **clearance rate** have been used as measures of "good" policing. A lower crime rate might be cited as evidence of an effective department, but critics note that this measure is affected by other factors beside policing.

The clearance rate is the percentage of crimes known to police that they believe they have solved through an arrest. Each type of offense has a different clearance rate. In the case of burglary, in which the police may learn about the crime hours or even days later, the clearance rate is only about 14 percent.

Police have much more success in handling violent crimes (46 percent), in which victims tend to know their assailants (FBI, 1996. *Crime in the United States—1995*:183). Proactive policing leads to even higher clearance rates because the police catch offenders in the act.

These measures of police productivity may be supplemented by other data, such as the numbers of traffic citations issued, illegally parked cars ticketed, and suspects stopped for questioning, and the value of stolen goods recovered. These additional ways of counting work performed reflect that an officer may work hard for many hours yet have no arrests to show for his or her efforts (Kelling, 1992:23). But society may benefit more when officers spend their time in activities that are hard to measure, such as calming disputes, becoming acquainted with people in the neighborhood, and providing services to those in need (Brady, 1996).

CHECKPOINT

2. What is "incident-driven policing"?
3. What is "differential response"?
4. What is the basic measure of police productivity?

DELIVERY OF POLICE SERVICES

line functions

Police components that directly perform field operations and carry out the basic functions of patrol, investigation, traffic, vice, juvenile, and so on.

In service bureaucracies like the police, a distinction is often made between line and staff functions. **Line functions** are those that directly involve field operations such as patrol, investigation, traffic control, vice, and juvenile crimes. By contrast, staff functions supplement or support line functions. Staff functions are based in the chief's office and the support or services bureau, as well as in the staff inspection bureau (see Figure 5.1). An efficient department has an appropriate balance between line and staff duties.

Patrol Functions

Patrol is often called the backbone of police operations. Every police department has a patrol unit. Even in large departments, patrol officers account for up to two-thirds of all **sworn officers**—those who have taken an oath and been given the powers to make arrests and use necessary force in accordance with their duties. In small communities, police operations are not specialized, and the patrol force *is* the department. The patrol officer must be prepared for any imaginable situation and must perform many duties.

sworn officers

Police employees who have taken an oath and been given powers by the state to make arrests and use necessary force, in accordance with their duties.

Television portrays patrol officers as always on the go—rushing from one incident to another and making a number of arrests in a single shift. A patrol officer may indeed be called to deal with a robbery in progress or to help rescue people from a burning building. However, while such activities are important, the patrol officer's life is not always so exciting. The officer may perform some challenging tasks, but he or she may also handle routine and even boring tasks such as directing traffic at accident scenes and road construction sites. To better understand patrol work, note how the police of Wilmington, Delaware, allocate time to various activities, as shown in Figure 5.2.

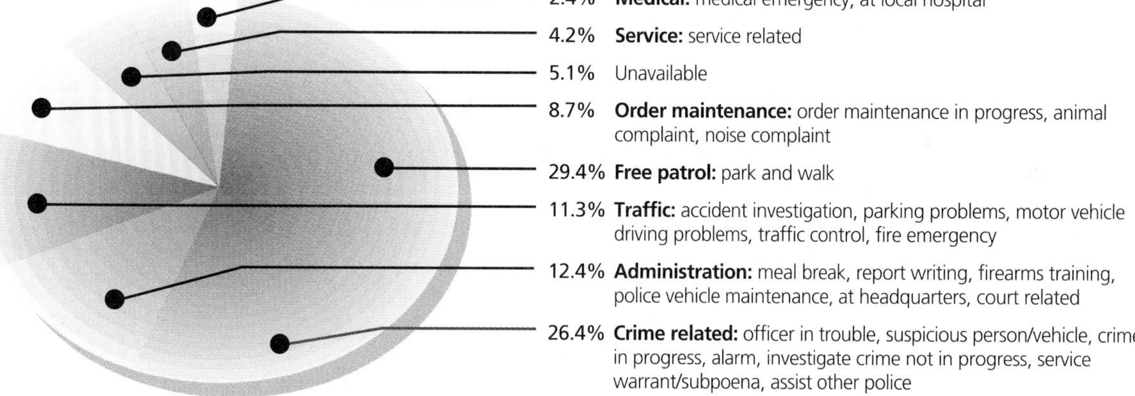

Figure 5.2
Time allocated to patrol activities by the police of Wilmington, Delaware

The time spent on each activity was calculated from records for each police car unit. Note the range of activities and the time spent on each.

SOURCE: Jack R. Greene and Carl B. Klockars, "What Police Do," in *Thinking about Police*, 2d ed., ed. Carl B. Klockars and Stephen D. Mastrofski (New York: McGraw-Hill, 1991), 279.

The patrol function has three parts: answering calls for help, maintaining a police presence, and probing suspicious circumstances. Patrol officers are well suited to answering calls because they usually are near the scene and can move quickly to provide help or catch a suspect. At other times, they engage in **preventive patrol**—that is, making the police presence known in an effort to deter crime and to make officers available to respond quickly to calls. Whether walking the streets or cruising in a car, the patrol officer is on the lookout for suspicious people and behavior. With experience, officers come to trust in their own ability to spot signs of suspicious activity that merit stopping people on the street for questioning.

preventive patrol

A form of patrolling that makes the police presence known in order to deter crime and to make officers available for quick response to calls.

Patrol officers also help maintain smooth relations between the police and the community. As the most visible members of the criminal justice system, they can have a profound effect on the willingness of citizens to cooperate. When officers earn the trust and respect of the residents of the neighborhoods they patrol, people are much more willing to provide information about crimes and suspicious activities. Effective work by patrol officers can also help reduce citizens' fear of crime and foster a sense of security.

Patrol officers' duties sound fairly straightforward, yet they often find themselves in complex situations requiring sound judgments and careful actions. As the first to arrive at a crime scene, the officer must comfort and give aid to victims, identify and question witnesses, control crowds, and gather evidence. All these responsibilities call for creativity and good communication skills.

Because the patrol officer has the most direct contact with the public, the image of the police and their relations with the community are based on patrol officers' actions. Moreover, successful investigations and prosecutions often depend on patrol officers' actions in questioning witnesses and gathering evidence after a crime.

Daylight basketball is just one aspect of the cops' increased presence in the Desire Housing Project in New Orleans. With a new police substation, gang bangers have fled.

CHECKPOINT

5. What is the difference between line and staff functions?
6. What are the three parts of the patrol function?

Because the patrol officer's job involves the most contact with the public, the best-qualified officers should do it. However, because of the low status of patrol assignments, many officers seek higher-status positions such as that of detective. A key challenge facing policing is to grant to patrol officers a status that reflects their importance to society and the criminal justice system. The next Workperspective describes a situation that involved Officer John Reilly.

Issues in Patrolling

In the last twenty years, much research has been done on methods of assigning tasks to patrol officers and various means of transportation and communication. Although the conclusions of these studies have been mixed, they have caused experts to rethink some aspects of patrolling. Yet even when researchers agree on the patrol practices that would be the most effective, those practices often run counter to the desires of departmental personnel. Police administrators therefore must deal with many issues, including (1) assignment of patrol personnel, (2) preventive patrol, (3) hot spots, (4) response time, (5) foot patrol versus motorized patrol, (6) one-person versus two-person patrol units, (7) aggressive patrol, (8) community-oriented policing, and (9) special populations. We will discuss each of these in turn.

WORK *Perspective*

John Reilly
Police Officer

Police Department
Bristol, Connecticut

While an undergraduate at the University of Connecticut I worked for the Caldor Department Stores as a private security officer. Upon graduation in 1992 I continued with that work, rising to the position of Caldor's loss prevention manager for the New York City area. Although I was quite successful in private security work, I always hoped to become a municipal police officer. That opportunity came in 1994 when I joined the Bristol Department.

As a patrol officer I have encountered a number of situations in which I had to think clearly, evaluate options, and use my discretion. In policing, decisions must be made according to the law *and* departmental policies. All of this usually takes place in an emotionally charged situation.

During my first few weeks on the job I was under the supervision of a field training officer. This "on-the-job training" was designed to supplement the lectures I had heard at the police academy.

One night we were dispatched to a "suspicious noise" complaint at a private home in a quiet area of the city. Officers must respond to such calls in an appropriate manner because you don't know what you are going to find. It could be nothing or it could be a dangerous situation. We responded without siren or flashing lights and searched the grounds. We found footprints below a rear window where the owner had heard the noise. There was no other evidence. At this point, an officer must decide whether to just leave the scene or give advice to the complainant. We chose to show the homeowner how to better protect his property and to increase physical security.

Soon after we left the scene we received a second call about a suspicious noise and person at the same address. We asked the dispatcher for more information and were told that a person driving a small, light-colored vehicle had approached the house and sped away. Just then the vehicle passed us at a high rate of speed.

Should we pursue the vehicle? On the surface there seems to be a logical answer: yes. But in fact making such a decision is not easy. Officers must be concerned for the safety of the public and the danger of a pursuit. But we must also be concerned that a crime has been committed and that the suspect is fleeing to escape arrest.

Bristol Police Department policies and Connecticut law help guide an officer's decision in determining whether the situation warrants pursuit. Officers are required to notify the street sergeant of the action they think should be taken and get his okay. As the vehicle is followed calls must be continually made to headquarters relaying direction, speed, and location. This is of great importance in case there is a problem. It is the responsibility of the pursuing officer to coordinate the response of other officers.

In this case we decided to follow the vehicle but at an appropriate speed because the suspect was driving slowly and not really trying to evade the police. The vehicle simply did not stop and eventually crossed over the city line and out of our jurisdiction. By this time the state police had heard our communications and began to pursue the vehicle. Farmington, Avon, and Canton Police Departments then joined in the pursuit as the suspect vehicle passed through their respective towns. Finally, the driver was stopped and cited for breach of the peace, failure to stop for an officer's signal, and operating without a license.

The 15-year-old driver had gone to visit his girlfriend, rapped on her bedroom window, got scared when he saw the police car approach the house, ran to his car, and drove off. He later told police that he did not stop because "he was afraid that he would get into trouble, because he had no license."

You might think of this as a minor incident, but it had the potential for escalating into a high-speed chase with the potential for loss of life. I learned the importance of making decisions according to departmental policies and in as rational and calm manner as possible. The discretion given police officers is great, and it must be used wisely.

WORK*Perspective*

Assignment of Patrol Personnel

In the past it was assumed that patrol officers should be assigned where and when they would be most effective in preventing crime, keeping order, and serving the public. For the police administrator, the question has been, Where should the officers be sent, when, and in what numbers? There are no guidelines to answer this question, and most assignments seem to be based on the notion that patrols should be concentrated in areas where crime rates are high or in "problem" neighborhoods. Thus, the assignment of officers is based on factors such as crime statistics, degree of urbanization, pressures from business and community groups, ethnic composition, and socioeconomic conditions.

Preventive Patrol

Preventive patrol has long been thought to help deter crime. It has been argued that the movement of patrol officers through an area will keep criminals from carrying out illegal acts. In 1974 this assumption was tested in Kansas City, Missouri. The results were surprising and shook the theoretical foundations of American policing (Sherman and Weisburd, 1995).

In the Kansas City Preventive Patrol Experiment, a fifteen-beat area was divided into three sections, each with similar crime rates, population characteristics, income levels, and numbers of calls to the police. In one area, labeled "reactive," all preventive patrol was withdrawn, and the police entered only in response to citizens' calls for service. In another section, labeled "proactive," preventive patrol was raised to as much as four times the normal level; all other services were provided at the same levels as before. The third section was used as a control, with the usual level of services, including preventive patrol, maintained. After observing events in the three sections for a year, the researchers concluded that the changes in patrol strategies had had no major effects on the amount of crime reported, the amount of crime as measured by citizen surveys, or citizens' fear of crime (Kelling et al., 1974).

Because of this study, many departments have shifted their focus from law enforcement to maintaining order and serving the public. Some have argued that if the police cannot prevent crime by changing their patrol tactics, they may serve society better by focusing patrol activities on other functions while fighting crime as best they can.

Those who support the professional crime-fighting model of policing have criticized this and other studies that question the effectiveness of preventive patrol.

They claim that the research attacks the heart of police work. But the research simply calls into question the inflexible aspects of preventive patrol.

Hot Spots

In the past, patrols were organized by "beats." It was assumed that crime can happen anywhere, and the entire beat must be patrolled at all times. Research shows, however, that crime is not spread evenly over all times and places. Instead, direct-contact predatory crimes, such as muggings and robberies, occur when three elements converge: motivated offenders, suitable targets, and the absence of anyone who could prevent the violation. This means that resources should be focused on "hot spots," places where crimes are likely to occur (Cohen and Felson, 1979:589).

In a study of crime in Minneapolis, researchers found that a small number of "hot spots"—3 percent of streets and intersections—produced 50 percent of calls to the police. By analyzing the places from which calls were made, they could identify those that produced the most crime (Sherman, Gartin, and Buerger, 1989:27). With this knowledge, officers can be assigned to **directed patrol**—a proactive strategy designed to direct resources to known high-crime areas. There is always a risk, however, that the extra police pressure will simply cause lawbreakers to move to another neighborhood. The premise of this argument is that "there are only so many criminals seeking outlets for the fixed number of crimes they are predestined to commit" (Sherman and Weisburd, 1995:629). Although this shifting of "the action" may be a factor in some public drug markets, it does not fit all crime or even all vice—such as prostitution (Sherman, 1990; Weisburd and Green, 1995).

directed patrol

A proactive form of patrolling that directs resources to known high-crime areas.

Many officers disliked the new tactics. Being a "presence" in a hot spot might deter criminals, but the officers were bored. Preventing crime is not as glamorous as catching criminals (Sherman and Weisburd, 1995:646).

Response Time

Modern patrol tactics are based on a system in which calls for help come to a communications center that dispatches the nearest officers by radio to the site of the incident. Because most citizens have access to phones, most cities have 911 systems; and because most officers are in squad cars linked to headquarters by two-way radios, police can respond quickly to calls. But are response times short enough to catch the offender?

Several studies have measured the impact of police response time on the ability of officers to intercept a crime in progress and arrest the criminal. In a classic study, William G. Spelman and Dale K. Brown found that the police were successful in only 29 per thousand cases. It made little difference whether they arrived two minutes or twenty minutes after the call. What did matter, however, was how soon the police were called (Spelman and Brown, 1984).

Although delayed arrival of the police is often due to slowness in calling, it seems unlikely that arrest rates would be improved merely by educating the public about their key role in stopping crime. As Spelman and Brown point out, there are three *decision-making* delays that slow the process of calling the police:

1. Ambiguity delays. Some people find the situation *ambiguous* and are not sure whether the police should be called. They may see an event but not know whether it is a robbery or two young men "horsing around."

IDEAS IN PRACTICE

Looking out the window of your room, you notice a young couple rolling on the ground beneath a large pine tree. You see books and a woman's purse scattered nearby. It is a beautiful spring day. You think, Isn't love wonderful! But a second thought enters your mind: Are these two lovers or is that woman in trouble? You stand up to get a better view. The woman's clothes seem disheveled. Is she being assaulted? Should I dial 911? No, I think I'd better call Jim; he'll know what to do since he's ridden with the campus police.

"Jim, there's a guy and girl rolling on the ground beneath my window. I can't make out if she's in trouble. Should I dial 911?"

"Of course. It can't do any harm and you may prevent a rape," replies Jim.

"Okay. I'll do it right now."

When the police arrive, they find a distraught young woman sobbing uncontrollably, her clothes torn and bloodied.

Are there any ways to shorten police response time to incidents such as this?

2. Coping delays. Other people are so busy *coping*—taking care of the victim or directing traffic—that they cannot leave the scene to call the police.
3. Conflict delays. Still other people must first resolve conflicts before they call the police. For example, they may call someone else for advice about whether to call the police.

Besides these delays, communication problems can slow response. For example, a telephone may not be available, the emergency number may have to be looked up, or the dispatcher may not be able to handle the incoming call because she or he is dealing with other problems.

Although delay is a major problem, reducing delay would only slightly increase arrest rates (Figure 5.3). In about three-quarters of crime calls, the police are reactive, in that the crimes (burglary, larceny, and the like) are "discovered" long after they have occurred. A much smaller portion are "involvement" crimes (robbery, rape, assault) that victims know about right away and for which they can call the police right away (Spelman and Brown, 1984:4).

In theory, rapid police response should prevent injury, increase arrests, and deter crime. However, as Lawrence Sherman says, "In practice, it seems to do none of these things." He notes that injuries occur during the first seconds of the event, and the chances of catching a criminal after a five-minute delay are not great. Rapid response time is valuable for only a small fraction of all calls. In sum, the costs of police resources and the danger created by high-speed response may outweigh any increase in effectiveness from faster response times (Sherman, 1995:334).

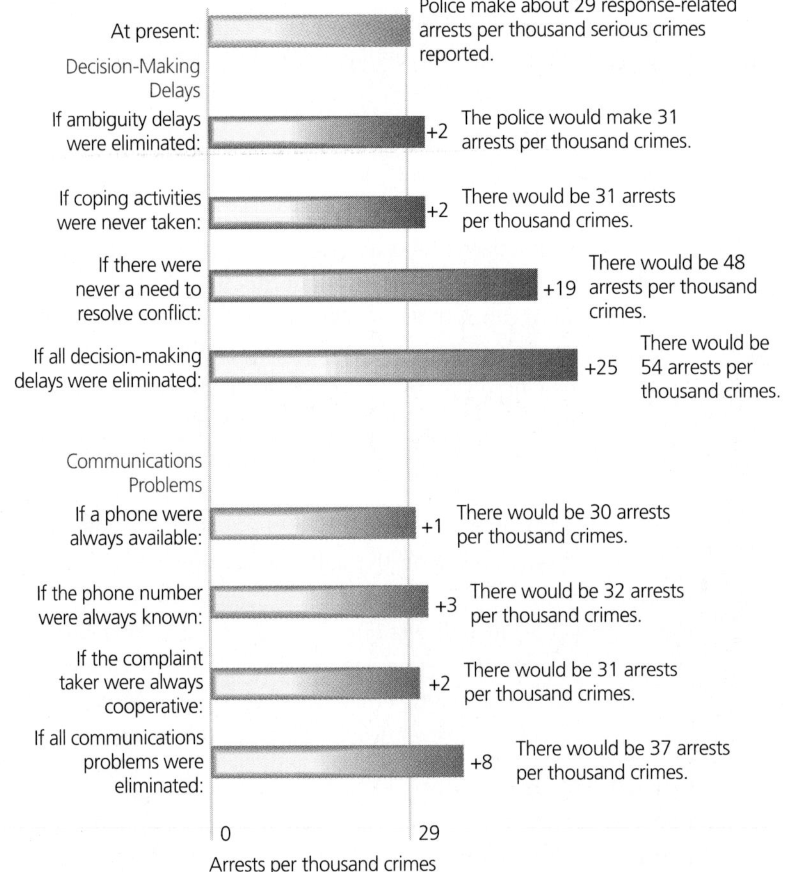

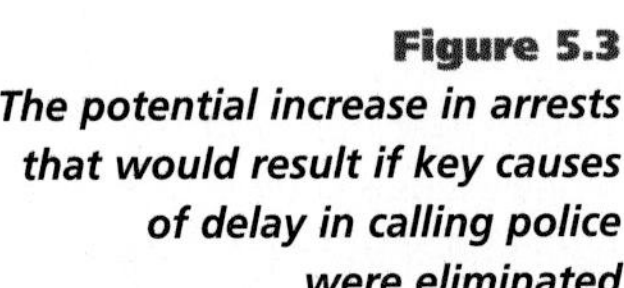

Figure 5.3
The potential increase in arrests that would result if key causes of delay in calling police were eliminated

Although citizens are encouraged to call the police quickly (through 911 numbers), research has shown that a major factor in police response time is the delay in recognizing that a crime has been committed and that the police should be called.

SOURCE: William Spelman and Dale Brown, *Calling the Police: Citizen Reports of Serious Crime* (Washington, D.C.: Police Executive Research Forum, 1984), xxix.

NOTE: Even if all reporting delays could be eliminated, no more than 70 crimes per thousand could result in response-related arrests.

*The total is more than the sum of the individual savings because of the nonlinear nature of the relationship between reporting time and arrest.

CHECKPOINT

7. What factors affect patrol assignments?
8. What did the Kansas City study show about preventive patrol?
9. What is a "hot spot"?
10. What is directed patrol?
11. What types of delays reduce response time?

Foot versus Motorized Patrol

One of the most frequent requests that citizens make is for officers to be put back on the beat. During the 1930s it was recognized that squad cars increase the amount of territory that officers can patrol and that two-way radios allow officers to be quickly sent where they are needed. A recent study found that in large cities almost 94 percent of patrol time is used in motorized patrol (Reaves, 1992).

However, many citizens and some researchers claim that patrol officers in squad cars have become remote from the people they protect and less aware of their needs and problems. As Sherman points out, motorized patrols and telephone dispatching have caused a shift from "watching to prevent crime" to "waiting to respond to crime" (Sherman, 1983:149). Because officers rarely leave the patrol car, citizens have few chances to tell them about suspicious activities within neighborhoods. In addition, patrol officers cannot mediate disputes, investigate suspected criminal activity, and make residents feel the police care about their well-being (Moore, 1992:113).

By contrast, officers on foot are close to the daily life of the neighborhood. Because they know the people of the area, they are better able to detect criminal activity and apprehend those who have broken the law. Further, patrol officers who are known to citizens are less likely to be viewed as symbols of oppression by poor or minority residents. In large cities, personal contact may help reduce racial tensions and conflict.

The past decade has seen a revived interest in foot patrol because of citizens' demands for a familiar figure walking through the neighborhood. Studies in a number of cities have shown that foot patrols are costly and do not greatly reduce crime, but that they make citizens less fearful of crime (Cohen, Miller, and Rossman, 1990).

One-Person versus Two-Person Patrol Units

The debate over one-person versus two-person patrol units has raged in police circles for years. Officers and their union leaders support the two-person squad car. They claim that police are safer and more effective when two officers work together in dangerous or difficult situations. However, police administrators contend that the one-person squad car is much more cost-effective and permits them to deploy more cars on each shift. With more cars to deploy, each can be assigned to a smaller area and response time can be decreased. They also contend that an officer working alone is more alert and attentive because he or she cannot be distracted by idle conversation with a colleague.

Aggressive Patrol

Aggressive patrol is a proactive strategy designed to maximize police activity in the community. It takes many forms, such as "sting" operations, firearms confiscation, raids on crack houses, programs that encourage citizens to list their valuables,

aggressive patrol

A patrol strategy designed to maximize the number of police interventions and observations in the community.

and the tracking of high-risk parolees. Studies have shown that patrol tactics that increase the risk of arrest are linked with lower crime rates. It is argued that the effect of the police on crime depends less on how many officers are deployed in an area than on what they do while they are there.

An aggressive patrol strategy does not mean that officers patrol in a hostile manner; rather, they often stop and ask people what they are doing. In San Diego, such a strategy led to large decreases in certain "suppressible" crimes: robbery, burglary, theft, auto theft, assault, sex crimes, malicious mischief, and disturbances. The strategy seemed to deter potential offenders, especially young opportunists who were ready to take advantage of a situation (Wilson, 1983:71). Officers in an "anti-crime patrol" in New York worked the streets of high-crime areas in civilian clothes. Although they accounted for only 5 percent of the officers assigned to each precinct, during one year they made more than 18 percent of the felony arrests, including more than half of the arrests for robbery and about 40 percent of the arrests for burglary and auto theft.

Handguns are the leading risk factor for criminal harm. Studies show a strong link between the number of guns in a community and rates of gun injury. James Q. Wilson argues that police should focus their gun-control efforts on guns being carried in high-risk places, by high-risk people, at high-risk times (Wilson, 1994:47).The police may legally seize firearms when they are carried without a permit, when they are concealed, and when the person carrying one is on probation or parole.

Some departments have begun to seize illegally possessed firearms as a way of getting guns off the street. In Kansas City, Missouri, aggressive traffic enforcement was used as a way to seize firearms in a beat with a high homicide rate. The police seized one gun for every twenty-eight traffic stops (Sherman and Rogan, 1995a:673). Aggressive patrol tactics were also used in raids on crack houses to seize firearms (Sherman and Rogan, 1995b:755). The result was a doubling of the gun recovery rate and a major reduction in gun violence (Sherman, 1995:340).

Antifencing efforts, often called "stings," are a widely used law enforcement technique. Typically police set up a storefront operation; then they pose as fences and buy stolen property from thieves. Large amounts of property are recovered and thieves are arrested and successfully prosecuted.

The most cost-effective of the aggressive patrol strategies seem to be those that encourage officers to carry out more field questioning and traffic stops. To implement such a strategy, the department must recruit certain kinds of officers, train them, and devise requirements and reward systems (traffic ticket quotas, required numbers of field interrogations, chances for promotion) that will encourage them to carry out the intended strategy.

Community Policing

To a great extent community policing has been seen as the solution to problems with the crime-fighter stance that prevailed during the professional era (Murphy, 1992). Community policing consists of attempts by the police to get residents involved in making their own neighborhoods safer. Based on the belief that citizens may be concerned about local disorder as well as crime in general, this strategy emphasizes cooperation between the police and citizens in identifying community needs and determining the best ways to meet them (Moore, 1992; Skogan and Hartnett, 1997).

Community policing has four components:

1. Community-based crime prevention
2. Changing the focus of patrol activities to nonemergency services

3. Making the police more accountable to the public
4. Decentralizing decision making to include residents (Skolnick and Bayley, 1988)

Community policing may be carried out by patrol officers assigned to walking neighborhood beats so they can get to know residents better. It may entail creating police mini-stations in the community and police-sponsored programs for youth and the elderly. Police departments may also survey citizens to find out about their problems and needs.

Associated with community policing, a method called **problem-oriented policing** tries to find out what is causing citizen calls for help (Goldstein, 1990). The police seek to identify, analyze, and respond to the conditions underlying the events that prompt people to call the police. Knowing those conditions, officers can enlist community agencies and residents to help resolve them. Officers may find that incidents will cease if street lighting is improved, aggressive measures are taken against streetwalkers, or the closing hours of a local bar are enforced. Whatever the solution, it usually means getting help from other agencies (Spelman and Eck, 1987). Police using this approach don't just fight crime; they address a broad array of problems that affect the quality of life in the community. As you read the Close-up "Hand-in-Hand: Police in the Community," consider whether you would like Officer Pasqurell's job.

problem-oriented policing

An approach to policing in which officers routinely seek to identify, analyze, and respond to the circumstances underlying the incidents that prompt citizens to call the police.

CLOSE-UP

Hand-in-Hand: Police in the Community

West End homeowner Chris Harper was growing more and more frustrated by the open drug sales, gunshots that pierced the night, piles of trash, and people urinating around his house. He'd repeatedly call the police. But they would show up hours later, and nothing would change.

Harper was tempted to take the law into his own hands, especially after a drug dealer spit in his face on the front lawn of his home while he was holding a summer barbecue.

Luckily, Officer Barry Pasqurell intervened.

Pasqurell, a community service officer assigned to Hartford's (Connecticut) West End, met with the homeowner, jotted down his concerns, and enlisted detectives in the intelligence, narcotics, and street crimes divisions to put some heat on the Warrenton Avenue building that seemed to be the source of Harper's agony. Pasqurell even set up his own field office in the building while Harper and others passed along the license plate numbers of motorists who did not belong in the area.

Soon drug dealers moved out of the building, and quiet was restored to the neighborhood.

"It was about time, but the police department was working," Harper said. "It takes people that want to work with police, and a cop that wants to work with them."

The partnership that developed between Pasqurell and the Warrenton Avenue block watch group is a prime example of how a community approach to policing can work. Pasqurell shared what he learned from residents with officers in patrol and other divisions, and residents invested their time to help police identify criminal suspects and conduct surveillance.

The community policing concept is basic—get police out of their cruisers and back on the streets, where they can get to know the people they serve and the problems they face. By focusing on quality-of-life complaints—vandalism, abandoned cars, noise—police can stave off more serious crimes.

With fourteen community service officers assigned to different city neighborhoods, the relationships between the cops and communities differ, depending on the size and problems of each neighborhood, the residents' involvement, each officer's commitment and responsiveness, and the mix of personalities.

The job of a community service officer is not an exalted position because it brings little of the high-profile, crime-fighting glory that a major drug bust might draw. Police now are considering ways to market the job better.

Being a community service officer is not a cushy assignment. The officers work days and nights to attend community meetings, and they field residents' complaints constantly. A cop has to want to do it.

Pasqurell wanted the job. He had spent nine years on patrol, another seven years in crime suppression, and a short time on the Asylum Hill task force. He was looking for a change.

In August 1995 he was assigned to the West End

neighborhood, a community he had few dealings with. After getting to know the people in the area, he quickly learned its problems. And, in between his jobs as a troubleshooter and community-police liaison, Pasqurell set up street and ice hockey programs for students in the Noah Webster School. Today the children there cry out, "Coach Barry!" when he visits them at recess.

SOURCE: Maxine Bernstein, "Hand-in-Hand: Police in the Community," *Hartford Courant*, December 22,1996, p. A1.

Community policing has spread across the country and gained a great deal of support from citizens, legislators, and Congress (Bayley, 1994). This support can be seen in the emphasis on community policing in the Violent Crime Control and Law Enforcement Act passed by Congress in 1994. Portions of the act call for increases in the numbers of officers assigned to community policing and for the development of new community policing programs.

As with any reform, change may not come easily. Police are used to dealing with problems according to established procedures and may feel that their authority is diminished when responsibility is given to precinct commanders (Kelling and Bratton, 1993). Another problem with implementing community policing is that it does not reduce costs; it requires either additional funds or redistribution of existing budgets. Measuring the success of this approach in reducing fear of crime, solving underlying problems, maintaining order, and serving the community also is difficult. Finally, there is the question of how far the police should extend their role beyond crime fighting to remedying other social problems.

Special Populations

Urban police forces must deal with a complex population. City streets contain growing numbers of mentally ill, homeless, runaways, public drunkards, drug addicts, and people with AIDS. Crowded jails, the release of mental health patients from institutions, the decriminalization of public drunkenness, and cutbacks in public assistance—all have increased the number of "problem" people on city streets. Most of these people do not commit crimes, but their presence is disturbing to residents, and they may contribute to disorder and fear of crime.

Patrol officers cooperate with social service agencies in helping individuals and responding to requests for order maintenance. The police must walk a fine line when requiring a person to enter a homeless shelter, obtain medical assistance, or be taken to a mental health unit (McCoy, 1986; Melekian, 1990). Police departments have developed various techniques for dealing with special populations. In New York City, Los Angeles, and Philadelphia, mobile units are equipped with restraining devices, Mace, and medical equipment to handle disturbed people. Madison, Wisconsin, has educated officers about special populations and ways of dealing with them. Birmingham, Alabama, uses social workers to deal with the mentally ill, freeing the police to respond to other problems (NIJ, 1988. *Research in Action*).

Clearly, dealing with special populations is a major problem for police in most cities. Each community must develop policies so that officers will know when and how they are to intervene when a person may not have broken the law but is upsetting residents.

The Future of Patrol

Preventive patrol and rapid response to calls for help have been the hallmarks of policing in the United States for the past half-century. However, research done in the past twenty years has raised many questions about patrol strategies that police should employ. The rise of community policing has shifted law enforcement toward problems that affect residents' quality of life. Police forces need to use patrol tactics that fit the needs of the neighborhood. Neighborhoods with crime "hot spots" may require different strategies than neighborhoods where residents are concerned mainly with order maintenance. Many researchers believe that traditional patrol efforts have focused too narrowly on crime control, neglecting the order maintenance and service activities for which police departments were originally formed. Critics have urged that the police become more community oriented and return to the first principle of policing: "to remain in close and frequent contact with citizens" (Williams and Pate, 1987).

CHECKPOINT

12. What are the advantages and disadvantages of foot patrol? of motorized patrol?
13. What are the advantages and disadvantages of one-person versus two-person patrol units?
14. What is aggressive patrol?
15. What are the major elements of community policing?

Investigation

All cities with a population of more than 250,000, and 90 percent of smaller cities, have officers (detectives) assigned to investigative duties. Detectives make up 15 percent of police personnel. They have a higher status in the department: their pay is higher, their hours are more flexible, and they are supervised less closely than patrol officers. Detectives do not wear uniforms, and their work is considered more interesting than that of patrol officers. In addition, they are engaged solely in law enforcement rather than in order maintenance or service work; hence, their activities conform more closely to the image of the police as crime fighters.

Detectives in small departments are generalists who investigate whatever crimes occur. But in large departments they are assigned to special units such as homicide, robbery, auto theft, forgery, and burglary. In recent years, because of public pressures, some departments have set up new special units to deal with bias crimes, child abuse, sexual assault, and computer crime (Bayley, 1994:26). The next Workpersective describes Officer David Blocker's job as a child abuse and neglect investigator.

A contaminated crime scene, in-fighting by the police, and conflict with the district attorney's office have been cited as some of the reasons why the murder of JonBenet Ramsey has not been solved.

Like patrol, criminal investigation is largely reactive. Detectives become involved after a crime has been reported and a patrol officer has done a preliminary investigation. The job of detectives is mainly to find out what happened by talking to people—victims, suspects, witnesses. On the basis of this information, detectives develop theories about who committed the crime and then set out to

WORK*Perspective*

David G. Blocker
Investigator,
Child Abuse and Neglect

Detroit Police Department

I became a police officer soon after my twenty-first birthday. I had attended Oakland Community College and possessed the basic requirements as to age, height, weight, vision, a high school diploma, and the absence of a criminal record. After attending the Detroit Police Academy I was appointed a patrol officer assigned to an emergency response unit. After six years I was transferred to the Youth Bureau with responsibilities for investigating, arresting, and processing delinquents in the juvenile court. In 1983 I was assigned to the Detroit Child Abuse Unit as an investigator. Child abuse investigation changed my outlook on how children should be raised. I know I'll always be an advocate for children in some capacity.

The case that changed me forever concerned a 6-month-old infant who was rushed to the Henry Ford Hospital in a comatose state with a fractured skull and broken leg. The mother, very neatly dressed and in her twenties, told the doctors that she left the child with her live-in boyfriend while she went to work. When she arrived home the boyfriend said that the baby was asleep and that he had to run off to do an errand. He had not returned. She explained that she had known the man for a few months and could provide only his name; she did not know his date of birth, family, or friends.

It appeared that this would be an easy case. Protective services would take responsibility for the child if the mother had been neglectful, and I would be responsible for tracking down the boyfriend and locking him up. The protective services caseworker told me that she did not feel comfortable with the mother's explanation as to how the child was injured. I thought the caseworker was totally off base with her suspicion, but she finally convinced me that we should visit the mother's apartment.

Arrangements were made to meet the mother. I still thought that she was being truthful but went along with the caseworker just to prove a point. At the apartment the caseworker pointed out that there was no evidence—clothes, personal belongings—suggesting that a man lived there. The more we questioned the mother about the boyfriend, the more vague were her responses. Finally, she admitted that there was no boyfriend; that the baby's father was married, would not leave his wife, and had denied responsibility for the child. She admitted that the baby had been wet and crying. She had smoked a joint to ease her nerves, but when she began to change the diaper she "lost it." She just couldn't take the crying anymore; she twisted the baby's leg and then slammed its head into the headboard of the bed.

I took a lot of teasing from the caseworker after we left the house, but it really opened my eyes to the importance of a thorough investigation. It's unfortunate that as police officers we must be suspicious of most things that people tell us, but the job requires it. We tend to stereotype people based on certain lifestyles, personal characteristics, and conditions. When you treat people according to a stereotype, you are subject to mistakes. I nearly made a big mistake because I had misjudged this woman. Initially I believed everything she told me. It was several days before I was willing to listen to the more experienced caseworker.

This case really whet my appetite for more knowledge on child abuse. I became a member of a hospital child protection team and of the State Court Administrator's Foster Care Review Board, and I have lectured throughout the state to college students and police recruits on how to investigate instances of child neglect and abuse.

WORK *Perspective*

gather the evidence that will lead to arrest and prosecution. Bayley notes that detectives do not maintain an open mind about the identity of the offender. They know that if the suspect cannot be identified by people on the scene, they are not likely to find him or her on their own. Detectives collect physical evidence to support testimony that identifies a suspect, not to *find* the suspect (Bayley, 1994:26).

Although detectives focus on serious crimes, they are not the only ones who investigate crimes. Patrol, traffic, vice, and juvenile units may also be involved. In small towns and rural areas, patrol officers must conduct investigations because police departments are too small to have separate detective bureaus. In urban areas, because they are likely to be the first police to arrive at the scene of a crime, patrol officers must do much of the initial investigative work. The patrol unit's investigation can be crucial. If patrol officers cannot obtain information from victims and witnesses right away, they have less chance of arresting and prosecuting the suspect.

Apprehension

The discovery that a crime has been committed sets off a chain of events leading to the capture of a suspect and the gathering of the evidence needed to convict that person. It may also lead to a number of dead ends, such as a lack of clues pointing to a suspect or a lack of evidence to link the suspect to the crime.

The process of catching a suspect has three stages: detection of a crime, preliminary investigation, and follow-up investigation. Depending on the outcome of the investigation, these three steps may be followed by a fourth: clearance and arrest. As shown in Figure 5.4, these actions are designed to use criminal justice resources to arrest a suspect and assemble enough evidence to support a charge.

1. **Detection of a Crime** Information that a crime has been committed usually comes in a call to the police. The patrol officer on the beat may also come upon a crime, but usually the police are alerted by others. The police may be informed of a crime on business premises by automatic alarms linked to police headquarters. Such direct communications help shorten response time and increase the chances of catching the suspect.
2. **Preliminary Investigation** The first law enforcement official on the scene is usually a patrol officer who has been dispatched by radio. The officer must give aid to the victim, secure the crime scene for investigation, and document the facts of the crime. If a suspect is present or nearby, the officer conducts a "hot" search and may apprehend the suspect. This initial work is crucial. The officer must gather the basic facts, including the name of the victim, a description of the suspect, and the names of witnesses. After the information is collected, it is sent to the investigation unit.
3. **Follow-up Investigation** After a crime has been brought to the attention of the police and a preliminary investigation has been made, the detective will decide what course of action to pursue. In big-city departments, incident reports

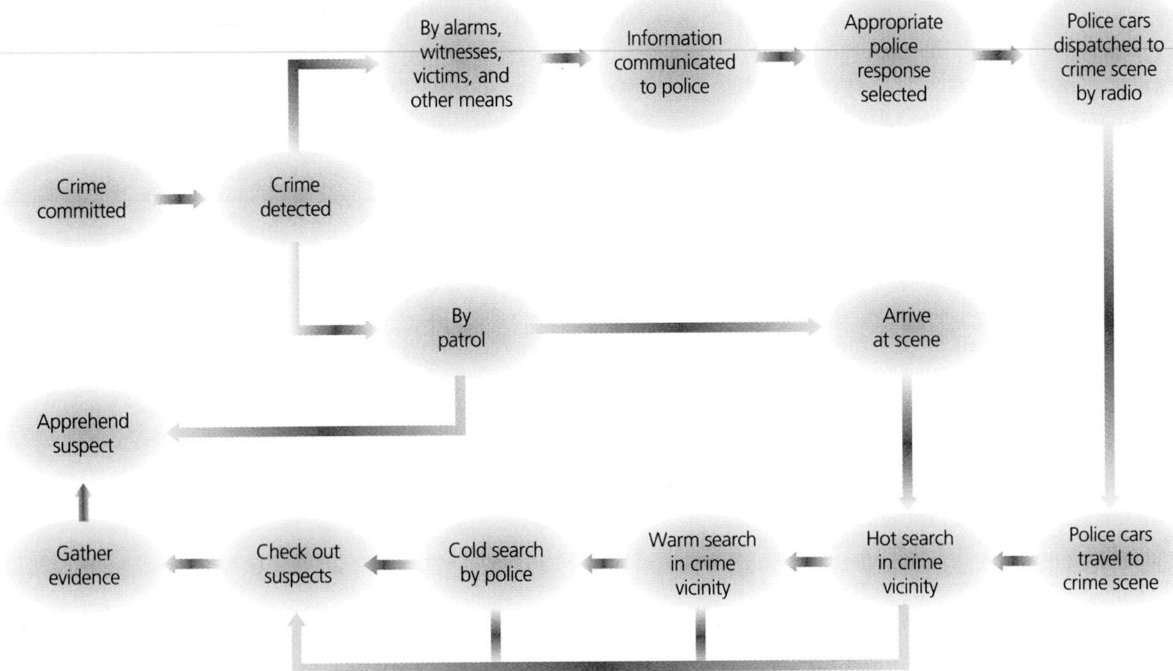

Figure 5.4
The apprehension process

Apprehension of a felony suspect may result from a sequence of actions by patrol officers and detectives. Coordination of these efforts is a key factor in solving major crimes.

from each day are analyzed the next morning. Investigators receive assignments based on their specialties. They study the information, weigh each factor, and decide whether the crime has a good chance of being solved.

Some departments have guidelines for making these decisions so that resources will be used efficiently. If the detectives decide there is little chance of solving the crime quickly, the case may be dropped. Steven Brandl found that in burglary and robbery follow-up investigations the value of the lost property and the detective's belief that the case could be resolved through an arrest were the main factors affecting how much time and effort were spent in solving the crime (Brandl, 1993:141).

When detectives decide that a full-scale investigation is warranted, they carry out a wider search—known as a "cold" search—for evidence or weapons. Witnesses may be questioned again, informants contacted, and evidence gathered. Because of the pressure of new cases, however, an investigation may be shelved so that resources may be directed toward "warmer" cases.

4. **Clearance and Arrest** The decision to arrest is a key part of the apprehension process. In some cases, further evidence or links between suspects and others are not discovered if arrests are made too soon. A crime is considered cleared when the evidence supports the arrest of a suspect. If a suspect admits having committed other unsolved crimes, those crimes are also "cleared." When a crime is cleared in police files, it does not always mean that the suspect will be found guilty.

Forensic Techniques

American police have long relied on science in gathering, identifying, and analyzing evidence. Scientific analysis of fingerprints, blood, semen, hair, textiles, and weapons has helped the police identify criminals. It has also helped prosecutors convince jurors of the guilt of defendants. There are forensic labs in all states and many large cities.

DNA "fingerprinting" is the latest weapon to be employed in investigating many kinds of crimes. This technique is used to identify people through their distinctive gene patterns (also called "genotypic features"). DNA, or deoxyribonucleic acid, is the basic component of all chromosomes and is the same for all the cells in a person's body, including skin, blood, organs, and semen. The characteristics of certain segments of DNA vary from person to person and thus form a genetic "fingerprint." It is therefore possible to analyze DNA from, say, samples of hair and compare them to those of suspects.

Use of the DNA technique has been hampered because few labs are equipped to perform DNA analysis. Moreover, many detectives and prosecutors do not make full use of these resources, and there is some concern that the method does not yet have a sound scientific foundation. Courts in most states now accept DNA results as evidence, but in some states, defense attorneys have successfully challenged the use of DNA evidence (Neufeld and Colman, 1990:46). One impact of the technology has been the release from prison of twenty-eight persons after post-trial DNA testing showed that they could not have committed the crimes for which they were imprisoned (Connors et al., 1996:2).

IDEAS IN PRACTICE

A formula for deciding the police department's response to burglary cases was developed in Fremont, California. Officers add the weighting factor for each information element. If the total score is 10 or less, further action on the case is suspended.

Information Element	Weighting Factor
Estimated time since occurrence:	
Less than 1 hour	5
1 to 12 hours	1
12 to 24 hours	0.3
More than 24 hours	0
Witness report of the offense	7
On-view report of the offense	1
Usable fingerprints	7
Suspect information developed:	
Description or name	9
Vehicle description	0.1
Other	0

Are there other factors that you think ought to be considered? Do the weightings look reasonable?

Research on Investigation

The results of several studies raise questions about the value of investigations and the role detectives play in apprehension. This research suggests that the police have attached too much importance to investigation as a means of solving crimes and shows that most crimes are cleared because of arrests made by the patrol force at or near the scene. Response time is a key factor in apprehension, as is the information given by the victim or witnesses.

A Rand Corporation study of 153 large police departments found that a key factor in solving crimes was identification of the perpetrator by the victim or witnesses. Of those cases that were not solved right away but were cleared later, most were cleared by routine procedures such as fingerprint searches, tips from informants, and mug-shot "show-ups." The report found that actions by the investigative staff were important in very few cases. In sum, about 30 percent of the crimes were cleared by on-scene arrest and another 50 percent through identification by victims or witnesses when the police arrived. Thus, detective work could have solved only about 20 percent. Even among this group, however, the study found that most crimes "were also solved by patrol officers, members of the public who spontaneously provide further information, or routine investigative practices" (Greenwood, Chaiken, and Petersilia, 1977:227).

Does this research show that detectives are not important? No. The detective's role is important in at least two ways in addition to solving crimes. First, the status of detective provides a goal to which patrol officers may aspire and gives them an incentive to excel in their work. Second, the public expects the police to conduct investigations. Citizens may have more trust in the police or feel more willing to cooperate with them when they see investigations being conducted, even if those investigations may not lead to arrests.

CHECKPOINT

16. What are the four steps of the apprehension process?
17. What is "DNA fingerprinting"?

Special Operations

Patrol and investigation are the two largest and most important units in a police department. In metropolitan areas, however, special units are set up to deal with specific types of problems. The most common such units specialize in traffic, vice, and juveniles. Some cities also have units to deal with organized crime and drugs. Even where these special units exist, however, patrol officers and investigators still deal with these problems in the course of their work.

Traffic

Traffic regulation is a major job of the police. On average 7 percent of officers are assigned to traffic units (Bayley, 1994:94). The police regulate the flow of vehicles, investigate accidents, and enforce traffic laws. This work may not seem to have much to do with crime fighting or order maintenance, but in fact it does. Besides helping to maintain order, enforcement of traffic laws educates the public in safe driving habits and provides a visible service to the community.

Traffic duty can also help the police catch criminals. In enforcing traffic laws, patrol officers can stop cars and question drivers. Stolen property and suspects linked to other criminal acts are often found in this way. Most departments can now automatically check license numbers against lists of wanted vehicles and suspects.

Enforcement of traffic laws is a good example of police discretion. Bayley (1986) has shown that when officers stop drivers for traffic violations they choose among five options:

1. Issue a citation (43 percent of stops).
2. Release the driver with a warning (20.7 percent).
3. Arrest the driver for intoxication or for another crime (14 percent).
4. Let the driver go (13.4 percent).
5. Issue a citation while also giving a stern lecture (12 percent).

Traffic work is mostly proactive, and the level of enforcement is linked to department policies. Guided by these policies, officers target certain kinds of violations or certain highways. Some departments expect officers to issue a certain number of citations during each shift. Although these norms may be informal, they are a way of gauging the productivity of traffic officers. For the most part, selective enforcement is the general policy, because the police have neither the desire nor the resources to enforce all traffic laws.

Vice

Enforcement of vice laws depends on proactive police work, which often involves the use of undercover agents and informers. Most large city police departments have a vice unit. Strict enforcement of these laws requires that officers be given wide discretion. They must often engage in degrading activities, such as posing as prostitutes or drug dealers, in order to catch lawbreakers. The special nature of vice work requires members of the unit to be well trained in the legal procedures that must be followed if arrests are to lead to convictions.

The potential for corruption in this type of police work presents some administrative dilemmas. Undercover officers are in a position to blackmail gamblers and drug dealers and may also be offered bribes. In addition, officers must be transferred when their identities become known.

The growth of undercover work and electronic surveillance troubles critics who favor more open policing. They fear that the use of these tactics violates civil liberties and increases government intrusion into the private lives of citizens, whether or not those citizens commit crimes.

Drug Law Enforcement

Many large cities have a bureau to enforce drug laws. Within these agencies may be task forces that deal with organized crime or gangs involved in drug dealing. Other groups may use sting operations to arrest drug sellers on the street or to provide drug education in the community.

Drug enforcement may reflect the goal of "aggressive patrol," assigning resources to get the largest number of arrests and stop street dealing. Police executives believe that showing dealers and the community that drug laws are enforced is important.

Various strategies have been used to attack drug dealing. One of these is building inspections of houses and buildings used by drug dealers. Those that do not meet city standards can be boarded up to rid the neighborhood of dealers. Streets where drugs are dealt openly may be flooded with officers who engage in proactive stops and questioning.

Another strategy is to disrupt the drug market. In Phoenix, Arizona, and other cities, police placed signs warning motorists entering "drug neighborhoods" that they may be stopped and questioned. In New York City's "Operation Pressure Point," a thousand police officers were moved into the Lower East Side to shut down the area's "drug supermarket." The police made thousands of arrests, abandoned buildings were torn down, and storefronts used by dealers were padlocked (Zimmer, 1987). This approach has been used in other parts of New York, in Los Angeles, and in other cities. But how effective is this approach? Do these efforts simply shift the drug market to another area, or do they actually reduce the availability of drugs?

Although arrests for drug sale or possession have increased dramatically, some observers believe that this is not the best way to deal with the problem. Many public officials argue that drugs should be viewed as a public health problem rather than as a crime problem. Critics of current policies believe society would benefit more if more resources were devoted to drug treatment programs, which can get some people to stop using drugs, than from police actions that fill prisons without doing much to reduce drug use.

POLICE ACTIONS AND THE RULE OF LAW

As we saw in Chapter 3, the police must work within the framework of the law; they are not free to use any means to fight crime. The law requires that the police investigate crimes by gathering information required to successfully prosecute a suspect and to free the innocent. To secure a conviction, the police must provide prosecutors with **admissible evidence**. Three police practices—search and seizure, arrest, and interrogation—are structured to ensure that the rule of law is upheld and the rights of citizens protected.

admissible evidence

Evidence that has been gathered by the police according to the law as specified in the Constitution, court decisions, and statutes.

The Supreme Court has devised two rules to make sure that police respect the rights of suspects. First, the exclusionary rule states that evidence seized by illegal means and confessions obtained in improper ways cannot be used in trials. Second, the Court has ruled that the Sixth Amendment right to counsel means that the defendant may have a lawyer present when he or she is questioned by police. Police departments have policies and procedures for searches, arrests, and interrogations that officers learn during training. Officers are keenly aware that prosecution of a case may be jeopardized if they do not follow proper procedures.

Search and Seizure

In *Mapp v. Ohio* (1961), the Supreme Court applied the exclusionary rule to all searches conducted by state and local police departments. Before that case, the rule had applied only to federal law enforcement officials and to the police in states that had their own rules about exclusion of improperly obtained evidence. Now all police officers must conduct investigations and arrests in accordance with the Fourth Amendment's rules against *unreasonable* searches and seizures.

Search Warrant

When a judge has issued a **search warrant**, the police may search a designated place for specific persons or items to be seized. To obtain the warrant, the officer must do two things:

search warrant

An order of a judge that allows a police officer to search a designated place for specific persons or items to be seized.

1. Provide reliable information showing that there is probable cause to believe that a crime has been or is being committed.
2. Identify the premises and pieces of property to be seized (the officer must swear under oath that the facts given are correct).

Warrantless Searches

In some circumstances, the interests of crime control require that the police conduct a search without a warrant. It is in this area that the courts have been most active in defining the term *unreasonable*. In this section we discuss five kinds of searches that may be legally conducted without a warrant and still be in accord with the Fourth Amendment. As we see in A Question of Ethics on page 121, warrantless searches raise a number of ethical concerns.

1. **Searches incident to a lawful arrest.** When an officer has observed a crime or believes that one has been committed, an arrest may be made and a search conducted without a warrant. Such searches are justified when they meet three requirements: (a) the officer has probable cause to arrest the suspect; (b) there is a need to prevent the loss of evidence or to protect officers and bystanders; and (c) the search is limited to that necessary to seize weapons or evidence.

   In *Chimel v. California* (1969), the Supreme Court ruled that such a search is limited to the person of the arrestee and the area within the arrestee's "immediate control," defined as that area "from within which he might [obtain] a weapon or something that could have been used as evidence against him" in order to destroy it. Thus, if the police are holding a person in one room of a house, they may not search and seize property in another part of the house.

2. **Field Interrogation** As a society, we want police to investigate people who behave in suspicious ways as well as those who disrupt public order. Thus, officers often stop people on the street to ask them who they are and what they are doing without knowing any facts that might justify an arrest. But officers must have a reasonable suspicion that the person may have committed or be about to commit a crime. These field interrogations, often called "threshold inquiries," allow for brief questioning and frisking: patting down the outside of the suspect's clothing to find out whether he or she has a concealed weapon.

   In the case of ***Terry v. Ohio*** (1968), the Supreme Court upheld the stop-and-frisk procedure when a police officer stopped and patted down three men who had been looking into store windows in a suspicious way. The officer found handguns during the patdown. The Court ruled that such a search could be conducted if the officer reasonably believed that the person might be dangerous.

   On the basis of this and later decisions, police officers now may stop and question a person if it is reasonable to assume that a crime is being committed, is about to be committed, or has been committed. The person may be frisked if the officer fears for his or her life and believes that the person has a weapon. The courts have concluded that an officer may conduct this kind of search in order to investigate suspicious persons without first showing probable cause. All that is required of the police is that they had a reasonable suspicion that the suspect may be armed and was considering criminal activity.

***Terry v. Ohio* (1968)**

A police officer may stop and frisk an individual if it is reasonable to suspect that a crime has been committed.

3. **Automobiles** Warrantless searches may be conducted when there is probable cause to believe that a vehicle contains criminal evidence. The Supreme Court permits officers to search cars more freely than houses because cars are mobile and evidence may be lost if officers must seek a warrant before conducting a search.

   The Supreme Court has struggled to define the conditions under which a vehicle may be searched. It has concluded that the search of a car without a warrant may include items within the car if there is probable cause to believe that they are evidence of a crime (***U.S. v. Ross***, 1982).

   The police cannot randomly stop vehicles to search for evidence of illegal activity (***Delaware v. Prouse***, 1979). However, stopping motorists at roadblocks to check licenses or safety equipment is legal if it is done in a systematic way (***Michigan Department of State Police v. Sitz***, 1990). Passengers may be asked to step out of the car when the driver has been stopped for an ordinary traffic violation (***Maryland v. Wilson***, 1997).

   Because of the importance of the automobile in American society, there will undoubtedly be further interpretation of the Fourth Amendment with regard to unreasonable search and seizure, including cases dealing with searches of passengers and drivers.

Warrantless searches of automobiles may be conducted when there is probable cause to believe that a vehicle contains criminal evidence. Lieutenant Tim Laun checks the inside and under a car seat after he and his colleagues arrested a suspect; they found marijuana in the vehicle on Midland Avenue, in Syracuse, New York.

4. **Plain View** Items that are in "plain view" may be searched and seized without a warrant when officers have reason to believe that they are linked to a crime. If an officer has a warrant to search a house for cocaine and finds guns in the course of the search, the guns may also be seized. For the plain-view doctrine

to apply, the officer must be legally entitled to be at the location, such as inside a house, and the item must be plainly visible. Moreover, the value of the item as evidence must be apparent.

Two decisions have further defined the plain-view doctrine. In *New York v. Class* (1986), the Supreme Court ruled that a gun protruding from under a seat, seen by an officer when he entered the car to look for the vehicle identification number, was within the bounds of the doctrine. However, in *Arizona v. Hicks* (1987), the Court ruled that an officer who moved a stereo system to find its identification number during a legal search for weapons had violated the Fourth Amendment ban on unreasonable search and seizure. The serial number was not in plain view, and the police did not have probable cause to believe that the stereo had been stolen.

5. **Consent** A person may waive the rights granted by the Fourth Amendment and allow the police to conduct a search or seize items without a warrant. The prosecution must be able to prove, however, that the consent was given voluntarily by the correct person. In some circumstances, as when security employees search the belongings of passengers before they board a plane, consent is implied.

Sometimes there are questions about who may give consent to search a location. May consent be given, for example, by a landlord or parent of the defendant? In *Illinois v. Rodriguez* (1990), the Supreme Court allowed police to use evidence obtained when officers reasonably, but mistakenly, believed that a defendant's girlfriend lived at his apartment and therefore could grant permission for a search of the premises.

IDEAS IN PRACTICE

While on routine patrol, you observe a speeding car. With lights flashing and siren wailing, you give chase. The car pulls over to the side of the road. You approach the vehicle from the rear, ask the driver for his license, and notice what smells like burnt marijuana. On the floor you see an envelope marked "Supergold." You arrest and handcuff the driver, then search the interior of the car. On the back seat, you find a black leather jacket. In the zippered pocket you find a glassine packet of what turns out to be cocaine.

What charges might you recommend? Have you violated the driver's Fourth Amendment rights?

Arrest

Arrest is the seizure of a person by a government official with the authority to take him or her into custody. Because the suspect is taken to the station house, an arrest is more intrusive on a person's freedom than a street stop or field questioning. The law of arrest requires that the officer show that there is probable cause to believe that a crime has been committed and that the person taken into custody is the perpetrator. Although courts prefer that officers seek warrants before making felony arrests, such warrants have not been required. Officers often make arrests without a warrant even when they had time to get one.

arrest

The physical taking of a person into custody on the ground that there is probable cause to believe that he or she has committed a criminal offense. Police may use only reasonable physical force in making an arrest. The purpose of arrest is to hold the accused for a court proceeding.

Interrogation

Protection against self-incrimination is one of the most important rights contained in the Fifth Amendment. People may not be forced to be witnesses against themselves. In our adversarial system, the government must prove the defendant's guilt. The prosecutor and police are not supposed to seek that proof by pressuring defendants to provide evidence of their guilt. Courts will exclude from evidence any confession obtained through undue pressure. In addition, the Sixth Amendment right to counsel protects suspects by allowing them to have the advice and assistance of an attorney during questioning.

As we saw in Chapter 3, the Supreme Court ruled that as soon as the investigation of a crime begins to focus on a particular suspect and he or she is taken into custody, the so-called *Miranda* warnings must be read aloud before questioning can begin (*Miranda v. Arizona*, 1966). Suspects must be told four things:

1. They have the right to remain silent.
2. If they decide to make a statement, it can and will be used against them in court.
3. They have the right to have an attorney present during interrogation or to have an opportunity to consult with an attorney.
4. If they cannot afford an attorney, the state will provide one.

The Controversy over Exclusion of Evidence

The Supreme Court's *Mapp* and *Miranda* rulings gave rise to much controversy. It was argued that (1) confessions are needed in order to apprehend and convict violators; (2) informing suspects of their rights would greatly reduce the ability of the police to obtain confessions; (3) few police would actually give the required warnings; (4) remedies other than exclusion of evidence could be used to punish officers who failed to observe rules; and (5) instead of deterring police misconduct, exclusion of evidence would punish society by letting guilty people go free.

A Question of ETHICS

Officer Mike Groton knocked on the apartment door. He and fellow officer Howard Reece had gone to this rundown part of town to arrest Richard Watson on the basis of evidence from an informer that Watson was a major drug seller. "Police officers, open up," said Groton. The door opened slowly, and a small, tense woman peered into the hallway.

"Ma'am, we have a warrant for the arrest of Richard Watson. Is he here?"

"No. I don't know any Watson," was the answer.

"Well, let us in so we can see for ourselves."

Groton and Reece entered the apartment. Reece quickly went to a back bedroom. The window leading to a fire escape was open and the bed looked as though someone had left it in a rush. Reece poked around the room, opening drawers and searching the closet. In the back of the closet he saw a woman's purse hanging on a hook. He opened it and found three glassine packages of a white powder.

"Hey, Mike, look what I found," he called. Groton came into the bedroom. "Looks like heroin to me," Reece remarked. "Too bad we can't use it."

"Why can't we use it? This is the place."

"But the warrant specifies the arrest of Watson. It doesn't say anything about searching his closet."

"Let's just keep those packets. When we catch him we can 'find' it in his pocket."

What are the issues here? Can the officers keep the heroin packets? Is bending the rules acceptable in some cases? If so, are they acceptable in the one just described? What should the officers do?

All of these arguments were challenged both by law enforcement officials and by social scientists studying the impact of the rulings. Upon reviewing the findings of a number of studies Nardulli was able to say that the exclusionary rule has had only a slight impact on the criminal court system (Nardulli, 1983:585).

In most cities the police solve crimes either by catching the suspect in the act or by finding witnesses who will testify. Because most departments have limited resources for investigation, suspects are not usually arrested until the crime is solved and conviction is likely. In these cases, interrogation is less essential than many critics of the *Miranda* rule believed. Instead of decreasing officers' ability to catch lawbreakers, rulings like *Miranda* and *Mapp* seem to have made officers more conscious of the legal rules that govern their decisions and actions.

Modifications of the Exclusionary Rule

In recent years the Supreme Court has created exceptions to the *Mapp* and *Miranda* decisions. Three of the most important exceptions to the exclusionary rule are the "public safety" exception, the inevitable discovery rule, and the "good-faith" exception.

The case of *New York v. Quarles* (1984) established a public safety exception to the *Miranda* warnings. Officers may ask arrested suspects questions before reading the *Miranda* warnings if the questions deal with an urgent situation affecting public safety. The suspect in the Quarles case had hidden a gun in a store as the police chased him, and when he was handcuffed, the police asked him where the gun was. The police were concerned that someone else might find the gun if they did not question the suspect as soon as possible.

The inevitable discovery exception was established by the Court in *Nix v. Williams* (1984). During the investigation of the murder of a 10-year-old girl, the police asked Robert Williams, the prime suspect, to show them where she was buried. Although officers had promised that they would not question Williams outside of his lawyer's presence, they did point out that the girl's parents had a right to hold a funeral for the little girl, who had been snatched from them on Christmas and murdered. In response Williams led the police to the burial site. Williams was convicted, but he appealed the ruling on the ground that he had been improperly questioned because his lawyer was not present. The Supreme Court accepted the prosecution's argument that the body would have been located inevitably even without the improper questioning of the defendant.

United States v. Leon (1984)

Evidence seized using a warrant that is later found to be defective is valid if the officer was acting in good faith.

Under the good-faith exception to the exclusionary rule, the Supreme Court has ruled that evidence may be used even though it was obtained under a search warrant that later proved to be technically invalid. In ***United States v. Leon*** (1984), police presented evidence to a judge concerning an informant's tip about drug activity at a certain house. The judge made an error in issuing a search warrant. The Supreme Court approved the search, despite the defective warrant, because the real error had been made by the judge. The police followed proper procedures by presenting evidence to the judge that they believed supported their request for a warrant. The Court ruled that the costs of enforcing the exclusionary rule, namely overturning the conviction, outweighed the benefits of seeking to deter police misconduct.

In large part, the Supreme Court decisions affecting the exclusionary rule reflect a continuing debate in American society. Civil libertarians argue that constitutional rights must protect all Americans, including criminal defendants, against excessive use of power by police and prosecutors. Critics say that the Supreme Court has gone too far and that too many guilty people have avoided prosecution and punishment. This debate will probably continue, and the relationship of police actions to the rule of law will always be a subject of controversy.

CHECKPOINT

18. What are the five kinds of searches that may be conducted without a warrant and still be in accord with the Fourth Amendment?
19. What is the exclusionary rule?
20. What are the three exceptions that the Supreme Court has made to the *Mapp* and *Miranda* decisions?

Summary

- Police operations are shaped by their formal organizational structures and also influenced by social and political processes both within and outside the department.
- The police are organized along military lines so that authority and responsibility can be located at appropriate levels.

- Police services are delivered through the work of the patrol, investigation, and specialized operations units.
- The patrol function has three components: answering calls for assistance, maintaining a police presence, and probing suspicious circumstances.
- Discussions of the future of policing are dominated by issues concerning the allocation of personnel, response time, foot versus motorized patrol, and community-oriented policing.
- The investigation function is the responsibility of detectives working in close coordination with patrol officers.
- The felony apprehension process is a sequence of actions that includes crime detection, preliminary investigation, follow-up investigation, clearance, and arrest.
- Specialized units dealing with traffic, drug, and vice are found in large departments.
- The police must work within the law so they do not violate the rights of citizens.
- Decisions by the Supreme Court over the past quarter-century have interpreted the Bill of Rights with regard to search and seizure, arrest, and interrogation.

Questions for Review

1. What are some of the issues that influence police administrators in their allocation of resources?
2. What is the purpose of patrol? How is it carried out?
3. What has research shown about the effectiveness of patrol?
4. Why do detectives have so much prestige on the force?
5. How do various amendments to the Bill of Rights affect police operations?

ANSWERS TO CHECKPOINTS

1. Patrol, investigation, traffic, vice, juvenile.
2. Citizen expectation that the police will respond quickly to *every* call.
3. Policy that gives priority to calls according to whether an immediate or a delayed response is warranted.
4. Clearance rate—the percentage of crimes known to the police that they believe they have solved through arrest.
5. Personnel assigned to line functions are directly involved in field operations. Personnel assigned to staff functions supplement and support the line function.
6. (a) Answering calls for help, (b) maintaining a police presence, and (c) probing suspicious circumstances.
7. Crime statistics, degree of urbanization, pressures from business and community groups, socioeconomic conditions.
8. Crime rates do not seem to be affected by changes in patrolling strategies, such as assigning more officers.
9. A hot spot is a location where there is a high number of calls for police response.
10. A proactive patrol strategy designed to direct resources to known high-crime areas.
11. Decision-making delays caused by ambiguity, coping activities, and conflicts.
12. Officers on foot patrol have greater contact with residents of a neighborhood, thus gaining their confidence and assistance. Officers on motorized patrol have a greater range of territory and can respond speedily to calls, but they may be less aware of needs and problems in the community.
13. One-person patrols are more cost-efficient; two-person patrols are thought to be safer.
14. Aggressive patrol is a proactive strategy to maximize police activity in the community.
15. Community policing emphasizes order maintenance and service. It attempts to involve members of the community in making their neighborhood safe. Foot patrol and the decentralization of command are usually part of community policing efforts.
16. The four steps in apprehension are (a) detection of crime, (b) preliminary investigation, (c) follow-up investigation, (d) clearance and arrest.
17. A technique that identifies individuals through their distinctive gene patterns.
18. (a) Incident to a lawful arrest, (b) field interrogation, (c) automobiles, (d) "plain view," (e) consent.
19. That evidence illegally seized by the police and confessions obtained in improper ways cannot be used in trials.
20. Public safety, inevitable discovery, and good faith.

Chapter 6

Policing: Issues and Trends

Who Are the Police?

- *Recruitment*
- *Training*
- *The Changing Profile of the Police*

The Police Subculture

- *The Working Personality*
- *Police Isolation*
- *Job Stress*

Police and the Community

- *Policing in a Multicultural Society*
- *Community Crime Prevention*

Police Abuse of Power

- *Use of Force*
- *Corruption*

Civic Accountability

- *Internal Affairs Units*
- *Civilian Review Boards*
- *Standards and Accreditation*
- *Civil Liability Suits*

Private Policing

- *Functions of Private Police*
- *Private Employment of Public Police*
- *The Public-Private Interface*
- *Recruitment and Training*

ON MONDAY, July 11, 1994, former New York City police officer Michael Dowd stood before Judge Kimba Wood in a federal courtroom. Dowd was about to be sentenced for a series of crimes in which he used his authority as a police officer to abuse people, steal money and goods, and obtain cocaine. His crimes ranged from stealing food intended for the needy from a church to plotting a kidnapping on behalf of drug dealers. Dowd had been the star witness in the city's Mollen Commission investigation, which uncovered the worst police corruption scandal in New York City in two decades.

Dowd had hoped that his cooperation would lead to a lenient sentence, but prosecutors found many of his statements to be false or misleading. When Judge Wood sentenced him to fifteen years in prison, a sentence just short of the maximum possible, Dowd was stunned and mumbled, "Oh, my God. Oh, my God." In issuing her sentence, Judge Wood said to Dowd, "You did not just fall prey to temptation and steal what was in front of you and take kickbacks or sell confidential law enforcement information. You also continually searched for new ways to abuse your position and at times you recruited fellow officers to join in your crimes."

Dowd's case illustrates a frequent problem in law enforcement. How can we make sure that those with authority do not use their power for their own gain? Police officers have sworn an oath to protect society against crime; thus, we are shocked and disappointed when they, of all people, violate the public trust. The bonds between the police and the community are often fragile, especially when racial, gender, or class bias comes into play.

In this chapter we discuss a number of issues concerning the police and their relationship to society. We first look at recruitment and training. Second, we examine the unique subculture of police officers. Third, the link between the police and the community is described. Fourth, we discuss the problem of abuse of power by the police and what is being done to make police more accountable. Finally, we look at a trend—private policing—that affects police operations today.

WHO ARE THE POLICE?

If you or someone you know plans a career in law enforcement, ask yourself what aspects of the job make it more appealing than other kinds of work. Some people may want the adventure and excitement of investigating crimes and catching suspects. Others may be drawn to the satisfactions that come from being a public servant. Still other people may be attracted to a civil service job with good benefits. Table 6.1 presents the reasons people give for choosing police work as a career.

Questions for Inquiry

Why do some people choose policing as a career?

How does the police subculture influence the behavior of officers?

What role does the link between the police and the community play in preventing crime?

In what ways do the police abuse their power, and how can they be controlled?

What methods can be used to make police more accountable to citizens?

What is the future of private policing?

Recruitment

How can departments recruit well-rounded, dedicated public servants? If pay scales are low, educational requirements minimal, and physical standards unrealistically rigid, police work will attract only those who are unable to enter other occupations. This was a problem in the past. Most departments now offer entrance salaries of more than $25,000 plus a great deal of overtime pay (BJS, 1997. Sourcebook:42). While many departments now expect at least two years of college, most require new members to have only a high school education. All departments require good physical condition and lack of a criminal record. To widen the pool of recruits and avoid discriminating against women and some ethnic groups, height and weight requirements have been changed, and many departments even overlook a minor criminal record if it was acquired when the applicant was under 18. Many departments now use written and psychological tests as well as physical fitness tests to identify the best candidates.

Today most recruits have had some college, although officers in rural areas and small cities may have less education. In the past twenty years, the educational levels of American police officers have risen. Now, as shown in Figure 6.1 (p. 127), about 60 percent of sworn officers have more than two years of college education.

While recruiting efforts and entry requirements affect the pool of potential officers, their training affects their attitudes.

Training

The performance of the police is not based solely on the types of people recruited; it is also shaped by their training. Most states require preservice training for all

Reason	Male	Female	Total
Variety	62.2%	92.1%	69.4%
Responsibility	50.4	55.3	51.6
Serve public	48.7	50.0	49.0
Adventure	49.6	39.5	47.1
Security	46.2	34.2	43.3
Pay	43.7	42.1	43.3
Benefits	36.1	31.6	35.0
Advancement	31.9	34.2	32.5
Retirement	27.7	5.3	22.3
Prestige	16.0	13.2	15.3

Table 6.1
Reasons for choosing police work as a career

How do the reasons for choosing police work differ from those that might be given for choosing other careers? What explains the different responses given by men and women?

SOURCE: Harold P. Slater and Martin Reiser, "A Comparative Study of Factors Influencing Police Recruitment," *Journal of Police Science and Administration* 16 (1988):170.

IDEAS IN PRACTICE

The following is excerpted from a recruiting brochure developed by the police department of Farmington, a suburban community outside of Hartford, Connecticut.

> As a police officer with the Town of Farmington, you will have ...
> - The opportunity to contribute to the community ...
> - A professional work environment ...
> - Merit-based growth opportunities ...
> - Excellent salary and benefits ...
> - Health and life insurance, Town-provided uniforms and equipment, cleaning allowance, and other benefits as determined by labor contract.

Farmington is a nationally accredited police department with a statewide reputation for excellence. The department enjoys strong support from the community, a history of progressive leadership, and high-quality personnel.

Always known for state-of-the-art police-work, the department is moving toward implementation of Problem-Oriented and Community-Based Policing. If you meet these qualifications ...

If you are 21 years of age or older, a United States citizen, have a valid Connecticut Driver's License and no significant criminal record, you are eligible to apply for the position of police officer.

Candidates must have earned an Associate's Degree or 60 college credits. ...

The Town of Farmington is an Equal Opportunity Employer. Women and members of minority groups are strongly encouraged to apply.

Judging by this brochure, what personal values and personality traits do you think Farmington is seeking in its recruits? How does the language in the brochure compare with recruitment language in your own community?

recruits. This is often a formal course at a police academy, but in some states candidates for police jobs must complete a basic training program, at their own expense, before being considered for employment. Large departments generally run their own programs, while state police academies train recruits from rural and small-town units. The courses range from two-week sessions that stress the handling of weapons to more academic six-month programs followed by fieldwork. Recruits hear lectures on social relations, receive foreign language training, and learn emergency medical treatment.

Formal training is needed to gain an understanding of legal rules, weapons use, and other aspects of the job. However, the police officer's job also demands skills in dealing with people that cannot be learned from a lecture or a book. Much of the most important training of police officers takes place during a probationary period when new officers work with and learn from experienced officers. When new officers finish their classroom training and arrive for their first day of patrol duty, they may be told by experienced officers, "Now, I want you to forget all that stuff you learned at the academy. You really learn your job on the streets."

The process of **socialization** as a police officer includes learning the informal rather than the rule-book ways of law enforcement. New officers must learn how to look "productive," how to take shortcuts in filling out forms, how to keep themselves safe in dangerous situations, how to analyze conflicts so as to maintain order, and a host of other bits of wisdom, norms, and folklore that define the subculture of a particular department. Recruits learn that loyalty to fellow officers, esprit de corps, and respect for police authority are highly valued.

In police work, the success of the group depends on the cooperation of its members. All patrol officers are under direct supervision, and their performance is measured by their contribution to the group's work. Supervisors are not the only people who evaluate the officers' contribution. Officers are also influenced by the ways their colleagues view them. Officers within a department may develop strong, shared views on the best way to "handle" various situations. How officers use their personal skills and judgment can mean the difference between defusing a conflict and making it worse so that it endangers citizens and other officers. In tackling their "impossible mandate," new recruits must learn the ways of the world from the other officers, who depend on them and on whom they depend.

The Changing Profile of the Police

The composition of American police forces has changed greatly in the last few decades. For most of the nation's history, almost all police officers were white men. Today, women and minorities are a growing percentage of police departments in many areas. One reason for this growth is the Equal Employment Opportunity Act of 1972, which bars state and local governments from discriminating in their hiring practices. Pressured by state and federal agencies as well as by lawsuits, most city police forces have mounted campaigns to recruit more

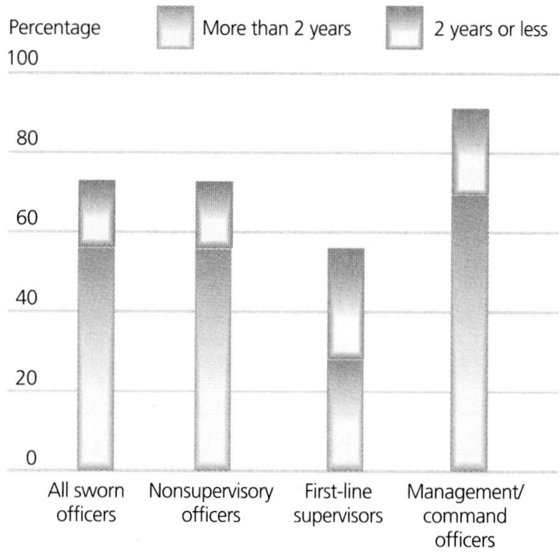

Figure 6.1
College education of sworn officers

During the past two decades the number of police officers with at least some college education has grown. However, about a quarter of all sworn officers have not gone to college.

SOURCE: David L. Carter, Allen D. Sapp, and Darrel W. Stephens, *The State of Police Education: Policy Direction for the Twenty-First Century* (Washington, D.C.: Police Executive Research Forum, 1989), 45.

minority and female officers (Martin, 1991). Figure 6.2 shows how the profile of the American police officer has changed.

socialization

The process by which the rules, symbols, and values of a group or subculture are learned by its members.

Minority Police Officers

Before the 1970s, many police departments did not hire nonwhites. As this practice declined, the makeup of police departments changed, especially in large cities. A study of the nation's fifty largest cities found that from 1983 to 1992, 29 percent of the departments reported an increase of 50 percent or more in the number of African-American officers, and 20 percent reported a similar increase in the number of Hispanic officers (Walker and Turner, 1992). A recent Bureau of Justice Statistics study found that minority police officers made up about 20 percent of all local departments (BJS, 1997. *Sourcebook*:39).

As political power shifts toward minorities in some American cities, the makeup of their police forces is changing as well. But the election of an African-American or a Hispanic-American mayor does not always produce an immediate change in the composition of the police force. However, three-quarters of Detroit's population

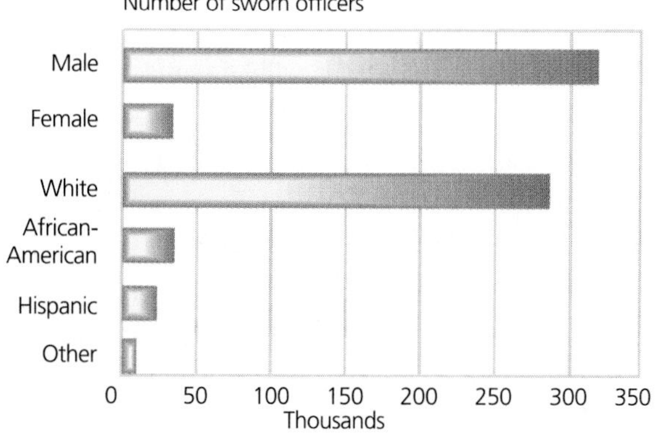

Figure 6.2
The changing profile of the American police officer

Today about 1 in 10 officers is female and 1 in 5 is a racial or ethnic minority.

SOURCE: U.S. Department of Justice, Office of Justice Programs, *Bureau of Justice Statistics Fiscal Year 1996: At a Glance* (Washington, D.C.: Government Printing Office, 1996), 25.

NOTE: Data from law enforcement agencies employing 100 or more sworn officers. This constitutes about half of the total number of officers.

is now African American, as are about half of the city's police officers. A survey of Detroit residents found that African Americans held more favorable attitudes toward the police than did whites. As the researchers note, "In Detroit, the people who perform the police function are not alien to African-Americans; instead they represent an indigenous force" (Frank et al., 1996:332).

Women on the Force

Women have been police officers since 1905, when Lola Baldwin was made an officer in Portland, Oregon. However, the number of women officers remained small for most of the twentieth century because of the belief that policing was "men's work." As this attitude changed, the percentage of female officers rose from 1.5 percent of sworn officers in 1970 to about 9 percent today. Interestingly, the larger the department, the higher the proportion of women as sworn officers. Nevertheless, about half of U.S. police agencies still employ no women.

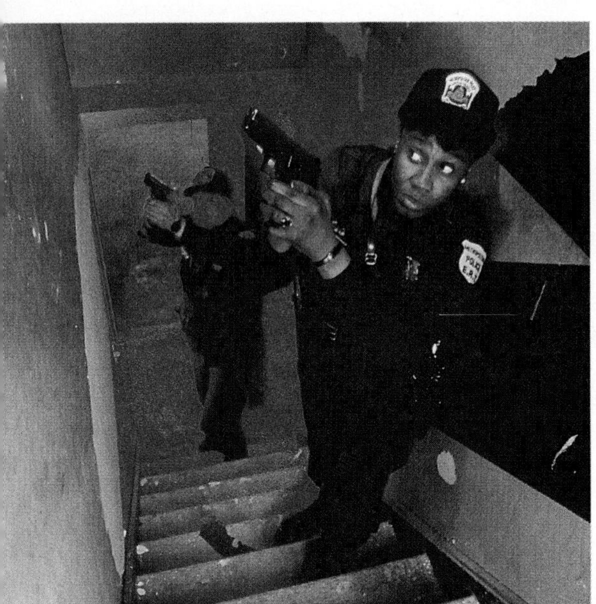

An increasing number of women have become police officers working alongside male partners. What are some of the problems they face? With the public? With their colleagues?

Although some male police officers still question whether women can handle dangerous situations and physical confrontations, most policewomen have easily met the expectations of their superiors. Indeed, studies have found that, in general, male and female officers perform in similar ways. In addition, research has found that most citizens have positive things to say about the work of policewomen (Bloch and Anderson, 1974; Sichel, 1978; Worden, 1993).

Despite these findings, women still have trouble breaking into police work. Cultural expectations of women often conflict with ideas about the proper behavior of officers, as the Close-up reveals. Once on the job, women often must contend with prejudice from their male colleagues and some citizens. In particular, they encounter resistance when they assert their authority. They are often subjected to sexist remarks and more overt forms of sexual harassment and may also find it hard to gain promotions. So despite the gains women have made, many male officers are upset by the entry of women into what they view as a male world. They complain that if their patrol partner is a woman, they cannot be sure of her ability to help them in times of danger—that she simply lacks the physical stature to act effectively when the going gets rough.

Few women have been promoted to supervisory jobs, so they are not yet able to combat the remaining barriers to the recruitment, retention, and promotion of female officers (Walker and Turner, 1992). However, the role of women in police work will undoubtedly evolve along with changes in the nature of policing, in cultural values, and in the organization of law enforcement. As citizens become accustomed to women on patrol, women officers will have an easier time gaining their cooperation. Finally, there are signs that more and more citizens and policemen are beginning to take it for granted that women will be found on patrol along with men (Martin, 1989).

THE POLICE SUBCULTURE

subculture

The symbols, beliefs, and values shared by members of a subgroup within the larger society.

A **subculture** is made up of the symbols, beliefs, values, and attitudes shared by members of a subgroup within the larger society. The subculture of the police helps define the "cop's world" and each officer's role in it. Like the subculture of any occupational group that sees itself as distinctive, police develop shared values that

CLOSE-UP

Patrol Officer Cristina Murphy

Jim Dyer was drunk out of his mind when he called the Rochester Police Department on a recent Saturday night. He wanted to make a harassment complaint; a neighbor, he claimed, was trying to kill him with a chair. Officer Cristina Murphy, 27, a petite, dark-haired, soft-spoken three-year veteran of the Rochester P.D., took the call.

"What's the problem here?" she asked when she arrived at the scene. A crowd had gathered. Dyer's rage was good local fun.

"You're a woman!" Dyer complained as Murphy stepped from her squad car. "All they send me is women. I called earlier and they sent me a Puerto Rican and she didn't do nothing either."

"Mr. Dyer, what exactly is the problem?"

"Dickie Burroughs is the problem. He tried to kill me." Through a drunken haze, Dyer made certain things clear: He wanted Dickie Burroughs locked up. He wanted him sent to Attica for life. He wanted it done that night. Short of all that, Dyer hoped that the police might oblige him by roughing up his foe, just a little.

"We don't do that sort of thing," Murphy explained in the voice she uses with drunks and children. "Mr. Dyer, I can do one of two things for you. I can go find Mr. Burroughs and get his side of the story; I can talk to him. The other thing I can do is take a report from you and advise you how to take out a warrant. You'll have to go downtown for that."

Later, in her squad car, Murphy would say that she isn't usually so curt to complaining citizens. "But it's important not to take crap about being a female. Most of the stuff I get, I just let slip by. This guy, though, he really did not want service on his complaint, he wanted retribution. When he saw a woman taking his call, he figured that I wouldn't give it to him; it never struck him that no male officer would either. You know, everyone has an opinion about women being police officers—even drunks. Some people are very threatened by it. They just can't stand getting orders from a woman. White males, I think, are the most threatened. Black males seem the least—they look at me and they just see blue. Now women, they sometimes just can't stand the idea that a woman exists who can have power over them. They feel powerless and expect all women to feel that way too. As I said, everyone has an opinion."

SOURCE: Claudia Driefus, "People Are Always Asking Me What I'm Trying to Prove," *Police Magazine* (March 1980). Reprinted by permission of the Edna McConnell Clark Foundation.

affect their view of human behavior and their role in society. There are three key issues in our understanding of the police subculture: the concept of the "working personality," the isolation of the police, and the stressful nature of much police work.

The Working Personality

Social scientists have demonstrated that there is a relationship between one's occupational environment and the way one interprets events. The police subculture produces a **working personality**—that is, a set of emotional and behavioral characteristics developed by members of an occupational group in response to the work situation and environmental influences. The police working personality thus influences the way officers view and interpret their occupational world.

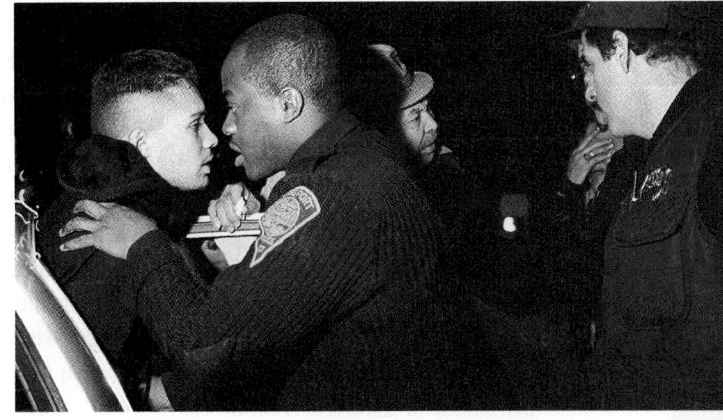

The occupational environment and working personality of officers are so interlocked that they greatly influence the daily experience of the police. How would you handle this situation?

The working personality of the police is defined by two elements of police work: (1) the threat of danger and (2) the need to establish and maintain one's authority (Skolnick, 1966:44).

1. External stress. This is produced by real threats and dangers, such as the need to enter a dark and unfamiliar building, respond to "man with a gun" alarms, and chase lawbreakers at high speeds.
2. Organizational stress. This is produced by the nature of work in a paramilitary structure: constant adjustment to changing schedules, irregular work hours, and detailed rules and procedures.
3. Personal stress. This may be caused by an officer's racial or gender status among peers, which may create problems in getting along with other officers and adjusting to group-held values that differ from one's own, as well as perceptions of bias and social isolation.
4. Operational stress. This reflects the total effect of dealing with thieves, derelicts, and the mentally ill; being lied to so often that all citizens become suspect; being required to face danger to protect a public that seems hostile; always knowing that one may be held legally liable for one's actions. (Cullen et al., 1985)

Police executives have been slow to deal with the problems of stress, but psychological and medical counseling has become more available. Some departments now offer stress prevention, group counseling, liability insurance, and family involvement programs. Many states have more liberal disability and retirement rules for police than for other public employees because their jobs are more stressful (Goolkasian, Geddes, and DeJong, 1989).

As we have seen, police officers face special pressures that can affect their interactions with the public and even harm their physical and mental health. How would you react to the prospect of facing danger and being on the lookout for crime at every moment even when you were not actually working? It seems understandable that police officers become a close-knit group, yet their isolation from society may decrease their understanding of other people. It may also strengthen their belief that the public is ungrateful and hostile. As a result, officers' actions toward members of the public may be hostile, gruff, and sometimes violent.

CHECKPOINT

1. What are the main requirements for becoming a police officer?
2. What type of training is required of police recruits?
3. Where does socialization to police work take place?
4. How has the profile of American police officers changed?
5. What are the two key elements of the police officer's working personality?
6. What are the four types of stress felt by the police?

(Answers are at the end of the chapter.)

POLICE AND THE COMMUNITY

The work of a police officer in an American city can be very hard. Hours of boring, routine work can be interrupted by short spurts of dangerous crime fighting. Although police work has always been frustrating and dangerous, officers today must deal with situations ranging from helping the homeless to dealing with domestic violence to confronting shoot-outs at drug deals gone sour. Yet police actions are often mishandled or misinterpreted, with the result that some people are critical of the police.

Policing in a Multicultural Society

Carrying out the complex tasks of policing efficiently and according to the law is a tough assignment even when the police have the support and cooperation of the public. But policing in a multicultural society presents further challenges.

In Detroit, Los Angeles, Miami, and other cities a police-citizen confrontation has led to a riot. In some minority neighborhoods police may be perceived as an "occupying force."

In the last quarter-century the racial and ethnic composition of the United States has changed. African Americans have continued to move from the South to northern cities. Hispanic immigrants from Puerto Rico, Cuba, Mexico, and South America have become the fastest growing minority. Immigrants from Eastern Europe, Russia, the Middle East, and Asia have entered the country in greater numbers. Between 1980 and 1990, the U.S. population increased by 23 million. Sixty percent of this increase was made up of nonwhite residents, including Hispanics (6.4 million), African Americans (4.3 million), and Asians and other nonwhites (3.4 million) (Bureau of the Census, 1991. *1990 Census*).

Policing requires trust, understanding, and cooperation between officers and the public. People must be willing to call for help and provide information about wrongdoing. But in a multicultural society, relations between the police and minorities are complicated by stereotypes, cultural differences, and language differences.

Officers often attribute undesirable traits to members of minority groups: "Asian Americans are shifty," "Arab Americans are terrorists," "African Americans are lazy," "Polish Americans are stubborn." But minorities may also stereotype the police as "fascist," "dumb," or "pigs." Treating people according to stereotypes, rather than as individuals, creates tensions that harden negative attitudes.

New immigrants often bring with them religious and cultural practices that differ from those of the dominant culture. Many times these practices, while accepted in the home country, are viewed as deviant or are even against the law in this country. The killing of animals by adherents of the Santaría religion has brought the police to churches in Florida. In Lincoln, Nebraska, arranged marriages of 13- and 14-year-old Iraqi-American sisters to new immigrants twice their ages brought charges of rape. In such cases the police must walk a fine line between upholding American law and respecting the customs of new residents (*New York Times*, December 2, 1996, p. A10).

Very few officers can speak a language other than English, and only in large urban departments are there officers who speak any of the many languages used by new immigrants. Limited English speakers who report crimes, are arrested, or are victimized may not be understood. Language can be a barrier for the police in responding to calls for help and dealing with organized crime. Language and cultural diversity make it harder for the FBI or local police to infiltrate the Russian, Vietnamese, and Chinese organized crime groups now found in East and West Coast cities.

Public opinion surveys have shown that race and ethnicity are key factors shaping attitudes toward the police. Polls show that 25 percent of white Americans say they have a great deal of confidence in the police and 11 percent say they have very little or none. Surprisingly, a greater portion (26 percent) of African Americans say they have a great deal of confidence, yet 21 percent say they have very little or none (BJS, 1997. *Sourcebook*: 119). Even so, most African Americans and Hispanic Americans are similar to most white Americans in their attitudes toward the

CLOSE-UP

Living under Suspicion

If you're white and confused about why so many blacks think O. J. Simpson is innocent of murder, try a simple exercise. Take a few minutes to sit down with an African American, preferably a male, and ask whether he has ever been hassled by the police. Chances are you'll get an education. . . .

He may have been pulled over for the offense of driving after dark through a white neighborhood, for the misdemeanor of driving with a white woman or for the felony of driving too fancy a car. He may have been questioned for making a suspicious late-night call from a public phone in a suburban mall or, as a boy, for flagrantly riding his new bike on his own street.

He may have been a student or a lawyer—even an off-duty policeman, threatened with drawn guns before he could pull out his badge. Some black parents warn their children never to run out of a store or a bank: better to be late than shot dead.

When you grow up in vulnerability and live at the margins of society, the world looks different. That difference, starkly displayed after Mr. Simpson's acquittal in the criminal trial, has been less passionate but no less definitive since he was found liable in his civil trial. . . .

For many African Americans, Mr. Simpson has become more symbol than individual. He is every black man who dared to marry a white women, who rose from deprivation to achievement, who got "uppity" and faced destruction by the white establishment that elevated him. He is every black man who has been pulled over by a white cop, beaten to the ground, jailed without evidence, framed for a crime he didn't commit.

Given that legacy, it is difficult for blacks not to doubt the police, and the doubts undermine law enforcement. In 1995 five Philadelphia policemen were indicted and pleaded guilty after years of fabricating evidence against poor blacks, calling into question some 1,500 prosecutions. One victim was Betty Patterson, a grandmother who spent three years in prison on a phony charge of selling crack; she later won a settlement of nearly $1 million from the city.

The indictments came as the Simpson jurors were hearing tapes of anti-black remarks by Detective Mark Fuhrman that reflected the endemic racism of the Los Angeles Police Department. As documented by the Christopher Commission, which investigated the department after the Rodney King beating in 1991, officers felt so comfortable in their bigotry that they typed racist computer messages to one another, apparently confident that they would face no punishment.

This is precisely the lesson of the black-white reactions to the Simpson case. Most policemen are not racist or corrupt, but most departments do not combat racism as vigorously as they do corruption. Many blacks have come to see the police as just another gang. Alarm bells should be going off, for the judicial system cannot function without credibility.

Of the country's institutions, police departments are probably furthest behind in addressing racism in their ranks. Some corporations are learning that a diverse work force enhances profits. The military knows that attracting volunteers and maintaining cohesion requires racial harmony. Police departments ought to understand that their bottom line is measured in legitimate convictions. They need to retrain officers and screen applicants for subtle bigotry. If morality is not argument enough, try pragmatism.

SOURCE: David K. Shipler, "Living under Suspicion," *New York Times*, February 7, 1997, p. A33.

police. It is young, low-income racial-minority males who have the most negative attitudes toward the police (Walker, Spohn, and DeLone, 1996:87, 89). As discussed in the Close-up, these attitudes help to explain why African Americans believed O. J. Simpson and not the police.

In inner-city neighborhoods—the areas that need and want effective policing—there is much distrust of the police; citizens therefore fail to report crimes and refuse to cooperate with the police. Encounters between officers and members of these communities are often hostile and sometimes lead to large-scale disorders.

Why do some urban residents resent the police? Studies have shown that this resentment stems from permissive law enforcement and police abuse of power (DiIulio, 1993a:3). In many cities the police have been charged with failure to give protection and services to minority neighborhoods and, as we will see in the next section, with abusing residents physically or verbally.

Almost all studies reveal the prejudices of the police toward the poor and racial minorities. These attitudes lead many officers to see all African Americans or Hispanic Americans as potential criminals, and as a result police tend to exaggerate the extent of minority crime. If both police and citizens view each other with hostility, then their encounters will be strained and the potential for conflict great.

Community Crime Prevention

There is a growing awareness that the control of crime and disorder cannot be achieved solely by the police. Social control requires involvement by all members of the community. Community crime prevention can be enhanced if government agencies and neighborhood organizations cooperate.

Community programs to help the police have greatly increased across the country. More than 6 million Americans are members of citizen crime-watch groups, which often have direct ties to police departments. Television and radio stations present the "unsolved crime of the week," and cash rewards are given for information that leads to conviction of the offender.

To what extent can such programs be relied upon to reduce crime and maintain social order? The results are mixed. Research on forty neighborhoods in six cities shows that while crime prevention efforts and voluntary community groups have had some success in more affluent neighborhoods, they are less likely to be found in poor neighborhoods with high levels of disorder. In such areas, "residents typically are deeply suspicious of one another, report only a weak sense of community, perceive they have low levels of personal influence on neighborhood events, and feel that it is their neighbors, not 'outsiders,' whom they must watch with care" (Skogan, 1990:130; McGabey, 1986:230).

However, Kelling and Coles have documented successful community-based crime prevention programs in Baltimore, Boston, New York, San Francisco, and Seattle (Kelling and Coles, 1996). In each city, community-based groups worked with the police and other governmental agencies to restore order and control crime. Ultimately, they say, the citizens of a community must take responsibility for maintaining civil and safe social conditions. Experience has shown that "while police might be able to *retake* a neighborhood from aggressive drug dealers, police could not *hold* a neighborhood without significant commitment and actual assistance from private citizens" (Kelling and Coles, 1996:248).

Law enforcement agencies need the support and help of the community for effective crime prevention and control. They need support when they take actions designed to maintain order. They need information about wrongdoing and cooperation with investigations. As we will see in the next section, that support will not be forthcoming if the police abuse their power.

CHECKPOINT

7. What three factors make policing in a multicultural society difficult?
8. What are the characteristics of people who have the most negative attitudes toward the police?
9. What are the two basic reasons that urban residents resent the police?
10. How are citizen watch groups and similar programs helpful to the police?

POLICE ABUSE OF POWER

The misconduct of the New York City police officer described at the beginning of this chapter is not unique. The beating of Rodney King by Los Angeles police officers drew national attention. The many recent police corruption scandals have made abuse of police power a major issue on the public agenda (Skolnick and Fyfe, 1993). Although such scandals have occurred throughout American history, only in the past quarter-century has the public been aware of the problems of police misconduct, especially illegal use of violence by law enforcement officers and criminal activities associated with police corruption. Most officers do not engage in misconduct, yet these problems deserve study because they raise questions about how much the public can control and trust the police.

Use of Force

Most people cooperate with the police, but there are times when officers must use force to arrest, control disturbances, and deal with the drunken or mentally ill. The police may use *legitimate* force to do their job. It is when they use *excessive* force that they violate the law. But what is excessive force? This is a question that has stumped both officers and experts.

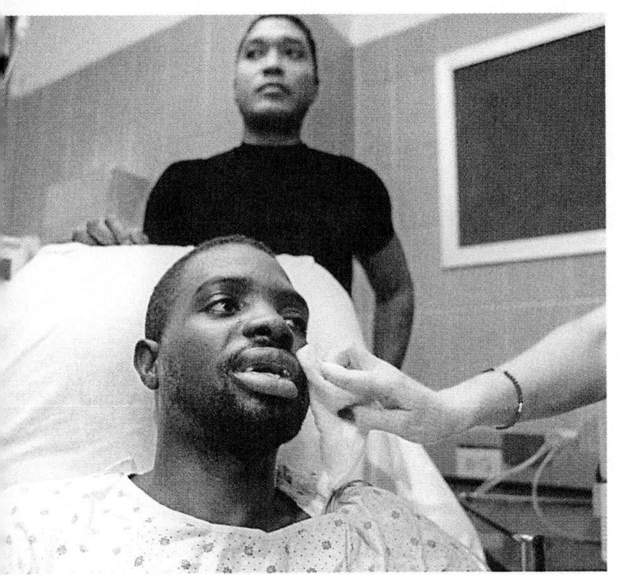

The beating of Haitian immigrant Abner Louima led to the arrest and prosecution of four New York officers. Louima said he was arrested in a late-night brawl outside a nightclub, pushed to the ground, handcuffed and kicked. He alleges he was beaten and sodomized with a toilet plunger.

In cities where racial tensions are high, conflicts between police and residents often result when officers are accused of acting in unprofessional ways. Citizens use the term *police brutality* to describe a wide range of practices, from the use of profane or abusive language to physical force and violence.

Stories of police brutality are not new. However, unlike the untrained officers of the early 1900s, today's officers are supposed to be professionals who know the rules and understand the need for proper conduct. Moreover, when abusive behavior by police comes to light, the public has no way of knowing how often police engage in such actions because most violence is hidden from public view. If a person looking on from a nearby window had not videotaped the beating of Rodney King, the officers could have claimed that they did not use excessive force and King would have had no way to prove that they did. How can we prevent such incidents, especially when they occur without witnesses?

The concept "use of force" takes many forms in practice. The various types of force can be arranged on a continuum ranging from most severe (civilians shot and killed) to least severe (come-alongs). Table 6.2 lists many of these forms of force according to their frequency of use.

How often must force be used? Most research has shown that in police contacts with suspects, force is used infrequently and the type of force used is usually at the low end of the continuum—toward the less severe. Research in Phoenix found that the single largest predictor of police use of force was use of force by the suspect, to which the police then responded (Garner et al., 1995). It is excessive use of force, in violation of department policies and state laws, that constitutes abuse of police power.

By law, the police have the right to use force if necessary to make an arrest, keep the peace, or maintain public order. But just how much force is necessary and under what conditions it may be used are very complex and debatable questions.

Type of Force	Rate per Thousand Sworn Officers
Handcuff/leg restraint	490.4
Bodily force (arm, foot, or leg)	272.2
Come-alongs	226.8
Unholstering weapon	129.9
Swarm	126.7
Twist locks/wrist locks	80.9
Firm grip	57.7
Chemical agents (Mace or Cap-Stun)	36.2
Batons	36.0
Flashlights	21.7
Dog attacks or bites	6.5
Electrical devices (TASER)	5.4
Civilians shot at but not hit	3.0
Other impact devices	2.4
Neck restraints/unconsciousness-rendering holds	1.4
Vehicle rammings	1.0
Civilians shot and killed	0.9
Civilians shot and wounded but not killed	0.2

Table 6.2
Reported uses of force by big-city police.

Police have the legal right to use force to make an arrest, keep the peace, and maintain order. Of the many types of force available to police, the less severe types are used the most often.

SOURCE: Drawn from U.S. Department of Justice, Bureau of Justice Statistics, *National Data Collection on Police Use of Force* (Washington, D.C.: Government Printing Office, 1996), 43.

In particular, the use of deadly force in the apprehending of suspects has become a deeply emotional issue with a direct connection to race relations. Research has shown that the greatest use of deadly force by the police is found in communities with high levels of economic inequality and large minority populations (Sorensen, Marquart, and Brock, 1993:493).

There are no accurate data on the number of people killed by the police. Estimates range between 300 and 600 a year, with about 1,500 more wounded (Sherman and Cohn, 1986). The number of people shot and killed by the police hit a high of 559 in 1975 and has since declined to 385 in 1990, the most recent year for which figures are available (Geller and Scott, 1992; Pate and Fridell, 1993). Even though the numbers have dropped, those killed are disproportionately young black men (Walker, Spohn, and DeLone, 1996:93).

Until the 1980s, the police had broad authority to use deadly force in pursuing suspected felons. Police in about half the states were guided by the common-law principle that allowed the use of whatever force was necessary to arrest a fleeing felon. In 1985 the Supreme Court set a new standard in ***Tennessee v. Garner***, ruling that the police may not use deadly force in apprehending fleeing felons "unless it is necessary to prevent the escape and the officer has probable cause to believe that the suspect poses a significant threat of death or serious physical injury to the officer or others" (*Tennessee v. Garner*, 1985). The case, which dealt with the killing of Edward Garner, a 15-year-old eighth-grader who was shot by a member of the Memphis Police Department, is examined in the accompanying Ideas in Practice.

***Tennessee v. Garner* (1985)**

Deadly force may not be used against an unarmed and fleeing suspect unless it is necessary to prevent the escape and unless the officer has probable cause to believe that the suspect poses a significant threat of death or serious injury to the officers or others.

The standard set by *Tennessee v. Garner* presents problems because it can be hard to judge how dangerous a suspect may be. Because officers must make quick decisions in stressful situations, creating rules that will guide them in every case is impossible. The Court tried to clarify its ruling in the case of *Graham v. Connor* (1989). Here the justices established the standard of "objective reasonableness," saying that the officer's use of deadly force should be judged in terms of the "reasonableness at the moment." This means that the reasonableness of the use of the deadly force should be judged on a case-by-case basis. In its decision, the Court noted that "officers are often forced to make split-second judgments—in circumstances that are tense, uncertain, and rapidly evolving—about the amount of force that is necessary in a particular situation."

The risk of lawsuits by victims of improper police shootings looms over police departments and creates a further incentive for administrators to set and enforce

IDEAS IN PRACTICE

Officer Elton Hymon and his fellow officer, Leslie Wright, of the Memphis Police Department were dispatched to answer a "prowler-inside" call. Arriving at the scene, they saw a woman standing on her porch and gesturing toward the adjacent house. She told them she heard glass breaking and someone was inside next door. While Wright radioed for help, Hymon went to the back of the house, heard a door slam, and saw someone run across the backyard toward a 6-foot chainlink fence. With his flashlight, Hymon was able to see that the fleeing young male was unarmed. The officer called out, "Police! Halt!" but the young man began to climb the fence. Convinced that if he made it over the fence he would escape, Hymon fired, hitting him in the back of the head. The fleeing suspect died on the operating table, the ten dollars he had stolen in his pocket. Hymon was acting under Tennessee law and Memphis Police Department policy.

Given the Supreme Court's decision in *Tennessee v. Garner*, what should police officers do in such situations? What if police do not know whether the fleeing suspect is armed?

standards for the use of force. However, as long as officers carry weapons, some improper shootings will occur. Training, internal review of incidents, and disciplining or firing trigger-happy officers may help reduce the use of unnecessary force (Fyfe, 1993:128; Blumberg, 1989:442).

Although progress has been made in reducing police brutality and misuse of deadly force, corruption is still a major problem. We turn to this issue next.

Corruption

Police corruption has a long history in America. Early in the twentieth century, city officials organized liquor and gambling businesses for their personal gain. In many cities ties were maintained between politicians and police officials so that favored clients would be protected and competitors harassed. Much of the Progressive movement to reform the police was designed to combat such corrupt arrangements. Although these political ties have been reduced in most cities, corruption still exists.

Sometimes corruption is defined so broadly that it ranges from accepting a free cup of coffee (see A Question of Ethics) to robbing businesses or beating suspects. Obviously, *corruption* is not easily defined, and there are disagreements about what it includes. As a useful starting point, we can focus on the distinction between corrupt officers who are "grass eaters" and those who are "meat eaters."

Grass Eaters and Meat Eaters

"Grass eaters" are officers who accept payoffs that the routines of police work bring their way. "Meat eaters" are officers who actively use their power for personal gain. Although meat eaters are few in number, their actions make headlines when they are discovered. By contrast, because "grass eaters" are numerous, they make corruption seem acceptable and promote a code of secrecy that brands any officer who exposes corruption as a traitor. Grass eaters are the heart of the problem and are often harder to detect.

In the past, low salaries, politics, and poor hiring practices have been cited as factors contributing to corruption. While some claim that a few "rotten apples" should not taint an entire police force, corruption in some departments has been so rampant that the rotten-apple theory does not fully explain the situation. Some explanations are based on the nature of police work. Much police work involves enforcement of laws in situations in which there is no complainant or it is unclear whether a law has been broken. Moreover, most police work is carried out at the officer's own discretion, without direct supervision. Thus, police officers may have many opportunities to gain benefits by using their discretion to protect people who engage in illegal conduct.

There will always be opportunities for corruption when police administrators do not monitor the activities of officers. Police departments in New York, Philadelphia, Miami, and New Orleans have been rocked by scandal. In Miami, ten officers pleaded guilty to murder, conspiracy, or drug-trafficking charges for participation in a $13-million theft of cocaine from a boat anchored in the Miami River. Three drug smugglers drowned when they jumped into the water as the officers were approaching. The officers later sold the cocaine they had taken. In New York's Thirtieth Precinct, investigators found officers involved in drug dealing. Further, ninety-eight convicted drug dealers were freed because it was shown that officers gave false testimony at their trials. Thirty-three officers have been convicted of perjury and are now serving prison terms (*New York Times*, January 5, 1997, p. A1).

Enforcement of vice laws, especially drug laws, creates major problems for police agencies. In many cities vice offenders can easily afford to make large payments to unethical officers to protect themselves against prosecution. Police operations against victimless crimes are proactive, making the problem worse. Unless drugs are being sold openly, upsetting the residents of a neighborhood, no one will complain if officers ignore or even profit from the activities of drug dealers.

Over time, illegal activity may become accepted as normal. Ellwyn Stoddard, who studied "blue-coat crime," has said that it can become part of an "identifiable informal 'code.'" He suggests that officers are socialized to the code early in their careers. Those who "snitch" on their fellow officers may be ostracized. When corruption comes to official attention, officers protect the code by distancing themselves from the known offender rather than stopping their own improper conduct (Stoddard, 1968:205).

Police corruption has three major effects on law enforcement: (1) suspects are left free to engage in further crime, (2) morale is damaged and supervision becomes lax, and (3) the image of the police suffers. The image of the police agency is very important in light of the need for citizen cooperation. When the police are seen as not much different from the "crooks," effective crime control is even farther out of reach.

What is startling is that many people do not equate police corruption with other forms of crime. Some believe that police corruption is tolerable as long as the streets are safe. This attitude ignores the fact that corrupt officers are serving only themselves and are not committed to serving the public.

A Question of ETHICS

Bianco's Restaurant is a popular, noisy place in a tough section of town. Open from 6:30 A.M. until midnight, it is usually crowded with regulars who like the low prices and ample portions, teenagers planning their next exploit, and people grabbing a quick bite to eat.

Officer Buchanan has just finished his late-night "lunch" before going back on duty. As he walks toward the cash register, Cheryl Bianco, the manager, takes the bill from his hand and says, "This one's on me, John. It's nice to have you with us."

Officer Buchanan protests, "Thanks, but I'd better pay for my own meal."

"Why do you say that? The other cops don't object to getting a free meal now and then."

"Well, they may feel that way, but I don't want anyone to get the idea that I'm giving you special treatment," Buchanan replies.

"Come off it. Who's going to think that? I don't expect special treatment; we just want you to know we appreciate your work."

What issues are involved here? If Buchanan refuses to accept Bianco's generosity, what is he saying about his role as a police officer? If he accepts the offer, what does that say? Might people who overhear the conversation draw other meanings from it? Is turning down a free $6.50 meal that important?

CHECKPOINT

11. What kinds of practices do citizens view as police brutality?
12. When may the police use force?
13. How did the Supreme Court rule in *Tennessee v. Garner*?
14. What is the difference between "grass eaters" and "meat eaters"?

CIVIC ACCOUNTABILITY

Relations between citizens and the police depend greatly on citizen confidence that officers will behave in accordance with the law and with department guidelines. Rapport with the community is enhanced when citizens feel sure that the police will protect their persons and property and the rights guaranteed by the Constitution. It is hard to strike a balance between making the police responsive to citizen complaints and burdening them with a flood of citizen complaints.

The main challenge in making the police more accountable is to use citizen input to force police to follow the law and department guidelines without placing too many limits on their ability to carry out their primary functions. At present, four less-than-perfect techniques are used in efforts to control the police: (1) internal affairs units, (2) civilian review boards, (3) standards and accreditation, and (4) civil liability lawsuits.

Internal Affairs Units

Controlling the police is mainly an internal matter that administrators must give top priority. The community must be confident that the department has procedures to ensure that officers will protect the rights of citizens. Nevertheless, many departments have no formal complaint procedures, and when such procedures do exist, they often seem to be designed to discourage citizen input.

internal affairs unit

A branch of a police department that receives and investigates complaints against officers alleging violation of rules and policies.

Depending on the size of the department, a single officer or an entire section may serve as an **internal affairs unit** that receives and investigates complaints against officers. An officer charged with misconduct can face criminal prosecution or disciplinary action that can lead to resignation, dismissal, or suspension. Officers assigned to the internal affairs unit have duties similar to those of the inspector general's staff in the military. They must investigate complaints against their fellow officers.

The internal affairs unit must be given enough resources to carry out its mission, as well as direct access to the chief. Some internal investigators may assume that a citizen complaint is an attack on the police as a whole and will shield officers against such complaints. When this happens, administrators do not get the information they need to correct a problem. The public, in turn, may come to believe that the department condones the practices they complain of and that filing a complaint is pointless. Moreover, even when the top administrator seeks to attack misconduct, it may be hard to persuade police to testify against fellow officers.

Civilian Review Boards

If a police department cannot show the public that it effectively combats corruption among officers, the public is likely to demand that a *civilian review board* investigate the department. These boards are organized so that complaints can be channeled through a committee of persons who are not sworn police officers. The organization and powers of civilian review boards vary, but all oversee and review how police departments handle citizen complaints. The boards may also recommend remedial action. They do not have the power to investigate or discipline individual officers (Walker and Bumphus, 1991).

During the 1980s, as minorities gained more political power in large cities, there was a revival of civilian review boards. A 1994 survey found that 66 law enforcement agencies had some form of civilian review. Of the 50 largest cities, 36 now have civilian review boards, as do 13 of the 50 next largest cities (Walker and Wright, 1995).

The main argument made by the police against civilian review boards is that people outside law enforcement do not understand the problems of policing. The police contend that civilian oversight lowers morale and hinders performance and that officers will be less effective if they are worried about possible disciplinary action. In reality, however, the boards have not been harsh (Kerstetter, 1985:162).

Review of police actions occurs some time after the incident has taken place and usually comes down to the officer's word against that of the complainant. Given the low visibility of the incidents that lead to complaints, a great many complaints are not substantiated. For example, only 8 percent of complaints against police in San Francisco in 1990 were upheld (Skolnick and Fyfe, 1993:229). The effectiveness of civilian review boards has not been tested, but their presence may improve police-citizen relations.

Standards and Accreditation

One way to increase police accountability is to require that police actions meet nationally recognized standards. The movement to accredit departments that meet these standards has gained momentum during the past decade. It has the support of the Commission on Accreditation for Law Enforcement Agencies (CALEA), a private nonprofit corporation formed by four professional associations: the International Association of Chiefs of Police (IACP), the National Organization of Black Law Enforcement Executives (NOBLE), the National Sheriffs Association (NSA), and the Police Executive Research Forum (PERF).

The *Standards*, first published by CALEA in 1983, have been updated from time to time. There are now 900 standards organized under forty-eight headings. Each standard is a statement, with a brief explanation, that sets forth clear requirements.

For example, under "Limits of Authority," Standard 1.2.2 requires that "a written directive governs the use of discretion by sworn officers." The explanation states: "In many agencies, the exercise of discretion is defined by a combination of written enforcement policies, training and supervision. The written directive should define the limits of individual discretion and provide guidelines for exercising discretion within those limits." (Commission on Accreditation, 1989. *Standards*:1-2). Because police departments have said almost nothing about their use of discretion, this is a major shift. However, the standard still is not specific enough. For example, does it cover stop-and-frisk actions, the handling of drunks, and the use of informants?

Police accreditation is voluntary. Departments contact CALEA, which helps them in their efforts to meet the standards. This process involves self-evaluation by department executives, the development of policies that meet the standards, and training of officers. CALEA personnel act like a military inspector general, visiting the department, examining its policies, and seeing if the standards are met in its daily operations. Certification is given to departments that meet the standards. The standards can be used as a management tool, with officers trained to know the standards and to be accountable for their actions.

Obviously, the standards do not guarantee that police officers in an accredited department will avoid misconduct. However, they are a major step toward providing

clear guidelines to officers about proper behavior. Accreditation can also show the public that the department is committed to making sure officers carry out their duties in an ethical, professional manner.

Civil Liability Suits

Civil lawsuits against departments for police misconduct can increase civic accountability. Only recently has it been possible for citizens to sue public officials. In 1961, the U.S. Supreme Court ruled that Section 1983 of the Civil Rights Act of 1871 allows citizens to sue public officials for violations of their civil rights. This right was extended in 1978 when the Supreme Court ruled in *Monell v. Department of Social Services for the City of New York* that individual officials and the agency may be sued when a person's civil rights are violated by the agency's "customs and usages." If an individual can show that harm was caused by employees whose wrongful acts were the result of these "customs, practices, and policies, including poor training and supervision," then he or she can sue.

Lawsuits charging brutality, false arrest, and negligence are being brought in both state and federal courts. Damage awards in the millions of dollars have been granted by courts in a number of states, and police departments have settled some suits out of court. For example, a Michigan court awarded $5.7 million to the heirs of a man who had been mistakenly shot by a Detroit officer, and Boston paid $500,000 to the parents of a teenager who was shot to death. The total amount paid by city governments in a year can be quite high. In 1990, Los Angeles paid $8 million in damages and Detroit paid $20 million (del Carmen, 1991).

Civil liability rulings by the courts tend to be simple and severe: officials and municipalities are ordered to pay a sum of money, and that judgment can be enforced by the courts. With the potential for costly judgments, police departments have an incentive to improve the training and supervision of officers. Smith and Hurst asked a sample of police executives to rank the policy issues most likely to be affected by civil liability decisions. The top-ranked issues were use of force, pursuit driving, and improper arrests (Smith and Hurst, 1996). Most departments have liability insurance, and many officers have their own insurance policies.

The courts have ruled that police work must follow generally accepted professional practices and standards. The potential for civil suits seems to have led to some changes in policy. Plaintiffs' victories in civil suits have spurred accreditation efforts because police executives believe that liability can be avoided or reduced if they can show that their officers are meeting the highest professional standards. In fact, insurance companies providing civil liability protection now offer discounts to accredited departments.

CHECKPOINT

15. What are the four methods used to increase the civic accountability of the police?
16. What is an internal affairs unit?
17. Why are civilian review boards not more common?
18. What is the importance of the decision in *Monell v. Department of Social Services for the City of New York*?

PRIVATE POLICING

Private security is assuming an increasingly large role in American society. Tim Hitt, security guard at the Poughkeepsie (N.Y.) Galleria mall, says he patrols so as to provide a "certain level of calmness" in the shopping center.

In recent years, more and more firms have employed private security forces to deal with shoplifting, employee pilfering, robbery, and airplane hijacking. Today, retail and industrial firms spend nearly as much for private protection as all localities spend for police protection. Many private groups, such as residents of wealthy suburbs, have hired private police to patrol their neighborhoods.

About 4,000 private agencies now employ a total of 1.5 million people in security operations. It has been estimated that by the year 2000 more than $100 billion will be spent annually on private security by businesses, organizations, and individuals. By then private security companies will employ more officers (1.9 million) than the federal, state, and local public police forces combined (700,000) (Cunningham, Strauchs, and Van Meter, 1991). Figure 6.3 compares this dramatic increase in private police to the numbers of public police.

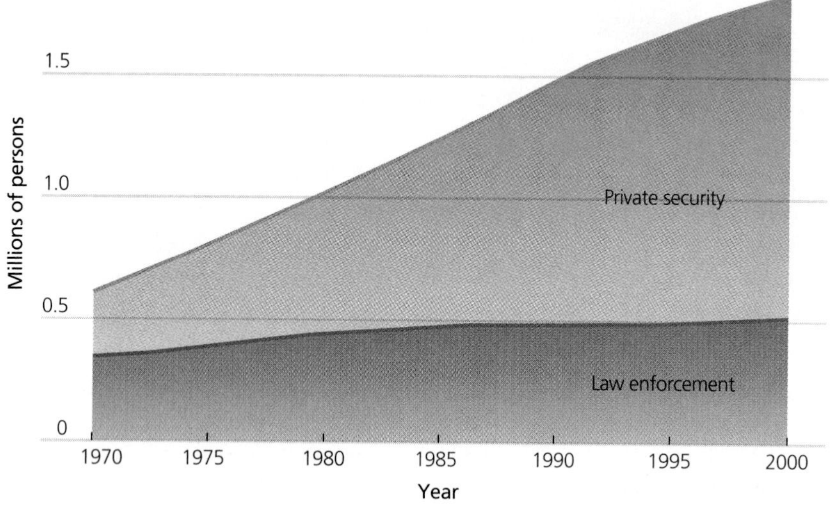

Private security and law enforcement employment

Figure 6.3
Employment in private and public protection, 1970-2000 (projected)

The number of people employed by private security firms has surpassed the number employed by the public police and is growing. Such a large private force presents questions for the criminal justice system.

SOURCE: William Cunningham, John Strauchs, and Clifford Van Meter, *Private Security: Patterns and Trends* (Washington, D.C.: National Institute of Justice, 1991), 3.

The rise of private agencies has occurred for a number of reasons, including (1) an increase in crimes in the workplace, (2) an increase in fear (real or perceived) of crime, (3) the fiscal crises of state and local governments, which have limited public protection, and (4) increased public and business awareness and use of more cost-effective private security services (Cunningham, Strauchs, and Van Meter, 1990:236).

Functions of Private Police

The activities of private security personnel vary greatly: some act as guards and call the police at the first sign of trouble; others have the power to carry out patrol and investigative duties similar to those of police officers; and still others rely on their

WORK*Perspective*

Radford W. Jones
Former Manager of Security and Fire Protection
Ford Motor Company

I wanted to be a Secret Service agent since writing a paper on the agency in high school. While a student in the School of Police Administration (now School of Criminal Justice) at Michigan State University, I applied to be a special agent. I later received my appointment after working for one year as a police officer.

During my twenty-six years with the U.S. Secret Service, I worked on criminal investigations and physical protection of the President, Vice President, presidential candidates, and visiting heads of state. My criminal investigations involved pursuing counterfeiters, check forgers, and people who made threats against the President and others under Secret Service protection. In my physical protection work, I worked for U.S. Presidents and Vice Presidents from John F. Kennedy through George Bush. When I retired from the Secret Service, I was a special agent in charge of the Detroit field office.

Upon my retirement from the Secret Service, I joined the Ford Motor Company to handle executive and personnel security matters around the world. Corporate executives and families are sometimes targets of kidnappers, political factions, or disturbed individuals, and thus corporations have become increasingly aware of the need to protect personnel. As manager of security and fire protection, I was responsible for a broad range of security issues: from reducing risks of burglary and fires or explosions at company facilities to preventing thefts of company property and materials by employees, to preventing competing companies and foreign countries from stealing information on new products and technologies. My training and experience in the Secret Service prepared me to handle the complex range of security responsibilities at Ford. I know other retired federal law enforcement officials who were also hired by various corporations to handle security matters.

The transition from a public law enforcement agency to corporate security can be difficult and requires adjustment. While law enforcement is an important national priority, security is not the core business function of a corporation. The primary focus of corporate executives is usually on issues other than security, so security managers can easily feel overlooked in the business organization. But despite the differences between public law enforcement and private security, many of the skills learned in law enforcement—planning, organizing, managing personnel, and investigating—are important for effectiveness in corporate security.

Professionalism and ethics are essential in both public law enforcement and private security. Just like law enforcement officers, private security officials must maintain the confidence and trust of the people they serve. Unfortunately, employees in any setting, including security, can lose sight of their important role and responsibilities. As a supervisor in government and the private sector, I sometimes encountered situations in which employees intentionally filed inaccurate reports, often to hide their own failure to follow proper procedures when some incident occurred, or violated procedures. In these situations I had to

face the decision of whether or not to dismiss the employee. Sometimes the details were misreported or the nature of the procedures ignored were only "small" violations in the minds of these employees, and when caught, they believed they should receive only a reprimand. Such thinking ignores the important responsibilities of security officials. They are trusted to keep keys to buildings, transport money and other valuable property, and control access to sensitive information. Because of these important responsibilities, they cannot pick and choose when they will behave professionally and ethically. I believe that they must always behave in ways that maintain trust and confidence, and I made personnel decisions based on that belief, even when it meant making the difficult decision to terminate someone's employment.

Private security personnel often do not view themselves in the same role as law enforcement officers. While their roles differ, my experiences convinced me that officials who are responsible for people's safety and for the security of valuable property must live up to the highest standards of ethics and professionalism, whether they work for the government or for a private corporation.

WORK*Perspective*

presence, and the ability to make a "citizen's arrest" to deter lawbreakers. In most cases, private persons are authorized by law to make an arrest only when a felony has been committed in their presence. Thus private security companies risk being held liable for false arrest and violation of civil rights.

Some states have passed laws that give civil immunity to store personnel who reasonably but mistakenly detain people suspected of shoplifting. More ambiguous is the search of the person or property of a suspect by a private guard. The suspect may resist the search and file a civil suit against the guard. If such a search yields evidence of a crime, the evidence may not be admitted in court. Yet the Supreme Court has not applied the *Miranda* ruling to private police. Federal law bars private individuals from engaging in wiretapping, and information so gathered cannot be entered as evidence at trial.

Security managers are willing to accept increased responsibility for minor criminal incidents that occur within their jurisdictions, according to a study sponsored by the National Institute of Justice (NIJ, 1984. *Research in Brief*). They may perform such tasks as responding to burglar alarms, investigating misdemeanors, and carrying out preliminary investigations of other crimes. Law enforcement administrators indicated in the same study that they might be willing to transfer some of these tasks to private security firms. They cited a number of police tasks that are "potentially more cost-effectively performed by private security," such as providing security in public buildings and enforcing parking regulations. In some parts of the country personnel from private firms are already performing some of these tasks.

Private Employment of Public Police

Private firms are often eager to hire public police officers on a part-time basis. These officers retain their full powers and status as police personnel even when they work for a private firm while off duty. Although 20 percent of departments forbid "moonlighting," about 150,000 police officers still work part-time for private firms (Reiss, 1988). While the use of off-duty officers expands the number and visibility of law enforcement officers, it also raises issues, two of which are discussed here.

Conflict of Interest

Police officers must avoid any appearance of conflict of interest when they accept private employment. They are barred from jobs that conflict with their public duties. For example, they may not work as process servers, bill collectors, repossessors, or preemployment investigators for private firms. They are also barred from working as investigators for criminal defense attorneys or as bail bondsmen. They may not work in places that profit from gambling, and many departments do not allow officers to work in bars or other places where regulated goods, such as alcohol, are sold. It is hard to know the full range of situations in which private employment of an officer might harm the image of the police or create a conflict with police responsibilities. Thus, departments need to be aware of new situations that might require that they refine their regulations for private employment of off-duty officers.

Management Prerogatives

Another issue concerns the impact of private employment on the capabilities of the local police department. Private employment cannot be allowed to tire officers and impair their ability to protect the public when they are on duty. Late-night duties as a private security officer, for example, may reduce an officer's ability to police effectively the next morning.

Departments require that officers request permission for outside work. Such permission may be denied for a number of reasons. Officers may not be allowed to perform work that lowers the dignity of the police, is too risky or dangerous, is not in the "home" jurisdiction, requires more than eight hours of off-duty service, or interferes with department schedules.

The Public-Private Interface

The relationship between public and private law enforcement is a concern for police officials. Private agents work for the people who employ them, and their goals may not always serve the public interest. Questions have been raised about the power of private security agents to make arrests, conduct searches, and take part in undercover investigations. A key issue is the boundary between the work of the police and that of private agencies. Lack of coordination and communication between public and private agencies has led to botched investigations, destruction of evidence, and overzealousness.

Growing awareness of this problem has led to efforts to have private security agents work more closely with the police. However, many security managers in private firms tend to treat crimes by employees as internal matters that do not concern the police. They report *UCR* index crimes to the police, but employee theft, insurance fraud, industrial espionage, commercial bribery, and computer crime tend not to be reported to public authorities. In such cases the chief concern of private firms is to prevent losses and protect assets. Although some such incidents are reported, most are resolved through internal procedures ("private justice"). When such crimes are discovered, the offender may be "convicted" and punished within the firm by forced restitution, loss of the job, and the spreading of information about the incident throughout the industry.

Private firms often bypass the criminal justice system so they don't have to deal with prosecution policies, administrative delays, rules that would open the firms' internal affairs to public scrutiny, and bad publicity. Thus, the question arises, To what extent does a parallel system of private justice exist with regard to some offenders and some crimes (Davis, Lundman, and Martinez, 1991)?

Recruitment and Training

A major concern of law enforcement officials and civil libertarians is the recruitment and training of private security personnel. Studies have shown that such personnel often have little education and training; because the pay is low, the work often attracts people who cannot find other jobs or who seek temporary work. This portrait has been challenged by William Walsh, who argues that differences between private and public police are not that striking (Walsh, 1989).

The growth of private policing has brought calls for the screening and licensing of its personnel. Less than half of the states have such requirements. In some states, security firms are licensed by the attorney general, while in others this is done by the local police. In general, however, there is little regulation of private security firms.

Private policing has grown in response to a perceived need. The need may stem from the higher crime rates, but it may also come from a belief that the police cannot effectively carry out certain tasks. It is important to distinguish between public and private policing and to ensure that private policing does not hamper the work of law enforcement or create new problems by recruiting unqualified personnel, misusing off-duty police officers, or failing to communicate with police departments.

CHECKPOINT

19. What is the significance of the growth of private policing?
20. When may a private person make an arrest?

Summary

- To meet current and future challenges, the police must recruit and train individuals who will uphold the law and receive citizen support.
- Improvements have been made during the past quarter-century in recruiting more officers who are women, racial and ethnic minorities, and well-educated applicants.
- The police work in an environment greatly influenced by their subculture.
- The concept of the working personality helps us understand the influence of the police subculture on how individual officers see their world.
- The isolation of the police strengthens bonds among officers but may also add to job stress.
- For the police to be effective they must maintain their connection with the community.
- Policing in a multicultural society requires an appreciation of the attitudes, customs, and languages of minority-group members.
- The problems of police misuse of force and corruption cause erosions of community support.

- Internal affairs units, civilian review boards, standards and accreditation, and civil liability suits are four approaches designed to increase police accountability to citizens.
- The expansion of private policing adds a new dimension to how order is maintained and laws are enforced.

Questions for Review

1. How do recruitment and training practices affect policing?
2. What is meant by the police subculture, and how does it influence an officer's work?
3. What elements in the police officer's "working personality" influence an officer's work?
4. What are the pros and cons of the major approaches to making the police accountable to citizens?
5. What has the Supreme Court ruled regarding police use of deadly force?
6. What are the problems associated with private policing?

ANSWERS TO CHECKPOINTS

1. High school diploma, good physical condition, lack of a criminal record.
2. Preservice training, usually in a police academy.
3. On the job.
4. Better educated, more women and minority officers.
5. Threat of danger, need to establish and maintain one's own authority.
6. External stress, organizational stress, personal stress, operational stress.
7. Stereotyping, cultural differences, language differences.
8. Young, low-income, racial-minority males.
9. Permissive law enforcement and police abuse of power.
10. Assist the police by reporting incidents and providing information.
11. Profane or abusive language, physical force, violence.
12. The police may use force if necessary to make an arrest, to keep the peace, or to maintain order.
13. Deadly force may not be used in apprehending a fleeing felon unless it is necessary to prevent the escape and unless the officer has probable cause to believe that the suspect poses a significant threat of death or serious physical injury to the officer or to others.
14. Grass eaters are officers who accept payoffs that police work brings their way. Meat eaters are officers who actively use their power for personal gain.
15. Internal affairs units, civilian review boards, standards and accreditation, civil liability suits.
16. A unit within the police department designated to receive and investigate complaints against officers.
17. Opposition by the police.
18. Allows citizens to sue individual officers and the agency when an individual's civil rights are violated by the agency's "customs and usages."
19. Public concern for order.
20. When a felony has been committed in his or her presence.

INSIDE THE CRIMINAL JUSTICE SYSTEM AND BEYOND: ONE MAN'S JOURNEY

Stepping into a New World: Arrested, Booked, Charged, Jailed, and Investigated

By the mid-1970s I had spent time in jail and was on probation for burglary. My probation officer, thinking I could never stay "clean" (not use heroin), thought I belonged in San Quentin and told me he'd do everything within his power to send me there. He tested my urine for drugs and checked my arms for needle marks with a magnifying glass two or three times a week until I couldn't take it anymore. Eventually I quit reporting and went "on the run." The fact that I had skipped probation and there was now an arrest warrant with my name on it left me feeling like a desperado. Now it was time to get really hooked.

I began selling dope to support my habit. I was living in a Manhattan Beach motel and selling about a thousand dollars' worth of heroin a week. For me this was "doing good," because I wasn't stealing. Not only that, my customers seemed to appreciate my services.

Arrest

One Thursday afternoon, while calling my connection from a phone booth in front of my motel, I noticed several men in suits knocking on the door of my room. I instantly knew they were cops and that I needed to get away from there fast. Trying to be discreet, I opened the booth door and quietly started walking away. Before I took two steps a woman came running out of the nearby motel office, pointing at me and yelling, "There he is! There he is!" Because of the many people she had observed coming and going from my room, she suspected me of dealing and called the Manhattan Beach City Police Department.

I started running but didn't get far. Besides the cops upstairs other officers were surrounding the motel. Though I hadn't noticed, two of them were within ten feet of where I stood. As soon as I realized that I had been spotted by the police, I bolted from that phone booth as if my life depended on it. Ignoring their commands to "halt," I ran as fast as I could. Before I had gone a hundred yards, they tackled me to the ground and cuffed me. At that moment I felt a sense of fear, helplessness, and anger that is difficult to describe. I was under arrest—again. While one cop held me from behind, the other went into my pockets and pulled out eleven balloons filled with heroin. The plainclothes cops found more heroin, other drugs, and several hundred dollars in my room. Next thing I knew somebody was reading me my Miranda rights ("You have the right to remain silent....") and I found myself sitting in the back seat of a cop car, alone, angry, scared, and cuffed, the crackling sounds and voices from the police radio relentlessly assaulting my ears. Welcome to my nightmare—live from Los Angeles County.

During the ride to the Manhattan Beach City Jail, the police lockup, I felt helpless and desperate, like a captured animal. The cops in the front seat seemed excited as they talked about what had just gone down—the chase, the bust. As I listened to their conversation I got a sense of what I must mean to them—a good catch, evidence of a job well done, but little else. They talked about me as if I were invisible. That my whole world had just caved in was apparently insignificant to them. Underneath all these feelings was the unquestionable certainty that I would soon become sick from heroin withdrawal.

Booking

We quickly arrived at the local police lockup—a small facility that functioned as a way station, a place where recently captured "suspects" are held until they can bail out or be transported to the county jail. Once inside I was promptly booked, a process that included being notified of my charges (given paperwork clarifying the specific crimes I was being accused of—possession of heroin with the intent to sell was the most serious) and the amount of my bail (which was high), photographed, fingerprinted, and strip-searched. Because I could not make bail, I was held for a court appearance and confined to a small cellblock (the tank), where I was given a blanket, toilet

ONE MAN'S JOURNEY (CONTINUED)

paper, and food twice a day. Because Friday was a holiday I would not be sent to the county jail until Monday. It was here that I began kicking a heroin habit that was so bad I did not sleep for the following three weeks.

For the next four days this cellblock was my home. I had never been so physically addicted or experienced such severe withdrawal. I was weak, couldn't eat, ached all over, and had the sweats, chills, and diarrhea.

While in the lockup a few other men came and went. Most had been arrested for crimes that were not as serious as mine—not paying traffic tickets and the like. But they say misery loves company, and having other people around *did* help. In such facilities there is usually a high level of camaraderie among inmates. Having been stripped of everything we take for granted "on the streets," like personal autonomy, heterosexual relations, jobs, safety, and loved ones, we are left with just about all there is to associate with and find meaning from on the inside—each other.

On the third day I was called out of the tank and placed inside a room with two men who looked like addicts. One was Chicano and the other white. They had tattoos, tracks on their arms (scars from needle marks), and talked like convicts. By this time I was extremely weak—neither my vision nor my perception was very sharp. To my surprise these guys turned out to be narcotics officers who worked for the local police department. I felt like I was in the Twilight Zone. They wanted me to tell on my connection. "We know you were scoring ounces. We figure if you tell us who your man is we can get to the guy who has the pounds." My head began to spin.

Even though it happens a lot, being a police informant is taboo among prisoners. Informants often spend years in protective custody (special sections of jails or prisons separated from the main population) or are killed for providing information that leads to further arrests. Nevertheless, police relentlessly seek new informants. Payment for cooperation varies. A good example of this is the witness protection programs that keep all sorts of people, including murderers, out of prison in exchange for the information they provide.

I was still consumed by my need for heroin as I sat facing these guys. Sick as I was, I would do just about anything for a shot. Except tell. They said if I cooperated they would give me enough dope to "get well." I told them I could never give up my connection because he was my friend. *How could I live with myself if I did that?* They told me they'd set it up so nobody would have to know (apparently they didn't understand *why* I couldn't do it). Their plan was for me to have my connection meet me on a street corner and sell me some dope while they watched from a hidden location. Once the buy was made they would rush in, arrest us, take us both to jail, *and then let me go*. All my charges would be dropped and they would cut me loose. Luckily, their offer did not tempt me. I knew what time it was. I went to bed in the tank that night sick as a dog, but I still had my dignity. The following Monday I was transported in chains to the county jail.

Part III

Courts

7 COURTS AND PRETRIAL PROCESSES

8 PROSECUTION AND DEFENSE

9 DETERMINATION OF GUILT: PLEA BARGAINING AND TRIALS

10 PUNISHMENT AND SENTENCING

IN A DEMOCRACY, the arrest of a person is only the beginning of a complex process designed to separate the guilty from the innocent. Part Three examines the process by which guilt is determined in accordance with the law's requirements, as well as the processes and underlying philosophies of the punishment that further separates the convicted from the acquitted.

Here we look at the work of prosecutors, defense attorneys, bondsmen, and judges to understand the contribution each makes toward the ultimate decision. It is during the adjudicatory stage that the goals of an administrative system blunt the force of the adversarial process prescribed by law. Although courtroom activities may get more attention in the media, much of the action doesn't appear in court. Most decisions relating to the disposition of a case are made in less-public surroundings. After studying these chapters, we should think about whether justice is served by processes that are more like bargaining than the adversarial combat between two lawyers that we expect. We may also consider whether the punishments our courts hand out are doing the job they are supposed to do in punishing offenders.

Chapter 7

Courts and Pretrial Processes

The Structure of American Courts

Effective Management of the State Courts

To Be a Judge

- *Who Becomes a Judge?*
- *Functions of the Judge*
- *How to Become a Judge*

From Arrest to Trial or Plea

Bail: Pretrial Release

- *The Reality of the Bail System*
- *Bail Bondsmen*
- *Setting Bail*
- *Reforming the Bail System*

Pretrial Detention

The Courtroom: How It Functions

- *The Courtroom Workgroup*
- *The Impact of Courtroom Workgroups*

ON SEPTEMBER 22, 1997, nationally known sportscaster Marv Albert entered the Circuit Court building in Arlington, Virginia, to begin his trial on sexual assault charges. Because he had spent three decades as the broadcast voice for the New York Knicks basketball team and New York Rangers hockey team as well as NBC network sports broadcasts, Albert and the allegations against him received tremendous publicity. From the moment allegations against him emerged, Albert insisted that he was completely innocent. Now he faced the possibility of life in prison for allegations that he assaulted a woman and forced her to have sex with him in a hotel room.

Courts are the ultimate destination for criminal cases, whether the alleged offenses involved poor people on a street corner or celebrities in expensive hotel rooms. In courts, formal procedures guide the determination of guilt. Even when cases end through plea bargaining, court procedures shape the outcome. During negotiations, attorneys think about rules of evidence and procedure that may strengthen or weaken their bargaining position if the opposing side actually decides to carry the case through to trial. Attorneys must also remain aware of the judge's viewpoint, since the judge must approve any plea agreement.

Judges are key figures in any criminal case, whether they preside over a trial or merely decide whether to approve a plea agreement. Some judges work within awe-inspiring court buildings, with marble columns and wood paneling. Others preside over a simple room filled with tables and chairs in a small town. In any setting, judges embody the authority and power of the courts. Judges try to be neutral and fair because they must uphold the image of the courts as institutions dedicated to justice.

The judge is important even before the defendant arrives to begin the jury selection process. Pretrial processes help lay the groundwork for the trial—or the plea bargain. In the Albert case, for example, defense attorney Roy Black filed pretrial motions asking Judge Benjamin Kendrick to dismiss the case. Black claimed that the allegations against Albert were not stated properly in court papers when he was formally charged with the crimes (*Washington Post*, September 17, 1997, p. B6).

Albert's attorney also asked the judge to permit presentation of evidence on the victim's past relationships and sexual history, apparently in an effort to show that she willingly engaged in sexual relationships and liked to get attention from her involvement with prominent men. Judge Kendrick denied Albert's requests.

The judge has an important role before trial in determining the admissibility of evidence and whether court procedures were followed properly. Judges' rulings prior to a trial can often lead one side or the other to offer a plea agreement if it appears that the trial will be unsuccessful for them. As it turned out, after two days of trial, Albert entered a guilty plea to misdemeanor charges in exchange for the prosecutor's dismissal of the pending felony charges. Albert's attorney claimed that his client pleaded guilty only because the judge rejected the evidence about the victim's past. The attorney indicated that if the jury knew about the alleged victim's involvement with various men, they would not believe that Albert forced himself upon her. Albert and his attorney feared that he would be convicted of felony charges if the case moved forward, especially because the prosecutor had presented evidence about Albert's past behavior with other women, which seemed to show a pattern of abusive actions consistent with the allegations in this case. As in many other cases, the judge's discretionary decisions about admissible evidence and other matters helped determine the outcome of the case.

In this chapter, we will examine courts, the setting in which criminal defendants' cases are processed. We will look at judges and their important role in criminal cases. In particular, we will look at the pretrial processes that help determine the fates of criminal defendants.

Questions for Inquiry

What is the structure of the American court system?

What qualities are desired in a judge, and how are judges chosen?

How does the bail system work, and how is bail set?

Why might an accused person be detained before trial?

What is the courtroom workgroup, and how does this concept help explain court actions?

THE STRUCTURE OF AMERICAN COURTS

The United States has a dual court system in which separate federal and state court systems handle matters from throughout the nation. Each system has its own **jurisdiction**, the authority it has over a particular geographic area and set of laws. Other countries have a single national court system, but American rules and traditions permit states to create their own court systems to handle most legal matters, including most crimes.

The federal courts oversee a limited range of criminal cases. For example, they deal with people accused of violating the criminal laws of the national government. Counterfeiting, kidnapping, smuggling, and drug trafficking are examples of federal crimes. But such cases account for only a small portion of the criminal cases that pass through American courts each year. For every criminal case filed in federal courts, nearly 300 are filed in state courts, because most crimes are defined by state laws (Administrative Office of the U.S. Courts, 1994. *Judicial Business of the U.S. Courts*:7-9). The U.S. Supreme Court oversees both court systems, and the Constitution protects the rights of defendants in federal and state criminal cases.

Both the federal and state court systems have trial and appellate courts. There are three levels of courts: **appellate courts, trial courts of general jurisdiction,** and **trial courts of limited jurisdiction.**

Cases begin in the trial courts, which handle determinations of guilt and sentencing. Cases move to appellate courts if defendants claim that errors by police or the trial court contributed to their convictions. Further appeals may be filed with a state supreme court or the U.S. Supreme Court, depending on which court system the case is in and what kind of legal argument is being made. Among the appellate

jurisdiction

The geographic territory or legal boundaries within which control may be exercised; the range of a court's authority.

appellate courts

Courts that do not try criminal cases but hear appeals of decisions of lower courts.

trial courts of general jurisdiction

Criminal courts with jurisdiction over all offenses, including felonies. In some states these courts may also hear appeals.

trial courts of limited jurisdiction

Criminal courts with trial jurisdiction over misdemeanor cases and preliminary matters in felony cases. Sometimes these courts hold felony trials that may result in penalties below a specified limit.

courts, all states have courts of last resort (usually called "state supreme courts"), and all but a few have an intermediate level (state courts of appeals). In the federal system, the U.S. Supreme Court is the court of last resort, and the U.S. Circuit Courts of Appeals are the intermediate appellate courts.

Although the basic, three-tier structure is found throughout the United States, the number of courts, their names, and their specific functions vary widely. For example, the federal system has no trial courts of limited jurisdiction. In state systems there are 13,000 trial courts of limited jurisdiction that handle traffic cases, small claims, misdemeanors, and other less serious matters. These courts handle 90 percent of all criminal matters. The federal system begins with the U.S. District Courts, its trial courts of general jurisdiction. In the states, these courts have a variety of names (Circuit, District, Superior, and others) and are reserved for felony cases or substantial lawsuits. These are the courts in which trials take place, judges rule on evidence, and juries issue verdicts. The basic structure of the dual court system is shown in Figure 7.1.

Some states have reformed their court systems by simplifying the number and types of courts, while others still have a confusing assortment of lower courts. Figure 7.2 contrasts the court structure of Alaska, a reformed state, with that of Georgia, where the court structure has not been reformed. Both follow the three-tier model, but Georgia has more courts and a more complex system—and potential confusion—for determining which court will handle which kind of case.

American trial courts are highly decentralized. Thus local political influences and community values are brought to bear on the courts: local officials determine their resources, residents make up the staff, and operations are managed to fit community needs. Only in a few small states is the court system organized on a statewide basis, with a central administration and state funding. In most of the country, the criminal courts operate under the state penal code but are staffed, managed, and financed by county or city government. The federal courts, by contrast, have central administration and funding, although judges in each district help shape their practices and procedures.

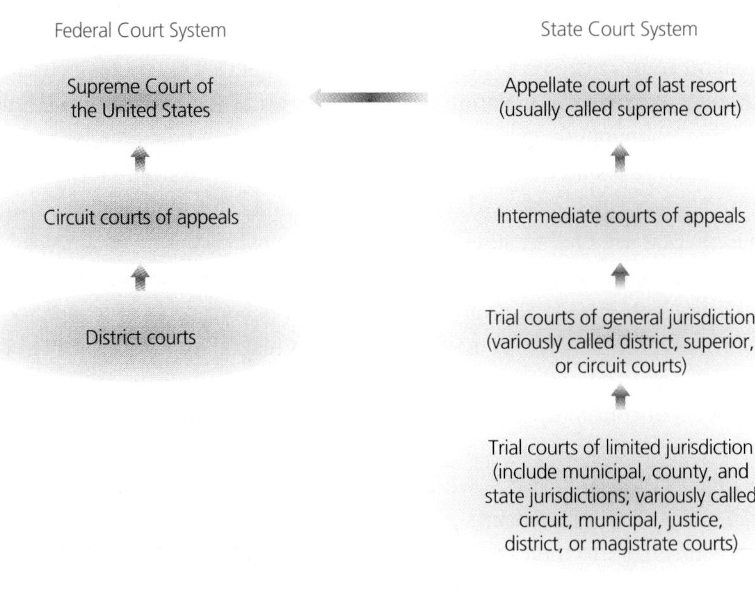

Figure 7.1
The dual court system of the United States and routes of appeal

Whether a case enters through the federal or the state court system depends on which law has been broken. The right of appeal to a higher court exists in either system.

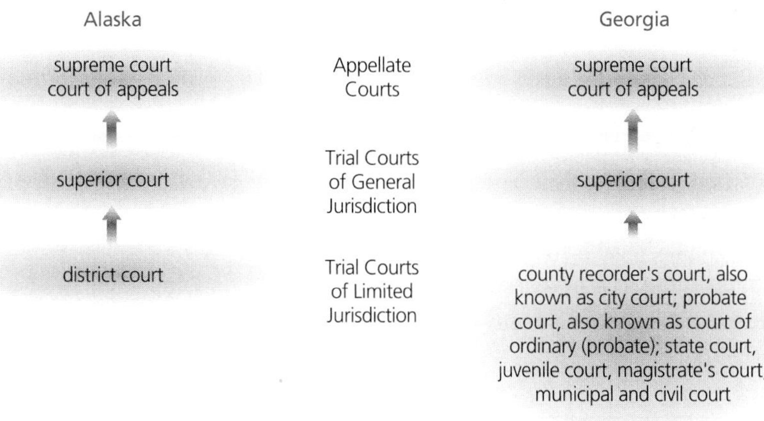

Figure 7.2
Court structures of Alaska (reformed) and Georgia (unreformed)

Reformers have called upon states to reduce the number of courts, standardize their names, and clarify their jurisdictions.

SOURCE: National Center for State Courts, *State Court Caseload Statistics: Annual Report* (Williamsburg, Va.: National Center for State Courts, 1989), 185, 194.

EFFECTIVE MANAGEMENT OF THE STATE COURTS

Throughout the twentieth century there have been efforts to reform the structure, administration, and financing of the state courts so they can deal more effectively with their huge caseloads. In addition to problems with inadequate resources and the uneven quality of politically appointed judges, the fragmented structure of state courts is often viewed as the biggest barrier to effective justice. Proposed solutions include the creation of a unified court system with four goals:

1. Eliminating overlapping and conflicting jurisdictional boundaries
2. Creating a hierarchical and centralized court structure with administrative responsibility held by a chief justice and a court of last resort
3. Funding the courts through state government
4. Creating a separate personnel system run by a state court administrator

These goals are at the forefront of the movement to make the state courts more efficient and able to dispense justice more effectively. However, local political interests often resist court reform. Local courts have long been used as a source of patronage jobs to reward people loyal to the political party in power. Centralization of court administration and professionalization of court personnel would eliminate the opportunities to use court jobs in this manner.

CHECKPOINT

1. What is the dual court system?
2. What different categories of courts exist within each court system?
3. What does it mean for courts to be decentralized?
4. What are the main goals of advocates of judicial reform?

TO BE A JUDGE

The judge's black robe and gavel are symbols of impartiality. Both within and outside the courthouse the judge is supposed to act according to a well-defined role.

We expect judges to make careful, consistent decisions that uphold the ideal of equal justice for all citizens. But this image of judges devoting themselves to careful and thoughtful decisions is not, in fact, the day-to-day reality for most American judges.

Lower-court judges can face large caseloads that require them to quickly exercise discretion in disposing and punishing minor offenses with little supervision from any higher court. Although judges are often portrayed as being forced to decide complex legal issues, in reality many of their tasks are routine. Because of the unending flow of cases, the courtroom is like an assembly line. By working under difficult conditions many judges, like assembly-line workers, soon tire of the repetition.

CHECKPOINT

5. What is the image of the judge in the eyes of the public?

Who Becomes a Judge?

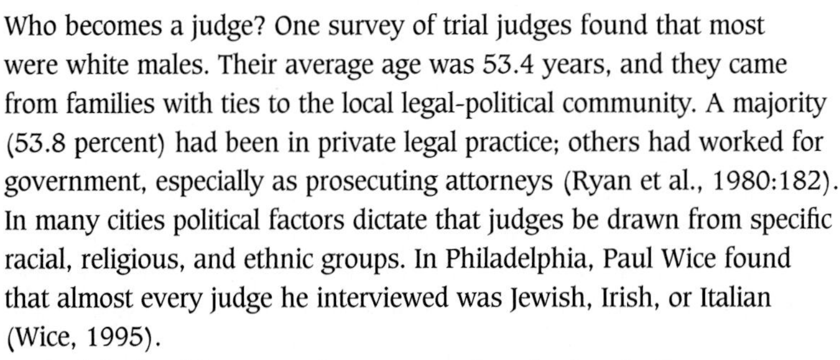

Like all judges, Honorable Sandra Townes, Syracuse City Court, is expected to "embody justice," ensuring that the right to due process is respected and that defendants are treated fairly.

Who becomes a judge? One survey of trial judges found that most were white males. Their average age was 53.4 years, and they came from families with ties to the local legal-political community. A majority (53.8 percent) had been in private legal practice; others had worked for government, especially as prosecuting attorneys (Ryan et al., 1980:182). In many cities political factors dictate that judges be drawn from specific racial, religious, and ethnic groups. In Philadelphia, Paul Wice found that almost every judge he interviewed was Jewish, Irish, or Italian (Wice, 1995).

Racial minorities are underrepresented on the bench. One study found that 3.6 percent of state court judges were African American, most of them serving in the lower criminal courts (Graham, 1995:219). Comparing the racial and ethnic makeup of the judiciary to the race and ethnicity of many defendants in urban courts raises many questions. Is there a risk that people will think punishment is being imposed on behalf of a privileged segment of society rather than on behalf of our entire, diverse society? Might people believe that decisions about guilt and punishment are being made in an unfair manner if middle-aged white males have nearly all the power to make judgments about people from other segments of society?

CHECKPOINT

6. Why might it be important for judges to represent different segments of society?

Functions of the Judge

We tend to think that the job of a judge is to preside at trials, but in reality the work of most judges extends to all aspects of the judicial process. A study of the criminal courts in New York City found that, on average, judges were on the bench only three hours and three minutes a day. Defendants see a judge whenever decisions about their future are being made: when bail is set, pretrial motions are made, guilty pleas are accepted, a trial is conducted, a sentence is pronounced, and appeals are filed (see Figure 7.3). However, judges' duties are not limited to making such decisions in the courtroom about criminal defendants. Judges also perform

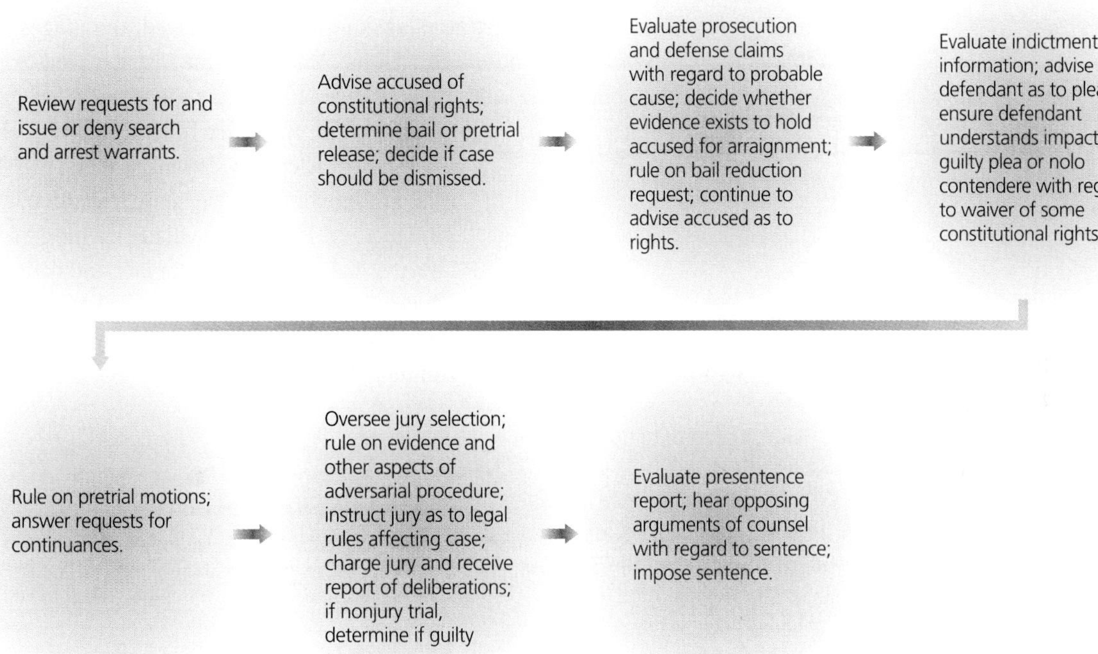

Figure 7.3
Actions of a trial court judge in processing a felony case

Throughout the process the judge ensures that legal standards are upheld; he or she maintains courtroom decorum, protects the rights of the accused, meets the requirement of a speedy trial, and ensures that case records are maintained properly.

administrative tasks outside the courtroom. Judges have three major roles: adjudicator, negotiator, and administrator. Let us look more closely at each of these.

Adjudicator

Judges must assume a neutral stance in overseeing the contest between the prosecution and the defense. They must apply the law so that the rights of the accused are upheld in decisions about detention, plea, trial, and sentence. Judges are given a certain amount of discretion in performing these tasks—for example, in setting bail—but they must do so according to law. They must avoid any conduct that may give an appearance or impression of bias.

Negotiator

Many decisions that determine the fates of defendants are made outside of public view in the judge's private chambers. These decisions about plea bargains, sentencing, and bail conditions are reached through negotiations between prosecutors and defense attorneys. Judges spend much of their time in their chambers talking with prosecutors and defense attorneys. Sometimes a judge actively takes part in the negotiations, suggesting terms for an agreement or even pressuring one side to accept an agreement.

Administrator

A seldom-recognized function of most judges is managing the courthouse. In urban areas a professional court administrator may direct the people who keep records, schedule cases, and do the many other jobs that keep a system functioning. But even in cities, judges are in charge of their own courtroom and staff. In rural areas, where professional court administrators are not usually employed, the judges' administrative tasks may be more burdensome. The judge may be required to manage labor relations, budgeting, and maintenance of the courthouse building. As administrator, the judge must deal with political actors such as county commissioners, legislators, and members of the state executive bureaucracy. For judges whose training as lawyers focused on learning law and courtroom advocacy skills, managing a complex organization with a sizable budget and many employees can be a major challenge.

A Question of ETHICS

Judge Harold Abrams of the Euclid District Court was angry. He had been sitting on the bench all Monday morning, arraigning, setting bail, and taking pleas from a stream of people who had been arrested over the weekend. Most of those who came before him were charged with offenses such as possession of a controlled substance, solicitation for prostitution, drunk and disorderly conduct—samples of the range of behaviors that had drawn the attention of the police on Saturday night. He had seen many of the accused before, and a steady banter came from the bench as the judge took each case.

"So it's you again, Lucille. When are you girls going to learn that you can't walk up and down First Avenue? In that eight-inch skirt you're a menace to traffic. We can't have every Tom, Dick, and Harry—and I mean mostly Dick—screwing their eyes on you and not on the road. Get what I mean?"

"But this time I was just going to the store to buy a loaf of bread."

"Sure. You mean you were walking to make some bread! In fact you don't do much walking, do you, Lucille: you're mainly on your back! How do you plead?"

"Guilty, but I didn't do no soliciting."

"Fifty dollars and costs. Now, I suppose you'll be back on the Avenue to earn the fine. See you again, Lucille."

The courtroom regulars grinned throughout this exchange. You could see quite a show in Judge Abrams's courtroom.

Is this the way justice should be carried out? Are Judge Abrams's banter and manner appropriate? What are the defendants learning about the justice system? Should the judge be removed from the bench?

Judges often are chosen for reasons that have little to do with either their legal qualifications or their judicial manner. Instead, they may be chosen because of their political ties, friendships with influential officials, or contributions to political parties. The character and quality of judges can depend on the method used for judicial selection.

CHECKPOINT

7. What are judges' main functions?

How to Become a Judge

The public image of the criminal justice system is shaped to a great extent by the trial judge's behavior in the courtroom. When a judge is rude or hasty or allows the courtroom to become noisy and crowded, the public may lose confidence in the fairness and effectiveness of the criminal justice process. In A Question of Ethics, the behavior of Judge Abrams raises this issue.

Methods of Selection

Six methods are used to select state trial court judges: gubernatorial appointment, legislative selection, merit selection, **nonpartisan election, partisan election**, and a mixture of methods. Table 7.1 shows the method used in each of the states. All the methods used raise persistent concerns about the desired qualities of judges.

Partisan Election	Nonpartisan Election	Gubernatorial Appointment	Legislative Election	Missouri Plan	Hybrid*
Alabama	Georgia	Delaware	South Carolina	Alaska	Arizona
Arkansas	Idaho	Maine	Virginia	Colorado	California
Illinois	Kentucky	Maryland		Connecticut	Florida
Mississippi	Louisiana	Massachusetts		Hawaii	Indiana
North Carolina	Michigan	New Hampshire		Iowa	Kansas
Pennsylvania	Minnesota	New Jersey		Nebraska	Missouri
Texas	Montana			New Mexico	New York
West Virginia	Nevada			Utah	Oklahoma
	North Dakota			Vermont	Rhode Island
	Ohio			Wyoming	South Dakota
	Oregon				Tennessee
	Washington				
	Wisconsin				

Table 7.1
Methods used by states to select trial judges

States use different methods to select judges. Note that many judges are initially appointed to fill a vacancy, giving them an advantage if they must run for election at a later date.

SOURCE: *The Book of the States, 1992-1993 Edition* (Lexington, Ky.: Council of State Governments, 1992), 233-235.

* States that use more than one method are classified as "Hybrid."

Selection by public voting occurs in more than half the states and has long been part of this nation's tradition (DuBois, 1980). Election campaigns for judgeships tend to be low-key contests marked by little controversy. Usually only a small portion of the voters participate, judgeships are not prominent on the ballot, and candidates are constrained by ethical considerations from discussing controversial issues. Judgeships may serve as a reward for attorneys who work loyally for a political party. Political parties also want judgeships to be elected posts because they can use courthouse staff positions to reward party loyalists. When a party member wins a judgeship, courthouse jobs may become available for campaign workers because the judge chooses clerks, bailiffs, and secretaries.

Some states have tried to reduce the influence of political parties in the selection of judges while still allowing voters to select judges. These states hold nonpartisan elections in which only the names of candidates, and not their party affiliations, are on the ballot. However, political parties are often strongly involved in these elections. In Ohio, for example, the Republican and Democratic Parties hold their own primary elections to choose the judicial candidates whose names will go on the nonpartisan ballot for the general election (Felice and Kilwein, 1992). In other states, party organizations raise and spend money on behalf of candidates in nonpartisan elections. When candidates' party affiliations are not listed on the ballot, voters may be unaware of which party is supporting which candidate, especially in low-visibility elections for local trial judgeships. These judgeships do not receive the same level of media attention as elections for state supreme court seats (Lovrich and Sheldon, 1994).

nonpartisan election

An election in which candidates without any party affiliation listed on the ballot are presented to voters for selection.

partisan election

An election in which candidates endorsed by political parties are presented to voters for selection.

Even in states that elect judges, many judges are first appointed by the governor to fill a vacancy occurring between elections. These appointed judges often gain name recognition that helps them keep their positions when they must later run for election. As you read the Workperspective of Justice Charles Smith, note his career path to the Washington State Supreme Court. Think about the difficulties that elected judges might face when they must make tough decisions that are unpopular with the voters.

merit selection

A reform plan by which judges are nominated by a commission and appointed by the governor for a given period. When the term expires, the voters are asked to approve or disapprove the judge for a succeeding term. If the judge is disapproved, the committee nominates a successor for the governor's appointment.

Merit selection, which combines appointment and election, was first used in Missouri in 1940 and has since spread to other states. When a judgeship becomes vacant, a nominating commission made up of citizens and attorneys evaluates potential appointees and sends the names of three nominees to the governor, who then chooses the replacement from among them. After one year, a referendum is

WORK*Perspective*

Charles Z. Smith
Justice

Supreme Court of Washington

I entered law school for a variety of personal reasons, but I did not really plan to become a lawyer. It was only after serving as a law clerk for a justice on the Washington State Supreme Court that I knew I wanted a career in law.

Initially, I never expected to become a judge. Early in my career I worked as a deputy prosecuting attorney for King County, Washington, and as special assistant to the U.S. Attorney General. Then, in 1965, I was appointed by the mayor of Seattle as a judge on the Seattle Municipal Criminal Court. One year later, the governor appointed me to a judgeship on the King County Superior Court. I presided over many criminal cases and also served in the juvenile court. When my term in office came to a close, I was elected unopposed to a full term on the court. In 1973, I left the court after experiencing "burnout," and I believed that I would not return to the judiciary.

I spent the next thirteen years as a professor at the University of Washington School of Law and then retired as professor emeritus. In 1988, a vacancy occurred on the state supreme court and the governor appointed me to fill the vacancy. Subsequently, I have been elected three times unopposed to retain my position on the Washington Supreme Court.

We are randomly assigned cases for which we will write opinions for the court. Many of our cases are criminal cases and I get my share. Our principal concern is determining whether a person had a fair trial under established rules and procedures, and under the Washington State Constitution and the U.S. Constitution.

I was assigned the opinion in a highly publicized case in which an arson fire at a warehouse resulted in the tragic deaths of four firefighters. The suspect traveled to Brazil and Washington officials sought to have him extradited—returned to the United States for trial—under the Brazil-United States Extradition Treaty. The Federal Supreme Court of Brazil authorized his extradition for the charge of arson only, but not for the murders of the firefighters. After the suspect was returned to Washington, the prosecutor charged him with four counts of murder as well as the arson. The case came to our court with the question of whether he could be charged with murder in light of the treaty and the Brazilian court's decision.

The case was difficult because we had to study the opinion of a foreign court as well as an international treaty. Ultimately, a slim majority of justices joined my opinion declaring that the State of Washington must respect the decision of the Federal Supreme Court of Brazil. Therefore the suspect could be charged only with arson and not with murder. There was a vigorous dissent by our chief justice and three other members of the court. The prosecutor unsuccessfully sought to have the U.S. Supreme Court review the decision.

This case focuses attention on the responsibility of an appellate court to reach a conclusion based upon the application of law and not upon our personal feelings or public sentiment in a case with such tragic consequences for the victims, their families, and our community. Our constitutions and laws are designed to achieve fairness for all persons in our great democratic society.

held to decide whether the judge will stay on the bench. The ballot asks, "Shall Judge X remain in office?" The judge who wins a majority vote serves out the term and can then be listed on the ballot at the next election.

Merit selection is designed to remove politics from the selection of judges and is also supposed to allow the voters to unseat judges. However, most judges selected by this means remain in office. Studies have shown that voters in merit selection states have removed only a handful (Hall and Aspin, 1987).

Despite the support of bar associations, merit selection has not gone unchallenged. Many lawyers see the system as favoring "blue bloods" (high-status attorneys with ties to corporations) over the "little guy" when lawyers are selected to be judges (Watson and Downing, 1969).

CHECKPOINT

8. Why do political parties often prefer that judges be elected?
9. What are the steps in the merit selection process?

FROM ARREST TO TRIAL OR PLEA

Gordon Mower is escorted into police headquarters in Sidney, New York, to be booked, fingerprinted, and photographed prior to being arraigned on two counts of second-degree murder.

Now that we have examined the court system and the important role of judges, let's trace the path of cases as they enter the courts and the processes that determine the fates of defendants. At each stage of the pretrial process, key decisions are made to move some defendants to the next stage of the process and to filter others out of the system.

After arrest, the accused is booked at the police station. This process includes taking photographs and fingerprints, which form the basis of the case record. Within forty-eight hours of an arrest without a warrant, the defendant must be taken to court for the initial appearance to hear which charges are being pursued, be advised of his or her rights, and be given the opportunity to post bail. The judge also has a chance to make sure that there is **probable cause** to believe that a crime has been committed and that the accused should be prosecuted for the crime.

Often, the first formal meeting between the prosecutor and the defendant's attorney is the **arraignment**: the formal court appearance in which the charges against the defendant are read and the defendant, advised by his or her lawyer, enters a plea of "guilty" or "not guilty." Most defendants will enter a plea of not guilty, even if they are likely to plead guilty at a later point. This is because, thus far, the prosecutor and defense attorney usually have had little chance to discuss a potential plea bargain.

probable cause

The criterion for deciding whether evidence is strong enough to uphold an arrest or to support issuing an arrest or search warrant. Also, the facts upholding the belief that a crime has been committed and that the accused committed the offense.

At the time of arraignment, prosecutors begin to evaluate the evidence. This screening process has a major impact on the lives of accused persons, whose fate is largely at the mercy of the prosecutor's discretion (Barnes and Kingsnorth, 1996). If the prosecutor believes the case against the defendant is weak, the charges may simply be dropped. Prosecutors do not wish to waste their limited time and resources on cases that will not stand up in court. A prosecutor may also drop charges if the alleged crime is minor, if the defendant is a first offender, or if the

As his parents look on, John Salvi, indicted for the murders of two Massachusetts abortion clinic nurses, is handcuffed at the end of the first day of his trial. Salvi was later convicted and sentenced to two life terms in prison. Eight months later he committed suicide in his cell.

prosecutor believes that the few days spent in jail before arraignment are enough punishment for the alleged offense. The decision to drop charges may also be influenced by jail overcrowding or the need to work on more serious cases. In making these decisions, prosecutors at times may discriminate against accused persons, based on race, wealth, or some other factor (Crew, 1991). As cases move through the system, prosecutors' decisions to reduce charges for some defendants greatly affect the punishment eventually applied (Miller and Sloan, 1994). Thus, individual prosecutors play a major role in deciding which defendants will receive criminal punishment.

As Figure 7.4 shows, prosecutors use their decision-making power to filter many cases out of the system. The 100 cases illustrated are typical felony cases. Obviously, the percentages of cases will vary from city to city, depending on such factors as the effectiveness of police investigations and prosecutors' policies about which cases to pursue. For example, nearly half of those arrested did not ultimately face felony prosecutions. A small number of defendants were steered toward diversion programs. A larger number had their cases dismissed for reasons that we have discussed—including lack of evidence, the minor nature of the charges, or first-time-offender status. Other cases were dismissed by the courts because the police and prosecutors did not present enough evidence to a grand jury or a preliminary hearing to justify moving forward.

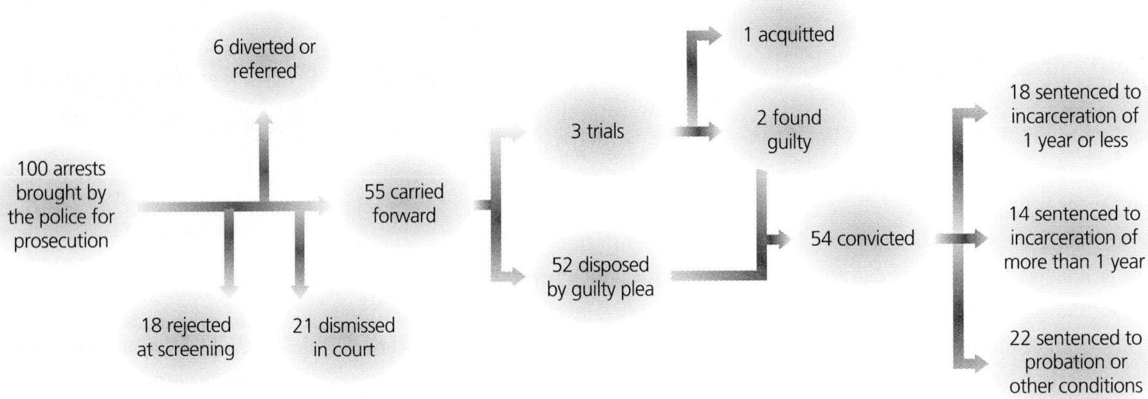

Figure 7.4
Typical outcomes of 100 urban felony cases

Prosecutors and judges make crucial decisions during the period before trial or plea. Once cases are bound over for disposition, guilty pleas are many, trials are few, and acquittals are rare.

SOURCE: Barbara Boland, Paul Mahanna, and Ronald Stones, *The Prosecution of Felony Arrests, 1988*, U.S. Department of Justice, Bureau of Justice Statistics (Washington, D.C.: Government Printing Office, 1992), 2.

The proportion of cases dropped at the various stages of the pretrial process varies from city to city. In some cities, many cases are dropped before charges are filed. Prosecutors evaluate the facts and evidence and decide which cases are strong enough to carry forward. The others are quickly dismissed. In other cities, formal charges are filed almost automatically on the basis of police reports, but many cases are dismissed when the prosecutor takes the time to closely examine each defendant's situation.

During the pretrial process defendants are exposed to the informal, "assembly-line" atmosphere of the lower criminal courts. Often, decisions are quickly made about bail, arraignment, pleas, and the disposition of cases. Moving cases as quickly as possible seems to be the major goal of many judges and attorneys during the pretrial process. American courts often have too little money, too few staff members, and not enough time to give detailed attention to each case, let alone a trial.

In American courts, the defense uses the pretrial period to its own advantage. Preliminary hearings are an opportunity for defense attorneys to challenge the prosecution's evidence and make **motions** requesting that the judge issue an order to bring about a specified action. Through pretrial motions, the defense may try to suppress evidence or learn about the prosecutor's case.

The large number of cases dismissed need not be viewed as a sign of weakness in the system. Instead, the strength of the system can be seen in the power of prosecutors and judges to dismiss charges when a conviction would be either unfair or unlikely. A close look at Figure 7.4 shows a high conviction rate for offenses that a prosecutor decides to pursue. Out of 55 typical cases carried forward, 52 will end with a guilty plea and 2 of the 3 defendants who had full trials will be convicted. These examples make it clear that the criminal justice system is effective in producing convictions when a prosecutor, with sufficient evidence, pursues a felony prosecution.

arraignment

The court appearance of an accused person in which the charges are read and the accused person, advised by a lawyer, pleads guilty or not guilty.

motion

An application to a court requesting that an order be issued to bring about a specified action.

CHECKPOINT

10. What are the purposes of preliminary hearings, arraignments, and defense motions?
11. Why and how are cases filtered out of the system?

BAIL: PRETRIAL RELEASE

We often say that defendants are presumed innocent until proved guilty. However, people who are arrested are taken to jail. If they cannot gain pretrial release, they are deprived of their freedom and, in many cases, subjected to miserable living conditions while they await the processing of their cases. The idea that people who are presumed innocent can lose their freedom—sometimes for many months—as their cases work their way toward trial clashes with the ideal of individual freedom. Yet we do not want defendants to flee or to commit additional crimes. We use bail and other methods to release defendants on the condition that they will appear in court as required.

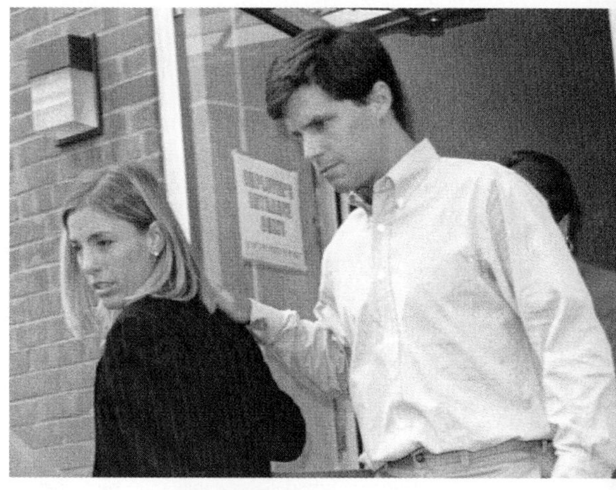

Alex Kelly leaves Stamford Superior Court with his girlfriend after being released on $1-million bail until sentencing. Kelly was convicted of raping a Darien High School student. Three days before he was to come to trial he jumped bail and lived in Europe for eight years before his return to Connecticut to face the charges.

Bail is a sum of money or property specified by the judge that the defendant presents to the court as a condition of pretrial release. The amount of bail should be high enough to ensure that the defendant appears in court for trial—but no higher. The bail will be forfeited if the defendant does not appear in court as scheduled. There is no constitutional right to release a defendant on bail, nor even a right to have the court set an amount as the condition of release. The Eighth Amendment to the U.S. Constitution forbids excessive bail, and state bail laws are usually designed to prevent discrimination in setting bail. They do not guarantee, however, that all defendants will have a realistic chance of being released before trial (Nagel, 1990).

Another purpose of bail is the need to protect the community from further crimes that some defendants may commit while out on bail. Congress and some of the states have passed laws that permit preventive detention of defendants who are believed by the judge to pose a threat to any other person or to the community while awaiting trial.

bail

An amount of money specified by a judge to be paid as a condition of pretrial release to ensure that the accused will appear in court as required.

A Question of ETHICS

Jim Rourke stood in front of Desk Sergeant Jack Sweeney at the Redwood City Police Station. Rourke was handcuffed and waiting to be booked. He had been caught by Officers Davis and Timulty outside a building in a wealthy neighborhood, soon after the police had received a 911 call from a resident reporting that someone had entered her apartment. Rourke was seen loitering in the alley with a flashlight in his back pocket. He was known to the police because of his prior arrests for entering houses at night. As Timulty held Rourke, Davis went around behind the desk and spoke to Sergeant Sweeney in a soft voice.

"I know we don't have much on this guy, but he's a bad egg and I bet he was the one who was in that apartment. The least we can do is set the bail high enough so that he'll know we are on to him."

"Davis, you know I can't do that. You've got nothing on him," said Sweeney.

"But how's it going to look in the press if we just let him go? You know the type of people who live in Littleton Manor. There will be hell to pay if it gets out that this guy just walks."

"Well, he did have the flashlight. ... I suppose that's enough to make him a suspect. Let's make the bail $1,000. I know he can't make that."

What is the purpose of bail? Was the amount set appropriate in this instance? Should Rourke be held merely because of the suspicion that he might have entered the apartment? Do you think the case would have been handled in the same way if the call had come from a poorer part of town?

In almost all courts, the amount of bail is based mainly on the judge's view of the seriousness of the crime and of the defendant's record. Because bail must be allowed within twenty-four to forty-eight hours after an arrest, there is no time to conduct a more thorough assessment. As a result, judges in many communities have developed standard rates: so many dollars for such-and-such an offense. In some cases, a judge may set a high bail if the police or prosecutor want a certain person to be kept off the streets.

Critics of the bail system argue that it discriminates against poor people. Imagine that you have been arrested and have no money. Should you be denied a chance for freedom before trial just because you are poor?

The Reality of the Bail System

The reality of the bail system is far from the ideal. For minor offenses, police officers may have a standard list of bail amounts. For serious offenses, bail will be set in court by a judge. In both cases, those setting bail may have discretion to set differing bail amounts for different suspects, depending on the circumstances of each case. As A Question of Ethics illustrates, this discretion creates the risk that officials will deprive some defendants of their freedom unfairly or for improper reasons.

Bail Bondsmen

The bail bondsman is a key figure in the bail process. Bail bondsmen (or women) are private businesspeople who are paid fees by defendants who lack the money to make bail. They are licensed by the state and are able to choose their own clients. In exchange for a fee, which may be 5 to 10 percent of the bail amount, the bondsman will put up the money (or property) to gain the defendant's release. Bondsmen are not obliged to provide bail money for every defendant who seeks to use their services. Rather, they decide which defendants are likely to return for court appearances. If the defendant skips town, it is the bondsman's money that is forfeited.

The use of bail bondsmen raises an important issue about the just treatment of all those entering the system, because there is a risk of corruption if bondsmen pay police officers to steer defendants to their business. More important, we face a serious question: Is it proper for a private, profit-seeking businessperson to decide who will gain pretrial release and to profit from a person who is "presumed innocent" but is threatened with the loss of his or her freedom?

Despite the seriousness of this issue, bondsmen may provide some benefits for the criminal justice system. Although bondsmen act in their own interest, they may help the courts by reminding defendants about court dates, calling defendants' relatives to make sure that the defendant will arrive on time, and warning defendants about the penalties for failing to appear.

Court and law enforcement officials could handle the same functions as well or better if they had the resources, time, and interest to make sure that released defendants return to court. With pretrial services offices like those in the federal courts (Marsh, 1994; Peoples, 1995), defendants could be monitored and reminded to return to court without the risks of discrimination and corruption associated with the use of bail bondsmen (Carr, 1993).

Setting Bail

When the police set bail at the station house for minor offenses, there is usually a standard amount for a particular charge. By contrast, when a judge sets bail, the amount of bail and conditions of release are a product of interactions among the judge, prosecutor, and defense attorney. These actors discuss the defendant's personal qualities and prior record. The prosecutor may stress the seriousness of the crime, the defendant's record, and negative personal characteristics. The defense attorney may stress the defendant's good job, family responsibilities, and ties to the community. Judges are often most concerned with the seriousness of the pending charge, the defendant's prior record, and defendant's personal qualities and community connections.

Research studies highlight the disadvantage of the poor in the bail process. A study of Hispanic-American arrestees in the southwestern United States found that those who could afford to hire their own attorneys were seven times more likely to gain pretrial release than those who were represented at public expense (Holmes et al., 1996). This result may reflect the fact that affluent defendants are better able to come up with bail money, as well as the possibility that private attorneys fight harder for their clients than public defenders do in the early stages of the criminal process.

The amount of bail may also reflect racial or ethnic discrimination by criminal justice officials, or the social class of the defendant. A study of bail in Connecticut showed that at each step in the process African-American and Hispanic-American males with clean records were given bail amounts double those of whites (see Figure 7.5). One reason may be that poor defendants often do not have jobs and a permanent residence, factors that strongly influence the amount of bail. The study also recognized that African Americans and Hispanics were more likely to be charged with a felony than whites, often influencing bail amounts. Yet the largest disparities in bail were in felony drug cases. In these cases the average bail for African Americans and Hispanic Americans was four times higher than for whites at the same courthouse.

Reformers have urged the courts to release more people without bail in order to reduce discrimination and avoid the harsh impact of detention on defendants who are still supposedly presumed innocent. A recent survey of the seventy-five most populous counties found that nearly two-thirds of felony defendants were released before disposition of their cases. Of those detained, 1 in 6 were held without bail (Reaves and Perez, 1994:1). These changes have occurred, in part, because of the use of certain pretrial release methods. These are listed in Table 7.2 (p. 165), and some of them are discussed in the following sections.

WORK*Perspective*

Hon. Virginia M. Morgan
U.S. Magistrate Judge

U.S. District Court,
Eastern District of Michigan

Growing up, I planned a career as a teacher and educator. After graduation from the University of Michigan, I taught math on the Navajo Indian Reservation and in California. I became aware of many public policy issues with respect to equal treatment and civil rights. Law presented the opportunity to work in these areas and to make a difference, with more flexibility than classroom teaching afforded. When I returned to Ohio, I taught during the day and attended law school at night and full-time in the summer.

I graduated from the University of Toledo College of Law and began work as assistant county prosecutor in Ann Arbor, Michigan. I was the first woman attorney there. For four years I prosecuted crimes from illegal entry to murder and handled mental health cases. The work was rewarding, my colleagues were wonderful, and I felt that we were making a difference in the community.

I left to become an assistant U.S. Attorney in Detroit and work with federal agencies, such as the FBI and Secret Service, to develop and prosecute increasingly complex federal criminal cases and defend the cases on appeal. I was promoted to chief of the General Crimes Unit and later transferred to the Civil Division. There I worked with agency lawyers to present cases involving environmental issues, labor union elections, and medical malpractice.

In 1985 a position as U.S. Magistrate opened in our district, and I applied. So did some 170 other lawyers. The process is a merit selection, and the committee recommended me based on my knowledge, experience, and writing. The district judges selected me for the position, which carries an eight-year renewable term of office. The title of the position was changed to United States Magistrate Judge in 1990, and I am now in my second term. I am active in professional associations and am a past-president of the national Federal Magistrate Judges Association. I was selected by the Chief Justice to serve on a committee of the Judicial Conference of the United States and as a member of the Federal Judicial Center Board.

U.S. magistrate judges are given broad authority and significant responsibilities. As a federal judicial officer, I preside over matters that extend to the full jurisdiction of the federal district court, with the exception of felony trials. I preside over matters, such as civil trials, that require consent of the parties and an order of reference. Routinely I hear and decide nondispositive civil motions, write opinions, called "Report & Recommendations," on dispositive motions such as summary judgments and petitions for habeas corpus, and conduct facilitative mediations. Both the bench and the bar recognize the increasing importance of magistrate judges in securing the just, speedy, and inexpensive determination of justice in the federal courts.

An important responsibility of U.S. magistrate judges is conducting initial appearances and setting bail for criminal defendants. Magistrate judges must use their judgment to decide if bail should be granted and, if so, what the terms should be. Under the federal Bail Reform Act, the magistrate judge must determine whether there are conditions of release that will reasonably assure the defendant's appearance and the safety of the community. The defendant is entitled to a hearing to decide if he or she should be detained pending trial. At this hearing testimony comes from witnesses and by proffer. Before the hearing, the defendant is interviewed by a Pretrial Services officer who obtains information about the factors bearing on release or detention. These factors include the defendant's community and family ties, employment, past criminal record, financial status, physical and mental health, and history of substance abuse. Pretrial Services tries to verify the information before the hearing, which may be only a few hours away. The decision to release or detain a defendant is a serious one that can greatly affect the defendant and the community.

For example, in a recent case a defendant was charged with illegally possessing firearms following his conviction for domestic assault two years earlier. He had only that prior misdemeanor, but he had violated probation. He still resided with the victim of the earlier domestic assault, and he had three loaded guns in the house at the time of his arrest. Complicating the decision was his claim that he rejects the authority of the government to regulate guns and the authority of the federal courts to enforce the law. I needed to assure myself that he would obey the conditions that I set for release. Ultimately, I set a bond of $100,000/10 percent, requiring him to post $10,000 with the court before release, to be returned to him at the conclusion of the case if he complied with his bond conditions. This amount, though large, was possible based on Pretrial Service's information. I also imposed electronic monitoring and a curfew. After a few days in jail he secured the funds and posted the bond. Without the information and suggestions by the Pretrial Services officer, the defendant may have remained in jail unnecessarily, at great cost to the taxpayers, or may have had no incentive to obey the conditions.

There is no easy formula for setting bond conditions or deciding to detain a defendant. It is an important decision that benefits from the experience and information provided by Pretrial Services, and it requires careful consideration of the interests of the parties and the public.

WORK*Perspective*

Table 7.2
Pretrial release methods

Financial Bond	Alternative Release Options
Fully secured bail. The defendant posts the full amount of bail with the court.	*Release on recognizance (ROR).* The court releases the defendant on his or her promise to appear in court as required.
Privately secured bail. A bondsman signs a promissory note to the court for the bail amount and charges the defendant a fee for the service (usually 10 percent of the bail amount). If the defendant fails to appear, the bondsman must pay the court the full amount. The bondsman frequently requires the defendant to post collateral in addition to the fee.	*Conditional release.* The court releases the defendant subject to his or her adherence to specific conditions set by the court, such as attendance at drug treatment therapy or staying away from the complaining witness.
Percentage bail. The courts allow the defendant to deposit a percentage (usually 10 percent) of the full bail with the court. The full amount of the bail is required if the defendant fails to appear. The percentage bail is returned after disposition of the case, although the court often retains 1 percent for administrative costs.	*Third-party custody.* The defendant is released into the custody of an individual or agency that promises to ensure his or her appearance in court. No monetary transactions are involved in this type of release.
Unsecured bail. The defendant pays no money to the court but is liable for the full amount of bail should she or he fail to appear.	

SOURCE: U.S. Department of Justice, Bureau of Justice Statistics, *Report to the Nation on Crime and Justice*, 2d ed. (Washington, D.C.: Government Printing Office, 1988), 76.

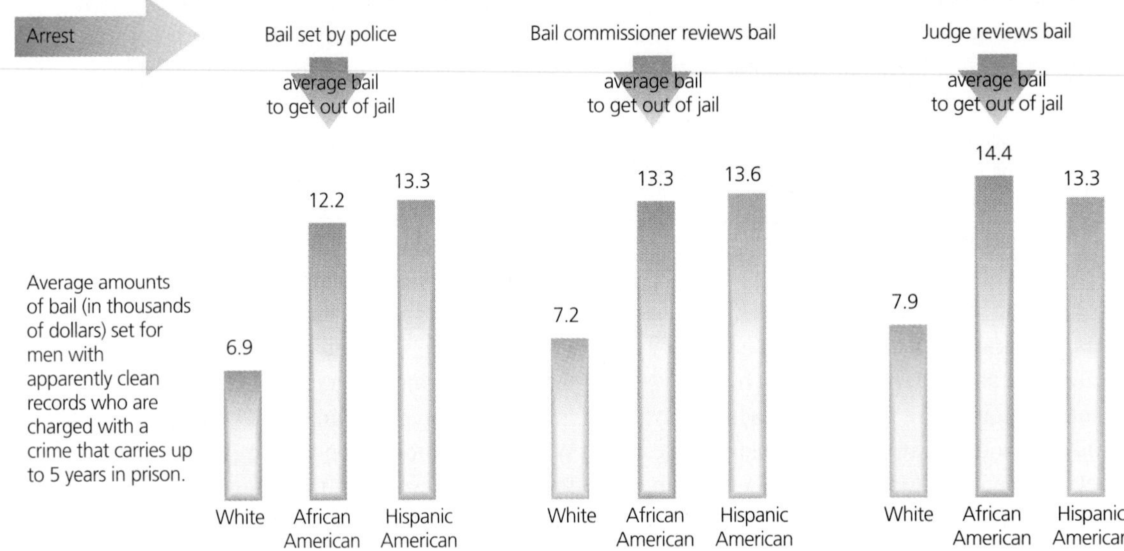

Figure 7.5
The price of freedom in Connecticut

Bail can be set by several actors in the justice system. A study of 150,000 cases showed that the bail amount for African Americans and Hispanic Americans was double that for whites. Is this a result of discrimination? What other factors might be at work here?

SOURCE: *Hartford Courant*, June 16, 1991, p. A1; data from State Bail Commission Records.

CHECKPOINT

12. What factors affect whether bail is set in serious cases, and how much money or property a defendant must provide to gain pretrial release?
13. What positive and negative effects does the bail bondsman have on the bail system?

Reforming the Bail System

Studies of pretrial detention in such cities as Philadelphia and New York raised questions about the need to hold defendants in jail. Criticisms of the bail system have focused on judges' discretion in setting bail amounts, the fact that the poor are deprived of their freedom while the affluent can afford bail, the negative aspects of bail bondsmen, and jail conditions for those detained while awaiting trial (Clark and Henry, 1997). Reform of the bail system has been attempted in response to these criticisms.

Citation

citation

A written order or summons issued by a law enforcement officer directing an alleged offender to appear in court at a specified time to answer a criminal charge.

A **citation**, or summons, to appear in court—a "ticket"—is often issued to a person accused of committing a traffic offense or some other minor violation. By issuing the citation the officer avoids taking the accused person to the station house for booking and to court for arraignment and setting of bail. Citations are now being used for more serious offenses, in part because the police want to reduce the amount of time they spend booking minor offenders and waiting in court for the cases to come up.

Release on Recognizance

Pioneered in the 1960s by the Vera Institute of Justice in New York City, the **release on recognizance** (ROR) approach is based on the assumption that judges will grant releases if the defendant is reliable and has roots in the community. Soon after the arrest, court personnel talk to defendants about their job, family, prior record, and associations. They then decide whether to recommend release. Today ROR programs exist in almost every major jurisdiction (Eskridge, 1986:27).

release on recognizance (ROR)

Pretrial release granted on the defendant's promise to appear in court because the judge believes that the defendant's ties in the community guarantee that he or she will appear.

Ten Percent Cash Bail

Although ROR is a useful alternative to money bail, judges are unwilling to release some defendants on their own recognizance. Some states (Illinois, Kentucky, Nebraska, Oregon, Pennsylvania) have started bail programs in which the defendants deposit with the court an amount of cash equal to 10 percent of their bail. When they appear in court as required, 90 percent of this amount is returned to them. Begun in Illinois in 1964, this plan is designed to release as many defendants as possible without the use of bondsmen.

IDEAS IN PRACTICE

As judge of the District Court of Northampton, Massachusetts, you are responsible for setting bail. In the following cases, indicate whether you would order release on recognizance (ROR), set bail at some specific amount (state the amount), or deny bail and order preventive detention. Explain your decision.

Tony Smith is charged with possession of cocaine with intent to distribute. He has one prior conviction for misdemeanor assault. He is twenty years old, works at a grocery store, and supports his wife and one child. He is a lifelong resident of Northampton.

Susan Claussen is charged with theft for ordering and consuming dinner at an expensive restaurant and then leaving without paying the bill. She has entered guilty pleas to this offense on five previous occasions over the past three years. She has been placed on probation several times and served one thirty-day jail sentence. She is unemployed, lives with her parents, and is a lifelong resident of Northampton.

Bail Guidelines

To deal with the problem of unequal treatment, reformers have written guidelines for setting bail. The guidelines specify the standards judges should use in setting bail and also list appropriate amounts. Judges are expected to follow the guidelines but may deviate from them in special situations. The guidelines take into account the seriousness of the offense and the defendant's prior record in order to protect the community and ensure that released persons can be trusted to return for court appearances.

Preventive Detention

Reforms have been suggested not only by those concerned with unfairness in the bail system but also by those concerned with stopping crime. Critics of the bail system point to a link between release on bail and the commission of crimes, arguing that the accused may commit other crimes while awaiting trial. A study of the nation's most populous counties found that 14 percent of felony defendants released on bail were rearrested for another crime while awaiting trial. Although only 9 percent of defendants with one prior conviction were rearrested during pretrial release, 29 percent of defendants with five or more prior convictions were rearrested (Reaves and Perez, 1994:1). To address this problem, legislatures have passed laws permitting detention of defendants without bail.

For federal criminal cases, Congress enacted the Bail Reform Act of 1984 (Scott, 1985), which authorizes **preventive detention**. Under the act, if the prosecutor recommends that the defendant be kept in jail, a federal judge holds a hearing to determine (1) if there is a serious risk that the person will flee; (2) if the person will obstruct justice or threaten, injure, or intimidate a prospective witness or juror; or (3) if the offense is one of violence or one punishable by life imprisonment or death. Upon finding that one or more of these factors makes it impossible to set bail without endangering the community, the judge can order the defendant held in jail until the case is completed (Smith, 1990:166-167).

preventive detention

Holding a defendant for trial based on a judge's finding that, if the defendant were released on bail, he or she would endanger the safety of any other person and the community or would flee.

Critics of preventive detention argue that it violates the Constitution's due process clause because the accused is held in custody until a verdict is rendered.

United States v. Salerno (1987)

Preventive detention provisions of the Bail Reform Act of 1984 are upheld as a legitimate use of governmental power designed to prevent people from committing crimes while on bail.

However, the Supreme Court has ruled that it is constitutional. The preventive detention provisions of the Bail Reform Act of 1984 were upheld in ***United States v. Salerno*** (1987). By upholding the federal law, the Court also upheld state laws dealing with preventive detention (Miller and Guggenheim, 1990). The Close-up, "Preventive Detention: Two Sides of an Issue," presents a case in support of preventive detention. Research has shown that the nature and seriousness of the charge, a history of prior arrests, and drug use have a strong bearing on the likelihood that a defendant will commit a crime while on bail (Institute for Law and Social Research, 1980. *Pretrial Release and Misconduct in the District of Columbia*).

Those who are unable to post bail and are not released on their own recognizance are held in pretrial detention in the local jail until their court appearance. As we will see, this has a major impact on these defendants.

CHECKPOINT

14. What methods are used to facilitate pretrial release for certain defendants?
15. How did the U.S. Supreme Court rule in cases involving preventive detention? Why?

CLOSE-UP

Preventive Detention: Two Sides of an Issue

For Ricardo Armstrong, there is the despair of trying to reunite his family after spending four months in a Cincinnati jail awaiting trial on bank robbery charges only to be acquitted of the crime.

For friends and family of Linda Goldstone, there is the anguish of knowing that she would still be alive if Hernando Williams had been kept in jail while he was facing rape and assault charges in Chicago.

Ricardo Armstrong was one of the first defendants held under the Bail Reform Act of 1984. The 28-year-old janitor, who had a prior burglary conviction, was denied bail after he was charged with robbing two Ohio banks.

From the start, Mr. Armstrong had insisted that bank robbery charges against him were part of some nightmarish mix-up.

A Cincinnati jury agreed. After viewing bank photographs of the robber, the jury acquitted Mr. Armstrong in what was apparently a case of mistaken identity.

Justice, it seemed, had been served—but not before Mr. Armstrong had spent four months in jail—and his wife left their home and moved with their children a thousand miles away.

"Who's going to get me back those four months?" he now asks bitterly. "Who's going to get me back my kids?" The Bail Reform Act makes no provision for compensating defendants who are jailed and later acquitted.

Proponents of the Bail Reform Act concede that some injustices inevitably occur. But they note that other cases, involving dangerous defendants set free on bond, ring just as tragically for victims of crimes that could have been prevented.

Prosecutors point to the release of Hernando Williams as the classic example of the need for preventive detention. Even as Mr. Williams, free on $25,000 bond, drove to court to face charges [of raping and beating a woman he abducted at a shopping mall], another woman lay trapped inside his car trunk. This victim, Linda Goldstone, a 29-year-old birthing instructor, was abducted by Mr. Williams as she walked to Northwestern Hospital and was forced at gunpoint to crawl into his trunk.

Over a four-day period, Mrs. Goldstone was removed from the trunk periodically to be raped and beaten until she was shot to death. Mr. Williams has been sentenced to death.

"Linda Goldstone might well be alive today if we'd had this law then," said Richard M. Daley, the Cook County state's attorney.

SOURCE: Excerpted from Dirk Johnston, "Preventive Detention: Two Sides of an Issue," *New York Times,* July 13, 1987, p. A13.

PRETRIAL DETENTION

People who are not released before trial must remain in jail. Often called the "ultimate ghetto," American jails hold almost a half million people on any one day. Most are poor, half are in pretrial detention, and the rest are serving sentences (normally of less than one year) or are waiting to be moved to state prison or to another jurisdiction (Clear and Cole, 1997:144).

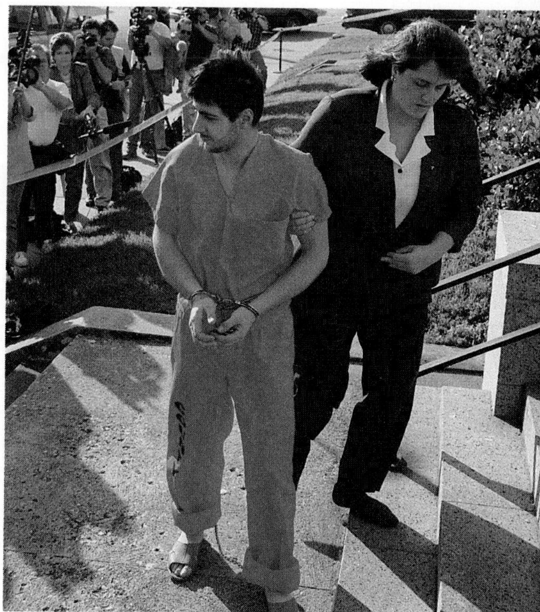

Suspects not able to make bail are held awaiting trial. What is the impact on the jury of an accused who rises from the audience when his case is called, compared to an accused who is escorted by the jailer to the defense table?

Urban jails also contain troubled people, many with mental health and drug abuse problems, that the police have swept off the streets. Michael Welch calls this process, in which the police remove socially offensive people from certain areas, "social sanitation" (Welch, 1994:262).

Conditions in jails are often much harsher than those in prisons. People awaiting trial are often held in barracks—like cells with sentenced offenders. Thus, a "presumed innocent" pretrial detainee might spend weeks in the same confined space with troubled people or sentenced felons (Perkins, Stephan, and Beck, 1995). Detainees may be threatened or harmed by their cellmates. They may also lose their jobs and homes while in jail.

In many cases, the period just after arrest is the most frightening and difficult time for suspects. Imagine freely walking the streets one minute and being locked in a small space with a large number of troubled and potentially dangerous cellmates the next. Suddenly you have no privacy and must share an open toilet with hostile strangers. You have been fingerprinted, photographed, and questioned—treated like the "criminal" that the police and the criminal justice system consider you to be. You are alone with people whose behavior you cannot predict. You are left to worry and wonder about what might happen. If you are female, you may be placed in a cell by yourself (Steury and Frank, 1990). Given the stressful nature of arrest and jailing, it is little wonder that most jail suicides and psychotic episodes occur during the first hours of detention.

Pretrial detention can last a long time. While most detainees have their cases adjudicated within three months, 12 percent must wait in jail for more than six months and 4 percent for more than a year (Reaves and Perez, 1994:13). Thus, the psychological and economic hardships faced by pretrial detainees and their families can be major and prolonged.

Pretrial detention not only imposes stresses and hardships that may reach crisis levels, but also can affect the outcomes of cases. People who are held in jail can give little help to their defense attorneys. They cannot help find witnesses and perform other useful tasks on their own behalf. In addition, they may feel pressured to plead guilty in order to end their indefinite stay in jail. Even if they believe that they should not be convicted of the crime charged, they may prefer to start serving a prison or jail sentence with a definite end point. Some may even gain quicker release on probation or in a community corrections program by pleading guilty, while—ironically—they might stay in jail for a longer period of time by insisting on their innocence and awaiting a trial.

CHECKPOINT

16. People are detained in jail for a number of reasons. What categories of people are found in jails?
17. What are the sources of stress for people in jail awaiting trial?

THE COURTROOM: HOW IT FUNCTIONS

After defendants move through the pretrial processes of arrest, bail hearings, and possible detention, their cases receive attention from the courts. In the courts, their fates are usually determined by the discretionary decisions, relationships, and interactions of lawyers and judges.

Although similar rules and processes are used in criminal cases throughout the nation, courts differ in the precise ways they apply these rules and procedures. A study of criminal courts in nine communities in three states showed that similar laws and procedures can have different results in the treatment of defendants (Eisenstein, Flemming, and Nardulli, 1988). Some courts sentence offenders to longer terms than do others. In some places, court delays and tough bail policies keep many accused persons in jail awaiting trial, while in other places defendants are more likely to be released before trial or have their cases resolved quickly. Guilty pleas may make up 90 percent of dispositions in some communities but only 60 percent in others. How can we explain these differences among courts—differences that are found even in the same city?

local legal culture

Norms shared by members of a court community as to how cases should be handled and how a participant should behave in the judicial process.

Researchers have identified a **local legal culture**—values and norms shared by members of a particular court community (judges, attorneys, clerks, bailiffs, and others)—about how cases should be handled and the way court officials should behave (Church, 1985). The local legal culture influences court operations in three ways:

1. Norms (shared values and expectations) help participants distinguish between "our" court and other courts. Often a judge or prosecutor will proudly describe how "we" do the job better than officials in a nearby county or city.
2. Norms tell members of a court community how they should treat one another. For example, mounting a strong adversarial defense may be viewed as not in keeping with the norms of one court, but it may be expected in another.
3. Norms describe how cases *should* be processed. The best example of such a norm is the **going rate**, the local view of the proper sentence, considering the offense, the defendant's prior record, and other factors. The local legal culture also includes attitudes on such issues as whether a judge should take part in plea negotiations, when continuances—lawyers' requests for delays in court proceedings—should be granted, and which defendants qualify for a public defender.

going rate

Local view of the appropriate sentence for the offense, the defendant's prior record, and other characteristics.

Differences among local legal cultures help explain why court decisions may differ even though the formal rules of criminal procedure are basically the same. Informal rules and practices arise in particular settings, and "the way things are done" differs from place to place. As one might expect, the local legal culture of San Francisco inevitably differs from that of Burlington, Vermont, or Baltimore, Maryland. The norms and customs of each jurisdiction also vary because local practices are influenced by factors such as size, politics, and demographics. Among these, differences between urban and rural areas are a major factor.

CHECKPOINT

18. How does the local legal culture affect criminal cases?

The Courtroom Workgroup

Our image of a courtroom may be based on those we see in television dramas. In these settings prosecutors and defense attorneys lock horns in verbal combat, each side trying to persuade a judge or jury to either convict or acquit the defendant. However, this image of adversarial proceedings does not reflect the actual scene in most American courtrooms. A more realistic portrayal would stress the interactions among the actors, who are guided by the norms and expectations of the local legal culture. Many of these interactions take the form of calm cooperation among the prosecutor, defense attorney, and judge, rather than the battle of adversaries portrayed in fictional accounts (Flemming, Nardulli, and Eisenstein, 1992).

Even in the most adversarial cases, such as the O. J. Simpson trial, courtroom participants form a workgroup that requires constant interaction, cooperation, and negotiation.

Decision making in criminal cases is influenced by the **workgroups** handling them. A workgroup consists of the judge, prosecutor, and defense attorney, along with the support staff (clerk, reporter, and bailiff) usually assigned to a specific courtroom. All members of the workgroup must work together if they are to dispose of cases. The workgroup concept is especially important in analyzing urban courts, where there are many courtrooms, large numbers of lawyers, judges, and other court personnel, and a heavy caseload.

Merely placing the major actors in the courtroom does not make them into a workgroup that can apply shared norms in a smooth, cooperative fashion. In order to become a functioning workgroup, the members must interact, share attitudes about their goals, and develop a set of norms about how they will treat each other and handle cases.

workgroup

A collection of individuals who interact in the workplace on a continuing basis, share goals, develop norms regarding how activities should be carried out, and eventually establish a network of roles that differentiates the group from others.

Considering the factors that define a workgroup, we can expect to see differences in workgroups from courthouse to courthouse depending on the strength of these factors in each setting. For example, a rotation system that moves judges among courtrooms in a large courthouse may limit the development of workgroup norms and roles. Although the same prosecutors and defense attorneys may be present every day, the arrival of a new judge every week or month will require them to learn and adapt to new ideas about how cases should be negotiated or tried. When shared norms cannot develop, cases are likely to proceed in a more formal manner. The actors in such a courtroom have fewer chances to follow agreed-upon routines than a workgroup with a well-developed pattern of interactions.

On the other hand, if the same actors are in the courtroom on a continuing basis, we may expect the relationships among the judge, prosecutor, and defense attorney, as well as the staff, to shape the way decisions are made. The defendant, a person from outside the workgroup, will face "an organized network of relationships, in which each person who acts on his case is reacting to or anticipating the actions of others" (Neubauer, 1996: 73). When there are shared expectations and consistent relationships, the business of the courtroom proceeds in a regular but informal manner, with many shared understandings among members easing much of the work (Worden, 1995). Through cooperation, each member can achieve his or her goals as well as those of the group. The prosecutor wants to gain quick convictions, the defense attorney wants fair and prompt resolution of the defendant's case, and the judge wants cooperative agreements on guilt and sentencing. All these actors want efficient processing of the steady flow of cases that burden their working lives.

Each actor—judge, prosecutor, and defense attorney—has a specific role. Each has unique duties and responsibilities because each represents a different "sponsoring organization." One organization, loosely called the court, sends judges; the prosecuting attorney's office sends assistant prosecutors; the public defender's office sends counsel for indigents. The sponsoring organizations provide the resources for the courtroom workgroup and—perhaps more important—regulate the behavior of their representatives in the courtroom. The policies of a sponsoring organization may stipulate rules to be followed, encourage or discourage plea bargaining, or insist that police evidence conform strictly to formal requirements.

The elements of the courtroom workgroup and the influences that bear on decision making are shown in Figure 7.6. Note that the workgroup operates in an environment in which decision making is influenced by the local legal culture, recruitment and selection processes, nature of the cases, and the socioeconomic, political, and legal structures of the broader community.

CHECKPOINT

19. How does a courtroom workgroup form and operate?

The Impact of Courtroom Workgroups

The classic research of James Eisenstein and Herbert Jacob (1977) on the felony disposition process in Baltimore, Chicago, and Detroit offers important insights into the workgroup's impact on decisions in felony cases and reveals differences in the criminal justice systems of three cities. The researchers found that the same type of felony case was handled very differently in each city, yet the outcomes of the dispositions were remarkably similar. Differences were not due to the law, rules of procedure, or crime rate. Instead, they emerged from the structure of the courtroom workgroups, the influence of the sponsoring organizations, and sociopolitical factors.

Many felony cases never reach a trial court because they are dismissed or the charges are reduced to a misdemeanor at a preliminary hearing. What impact did the courtroom workgroups have on these preliminary hearings? Eisenstein and Jacob (1977) found that the stable courtroom workgroups in Chicago had informal procedures for screening cases. Because the groups work in the same courtrooms on a fairly regular basis, they felt pressure to screen out many cases and thus spare the resources of the judges and the courts. This led to a very high dismissal rate. In Detroit, also a city with stable workgroups, the prosecutors had discretion to screen cases before they reached the courtroom; hence most of the defendants who appeared at preliminary hearings were sent to trial. Baltimore had less stable workgroups, in part because members were rotated, and sponsoring organizations did not supervise assistant prosecutors and defense attorneys very closely. The unstable workgroups lacked close working relationships, shared values, or reasons

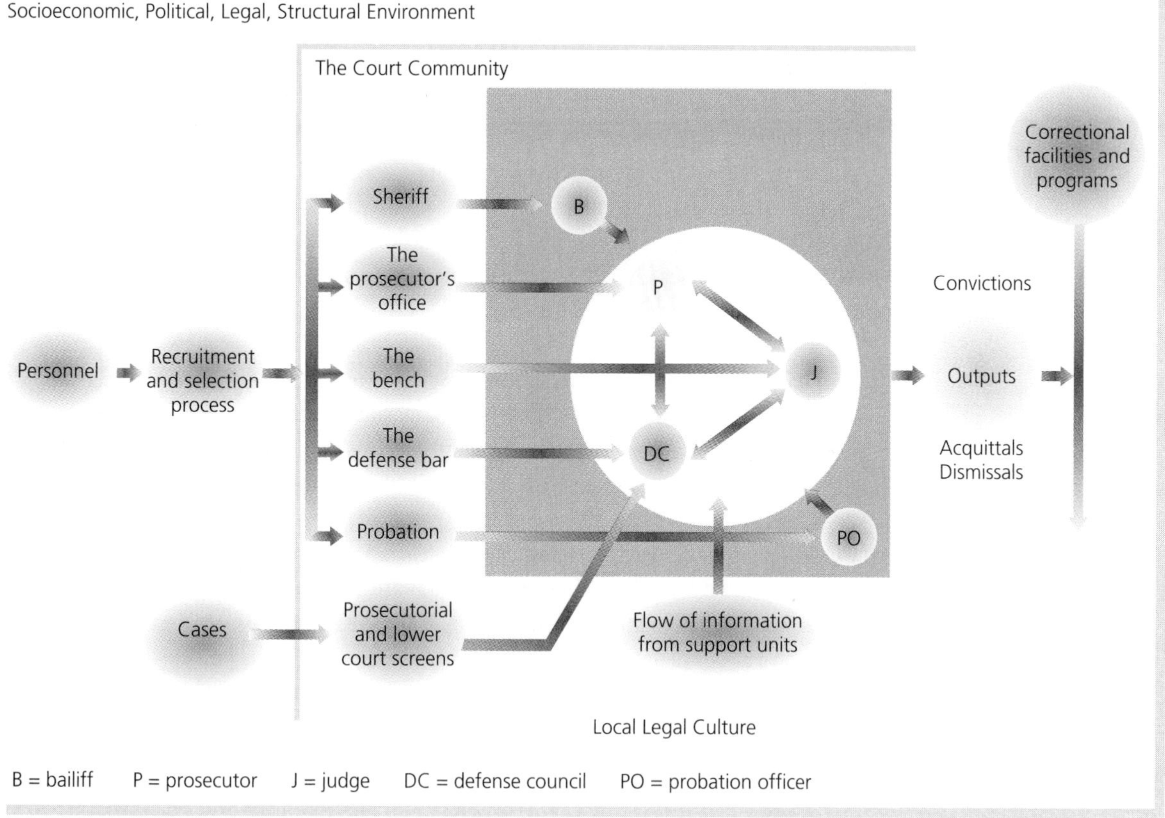

Figure 7.6
Model of criminal court decision making

This model ties together the elements of the courtroom work-group, sponsoring organizations, and local legal culture. Note the effects on decision making. What other factors should be taken into account?

SOURCE: Adapted from Peter Nardulli, James Eisenstein, and Roy Flemming, *Tenor of Justice: Criminal Courts and the Guilty Plea Process* (Urbana: University of Illinois Press, 1988). Copyright © 1988 by the Board of Trustees of the University of Illinois. Reprinted by permission of the University of Illinois Press.

to cooperate. As a result, there were fewer guilty pleas and most defendants were sent on to the grand jury and thence to trial.

According to the study, the interaction of members of the courtroom workgroup determine the outcomes of felony cases. The decisions made by each member are influenced by the policies of their sponsoring organizations. These interactions and policies may vary from courthouse to courthouse.

CHECKPOINT

20. Why are courtroom workgroups different in different cities?

Summary

- The United States has a dual court system consisting of state and federal courts that are organized into separate hierarchies.
- Trial courts and appellate courts have different jurisdictions and functions.
- Despite resistance from local judges and political interests, reformers have sought to improve state court systems through centralized administration, state funding, and a separate personnel system.
- The judge is a key figure in the criminal justice process and has the roles of adjudicator, negotiator, and administrator.

- State judges are selected through various methods, including partisan elections, nonpartisan elections, gubernatorial appointment, and merit selection.
- Merit selection methods for choosing judges have gradually spread to many states. Such methods normally use a screening committee to make recommendations of potential appointees who will, if placed on the bench by the governor, go before the voters for approval or disapproval of their performance in office.
- Pretrial processes determine the fates of nearly all defendants through case dismissals, decisions defining the charges, and plea bargains that affect more than 90 percent of cases.
- Defense attorneys use motions to suppress evidence and to learn about the prosecution's case.
- The bail process provides opportunities for many defendants to gain pretrial release, but poor defendants may be disadvantaged by their inability to come up with the money or property needed to secure release. New preventive detention statutes may permit judges to hold defendants considered dangerous or likely to flee.
- Bail bondsmen are private businesspeople who provide money for defendants' pretrial release for a fee. Their activities create risks of corruption and discrimination in the bail process, but they may help the system by reminding defendants about court dates and tracking down defendants who disappear.
- Although judges bear primary responsibility for setting bail, prosecutors are especially influential in recommending amounts and conditions for pretrial release.
- Initiatives to reform the bail process include release on recognizance (ROR), police-issued citations, and bail guidelines.
- Pretrial detainees, despite the presumption of innocence, are held in difficult conditions in jails containing mixed populations of convicted offenders, detainees, and troubled people. The shock of being jailed creates risks of suicide and depression.
- The outcomes in criminal cases are significantly influenced by a court's local legal culture, which defines the "going rates" of punishment for various offenses.
- Courtroom workgroups are made up of judges, prosecutors, and defense attorneys who work together to smoothly and efficiently handle cases through cooperative plea bargaining processes.
- The cohesion of a workgroup is enhanced by the physical setting of the courtroom, the different roles performed by each actor—judge, prosecutor, and defense attorney—in the group, and the exchange relationships that develop among these actors.

Questions for Review

1. Why have reformers sought to centralize the administration of courts through unified court systems?
2. Can any judicial selection method expect to remove politics from the process? Is it necessarily harmful to have political aspects in the judicial selection process?
3. What roles do judges play? Do any of these roles conflict?
4. What is the bail-setting process?
5. What are the purposes of pretrial detention? Does pretrial detention violate American beliefs in individual liberty and the presumption of innocence?
6. Who makes up the courtroom workgroup?

ANSWERS TO CHECKPOINTS

1. Separate federal and state court systems handle cases from throughout the land.
2. Most state court systems have trial courts of limited jurisdiction, trial courts of general jurisdiction, intermediate appellate courts, and a court of last resort. The federal system is similar except that it has no trial courts of limited jurisdiction.
3. Most state and county courts are decentralized because they are operated and controlled by the local communities, not a statewide administration.
4. To create a unified court system that has consolidated and simplified structures, centralized management, full funding by the state, and a central personnel system.
5. That judges carefully and deliberately weigh the issues in a case before making a decision. Judges embody justice and dispense it impartially.
6. So that all segments of society will view the decisions as legitimate and fair.

7. Adjudicator, negotiator, administrator.
8. To secure the support of attorneys who aspire to become judges and to ensure that courthouse positions are allocated to party workers.
9. When a vacancy occurs, a nominating commission sends the governor the names of approved candidates. The governor must fill the vacancy from this list. After a year's term, a referendum is held to ask the voters whether the judge should be retained.
10. Arraignments involve the formal reading of charges and the entry of a plea. Preliminary hearings inform defendants of their rights, challenge the evidence, and determine if there is probable cause. Motions seek to bring about a specific action—to suppress evidence and learn about the prosecution's case.
11. Cases are filtered out through the discretionary decisions of prosecutors and judges when they believe that the case is weak, the charges are minor, the defendant is a first offender, there is jail overcrowding, or when prosecutors believe there is inadequate evidence to proceed, or when prosecutors believe that their scarce resources are best directed to other cases.
12. Bail decisions are based primarily on the judge's view of the seriousness of the crime and the defendant's prior record. The decisions are influenced by the prosecutor's recommendations and the defense attorney's counterarguments about the defendant's prior record and ties to the community.
13. Bondsmen may help the system by reminding defendants about their court dates and finding them if they fail to appear. However, bondsmen also may contribute to corruption and discrimination.
14. Bail reform alternatives include police citations, release on recognizance, and 10 percent cash bail.
15. The U.S. Supreme Court ruled that preventive detention did not violate the Constitution's ban on excessive bail because such detentions are not punishment and are merely a way to protect the public.
16. The jail population includes pretrial detainees for whom bail was not set or those who are too poor to pay the bail amount required. People convicted of misdemeanors are also in jail, serving short sentences, along with people convicted of felonies awaiting transfer to prison, and people with psychological or substance abuse problems who have been swept off the streets.
17. Pretrial detainees face the stress of living with difficult and potentially dangerous cellmates. They also face uncertainty about what will happen to their case, their families, their jobs and homes, and their ability to contribute to the preparation of their defense.
18. The local legal culture consists of norms that distinguish between "our" court and other jurisdictions, that stipulate how members should treat one another, and that describe how cases should be processed.
19. The courtroom workgroup is made up of judge, prosecutor, defense counsel, and support staff assigned to a specific courtroom. Through interaction of these members, goals and norms are shared and a set of roles becomes stabilized.
20. Several factors can vary in different cities: the structure of the courtroom workgroups, the influence of the sponsoring organizations, and the sociopolitical environment of the city.

Chapter 8

Prosecution and Defense

The Prosecutorial System

- *Politics and Prosecution*
- *The Prosecutor's Influence*
- *The Prosecutor's Roles*
- *Discretion of the Prosecutor*
- *Key Relationships of the Prosecutor*
- *Decision-Making Policies*
- *Implementing Prosecution Policy*

The Defense Attorney: Image and Reality

- *The Role of the Defense Attorney*
- *Realities of the Defense Attorney's Job*
- *Private Counsel: An Endangered Species?*
- *The Environment of Criminal Practice*
- *Counsel for Indigents*
- *Methods of Providing Indigents with Counsel*
- *Private versus Public Defense*
- *Defense Counsel in the System*
- *Attorney Competence*

ON OCTOBER 25, 1994, a caller dialed 911 in Union, South Carolina, to say that a distraught woman had appeared on the doorstep seeking help because her two young sons had been kidnapped. The frantic mother, Susan Smith, described the kidnapper as an African-American man wearing a knit cap and armed with a gun who had approached her stopped car at a traffic light, forced her out of the car, and sped off with her children. Law enforcement officials quickly mounted an intensive search throughout the country and the case received national attention as Smith stood before television cameras issuing emotional pleas for the return of her children.

Two weeks later, Smith's story crumbled. She failed two lie-detector tests, and eventually confessed that the car—and her sons—could be found in a nearby lake. Divers found the young boys' bodies, still strapped into their car seats, in the upside-down vehicle at the murky bottom of the lake. The chilling conclusion of the kidnapping hoax generated troubling questions for observers throughout the country. How could a mother kill her own children? Why would she do such a thing? Why did this white woman arouse racial tensions by falsely claiming that she was victimized by a menacing black kidnapper? Most difficult of all, perhaps, how should society punish someone who commits such a terrible act?

County prosecutor Thomas Pope faced difficult decisions. As part of his responsibilities as prosecutor, Pope could use his discretion to decide whether to charge Smith with first-degree murder for committing planned, intentional killings. As information emerged about Smith's troubled life he also had the option of charging her with a lesser homicide offense, such as manslaughter, if he believed that she committed a rash act, produced by emotion rather than premeditation. In addition, he had to decide whether this was an appropriate case in which to seek society's ultimate punishment: the death penalty.

Eventually, he charged Smith with premeditated murder and he decided to ask the jury to recommend that Smith be executed for this terrible crime. Pope argued that Smith had intentionally committed the most horrible of all crimes against the most vulnerable of all victims, small children who place complete trust in their parents. Moreover, she had manipulated law enforcement officials and, indeed, the entire nation through the news media, by creating a phony story about a kidnapping. Thus, according to Pope, Smith deserved the ultimate punishment because she demonstrated her intentions to commit—and get away with—the most horrible of crimes.

Susan Smith was represented by David Bruck, a South Carolina attorney who was nationally known for his opposition to the death penalty. Bruck painted a picture of a troubled woman who had become overwhelmed by the emotional scars of her difficult life. A woman who, according to Bruck, could feel pushed to attempt suicide by driving her car into a lake. Perhaps it was only by tragic chance that she panicked and survived by escaping from the car, yet could do nothing to save the children whom she had sought to take with her in ending her own life. In his role as defense attorney, Bruck wanted the jury to ask itself what society would accomplish by putting to death a mother who was consumed and tortured by the guilt of causing her own children's deaths. An execution would mean one more death, but it would do nothing to bring back the children for whom society felt such painful sadness.

The prosecutor and the defense attorney each played their proper roles. Their strong arguments on behalf of the state and defendant presented the judge and jury with choices about how to answer the difficult question of appropriate punishment. Ultimately, the jury declined to recommend the death penalty and Smith was sentenced to life in prison. Was this result a clear-cut "victory" for the defense? Not necessarily so. The outcome of Smith's case may be viewed as the attainment of a measure of justice through the criminal court process.

A key difference between Smith's case and most criminal justice cases is that the important decisions about how to address the tragic murder occurred under the glare of news camera lights and public scrutiny. The attorneys' decisions and strategies were visible. In most cases, however, the attorneys' decisions, strategies, and agreements take place behind closed doors. Thus it is often difficult to assess the basis for prosecutors' and defense attorneys' decisions. Moreover, it is hard to evaluate whether each lawyer enthusiastically represented his or her side in the case when the public only hears about the results of the plea bargaining agreement and cannot monitor the lawyers' interactions and negotiations.

In essence, our system places tremendous power and responsibility in the hands of attorneys for each side in a criminal case. As a result, the justice system's ability to handle cases and produce fair results depends on the dedication, skill, and enthusiasm that these lawyers bring to the tasks and decisions that they control in the private meetings that determine the fates of most criminal defendants.

Questions for Inquiry

What are the roles of the prosecuting attorney?

What is the process by which criminal charges are filed, and what role does the prosecutor's discretion play in that process?

With whom does the prosecutor interact in decision making?

What is the day-to-day reality of criminal defense work in the United States?

Who becomes a defense attorney?

How is counsel provided for defendants who cannot afford a private attorney?

What role does the defense attorney play in the system, and what is the nature of the attorney-client relationship?

THE PROSECUTORIAL SYSTEM

Prosecuting attorneys make discretionary decisions about whether to pursue criminal charges, which charges to make, and what sentence to recommend. Except in a few states, no higher authority can second-guess or change these decisions. Because the prosecutor has significant discretion to make such decisions without direct interference from either the law or other actors in the justice system, prosecu-

prosecuting attorney

A legal representative of the state with sole responsibility for bringing criminal charges. In some states referred to as district attorney, state's attorney, commonwealth attorney, or county attorney.

tors are more independent than almost all other public officials (Caulfield, 1994). Because their decisions are made in private, gaining a firm understanding of the power, function, and role of this key actor is important.

Most crimes are violations of state laws, so the vast majority of criminal cases are handled in the 2,343 county-level offices of the prosecuting attorney, who pursues cases that violate state law. In various states the prosecuting attorney is known as the district attorney, state's attorney, commonwealth attorney, or county attorney (BJS, 1996. *Bulletin*, October).

In rural areas the prosecutor's office may be composed solely of the prosecuting attorney and a part-time assistant. By contrast, in some urban jurisdictions, such as Los Angeles, which employs 500 assistant prosecutors and numerous legal assistants and investigators, the office is organized according to various types of crimes. Many assistant prosecutors seek to use the trial experience gained in the prosecutor's office as a means of moving on to a more highly paid position in a private law firm.

United States attorney

Officials responsible for the prosecution of crimes that violate the laws of the United States. Appointed by the president and assigned to a U.S. district court jurisdiction.

For cases that involve violation of federal criminal laws, prosecutions are handled in federal court by **United States attorneys**. These attorneys are responsible for a large number of drug-related and white-collar crime cases. They are appointed by the president and are part of the Department of Justice. One U.S. attorney and a staff of assistant U.S. attorneys prosecute cases in each of the ninety-four U.S. district courts.

state attorney general

Chief legal officer of a state responsible for both civil and criminal matters.

Each state has an elected **attorney general**, who usually has the power to bring prosecutions in certain cases. A state attorney general may, for example, handle a statewide consumer fraud case if a chain of auto repair shops is suspected of overcharging customers. In Alaska, Delaware, and Rhode Island, the state attorney general also directs all local prosecutions.

Politics and Prosecution

In all states except Connecticut and New Jersey, prosecutors are elected, usually for a four-year term; the office thus is heavily involved in local politics. By seeking to please voters many prosecutors have tried to use their local office as a springboard to higher office—such as state legislator, governor, or member of Congress. They may hire particular assistant prosecutors or make choices about what crimes to emphasize based on political considerations and the need to gain reelection.

CHECKPOINT

1. What are the titles of the officials responsible for criminal prosecution at the federal, state, and local levels of government?

(Answers are at the end of the chapter.)

The Prosecutor's Influence

Prosecutors have great influence because they are concerned with all aspects of the criminal justice process (Jacoby, 1995). By contrast, other decision makers are involved in only part of the process. From arrest to final disposition of a case, prosecutors can make decisions that will largely determine the defendant's fate. The prosecutor chooses the cases to be prosecuted, selects the charges to be brought, recommends the bail amount, approves agreements with the defendant, and urges the judge to impose a particular sentence. The other actors in the system may adjust their decisions and actions to match the preferences of the prosecutor. For example, police officers' investigation and arrest practices are likely to reflect the prosecutor's priorities. Thus, prosecutors influence the decisions of others while also shaping their own actions in ways that reinforce their relationships with police, defense attorneys, and judges.

Prosecutors gain additional power from the fact that their decisions and actions are hidden from public view. For example, a prosecutor and a defense attorney may strike a bargain whereby the prosecutor reduces a charge in exchange for a guilty plea or drops a charge if the defendant agrees to seek psychiatric help. In such instances a decision on a case is reached in a way that is nearly invisible to the public.

CHECKPOINT

2. What are the powers of the prosecuting attorney?

The Prosecutor's Roles

As "lawyers for the state," prosecutors must do everything they can to win a conviction; yet as members of the legal profession they must see that justice is done even if it means that the accused is not convicted. These pressures are often called "the prosecutor's dilemma." Another source of conflict is "prosecutor's bias," sometimes called a "prosecution complex." Although they are supposed to represent all the people, including the accused, prosecutors may view themselves as instruments of law enforcement. Thus, as advocates on behalf of the state, their strong desire to close each case with a conviction may keep them from recognizing unfair procedures or evidence of innocence.

As lawyers for the state, prosecutors are expected to do everything to win each case, but they are also expected to see that justice is done.

Because of their personal values and professional goals, and the political climate of their city or county, prosecutors may define their roles differently from those of their counterparts in other places. For example, a prosecutor who believes that young offenders can be rehabilitated might send them to counseling programs; one who believes that young offenders should be prosecuted as adults might seek to process them through the adult system of courts and corrections. A prosecutor with no assistants and few resources for conducting full-blown jury trials may be forced to stress effective plea bargaining, while a prosecutor in a wealthier county may have more options when deciding whether to take cases to trial.

When prosecutors are asked about their roles, they often mention these four, each quite distinct from the others:

1. Trial counsel for the police. Prosecutors who see their main function in this light believe they should reflect the views of law enforcement in the courtroom and take a crime-fighter stance in public.

2. House counsel for the police. These prosecutors believe their main function is to give legal advice so that arrests will stand up in court.
3. Representative of the court. Such prosecutors believe their main function is to enforce the rules of due process to ensure that the police act according to the law and uphold the rights of defendants.
4. Elected official. These prosecutors may be most responsive to public opinion. The political impact of their decisions is one of their major concerns.

Each of these roles involves a different view of the prosecutor's "clients" as well as his or her own responsibilities. In the first two roles, prosecutors appear to believe that the police are the clients of their legal practice. The third role may emphasize the prosecutor's responsibilities as guardian of justice instead of leader in crime control. The final role may involving representing the public in the courts as well as self-interest in aspiring to gain reelection or seek higher office.

IDEAS IN PRACTICE

Lieutenant Roger Cirella of the police drug task force of Northwest City entered the office of Chief Deputy Prosecutor Michael Ryan. Cirella reported that during questioning a well-known drug dealer hinted that he could provide evidence against a pharmacist suspected of illegally selling drugs. The officer wanted to transfer the case to the friendlier hands of a certain deputy prosecutor and to arrange for a reduction of charges and bail.

Cirella: Yesterday we got a break in the pharmacy case. We had arrested Sam Hanson after an undercover buy down on First Avenue. He says that a druggist at the Green Cross Pharmacy is selling out the back door. We thought that something like that was happening because we had seen these bums standing around there, but we've not been able to prove it. Hanson says he will cooperate if we'll go easy on him. Now, I'd like to get this case moved to Wadsworth, he's worked with us before, and that new guy who's on it now just doesn't understand our problems.

Ryan: O.K., but what's that going to accomplish?

Cirella: We also need to be able to fix it so Hanson gets out on bail without letting the druggies out there know he has become an informer. If we can get Judge Griffin to reduce bail, Hanson can probably put up the bond. Now we also need to reduce the charges yet keep him on the string so that we can bring him right back if he doesn't play our game.

Ryan: I want to cooperate with you guys, but I can't let the boss get a lot of heat for letting a pusher out on the street. How are we going to know that he's not going to screw up?

Cirella: Believe me, we will keep tabs on him.

Ryan: O.K. But don't come here telling me we're going to get splashed with mud in the press.

What does this scenario tell us about the problem of enforcing drug laws?

CHECKPOINT

3. What are the roles of the prosecutor?

Discretion of the Prosecutor

Because they have such broad discretion, prosecutors can shape their decisions to fit different interests. Their decisions might be based on a desire to impress voters through tough "throw-the-book-at-them" charges in a highly publicized case (Maschke, 1995). Their decisions might stem from their personal values, such as an emphasis on leniency and rehabilitation for young offenders. They may also shape their decisions to please local judges by, for example, accepting plea agreements that will keep the judges from being burdened by too many time-consuming trials. The prosecutor has almost complete control over decisions about dropping or pursuing charges and making plea agreements. The discretion of the prosecutor is illustrated in the Ideas in Practice.

While the rate of such dismissals varies from place to place, in most cities up to half of all arrests do not lead to formal charges. Prosecutors may decide not to press charges because of factors related to a particular case or because they have a policy of not bringing charges for certain offenses.

Even after deciding that a case should be prosecuted, the prosecutor has great freedom in deciding what charges to file. Criminal incidents may involve a number of laws, so the prosecutor can bring a single charge or more than one. For example, suppose that Smith, who is armed, breaks into a grocery store, assaults the proprietor, and robs the cash drawer. What charges may the prosecutor file?

By virtue of having committed the robbery, the accused can be charged with at least four crimes: breaking and entering, assault, armed robbery, and carrying a dangerous weapon. Other charges, or **counts**, may be added, depending on the nature of the incident. A forger, for instance, may be charged with one count for each act of forgery committed. By filing as many charges as possible, the prosecutor strengthens his or her position in plea negotiations by increasing the supply of "bargaining chips."

The discretionary power to set charges does not give the prosecutor complete control over plea bargaining. Defense attorneys strengthen their position through the **discovery** process, in which information from the prosecutor's case file must be made available to the defense. For example, the defense has the right to see any statements made by the accused during interrogation by the police and the results of any physical or psychological tests. This information tells the defense attorney about the strengths and weaknesses of the prosecution's case.

After the charge has been made, the prosecutor may reduce it in exchange for a guilty plea or enter a notation of ***nolle prosequi*** (nol. pros.). The latter is a freely made decision to drop charges, either all of them or one or more counts. When a prosecutor decides to drop charges, no higher authorities can force him or her to reinstate them.

count

Each separate offense of which a person is accused in an indictment or an information.

discovery

A prosecutor's pretrial disclosure to the defense of facts and evidence to be introduced at trial.

nolle prosequi

An entry made by a prosecutor on the record of a case and announced in court to indicate that the charges specified will not be prosecuted. In effect, the charges are thereby dismissed.

CHECKPOINT

4. How does a prosecutor use discretion to decide how to treat each defendant?

Key Relationships of the Prosecutor

Prosecutors' decisions are not based solely on formal policies and their conception of their role (Fridell, 1990). They are also influenced by relationships with other actors in the justice system. Despite their independent authority, prosecutors must consider how police, judges, and others will react. They depend on these other officials in order to prosecute cases successfully. In turn, the success of police, judges, and corrections officials depends on prosecutors' effectiveness in identifying and convicting lawbreakers. Consequently these officials build exchange relationships in which they cooperate with each other.

For example, prosecutors depend on the police to provide both the suspects and the evidence needed to convict lawbreakers. Prosecutors cannot control the types of cases brought to them because they cannot investigate crimes on their own. Thus the police control the initiation of the criminal justice process through their actions and in investigating crimes and arresting suspects. Police actions may create problems for prosecutors if, for example, the police make arrests without gathering enough evidence to ensure conviction. Prosecutors and police have an exchange relationship in which the success of each depends on cooperation with the other (Buchanan, 1989).

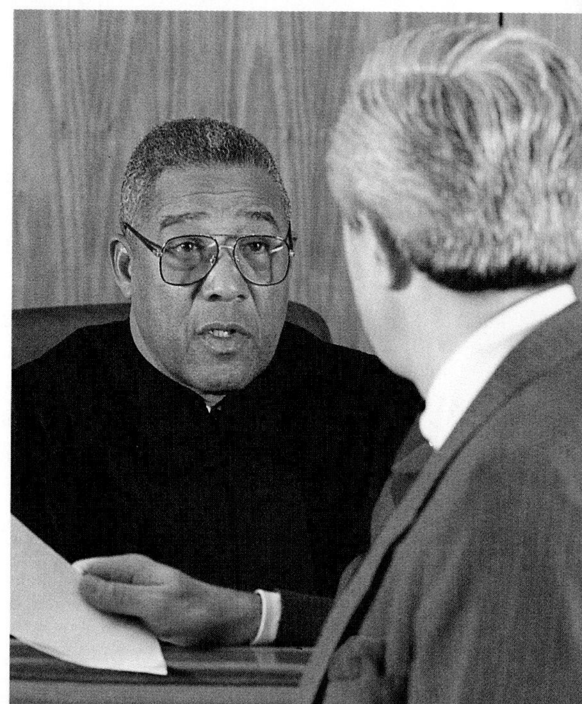

Prosecutors' decisions are influenced by their knowledge and relationships with judges. For example, knowing that a judge imposes exceptionally lenient sentences for particular offenses may discourage the prosecutor from pursuing such cases.

Prosecutors also depend on the cooperation of victims and witnesses. Although a case can be prosecuted whether or not a victim wishes to press charges, many prosecutors will not pursue cases in which a victim who is unwilling to cooperate must provide the key testimony and other necessary evidence. Prosecutors need the cooperation of people who have witnessed crimes.

Prosecutors may also base their decisions on whether or not the victim and defendant had a prior relationship. Studies have shown that prosecutions are most successful when they are aimed at defendants accused of committing crimes against strangers (Boland et al., 1983). When the victim is an acquaintance, a friend, or even a relative of the defendant, he or she may refuse to act as a witness, and prosecutors and juries may view the offense as less serious.

The decision to prosecute is often based on an assessment of the victim's role in his or her own victimization and the victim's credibility as a witness. If a victim has a criminal record, the prosecutor may choose not to pursue the case in the belief that a jury would not consider the victim a credible witness—even though the jury will never learn that the victim has a criminal record. In fact, the decision not to prosecute may actually reflect the prosecutor's belief that someone with a criminal record is untrustworthy or does not deserve the protection of the law. In other words, the prosecutor's own biases may affect which cases he or she pursues (Frohmann, 1997). If a victim is poorly dressed, uneducated, or a poor communicator, the prosecutor may be inclined to dismiss charges out of fear that a jury would find the victim unpersuasive (Stanko, 1988).

In recent years, many people have called for measures that would force prosecutors to make victims more central to the prosecution. Because in criminal cases it is the state that pursues charges against the accused, the victim is often forgotten in the process. The victims' rights movement produced proposals to give victims a chance to comment on plea bargains, sentences, and parole decisions. In June 1996 President Bill Clinton endorsed a proposed constitutional amendment that, if ratified, would require prosecutors to keep victims informed on the progress of criminal cases and allow them to have some input in decisions on bail, plea bargains, and sentencing.

Although plea bargaining is often controversial, it keeps cases moving through the overburdened court system. Prosecutors depend on defense attorneys and judges to cooperate in plea bargaining. It is hard for prosecutors to persuade defendants and their attorneys to accept plea agreements unless judges' sentencing patterns are predictable. If the defendants and their lawyers are to accept a lesser charge or a promise of a lighter sentence in exchange for a guilty plea, there must be some basis to believe that the judge will support the agreement. Although some judges will informally approve plea agreements before the plea is entered, other judges believe that it is improper for them to take part in plea bargaining. Because these judges are unable to state their agreement with the details of any bargain, the prosecutor and defense attorney use the judge's past performance as a guide in arranging a plea that the court will accept.

Prosecutors also depend on positive relationships with the public and the news media, both to gain public cooperation in fighting crime and to keep their jobs as public officials. Prosecuting attorneys, like police chiefs and school superintendents, will not remain in office long if they are out of step with community values. The prosecutor's office usually has the public in mind when it makes its decisions.

CHECKPOINT

5. What are the prosecutor's key exchange relationships?

Decision-Making Policies

Despite the many factors that may affect prosecutors' decisions in each case, we can draw some general conclusions about how prosecutors approach their jobs. Prosecutors develop their own policies on how cases will be handled. These policies shape the decisions made by the assistant prosecutors and thus have a major impact on the administration of justice. In different counties, prosecutors may pursue different goals in forming policies on which cases to pursue, which ones to drop, and which ones to plea bargain. For example, some prosecutors may wish to maintain a high conviction rate and therefore will drop cases with weak evidence. Others may be concerned about using limited resources effectively. They will focus most of their time and energy on the most serious crimes.

Figure 8.1 shows how prosecutors handle felony cases in two different jurisdictions. Some make extensive use of screening and are less inclined to press charges. Guilty pleas are the main method of processing cases in some offices, while pleas of not guilty strain the courts' trial resources in others. Some offices remove cases—by diverting or referring them to other agencies—soon after they are brought to the prosecutor's attention by the police; in others, disposition occurs as late as the first day of trial. The period from the receipt of the police report to the start of the trial therefore is a time of review in which the prosecutor uses discretion to decide what actions should be taken.

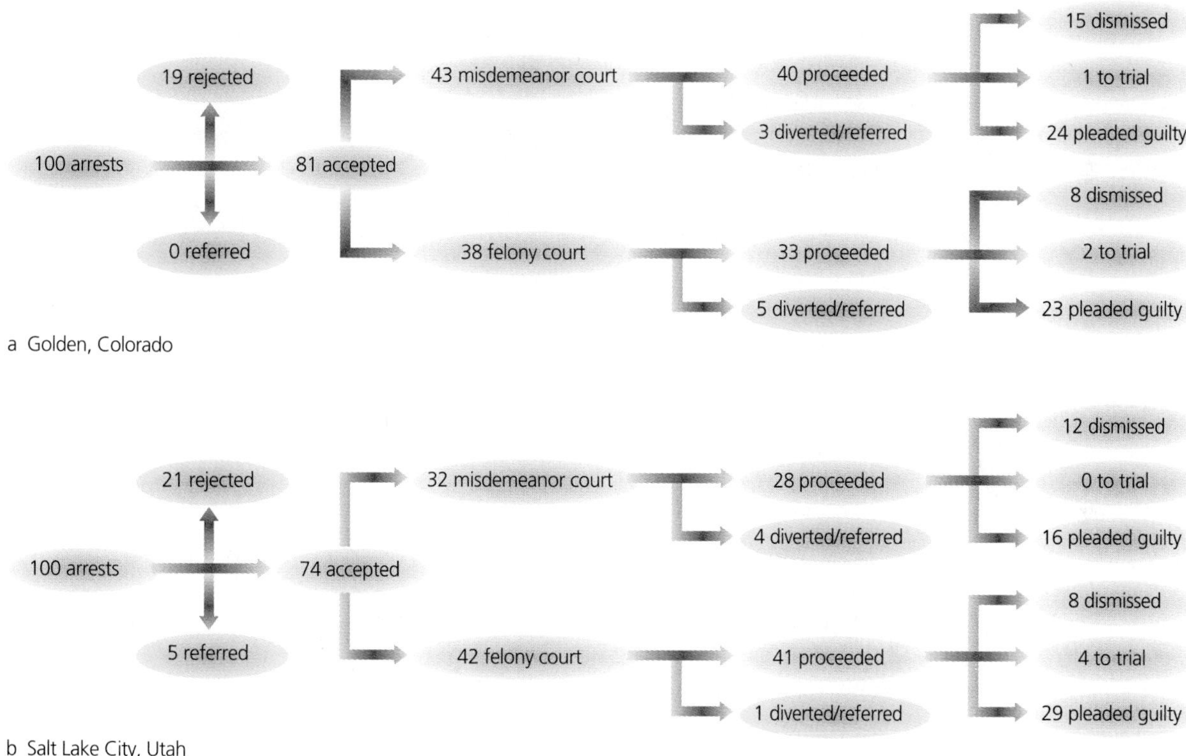

Figure 8.1
Differences in how prosecutors handle felony cases in two jurisdictions

The discretion of the prosecutor is evident in these two flowcharts. Note that different screening policies seem to be in operation: cases are referred earlier in the process in Utah and later in Colorado.

SOURCE: U.S. Department of Justice, Bureau of Justice Statistics, *Report to the Nation on Crime and Justice,* 2d ed. (Washington, D.C.: Government Printing Office, 1988), 71.

Implementing Prosecution Policy

Joan Jacoby analyzed the management policies that prosecutors use during the pretrial process and how they staff their offices to achieve their goals. On the basis of data from more than 3,000 prosecutors, she described three policy models: legal sufficiency, system efficiency, and trial sufficiency. The choice of a policy model is shaped by personal aspects of the prosecutor (such as role conception), external factors such as crime levels, and the relationship of prosecution to the other parts of the criminal justice system (Jacoby, 1979).

The policy model adopted by a prosecutor's office affects the screening and disposing of cases. According to the policy models shown in Figure 8.2, prosecutors select certain points in the process to dispose of most of the cases brought to them by the police. Each model identifies the point in the process at which cases are filtered out of the system. A particular model may be chosen to advance specific goals, such as saving the prosecutor's time and energy for the most clear-cut or serious cases. Each model also affects how and when prosecutors interact with defense attorneys in exchanging information or discussing plea bargain options.

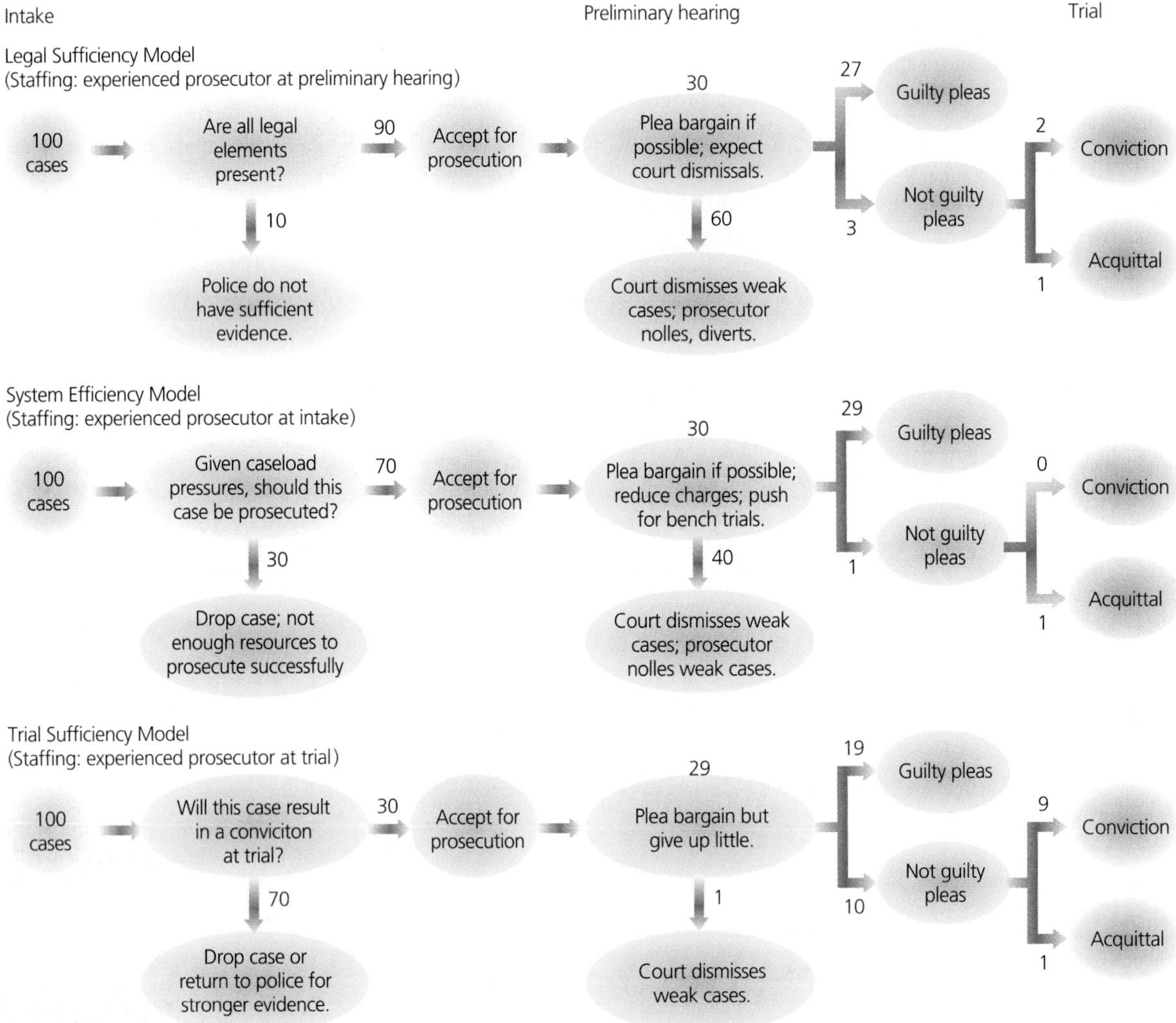

Figure 8.2
Three policy models of prosecutorial case management

Prosecutors develop policies to guide the way their offices will manage cases. All of these models assume that a portion of arrests will be dropped at some point in the system so that few cases reach trial.

In the **legal sufficiency model**, prosecutors are merely asking whether there is enough evidence to serve as a basis for prosecution. Some prosecutors believe they should pursue any case for which they think they can prove that the minimum legal elements of the charge are met. Because of limited resources, assistant prosecutors, especially those assigned to misdemeanor courts, make extensive use of plea bargains to keep cases flowing through the courts. In this model judges may dismiss many cases after determining that there is not enough evidence for prosecution to continue.

The **system efficiency model** aims at speedy and early disposition of a case. Each case is evaluated in light of current caseload pressures. To close cases quickly, the prosecutor might charge the defendant with a felony but agree to reduce the charge to a misdemeanor in exchange for a guilty plea. According to Jacoby's research, this model is usually followed when the trial court is backlogged and the prosecutor has limited resources.

In the **trial sufficiency model**, (defined on p. 188) a case is accepted and charges are made only when there is enough evidence to ensure conviction. For each case the prosecutor asks, "Will this case result in a conviction?" The prosecutor's prediction about the likelihood of conviction may not be correct in every case. However, the prosecutor will make every effort to win a conviction when he or she believes there is evidence to prove that all necessary legal elements for a crime are present. This model requires good police work, a prosecution staff with trial experience, and—because there is less plea bargaining—courts that are not too crowded to handle trials on a regular basis.

Prosecution policies are not made in isolation but are created within the context of political and community pressures. Here, Boundary County Prosecutor Denise Woodbury, with Sheriff Greg Sprungl at her side, announces that she has filed charges against former Ruby Ridge resident Kevin Harris and FBI Sharpshooter Lon Horiuchi during a news conference in Bonners Ferry, Idaho.

Clearly, these three models lead to different results. While a suspect's case may be dismissed for lack of evidence in a "trial sufficiency" court, the same case may be prosecuted and the defendant pressured to enter a guilty plea in a "legal sufficiency" court. In the Workperspective by former Deputy District Attorney Kathryn Zoglin, which prosecution policy guided her discretionary decisions about whom to prosecute?

Case Evaluation

The **accusatory process** is the series of activities that take place from the moment a suspect is arrested and booked by the police to the moment the formal charge—in the form of an indictment or information—is filed with the court.

In an indictment, evidence is presented to a grand jury made up of citizens who determine whether to issue a formal charge. In an information, the prosecutor files the charge. Although these two charging processes seem clear-cut, in practice variations can mix the roles of the city police, prosecutor, and court. In some places the prosecutor has full control of the charging decision; in others, the police informally make the decision, which is then approved by the prosecutor; in still others, the prosecutor not only controls the charging process but also is involved in functions such as setting the court calendar, appointing defense counsel for indigents, and sentencing.

legal sufficiency

The presence of the minimum legal elements necessary for prosecution of a case. When a prosecutor's decision to prosecute a case is customarily based on legal sufficiency, a great many cases are accepted for prosecution, but the majority of them are disposed of by plea bargaining or dismissal.

A prosecutor's decision will be influenced by the policy model that his or her office uses. Each model requires an evaluation of the quality and quantity of evidence for a particular case. Each may also include assessments of the resources of the prosecutor's office and trial court. For example, if the court is overcrowded and the prosecutor does not have enough lawyers, the prosecutor may be forced to use the system efficiency model even if he or she would prefer to use another approach.

system efficiency

Policy of the prosecutor's office that encourages speedy and early disposition of cases in response to caseload pressures. Weak cases are screened out at intake, and other nontrial alternatives are used as the primary means of disposition.

In evaluating cases, prosecutors may knowingly or unknowingly permit their personal biases to affect their decisions. A study in Los Angeles County found that men were more likely to be prosecuted than women and that Hispanics were prosecuted more often than African Americans, who were prosecuted more often than Anglos. The researchers believed that in borderline cases—those that could either be pursued or dismissed—the scale was often tipped against minorities (Spohn, Gruhl, and Welch, 1987).

Clearly the prosecutor's established policies and decisions play a key role in determining whether charges will be filed against a defendant. Keep in mind,

WORK*Perspective*

Kathryn Zoglin
Former Deputy District Attorney
Santa Clara County, California

While working on my undergraduate degree in psychology, I decided to go to law school. Although I planned to work in the public sector, I had no particular interest in criminal justice. In fact, I took only one criminal law course during law school. As it turned out, my career as a lawyer led me into the criminal justice system. I have represented the government in a wide range of cases involving criminal justice issues: prosecution of misdemeanors and felonies; jail conditions; excessive use of force by police; and employment discrimination in criminal justice jobs.

After law school, I worked as an attorney for a San Francisco law firm. I handled matters related to lawsuits involving major corporations, but I had few opportunities to present arguments in court. A friend of mine worked for the Santa Clara County District Attorney and told me how much she enjoyed her job. Based on my friend's experience, I applied for a job with the district attorney in order to gain courtroom experience and tackle the challenge of handling a large, fast-paced caseload. I also wanted to return to my original career objective of working in the public sector in order to devote my energies to serving society. In particular, I saw my work as a prosecutor as a chance to help crime victims.

During my first week as a deputy district attorney, I observed prosecutors handling cases. The second week I was handed my own caseload. Like other prosecutors, I learned through on-the-job experience rather than formal training. I spent my first year prosecuting misdemeanor cases. Then, after a few months handling preliminary hearings, I joined the narcotics prosecution team, where I worked closely with undercover police officers. After one year handling drug prosecutions, I transferred to the robbery and assault team. I spent two years prosecuting robbery and assault cases, including domestic violence cases.

I left the Santa Clara County District Attorney's Office to become an assistant city attorney for San Francisco. In that position, I handled a variety of lawsuits, including allegations that police officers used excessive force in making arrests. I also represented the city in a long-standing case concerning allegations of overcrowded conditions and lack of medical care for inmates in the city's jail. Because the city had agreed to make changes at the jail, much of my time was spent talking to jail officials, inmates' attorneys, and the court about whether the city was fulfilling its obligations properly. After a few years in San Francisco, I returned to Santa Clara County government, where I now handle civil litigation, including lawsuits alleging employment discrimination in the hiring and promotion of corrections officers at the county jail.

In both civil and criminal cases, attorneys possess significant discretion in deciding how to handle a case. Discretion is particularly important in criminal cases because prosecutors decide whether to dismiss charges, reduce charges, or take a case to trial. Some prosecutors will take cases to trial even if the evidence has significant weaknesses because they are willing to let the jury decide guilt. By contrast, I would not take a case forward unless I actually believed that the evidence established that the defendant was guilty. I felt that I was responsible for using the government's power to prosecute and punish only when I was confident about the defendant's guilt. In one robbery case, I decided against pursuing charges because I had doubts about the evidence. The camera at an ATM machine took pictures of the robbery, but it was not clear from the grainy pictures if our suspect was actually the robber. I declined to prosecute even though I knew other prosecutors in the office probably disagreed with my decision.

WORK*Perspective*

though, that the prosecutor's decision-making power is not limited to decisions about charges. As illustrated in Figure 8.3, the prosecutor makes important decisions at each stage, both before and after a defendant's guilt is determined. Because the prosecutor's involvement and influence span the justice process, from seeking search warrants during early investigations to arguing against post-conviction appeals, the prosecutor is a highly influential actor in criminal cases. No other participant in the system is involved in so many different stages of the criminal process.

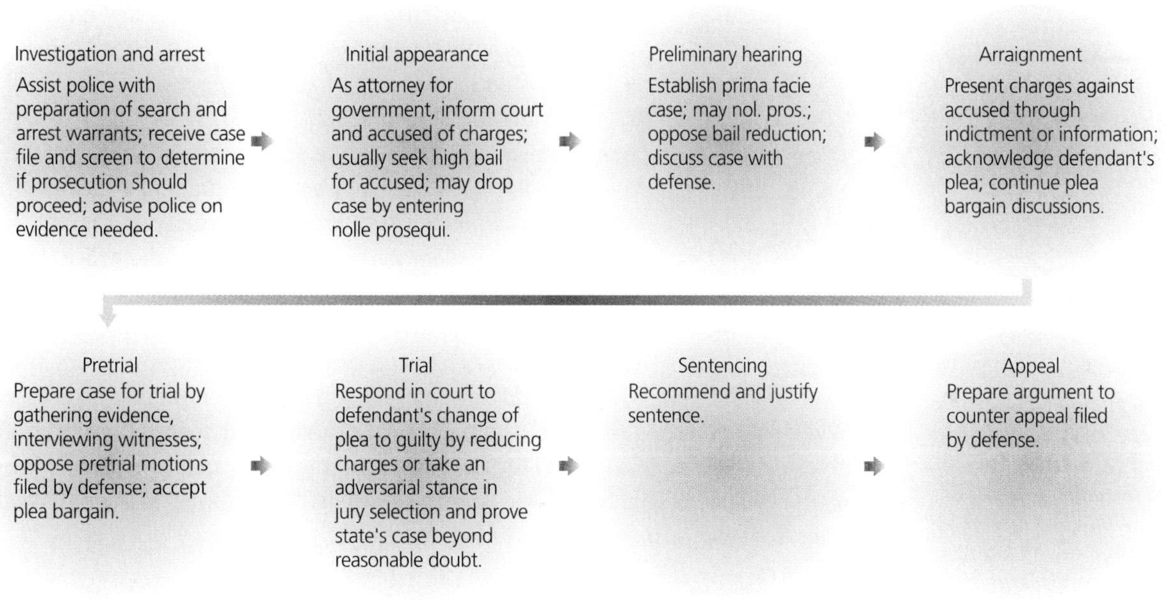

Investigation and arrest
Assist police with preparation of search and arrest warrants; receive case file and screen to determine if prosecution should proceed; advise police on evidence needed.

Initial appearance
As attorney for government, inform court and accused of charges; usually seek high bail for accused; may drop case by entering nolle prosequi.

Preliminary hearing
Establish prima facie case; may nol. pros.; oppose bail reduction; discuss case with defense.

Arraignment
Present charges against accused through indictment or information; acknowledge defendant's plea; continue plea bargain discussions.

Pretrial
Prepare case for trial by gathering evidence, interviewing witnesses; oppose pretrial motions filed by defense; accept plea bargain.

Trial
Respond in court to defendant's change of plea to guilty by reducing charges or take an adversarial stance in jury selection and prove state's case beyond reasonable doubt.

Sentencing
Recommend and justify sentence.

Appeal
Prepare argument to counter appeal filed by defense.

Figure 8.3
Typical actions of a prosecuting attorney in processing a felony case

The prosecutor has certain responsibilities at various points in the process. At each point the prosecutor is an advocate for the state's case against the accused.

CHECKPOINT

6. What are the three models of prosecution policy and how do they differ?

THE DEFENSE ATTORNEY: IMAGE AND REALITY

While the prosecutor has impressive powers, the **defense attorney** has major responsibilities. Defense attorneys must monitor and protect the constitutional rights of defendants. They must also present any available evidence and arguments in an effort to poke holes in the prosecution's case or to gain a favorable plea agreement for the accused. Because many of these tasks are carried out in closed-door plea negotiations with prosecutors, evaluating the quality of the defense attorney's performance isn't easy. Like prosecutors, defense attorneys cannot be readily observed or controlled by the public.

Television usually portrays defense attorneys as fiery advocates whose passionate arguments sway the jury. In reality, however, most cases are processed through plea bargaining, discretionary dismissals, and other decisions by actors in the justice system. In these cases the defense attorney may seem less like the prosecutor's adversary and more like a partner in the effort to dispose of cases as quickly and efficiently as possible through negotiation.

trial sufficiency

The presence of sufficient legal elements to ensure successful prosecution of a case. When a prosecutor's decision to prosecute a case is customarily based on trial sufficiency, only cases that seem certain to result in conviction at trial are accepted for prosecution. Use of plea bargaining is minimal; good police work and court capacity to go to trial are required.

The Role of the Defense Attorney

Nationally known criminal defense specialist Gerry Spence, conferring with Randy Weaver, is one of the small number of attorneys who have built their reputations on taking highly publicized cases for large fees.

Defense attorneys have knowledge of law and procedure, skill in investigation, experience in advocacy, and, in many cases, relationships with prosecutors and judges that will help a defendant obtain the best possible outcome. In the American legal system the defense attorney performs the key function of making sure that the prosecution proves its case in court or has substantial evidence of guilt before a guilty plea leads to conviction and punishment.

As shown in Figure 8.4, the defense attorney advises the defendant and protects his or her constitutional rights at each stage of the criminal justice process. The defense attorney advises the defendant during questioning by the police, represents him or her at each arraignment and hearing, and serves as advocate for the defendant during the appeal process if there is a conviction. Without a defense attorney, prosecutors and judges would not necessarily respect the rights of the accused. While filling these roles in the criminal justice system, the defense attorney also gives psychological support to the defendant and his or her family. Relatives are often bewildered, frightened, and confused. The defense attorney is the only legal actor available to answer the question, "What will happen next?"

Realities of the Defense Attorney's Job

accusatory process

The series of events from the arrest of a suspect to the filing of a formal charge (through an indictment or information) with the court.

defense attorney

The lawyer who represents the accused and the convicted offender in their dealings with criminal justice officials.

How well do defense attorneys represent their clients? Contrary to the television image of defense attorneys as strong advocates, the enthusiasm and effectiveness of defense attorneys' efforts may vary. Several factors affect the performance of defense attorneys. Attorneys who are inexperienced, uncaring, or overburdened have trouble representing their clients effectively. The attorney may quickly agree to a plea bargain and then work to persuade the defendant to accept it. The attorney's self-interest in disposing of cases quickly, receiving payment, and moving on to other cases may cause the attorney to, in effect, work with the prosecutor to pressure the defendant to plead guilty.

Although skilled defense attorneys will also consider a plea bargain in the earliest stages of a case, their role as an advocate for the defendant will guide their use of plea bargaining. An effective defense attorney does not try to take every case all

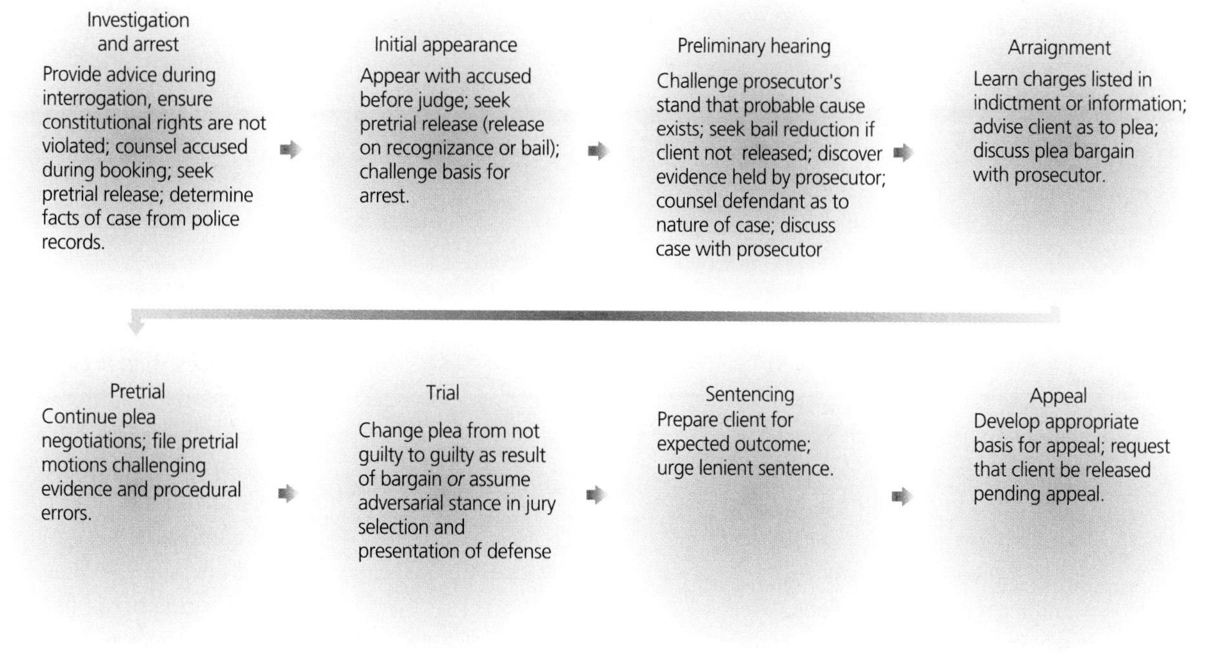

Investigation and arrest
Provide advice during interrogation, ensure constitutional rights are not violated; counsel accused during booking; seek pretrial release; determine facts of case from police records.

Initial appearance
Appear with accused before judge; seek pretrial release (release on recognizance or bail); challenge basis for arrest.

Preliminary hearing
Challenge prosecutor's stand that probable cause exists; seek bail reduction if client not released; discover evidence held by prosecutor; counsel defendant as to nature of case; discuss case with prosecutor

Arraignment
Learn charges listed in indictment or information; advise client as to plea; discuss plea bargain with prosecutor.

Pretrial
Continue plea negotiations; file pretrial motions challenging evidence and procedural errors.

Trial
Change plea from not guilty to guilty as result of bargain *or* assume adversarial stance in jury selection and presentation of defense

Sentencing
Prepare client for expected outcome; urge lenient sentence.

Appeal
Develop appropriate basis for appeal; request that client be released pending appeal.

Figure 8.4
Typical actions of a defense attorney processing a felony case

Defense attorneys are advocates for the accused. They have an obligation to challenge points made by the prosecution and advise clients about legal rights.

the way to trial. In many cases, a negotiated plea with a predictable sentence will serve the defendant better than a trial spent fending off more serious charges. As you read attorney Abraham Hutt's Workperspective, consider how the attorney's responsibilities can require difficult decisions.

The defense attorney's job is made all the more difficult because neither the public nor defendants fully understand the attorney's duties and goals. The public often views defense attorneys as protectors of criminals. In fact, the attorney's basic duty is not to save criminals from punishment but to protect constitutional rights, keep the prosecution honest in preparing and presenting cases, and prevent innocent people from being convicted. In performing these tasks, which ultimately benefit both the defendant and society, the attorney must evaluate and challenge the prosecution's evidence. The defense attorney often negotiates the most appropriate punishment in light of the resources of the court, the strength of the evidence, and the defendant's prior criminal record.

Defendants who, like the public, have watched hours of courtroom drama on television often expect their attorneys to fight vigorous battles against the prosecutor at every stage of the justice process. They do not realize that plea agreements negotiated in a friendly, cooperative way may be in their best interest. Public defenders in particular are often criticized because the defendants cannot choose their legal representatives. The defendants often assume that if the state provided an attorney for them, the attorney must be working for the state rather than on their behalf.

CHECKPOINT

7. How does the image of the defense attorney differ from the attorney's actual role?

WORK*Perspective*

Abraham V. Hutt
Criminal Defense Attorney, Private Practice
Denver, Colorado

After working a manual labor job one summer during college, I knew I needed to make a greater effort to gain experience that would help me choose a career. Because I had long been interested in becoming a lawyer, I wrote letters to law firms, government agencies, and legal aid organizations seeking a summer job the following year. The Colorado State Public Defender's Office offered to give me an unpaid internship. For the next two summers I worked as an investigator interviewing witnesses and helping lawyers prepare to defend poor people accused of crimes. The experience brought me into close contact with trial lawyers and courtrooms as well as police officers, jailed defendants, judges, and jurors. I was hooked by the drama of the criminal justice process that would decide the fates of the individual clients whom I got to know. I was also motivated by my belief that one of our Constitution's most enlightened and inspiring principles is that everyone, no matter what he is accused of, deserves to have an attorney who will fight to protect his rights and help present his case.

Upon graduating from college, I worked for one year as an investigator for a former public defender who had moved to private practice. During law school at the University of Southern California, I returned to the Denver law office for two summers to gain additional experience in criminal defense practice. I spent one summer with a large Los Angeles law firm that handled copyright litigation for movie studios and other commercial matters. Although attorneys for corporations make more money than public defenders, the experience of working with these other areas of law convinced me that I'd rather work on criminal cases than seek the highest possible starting salary.

I spent my first decade as a lawyer working in a three-member law firm that specialized in criminal defense. Then I started my own solo practice. Most of my clients can pay me, although this does not necessarily mean they are wealthy. Many must borrow money to pay their legal bills. Sometimes the court appoints me to represent indigent defendants at state expense. I have defended everything from traffic tickets to death penalty homicides.

One of the many difficult things about counseling clients in the criminal justice system is advising clients to accept plea bargains even when I believe they are innocent. I may advise them to plead guilty and accept a lesser punishment when they face the realistic possibility of horrendous consequences from a mandatory sentence if convicted at trial. For example, I once represented a 16-year-old boy charged with first-degree murder. He had been at a big high school party when a fight broke out. Many of the seventy or so kids at the party had guns and you could hear the sound of gunfire throughout the police tapes of 911 calls made by the neighbors. Kids who didn't have guns used bricks, bottles, rakes, and fence posts to either defend themselves or join in the fray. It was obvious that there was complete confusion, because the testimony of various kids at the party demonstrated that no two of them provided the same account of events. However, one participant in the fight said he saw my client fire a pistol at three boys who were attacking with rakes and fence posts.

Other witnesses said they had seen my client with a gun, but they never saw him fire it. One youth was shot and killed in the chaos.

This tragic event occurred at a moment when people in Denver were frightened about gang violence and many people were urging authorities to treat juvenile offenders more like adults. Consequently, my client was charged with first-degree murder as an adult, meaning that if we lost the trial he would have to serve a mandatory sentence of life in prison with absolutely no possibility of parole. My client said that he brought a gun to the party but he dropped it when he was hit on the head with a brick, and he never saw the gun again as his friends helped him to his car and drove away.

Ultimately the prosecution offered a plea bargain in which my client could plead guilty to manslaughter, which, although it carried a maximum possible penalty of sixteen years in prison, made him eligible for a new Youth Offender program. Under this program, he would be housed with other juvenile offenders serving adult sentences in a "boot camp" program. He would not be locked up with hardened adult offenders. He also would have the opportunity to be in educational programs. How can you advise a kid to turn down that deal, in which he might get out in as little as five years, as opposed to the risk of spending the rest of his life in prison? But how can you tell a kid to plead guilty and go to prison when you don't believe he committed the crime? How do you explain to his parents that the justice system has forced their son to make this choice? How do you stand next to him in court while a judge asks him if he is entering his guilty plea freely and voluntarily? People ask me how I can sleep at night defending guilty people and helping some of them remain free. They don't realize how common it is for defense lawyers to deal with other troubling issues in defending people who are wrongly accused but who face overwhelming odds in trying to prove their innocence.

In this case, I tell myself that my client's chance of survival and success in life are much greater with the plea bargain. He might have been seriously victimized or killed serving hard time as a teenage lifer among hardened adult offenders. Even if we went to trial and I managed to win his case, there was a significant risk that the victim's family would be gunning for him as a matter of revenge. Perhaps when he gets out, enough time will have passed for this teenager to mature so that he can survive and build a life of his own.

WORK*Perspective*

Private Counsel: An Endangered Species?

Of an estimated 800,000 practicing lawyers in the United States, only between 10,000 and 20,000 accept criminal cases on a "more than occasional" basis, and of these only 14,000 work as public defenders. One study found that the number and quality of privately retained lawyers varied among cities, depending on legal, institutional, and political factors (Wice, 1978).

According to Wice, the average criminal lawyer practices alone, not as a member of a law firm, comes from a middle-class, nonprofessional background, and graduated from a lesser law school. Many entered private criminal practice after working as public lawyers. Wice found that 38 percent of his sample of private criminal lawyers had been prosecutors and that 24 percent had been public defenders, had worked for legal services (doing civil law work), or had held civil service positions (Wice, 1978:75).

Three kinds of lawyers handle criminal cases on a regular basis. The first group is composed of nationally known attorneys who charge large fees in highly publicized cases. In the murder trial of former football star O. J. Simpson, the defense team included two attorneys who had built their reputations by defending famous clients: F. Lee Bailey, who defended heiress Patricia Hearst, and Alan Dershowitz, who handled the appeal for boxer Mike Tyson. Each large city has a small group of defense attorneys who are the lawyers of choice for defendants who can afford to pay high fees. O. J. Simpson's other attorneys, Johnnie Cochran and Robert Shapiro, were well known in Los Angeles for their success in big cases. These attorneys make handsome incomes by representing white-collar criminals, drug dealers, and affluent people charged with crimes. When business executives are charged with drunk driving, for example, they may be willing to pay top dollar to attorneys who can help them avoid conviction and the loss of their license. Attorneys may join this select group by winning highly publicized cases, but usually there are not enough clients who can pay high fees to permit many lawyers to make large amounts of money.

The largest group of attorneys in full-time criminal practice are courthouse regulars who accept many cases for small fees and who participate daily in the criminal justice system as either retained or assigned counsel. These attorneys handle a large volume of cases quickly. They negotiate guilty pleas and try to convince their clients that these agreements are good deals. They depend on the cooperation of prosecutors, judges, and other courtroom actors, with whom they form exchange relationships in order to reach plea bargains quickly.

In addition to these defense specialists, many private attorneys handle criminal cases occasionally. These attorneys often have little trial experience and lack well-developed relationships with other actors in the criminal justice system. In fact, their clients might be better served by a courthouse regular who has little interest in each case but whose relationships with prosecutors and judges will produce more favorable plea bargains.

The Environment of Criminal Practice

Defense attorneys have a difficult job. Much of their work involves preparing clients and their relatives for the likelihood of conviction and punishment. Although they may know that their clients are guilty, they may become emotionally involved because they are the only judicial actors who know the defendants as human beings and see them in the context of their family and social environment.

Most defense lawyers constantly interact with lower-class clients whose lives and problems are depressing. They may also visit the local jail at all hours of the day and night. Thus, their work setting is far removed from the fancy offices and expensive restaurants of the world of corporate attorneys.

Defense lawyers must also struggle with the fact that criminal practice does not pay well. Public defenders have relatively low salaries, and attorneys appointed to represent poor defendants are paid small sums. Private attorneys must demand payment from their clients at the start of the case because there is no incentive for clients to pay for legal services while sitting in a prison cell after the case. To perform their jobs well and gain satisfaction from their careers, defense attorneys must focus on goals other than money, such as their key role in protecting people's constitutional rights. However, the fact that they are usually on the losing side can make it hard for them to feel like professionals—with high self-esteem and satisfying work.

CHECKPOINT

8. How is the private defense bar organized?
9. What special pressures do defense attorneys face?

Counsel for Indigents

Clark Elmore talks with his lawyer, Public Defender Jon Komorowski, right, and Investigator Michael Sparks, center, before being sentenced to death for the murder of his girlfriend's daughter in Bellingham, Washington.

Since the 1960s, the Supreme Court has interpreted the "right to counsel" in the Sixth Amendment to the Constitution as requiring that attorneys be provided to indigent criminal defendants—that is, those who are too poor to afford their own lawyers. The Court has also required that attorneys be provided early in the criminal justice process to protect suspects' rights during questioning and pretrial proceedings. A summary of key rulings on the right to counsel is set forth in Table 8.1.

In a recent study of inmates, 76 percent of those serving time in state prisons and half of those in federal prisons said that they had received publicly provided legal counsel. An additional 83 percent of those in county jails said that they were provided with counsel by the state (BJS, 1996. *Selected Findings*, February). The portion of defendants who are provided with counsel because they are indigent has increased greatly in the past three decades.

Case	Year	Ruling
Gideon v. Wainwright	1963	The Fourteenth Amendment gives defendants in state noncapital felony cases the right to counsel.
Escobedo v. Illinois	1964	The accused has the right to counsel during interrogation by the police.
Miranda v. Arizona	1966	The right to counsel begins when investigation of a crime focuses on a suspect. The suspect must be informed of the right to remain silent and to have counsel and be informed that any statement made may be used against him or her.
United States v. Wade	1967	The defendant has the right to be assisted by counsel during a police lineup. (Extended to state defendants in *Gilbert v. California* [1967]).
Coleman v. Alabama	1970	Counsel must be present at a preliminary hearing.
Argersinger v. Hamlin	1972	Whenever a criminal charge may result in a prison sentence, the accused has the right to counsel.
Ross v. Moffitt	1974	States are not required to provide counsel for indigents beyond one appeal.
Moore v. Illinois	1977	The defendant has the right to counsel at a preliminary court hearing at which he or she appears to be identified by a witness.
United States v. Henry	1980	Government agents may not solicit a statement from a defendant covertly and then introduce the statement at trial.
Strickland v. Washington	1984	The defendant has the right to the *effective* assistance of counsel, whether privately retained or publicly provided.

Table 8.1
The right to counsel: major Supreme Court rulings

Marea Beeman (1995:49), "There are serious potential dangers with the contract model, such as expecting contract defenders to handle an unlimited caseload or awarding contracts on a low-bid basis only, with no regard to qualifications of contracting attorneys."

Public defender. The most recent national survey found that public defender systems exist in 1,144 counties, covering more than 70 percent of the U.S. population (BJS, 1988. *Bulletin*, September). The public defender system, which is growing fast, is used in 43 of the 50 most populous counties and in most large cities. There are about twenty statewide, state-funded systems; in other states they are organized and paid for by counties. Only two states, North Dakota and Maine, do not have public defenders.

A Question of ETHICS

The call to attorney Susan Chaplin came from Judge Henry.

"Sue, you're on the bar association's list for assigned counsel, and I want to assign an indigent defense case to you. It's going to be a hard case, but I hope you'll be willing to take it."

"Sure, Your Honor, what's the case?"

"Well, Sue, it's the Scott case. You may have read about it in the papers. Alan Scott has been charged with ten counts of child molestation."

"Oh, no! Not that one. You want me to defend the guy who's accused of sexually abusing his two young stepdaughters? From what I've seen of him on television, he's rotten to the core. Judge, as a woman I would have hard time dealing with him as a client."

"But you are also an attorney, and Scott has a right to a defense. I know it's going to be hard, but just let me put you down as the counsel. You can pick up the case file from the D.A.'s office."

Is Chaplin obliged to take Scott's case? Because she already has an opinion about the case, should Judge Henry look for another defense lawyer? Given the nature of the case, does it make a difference if the defense attorney is a man or a woman? Does it matter if the defense attorney has children? Can Chaplin provide a full and vigorous defense?

The public defender system is often viewed as better than the assigned counsel system because public defenders are specialists in criminal law. Because they are full-time government employees, public defenders, unlike appointed counsel and contract attorneys, do not sacrifice their clients' cases to protect their own financial interests. Public defenders do face certain special problems, however.

Public defenders may have trouble gaining the trust and cooperation of their clients. Criminal defendants may assume that attorneys on the state payroll, even with the title "public defender," have no reason to protect the defendants' rights and interests. Lack of cooperation from the defendant may make it harder for the attorney to prepare the best possible arguments for use during hearings, plea bargaining, and trials.

Public defenders may also face heavy caseloads. In New York City's public defender program, for example, Legal Aid lawyers may handle as many as a hundred felony cases at any time. A public defender in Atlanta may be assigned as many as forty-five new cases *at a single arraignment* (Bright, 1994). Such heavy caseloads do not allow time for attorneys to become familiar with each case. Overburdened public defenders may find it difficult to avoid making routine decisions. One case may come to be viewed as very much like the next, and the process can become routine and repetitive.

Public defender programs are most effective when they have enough money to keep caseloads manageable. However, these programs do not control their own budgets and usually are not seen as high priorities by state and local governments. Thus it is hard for them to gain the funds they need to give adequate attention to each defendant's case.

Because state and local governments can decide how to provide defense attorneys for indigent defendants, the amount budgeted for criminal defense can vary from county to county. So, too, can the quality of counsel provided to poor defendants. Because state and local governments have limited funds, scholars have noted a "tendency to provide representation on the cheap," which raises concerns about the quality of representation (Spangenberg and Beeman, 1995:48).

CHECKPOINT

10. What are the three main methods of providing attorneys for indigent defendants?

Private versus Public Defense

Publicly funded defense attorneys now handle up to 85 percent of the cases in many places. Does the small percentage of defendants who can afford their own counsel get better legal services? Many convicted offenders say "you get what you pay for," meaning that they would have received better counsel if they had been able to pay for their own attorneys. At one time, researchers thought public defenders entered more guilty pleas than did lawyers who had been either privately retained or assigned to cases. However, studies show little variation in case outcomes by various types of defense. For example, in a study of plea bargains in nine medium-sized counties in Illinois, Michigan, and Pennsylvania, the type of attorney representing the client appeared to make no difference in the nature of plea agreements (Nardulli, 1986). Other studies have also found few differences among assigned counsel, contract counsel, public defenders, and privately retained counsel with respect to case outcomes and length of sentence (Hanson and Chapper, 1991). Table 8.2 lists data on the relationship between type of counsel and case results in four cities.

	Detroit, Michigan			Denver, Colorado		Norfolk, Virginia		Monterey, California		
Type of Disposition	**Public Defender**	**Assigned Counsel**	**Private Counsel**	**Public Defender**	**Private Counsel**	**Assigned Counsel**	**Private Counsel**	**Public Defender**	**Assigned Counsel**	**Private Counsel**
Dismissals	11.9%	14.5%	12.8%	21.0%	24.3%	6.4%	10.4%	13.5%	8.9%	3.0%
Trial acquittals	9.5	5.7	10.3	1.8	0.0	3.3	5.2	1.7	1.3	0.0
Trial convictions	22.6	14.5	24.4	5.1	9.5	5.2	2.2	7.1	11.4	18.2
Guilty pleas	54.8	64.9	52.6	72.1	66.2	85.1	81.3	76.8	78.5	78.8
Diversion	1.2	0.3	0.0	0.0	0.0	0.0	0.7	1.0	0.0	0.0
	100.0%	99.9%	100.1%	100.0%	100.0%	100.0%	99.8%	101.1%	101.1%	100.0%
Total number of cases	84	296	78	276	74	329	134	294	79	33

Table 8.2
Case disposition and types of defense attorneys

There are few variations in case disposition among the defense systems used in each jurisdiction. Why do the cities differ in case outcomes?

SOURCE: Roger Hanson and Joy Chapper, Indigent Defense Systems, Report to the State Justice Institute. Copyright ©1991 by National Center for State Courts (Williamsburg, Va.: National Center for State Courts, 1991).

CHECKPOINT

11. Are public defenders more effective than private defense attorneys?

Defense Counsel in the System

Most of the criminal lawyers in urban courts work in a difficult environment. They work very hard for small fees in unpleasant surroundings and often are not accorded respect by other lawyers or the public. Because plea bargaining is the main method of deciding cases, defense attorneys believe they must maintain close personal ties with the police, prosecutor, judges, and other court officials. Critics point out that the defenders' independence is undermined by daily interaction with the same prosecutors and judges. There are risks that when the supposed adversaries become close friends as a result of daily contact, the defense attorneys no longer fight vigorously on behalf of their clients.

For the criminal lawyer who depends on a large volume of petty cases from poor clients and assumes that they are probably guilty, the incentives to bargain are strong. If the attorney is to be assigned other cases, he or she must help make sure that cases flow smoothly through the courthouse. This requires a cooperative relationship with judges, prosecutors, and others in the justice system.

It is often hard for defendants to understand the benefits of plea bargaining and friendly relationships between defense attorneys and prosecutors. In many cases the evidence of the defendant's guilt simply cannot be overcome by skilled lawyering. Thus good relationships can benefit the defendant by gaining a less-than-maximum sentence. At the same time, however, these relationships pose the risk that if the defense attorney and prosecutor are too friendly, the defendant's case will not be presented in the best possible way in plea bargaining or at trial.

Some scholars have called defense attorneys "agent-mediators" because they often work to prepare the defendant for the likely outcome of the case—usually conviction (Blumberg, 1967). According to this view, the attorney's efforts may help the defendant gain a good plea bargain and become mentally prepared to accept the sentence, but they are primarily geared to advance the needs of the attorney and the legal system. By mediating between the defendant and the system—for example, by encouraging a guilty plea—the attorney helps save time for the prosecutor and judge in gaining a conviction and completing the case. In addition, appointed counsel and contract attorneys may have a financial interest in getting the defendant to plead guilty quickly so that they can receive payment and move on to the next case.

A more sympathetic view of defense attorneys labels them "beleaguered dealers" who cut deals for defendants in a tough environment (Uphoff, 1992). While many of their actions help push cases through the courts, defense attorneys are under tremendous pressure to manage large caseloads in a difficult court environment. From this perspective, their actions in encouraging clients to plead guilty result from the difficult aspects of their jobs rather than from self-interest. Yet, as described in the Close-up, some public defenders are able to maintain a personal interest in their clients.

CLOSE-UP

The Public Defender: Lawyer, Social Worker, Parent

Eddie, a nervous-looking heroin abuser with a three-page police record, isn't happy with his lawyer's news about his latest shoplifting arrest.

"The prosecutor feels you should be locked up for a long time," public defender William Paetzold tells Eddie in a closet-sized interview room in superior court. Barely big enough for a desk and two chairs, the room is known as "the pit."

Eddie, 34 and wide-eyed with a blond crew cut, twists a rolled-up newspaper in his hands. And as Paetzold goes over the evidence against him for the theft of $90.67 worth of meat from a supermarket, the paper gets tighter and tighter.

"So, you basically walked right through the doors with the shopping carriage?" Paetzold asks, scanning the police report.

"Well, there was another person involved, and we really never got out of the store," Eddie replies quickly, now jingling a pocketful of change.

Eddie wants to take his case to trial. Paetzold doesn't like his chances with a jury.

"If you're going to base your whole case on that statement about not leaving the store, you're going to lose," he says. "If you lose, you're going to get five years."

Paetzold advises Eddie to consider pleading guilty in exchange for a lesser sentence.

Eddie rolls his eyes and grumbles. He thinks he deserves a break because he has been doing well in a methadone clinic designed to wean him from heroin.

"I'm not copping to no time," he says, shifting in his seat. "I'm not arguing the fact that I've been a drug addict my whole life, but I haven't been arrested since I've been in that program. I'm finally doing good and they want to bury me."

Paetzold says he will talk to the prosecutor and see what can be done.

"I'll be waiting upstairs," Eddie says, grabbing his newspaper and walking out past a small crowd of other clients waiting to see Paetzold or public defender Phillip N. Armentano.

Every client wants individual attention. Many expect Paetzold or Armentano to resolve their case with little or no punishment. And they don't care that the lawyers may have twenty-five other clients to see that morning demanding the same.

"A lot of what we do is almost like social work," says Armentano. "We have the homeless, the mentally ill, the drug addicts, and the alcoholics. Our job just isn't to try to find people not guilty, but to find appropriate punishment, whether that be counseling, community service or jail time."

"It's like being a parent," says Paetzold. "These clients are our responsibility, and they all have problems and they want those problems solved now."

And like many parents, the lawyers often feel overwhelmed. Too many cases, not enough time or a big enough staff. Those obstacles contribute to another—the stigma that overworked public defenders are pushovers for prosecutors and judges.

"There's a perception that public defenders don't stand up for their clients," Armentano says. "We hear it all the time, 'Are you a public defender or a real lawyer?' There's a mistrust right from the beginning because they view us as part of the system that got them arrested."

With a caseload of more than a thousand clients a year, Paetzold and Armentano acknowledge that they cannot devote as much time to each client as a private lawyer can. But they insist that their clients get vigorous representation.

"Lawyers are competitors, whether you're a public defender or not," Paetzold says. "I think that under the conditions, we do a very good job for our clients."

SOURCE: Steve Jensen, "The Public Defender: He's One Part Lawyer, One Part Social Worker and One Part Parent," *Hartford Courant*, September 4, 1994, p. H1.

CHECKPOINT

12. What special pressures face defense attorneys, and how do these affect their work?

Attorney Competence

The right to counsel is of little value when the counsel is not competent or effective. The adequacy of counsel provided to both private and public clients is a matter of concern to defense groups, bar associations, and the courts (Goodpaster, 1986). There are, of course, many examples of incompetent counsel (Gershman, 1993). Even in death penalty cases, attorneys have shown up drunk in court or made major errors that contributed to their clients' convictions (Bright, 1994; Smith and Jones, 1993).

The U.S. Supreme Court has examined the question of what requirements must be met if defendants are to receive effective counsel. In two 1984 cases, *United States v. Cronic* and *Strickland v. Washington*, the Court set standards for effective assistance of counsel. The Supreme Court indicated its reluctance to second-guess defense attorney's actions. Errors by an attorney are not enough to establish ineffective assistance. The errors must be so bad that they make the trial result unreliable and deny a fair trial to the defendant. The Court has made it hard for defendants to prove that they were denied effective counsel, even when defense attorneys perform very poorly. As a result, innocent people who were poorly represented have been convicted, even in death penalty cases (Radelet, Bedeau, and Putnam, 1992).

When imprisoned people are proved innocent and released—sometimes after losing their freedom for many years—we are reminded that the American justice system is imperfect. In 1996 four men, including two who had been on death row, were released from prison in Illinois after serving eighteen years for murders they did not commit (*New York Times*, July 3, 1996, p. A8). Such reminders highlight the importance of having quality legal counsel for criminal defendants. However, because state and local governments have limited funds, there will continue to be concerns about the quality of defense attorneys' work.

CHECKPOINT

13. How has the U.S. Supreme Court addressed the issue of attorney competence?

Summary

- American prosecutors, both state and federal, have significant discretion to determine how to handle criminal cases.
- There is no higher authority over most prosecutors that can overrule a decision to decline to prosecute (*nolle prosequi*) or to pursue multiple counts against a defendant.
- The prosecutor can play various roles, including trial counsel for the police, house counsel for the police, representative of the court, and elected official.
- Prosecutors' decisions and actions are affected by their exchange relationships with many other important actors and groups, including police, judges, victims and witnesses, and the public.
- Three primary models of prosecutors' decision-making policies are legal sufficiency, system efficiency, and trial sufficiency.
- The image of defense attorneys as courtroom advocates is often vastly different from the reality of pressured, busy negotiators constantly involved in bargaining with the prosecutor over guilty plea agreements.
- Relatively few private defense attorneys make significant incomes from criminal work, but larger numbers of private attorneys accept court appointments to handle indigent defendants' cases quickly for relatively low fees.
- Three primary methods for providing attorneys to represent indigent defendants are appointed counsel, contract counsel, and public defenders.
- Defense attorneys must often wrestle with difficult working conditions and uncooperative clients as they seek to provide representation, usually in the plea negotiation process.
- The quality of representation provided to criminal defendants is a matter of significant concern, but U.S. Supreme Court rulings have made it difficult for convicted offenders to prove that their attorneys did not provide a competent defense.

ANSWERS TO CHECKPOINTS

1. United States attorney, state attorney general, prosecuting attorney (the prosecuting attorney is also called district attorney, state's attorney, county attorney).
2. Chooses the cases to be prosecuted, what bail amounts to recommend, approves agreements with the defendant, and what sentence to recommend to the judge.
3. Trial counsel for the police, house counsel for the police, representative of the court, elected official.
4. The prosecutor can determine the type and number of charges, reduce the charges in exchange for a guilty plea, enter a nolle prosequi (thereby dropping some or all of the charges), and recommend sentence.
5. Police, victims and witnesses, defense attorneys, judges.
6. Legal sufficiency: Is there sufficient evidence to pursue a prosecution? System efficiency: What will be the impact of this case on the system with respect to caseload pressures and speedy disposition? Trial sufficiency: Does sufficient evidence exist to ensure successful prosecution of this case through a trial?
7. The public often views defense attorneys as protectors of criminals. Defendants believe that defense attorneys will fight vigorous battles at every stage of the process. The defense attorney's role is to protect the defendant's rights and to make the prosecution prove its case.
8. There is a status hierarchy of private defense attorneys with a few nationally known specialists at the top; each city has a small group of attorneys for clients who can afford to pay high fees; at the bottom are courthouse regulars who accept small fees from many clients, including indigents whose cases are assigned by the court.
9. Securing cases, collecting fees, poor working conditions, persuading clients to accept pleas, accepting that they will lose most cases.
10. Assigned counsel, contract counsel system, public defender.
11. There seems to be little difference in outcomes.
12. They work very hard for small fees in unpleasant surroundings and are viewed negatively by the public.
13. The Supreme Court has addressed the issue of "ineffective assistance of counsel" in two 1984 cases: *United States v. Cronic* and *Strickland v. Washington*.

Questions for Review

1. What are the formal powers of the prosecuting attorney?
2. How are prosecutors affected by politics?
3. What considerations influence the prosecutor's decision about whether to bring charges and what to charge?
4. Why is the prosecuting attorney often cited as the most powerful office in the criminal justice system?
5. What are some of the problems faced by attorneys who engage in private defense practice?
6. What are the methods by which defense services are provided to indigents?
7. In what way is the defense attorney an agent-mediator?
8. Why might it be argued that publicly financed counsel serves defendants better than privately retained counsel?

Chapter 9

Determination of Guilt: Plea Bargaining and Trials

Plea Bargaining

- *Exchange Relationships in Plea Bargaining*
- *Legal Issues in Plea Bargaining*
- *Justifications for Plea Bargaining*
- *Criticisms of Plea Bargaining*
- *Reforming Plea Bargaining*

Trial: The Exceptional Case

- *Jury Trial*
- *The Trial Process*
- *Evaluating the Jury System*

Appeals

- *Basis for Appeals*
- *Habeas Corpus*
- *Evaluating the Appellate Process*

IN NOVEMBER 1997, public attention focused on the trial of Louise Woodward, a British teenager working for a Massachusetts family as a live-in baby sitter. A jury convicted Woodward of second-degree murder for causing the death of 9-month-old Matthew Eappen. She was given the mandatory sentence of life in prison with parole eligibility after fifteen years.

Woodward was accused of shaking the baby and causing a fatal head injury. Because her defense attorneys presented expert testimony indicating that the infant had suffered an undetected head injury several weeks before the day he was allegedly shaken by Woodward, many people in Britain and the United States believed that Woodward was wrongly convicted.

A few days after the verdict, amid public debates about her guilt, Judge Hiller Zobel, the state judge who presided over the trial, used his discretionary authority to reduce the conviction to manslaughter and free Woodward. He set her sentence as the 279 days she had already spent in jail awaiting trial. Millions of people in countries throughout the world watched on television as the judge made his extraordinary decision (Ferdinand, 1997).

Such cases comprise the top layer of Walker's wedding cake model and are the exception, not the rule. Skilled attorneys for the prosecution and defense battle in front of the jury while closely monitored by news reporters and the public. In Woodward's case, the agency that placed her with the family reportedly spent hundreds of thousands of dollars to pay for her defense attorneys. Most defendants do not have such resources. Moreover, few trials receive such attention. Yet these less-noticed trials are still exceptional, because most cases terminate through discretionary dismissals or guilty pleas.

Pick up your local newspaper on a typical day. See what kinds of cases end with a trial and compare them with those ending with a guilty plea. For example, on October 9, 1997, the local newspaper in Lansing, Michigan, featured side-by-side articles on two homicide cases that produced convictions. In one case, a jury trial resulted in a first-degree murder conviction for a defendant who fired shots through the screen door of a home and killed a 15-year-old youth (Bauza, 1997a). Under Michigan law, this defendant was certain to receive a mandatory sentence of life without parole just as a codefendant had previously been given a life sentence for the killing. By contrast, a 20-year-old woman was sentenced to four years' probation and agreed to finish high school as part of a plea agreement for third-degree child abuse after her baby drowned when left alone in the bathtub (Bauza, 1997b).

In the first case, the defendant faced a life sentence because the homicide involved intent, premeditation, and the use of firearms. Thus he went to trial because of the prospect of severe punishment. In the second case, the tragic death resulted from the mother's negligence. Because the prosecutor and the judge viewed the defendant as making a tragic error rather than causing an intentional harm, the prosecution and defense were able to agree on a guilty plea and sentence. The sentence did not include any time in jail or prison.

In earlier chapters we considered the actors in the court system—judges, prosecutors, and defense attorneys—as well as the way in which they may form courtroom workgroups. In this chapter we will examine the two methods for determining guilt: plea bargaining and trials. Both situations involve prosecutors, defense attorneys, and judges in strategic decisions and interactions.

Although trials are exceptional, they are important because they do more than simply decide the fate of a small percentage of defendants. Trial verdicts also help shape plea bargains. When prosecutors and defense attorneys discuss guilty pleas, each side is calculating a prediction about what might happen to the case if it actually proceeds to trial. If a defense attorney believes that the evidence is so strong that an unfavorable jury verdict is certain, then the attorney may be more willing to discuss a plea. Likewise, if a prosecutor fears that a jury might find a defendant "not guilty," the prosecutor may be willing to plea bargain in order to gain a sure conviction.

Questions for Inquiry

What is plea bargaining, and how does it affect the criminal justice system?

What legal rules limit plea bargaining?

What are the stages of a criminal trial?

How are juries chosen?

What is the basis for an appeal of a conviction?

PLEA BARGAINING

For the vast majority of cases, **plea bargaining**—also known as "negotiating a settlement," "copping a plea," or "copping out"—is the most important step in the criminal justice process. Very few cases go to trial. Most studies report that up to 90 percent of felony defendants in the United States plead guilty. Plea agreements vary. Some involve a sentence recommendation; others involve dismissal or reduction of charges.

plea bargaining

Entering a plea of guilty to a criminal charge with the expectation of receiving a penalty lighter than the one carried by the original offense.

Quick resolution of cases through negotiated guilty pleas has been common since at least the late 1800s, although only in the past thirty years have lawyers and judges publicly acknowledged its widespread existence (Friedman, 1993). In the 1960s scholars began to examine plea bargaining, and the U.S. Supreme Court endorsed the process in the 1970s. In 1971, for example, in ***Santobello v. New York***, Chief Justice Warren Burger ruled that prosecutors were obliged to fulfill promises made during plea negotiations. Burger also listed a number of reasons that plea bargaining was a "highly desirable" part of the criminal justice process:

***Santobello v. New York* (1971)**

When a guilty plea rests on a promise of a prosecutor, it must be fulfilled.

- If every case went to trial, federal and state governments would need many times more courts and judges than they now have.
- Plea bargaining leads to the prompt and largely final disposition of most criminal cases.
- Plea bargaining reduces the time that pretrial detainees must spend in jail. If they plead guilty to serious charges, they can be moved to prisons with

recreational and educational programs instead of enduring the enforced idleness of jails.

- By disposing of cases more quickly than trials would, plea bargaining reduces the amount of time that released suspects spend free on bail. Therefore, the public is better protected from crimes that such suspects may commit while on pretrial release.
- Offenders who plead guilty to serious charges can move more quickly into prison counseling, training, and education programs designed to rehabilitate offenders.

As Justice Potter Stewart revealed in *Blackledge v. Allison* (1976), plea bargaining "can benefit all concerned" in a criminal case. There are advantages for defendants, prosecutors, defense attorneys, and judges. Defendants can have their cases completed more quickly and know what the punishment will be, rather than facing the uncertainty of a judge's sentencing decision. Moreover, the defendant is likely to receive less than the maximum punishment that might have been imposed after a trial. Prosecutors gain an easy conviction, even in cases in which there may not be enough evidence to convince a jury to convict the defendant. They also save time and resources by disposing of cases without having to prepare for a trial. Private defense attorneys also save the time needed to prepare for a trial. They earn their fee quickly and can move on to the next case. Likewise, plea bargaining helps public defenders cope with large caseloads. Judges avoid time-consuming trials and can rely on prosecutors' sentencing recommendations.

Because plea bargaining benefits all involved, it is little wonder that it existed long before it was publicly acknowledged by the legal community and that it still exists, even when prosecutors, legislators, or judges claim that they wish to abolish it. Efforts to abolish plea bargaining result in bargaining over the *charges* instead of over the sentence recommendation or simply move plea bargaining to an earlier stage in the judicial process (McCoy, 1993). If a prosecutor forbids his or her staff to plea bargain, judges may become more involved in negotiating and facilitating guilty pleas that result in predictable punishments for offenders.

Plea bargaining is no longer a hidden "secret" of the legal profession. Today prosecutors and defense attorneys often include judges in their negotiations.

Exchange Relationships in Plea Bargaining

Plea bargaining is a set of exchange relationships in which the prosecutor, the defense attorney, the defendant, and sometimes the judge participate. All have specific goals, all try to use the situation to their own advantage, and all are likely to see the exchange as a success.

Plea bargaining does not always occur in a single meeting between prosecutor and defense attorney. Prosecutors and defense attorneys interact again and again as the case moves farther along in the judicial process. As time passes, the prosecutor's hand may be strengthened by the discovery of more evidence or new information about the defendant's background (Emmelman, 1996). Often it is the prosecution rather than the defense that is in the best position to obtain new evidence (Cooney, 1994). However, the defense attorney's position may gain strength if the prosecutor does not wish to spend time going farther down the path toward a trial.

Tactics of Prosecutor and Defense

While talking in a friendly manner, each side tries to impress the other with its confidence in its own case while pointing out weaknesses in the opponent's case. Defense attorneys also try to make the prosecutor see the defendant as a human being rather than as just a faceless criminal suspect. There is an unspoken rule of openness and honesty designed to keep the relationship on good terms. As A Question of Ethics shows, there seems to be a rule that confidences shared during plea bargaining will not be used in court. Attorneys who violate this understanding harm their relationships with other attorneys and are less likely to receive cooperation in future negotiations (Champion, 1989).

Each side has tools available to pressure the opponent. Prosecutors can use multicount indictments, giving them a large number of charges to negotiate with. By contrast, defense attorneys may threaten to ask for a jury trial if concessions are not made. Their hand is further strengthened if they have filed pretrial motions that require a formal response by the prosecutor. Another tactic is to request **continuances**, a judge's permission to delay various pretrial processes or court proceedings. Attorneys seek to reschedule pretrial activities in the hope that witnesses will become unavailable, media attention will die down, and memories of the crime will be weakened by the time of trial. Rather than resort to such legal tactics, however, some attorneys prefer to bargain on the basis of friendship and cooperation.

A Question of ETHICS

Defense attorney Jonathan Bowman came bustling into the office of Assistant Prosecutor Wayne Charro with an armload of case files. Charro had been expecting the visit and knew what Bowman was likely to do.

"Wayne, I'd like to talk with you about these ten cases that I have for tomorrow. Most of them are just garbage, so I think we can get rid of them quickly. For example, here is the Buckley and Dickens case. They're codefendants and I've got them both. They're each charged with armed robbery, but Dickens says he did not have the gun. You've got to admit that the whole case is pretty flimsy, since the victim is confused as to what happened. How about a guilty plea on a reduced charge of Robbery 2 for Dickens? He's a young kid and deserves a break. He told me that Buckley actually planned this whole thing and held the gun to the woman's head. Buckley's not been very cooperative with me. I just don't like his attitude."

"Well, Jon, I don't know. These guys have been in trouble before. If I go for the plea for Dickens, where does that place Buckley?"

How should Charro react to Bowman's statement? What ethical questions might arise from this case should Charro accept the offer of a guilty plea and reduced charge for Dickens? What should happen to Buckley? How might the disposal of this case affect future bargaining between Charro and Bowman?

continuance

An adjournment of a scheduled case until a later date.

Pleas without Bargaining

Studies have shown that in many courts give-and-take plea bargaining does not occur for certain types of cases, yet there are as many guilty pleas as in other courts (Eisenstein, Flemming, and Nardulli, 1988). The term *bargaining* in these situations may be misleading in that it implies haggling. Indeed, many scholars argue that in most plea bargaining guilty pleas emerge after the prosecutor, the defense attorney, and sometimes the judge reach an agreement to "settle the facts" (Utz, 1978). In this view the parties first study the facts of a case. What were the circumstances of the event? Was it really an assault or was it more of a shoving match? Did the victim antagonize the accused? Each side may hope to persuade the other that provable facts back up its view of the defendant's actions. The prosecution wants the defense to believe that strong evidence proves its version of the event. The defense attorney wants to convince the prosecution that the evidence is not solid and that in fact there is a risk of acquittal if a jury hears the case.

In some cases, the evidence is strong and the defense attorney has little hope of persuading the prosecutor otherwise. Instead, the prosecutor and defense attorney seek to reach a shared view of the provable facts in the case. Once they agree on the facts, they will both know the appropriate charge, and they can agree on the sentence according to the locally defined going rate (the usual sentence for such an offense). This process may be thought of as "implicit plea bargaining" because the shared understandings of the prosecutor and defense create the expectation that a guilty plea will lead to a less-than-maximum sentence, even without any actual exchange or bargaining.

The going rates for sentences for particular crimes and offenders depend on local values and sentencing patterns (Worden, 1995). Prosecutors and defense attorneys who work within the same court community and legal culture need to share an understanding of these prevailing rates for several reasons. *First*, if both sides understand what sentences should be, plea bargaining is more effective because both sides know which sentences apply to which cases. Instead of debating about whether a burglary case should be punished by a short prison term, both sides already know whether a prison term is part of the going rate for burglary. *Second*, shared understandings between the two sides help create a cooperative climate for plea bargaining, even if there are bad feelings between the prosecutor and the defense attorney. The local legal culture dictates how attorneys are expected to treat each other and thereby reach agreements. And *third*, these shared understandings between the attorneys help maintain their relationship.

Just as the local legal culture and going rates may vary from courthouse to courthouse, so too can the routine procedures that affect plea bargaining. In some courts a "slow plea" process is dominant: defendants plead not guilty at first but change their pleas as the trial progresses, just as broadcaster Marv Albert did in the example presented in Chapter 7. In other courts, prosecutors may filter out part of the caseload by dropping cases or diverting offenders.

CHECKPOINT

1. Why does plea bargaining occur?
2. What is implicit plea bargaining?

(Answers are at the end of the chapter.)

Legal Issues in Plea Bargaining

***Boykin v. Alabama* (1969)**

Defendants must state that they are voluntarily making a plea of guilty.

***North Carolina v. Alford* (1970)**

A plea of guilty may be accepted for the purpose of a lesser sentence by a defendant who maintains his or her innocence.

Over the last few decades the United States Supreme Court has faced legal questions about plea bargaining. In ruling on these questions the Court has upheld the constitutionality of plea bargaining and sought to ensure that due process rights are upheld in plea agreements.

A central concern is whether the defendant enters a guilty plea voluntarily. In ***Boykin v. Alabama*** (1969) the Court ruled that defendants must state that the plea was made voluntarily before a judge may accept it. Judges use standard questions to ask the defendant whether the plea is voluntary and whether the consequences of the plea are understood. The Supreme Court also has stated (***North Carolina v. Alford***, 1970) that trial judges should not accept a plea unless there is a factual basis for believing that the defendant is in fact guilty, even when the person entering the plea maintains his or her innocence (Whitebread and Slobogin, 1993:647).

A second issue is whether the plea agreement is fulfilled. If the prosecutor has promised a lenient sentence, the promise must be kept (***Santobello v. New York***,

1971). The Court also decided that defendants must keep their side of the bargain, such as an agreement to testify against codefendants (***Ricketts v. Adamson,*** 1987).

May prosecutors threaten to penalize defendants who insist upon their right to a jury trial? Yes. Prosecutors may, for example, threaten repeat offenders with life sentences under habitual offender statutes if they do not agree to plead guilty and accept specified terms of imprisonment (***Bordenkircher v. Hayes***, 1978). A threat of more serious charges, as long as such charges are legitimate and supported by evidence, is not considered improper pressure that makes a guilty plea involuntary and hence invalid.

***Ricketts v. Adamson* (1987)**

Defendants must uphold the plea agreement or suffer the consequences.

***Bordenkircher v. Hayes* (1978)**

A defendant's rights were not violated by a prosecutor who warned that failure to accept a guilty plea would result in a harsher sentence.

Justifications for Plea Bargaining

Plea bargaining is justified on the grounds that it individualizes justice and that it is necessary from an administrative standpoint because there are not enough courts, prosecutors, and judges to handle an ever-larger number of trials.

Individualized Justice

This justification suggests that if the criminal law is to be fair, the prosecutor's office must be able to determine the proper charge and punishment on the basis of the facts of the case, the defendant's willingness to show remorse, and other factors. In addition, judges may individualize justice by fashioning sentences according to the severity of the offense and the characteristics of the offender. The use of discretion by prosecutors and judges to individualize justice can, however, undercut the intent of legislatures in mandating specific sentences for particular crimes.

Administrative Necessity

A second justification for plea bargaining is administrative necessity. As we have seen, many, many defendants must be processed quickly in order for the courts to keep up with the arrests made by the police, especially in large cities. The demands on the judicial process—crowded court calendars and strains on judicial personnel—are overwhelming. Thus some observers argue that plea bargaining saves the courts from being swamped and paralyzed by an excessive number of trials.

Studies cast doubt on the assumption that plea bargaining is a contemporary practice that arose in response to increased caseloads. In fact, one study found that plea bargaining was practiced in both high- and low-volume courts as early as 1880 and that since then fewer than 10 percent of indictments have led to trials (Heumann, 1978). It appears that plea bargaining developed for other reasons, such as its benefits for everyone involved in a case, rather than out of administrative necessity.

Criticisms of Plea Bargaining

A number of scholars and groups like the American Bar Association criticize the use of plea bargaining, arguing that it is unfair because defendants give up some of their constitutional rights, especially the right to trial by jury. A second criticism points out that society's interest in appropriate punishments for crimes is reduced by plea bargaining. In urban areas with high caseloads, harried prosecutors and judges are said to make concessions based on administrative need, resulting in lighter sentences than those required by the penal code.

Plea bargaining also comes under fire because it is hidden from judicial scrutiny. Because the agreement is most often made at an early stage, the judge has little information about the crime or the defendant and cannot evaluate the case. Nor can the judge review the terms of the bargain—that is, check on the amount of pressure put on the defendant to plead guilty. The result of "bargain justice" is that the judge, the public, and sometimes even the defendant cannot know for sure who got what from whom in exchange for what.

Other critics believe that overuse of plea bargaining breeds disrespect and even contempt for the law. They say criminals look at the judicial process as a game or a sham, much like other "deals" made in life.

Critics also contend that it is unjust to penalize persons who assert their right to a trial by giving them stiffer sentences than they would have received if they had pleaded guilty. The evidence here is unclear, although it is widely believed that an extra penalty is imposed on defendants who take up the court's time by asserting their right to a trial (Spohn, 1992; Cuniff, 1987). Critics note that federal sentencing guidelines encourage avoidance of trial because they include a two-point deduction from an offender's base score—thus lowering the sentence—for "acceptance of responsibility" (McCoy, 1995).

Finally, another concern about plea bargaining is that innocent people will plead guilty to acts that they did not commit. Although it is hard to know how often this happens, there is evidence that some defendants have indeed entered guilty pleas when they have not committed the offense. It may be hard for middle-class people to understand how anyone could possibly plead guilty when they are innocent. However, people with little education and low social status may lack the confidence to say "no" to an attorney who pressures them to plead guilty. Poor people may feel helpless in the stressful climate of the courthouse and jail. If they lack faith in the system's ability to protect their rights and find them not guilty, they may accept a lighter punishment rather than risk conviction for a serious offense.

Reforming Plea Bargaining

In some jurisdictions (Honolulu, New Orleans, El Paso, and the Bronx), efforts have been made to ban plea bargaining (*Wall Street Journal*, December 10, 1992). In Alaska, the state attorney general told district attorneys to cease the practice. Judges feared that as a result the courts would be flooded with cases and the justice process would be bogged down. Neither fear was realized. While direct bargaining ceased, "implicit" bargaining remained. Prosecutors also screened more cases so that only the strongest ones went to trial. There was some increase in the punishment given in minor cases but little impact on the sentences received for serious ones (Rubenstein and White, 1979:367; Carns and Kruse, 1991).

In 1982 California voters passed Proposition 8, a victims' bill of rights. Included in this new law was a ban on plea bargaining in cases involving serious crimes. However, the ban did not extend to cases decided in the municipal court. Candace McCoy (1993) has shown how Proposition 8 shifted plea bargaining to the lower courts, with only the most serious and disputed felonies being bound over to the superior court. Brian Forst concludes:

It is clear that little good would be served by attempting to force all cases through the court [in trials]; many, perhaps most, pleas involve cases in which an offender has no defense and simply wishes to expedite the process, often in exchange for minor concessions by the prosecutor. (Forst, 1995:336)

CHECKPOINT

3. What issues concerning plea bargaining has the Supreme Court examined?
4. What are justifications for plea bargaining?
5. What are criticisms of plea bargaining?

TRIAL: THE EXCEPTIONAL CASE

Eighty percent of all jury trials worldwide take place in the United States. Here, jurors in Rockville, Maryland, are sworn in after having been scrutinized through the voir dire process.

If cases are not dismissed or terminated through plea bargaining, they move forward for trial. A case often will go to trial when defendants face very serious charges or are sufficiently wealthy to pay an attorney to take the case through the entire judicial process.

Most Americans are familiar with the image of the criminal trial. As portrayed in so many movies and television shows, the prosecutor and defense attorney face off in a tense courtroom conflict. Each attorney attempts to use evidence, persuasion, and emotion to convince a **jury** of citizens to favor its arguments about the defendant's guilt or innocence.

The trial process is based on the assumption that an open battle between opposing lawyers is the best way to discover the truth. The authors of the U.S. Constitution apparently shared this assumption: the Sixth Amendment says the accused shall enjoy a speedy and public trial by an impartial jury "in all criminal prosecutions" (Langbein, 1992). In theory, each side will present the best evidence and arguments it can muster for its side, and the jury will make a decision based on thorough consideration of the available information about the case.

But trials are very human processes, and the truth is not guaranteed to emerge in the final verdict. Many factors may keep a trial from achieving its goal of revealing the truth. The rules of evidence—which govern what evidence the court may hear during the trial—may prevent one side from presenting the most useful evidence. One side may have impressive expert witnesses whom the other side cannot afford to counter with its own experts. One side's attorney may be more persuasive and likable and thus may sway the jury in spite of the evidence. The judge or jurors may bring into the courtroom their own prejudices, which cause them to favor some defendants or automatically assume the worst about others. Fundamentally, we place great faith in the trial process as the best means we have for giving complete consideration of a defendant's potential guilt, yet we cannot have confidence that the process will always work as it should.

Only 11 percent of felony cases go to trial. Of these, 6 percent are jury trials, and 5 percent are **bench trials** presided over by a judge without a jury (BJS, 1997. *Sourcebook*:476). Defendants may choose a bench trial if they believe a judge will

jury

A panel of citizens selected according to law and sworn to determine matters of fact in a criminal case and to deliver a verdict of guilty or not guilty.

bench trial

Trial conducted by a judge who acts as finder of fact and determines issues of law. No jury participates.

be more capable of making an objective decision, especially if the charges or evidence are likely to arouse emotional reactions in jurors.

As noted earlier in this chapter, the seriousness of the charge and the wealth of the defendant may be particularly important in determining whether a case will go to trial. Therefore the severity of the potential sentence makes murder defendants more likely than other defendants to go to trial. Nevertheless, courts differ in the percentage of murder and other kinds of cases going to trial, as shown in Table 9.1. What might be the reasons for differences from one city to another and for one offense or another? Think about how prosecutors' policies or sentencing practices in different cities may increase or decrease the incentives for a defendant to plead guilty.

Table 9.1
Percentage of indicted cases that went to trial, by offense

The percentages of cases that went to trial differ both by offense and by jurisdiction. It seems that the stiffer the possible penalty, the greater the likelihood of a trial.

SOURCE: Adapted from U.S. Department of Justice, Bureau of Justice Statistics, *Report to the Nation on Crime and Justice*, 2d ed. (Washington, D.C.: Government Printing Office, 1988), 84.

Jurisdiction	Homicide	Sexual Assault	Robbery	Larceny	Drug Offenses
Indianapolis, Ind.	38%	18%	21%	12%	9%
Los Angeles, Calif.	29	20	12	5	7
Louisville, Ky.	57	27	18	10	11
New Orleans, La.	22	18	16	7	7
St. Louis, Mo.	36	23	15	6	6
San Diego, Calif.	37	2	12	5	3
Washington, D.C.	43	32	22	12	10

Jury Trial

The rules of criminal law, procedure, and evidence govern the conduct of trials. While the prosecution and defense present their sides of the case, the judge sees to it that the rules are followed and that the jury evaluates the evidence fairly and reflects the community's interest. The jury is the sole evaluator of the facts in a case.

Eighty percent of all jury trials worldwide take place in the United States (Hans and Vidmar, 1986:109). Among the legal systems of the world, it is only in common-law countries such as Great Britain, Canada, Australia, and the United States that a group of citizens drawn from the community determines the guilt of criminal defendants. In civil-law countries such as France, Russia, and Japan, a judge or judges, often assisted by two or three nonlawyers serving as "assessors," usually perform this function.

Juries perform six vital functions in the criminal justice system:

1. Prevent government oppression by safeguarding citizens against arbitrary law enforcement.
2. Determine whether the accused is guilty on the basis of the evidence presented.
3. Represent diverse community interests so that no single set of values or biases dominates decision making.
4. Serve as a buffer between the accused and the accuser.
5. Educate citizens selected for jury duty about the criminal justice system.
6. Symbolize the rule of law and the community foundation that supports the criminal justice system.

As a symbol of law, juries demonstrate to the public—and to defendants—that decisions about depriving individuals of their liberty will be made carefully by a group of citizens who represent the community's values. In addition, juries provide the primary element of direct democracy in the judicial branch of government. Through participation on juries citizens use their votes to determine the outcomes of cases (Smith, C.E., 1994). This branch of government, which is dominated by judges and lawyers, offers few other opportunities for citizens to shape judicial decisions directly.

Every year nearly 2 million Americans respond to the call to perform this civic duty, even though doing so usually entails personal and financial hardship. They must miss time from work, arrange for child care, drive through downtown traffic, and pay for parking. The court's daily pay rate for jurors is usually minimal. In addition, not all employers pay for time lost from the job. (See A Question of Ethics.)

Most jurors experience great frustration with the system as they wait endless hours in barren courthouse rooms. Often they are placed on a jury only to have their function preempted by a sudden change of plea to guilty during the trial. The result is wasted juror time and wasted money. Unfortunately, what could be a valuable civic education often leaves jurors with an unnecessarily negative impression of the entire criminal justice system.

A Question of ETHICS

The return address on the official-looking envelope read "Jury Commissioner, District Court, Plainville, Massachusetts." Having a good idea of the contents, Donald Rotman tore open the envelope and pulled out a computer-generated form that read: "Donald A. Rotman, You are hereby summoned to be available for duty as a trial juror and are directed to report to the District Court of the Commonwealth of Massachusetts, 61 South Street, Plainville, at 9:00 A.M. on July 10. Failure to appear as instructed by law may subject you to a penalty as provided by law. Your juror number is 89367. The term of your jury duty will be one day or one trial."

"Hell! I can't do that. I want to go to Cape Cod that week. There must be some way out of this." Rotman looked at the bottom of the form and read, "You may apply to be excused if you are: an attorney; caring for a child under three; student or teacher during the school year ... " and about five other categories, none of which applied to him.

"This is no big deal. Everyone does it. I'll just tell them I'm going to summer school. They won't check."

Is getting out of jury duty no big deal? What are the implications of Donald's action? If Donald is required to serve on a jury, how might justice be affected by the fact that he had planned to spend a week on vacation? What exemptions to service should exist?

To deal with some of the more negative aspects of jury duty, some courts have introduced the "one-day-one-trial" system. Traditionally, citizens are asked to be jurors for a thirty-day term, and although only a few may be needed on a particular day, the entire pool may be present in the courthouse for the full thirty-day period. In the new system, jurors serve for either one day or the duration of one trial. Prospective jurors who are challenged at voir dire or who are not called to a courtroom are dismissed at the end of their first day and have thus fulfilled their jury duty for the year. Those who are accepted on a jury are required to serve for the duration of that trial, normally about three days. The consensus of jurors, judges, and court administrators is that the one-day-one-trial system is a great improvement to traditional jury service.

In the United States, a jury in a criminal trial traditionally comprises twelve citizens, but some states now allow as few as six citizens to make up a jury. This reform was recommended to modernize court procedures and reduce expenses. It costs less for the court to contact, process, and pay a smaller number of jurors. The Supreme Court upheld the use of small juries in ***Williams v. Florida*** (1970) although twelve-person juries are still required in death penalty cases. In *Burch v. Louisiana* (1979), the Supreme Court ruled that six-member juries must vote unanimously to convict a defendant, but unanimity is not required for larger juries. Some states permit juries to convict defendants by votes of 10 to 2 or 9 to 3 (see Figure 9.1 for jury-size requirements in each state). The change to six-person juries has its critics, who charge that the smaller group is less representative of the conflicting views in the community and too quick to bring in a verdict (Sperlich, 1980).

***Williams v. Florida* (1970)**

Juries of fewer than twelve members are constitutional.

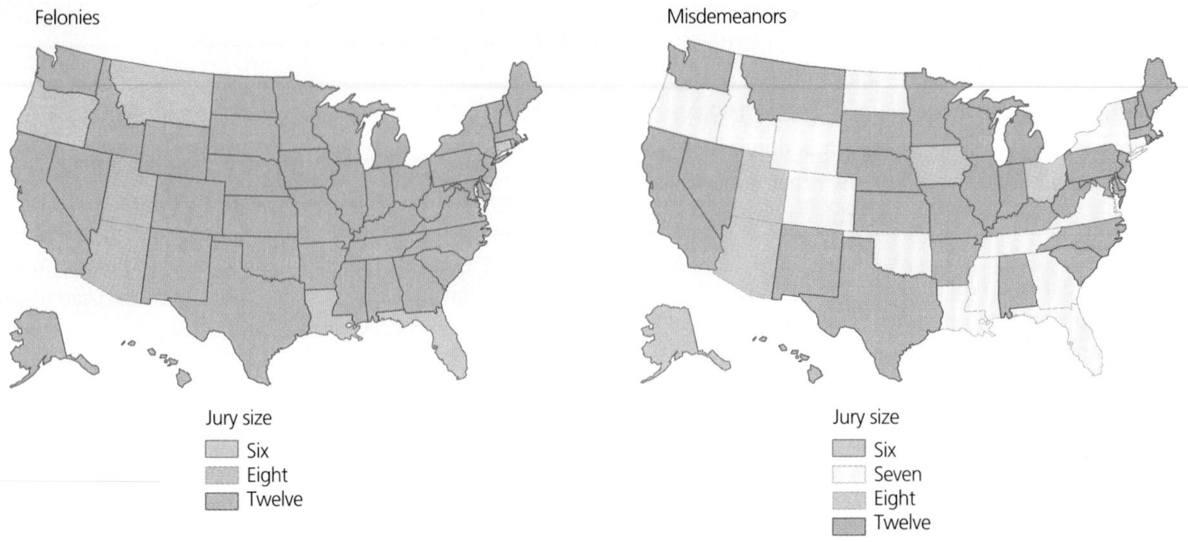

Figure 9.1
Jury size for felony and misdemeanor trials

All states require twelve-member juries in capital cases; six states permit juries of fewer than twelve members in felony cases. Does a smaller jury have advantages or disadvantages? Would you rather have your case decided by a twelve- or six-person jury?

SOURCE: U.S. Department of Justice, Bureau of Justice Statistics, *Report to the Nation on Crime and Justice*, 2d ed. (Washington, D.C.: Government Printing Office, 1988), 86.

CHECKPOINT

6. What are three functions that juries serve in the criminal justice system?
7. What reform has improved jurors' experience with the court system and reduced the frustrations of jury service?
8. What has the Supreme Court decided concerning the size and unanimity requirements of juries?
9. Approximately what percentage of criminal cases reach their conclusion through a trial?

The Trial Process

Barry Sheck, attorney for Louise Woodward, presents evidence that an earlier skull fracture, and not a shaking of 8-month-old Matthew Eappens by his client, had caused the death.

The trial process generally follows nine steps: (1) selection of the jury, (2) opening statements by prosecution and defense, (3) presentation of the prosecution's evidence and witnesses, (4) presentation of the defense's evidence and witnesses, (5) presentation of rebuttal witnesses, (6) closing arguments by each side, (7) judge's instructions to the jury, (8) decision by the jury, and (9) sentencing. The details of each step may vary according to each state's rules. Although the proportion of trials may be small, it is important to understand each step in the process and to consider the broader impact of this institution.

Jury Selection

The selection of the jury, which is outlined in Figure 9.2, is a crucial first step in the trial process. Because people always apply their experiences, values, and biases in their decision making, prosecutors and defense attorneys actively seek to identify potential jurors who may be automatically sympathetic or hostile to their side. When they believe they have identified such jurors, they try to find ways to exclude those who may sympathize with the other side and to keep those who may favor their side. Lawyers do not necessarily achieve these goals because the selection of jurors involves the decisions and interactions of prosecutors, defense attorneys, and judges, each of whom has different objectives in the selection process.

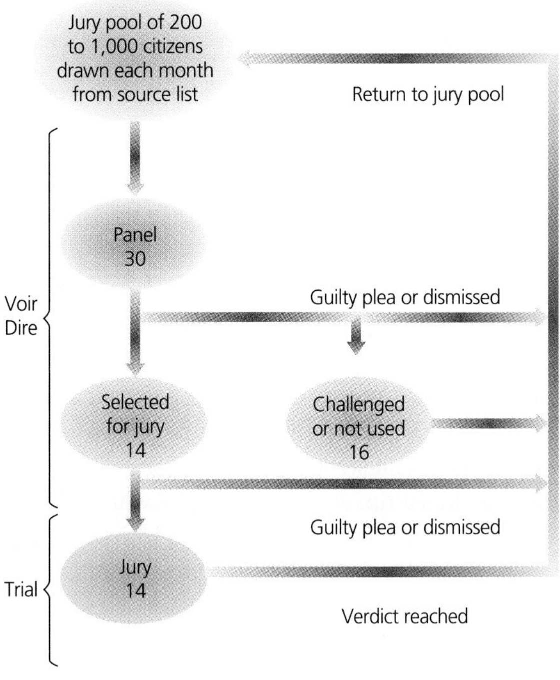

Figure 9.2
Jury selection process for a twelve-member jury

Potential jurors are drawn at random from a source list. From this pool a panel including two alternate jurors is selected and presented for duty. The voir dire examination may remove some panel members.

Jurors are selected from among the citizens whose names have been placed in the jury pool. The composition of the jury pool has a tremendous impact on the ultimate composition of the trial jury. In most states the jury pool is drawn from lists of registered voters, but research has shown that nonwhites, the poor, and young people register to vote at much lower rates than the rest of the population. As a result, members of these groups are underrepresented on juries (Fukurai, 1996). In many cases, the presence or absence of these groups may make no difference in the ultimate verdict. In some situations, however, their interpretation of evidence may differ from that of the older, white, middle-class segment of the population, who dominate the composition of juries (Cowan, Thompson, and Ellsworth, 1984:60).

Some jurisdictions have addressed the problem of unrepresentative jury pools by seeking to broaden the sources from which the jurors' names are drawn (Kairys, Kadane, and Lehoczky, 1977). Today courts may use lists of driver's and hunting license applicants and utility customers as well as lists of registered voters (Newman, 1996).

Only about 15 percent of adult Americans have ever been called for jury duty. Many people, such as doctors, police officers, and lawyers, are frequently excused from jury service because of the demands of their jobs. Others are excused because they have child-care responsibilities or medical problems or because jury service would cause an economic hardship when they miss work. Because of the exclusions from service, retired people and homemakers with grown children tend to be overrepresented on juries because they are less inconvenienced by serving.

voir dire

A questioning of prospective jurors in order to screen out persons the attorneys think may be biased or incapable of delivering a fair verdict.

challenge for cause

Removal of a prospective juror by showing that he or she has some bias or some other legal disability. The number of such challenges permitted to attorneys is unlimited.

peremptory challenge

Removal of a prospective juror without giving a reason. Attorneys are allowed a limited number of such challenges.

The courtroom process of **voir dire** (which means "to speak the truth") is used to question prospective jurors in order to screen out those who might be biased or incapable of making a fair decision. Attorneys for each side, as well as the judge, may question jurors about their background, knowledge of the case, and acquaintance with any participants in the case. Jurors are also asked whether they or their immediate family members have been crime victims or otherwise involved in a criminal case in a manner that may prevent them from making open-minded decisions about the evidence and the defendant. If a juror's responses indicate that he or she will not be able to make a fair decision, the juror may be **challenged for cause**. The judge must rule on the challenge, but if the judge agrees with the attorney, the juror is excused from the case. There is usually no limit on the number of jurors that the attorneys may challenge for cause. It is not easy, however, for attorneys to identify all of a juror's biases through brief questioning (Dillehay and Sandys, 1996).

Although challenges for cause are ultimately under the judge's control, the prosecution and defense can exert their own control over the jury's composition through the use of **peremptory challenges**. Using these challenges, the prosecution and defense can exclude prospective jurors without giving specific reasons. Attorneys use peremptory challenges to exclude jurors whom they think will be unsympathetic to their arguments. Attorneys usually use hunches about which jurors to challenge; there is little evidence that they can accurately identify which jurors will be sympathetic or unsympathetic to their side (White, 1995). Normally, the defense is allowed eight to ten peremptory challenges, the prosecution six to eight.

In applying peremptory challenges, attorneys are not necessarily seeking to seat a jury made up of the most open minded people. Instead, they would prefer to have people who lean toward their position. Wealthy defendants may hire jury consultants—psychologists who advise them on what kinds of people are likely to be on their side. For example, in the O. J. Simpson murder trial, the defense attorneys were happy to have African Americans well represented on the jury, thinking they would be likely to listen sympathetically to arguments about allegedly discriminatory actions by the Los Angeles police in investigating the case. Although jury consultants claim credit when their clients are acquitted, research has questioned whether consultants can accurately predict how different people are likely to decide a particular case (Diamond, 1990).

The use of peremptory challenges has raised concerns that attorneys can use them to exclude, for example, African-American jurors when an African American is on trial. In a series of decisions in the late 1980s and early 1990s, the Supreme Court prohibited using peremptory challenges to systematically exclude potential jurors because of their race or gender (*Batson v. Kentucky*, 1986; *Georgia v. McCollum*, 1992; *J.E.B. v. Alabama* ex rel. T.B., 1994). This does not mean that prosecutors and defense attorneys cannot use a peremptory challenge to exclude a nonwhite or female juror. However, if the opposition accuses the prosecution or defense of excluding prospective jurors based on race or gender, the attorney must give the judge a reason for the exclusion that has nothing to do with race or gender. Nevertheless, in practice the enforcement of this prohibition is up to the trial judge (Smith, C. E., and Ochoa, 1996). If a trial judge is willing to accept flimsy excuses for race-based and gender-based exclusions, such as "I don't like the way this juror looked with the way his hair is cut" (*Purkett v. Elem*, 1995), the attorneys can ignore the ban on discrimination (Bray, 1992).

The jury selection process sets the stage for the trial by putting into place the decision makers who will decide the defendant's fate. Although voir dire takes place before the trial begins, jury selection can be viewed as the first step in trial.

Some lawyers say that trials are won or lost in jury selection. If a lawyer succeeds in seating a favorable jury, she may have a receptive audience who will readily support her side's arguments and evidence.

CHECKPOINT

10. What is voir dire?
11. What is the difference between a peremptory challenge and a challenge for cause?

Opening Statements

After the jury has been selected, the trial begins. The clerk reads the complaint (indictment or information) detailing the charges, and the prosecutor and the defense attorney may, if they desire, make opening statements to the jury to summarize the position they intend to take. The jury is not supposed to regard the attorneys' statements as evidence that proves or disproves anything about the case. Judges normally keep tight control over opening statements so that the attorneys will not make prejudicial or inflammatory remarks that may improperly sway the jury. Lawyers use this phase of the trial to establish themselves with the jurors and emphasize points they intend to make later.

real evidence

Physical evidence such as a weapon, records, fingerprints, stolen property—objects actually involved in the crime.

Presentation of the Prosecution's Evidence

One of the basic protections of the American criminal justice system is the assumption that the defendant is innocent until proved guilty. The prosecution has the burden of proving beyond a reasonable doubt, within the demands of court procedures and rules of evidence, that the individual named in the indictment committed the crime. That does not mean absolute certainty is required, only that the evidence is such that there is no reasonable doubt.

By presenting evidence to the jury, the prosecution must establish a case showing that the defendant is guilty. Evidence is classified as real evidence, demonstrative evidence, testimony, direct evidence, and circumstantial evidence. Real evidence might include such objects as a weapon, business records, fingerprints, or stolen property. These are real objects actually involved in the crime. Demonstrative evidence is presented for jurors to see and understand without testimony. **Real evidence** is one form of demonstrative evidence, but there are other forms of **demonstrative evidence**, such as maps, X-rays, photographs, models, and diagrams, that demonstrate points to jurors even though they are not items actually involved in the crime.

demonstrative evidence

Evidence that is not based on witness testimony but that demonstrates information relevant to the crime, such as maps, X-rays, and photographs; includes real evidence involved in the crime.

testimony

Oral evidence provided by a legally competent witness.

Most evidence in a criminal trial consists of the **testimony** of witnesses. Witnesses at a trial must be legally competent. Thus the judge may be required to determine whether the witness whose testimony is challenged has the intelligence to tell the truth and the ability to recall what was seen. Witnesses with inadequate intelligence or mental problems may not be regarded as qualified to present testimony. **Direct evidence** refers to eyewitness accounts—for example, "I saw John Smith fire the gun." **Circumstantial evidence** requires that the jury infer a fact from what the witness observed: "I saw John Smith walk behind his house with a gun. A few minutes later I heard a gun go off, and then Mr. Smith walked toward me holding a gun." The witness's observation that Smith had a gun and that the witness then heard a gun go off does not provide the direct evidence that Smith fired his gun; yet the jury may link the described facts and infer that Smith fired

direct evidence

Eyewitness accounts.

circumstantial evidence

Evidence provided by a witness from which a jury must infer a fact.

his gun. After a witness has given testimony, he or she may be cross-examined by counsel for the other side.

The rules of evidence govern the facts that may be admitted into court for the judge and jury to consider. Real evidence that has been illegally seized, for example, may be excluded under the Fourth Amendment's protection against unreasonable searches and seizure. The judge decides, with reference to these rules, what evidence may be heard. In making such decisions, the judge must weigh the importance of the evidence and balance it against the need for a fair trial. The attorney for each side challenges the other side's presentation of evidence. If evidence violates the rules, reflects untrustworthy hearsay or opinion statements, is not relevant to the issues in the case, or will prejudice the jury, an attorney will object to its presentation.

After the prosecution has presented all of the state's evidence against the defendant, the court is informed that the People's case rests. It is common for the defense then to ask the court to direct the jury to bring forth a verdict of not guilty based on the argument that the state has not presented enough evidence to prove its case. The judge rules on this motion, sustaining or overruling it. If the motion is sustained (which is rare), the trial ends; if it is overruled, the defense presents its evidence.

Presentation of the Defense's Evidence

The defense is not required to answer the case presented by the prosecution. As it is the state's responsibility to prove the case beyond a reasonable doubt, it is theoretically possible—and in fact sometimes happens—that the defense rests its case immediately. Usually the accused's attorney employs one strategy or a combination of three strategies: (1) contrary evidence is introduced to rebut or cast doubt on the state's case; (2) an alibi is offered; or (3) an affirmative defense is presented. An affirmative defense is a legal excuse that permits the jury to find the defendant not responsible for the crime. As you recall from Chapter 3, defenses include self-defense, insanity, duress, and necessity.

A key issue for the defense is whether the accused will take the stand. The Fifth Amendment protection against self-incrimination means that the defendant does not have to testify. The Supreme Court has ruled that the prosecutor may not comment on, nor can the jury draw inferences from, the defendant's decision not to appear in his or her own defense. The decision is not made lightly, because if the defendant does testify, the prosecution may cross-examine. If the defendant testifies and thereby submits to cross-examination, the prosecutor often is able to introduce testimony about prior convictions.

Presentation of Rebuttal Witnesses

When the defense's case is complete, the prosecution may present witnesses whose testimony is designed to discredit or counteract testimony presented on behalf of the defendant. Evidence previously introduced by the prosecution may not be rehashed, but new evidence may be presented. If the prosecution brings rebuttal witnesses, the defense has the opportunity to question them and to present new witnesses in rebuttal.

Closing Arguments by Each Side

When each side has completed its presentation of the evidence, prosecution and defense make closing arguments to the jury. Veteran attorneys feel that the closing argument is a major chance to appeal directly to the members of the jury. The attorneys review the evidence of the case for the jury, presenting interpretations of the evidence that are favorable to their own side. The prosecutor may use the summation to show that the individual pieces of evidence together form a basis for concluding that the defendant is guilty. The defense, on the other hand, may set forth the applicable law and try to show that (1) the prosecution has not proved its case beyond a reasonable doubt and (2) the testimony raised questions but did not provide answers. Each side may remind the jury of its duty not to be swayed by emotion and to evaluate the evidence impartially. Even so, some attorneys may actually hope that the jurors react emotionally, especially if they think that those emotions will benefit their side.

Judge's Instructions to the Jury

The jury decides the facts of the case, but the judge determines the law. Before the jurors depart for the jury room to decide the defendant's fate, the judge instructs them on how the law should guide their decision. The judge may discuss basic legal principles such as proof beyond a reasonable doubt, the legal requirements necessary to show that all the elements have been proved by the prosecution, or the rights of the defendant. More specific aspects of the law bearing on the decision—such as complicated court rulings on the nature of the insanity defense or the ways certain types of evidence have been gathered—may be included in the judge's instructions. In complicated trials, the judge may spend an entire day instructing the jury.

The concept of **reasonable doubt** is at the heart of the jury system. The prosecution is not required to prove the guilt of the defendant beyond all doubt. Jurors should vote for conviction if they feel the evidence gives them a sense of certainty about guilt and if they do not find themselves wavering between conviction and acquittal. A vote for acquittal should not be based on sympathy or the reluctance of a jury to perform a disagreeable task.

reasonable doubt

The standard used by a juror to decide if the prosecution has provided enough evidence for conviction. Jurors should vote for acquittal if they think there is a reasonable doubt.

The experience of listening to the judge may become an ordeal for the jurors, who must hear and understand perhaps two or three hours of instruction on the law and the evidence (Bradley, 1992). It is assumed that somehow jurors will fully absorb these details upon first hearing them, so that they will thoroughly understand how they are supposed to decide the case in the jury room (Kramer and Koenig, 1990). Finally, the judge explains the charges and the possible verdicts. Trials usually involve multiple charges, and the judge must instruct the jurors in such a way that their decisions will be consistent with the law and the evidence.

Decision by the Jury

After they have heard the case and have been instructed by the judge, the jurors retire to a room where they have complete privacy. They elect a foreperson to run the meeting, and deliberations begin. Until now, the jurors have been passive observers of the trial, unable to question witnesses or to discuss the case among themselves; now they can discuss the facts that have been presented. Throughout their deliberations the jurors may be sequestered—kept together day and night, away from the influences of newspapers and conversations with family and friends. If jurors are allowed to spend nights at home, they are ordered not to discuss the case with anyone. The jury may request that the judge reread to them portions of the instructions, ask for additional instructions, or hear portions of the transcript detailing exactly what was said by specific witnesses.

In almost every state and in the federal courts, the verdict must be unanimous in criminal cases. Only Louisiana, Montana, Oregon, Oklahoma, and Texas permit majority decisions in a criminal case whose jury is composed of twelve people. If the jury becomes deadlocked and cannot reach a verdict, the trial ends with a hung jury and the prosecutor must decide whether to try the case all over again in front of a new jury.

When a verdict is reached, the judge, prosecution, and defense reassemble in the courtroom to hear it. The prosecution or the defense may request that the jury be polled, in which case each member individually tells his or her vote in open court. This procedure presumably ensures that no juror has felt pressured to agree with the other jurors. If the verdict is guilty, the judge may continue bail or may incarcerate the convicted person to await a presentence report. If the verdict is not guilty, the defendant is freed. Because the Fifth Amendment guarantees that a person shall not be "twice put in jeopardy of life or limb," prosecutors may not appeal a jury's finding or again prosecute the same charges against the defendant.

Sentencing

If the jury finds the defendant guilty, the judge must determine the appropriate sentence. Death penalty cases in some states require the jury to make the decision about the defendant's fate or to make a sentencing recommendation to the judge. Many judges say that sentencing is their most difficult responsibility. Prior to sentencing, a probation officer usually prepares a **presentence report** to help the judge select a punishment that will reflect the seriousness of the crime and the record of the defendant. In Chapter 10 we will closely examine judges' sentencing decisions. Sentencing is a particularly important stage of the trial process because of its impact on the lives of criminal offenders.

presentence report

Report prepared by a probation officer, who investigates a convicted offender's background to help the judge select an appropriate sentence.

Evaluating the Jury System

The question of which factors in a trial lead to the jury's verdict is always intriguing. Social scientists have been hampered in studying the process of juror decision making because of the secrecy of the jury room (Levine, J. P., 1996). Instead researchers must study simulated juries—groups of people who hear and decide a case presented to them as part of a research study.

Early research found that, consistent with theories of group behavior, participation and influence in the process are related to social status. Men were found to be more active participants than women, whites more active than minority members, and the better educated more active than those less educated. Much of the discussion in the jury room was not directly concerned with the testimony but rather with trial procedures, opinions about the witnesses, and personal reminiscences (Strodtbeck, James, and Hawkins, 1957). In 30 percent of the cases, a vote taken soon after entering the jury room was the only one necessary to reach a verdict; in the rest of the cases, the majority on the first ballot eventually prevailed in 90 percent of the cases (Broeder, 1959). Because of group pressure, only rarely did a single juror produce a hung jury. Although some individual jurors may view the case differently, they may doubt their own views or go along with the others if everyone else disagrees. More recent findings have upheld the importance of group pressure on decision making (Hastie, Penrod, and Pennington, 1983).

Researchers have attempted to discover whether judges view cases differently from juries. Studies have reached conflicting conclusions about whether judges are more likely to convict defendants (Kalven and Zeisel, 1966; Roper and Flango, 1983). Juries are likely to be impressed by defendants who testify in court. Juries tend to take a more liberal view of such issues as self-defense than judges and are likely to minimize the seriousness of an offense if they dislike some characteristic of the victim (Adler, 1994:200-207). For example, if the victim of an assault is a prostitute, the jury may minimize the assault. Judges have more experience with the justice process. Thus, they appear more likely to label as guilty defendants whose cases were sent forward by police and prosecutors who believed that there was strong evidence of guilt.

CHECKPOINT

12. What are the stages in the trial process?
13. What are the kinds of evidence presented during a trial?
14. What factors may affect a jury's decision differently from that of judges?

APPEALS

Imposition of a sentence does not mean that it must be served immediately; the defendant has the right to appeal the verdict to a higher court. An **appeal** is based on a claim that one or more errors of law or procedure were made during the investigation, arrest, or trial process. Such claims usually assert that the trial judge made errors in courtroom rulings or in improperly admitting evidence that was gathered by the police in violation of some constitutional right. A defendant might base an appeal, for example, on the claim that the judge did not instruct the jury correctly or that a guilty plea was not made voluntarily. Appeals are based on questions of law or procedure, not on issues of the defendant's guilt or innocence. The appellate court will not normally second-guess a jury. Instead it will check to make sure that the trial followed proper procedures.

appeal

A request to a higher court that it review actions taken in a completed trial.

Most criminal defendants must file an appeal shortly after trial in order to have an appellate court review the case. By contrast, many states provide for an automatic appeal in death penalty cases. The quality of defense representation is important because the appeal must usually meet short deadlines and carefully identify appropriate issues (Wasserman, 1990).

Correcting errors through the appeals process encourages trial judges to be careful in making decisions. Appellate courts also encourage consistent application of the law throughout a state, region or, in U.S. Supreme Court cases, the entire nation. If judges in different parts of a state are interpreting a provision of the criminal code differently, the appellate court can issue a decision to clarify the issue and ensure consistent application of the law.

Basis for Appeals

Unlike almost all other Western countries, the United States does not allow the terms of the sentence to be appealed in most circumstances. An appeal may be filed when it is contended that the judge selected penalties not in accord with the law or that there were violations of either due process or equal protection. But if the law gave the judge the discretion to impose a sentence of, for example, ten years in a particular case, and the defendant thought that the offense warranted only eight, overturning the sentence on appeal would be quite unusual unless an improper sentencing procedure was followed. A showing that the decision was illegal, unreasonable, or unconstitutional would be necessary.

A case originating in a state court is usually appealed through that state's judicial system. When a state case involves a federal constitutional question, it may be appealed to the U.S. Supreme Court. State courts decide almost four-fifths of all appeals.

The number of appeals in both the state and federal courts has increased during the past decade. What is the nature of these cases? A five-state study by Joy Chapper and Roger Hanson (1989) showed that (1) although a majority of appeals occur after convictions at trial, about a quarter result from nontrial proceedings such as guilty pleas and probation revocations; (2) homicides and other serious crimes against persons account for more than 50 percent of appeals; (3) most appeals arise from cases in which the sentence is five years or less; and (4) the issues raised at appeal tend to concern the introduction of evidence, the sufficiency of evidence, and jury instructions.

Table 9.2
Percentage distribution of alternative outcomes in five state appellate courts

Although the public thinks defendants exercising their right of appeal will be released, this study shows that 20 percent have their convictions reversed, but only a few are acquitted by the appellate court.

SOURCE: Joy Chapper and Roger Hanson, *Understanding Reversible Error in Criminal Appeals* (Williamsburg, Va.: National Center for State Courts, 1989).

Appeal Outcome	Percentage of Appeals	Percentage of Appeals Reversed
Conviction affirmed	79.4	—
Conviction reversed	20.6	100.0
Acquittal	1.9	9.4
New trial	6.6	31.9
Resentencing	7.3	35.3
Other	4.8	23.4

Most appeals are unsuccessful. In almost 80 percent of the cases Chapper and Hanson examined, the decision of the trial courts was affirmed. Most of the other decisions produced new trials or resentencing; relatively few decisions (1.9 percent) actually produced acquittals on appeal. Table 9.2 shows the percentage distribution of outcomes from the appellate process. The appellate process rarely provides a ticket to freedom for someone convicted of a crime.

habeas corpus

A writ or judicial order requesting the release of a person being detained in a jail, prison, or mental hospital. If a judge finds the person is being held improperly, the writ may be granted and the person released.

Habeas Corpus

After people use their avenues of appeal, they may pursue a writ of habeas corpus if they claim that their federal constitutional rights were violated during the lower-court processes. Known as "the great writ" from its traditional role in English law and its enshrinement in the U.S. Constitution, **habeas corpus** is a judicial order requesting that a judge examine whether an individual is being properly detained in a jail, prison, or mental hospital. If there is no legal basis for the person to be held, then the judge may grant the writ and order the person to be released. In the context of criminal justice, convicted offenders claim that their imprisonment is improper because one of their constitutional rights was violated during the investigation or adjudication of their case. Statutes permit offenders convicted in both state and federal courts to pursue habeas corpus actions in the federal courts. After first seeking favorable decisions by state appellate courts, convicted offenders can start their constitutional claims anew in the federal trial-level district courts and subsequently pursue their habeas cases in the federal circuit courts of appeal and the U.S. Supreme Court.

Only about 1 percent of habeas petitions are successful (Flango, 1994b). One reason may be that an individual has no right to be represented by counsel when pursuing a habeas corpus petition. Few offenders have sufficient knowledge of law and legal procedures to identify and present constitutional claims effectively in the federal courts.

In the late 1980s and early 1990s, the U.S. Supreme Court issued many decisions that made it more difficult for convicted offenders to file habeas corpus petitions (Alexander, 1993). The Court created tougher procedural rules that are more difficult for convicted offenders to follow. The rules also unintentionally created some new problems for state attorneys general and federal trial courts that must examine the procedural rule affecting cases rather than simply addressing the constitutional violations that the offender claims occurred (Smith, 1995a). In 1996, Congress enacted and President Bill Clinton signed the Antiterrorism and Effective Death Penalty Act, which placed additional restrictions on habeas corpus petitions. The U.S. Supreme Court quickly approved the statute (*Felker v. Turpin*, 1996). These reforms were based, in part, on a belief that prisoners' cases are clogging the federal courts (Smith, 1995a).

Evaluating the Appellate Process

The public seems to believe that many offenders are being "let off" through the appellate process. However, consider what follows a defendant's successful appeal, which is by no means a total and final victory. An appeal that results in reversal of the conviction normally means that the case is remanded to the lower court for a new trial. At this point the state must consider whether the procedural errors in the original trial can be overcome and whether it is worth additional expenditure to bring the defendant into court again. Frequently, the prosecutor pursues the case again and gains a new, proper conviction of the defendant. Moreover, the appeal process sometimes generates new plea negotiations that produce a second conviction with a lesser sentence that reflects the reduced strength of the prosecutor's case.

The appeals process performs the important function of righting wrongs. Beyond that, its presence is a constant influence on the daily operations of the criminal justice system as prosecutors and trial judges must consider how a higher court will later evaluate their decisions and actions.

CHECKPOINT

15. How does the appellate court's job differ from that of the trial court?
16. What is a habeas corpus petition?

Summary

- Most convictions are obtained through plea bargains, a process that exists because it fulfills the self-interest of prosecutors, judges, defense attorneys, and defendants.
- Plea bargaining is facilitated by exchange relations between prosecutors and defense attorneys. In many courthouses, there is little actual bargaining. Outcomes are determined through the implicit bargaining process of settling the facts and assessing the "going rate" punishment according to the values of the local legal culture.
- The U.S. Supreme Court has endorsed plea bargaining and addressed legal issues concerning the knowing and voluntary nature of pleas, guilty pleas by defendants who still claim to be innocent, and the obligations of prosecutors and defense attorneys to uphold the plea bargain agreement.
- Plea bargaining has been justified by its ability to individualize justice and ease administrative burdens on courts. It has been criticized for pressuring defendants to surrender their rights and for reducing the sentences imposed on offenders.
- Only 11 percent of felony cases go to trial, and nearly half of these are bench trials in front of a judge rather than jury trials.
- Cases go to trial because they involve defendants who are wealthy enough to pay attorneys to fight to the very end, they involve charges that are too serious to create incentives for plea bargaining, or they involve serious disagreements between the prosecutor and defense attorney about the provable facts and appropriate punishment.
- The U.S. Supreme Court has ruled that juries need not be made up of twelve members, and twelve-member juries can, if permitted by state law, convict defendants by a majority vote rather than a unanimous vote.
- Juries serve vital functions for society by preventing arbitrary action by prosecutors and judges, educating citizens about the justice system, symbolizing the rule of law, and involving citizens from diverse segments of the community in judicial decision making.
- The jury selection process, especially in the formation of the jury pool and the exercise of peremptory challenges, often creates juries that do not fully represent all segments of a community.
- The trial process consists of a series of steps: opening statements, presentation of prosecution's evidence, presentation of defense evidence, presentation of rebuttal witnesses, closing arguments, judge's jury instructions, and the jury's decision.
- Rules of evidence dictate what kinds of information may be presented in court for consideration by the jury. Types of evidence include real evidence, demonstrative evidence, testimony, direct evidence, and circumstantial evidence.
- Convicted offenders have the opportunity to appeal, although defendants who plead guilty—unlike those convicted through a trial—often have few grounds for an appeal.
- Appeals focus on claimed errors of law or procedure in the investigation by police and prosecutors or the decisions by trial judges. Relatively few offenders win their appeals, and most of those simply gain an opportunity for a new trial rather than release from jail or prison.
- After convicted offenders have used all of their appeals, they may file a habeas corpus petition to seek federal judicial review of claimed constitutional rights violations in their cases. Very few petitions are successful.

ANSWERS TO CHECKPOINTS

1. Plea bargaining occurs because it serves the self-interest of all relevant actors: defendants gain a certain, less-than-maximum sentence; prosecutors gain swift, sure convictions; defense attorneys get prompt resolution of cases; judges do not have to preside over as many time-consuming trials.
2. Implicit plea bargaining occurs when prosecutors and defense attorneys reach a shared view of the facts of the case and agree on a resolution based on the going rate for sentences in the local legal culture.
3. The U.S. Supreme Court has examined whether the defendant pleads guilty in a knowing and voluntary way, guilty pleas come from defendants who still claim to be innocent; and prosecutors and defendants fulfill their plea agreements.
4. Justifications for plea bargaining are (1) the opportunity to individualize justice during an era when legislatures mandate specific punishments, and (2) administrative necessity because of overcrowded courts.
5. The criticisms of plea bargaining include concerns about pressures on defendants to surrender their rights and concerns that society's mandated criminal punishments are improperly reduced.
6. The six functions of juries are to safeguard citizens against arbitrary law enforcement, determine the guilt of the accused, represent diverse community interests and values, serve as buffer between accused and accuser, educate citizens about the justice system, and symbolize the law.
7. The one-day-one-trial reform has improved the jury system in the minds of jurors, judges, and court administrators.
8. The Supreme Court has said that juries can have as few as six jurors, except in death penalty cases, in which twelve are required, and convictions can occur through less-than-unanimous verdicts.
9. Only 11 percent of felony cases go to trial; 6 percent are jury trials and 5 percent are bench trials.
10. Voir dire is the jury selection process in which lawyers and judges ask questions of prospective jurors and make decisions about using peremptory challenges and challenges for cause to shape the jury's composition.
11. A challenge for cause is based on an indication that a prospective juror cannot make a fair decision. The judge must approve such challenges. A peremptory challenge can be made by the attorney without giving a specific reason, unless there is an allegation that the attorney is using such challenges systematically to exclude people because of race or gender.
12. The stages in the trial process are attorneys' opening statements, presentation of prosecution's evidence, presentation of defense's evidence, presentation of rebuttal witnesses, closing arguments by each side, judge's instructions to the jury, and the jury's decision.
13. The kinds of evidence are real evidence, demonstrative evidence, witness testimony, direct evidence, and circumstantial evidence.
14. Jurors may be impressed with defendants who take the stand or those who have no criminal record, tend to take a more liberal view of issues such as self-defense, and may discount cases in which they dislike the victims.
15. Unlike trial courts, which have juries, hear evidence, and decide if the defendant is guilty or not guilty, appellate courts focus only on claimed errors of law or procedure in trial court proceedings. Victory for a defendant in a trial court means an acquittal and instant freedom. Victory in an appellate court may mean only a chance at a new trial—which often leads to a new conviction.
16. After all appeals have been filed and lost, convicted offenders ask a federal court to review whether any constitutional rights were violated during the course of a case investigation and trial. If rights were violated, the person's continued detention in prison or jail may be improper.

Questions for Review

1. What has the U.S. Supreme ruled about plea bargaining?
2. What tactics are used in plea bargaining?
3. How are jurors selected?
4. What is the purpose of appeals?
5. What is a habeas corpus petition?

Chapter 10

Punishment and Sentencing

The Goals of Punishment

- *Retribution—Deserved Punishment*
- *Deterrence*
- *Incapacitation*
- *Rehabilitation*

Forms of the Criminal Sanction

- *Incarceration*
- *Intermediate Sanctions*
- *Probation*
- *Death*

The Sentencing Process

- *The Administrative Context of the Courts*
- *Attitudes and Values of Judges*
- *Presentence Report*
- *Sentencing Guidelines*
- *Who Gets the Harshest Punishment?*

"ALL RISE!" Everyone stands as Los Angeles County Superior Court Judge Stanley Weisberg strides into the courtroom. On this day in July 1996 the courtroom is packed with attorneys, reporters, and members of the defendants' family. Judge Weisberg is about to sentence Erik and Lyle Menendez for murdering their parents. After two trials, a jury had convicted the brothers of killing Jose and Kitty Menendez as they watched television in their Beverly Hills mansion in 1989. The brothers admitted the murders. But they said their parents had sexually and psychologically abused them throughout their childhood, and they had feared for their lives. Prosecutors had described the killings as cold-blooded executions. They said the brothers were motivated by greed for the family's $14-million fortune.

In California, trials are divided into two separate phases when the death penalty is a possible punishment. During the first phase the jury determines guilt or innocence. In the second phase it determines the penalty. Having found the defendants guilty, the jury spent sixteen hours considering whether the brothers should die by lethal injection as the prosecution demanded or spend their lives in prison. There would be no chance for parole. The jury recommended that the brothers be sent to prison. After the announcement, defense attorneys expressed relief. They said they would present the judge with motions for a new trial.

The law recognizes that it is the judge who must decide the sentence. The jury's decision is only a recommendation. But California law specifies that the judge may not impose a death sentence against a jury's recommendation. Nor can Judge Weisberg reduce the life sentence. Thus, as the judge begins to address the defendants, they already know the outcome.

Rather than simply announcing the terms of the punishment, Judge Weisberg takes pains to review the case and to explain the reasons for the sentence. He says that he believes the brothers carefully decided to kill their parents and discussed the means for carrying out the murders. He then imposes the required two consecutive life terms without possibility of parole. As the judge speaks, the defendants show no reaction. Their relatives and friends remain silent. Upon leaving the courthouse, Lyle Menendez waves to his fiancée, Anna Eriksson, their plans for marriage now in disarray (*New York Times*, July 3,1996, p. A8).

Sentencing is a crucial point in the criminal justice system. After guilt is established, a decision must be made about what to do with the defendant. The interest of the public—even in a highly publicized case—seems to drop at this point. Usually the convicted criminal is out of sight and the case is out of the public's mind. But for the offender, sentencing is the beginning of corrections.

The criminal justice system aims to solve three basic questions: What conduct is criminal? What determines guilt? What should be done with the guilty? Earlier chapters discussed the first two questions. The answers given by the legal system to the first question are the basic rules of society: do not murder, rob, sell drugs, commit treason. The process for determining guilt or innocence is spelled out in the law, but it is greatly influenced by administrative and interpersonal considerations of the actors in the criminal justice system. In this chapter we will begin to examine the third question, sanction and punishment. We will consider the four goals of punishment: retribution, deterrence, incapacitation, and rehabilitation. We will then explore the forms that punishment takes to achieve its goals. These are incarceration, intermediate sanctions, probation, and death.

Questions for Inquiry

What are the goals of punishment?

What really happens in sentencing?

What types of sentences may judges impose?

Does the system treat wrongdoers equally?

THE GOALS OF PUNISHMENT

Criminal sanctions in the United States have four goals: retribution (deserved punishment), deterrence, incapacitation, and rehabilitation. Throughout the history of Western civilization the design of criminal punishments has been shaped by the dominant philosophical and moral orientations of the time. Ultimately, all criminal punishment is aimed at maintaining the social order. However, each goal represents a different approach to advancing society's interests.

Punishments reflect the dominant values of a particular moment in history. By the end of the 1960s, for example, the number of Americans who were sentenced to imprisonment decreased because of a widespread commitment to rehabilitating offenders through counseling, education, and other forms of assistance. By contrast, record numbers of offenders are being sentenced to prison during the late 1990s because of an emphasis on imposing strong punishments for the purposes of retribution, deterrence, and incapacitation.

Richard Allen Davis was convicted of the kidnapping and murder of 12-year-old Polly Klaas of Petaluma, California, while he was on parole. What should be the goal of his punishment?

Retribution—Deserved Punishment

Retribution refers to punishment inflicted on a person who has infringed on the rights of others and so deserves to be penalized. The biblical expression "An eye for an eye, a tooth for a tooth" illustrates the philosophy underlying retribution. Retribution means that those who commit a particular crime should be punished alike, in proportion to the gravity of the offense or to the extent to which others have been made to suffer. Retribution is deserved punishment; offenders must "pay their debts."

retribution

Punishment inflicted on a person who has infringed on the rights of others and so deserves to be penalized. The severity of the sanction should fit the seriousness of the crime.

Some scholars claim that the desire for retribution is a basic human emotion. They maintain that if the state does not provide retributive sanctions to reflect community revulsion at offensive acts, citizens will take the law into their own hands to punish offenders. Under this view, the failure of government to satisfy the people's desire for retribution could produce social chaos.

This argument may not be valid for all crimes, however. If a rapist is inadequately punished, then the victim's friends, family, and other members of the community may be tempted to exact their own retribution. But what about a young adult smoking marijuana? If the government failed to impose retribution for this offense, would the community really care? The same apathy may hold true for offenders who commit other nonviolent crimes that have a modest impact on society. Yet in these seemingly trivial situations, retribution may be useful and necessary to remind the public of the rule of law and the important values it protects.

In recent years retribution as a justification for the criminal sanction has aroused new interest, largely because of dissatisfaction with the philosophical basis and practical results of rehabilitation. Using the concept of "just deserts or deserved punishment" to define retribution, some theorists argue that one who infringes on the rights of others deserves to be punished. This approach is based on the philosophical view that punishment is a moral response to harm inflicted on society. In effect, these theorists believe that basic morality demands that wrongdoers be punished. Andrew von Hirsch, a leading contemporary writer on punishment, has said that "the sanctioning authority is entitled to choose a response that expresses moral disapproval: namely, punishment" (von Hirsch, 1976:49). According to von Hirsch and others, punishment should be applied only for the wrong inflicted and not primarily to achieve other goals such as deterrence, incapacitation, or rehabilitation.

Deterrence

Many people see criminal punishment as a basis for affecting the future choices and behavior of individuals. Politicians frequently talk about being tough on crime in order to send a message to would-be criminals. This deterrence approach has its roots in eighteenth-century England among the followers of the social philosopher Jeremy Bentham.

Bentham was struck by what seemed to be the pointlessness of retribution. His fellow reformers adopted Bentham's theory of utilitarianism, which holds that human behavior is governed by the individual's calculation of the benefits versus the costs of performing an act. Before stealing money or property, for example, potential offenders would consider the punishment that others have received for similar acts and would thereby be deterred.

general deterrence

Punishment of criminals that is intended to be an example to the general public and to discourage the commission of offenses by others.

There are two types of deterrence (Stafford and Warr, 1993). **General deterrence** presumes that members of the general public will be deterred by the punishments that others receive and conclude that the costs of crime outweigh the benefits. For general deterrence to be effective, the public must be constantly reminded about the likelihood and severity of punishment for various acts. They must believe that they will be caught, prosecuted, and given a specific punishment if they commit a particular crime. Moreover, the punishment must be severe enough that they will be impressed by the consequences of committing crimes. For example, public hanging was once considered to be an effective general deterrent.

By contrast, **special deterrence**, also called "specific" or "individual deterrence," targets the decisions and behavior of offenders who have already been convicted. Under this approach, the amount and kind of punishment are calculated to discourage the criminal from repeating the offense. The punishment must be sufficiently severe to cause the criminal to say, "The consequences of my crime were too painful. I will not commit another crime because I do not want to risk being punished again."

special deterrence

Punishment that is inflicted on criminals to discourage them from committing future crimes.

There are obvious difficulties with the concept of deterrence (Stafford and Warr, 1993). Deterrence assumes that all people act rationally and think before they act. Deterrence does not account for the many people who commit crimes while under the influence of drugs or alcohol or those whose harmful behavior stems from psychological problems or mental illness. Deterrence also does not account for people who act impulsively in stealing or damaging property. In other cases, the low probability of being caught defeats both general and special deterrence. In order to be generally deterrent, punishment must be perceived as relatively fast, certain, and severe. That, of course, is not always the case.

Social science is unable to measure the effects of general deterrence; only those who are *not* deterred come to the attention of researchers. A study of the deterrent effects of punishment would have to examine the impact of different forms of the criminal sanction on various potential lawbreakers. How can we ever know how many people—or even if *any* people—stopped themselves from committing a crime because they were deterred by the prospect of prosecution and punishment? Therefore, while legislators often cite deterrence as a rationale for certain sanctions, we do not really know the extent to which sentencing policies based on deterrence achieve their objectives. Because contemporary American society has shown little ability to reduce crime by imposing increasingly severe sanctions, we have strong reason to question the effectiveness of deterrence for many crimes and criminals.

Incapacitation

Incapacitation assumes that society can remove an offender's capacity to commit further crimes by detention in prison or by execution. Many people express such sentiments, urging that we should "lock 'em up and throw away the key!" In primitive societies, banishment from the community was the usual method of incapacitation. In early America, offenders often agreed to move away or to join the army as an alternative to some other form of punishment. In contemporary America, imprisonment is the usual method of incapacitation. Offenders can be confined within secure institutions and effectively prevented from inflicting additional harm against society for the duration of their sentences. Capital punishment is the ultimate method of incapacitation.

Since the early 1800s confinement in a prison or jail has been the usual method of incapacitation. It is assumed that while incapacitated an offender cannot commit additional harm to society.

Any sentence that physically restricts an offender can have the effect of incapacitating the person, even when the underlying purpose of the sentence is retribution, deterrence, or rehabilitation. Sentences based on incapacitation are future oriented. Whereas retribution focuses on the harmful act of the offender, incapacitation looks at the offender's potential future actions. If the offender is likely to commit future crimes, then a severe sentence may be imposed—even for a relatively minor crime.

For example, under the incapacitation theory, a woman who kills her abusive husband as an emotional reaction to his verbal insults and physical assaults could receive a light sentence. As a one-time impulse killer who felt driven to kill by unique circumstances, she is not likely to commit additional crimes. By contrast, someone who shoplifts merchandise from a store and has been convicted of the offense on ten previous occasions may receive a severe sentence. The criminal record and type of crime indicate that he or she will commit additional crimes if released. Thus incapacitation focuses on characteristics of the offenders rather than characteristics of their offenses.

incapacitation

Depriving an offender of the ability to commit crimes against society, usually by detaining the offender in prison.

Does it offend our sense of justice that a person could receive a more severe sentence for shoplifting than for manslaughter? This is one of the criticisms of incapacitation. There are also questions about how to determine the length of sentence. Presumably, offenders will not be released until the state is reasonably sure that they will no longer commit crimes. But can we accurately predict any person's behavior? Moreover, on what grounds can we punish people for anticipated future behavior that we cannot accurately predict?

In recent years greater attention has been paid to the concept of **selective incapacitation**, whereby offenders who repeat certain kinds of crimes are sentenced to long prison terms. Research has suggested that a relatively small number of offenders are responsible for a large number of violent and property crimes (Clear, 1994:103). Burglars, for example, tend to commit many offenses before they are caught. Thus, it is argued, these "career criminals" should be locked up for long periods. Such policies could be costly, however. Not only would correctional facilities have to be expanded, but the number of expensive, time-consuming trials might also increase if more severe sentences caused more repeat offenders to plead not guilty. Another difficulty with this policy is that we are unable to accurately predict which offenders will, in fact, commit more crimes upon release.

selective incapacitation

Making the best use of expensive and limited prison space by targeting for incarceration those individuals whose incapacity will do the most to reduce crime in society.

Rehabilitation

Rehabilitation refers to the goal of restoring a convicted offender to a constructive place in society through some form of vocational or educational training or therapy. Many find rehabilitation the most appealing modern justification for use of the criminal sanction. Americans want to believe that offenders can be treated and resocialized so that they will lead a crime-free, productive life. Throughout the twentieth century, many people have argued that techniques are available to identify and treat the causes of criminal behavior. If the offender's criminal behavior is assumed to result from some social, psychological, or biological imperfection, treatment of the disorder becomes the primary goal of corrections.

rehabilitation

The goal of restoring a convicted offender to a constructive place in society through some form of vocational or educational training or therapy.

Rehabilitation is focused on the offender. Its objective does not imply any consistent relationship between the severity of the punishment and the gravity of the crime. People who commit lesser offenses can receive long prison sentences if experts believe that a long period of time will be required to successfully rehabilitate them. By contrast, a murderer might win early release by showing signs that the psychological or emotional problems that led to the killing have been corrected.

According to the concept of rehabilitation, offenders are treated, not punished, and they will return to society when they are "cured." Consequently, judges should not set fixed sentences but rather maximum and minimum terms so that parole boards may release inmates when they have been rehabilitated. Such sentences are known as **indeterminate sentences** because no fixed release date is set by the judge. The underlying principle of indeterminate sentencing is that if prisoners know when they are going to be released, they will not make an effort to engage in

indeterminate sentence

An indefinite period set by a judge that specifies a minimum and a maximum time served in prison. Sometime after serving the minimum sentence, the offender may be eligible for parole. Because it is based on the idea that the time necessary for treatment cannot be set, the indeterminate sentence is closely associated with rehabilitation.

the treatment programs prescribed for their rehabilitation. If, however, they know that they will be held until they are cured, they will cooperate with counselors, psychologists, and other professionals seeking to treat their problems.

From the 1940s until the 1970s the goal of rehabilitation was so widely accepted that treatment and reform of the offender were generally regarded as the only issues worth serious attention. Crime was assumed to be caused by problems affecting individuals, and modern social sciences had given us the tools to address those problems. During the past twenty years, however, the assumptions of the rehabilitation model have been questioned. Studies of the results of rehabilitation programs have challenged the idea that we really know how to cure criminal offenders (Martinson, 1974). Moreover, it is no longer taken for granted that crime is caused by identifiable, curable problems such as poverty, lack of job skills, low self-esteem, and hostility toward authority. Instead, some scholars argue that we cannot expect to identify the cause of individual offenders' criminal behavior. Clearly, many legislatures, prosecutors, and judges have abandoned the rehabilitation goal in favor of

Goal	Judge's Possible Statement
Retribution	I am imposing this sentence because you deserve to be punished for murdering your parents. Your criminal behavior is the basis of the punishment. Justice requires that I impose a sanction at a level that illustrates the importance that the community places on the sanctity of life.
Deterrence	I am imposing this sentence so that your punishment for murdering your parents will serve as an example and deter others who may contemplate similar actions. In addition, I hope that this sentence will deter you from ever again committing an illegal act.
Incapacitation	I am imposing this sentence so that you will be incapacitated and hence unable to murder a person in the free community during the length of this term.
Rehabilitation	The trial testimony and information contained in the presentence report make me believe that aspects of your personality led you to murder your parents. I am therefore imposing this sentence so that you can receive treatment that will rectify your behavior and you will not commit another crime.

Table 10.1
The goals of punishment

At sentencing the judge usually gives reasons for the punishments imposed. Here are statements that Judge Stanley Weisberg might have given to Erik and Lyle Menendez, each promoting a different goal for the sanction. Remember, however, that in this case California law did not give the judge sentencing discretion.

retribution, deterrence, or incapacitation. Yet on the basis of opinion polls Richard McCorkle has found public support for rehabilitative programs (McCorkle, 1993:240). Prison wardens have also supported such programs (Cullen et al., 1993:69). The various goals of punishment are summarized in Table 10.1.

Although the four goals of the criminal sanction are often discussed as if they were distinct, they overlap a great deal. A sentence of life imprisonment can be philosophically justified in terms of its primary goal of incapacitation, but the secondary functions of retribution and deterrence are also present. Deterrence is such a broad concept that it mixes well with all the other purposes. The next section explores the ways that these goals are applied through the various forms of punishment. As you read it, keep in mind the underlying goal—or mix of punishment goals—that justifies each form of sanction.

CHECKPOINT

1. What are the four goals of the criminal sanction?
2. What are the difficulties in showing that punishment acts as a deterrent?

(Answers are at the end of the chapter.)

FORMS OF THE CRIMINAL SANCTION

Incarceration, intermediate sanctions, probation, and death are the basic ways that the criminal sanction, or punishment, is applied in the United States. Most people think of incarceration as the usual punishment. As a consequence, much of the public thinks that using alternatives to incarceration, such as probation, means that offenders are "getting off." However, community-based punishments such as probation and intermediate sanctions are imposed almost three times as often as prison sentences.

As we examine the various forms of criminal sanctions, bear in mind that applying these legally authorized punishments is complex. Judges are given wide discretion in determining the appropriate sentence within the parameters of the penal code.

Incarceration

Imprisonment is the most visible penalty imposed by U.S. courts. Although fewer than 30 percent of persons under correctional supervision are in prisons and jails, incarceration remains the standard for punishing those who commit serious crimes. Imprisonment is thought to have a significant effect in deterring potential offenders. However, incarceration is expensive. It also creates the problem of reintegrating offenders into society upon release.

In penal codes, legislatures stipulate the type of sentences and the amount of prison time that may be imposed for each crime. Three basic sentencing schemes are used: (1) indeterminate sentences, (2) determinate sentences, and (3) mandatory sentences. Each type of sentence makes certain assumptions about the goals of the criminal sanction, and each provides judges with varying degrees of discretion.

Indeterminate Sentences

When the goal of rehabilitation dominated corrections, legislatures enacted indeterminate (often termed "indefinite") sentences. In keeping with the goal of treatment, indeterminate sentences give correctional officials and parole boards significant control over the amount of time a prisoner serves. Penal codes with indeterminate sentences specify a minimum and a maximum amount of time to be served in prison (for example, one to five years, three to ten years, or one year to life). At the time of sentencing, the judge informs the offender of the range of the sentence. The offender also learns that he or she will probably be eligible for parole at some point after the minimum term has been served. "Good time" may be subtracted from either the minimum or maximum; good time is earned by good behavior in prison or participation in a rehabilitation program. The parole board decides the actual release date.

Determinate Sentences

Growing dissatisfaction with the rehabilitation goal and support for the concept of deserved punishment led many legislatures to shift to **determinate sentences**. With a determinate sentence, a convicted offender is imprisoned for a specific period of time (for example, two years, five years, ten years). At the end of the term, minus credited "good time," the prisoner is automatically freed. The time of release is not tied to participation in treatment programs or to the offender's likelihood of returning to criminal activities, as judged by the parole board.

determinate sentence

A sentence that fixes the term of imprisonment to a specific period of time.

As states have moved toward determinate sentences, some have adopted penal codes that stipulate a specific term for each crime category; others still allow the judge to choose a range of time to be served. Some states emphasize a determinate **presumptive sentence**: the legislature or often a commission specifies a term based on a time range (for example, fourteen to twenty months) into which most cases should fall. Only in special circumstances should judges deviate from the presumptive sentence. Whichever variation is used, however, the offender theoretically knows at sentencing the amount of time to be served. One result of determinate sentencing is that by reducing the judge's discretion, legislatures have tended to limit sentencing disparities and to ensure that the terms will correspond to those the elected body thinks are appropriate (Griset, 1993).

presumptive sentence

A sentence for which the legislature or a commission sets a minimum and maximum range of months or years. Judges are to fix the length of the sentence within that range, allowing for special circumstances.

Mandatory Sentences

Politicians and the public have continued to complain that offenders are released before serving long enough terms, and legislatures have responded to the outcry. All but two states now require **mandatory sentences**, which state some minimum period of incarceration that persons convicted of selected crimes must serve. As with determinate sentences, mandatory sentences eliminate judicial discretion. The judge cannot consider the circumstances of the offense or the background of the offender, and may not impose sentences that do not involve imprisonment. Mandatory prison terms are most often specified for violent crimes, drug violations, habitual offenders, or crimes in which a firearm was used.

mandatory sentence

A sentence determined by statutes and requiring that a certain penalty be imposed and carried out for convicted offenders who meet certain criteria.

The "three strikes and you're out" laws adopted by several states and the federal government are an example of mandatory sentencing (Turner et al., 1995). These laws require that judges sentence offenders with three felony convictions to long prison terms, sometimes to life without parole. In Washington state and California the laws have had the unintended consequences of clogging the courts, lowering rates of plea bargaining, and causing desperate offenders to violently resist arrest (Edna McConnell Clark Foundation, Seeking Justice, 1997:20). Experience with a "three-strikes" law in the state of Washington is discussed in the Close-up.

CLOSE-UP

A Three-Strike Penal Law Shows It's Not as Simple as It Seems

In the fight against violent crime, perhaps no idea is more popular than "three strikes and you're out"—locking up repeat offenders for life without parole. ... But two months after the state of Washington established a law requiring criminals to spend life in prison without parole if they are convicted of three felonies, the first faces of "three strikes" are emerging. And they present a picture that is more complicated than the baseball slogan that inspired 76 percent of Washington state voters to back the measure last fall.

Prosecutors and police officers say the law has had some unintended side effects. With nothing to lose, some criminals are showing a tendency to be more violent or desperate when officers try to arrest them. And prosecutors say first- and second-time offenders are less willing to plea bargain, which would mean pleading to a felony—the first or second "strike." These offenders are instead forcing full trials in a court system that has neither the staff nor the space to take on the extra load.

Among the first candidates for life in prison under the three-strikes law, several seem to fit the profile of violent predators with long criminal histories. But other cases may not be what voters here had in mind. ...

The case most troubling to the law's critics is that of Larry Lee Fisher, 35, who has been in and out of jail since he was a teenager. His first strike was in 1986, when he was convicted of robbery in the second degree—pushing his grandfather down and taking $390 from him. Mr. Fisher served four months in jail. Two years later came his second strike, a $100 robbery of a pizza parlor in which he concealed his finger and said it was a gun. He served seventeen months on a work farm.

Last month Mr. Fisher was arrested for holding up a sandwich shop in Everett, again without a gun but pretending he had one, pointing his finger inside his coat pocket. The police found him an hour after the holdup drinking beer in a nearby tavern. Normally, he would face about twenty-two months in jail. But now, if convicted, he will spend the rest of his life in prison. ...

Dave LaCourse, a leader of the three-strikes initiative, said Mr. Fisher's case was unusual but not unintended. "Here's a guy with ten misdemeanors on his record, he's 35 years old, and he hasn't learned his lesson yet," Mr. LaCourse said. "What's it going to take? He seems to be one of those people who's making crime a career."

Washington prosecutors said states now considering three-strikes laws would do well not to put too many crimes in the mix of what qualifies. Because of cases like Larry Lee Fisher's, Washington's law may have to be refined, they said.

"Don't assume this will have a dramatic effect on crime," said John Ladenburg, Pierce County prosecutor. "This is not a cure-all. This is not going to fix crime. What it will do is get some of the worst offenders off of the street forever."

SOURCE: Condensed from Timothy Egan, "A Three-Strike Penal Law Shows It's Not as Simple as It Seems," *New York Times*, February 15, 1994, p. 1.

Although many criminal justice scholars believe that mandatory sentences do not achieve their purpose (Tonry, 1992), research conducted on Florida's mandatory minimum sentences does support their effectiveness (Florida, Department of Corrections, 1991. *Mandatory Minimum Sentences in Florida*). The Florida law is designed to ensure that certain offenders are not released early (through good time and other provisions) before a certain portion of their sentence has been served. Eleven categories of offenders—for example, those convicted of capital offenses and certain drug and firearms offenses, and those labeled habitual offenders—come under the mandatory provisions. These laws have been cited as a major cause of the longer prison terms that have in turn led to increases in the prison population.

The Sentence versus Actual Time Served

Regardless of the discretion judges have to fine-tune the sentences they give, the prison sentences that are imposed may bear little resemblance to the amount of time actually served. In reality, parole boards in states with indeterminate-sentencing laws have broad discretion in release decisions once the offender has served a minimum portion of the sentence. In addition, convicts can have their prison sentences reduced by earning "good time," at the discretion of the prison administrator.

All but four states have policies that take good time into account. Days are subtracted from prisoners' minimum or maximum term for good behavior or for participation in various types of vocational, educational, or treatment programs. Corrections officials consider these sentence-reduction policies necessary for maintaining institutional order and reducing crowding. The possibility of receiving good-time credit is an incentive for prisoners to follow institutional rules. Prosecutors and defense attorneys also consider good time during plea bargaining. In other words, they think about the actual amount of time a particular offender is likely to serve.

The amount of good time that one can earn varies among the states, usually from five to ten days a month. In some states, once ninety days of good time are earned, they are vested; that is, the credits cannot be taken away as a punishment for misbehavior. Prisoners who then violate the rules risk losing only days not vested.

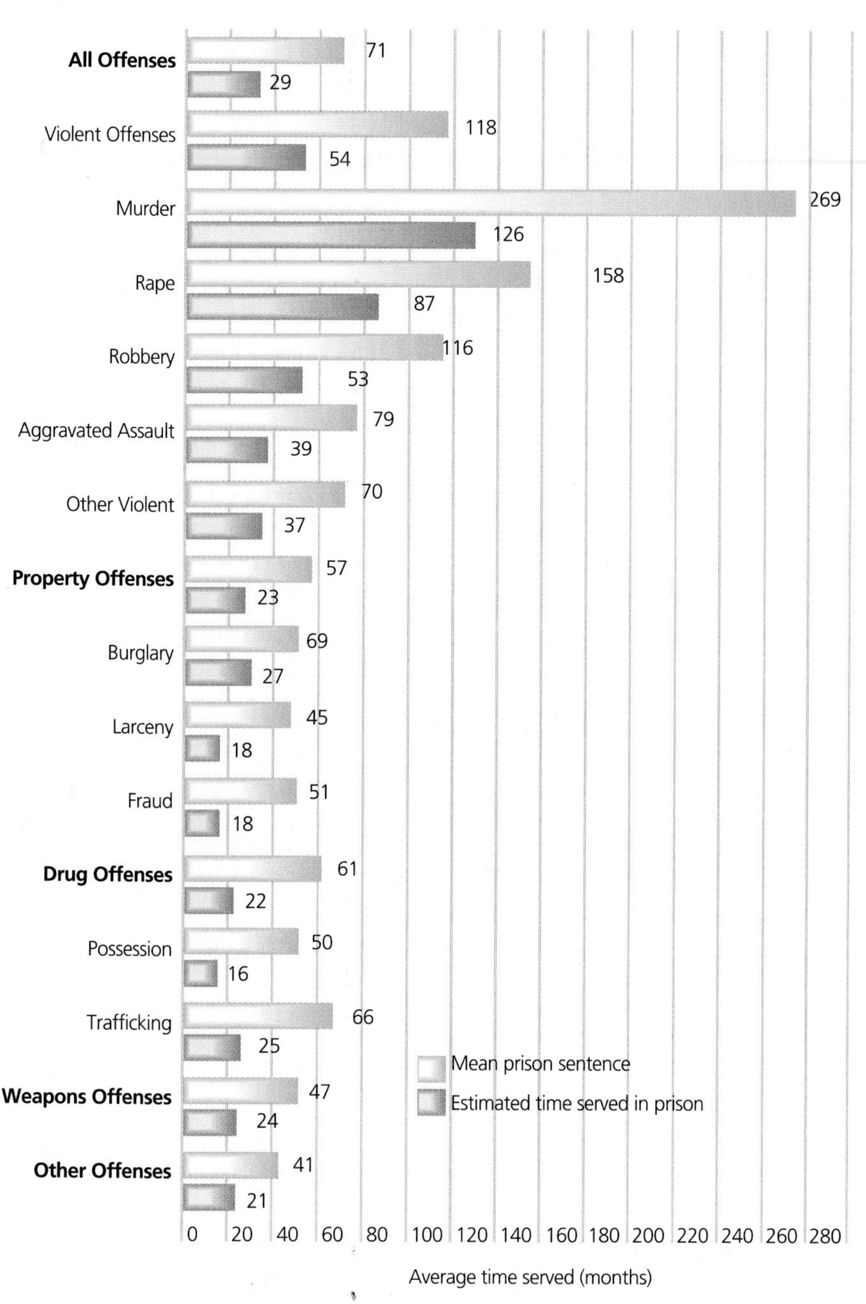

Figure 10.1
Estimated time served in state prison compared to mean length of sentence

Most offenders serve a third or less of their mean sentences. Why is there such a difference between the sentence and actual time served?

SOURCE: U.S. Department of Justice, Bureau of Justice Statistics, *Bulletin* (July 1997), 9.

Good time and parole reduce the amount of time spent in prison. Figure 10.1 shows the estimated time actually served by offenders sent to state prisons versus the average sentence imposed. Note that the national average for time served by state prisoners is twenty-nine months, or 41 percent of the mean sentence of seventy-one months. This type of national data often hides the impact of variations in sentencing and releasing laws in individual states. In many states, because of prison crowding and release policies, offenders are serving less than 20 percent of their sentences. Calls for "truth-in-sentencing laws" have arisen when the public has learned that the actual time served is much less than expected.

Intermediate Sanctions

Community service, such as assisting in a homeless shelter, is one form of intermediate punishment. Advocates of these sanctions stress that offenders need to recognize responsibility for their acts.

Prison crowding and the low levels of probation supervision have spurred interest in the development of **intermediate sanctions**, punishments that are less severe and costly than prison but more restrictive than traditional probation (Morris and Tony, 1990). Intermediate sanctions give judges a greater range of sentencing alternatives by providing a variety of restrictions on freedom, such as fines or other monetary sanctions, home confinement, intensive probation supervision, restitution to victims, community service, boot camp, and forfeiture of possessions or stolen property. It has been estimated that even if murderers and rapists, those offenders who had been previously incarcerated, and those with a prior sentence for violence were excluded from consideration for intermediate punishments, 29 percent of those who are now headed for prison could be sanctioned in the community (Petersilia and Turner, 1989).

In advocating intermediate punishments, Morris and Tonry specify that these sanctions should be not be used in isolation, but rather in combination to reflect the severity of the offense, the characteristics of the offender, and the needs of the community (Morris and Tonry, 1990:37). In addition, intermediate punishments must be supported and enforced by mechanisms that take seriously any breach of the conditions of the sentence. Too often criminal justice agencies have devoted few resources to enforcing sentences that don't involve incarceration. If the law does not fulfill its promises, offenders may feel that they have "beaten" the system, which makes the punishment meaningless. Citizens viewing the ineffectiveness of the system may develop the attitude that nothing but stiffer sentences will work. Intermediate sanctions are discussed fully in Chapter 12.

intermediate sanctions

A variety of punishments that are more restrictive than traditional probation but less severe and less costly than incarceration.

Probation

probation

A sentence that the offender is allowed to serve in the community under supervision.

The most frequently applied criminal sanction is **probation**, a sentence that an offender serves in the community under supervision. Nearly 65 percent of adults under correctional supervision are on probation. Probation is designed to maintain supervision of offenders while they attempt to straighten out their lives. Probation is a judicial act, granted by the grace of the state rather than extended as a right. Conditions of probation specify how an offender will behave through the length of the sentence. Probationers may be ordered to undergo regular drug tests, abide by curfews, enroll in educational programs or remain employed, stay away from certain parts of town or certain people, or meet regularly with probation officers. If the conditions of probation are not met, the supervising officer recommends to the court that the probation be revoked and that the remainder of the sentence be served in prison. Probation may also be revoked for commission of a new crime.

shock probation

A sentence in which the offender is released after a short incarceration and resentenced to probation.

Although probationers serve their sentences in the community, the sanction is often tied to incarceration. In some jurisdictions, the court is authorized to modify an offender's prison sentence after a portion is served by changing it to probation. This is often referred to as **shock probation** (or "split probation"): an offender is released after a period of incarceration (the "shock") and resentenced to probation. An offender on probation may be required to spend intermittent periods, such as weekends or nights, in jail. Whatever the specific terms of the probationary sentence, it emphasizes guidance and supervision in the community.

Probation is generally advocated as a way of rehabilitating offenders whose crimes are less serious or whose past records are clean. It is viewed as less expensive than imprisonment, and more effective. Imprisonment may embitter youthful or first-time offenders and mix them with hardened criminals so that they learn more sophisticated criminal techniques.

Death

Although other Western democracies abolished the death penalty years ago, the United States continues to use it. Capital punishment was imposed and carried out regularly prior to the late 1960s. Amid debates about the constitutionality of the death penalty and with public opinion polls increasingly showing opposition to it, the U.S. Supreme Court suspended its use from 1968 to 1976 (Keil and Vitto, 1991). Eventually, the Court decided that capital punishment does not violate the Eighth Amendment's prohibition on cruel and unusual punishment. Executions resumed in 1977 as a majority of states began, once again, to sentence murderers to death.

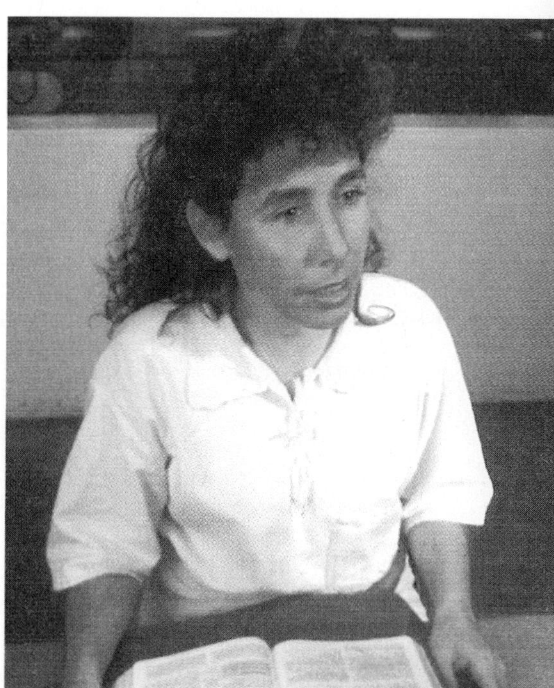

Condemned killer Karla Faye Tucker reads her Bible prior to becoming the first woman in 135 years to be executed in Texas for participating in double pick ax murders. The fact that she was a woman and had become a "born-again" Christian drew support for clemency from around the world, including Pope John Paul II and television evangelist Pat Robertson.

The numbers of persons facing the death penalty has increased dramatically in the past decade, as Figure 10.2 reveals. There are now more than 3,000 persons awaiting execution in thirty-five of the thirty-eight death penalty states. Two-thirds of those on death row are in the South, with the greatest number found in Texas, Georgia, Alabama, and Florida (see Figure 10.3). Yet since 1976, when the Supreme Court allowed the resumption of capital punishment, the number of executions has never exceeded 74, the number in 1997, in any one year. From 1930 through 1967, in contrast, more than 3,800 men and women were executed in the United States, 199 of them in 1935, the deadliest year. The 74 executions that took place in 1997 were the greatest number since 1957, when 65 people were executed. Use of the penalty has spread in recent years from its southern base to states around the country (*New York Times*, October 14, 1997, p. 1).

The Death Penalty and the Constitution

Death obviously differs from other punishments in that it is final and irreversible. The Supreme Court has therefore examined the decision-making process in capital cases to ensure that the Constitution's requirements regarding due process, equal protection, and cruel and unusual punishment are fulfilled. Because life is in the balance, capital cases must be conducted according to higher standards of fairness and more careful procedures than other kinds of cases. Several important Supreme Court cases illustrate this concern.

Key Supreme Court Decisions

Furman v. Georgia (1972)

The death penalty, as administered, constituted cruel and unusual treatment.

In ***Furman v. Georgia*** (1972), the Supreme Court ruled that the death penalty, as administered, constituted cruel and unusual punishment. The decision invalidated the death penalty laws of thirty-nine states and the District of Columbia. Although a majority of justices objected to the way in which the death penalty was applied,

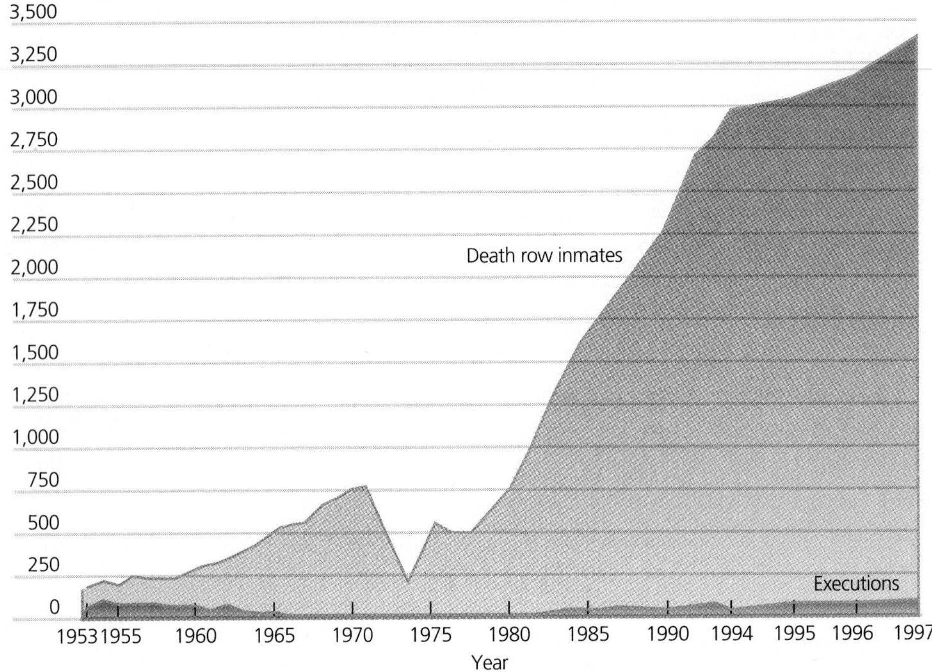

Figure 10.2
Persons under sentence of death and persons executed, 1953–1997

Since 1976 approximately 250 new offenders have been added to death row each year, yet the number of executions has never been greater than 74. What explains this situation?

SOURCE: NAACP Legal Defense and Education Fund, *Death Row, USA* (Winter 1998); Fox and Butterfield, *New York Times*, January 25, 1998, p. WK1.

they could not agree on the reasons that it was unconstitutional. Two justices argued that the death penalty *always* violates the Eighth Amendment's prohibition on cruel and unusual punishment, but other members emphasized that the *procedures* used to impose death sentences were arbitrary and unfair.

Over the next several years, thirty-five states enacted new capital punishment statutes that provided for more careful decision making and more modern methods of execution, such as lethal injection. The new laws were tested before the Supreme Court in 1976 in the case of ***Gregg v. Georgia***. The Court upheld those laws that required the sentencing judge or jury to take into account specific aggravating and mitigating factors in deciding which convicted murderers should be sentenced to death.

Gregg v. Georgia (1976)

Death penalty laws are constitutional if they require judge and jury to consider certain mitigating and aggravating circumstances in deciding which convicted murderers should be sentenced to death.

As a result of *Gregg,* instead of deciding the defendant's guilt and imposing the death sentence in the same proceeding, states created "bifurcated" proceedings. This two-part process consists of a trial that determines guilt or innocence and then a separate hearing that focuses exclusively on the issues of punishment. Under the *Gregg* decision, the prosecution uses the punishment-phase hearing to focus attention on the existence of "aggravating factors," such as excessive cruelty or a defendant's prior record of violent crimes. The decision makers must also focus on "mitigating factors," such as the offender's youthfulness, mental retardation, or lack of a criminal record. These aggravating and mitigating factors must be weighed together before the judge or jury can make a decision about whether to impose a death sentence. The purpose of the two-stage decision-making process is to ensure thorough deliberation before the defendant is given the ultimate punishment.

Despite the Supreme Court's endorsement of the constitutionality of capital punishment, opponents of the death penalty have continued to challenge it with new cases. Instead of making the broad claim that capital punishment is unconstitutional, these cases challenged aspects of it—such as racial discrimination in capital sentencing and the execution of minors and the mentally retarded.

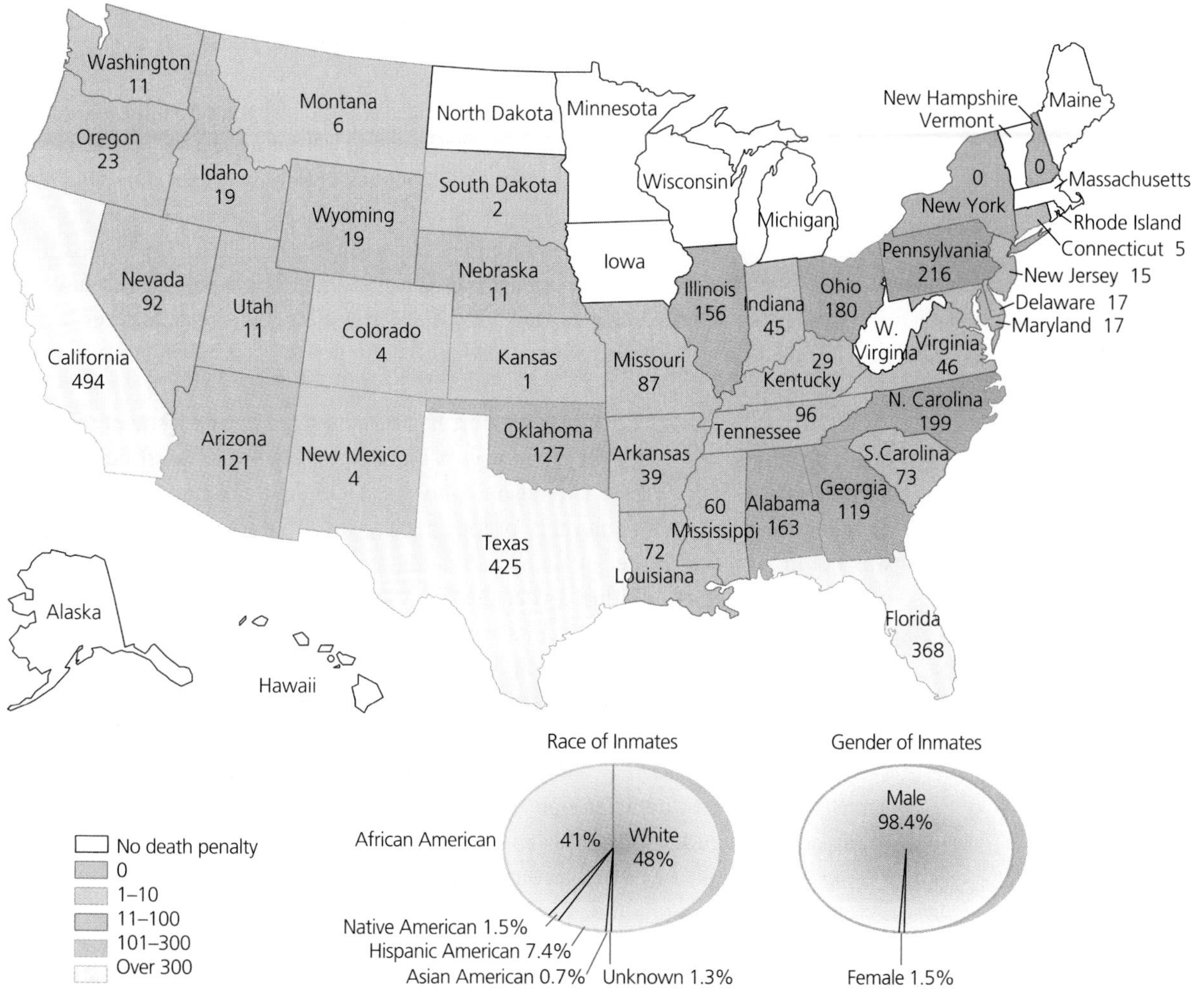

Figure 10.3
Death row census, 1998

Many of the inmates on death row are concentrated in certain states. African Americans make up about 13 percent of the U.S. population and yet make up 41 percent of the death row population. How might you explain this higher rate in proportion to the population?

SOURCE: NAACP Legal Defense and Education Fund, *Death Row, USA* (Winter 1998); U.S. Department of Justice, Bureau of Justice Statistics, *Bulletin* (December 1966), 4.

The U.S. Supreme Court may have dealt a fatal blow to the hopes of death penalty opponents in 1987. In the case of ***McCleskey v. Kemp***, the Court rejected a constitutional challenge to Georgia's death penalty law on the grounds of racial discrimination. Warren McCleskey, an African American, was sentenced to death for the killing of a white police officer during a furniture store robbery. Before the U.S. Supreme Court McCleskey's attorney cited research that showed a disparity in the imposition of the death penalty in Georgia based on the race of the victim and, to a lesser extent, the race of the defendant (Baldus, Woodworth, and Pulaski, 1994).

By a 5-to-4 vote the justices rejected McCleskey's assertion that Georgia's capital sentencing practices violated the equal protection clause of the Constitution by producing racial discrimination. A slim majority of justices declared that McCleskey would have to prove that the decision makers acted with a discriminatory purpose in deciding his case. The Court also concluded that statistical evidence showing discrimination throughout the Georgia courts did not provide adequate proof. McCleskey was executed in 1991.

***McCleskey v. Kemp* (1987)**

Rejected a challenge of Georgia's death penalty on grounds of racial discrimination.

What Is the Future of the Death Penalty?

The *McCleskey* case was the most recent opportunity for opponents of capital punishment to seek its abolition. Other cases continue to challenge specific aspects of capital punishment, such as the execution of minors and the retarded and the length of the appeals process.

Capital punishment is an enduring public issue that elicits strong emotions both pro and con. Even though public opinion polls show strong support for the death of murderers, this support falls when life imprisonment without parole is presented as an alternative.

Execution of minors. The laws of thirteen states do not specify a minimum age for offenders receiving capital punishment. Since 1642, when the Plymouth Colony in Massachusetts hanged a teenage boy for bestiality, 281 juveniles have been executed in the United States (Rosenbaum, R., 1989). Death penalty opponents have argued that adolescents do not have the same capacity as adults to understand the consequences of their actions.

The Supreme Court has been divided on the issue of the death penalty for juveniles. In *Thompson v. Oklahoma* (1988) the Court narrowly decided that William Wayne Thompson, who was 15 when he committed murder, should not be executed. A plurality of four justices held that executing juveniles was not in accord with the "evolving standards of decency that mark the progress of a maturing society." Within a year the Court again considered the issue in *Stanford v. Kentucky* (1989) and *Wilkins v. Missouri* (1989). This time the justices upheld the death sentences imposed on offenders who were 16 and 17 years old at the time of their crimes. These decisions effectively set the minimum age for execution at 16.

With the Supreme Court evidently sanctioning executions of juveniles under some circumstances, Louisiana put to death Dalton Prejean, a juvenile at the time of the offense, on May 18, 1990. There are currently forty-one males on death rows who were under the age of 18 at the time their offenses occurred (NAACP Legal Defense and Education Fund, 1997. *Death Row USA*).

Execution of the retarded. An estimated 250 offenders on the nation's death rows are classified as retarded. Opponents of the death penalty for this group argue that retarded people have difficulty defending themselves in court because they have problems remembering details, locating witnesses, and testifying credibly in their own behalf. It is also asserted that executing the retarded serves neither retributive nor deterrent purposes, because the general public (the group being deterred from committing crime) may believe that the mental disability caused the offender to commit the crime (Fetzer, 1989).

In 1989 the Supreme Court decided that the Eighth Amendment does not prohibit execution of the mentally retarded. The case involved Johnny Paul Penry, a convicted killer with an IQ of about 70 and the mental capacity of a 7-year-old. The court noted that only Georgia and Maryland prohibited execution of the mentally retarded. Now, years after the Supreme Court decision, Penry is still on death row in Texas, in part because of the lengthy appeals process. In contrast, Alabama executed Horace Dunkins, Jr., who had an IQ of 69 (*New York Times*, July 15, 1989, p. 6).

Appeals. The long appeals process for death penalty cases is a source of ongoing controversy. The average length of time between sentencing by a trial court and the date that the sentence is carried out is between seven and eight years. During this time sentences are reviewed by the state courts and through the writ of habeas corpus by the federal courts.

Chief Justice William H. Rehnquist has actively sought to reduce the opportunities for capital punishment defendants to have their appeals heard by multiple courts (Pursley, 1995). In 1996 President Clinton signed a new law that required death row inmates to file habeas appeals within one year and required federal judges to issue their decisions within strict time limits (*Newsweek*, May 6, 1996, p. 72).

Appellate review is a time-consuming and expensive process, but it also has an impact. From 1973 to 1996, 5,580 persons were sentenced to death and 313 people executed. Of the remaining, 3,054 were still on death row at the end of 1995. However, 2,213 were removed from death row as a result of appeal, commutation (change of sentence) by a governor, or death while awaiting execution (BJS, 1996. *Bulletin*, February:14). Had the expedited appeals process and limitations on habeas corpus been in effect, would these death sentences have been overturned?

The Death Penalty: A Continuing Controversy

The philosophical and legal arguments over capital punishment continue. More than 250 new death sentences are being given out each year, yet the number of executions remains low. Is this situation the result of a complicated appeals process or the uncertainty of both political leaders and society about the taking of human life? Why is public opinion in support of capital punishment growing? Does the death penalty have more significance as a political symbol than as a deterrent to crime?

As we have seen, the criminal sanction takes many forms, and offenders are punished in various ways to serve various purposes. Table 10.2 summarizes how these sanctions operate and how they reflect the underlying philosophies of punishment.

CHECKPOINT

3. What are the three types of sentences used in the United States?
4. What are thought to be the advantages of intermediate sanctions?
5. What requirements specified in *Gregg v. Georgia* must exist before a death sentence may be imposed?

THE SENTENCING PROCESS

Now that we have examined the goals and forms of the criminal sanction, let's take a close look at the process for deciding the punishment to be imposed. Regardless of how and where the decision has been made—misdemeanor court or felony court, plea bargain or adversarial context, bench or jury trial—judges have the responsibility for imposing sentences.

Sentencing, which is often a difficult task, is frequently not merely a matter of applying clear-cut principles to individual cases. In one case, a judge may decide to sentence a forger to prison as an example to others, even though he is no threat to community safety and probably does not need rehabilitative treatment. In another case, the judge may impose a light sentence on a youthful offender who, although he has committed a serious crime, may be a good risk for rehabilitation if he can be quickly moved back into society.

Legislatures establish the penal codes that specify the sentences judges may impose. These laws generally give judges wide powers of discretion in sentencing. They may combine various forms of punishment so that the judge can tailor the

Form of Sanction	Description	Purposes
Incarceration	Imprisonment	
Indeterminate sentence	Specifies a maximum and minimum length of time to be served	Incapacitation, deterrence, rehabilitation
Determinate sentence	Specifies a certain length of time to be served	Retribution, deterrence, incapacitation
Mandatory sentence	Specifies a minimum amount of time for given crimes that must be served	Incapacitation, deterrence
Good time	Subtracts days from an inmate's sentence because of good behavior or participation in prison programs	Rewards behavior, relieves prison crowding, helps maintain prison discipline
Intermediate sanctions	Punishment for those requiring sanctions more restrictive than probation but less restrictive than prison	Retribution, deterrence
Administered by the judiciary		
Fine	Money paid to state by offender	Retribution, deterrence
Restitution	Money paid to victim by offender	Retribution, deterrence
Forfeiture	Seizure by the state of property illegally obtained or acquired with resources illegally obtained	Retribution, deterrence
Administered in the community		
Community service	Requires offender to perform work for the community	Retribution, deterrence
Home confinement	Requires offender to stay in home during certain times	Retribution, deterrence, incapacitation
Intensive probation supervision	Requires strict and frequent reporting to probation officer	Retribution, deterrence, incapacitation
Administered institutionally		
Boot camp/shock incarceration	Short-term institutional sentence emphasizing physical development and discipline, followed by probation	Retribution, deterrence, rehabilitation
Probation	Allows offender to serve a sentence in the community under supervision	Retribution, incapacitation, rehabilitation
Death	Execution	Incapacitation, deterrence, retribution

Table 10.2
The punishment of offenders

The goals of the criminal sanction are carried out in a variety of ways depending upon the provisions of the law, the characteristics of the offender, and the discretion of the judge. Judges may impose sentences that combine several forms to achieve punishment objectives.

sanction to the offender. The judge may specify, for example, that the prison terms for two charges are to run either concurrently (at the same time) or consecutively (one after the other), or that all or part of the period of imprisonment may be suspended. In other situations, the offender may be given a combination of a suspended prison term, probation, and a fine. Judges may also suspend a sentence as long as the offender stays out of trouble, makes restitution, or seeks medical treatment. The judge may delay imposing any sentence but retain the power to set penalties at a later date if the offender misbehaves.

Within the discretion allowed by the code, various elements in the sentencing process influence the decisions of judges. Let's look at several factors that social scientists believe influence the sentencing process: (1) the administrative context of the courts, (2) the attitudes and values of judges, (3) the presentence report, and (4) sentencing guidelines.

The Administrative Context of the Courts

Judges are strongly influenced by the administrative context within which they impose sentences. This factor accounts for the differences we see between, say, the assembly-line style of justice in the misdemeanor courts and the more formal proceedings found in felony courts.

Misdemeanor Courts: Assembly-Line Justice

Misdemeanor or lower courts have limited jurisdiction because they normally can only impose prison sentences of less than one year. These courts hear about 90 percent of criminal cases. While felony cases are processed in lower courts only for arraignments and preliminary hearings, every aspect of misdemeanor cases is processed in the lower courts, all the way through dismissals, guilty pleas, or convictions. Only a minority of cases adjudicated in lower courts end in jail sentences; most cases result in fines, probation, community service, or restitution.

Most lower courts are overloaded and allot minimal time to each case. Judicial decisions are mass produced because actors in the system share three assumptions. *First*, any person appearing before the court is guilty because the police and prosecution have presumably filtered out doubtful cases. *Second*, the vast majority of defendants will plead guilty. *Third*, those charged with minor offenses will be processed in volume, with dozens of cases being decided in rapid succession within a single hour. The citation will be read by the clerk, a guilty plea entered, and the sentence pronounced by the judge for one defendant after another.

Although the lower criminal courts have been criticized for their assembly-line characteristics, social scientists are now beginning to see redeeming features in this style of justice. They argue that the informality, availability, and diversity of the lower courts are their most valuable qualities. The lower courts have a unique capacity to resolve cases effectively because they are placed at the entry point of the system and are embedded within local communities. Lower court judges appear to be more interested in responding to "problems" than to formally defined "crimes." This makes them try to use their discretion to impose sentences that will fit the needs of the offender and the community, rather than simply imposing the sentences provided by law.

Defendants whose cases are processed through the lower court assembly line may appear to receive little or no punishment. However, people who get caught in the criminal justice system experience other punishments, whether or not they are ultimately convicted. A person who is arrested but then released at some point in the process still incurs various tangible and intangible costs. Time spent in jail awaiting trial, the cost of a bail bond, and days of work lost have immediate and concrete impact. Poor people may lose their jobs or be evicted from their homes if they fail to work and pay their bills for even a few days. For most people, simply being arrested is a devastating experience. It is impossible to measure the psychic and social price of being stigmatized, separated from family, and deprived of freedom.

As Malcolm Feeley has noted, such pretrial costs not only have a detrimental impact on unconvicted arrestees, but also encourage perfunctory practices in the courtroom and accelerated guilty pleas (Feeley, 1979). In order to get out of jail quickly, on probation, and back to their jobs and families, defendants plead guilty as early as possible, whether or not they are in fact guilty. People who insist that they are innocent incur additional costs to their lives and families as they sit in jail or repeatedly return to court for various proceedings.

Felony Courts

Felony cases are processed and offenders are sentenced in courts of general jurisdiction. Because of the seriousness of the crimes, the atmosphere is more formal and generally lacks the chaotic, assembly-line environment of misdemeanor courts. Even so, caseload burdens can affect how much time is devoted to individual cases. Exchange relationships among courtroom actors can facilitate plea bargains and

Most Serious Conviction Offenses	Percentage of Felons Sentenced to Prison	Jail	Probation
All offenses	45%	26%	29%
Violent offenses	62	20	18
Murder	95	2	3
Rape	71	17	12
Robbery	77	11	12
Aggravated assault	48	27	25
Other violent	45	30	25
Property offenses	42	26	32
Burglary	53	22	25
Larceny	38	28	34
Fraud	32	28	40
Drug offenses	83	8	9
Possession	42	27	31
Trafficking	48	23	29
Weapons offenses	42	27	31
Other offenses	36	30	34

Table 10.3
Types of felony sentences imposed by state courts

Although we often equate a felony conviction with a sentence to prison, almost a third of felony offenders are given probation.

SOURCE: U.S. Department of Justice, Bureau of Justice Statistics, Bulletin (July 1997).

shape the content of prosecutors' sentencing recommendations. Sentencing decisions are ultimately shaped, in part, by the relationships, negotiations, and agreements among the prosecutor, defense attorney, and judge. Table 10.3 shows the types of felony sentences imposed for different offenses.

Attitudes and Values of Judges

All lawyers recognize that judges differ from one another in their sentencing decisions. The differences can be explained in part by the conflicting goals of criminal justice, administrative pressures, and the influence of community values. Sentencing decisions also depend on the judges' own attitudes toward the law, toward a particular crime, or toward a type of offender.

Judges are products of different backgrounds and have different social values. Martin Levin's now-classic study of the criminal courts of Pittsburgh and Minneapolis showed the influence of judges' values on sentencing behavior. Pittsburgh judges, all of whom came from humble backgrounds, exhibited a greater empathy toward defendants than did judges in Minneapolis, who tended to come from upper-class backgrounds. While the Pittsburgh judges tried to make decisions that they believed would help straighten out the troubled defendants' lives, the Minneapolis judges were more inclined to follow the law precisely and to emphasize society's need for protection from crime (Levin, 1994). In the Workperspective, Judge James Batzer describes his work in a small-town courthouse. How might his approach to sentencing differ from that of a judge in an urban community?

WORK *Perspective*

Hon. James Batzer
State Trial Judge

Circuit Court
Manistee, Michigan

Although I was an English Literature major at the University of Michigan, I took many social science courses. I found myself very interested in public policy issues affecting people's lives. The professor who taught my course on juvenile delinquency strongly encouraged me to consider further study in that subject. As it happened, after I took the state civil service examination, the first job offered to me was as the state delinquency worker for Washtenaw County, which includes the city of Ann Arbor. For two years I worked with a variety of juvenile offenders, including those who committed serious crimes such as murder and armed robbery.

As the delinquency worker, I worked closely with judges, police officers, juvenile corrections officials, and others in the justice system. At that time the country was experiencing political conflicts concerning the Vietnam war and the civil rights movement. I was deeply troubled at hearing law enforcement officers in the courthouse express hatred toward college students involved in political protests. Although I could see that I had an impact on the lives of individual juvenile offenders, I wanted to have a greater impact on the development of public policy to address society's many conflicts and problems. I decided that I needed further education to advance professionally. Thus I earned a master's degree in criminal justice at Michigan State University and a law degree at Wayne State University in Detroit. I earned my graduate degrees on a part-time basis as I worked in various state positions in Lansing and Detroit dealing with juveniles offenders and abused children.

For one year after law school I worked as a law clerk for the U.S. District Court in Detroit researching prisoners' cases and making recommendations to judges about whether or not the cases should be dismissed. I decided that I really wanted to experience the rough-and-tumble of the courtroom, so I took a position as an assistant attorney general for the State of Michigan. In that position I spent five years representing the state in a variety of cases, including lawsuits challenging the conditions in state mental institutions.

In thinking about my experiences as a juvenile caseworker and an attorney, I recognized that I could have my greatest positive impact on society as a judge. I knew that I had no chance of winning a judicial election in Detroit, Lansing, or Ann Arbor, the cities in which I had worked and lived as an adult. Although Michigan has a system of nonpartisan elections for judges, election to urban judgeships requires political support, the ability to raise campaign funds, and connections to political parties. As a civil servant I had none of those things. So I returned to my small hometown, Manistee, Michigan, where I had always maintained my legal residence for voting purposes. I ran for circuit court judge against an incumbent who had been on the bench for eighteen years. I went door to door and set up a booth at the county fair in order to meet people. Despite the opposition of local attorneys who did not want to see change take place at the courthouse, I won the election. I was helped by my family's good reputation in the community and by some controversial decisions of the incumbent judge, who gave very light sentences to sex offenders.

As the circuit judge for two rural counties, I handle a wide array of civil lawsuits and criminal cases. I also handle appeals from the lower-level trial court—the district court—and prisoners' cases filed in circuit court under state law. Periodically I am also asked to sit by special designation as a visiting judge on the Michigan Court of Appeals. As a judge on the trial court of general jurisdiction, I probably have a broader range of cases and responsibilities than any other kind of state judge. Yet I must handle my responsibilities without all of the staff support that is available to court of appeals judges and federal judges.

Sentencing criminal offenders is one of my most difficult responsibilities. I must use my judgment to provide appropriate punishment while also thinking about what will become of the offender if he or she returns to society. In one difficult case, three teenage boys were drinking and crashed their car into some trees while driving at a high rate of speed. The two passengers were killed, but the driver survived. The prosecutor permitted the driver to plead guilty to negligent vehicular manslaughter rather than pursuing a manslaughter charge. I then faced the prospect of fashioning a sentence, which could entail anything up to two years in prison.

I received a variety of letters from people who wanted me to hand out the maximum sentence and from those who argued that he was a good kid who had simply made a terrible mistake. In a small town, a judge is often acquainted with family members of offenders and victims. Some judges may feel pressured by the thought of encountering victims' or offenders' family members at social events or elsewhere. In this case there was no easy answer. The offender was not evil but had committed a crime because he was young and used terrible judgment by drinking and driving. As in other such tragic cases, you look for the best way to impose appropriate punishment without destroying the young person's life in the process. I opted to send him for ninety days to a "boot camp" in the state prison system and then two months at an out-of-town halfway house. This punishment was followed by five years of probation with restrictions on his ability to drive and a prohibition on drinking. Although I later placed him in jail for three months for violating probation conditions by drinking, ultimately I believe he was appropriately punished yet still had the opportunity to straighten out his life by going to college.

WORK*Perspective*

It is widely assumed that judges are predisposed to treat female offenders less severely than men. Research on sentencing in Pennsylvania suggests that judges are concerned not only with an offender's prior record and level of involvement in the crime, but also such practical considerations as the responsibility for children, pregnancy, and availability of prison space (Steffensmeier, Kramer, and Streifel, 1993). Kathleen Daly and Rebecca Bordt found that gender effects are more likely to be found for felony offenses, in urban courts, and in the decision to incarcerate, rather than in the length of sentence (Daly and Bordt, 1995).

Presentence Report

Even though sentencing is the judge's responsibility, the presentence report has become an important ingredient in the judicial mix. Usually a probation officer investigates the convicted person's background, criminal record, job status, and mental condition in order to suggest a sentence that is in the interests of both the offender and society. Although the primary purpose of the presentence report is to help the judge select the sentence, it also assists in the classification of probationers, prisoners, and parolees for treatment planning and risk assessment. In the report, the probation officer makes judgments about what information to include and what conclusions to draw from that information. In some states, however, probation officers present only factual material to the judge and make no sentencing recommendation. The probation officer may not follow evidentiary rules and may include hearsay statements as well as firsthand information. The Close-up gives an example of a presentence report.

CLOSE-UP

Sample Presentence Report

STATE OF NEW MEXICO
Corrections Department
Field Service Division
Santa Fe, New Mexico 87501
Date: January 4, 1998

To: The Honorable Manuel Baca
From: Presentence Unit, Officer Brian Gaines
Re: Richard Knight

Evaluation

Appearing before Your Honor for sentencing is 20-year-old Richard Knight, who, on November 10, 1997, pursuant to a Plea and Disposition Agreement, entered a plea of guilty to Aggravated Assault Upon a Peace Officer (Deadly Weapon) (Firearm Enhancement), as charged in Information Number 95-5736900. The terms of the agreement stipulate that the maximum period of incarceration be limited to one year, that restitution be made on all counts and charges whether dismissed or not, and that all remaining charges in the Indictment and DA Files 39780 be dismissed.

The defendant is an only child, born and raised in Albuquerque. He attended West Mesa High School until the eleventh grade, at which time he dropped out. Richard declared that he felt school was "too difficult" and that he decided that it would be more beneficial for him to obtain steady employment rather than to complete his education. The defendant further stated that he felt it was "too late for vocational training" because of the impending one-year prison sentence he faces, due to the Firearm Enhancement penalty for his offense.

The longest period of time the defendant has held a job has been for six months with Frank's Concrete Company. He has been employed with the Madrid Construction Company since August 1997 (verified). Richard lives with his parents, who provide most of his financial support. Conflicts between his mother and himself, the defendant claimed, precipitated his recent lawless actions by causing him to "not care about anything." He stressed the fact that he is now once again "getting along" with his mother. Although the defendant contends that he doesn't abuse drugs, he later contradicted himself by declaring that he "gets drunk every weekend." He noted that he was inebriated when he committed the present offense.

In regard to the present offense, the defendant recalled that other individuals at the party attempted to stab his friend and that he and his companion left and returned with a gun in order to settle the score. Richard claimed remorse for his offense and stated that his past family problems led him to spend most of his time on the streets, where he became more prone to violent conduct. The defendant admitted being a member of the 18th Street Gang.

Recommendation

It is respectfully recommended that the defendant be sentenced to three years' incarceration and that the sentence be suspended. It is further recommended that the defendant be incarcerated for one year as to the mandatory Firearm Enhancement and then placed on three years' probation under the following special conditions:

1. That restitution be made to Juan Lopez in the amount of $622.40.
2. That the defendant either maintain full-time employment or obtain his GED, and
3. That the defendant discontinue fraternizing with the 18th Street Gang members and terminate his own membership in the gang.

The impression that the presentence report conveys about the offender is important. The language it uses is crucial. Summary statements may be written in a noncommittal style or instead may convey the notion that the defendant is either well behaved and worth favoring or unruly and worth punishing. Judges say that they read the report to get an understanding of the defendant's attitude. A comment such as "the defendant appears unrepentant" can send a person to prison. A Question of Ethics illustrates some of the difficulties faced by a judge who must impose a sentence with little more than the presentence report to go on.

Given the crucial role of the presentence report and the manner in which its information is collected, one might expect that the offender would have a right to examine it and to challenge the contents. In fact, the Supreme Court ruled that while a convicted person did not have a right to cross-examine persons who supplied the information in the report, he or she must be given the opportunity to deny or explain the information (*Williams v. New York*, 1949; *Gardner v. Florida*, 1977).

A Question of ETHICS

Seated in her chambers, Judge Ruth Carroll read the presentence investigation report of the two young men she would sentence when court resumed. She had not heard these cases. As often happens in this overworked courthouse, the cases had been given to her only for sentencing. Judge Harold Krisch had handled the arraignment, plea, and trial.

The codefendants had held up a convenience store in the early morning hours, terrorizing the young manager and taking $47.50 from the till.

As she read the reports, Judge Carroll noticed that they looked pretty similar. Each offender had dropped out of high school, had held a series of low-wage jobs, and had one prior conviction for which probation was imposed. Each had been convicted of Burglary 1, robbery at night with a gun.

Then she noticed the difference. David Bukowski had pleaded guilty to the charge in exchange for a promise of leniency. Richard Leach had been convicted on the same charge after a one-week trial. Judge Carroll pondered the decisions that she would soon have to make. Should Leach receive a stiffer sentence because he had taken the court's time and resources? Did she have an obligation to impose the light sentence that the prosecutor and the defender had recommended for Bukowski?

There was a knock on the door. The bailiff stuck his head in. "Everything's ready, Your Honor."

"Okay, Ben, let's go."

How would you decide? What factors would weigh in your decision? How would you explain your decision?

The presentence report is one tool judges use to ease the strain of decision making. The report lets judges shift partial responsibility to the probation department. Because a substantial number of sentencing alternatives are open to judges, they often rely on the report for guidance. Research has shown that judges follow the recommendation of the probation officer over 90 percent of the time.

Sentencing Guidelines

In recent years **sentencing guidelines** have been established in the federal courts and in seventeen states, and they are being developed in five other states (Frase, 1995). The guidelines are a mechanism designed to indicate to judges the expected sanction for particular types of offenses. They are intended to limit the sentencing discretion of judges and to reduce the disparity among sentences given for similar offenses. Although statutes provide a variety of sentencing options for particular crimes, guidelines attempt to direct the judge to more specific actions that should be taken. The range of sentencing options provided for most offenses is based on the seriousness of the crime and the offender's criminal history.

sentencing guidelines

A mechanism to indicate to judges the expected sanction for certain offenses, in order to reduce disparities in sentencing.

Legislatures—and commissions in some states and the federal government—formulate their sentencing guidelines as a grid (Tonry, 1993:140). As shown in Table 10.4, the grid identifies the range of the sentence according to the seriousness of the offense and the likelihood of offender recidivism (return to criminal behavior). The offender's score is obtained by totaling the points given to data such as the number of juvenile, adult misdemeanor, and adult felony convictions; the number of times incarcerated; the status of the accused at the time of the last offense, whether the accused is on probation or parole or has escaped from confinement; and employment status or educational achievement. Judges look at the grid to see what sentence should be imposed on a particular offender who has committed a specific offense. Judges may go outside of the guidelines if aggravating or

Severity of Offense (Illustrative Offenses)	Criminal History Score 0	1	2	3	4	5	6 or more
Sale of simulated controlled substance	12	12	12	13	15	17	19 *18–20*
Theft-related crimes ($2,500 or less) Check forgery ($200–$2,500)	12	12	13	15	17	19	21 *20–22*
Theft crimes ($2,500 or less)	12	13	15	17	19 *18–20*	22 *21–23*	25 *24–26*
Nonresidential burglary, theft crimes (over $2,500)	12	15	18	21	25 *24–26*	32 *30–34*	41 *37–45*
Residential burglary, simple robbery	18	25	27	30 *29–31*	38 *36–40*	46 *43–49*	54 *50–58*
Criminal sexual conduct, second degree	21	26	30	34 *33–35*	44 *42–46*	54 *50–58*	65 *60–70*
Aggravated robbery	48 *44–52*	58 *54–62*	68 *64–72*	78 *74–82*	88 *84–92*	98 *94–102*	108 *104–112*
Criminal sexual conduct, first degree Assault first degree	86 *81–91*	98 *93–103*	110 *105–115*	122 *117–127*	134 *129–139*	146 *141–151*	158 *153–163*
Murder, third degree Murder, second degree (felony murder)	150 *144–156*	165 *159–171*	180 *174–186*	195 *189–201*	210 *204–216*	225 *219–231*	240 *234–246*
Murder, second degree (with intent)	306 *299–313*	326 *319–333*	346 *339–353*	366 *359–373*	386 *379–393*	406 *399–413*	426 *419–433*

Less Serious ← Criminal History Score → More Serious (columns); Less Serious ↕ More Serious (rows)

At the discretion of the judge, up to a year in jail and/or other nonjail sanctions can be imposed instead of prison sentences as conditions of probation for most of these offenses. If prison is imposed, the presumptive sentence is the number of months shown.

Presumptive commitment to state prison for all offenses.

Table 10.4
Minnesota sentencing guidelines grid (presumptive sentence length in months)

The italicized numbers in the grid are the range of the sentence the judge may impose without the sentence considered a departure from the guidelines. The criminal history score is computed by adding one point for each prior felony conviction, one-half point for each prior gross misdemeanor conviction, and one-quarter point for each prior misdemeanor conviction.

SOURCE: *Seeking Justice: Crime and Punishment in America* (New York: Edna McConnell Clark Foundation, 1997):24.

NOTE: First-degree murder is excluded from the guidelines by law and is punished by life imprisonment.

mitigating circumstances exist; however, they must provide a written explanation of their reasons (Kramer and Ulmer, 1996).

Sentencing guidelines are to be reviewed and modified periodically to include recent decisions. Some critics argue that, because the guidelines reflect only what has been done in the past, they do not reform sentencing. Others question the choice of characteristics included in the offender scale and wonder whether some are used to mask racial criteria (Petersilia and Turner, 1987). However, as noted by Terance Miethe and Charles Moore, the Minnesota guidelines have resulted in sentences that are "more uniform, more predictable, and more socioeconomically neutral than before" (Miethe and Moore, 1989). Although the use of guidelines has been found to make sentences more uniform, many judges object to having their discretion limited in this manner (Weinstein, 1992).

CHECKPOINT

6. What are the four factors thought to influence the sentencing behavior of judges?

Leaving the Kankakee County Courthouse, Illinois after the state dropped murder charges are Joe Burrows and his wife, Shari. Burrows spent eight years on death row for the murder of an 88-year-old farmer before new evidence overturned his conviction.

Who Gets the Harshest Punishment?

The prison population in most states contains a higher proportion of African Americans and Hispanic Americans than is found in the general population. In addition, poor people are more likely to be convicted of crimes than those with higher incomes. Is this situation a result of the prejudicial attitudes of judges, police officers, and prosecutors? Are poor people more likely to commit crimes that elicit a strong response from society? Are enforcement resources distributed so that certain groups are subject to closer scrutiny than other groups? As discussed in Chapter 1, research on these and similar questions is inconclusive. Some studies have shown that members of racial minorities and the poor are treated more harshly by the system; other research has been unable to demonstrate a direct link between harshness of sentence and race or social class (Walker, Spohn, and DeLone, 1996:154).

Another serious dilemma for the criminal justice system concerns those who are falsely convicted and sentenced. While much public concern is expressed over those who "beat the system" and go free, comparatively little attention is paid to those who are innocent yet convicted. Each year several cases of the conviction of innocent persons come to national attention. For example, Randall Dale Adams, whose story was portrayed in the movie *The Thin Blue Line*, had his murder conviction overturned after he spent twelve years on death row. Likewise, Kevin Byrd was released and pardoned after serving twelve years in a Texas prison for a rape that DNA tests showed he had not committed (*New York Times*, October 9, 1997, p. A18).

How prevalent are such miscarriages of justice? It has been estimated that about 1 percent of felony convictions are in error (Huff and Rattner, 1988). Eyewitness error, unethical conduct by police and prosecutors, community pressure, false accusations, inadequacy of counsel, and plea bargaining pressures are usually cited as contributing to wrongful convictions. Beyond the fact that the real criminal is presumably still free in such cases, the standards of our society are damaged when an innocent person has been wrongfully convicted.

IDEAS IN PRACTICE

Standing before you for sentencing is William Arnette, who has been found guilty of unauthorized use of a motor vehicle. Arnette has one prior felony conviction (simple robbery) and two prior misdemeanors (trespassing, shoplifting). Using the Minnesota guidelines, what is the appropriate sentence for Arnette?

Summary

- Four goals of the criminal sanction are acknowledged in the United States—retribution, deterrence, incapacitation, and rehabilitation.
- These goals are carried out through incarceration, intermediate sanctions, probation, and death.
- Penal codes vary as to whether the permitted sentences are indeterminate, determinate, or mandatory. Each type of sentence makes certain assumptions about the goals of the criminal sanction.

- Good time allows correctional administrators to reduce the sentence of prisoners who live according to the rules and participate in various vocational, educational, and treatment programs.
- Capital punishment is allowed by the U.S. Supreme Court if the judge and jury are allowed to take into account mitigating and aggravating circumstances.
- Judges have considerable discretion in fashioning sentences to take into account factors such as the seriousness of the crime, the offender's prior record, and mitigating and aggravating circumstances.
- The sentencing process is influenced by the administrative context of the courts, the attitudes and values of the judges, and the presentence report.
- Sentencing guidelines have been formulated in many states as a way of reducing disparity among the sentences given offenders in similar situations.

Questions for Review

1. What are the major differences among retribution, deterrence, incapacitation, and rehabilitation?
2. What are the forms of the criminal sanction?
3. What purposes do intermediate sanctions serve?
4. What has been the Supreme Court's position on the constitutionality of the death penalty?
5. Is there a link between sentences and social class and race?

ANSWERS TO CHECKPOINTS

1. Retribution, deterrence, incapacitation, rehabilitation.
2. It is impossible to show who has been deterred from committing crimes; punishment isn't always certain; people act impulsively rather than rationally; people commit crimes while on drugs.
3. Determinate, indeterminate, and mandatory sentences.
4. Intermediate sanctions give judges a greater range of sentencing alternatives, reduce prison populations, cost less than prison, and increase community security.
5. Judge and jury must be able to consider mitigating and aggravating circumstances; proceedings must be divided into a trial phase and a punishment phase.
6. The administrative context of the courts, the attitudes and values of judges, the presentence report, and sentencing guidelines.

INSIDE THE CRIMINAL JUSTICE SYSTEM AND BEYOND: ONE MAN'S JOURNEY

Prosecution, Adjudication, and Sentencing

Los Angeles County has the largest jail system in the country. On any given day it houses roughly 20,000 inmates. As I walked into the main jail I was so sick I could hardly stand. Once the chains were removed I was placed in a holding tank with other "new arrivals." Whereas getting booked at the city jail took less than an hour, here it took two days. Remember, I had yet to be formally charged and had not had contact with an attorney.

As time passed more and more bodies were packed inside the tank. Before long we were standing shoulder to shoulder, butt to butt, like sardines in a can. My nightmare was at a high point. I felt like I wouldn't be able to do this much longer—like I might collapse or lose consciousness. Right then this guy looked at me and said, "Hey, brother, you're sick as hell aren't you?" When I said yes, he directed those around me to move over just enough so I could sit down. Never have I been so glad to sit.

We were eventually herded into a larger holding tank that had one seatless toilet and a sink for everyone. In this world privacy does not exist. Hours are spent in these concrete enclosures with others who are arrested for everything from public drunkenness to robbery. Most are addicts, skid-row winos, homeless people, or a mixture of all three. Many have mental problems. Within these rooms one hears a constant mixture of echoes from slamming cell doors, people yelling, wailing, vomiting, and laughing. Strange how, over time, I got used to it.

The next step of the journey involved being strip-searched. As our clothes were removed, the stench of body odor permeated the room. It took effort not to gag. After having every orifice of our naked bodies examined by deputies, we were steered to a shower area, given about thirty seconds to wash, and then sprayed with bug repellent. Next came jail clothing, a wool blanket, and a towel.

Before being assigned to a cell we were photographed, fingerprinted, and given receipts for our property. Finally, after nearly two days, I was led to a four-man cell—my next temporary home. There were already six men living there—two sleeping on the floor (these cells had enough space for two bunks, a toilet, a sink, and about thirty inches between the bunks). I, along with two of the others, slept on the concrete floor. Whereas they slept directly underneath each of the bunks, I took the space between them—and was glad to have it. No mattress. No pillow. But the blanket and the space sure were nice.

I welcomed the chance to rest. I still couldn't sleep, but it felt good to just lie there. Around 3:30 A.M. a guard came down the tier (the walkway in front of the rows of cells), waking up people whose names were on the daily court list. I was one of the fortunate few. Within a few minutes the cell door opened and I was guided to a holding tank where I waited with other court-bound men to be taken downstairs for breakfast. Once given food and seated, we had about three minutes to eat.

Our next stop was an area containing dozens of holding tanks—each acting as way stations for different courts. Deputies, reading names and court destinations from printouts, directed us to the appropriate tanks. I soon learned that I'd be going to the Torrance court. Before long we could hear the rattling of chains—a signal that we would soon be departing. As our names were called, we walked forward and placed our wrists in cuffs. After we were chained, we were led out of the jail into a parking lot where a huge fleet of black-and-white buses sat, waiting to take us to courts all over the county.

A jail bus ride can be an eventful occasion. For a short time you are almost in the world. Through steel-meshed windows you see cars, buildings, parks, streetlights, and people who are free—including women. Many of the men yell and joke about whatever crosses their mind. Others stare idly through the steel grillwork—silent and serious looking.

ONE MAN'S JOURNEY (CONTINUED)

Five days after my arrest I was finally going before a judge.

After arriving at the Torrance courthouse, we were taken to a basement holding tank and unchained. Because I didn't have money for a lawyer I was assigned a public defender (PD), whom I met through the bars of a holding cell located next to the courtroom. His name was Robert Harrison. Like every other lawyer I ever had, he was white. He carried a briefcase packed with papers, had a suit on, and looked like he was in his late twenties. Although clearly hurried, he treated me with respect. After introducing himself he informed me that this would be my initial appearance and that I'd be back in two weeks for a preliminary hearing. Our meeting took about three minutes.

During the initial appearance I was arraigned in municipal court (the lower, or misdemeanor, court), which meant being legally charged, given a set amount of bail, and a date on which to return. The district attorney (DA) and public defender introduced themselves to the judge as participants in the case. The entire proceeding took less than a minute. Afterward, as bailiffs escorted me from the courtroom, my PD told me, "See you soon."

Two weeks later, still in jail and running on no sleep, I returned for my preliminary hearing—the phase of the process in which the district attorney tries to convince the court that a felony has been committed while the PD shoots for dismissal based on lack of evidence or an unlawful arrest. The woman who called the police testified that she had seen suspicious activity around my room—strangers coming and going. The police testified that I evaded arrest. The heroin, money, and other drugs taken from my pockets and room were used as evidence. My PD tried to get the case dismissed by arguing that the police searched me without probable cause. The DA said the search had been lawful. The court ruled against me, and I was bound over for arraignment in the superior court (felony court). After the hearing, my lawyer told me, "It doesn't look good." I asked him, "How much time do you think I'll have to do?" He said I'd "better plan on doing five" (that meant years and that meant prison).

Arraignment in the superior court came two weeks later. This time, as well as being told what I was charged with, I made a plea. In another brief meeting before the hearing, my lawyer told me, "When they ask you to plead, say 'Not guilty.' The judge will then set a trial date. Before that time arrives I hope to know more about what the DA wants from this case." I did as he suggested and a trial date was set. Within a few weeks my PD came to visit me in the county jail to tell me about a deal being offered by the district attorney. If I pled guilty to possession of a controlled substance (heroin), the rest of the charges would be dropped and I would be sent to the Southern California Regional Guidance Center at Chino—state prison— for a ninety-day evaluation—a process designed to assist the court at sentencing. He said, "Because of the evidence in this case I don't think we'd have a chance to win at trial. If you take the deal there is the possibility that a positive evaluation by the people at Chino might influence the judge to send you to a drug program. The worst-case scenario, though, is two to ten years for possession. On the other hand, if you go to trial and lose, you will most likely get five to fifteen years for possession with the intent to sell."

I knew my situation was bleak. The court already had a presentence investigation (PSI) report from my last case in which I received jail time and probation. I didn't think I had a chance of being found not guilty for my current charges. Plus I had heard about guys getting breaks after going to Chino. So the deal sounded good and I went for it.

To formally accept the deal I had to plead guilty in court to the charge of possession of heroin. My PD told me I needed to understand that doing so must be a decision I willingly make and that the judge possibly would not accept the deal. Finally, there were no guarantees as to what type of sentence I'd get. He said he'd recommend a drug program, but the chances were good that I'd have to do prison time, regardless of what type of evaluation I received from Chino.

When the court date arrived I appeared in Judge Barrett's courtroom. The district attorney told the judge that in exchange for a guilty plea to possession of a controlled substance, the people would agree to drop the rest of the charges. My PD said that

ONE MAN'S JOURNEY (CONTINUED)

we agreed. Then the judge said, "Mr. Terry, before accepting this plea I must ensure that you are doing so voluntarily. Has anyone coerced you in any way to plead guilty to this charge?" I said, "No." "Has anyone promised that you will receive a specific sentence if you plead guilty?" "No." "Do you understand that you do not have to make this plea and that you have a right to a trial by a jury of your peers?" "Yes." "And understanding all this, do you waive that right at this time?" By now I was wondering if I was making a mistake. It seemed as if the judge was trying to talk me out of it. I looked at my PD for assurance. He nodded his head, indicating it was okay. I said, "Yes." After accepting my plea of guilty the judge sent me to Chino as expected and said that sentencing would take place upon my return to court.

The "evaluation" from the ninety-day observation came from a twenty-minute interview by a counselor who recommended a drug program and a fifteen-minute interview by a psychologist (nicknamed San Quentin Sally) who said I was a threat to society and belonged in prison. Within three months I was back in the county jail awaiting my final court date.

Finally, five days after I returned from Chino, I was again taken before Judge Barrett for sentencing. Inside the courtroom, before the actual hearing took place, my PD showed me a copy of the evaluation from Chino that clearly indicated the likelihood of a prison sentence. San Quentin Sally not only recommended prison but also said I was a chronic liar with a dismal future. Once I read that I lost all hope for a drug program. Right then I also felt alone, isolated, like it was me against the world and I was definitely losing. I had no friends or family in the courtroom, I was surrounded by strangers dressed in suits and fancy dresses, and the only person who seemed to care about my well-being was my PD.

When the hearing began, the DA used my criminal history and the evaluation from Chino as justification for a prison sentence. My PD suggested a drug program because I had an extensive history of addiction and no arrests for violent crimes. He pointed out that this was also the conclusion of the counselor at Chino. Before imposing the sentence, the judge asked me if I had anything to say. I said no. Then he said, "After considering all sides of this matter I feel little choice but to send you to the department of corrections for the term prescribed by law. I understand you have a problem with drugs, but you've had your chances in the past. It is my hope that when you get to prison you do something to better yourself so when you get out you can live a normal, decent life. With this said, I sentence you to do not less than two but no more than ten years in the California Department of Corrections for possession of narcotics."

I felt good that day when they chained me up to take me back to the county jail. It had been a while since I got arrested, and I was finally headed for the last leg of my journey. I figured that with the time I had already spent in custody, plus good time, I would be out within eighteen months to two years.

Part IV

Corrections

11 CORRECTIONS

12 COMMUNITY CORRECTIONS: PROBATION AND INTERMEDIATE SANCTIONS

13 INCARCERATION AND PRISON SOCIETY

14 RELEASE AND SUPERVISION IN THE COMMUNITY

DEBATE about the most appropriate and effective ways to punish lawbreakers has continued throughout history. Over time the corrections system has risen to peaks of excited reform only to drop to valleys of despairing failure. In Part Four we look at how the American system of criminal justice now deals with offenders. Chapters 11 through 14 discuss how offenders are punished and how various influences have structured our correctional system. As these chapters unfold, recall the processes that have occurred before sentence is imposed and how these are linked to the ways offenders are punished.

Chapter 11

Corrections

Development of Corrections

- *The Invention of the Penitentiary*
- *Reform in the United States*
- *The Reformatory Movement*
- *Improving Prison Conditions for Women*
- *The Reforms of the Progressives*
- *The Rehabilitation Model*
- *The Community Model*
- *The Crime Control Model*

Organization of Corrections in the United States

- *Federal Corrections System*
- *State Corrections Systems*
- *Jails: Local Correctional Facilities*

Issues in Corrections

- *Incarceration Trends*
- *Who Is in Prison?*

TWO TEENAGE Native Americans, convicted of robbing and beating a pizza delivery driver in Everett, Washington, were sentenced by the Tlingit Tribal Court to spend twelve to eighteen months on separate uninhabited islands off the Alaskan coast. Such a banishment was not an option according to the Washington State penal code, which required that the Superior Court of Snohomish County sentence first-time robbery offenders to three to five years in prison. With the court's approval, however, the alternative punishment was arranged by Rudy James, a Tlingit trial elder. The Tlingit offenders, Adrian Guthrie and Simon Roberts, were given only sleeping bags, forks for digging clams, axes, and enough food to carry them through the first five days. They were expected to live alone without modern conveniences (*New York Times*, September 1, 1994, p. 1).

Banishment is an ancient punishment that has not been formally imposed by a U.S. court since the beginning of the republic. As the punishment of these two young offenders makes us aware, prison is not the only form of corrections. Students of criminal justice are not surprised to learn that fewer than two-thirds of offenders under supervision are in prisons and jails. Most offenders are punished in the community through probation, intermediate sanctions, and parole. But because of the folklore, films, and songs about prison life in our culture, most Americans understandably think of incarceration when they think of corrections.

Corrections refers to the great number of programs, services, facilities, and organizations responsible for the management of people accused or convicted of criminal offenses. In addition to prisons and jails, corrections includes probation, halfway houses, education and work release, parole supervision, counseling, and community service. Correctional programs operate in Salvation Army hostels, forest camps, medical clinics, and urban storefronts. More than 5.5 million adults and juveniles receive correctional supervision from more than 500,000 administrators, psychologists, officers, counselors, social workers, and other professionals. An astounding 2.7 percent of U.S. adults (1 of every 21 men and 1 out of every 100 women) are incarcerated or on probation or parole. (Donziger, 1996:35).

Corrections is authorized by all levels of government, is administered by both public and private organizations, and costs more than $30 billion a year (BJS, 1997. *Sourcebook*:4). In this chapter we will examine (1) the history of corrections, (2) the organization of corrections, and (3) the future of incarceration.

Questions for Inquiry

How has the American system of corrections developed?

What roles are played by federal, state, and local governments in corrections?

Why has the prison population more than doubled in the last ten years?

What are the characteristics of persons incarcerated?

DEVELOPMENT OF CORRECTIONS

How did we get where we are in corrections today? Why are offenders now placed on probation or incarcerated rather than whipped or burned as in colonial times? Over the past two hundred years, ideas about punishment have moved like a pendulum from one direction to another. As we view the development of present-day policies, think about how future changes in society may lead to new forms of corrections.

The Invention of the Penitentiary

Until the early 1800s Americans followed the European practice of relying upon punishment that was physically brutal, such as death, flogging, and branding. This whipping post and pillory in New Castle, Delaware, continued to be used well into the 19th century.

The late eighteenth century stands out as a remarkable period. At that time scholars and social reformers in Europe and America were rethinking the nature of society and the place of the individual in it. During the **Enlightenment**, as this period was called, philosophers and reformers challenged tradition with new ideas about the nature of society and the place of the individual in the world, about limitations on government, and about rationalism. Such thinking was the major intellectual force behind the American Revolution, and it also affected the new nation's views on the nature of criminality and methods of punishment.

Before 1800, America copied Europe in using physical punishment as the main criminal sanction. Flogging, branding, and maiming were the methods of controlling deviance and maintaining public safety. For more serious crimes, offenders were hanged on the gallows. For example, in the state of New York about 20 percent of all crimes on the books were capital offenses. Criminals were regularly sentenced to death for picking pockets, burglary, robbery, and horse stealing (Rothman, 1971:49). Jails existed throughout the country, but they were only for holding people awaiting trial or punishment or people unable to pay their debts.

The French scholar Michel Foucault has written about the spread of Enlightenment ideas during the late eighteenth century (Foucault, 1977). Before the French Revolution of 1789, European governments tried to control crime by making punishments such as torture and hanging into public spectacles. Criminals were often branded to display their offenses. The dismembered bodies of capital offenders were put on display. In the early nineteenth century, such practices gradually were replaced by "modern" penal systems that emphasized punishments appropriate to the individual offender. The new goal was not to inflict pain on the offender's body but to change the individual and set him or her on the right path.

Clearly, this constituted a major shift in policy. The change from physical (corporal) punishment to correction of the offender reflected new ideas about the causes of crime and the possibility of reforming behavior.

Many people promoted the reform of corrections, but John Howard (1726-1790), sheriff of Bedfordshire, England, was especially influential. His book, *The State of*

corrections

The variety of programs, services, facilities, and organizations responsible for the management of people who have been accused or convicted of criminal offenses.

Prisons in England and Wales, published in 1777, described his observations of the prisons he visited (Howard, 1929). Among generally horrible conditions he was particularly concerned about the lack of discipline.

Enlightenment

A movement during the eighteenth century in England and France, in which concepts of liberalism, rationalism, equality, and individualism dominated social and political thinking.

Public response to the book resulted in Parliament's passage of the Penitentiary Act of 1779, which called for the creation of a house of hard labor where offenders would be imprisoned for up to two years. The institution would be based on four principles:

1. A secure and sanitary building
2. Inspection to ensure that offenders followed the rules
3. Abolition of the fees charged offenders for their food
4. A reformatory regime

At night prisoners were to be confined to individual cells. During the day they were to work silently in common rooms. Prison life was to be strict and ordered. Influenced by his Quaker friends, Howard believed that the new institution should be a place of industry. But more important, it was to be a place where criminals could have an opportunity for penitence (sorrow and shame for their wrongs) and repentance (willingness to change their ways). In short, the purposes of this **penitentiary** were to punish and to reform.

penitentiary

An institution intended to punish criminals by isolating them from society and from one another so they can reflect on their past misdeeds, repent, and reform.

Howard's idea of the penitentiary was not implemented in England until 1842, a half-century after his death. However, although Great Britain was slow to act, the United States applied Howard's theories much more quickly.

CHECKPOINT

1. What was the Enlightenment, and how did it influence corrections?
2. What were the main goals of the penitentiary?

(Answers are at the end of the chapter.)

Reform in the United States

Eastern Penitentiary, which opened outside of Philadelphia in 1829, was designed to insure that prisoners were confined separately so that they could reflect on their misdeeds and thus become rehabilitated.

From 1776 to around 1830, a new revolution occurred in the American idea of criminal punishment. Although based on the work of English reformers, the new correctional philosophy reflected many ideas expressed in the Declaration of Independence, including an optimistic view of human nature and of individual perfectibility. Emphasis shifted from the assumption that deviance was part of human nature to the belief that crime was a result of environmental forces. The new nation's humane and optimistic ideas were to be applied to reform of the criminal.

In the first decades of the nineteenth century, the creation of penitentiaries in Pennsylvania and New York attracted the attention of legislators in other states and investigators from Europe. Even travelers from abroad with no special interest in corrections made it a point to include a penitentiary on their itinerary. By the mid-1800s, the U.S. penitentiary had become world famous.

The Pennsylvania System

A number of groups in the United States dedicated themselves to reforming the institutions and practices of criminal punishment. One of these groups was the Philadelphia Society for Alleviating the Miseries of Public Prisons, formed in 1787. This group, which included many Quakers, was inspired by Howard's ideas. They argued that criminals could best be reformed if they were placed in penitentiaries—isolated from one another and from society to consider their crimes, repent, and reform.

In 1790 the Pennsylvania legislature authorized construction of two penitentiaries for the solitary confinement of "hardened and atrocious offenders." The first, created out of an existing three-story stone structure in Philadelphia, was the Walnut Street Jail. This building, 40 by 25 feet, had eight dark cells, each measuring 6 by 8 by 9 feet, on each floor. A yard was attached to the building. Only one inmate occupied each cell, and no communications of any kind were allowed. From a small, grated window high on the outside wall prisoners "could perceive neither heaven nor earth."

From this limited beginning the Pennsylvania system of **separate confinement** evolved. It was based on five principles:

separate confinement

A penitentiary system, developed in Pennsylvania, in which each inmate was held in isolation from other inmates. All activities, including craft work, took place in the cells.

1. Prisoners would not be treated vengefully but should be convinced that through hard and selective forms of suffering they could change their lives.
2. Solitary confinement would prevent further corruption inside prison.
3. In isolation, offenders would reflect on their transgressions and repent.
4. Solitary confinement would be punishment because humans are by nature social animals.
5. Solitary confinement would be economical because prisoners would not need long periods of time to repent, fewer keepers would be needed, and the costs of clothing would be lower. (Sellin, 1970)

The opening of the Eastern Penitentiary near Philadelphia in 1829 culminated forty-two years of reform activity by the Philadelphia society. On October 25, 1829, the first prisoner, Charles Williams, arrived. He was 18 years old and had been sentenced to two years for larceny. He was assigned to a cell 12 by 8 by 10 feet with an individual exercise yard 18 feet long. In the cell was a fold-up steel bed, a simple toilet, a wooden stool, a workbench, and eating utensils. Light came from an eight-inch window in the ceiling. Solitary labor, Bible reading, and reflection were the keys to the moral rehabilitation that was supposed to occur within the penitentiary. Although the cell was larger than most in use today, it was the only world the prisoner would see throughout the entire sentence. The only other human voice heard would be that of a clergyman who would visit on Sundays. Nothing was to distract the penitent prisoner from the path toward reform.

Unfortunately, the system did not work. The Walnut Street Jail became overcrowded as more and more offenders were held for longer periods. It became a "warehouse of humanity." Politicians influenced operation of the jail. A second Pennsylvania penitentiary near Pittsburgh was soon declared outmoded because isolation was not complete and the cells were too small for solitary labor. As in the other institutions, overcrowding became a problem, and the Pittsburgh institution was demolished in 1833.

The New York System

congregate system

A penitentiary system, developed in Auburn, New York, in which each inmate was held in isolation during the night but worked and ate with fellow prisoners during the day under a rule of silence.

In 1819 New York opened a penitentiary in Auburn that evolved as a rival to Pennsylvania's concept of separate confinement. Under New York's **congregate system**, prisoners were held in isolation at night but worked with fellow prisoners in shops during the day. They worked under a rule of silence and were even forbidden to exchange glances while on the job or at meals. The men were to experience the benefits of labor as well as meditation. They lived under tight control, had a simple diet, and worked to pay for a portion of their keep.

American reformers, seeing the New York approach as a great advance, copied it throughout the Northeast. Because the inmates produced goods for sale, advocates said operating costs would be covered.

During this period, advocates of the Pennsylvania and New York plans debated on public platforms and in the nation's periodicals. Advocates of both systems agreed that the prisoner must be isolated from society and placed on a disciplined routine. They believed that criminality was a result of corruption pervading the community that the family and the church did not sufficiently counterbalance. Only when offenders were removed from the temptations and influences of society and kept in a silent, disciplined environment could they reflect on their sins and offenses and become useful citizens. The convicts were not inherently depraved; rather, they were victims of a society that had not protected them from vice. While offenders were being punished, they would become penitent and motivated to place themselves on the right path.

The Reformatory Movement

By the middle of the nineteenth century, reformers had become disillusioned with the penitentiary. Neither the New York nor the Pennsylvania systems nor any of their imitators had achieved rehabilitation or deterrence. This failure was seen as the result of poor administration rather than as a sign of the basic concept's weakness. Within forty years of being built, penitentiaries had become overcrowded, understaffed, and minimally financed. Discipline was lax, brutality was common, and administrators were viewed as corrupt. For example, at Sing Sing Penitentiary in Ossining, New York, in 1870 investigators discovered "that dealers were publicly supplying prisoners with almost anything they could pay for" and that convicts were "playing all sorts of games, reading, scheming, trafficking" (Rothman, 1980:18).

The Cincinnati Declaration of Principles

penology

A branch of criminology dealing with the management of prisons and the treatment of offenders.

In 1870 the newly formed National Prison Association (predecessor of today's American Correctional Association) met in Cincinnati. The association issued a Declaration of Principles signaling a new round of penal reform. Progressive reformers advocated a new design for **penology**. The goal of punishment should be the moral regeneration of criminals, but the means to achieve this goal should be changed. Like the Quakers, these reformers also believed that rehabilitation should be done behind walls. However, the Cincinnati Declaration stated that prisons should reward offenders who reformed with release. Fixed sentences should be replaced by sentences of indeterminate length, and proof of reformation should replace the "mere lapse of time" in decisions about when to release a prisoner. This program of reformation required a progressive classification of prisoners based on improvements in their character.

Elmira Reformatory

The new approach took shape in 1876 at Elmira Reformatory in New York, when Zebulon Brockway was appointed superintendent. Brockway believed that diagnosis and treatment were the keys to reform and rehabilitation. He questioned each new inmate to explore the social, biological, psychological, and "root cause" of the offender's deviance. An individualized work and education treatment program was then prescribed. Inmates followed a rigid schedule of work during the day, followed by courses in academic, vocational, and moral subjects during the evening.

Designed for first-time felons aged 16 to 30, the approach at Elmira incorporated a "mark" system of classification, indeterminate sentences, and parole. Each offender entered the institution at grade 2, and if he earned nine marks a month for six months by working hard, completing school assignments, and causing no problems, he could be moved up to grade 1, which was necessary for release. If he failed to cooperate and violated the rules, he would be demoted to grade 3 and could not return to the path toward eventual release until he had completed three months of satisfactory behavior. This system placed "the prisoner's fate, as far as possible, in his own hands" (Pisciotta, 1994:20).

By 1900 the reformatory movement had spread throughout the nation, yet by the outbreak of World War I in 1914, it was already in decline. In most institutions the architecture, the attitudes of the guards, and the emphasis on discipline differed little from past orientations. Too often the educational and rehabilitative efforts took a back seat to the traditional emphasis on punishment. Even Brockway admitted that it was difficult to distinguish between inmates whose attitudes had changed and those who merely lived by prison rules. Being a good prisoner became the way to win parole, but this did not guarantee that the prisoner had truly changed.

CHECKPOINT

3. How did the New York and Pennsylvania systems differ?
4. What was the significance of the Cincinnati Declaration of Principles?

Improving Prison Conditions for Women

Until 1870 most women inmates were housed in the same prisons as men and treated essentially the same. The first separate, female-run prison was established in Indianapolis in 1873.

Until the beginning of the nineteenth century, female offenders in Europe and North America were treated no differently from males and were not separated from them when they were incarcerated. Only with John Howard's exposé of prison conditions in England and the development of the penitentiary in Philadelphia did attention begin to focus on the plight of the female offender. Among the English reformers, Elizabeth Gurney Fry, a middle-class Quaker, was the first of the reformers to press for changes. When she and fellow Quakers visited London's Newgate Prison in 1813, they were shocked by the conditions in which the female prisoners and their children were living (Zedner, 1995:333).

News of Fry's efforts spread to the United States, and the Women's Prison Association was formed in New York in 1844 with the goal of improving the treatment of female prisoners and separating them from males. Elizabeth Farnham, head matron of the women's wing at Sing Sing from 1844 to 1848, sought to implement Fry's ideas but was thwarted by the male overseers and legislators and was forced to resign.

Although the House of Shelter, a reformatory for women, was created in Detroit following the Civil War, not until 1873 was the first independent female-run prison opened, in Indiana. Within fifty years thirteen other states opened their own.

Three principles guided female prison reform during this period: (1) the separation of women prisoners from men, (2) the provision of care in keeping with the needs of women, and (3) the management of women's prisons by female staff. "Operated by and for women, female reformatories were decidedly 'feminine' institutions'" (Rafter, 1983:147).

As time passed, the original ideas of the reformers faltered. In 1927 the first federal prison for women was opened in Alderson, West Virginia, with Mary Belle Harris as warden. Yet by 1935 the women's reformatory movement had "run its course, having largely achieved its objective (establishment of separate prisons run by women)" (Rafter, 1983:165).

The Reforms of the Progressives

In the first two decades of the twentieth century, reformers known as the "Progressives" attacked the excesses of big business and urban society and advocated government actions against the problems of slums, vice, and crime. The Progressives believed that science could help solve social problems. The two main goals of the Progressives were to improve social conditions thought to be the breeding grounds of crime and to improve ways of rehabilitating individual deviants.

By the 1920s probation, indeterminate sentences, the presentence report, parole, and treatment programs were being promoted as a more scientific approach to criminality. All these components remain in corrections today, although they are not necessarily used strictly in accordance with the Progressives' goals and methods.

CHECKPOINT

5. What were the principles guiding reform of corrections for women in the nineteenth century?

The Rehabilitation Model

rehabilitation model

A model of corrections that emphasizes the need to restore a convicted offender to a constructive place in society through some form of vocational or educational training or therapy.

Although the Progressives were instrumental in advancing the new penal ideas, not until the 1930s were attempts made to fully implement what became known as the **rehabilitation model** of corrections. Taking advantage of the new prestige of the social sciences, penologists helped shift the emphasis of corrections. According to this approach, the social, intellectual, or biological deficiencies of criminals were the causes of their crimes. The essential elements of parole, probation, and the indeterminate sentence were already in place in most states, so incorporating the rehabilitation model meant adding classification systems to diagnose offenders and treatment programs to rehabilitate them.

Because penologists likened the new correctional methods to those used by physicians in hospitals, this approach was often referred to as the **medical model**.

Correctional institutions were to be staffed with clinicians who could diagnose the causes of an individual's criminal behavior, prescribe a treatment program, and determine when the offender was cured and could be safely released to the community.

medical model

A model of corrections based on the assumption that criminal behavior is caused by biological or psychological conditions that require treatment.

Following World War II, rehabilitation won new followers. Group therapy, behavior modification, counseling, and several other approaches became part of the "new penology." Yet even during the 1950s, when the medical model was at its height, only a small proportion of state correctional budgets was allocated for rehabilitation. What frustrated many persons committed to treatment was that, even while states adopted the rhetoric of the rehabilitation model, the institutions were still run with custody as the overriding goal.

The rehabilitation model failed to achieve its goals and became discredited in the 1970s. The problem was that it presumed corrections officials and psychologists could make consistent, accurate judgments about when particular prisoners had been rehabilitated. Studies of treatment programs showed that some prisoners successfully reentered society while others returned to their criminal ways. Corrections officials apparently did not know precisely which techniques would be effective or whether every prisoner had the potential to be rehabilitated. As a result of dissatisfaction with the rehabilitation model, new reforms emerged.

The Community Model

As we have seen, social and political values of particular periods have influenced correctional goals and methods. During the 1960s and early 1970s, U.S. society experienced the civil rights movement, the war on poverty, and resistance to the war in Vietnam. It was a time that challenged the conventional ways of government. In 1967 the President's Commission on Law Enforcement and the Administration of Justice (7) reported that

> crime and delinquency are symptoms of failures and disorganization of the community. ... The task of corrections, therefore, includes building or rebuilding social ties, obtaining employment and education, securing in the larger sense a place for the offender in the routine functioning of society.

This model of **community corrections** was based on the assumption that the goal of corrections should be to reintegrate the offender into the community. It did not represent a complete break with the Progressives' original emphasis on rehabilitation, but it embodied new thinking about the context in which offenders could best be reintegrated.

community corrections

A model of corrections based on the goal of reintegrating the offender into the community.

Proponents of community corrections advocated the rehabilitation of offenders in the community rather than in prisons. The emphasis was on increasing opportunities for offenders to be successful citizens rather than on providing psychological treatment. Programs were supposed to help offenders find jobs and remain connected to their families and the community. Imprisonment was to be avoided, if possible, in favor of probation, so that offenders could seek education and vocational training that would help their adjustment. The small proportion of offenders who had to be incarcerated would spend a minimal amount of time in prison before release on parole. To promote reintegration, correctional workers were to serve as advocates for offenders in dealing with governmental agencies providing employment counseling, medical treatment, and financial assistance.

This community model did not last long as the dominant emphasis of corrections. Significant numbers of offenders continued to commit additional crimes, the crime rate did not fall, and critics complained that lawbreakers were not being adequately punished. By the end of the 1970s, many penologists despaired over their inability to develop and implement effective programs.

The Crime Control Model

crime control model of corrections

A model of corrections based on the assumption that criminal behavior can be controlled by more use of incarceration and other forms of strict supervision.

As the political climate changed in the 1970s and 1980s, legislators, judges, and officials responded with a renewed emphasis on a **crime control model** of corrections. This more punitive approach to criminality makes greater use of incarceration, longer sentences, and strict supervision of probationers and parolees.

Some states have added "supermax" prisons such as Pelican Bay, California, for violent offenders or those with chronic behavior problems. In such institutions inmates spend up to twenty-three hours a day in their cells. They are shackled whenever they are out of their cells, during recreation, showers, and telephone calls. All these measures are designed to send a message to other inmates.

By 1998, the success of these "get-tough" policies was demonstrated by the record number of persons incarcerated, the greater amount of time being served, and the huge size of the probation population. In some states the political fervor to be tough on criminals has resulted in the reinstitution of chain gangs and the removal of television sets, body-building equipment, and college courses from prisons. Some advocates point to crime control policies as the reason the crime rate has begun to fall. Critics of these policies question whether crime control has really made a difference. Whatever the future holds, as the Close-up shows, we must remember that corrections consists of much more than impersonal fortresses.

CHECKPOINT

6. What are the underlying assumptions of the rehabilitation, community, and crime control models of corrections?

ORGANIZATION OF CORRECTIONS IN THE UNITED STATES

The organization of corrections in the United States is fragmented: each level of government has some responsibility for corrections. The federal government, the fifty states, the District of Columbia, the 3,047 counties, and most cities—each has at least one correctional facility and many correctional programs. State and local governments pay about 95 percent of the cost of all correctional activities in the nation (BJS, 1997. *Sourcebook*:4).

Federal Corrections System

The correctional responsibilities of the federal government are divided between the Department of Justice, which operates prisons through the Federal Bureau of Prisons, and the Administrative Office of the United States Courts, which is responsible for probation and parole supervision.

CLOSE-UP

Corrections Is More than Prison

The blue van passes through a small town and then veers off the highway onto a secondary road where only occasional houses punctuate the fields and woods. We are heading toward a looming fortress. As we approach it we see gray stone walls, barbed-wire fences, gun towers, steel bars. The van passes through opened gates and comes to a stop. Blue-uniformed guards move briskly to the rear doors, and in a moment four men, linked by wrist bracelets on a chain, stand on the asphalt and look about nervously.

For most Americans, prison comes to mind when they think of corrections. This is perhaps understandable, given the history of corrections in this country, the folklore, films, and songs about prison life, and the fact that incarceration is the most visible aspect of the process. But corrections is much more than prisons.

Consider the following:

It is 11:00 A.M. in New York City. A five-man crew has been removing trash from a park in the Bronx for several hours. Across town in Rikers Island, the view down a corridor of jail cells is of the hands of the incarcerated, gesturing through the bars as they converse, play cards, share cigarettes—the hands of people doing time. About a thousand miles to the south, over two hundred inmates sit on Florida's death row. In the same state, a woman on probation reports to a "community-control officer." She is wearing an electronic monitoring device on her ankle; it signals the officer if she leaves her home at night without permission. On the other side of the Gulf of Mexico, crops are tended by sunburned Texans dressed in stained work clothes. Almost due north in Kansas, an inmate grievance committee in a maximum security prison reviews complaints of guard harassment. Beside the Pacific, in San Francisco, a young man leaves a center-city office building on his way to work after dropping off a urine sample and talking with his parole officer. All these activities are part of corrections. And all of the central actors are offenders.

Federal Bureau of Prisons

The Federal Bureau of Prisons, which Congress created in 1930, now operates a system of prisons located throughout the nation and housing more than 100,000 inmates (BJS, 1997. *Bulletin*, June:1). Facilities and inmates are classified by a security level, ranging from Level l (the least secure, with camp-type settings like the Federal Prison Camp in Tyndall, Florida) through Level 6 (the most secure, such as the U.S. Penitentiary in Florence, Colorado). Between these extremes are Levels 2 through 5 federal correctional institutions—other U.S. penitentiaries, administrative institutions, medical facilities, and specialized institutions for women and juveniles.

Federal Probation and Parole Supervision

Probation and parole supervision for federal offenders are provided by the Federal Probation and Pretrial Services System, a branch of the Administrative Office of the United States Courts. Probation officers, 3,700 strong, are appointed by the federal judiciary, and are assigned to judicial districts across the country. They assist with presentence investigations but are primarily involved in supervising those on probation and offenders released either on parole or mandatory release.

State Corrections Systems

Although states vary considerably in how they organize corrections, in all states the administration of prisons is part of the executive branch. This point is important because probation is often part of the judiciary, parole may be separate from corrections, and in most states county governments operate jails.

In many states prisons are so crowded that offenders are backed up in county jails awaiting transfer. These inmates in the Franklin County, North Carolina jail have little to do but wait for prison space to open up.

Community Corrections

Probation, intermediate sanctions, and parole are the three major ways that offenders are punished in the community. In many states the judiciary, often through county and municipal governments, administer probation and intermediate sanctions. By contrast, parole is a function of state government. The decision to release an offender from prison is made by the state parole board in those states with discretionary release. Parole boards are a part of either the department of corrections or an independent agency. In states with mandatory systems (see Chapter 14), release is made by the department of corrections. Supervision of parolees in the community is also by an agency of state government.

State Prison Systems

A wide range of state correctional institutions, facilities, and programs exists for adult felons, including prisons, reformatories, prison farms, forestry camps, and halfway houses. This variety does not exist for women because the female prisoner population is smaller than the male population.

The maximum security prison (where 24 percent of inmates are confined) is built like a fortress, usually surrounded by stone walls with guard towers and designed to prevent escape. New facilities are surrounded by double rows of chainlink fences with rolls of razor wire in between and along the top of the fences. Inmates live in cells that include sanitary facilities. The barred doors may be operated electronically so that an officer can confine all prisoners to their cells with the flick of a switch. The purpose of the maximum security facility is custody and discipline; there is a military-style approach to order. Prisoners follow a strict routine. Some of the most famous prisons, such as Stateville, Attica, Yuma, and Sing Sing, are maximum security facilities.

The medium security prison (where 49 percent of inmates are confined) resembles the maximum security prison in appearance. Because it is organized on a somewhat different basis, its atmosphere is less rigid and tense. Prisoners have more privileges and contact with the outside world through visitors, mail, and access to radio and television.

The minimum security prison (where 43 percent of inmates are confined) houses the least violent offenders, long-term felons who have clean disciplinary records, and inmates who have nearly completed their terms. The minimum security prison does not have the guard towers and stone walls of correctional institutions. Often chainlink fencing surrounds the buildings. Prisoners usually live in dormitories or small private rooms rather than in barred cells. There is more personal freedom: inmates may have television sets, choose their own clothes, and move about casually within the buildings. The system offers opportunities for education and work release. Although outsiders may think that little punishment goes on inside the minimum security facility, it is still a prison; restrictions are placed on inmates, and they remain segregated from society.

State Institutions for Women

Because only 6 percent of the incarcerated population are women, there are relatively few women's facilities. A higher proportion of women defendants is sentenced to probation and intermediate punishments, partly as a result of male offenders' tendency to commit most of the violent crimes. However, since 1980 there has been a 600 percent increase in the number of women behind bars, a much faster rate of increase than that for men (BJS, 1997. *Sourcebook*:516).

Female offenders are incarcerated in fifty-three institutions for women and twenty-nine coed facilities. In some states with no separate facilities for women, offenders are assigned to a separate section of the state prison; other women offenders are housed in neighboring states by intergovernmental contract. The number of prisons for women has increased in the last decade.

CHECKPOINT

7. What agencies of the U.S. government are responsible for prisons and probation?
8. What agencies of state government are responsible for incarceration, probation, intermediate sanctions, and parole?

Private Prisons

One response to prison crowding has come from private entrepreneurs who argue that they can build and run prisons at least as effectively, safely, and humanely as any level of government. Their efficiency, they believe, can lower costs for taxpayers while allowing a profit for themselves. The contracting of correctional services such as food service, medical care, education, and vocational training is not new. What is new is the management of entire institutions for adult felons under private contract (Shichor, 1995; Lilly, 1993).

By the end of 1994, eighty-eight private prisons for adults were in operation, with a total capacity of 49,000 inmates in the eighteen states that allow them. The $250-million-a-year private prison business is dominated by Corrections Corporation of America and Wackenhut Corrections Corporation, which together hold more than half of the private prison population (Thomas, 1995).

The major advantages claimed by advocates of privately operated prisons are that they provide the same level of care as the states but more cheaply and flexibly. But this is difficult to determine. One problem is that many of the "true costs" (fringe benefits, contracting supervision, federal grants) are not taken into consideration. The quoted rates of existing private facilities vary widely; however, Corrections Corporation of America reported that it collected just under $40 per day on average for each prisoner held (*New York Times*, August 8, 1994, p. 6). This rate, equivalent to $14,600 per year, is much less than the costs per inmate held in most state prisons.

Political, fiscal, ethical, and administrative issues must be examined before corrections can become too heavily committed to the private ownership and operation of prisons. One ethical question is the propriety of delegating social-control functions to entities other than the state. Some people believe that the administration of justice is a basic function of government that should not be delegated. They fear that contractors may use their political influence to maintain high occupancy levels and would attempt to skim off the best inmates, leaving the most troublesome to the public correctional system.

We cannot yet demonstrate the fiscal value of private corrections; however, labor unions have opposed these incursions into the public sector, pointing out that the salaries, benefits, and pensions of workers in other spheres such as private security are lower than those of their public counterparts. Finally, there are questions about quality of services, accountability of service providers to corrections officials, and problems related to contract supervision. Opponents cite the many instances in which privately contracted services in group homes, day-care centers, hospitals, and schools have been terminated because of reports of corruption, brutality, or substandard services.

Nevertheless, the controversy about privatization has forced corrections to rethink some strongly held beliefs. In this regard the possibility of competition from the private sector may have a positive impact.

CHECKPOINT

9. What are the arguments in favor of and opposed to privately run prisons?

Jails: Local Correctional Facilities

Most Americans do not distinguish between jails and prisons, but there is an important distinction. The jail is a strange correctional hybrid: part detention center for people awaiting trial, part penal institution for sentenced misdemeanants, and part holding facility for social misfits. There are approximately 3,300 jails in the United States with the authority to detain individuals for more than forty-eight hours. The twenty-five largest hold 28 percent of the nation's jailed inmates. The Los Angeles County Men's Central Jail holds more than 6,000 people. Most jails, however, are much smaller: 67 percent hold fewer than fifty persons. Small jails are becoming less numerous because of new construction and new regional, multi-county facilities.

The most recent one-day census of the jail population found 509,828 inmates (193 per 100,000 adult residents), a 100 percent increase in ten years (BJS, 1995. *Bulletin*, April:1). But the number of persons held at any one time in jail does not tell the complete story. Many people are held for less than twenty-four hours; others may reside in jail as sentenced inmates for up to one year; a few may await their trial for more than a year. In fact, the turnover rate is so great that more than 13 million Americans are jailed in one year. More citizens see the inside of jails than see the inside of prisons, mental hospitals, and halfway houses combined.

Jails are usually locally administered by elected officials (sheriffs or county administrators). Jails have traditionally been run by law enforcement agencies. It seems reasonable that the agency that arrests and transports defendants to court should also administer the facility that holds them, but generally neither sheriffs nor their deputies have much interest in corrections. However, almost half the jail inmates are sentenced offenders under correctional authority.

The primary function of jails is to hold persons awaiting trial and persons who have been sentenced for misdemeanors to terms of no more than one year. On a national basis about 50 percent of jail inmates are persons awaiting trial. In some states, convicted felons may serve more than one year in jail rather than in prison. But for 87 percent of the sentenced population, stays in jail are less than one month.

Jails and police lockups shoulder responsibility for housing not only criminal defendants and offenders but also those persons viewed as problems by society. Here we can see how the criminal justice system is linked to other agencies of government. People with mental problems have become a new part of the jail population. They are often reported to the police when they act in a deviant manner that, although not illegal, is upsetting to the citizenry (urinating in public, appearing disoriented, shouting obscenities, and so on). The police must handle such situations, and temporary confinement in the lockup or jail may be necessary if no appropriate social service facilities are available. This situation has been likened to a revolving door that shifts these "street people" from the police station to the jail. After an appearance in court, they are often released to the streets to start their cycle through the system all over again.

Because of constant inmate turnover and because local control provides an incentive to keep costs down, correctional services are usually lacking. Recreational facilities and treatment programs are not found in most jails. Medical services are generally minimal. Such conditions add to the idleness and tensions of time spent in jail. Suicides and high levels of violence are hallmarks of many jails. In any one year almost half the people who die while in jail have committed suicide.

The mixture of offenders of widely diverse ages and criminal histories is another often-cited problem in U.S. jails. Because most inmates are viewed as temporary residents, little attempt is made to classify them for either security or treatment purposes. Horror stories of the mistreatment of young offenders by older, stronger, and more violent inmates occasionally come to public attention. The physical condition of most jails aggravates the situation, because most are old, overcrowded, and lacking basic facilities. Many sentenced felons prefer to move on to state prison, where the conditions are likely to be better.

As criminal justice policy has become more punitive, jails, like prisons, have become crowded. Surveys have documented increases averaging 6 percent during each of the past five years. With the cost of building new facilities as high as $100,000 per cell and the cost of incarcerating an inmate about $20,000 per year, the $4.5 billion annual cost of operating jails is a great financial burden for local governments.

CHECKPOINT

10. What are the functions of jails?
11. List three of the problems affecting jails.

ISSUES IN CORRECTIONS

For most of the past fifty years the number of persons incarcerated in the United States remained fairly stable and the characteristics of those individuals changed little. During the 1940s and 1950s, the incarceration rate was maintained at about 110 per 100,000 population. For a brief period in the late 1960s, when the trend was to stress rehabilitation and community corrections, the incarceration rate actually decreased. However, since 1973, when the overall crime rate started to level off, the number of people in prison has increased dramatically.

Incarceration Trends

Every June and December a census of the U.S. prison population is taken by the Bureau of Justice Statistics. As shown in Figure 11.1, from a low of 98 per 100,000 population in 1972 the incarceration rate has steadily risen, and by the middle of

1997 it was 436 per 100,000 (BJS, 1998. *Bulletin*: January). The census found that there were 1,158,763 men and women in state and federal prisons, an increase of more than double in a decade.

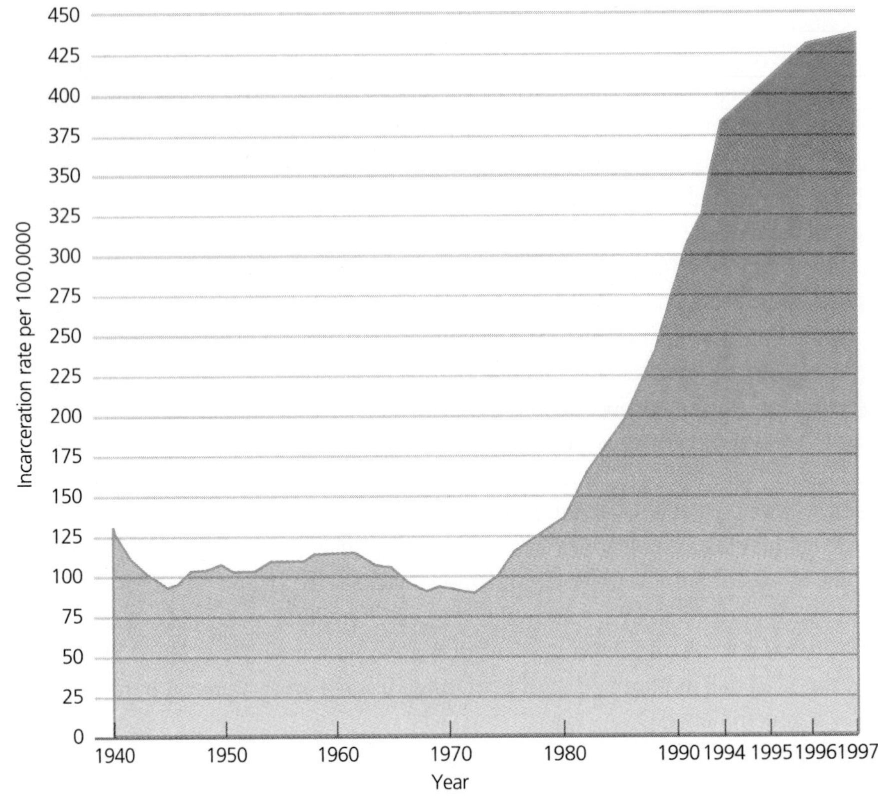

Figure 11.1 ***Incarceration per 100,000 population, 1940-1997***

Between 1940 and 1970 the incarceration rate was steady. Only since 1975 has there been a continuing increase. The rate today is about double what it was in 1985.

SOURCE: U.S. Department of Justice, Bureau of Justice Statistics, *Bulletin* (January 1998).

The skyrocketing prison population has created a correctional crisis of overcrowding. In many states new inmates have been crowded into already-bulging institutions; some offenders are held in county jails and temporary quarters. Faced with such conditions, courts in some states have demanded that changes be made, because they believe overcrowding violates the Constitution.

In most states prison construction has become a growth industry, with massive public expenditures for new facilities. Since 1976 state budgets for corrections have increased faster than any other spending category. Five states have corrections budgets of more than a billion dollars per year. California is the leader, spending $3.6 billion on operations and another $500 million per year on new prison construction (Donziger, 1996:48). Why this increase? Does the growth in the correctional population reflect higher crime rates?

In fact, during the 1980s crime rates increased only marginally, not enough to account for the major surge in the number of people incarcerated. We will next explore five reasons often cited for the growth.

Regional Factors

As Figure 11.2 shows, some of the highest ratios of prisoners to the civilian population are found in the southern states. In 1997 that region incarcerated 495 persons for each 100,000 inhabitants, a ratio much higher than the national average of 436. The penal codes in many southern states provide for the longest sentences. It is also a region with high levels of violence and the highest African-American population, a group that has experienced more punishment (McGarrell, 1993:23). But, as the figure also reveals, there are exceptions to the regional hypothesis: Arizona, California, and Nevada are among the ten states with the highest incarceration rates.

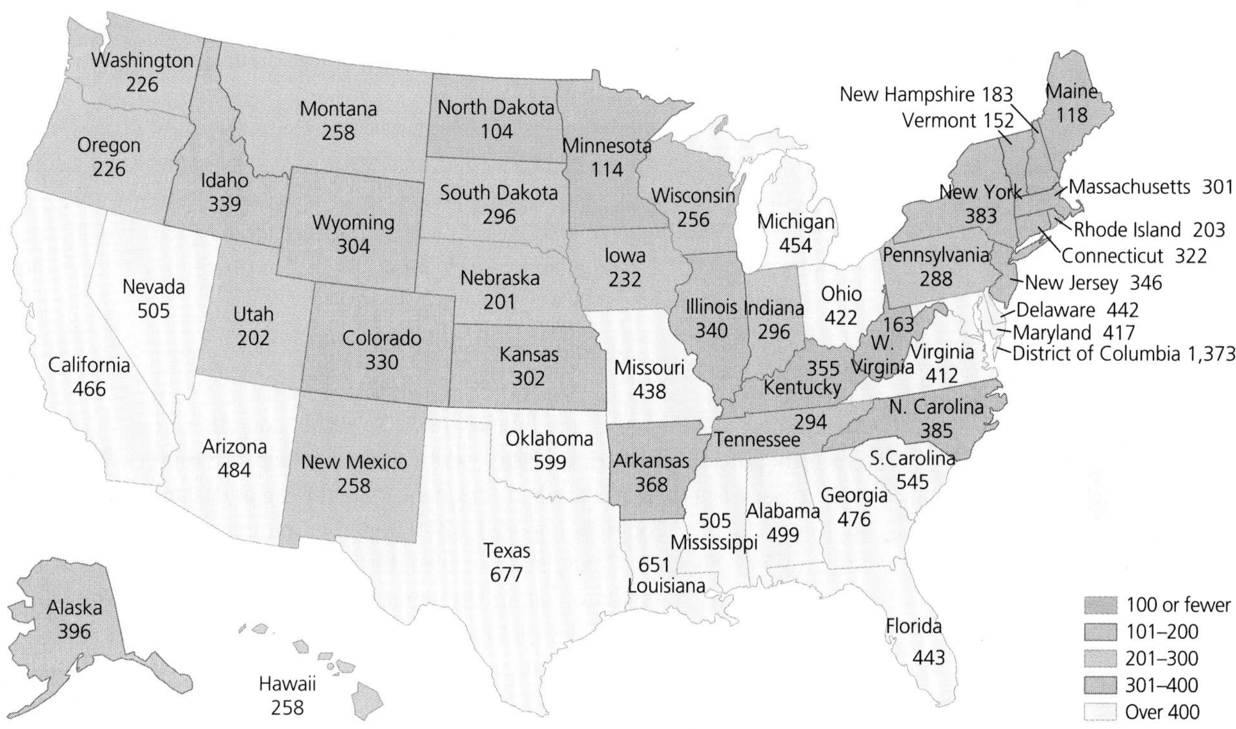

Figure 11.2
Sentenced prisoners in state institutions per 100,000 civilian population, June 30, 1997

What can be said about the differences in incarceration rates among the states? There are not only regional differences but also differences between adjacent states that seem to have similar socioeconomic and crime characteristics.

SOURCE: U.S. Department of Justice, Bureau of Justice Statistics. *Bulletin* (January 1998).

Better Police and Prosecution

Some analysts have argued that the billions of dollars spent on the crime problem may be paying off. Although crime rates overall have been fairly steady during the last decade, adult arrest rates for serious offenses have gone up nearly 41 percent between 1980 and 1993.

In addition to this increase in arrest rates has been an increase in the probability that those arrested for serious offenses will go to prison. Between 1980 and 1994 the likelihood of incarceration upon arrest increased fivefold for drug violations, threefold for weapons offenses, and twofold for larceny-theft, motor vehicle theft, and sexual assault other than rape (Beck, 1997:9).

Tougher Sentencing

Some observers think that a hardening of public attitudes toward criminals is reflected in longer sentences, in a smaller proportion of those convicted getting probation, and in fewer being released at the first parole hearing. However, Beck argues that the growth in the prison population is not the result of longer sentences. He finds that it is the amount of time served that has risen, a factor contributing to the number incarcerated (Beck, 1997:11).

Prison Construction

The increased rate of incarceration may be related to the creation of additional space in the nation's prisons. Public attitudes in favor of more punitive sentencing policies influence legislators to approve prison construction. After new cells are built, judges may feel little hesitation in sentencing offenders to prison. When space was short, the same judges reserved incarceration for only the most violent convicts. Consequently, the escalating incarceration rate may reflect the impact of prison expansion programs in some states. Theorists say that, once built, prisons will stay at capacity because of the organizational needs of the correctional bureaucracy. In other words, "beds will be filled."

Building costs are perhaps one of the greatest deterrents to prison expansion. The average cost of a new cell is $54,000, but because states borrow construction money, the interest on this debt means that a new cell actually costs well over $100,000. A Department of Justice study points out that for every $100 million a legislature commits to new prison construction, the cost to the taxpayers over the next three decades is $1.6 billion (Moore, J. W., 1994).

The War on Drugs

Crusades against the use of marijuana, heroin, cocaine, and other drugs have been a recurring theme of American society since the late nineteenth century. The last such crusade began in 1982, when President Ronald Reagan declared another "war on drugs." In 1987 Congress imposed stiff mandatory minimum sentences for federal drug law violations. Many states copied these sentencing laws. The war continued into the Bush and Clinton administrations, with Congress appropriating billions more to assist in the all-out law enforcement campaign against drugs.

The war on drugs succeeded on one front by packing the nation's prisons with drug law offenders. In 1980 only 8 percent of all state and federal prisoners were incarcerated for drug offenses, but this number had risen to 30 percent by 1996. The percentage of individuals incarcerated in federal prisons for drug offenses is even higher, at 60 percent of inmates (BJS, 1997. *Bulletin*, June:11).

What of the Future?

Given current public attitudes about crime and punishment, continued high crime rates, and the expansion of prison space, incarceration rates are likely to remain high (Blumstein, 1995). Perhaps only when the costs of punishment have a direct impact on taxpayer's pocketbooks will there be a shift in policies. Yet Alfred Blumstein notes that by imprisoning such a large number of people, especially young African-American males, "we have disrupted families and built up strong connections between criminal groups in prison and on the street." He argues that we have "now locked up so many people that we have lost the stigmatizing effect" (*New York Times*, September 28, 1997, p. D1).

CHECKPOINT

12. List five explanations for the great increase in the incarcerated population.
13. Why might additional construction only aggravate the problem?

Who Is in Prison?

What are the characteristics of inmates in our nation's prisons? Do most offenders have long records of serious offenses, or are significant numbers of inmates first-time offenders who have committed minor crimes? Do all prisoners "need" incarceration? These questions are crucial to an understanding of the work of wardens and correctional officers.

As shown in Figure 11.3, most prisoners are males in their late twenties to early thirties, have less than a high school education, and are disproportionately members of minority groups.

Recent studies indicate that inmates who are recidivists and who are convicted of violent crimes make up an overwhelming portion of the prison population. More than 60 percent of inmates have been either incarcerated or on probation at least twice; 45 percent of them, three or more times; and nearly 20 percent, six or more times. Two-thirds of inmates were serving a sentence for a violent crime or had previously been convicted of a violent crime. These are major shifts from the prison populations of earlier decades, when only about 40 percent of all inmates had committed such offenses (BJS, 1993. *Survey of State Prison Inmates*:3).

In addition to these shifts in the prison population, three other factors affect correctional operations: the increased number of elderly prisoners, the many prisoners with HIV/AIDS, and the increase in the number of prisoners sentenced to long terms of incarceration.

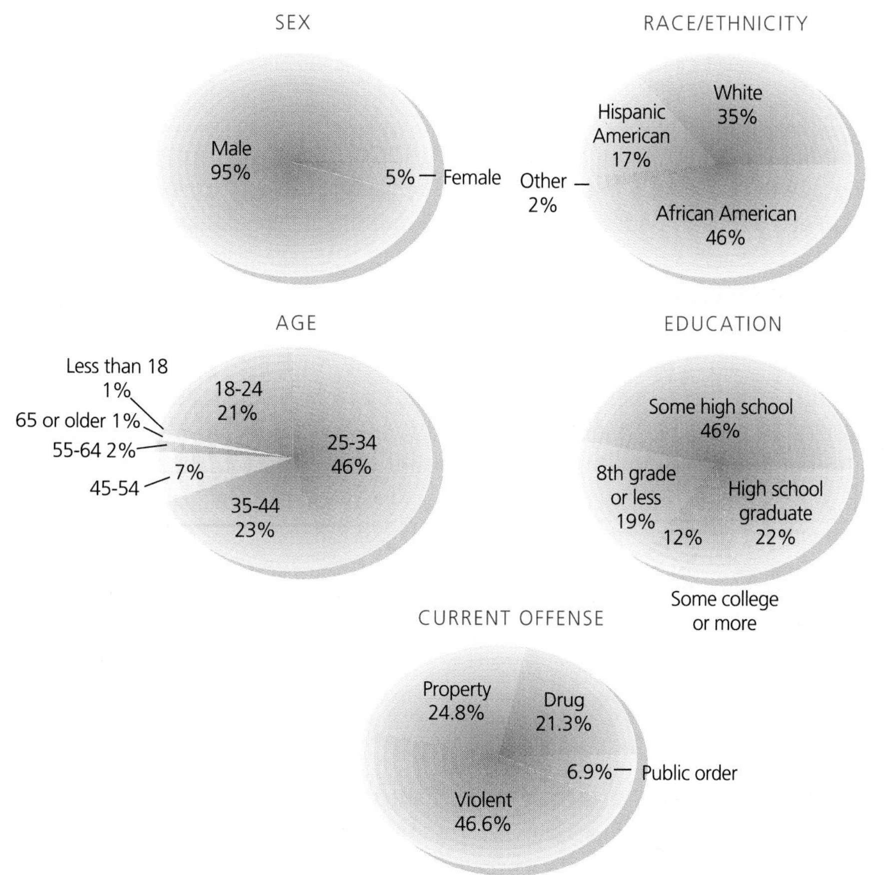

Figure 11.3
Sociodemographic and offense characteristics of state prison inmates

These data show the types of people found in state prisons. What do they indicate about the belief that many offenders do not "need" to be incarcerated?

SOURCE: U.S. Department of Justice, Bureau of Justice Statistics, *Survey of State Prison Inmates* (Washington, D.C.: Government Printing Office, 1993), 3.

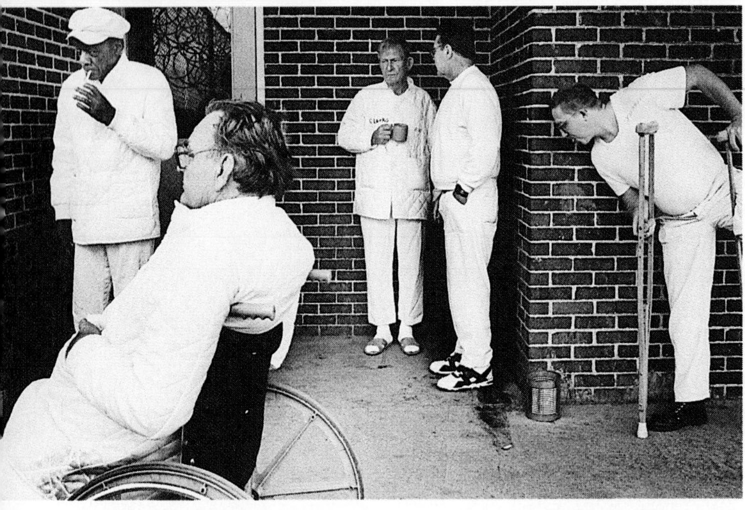

With longer sentences and stricter parole policies prisoners are getting older. Elderly inmates have extensive health problems such that some states are having to create correctional nursing homes.

Elderly Prisoners

Correctional officials have recently become aware of the increasing number of inmates over age 55. That number is now about 30,000, with about 700 over 75 years old. About half of these inmates are serving long sentences; the other half committed crimes late in life. Two-thirds of elderly offenders have been imprisoned for crimes of violence (*New York Times*, November 1, 1995, p. A1). Although older prisoners still make up a small proportion of the total inmate population, their numbers are doubling every four years.

Elderly prisoners have security and medical needs that differ from those of the average inmate. In a number of states, special sections of the institution have been designated for this older population so they will not have to mix with younger, tougher inmates. Elderly prisoners are more likely to develop chronic illnesses such as heart disease, stroke, and cancer (Zimbardo, 1994). The average yearly maintenance and medical costs for inmates over age 55 is about $69,000, triple that of the norm (Camp and Camp, 1994). A paradox of the incarceration of the elderly is that while in prison the offender's life will be prolonged and his medical care will be much better than if he is discharged (Morris, 1995:253). With longer sentences and the abolition of parole in some states, the number of aged prisoners will explode in the next ten to twenty years. Already Pennsylvania has 3,000 inmates serving life sentences without the possibility of parole. Will some prisons eventually have to be renamed Centers for the Correctional Treatment of Old Folks?

Prisoners with HIV/AIDS

In the coming years, AIDS is expected to be the leading cause of death among males aged 35 and younger. With 68 percent of the adult inmate population under age 35, correctional officials must cope with the problem of HIV—the human immunodeficiency virus that causes AIDS—as well as AIDS itself and related health issues. The rate of confirmed AIDS cases among prison inmates is six times higher than in the total U.S. population. More than 1,000 inmates die of AIDS each year. AIDS-related deaths make up over a third of all deaths of state prisoners (BJS, 1997. *Bulletin*, August:1). Because many inmates who are HIV infected are undiagnosed, these numbers underestimate the scope of the problem.

To deal with these offenders, prison officials have had to develop policies concerned with transmission of the disease, housing of those infected, and medical care for inmates with the full range of symptoms. Administrators are confronting legal, political, medical, budgetary, and attitudinal factors as they decide what actions their institutions should take. One such policy issue is addressed in A Question of Ethics.

Long-Term Inmates

More prisoners serve long sentences in the United States than in any other Western nation. While the average first-time offender serves about twenty-two months, an estimated 11 to 15 percent of all prisoners—well over 100,000—will serve more than seven years in prison. About 9 percent are serving life sentences, and another 24 percent are serving sentences of more than twenty-five years. These long-term prisoners are often the same people who will become elderly inmates, with all of the attendant problems (Flanagan, 1995:10).

Long-term prisoners represent a management problem for administrators, who must find ways of making prison life livable for those who are going to be there a long time. Administrators need to adhere to three main principles: (1) maximize opportunities for the inmate to exercise choice in living circumstances, (2) create opportunities for meaningful living, and (3) help the inmate maintain contact with the outside world (Flanagan, 1991).

In the context of overcrowded facilities, the contemporary inmate population presents several challenges to correctional workers. Resources may not be available to provide rehabilitative programs for most inmates. Even if the resources exist, the goal of maintaining a safe and healthy environment may tax the staff's abilities. These difficulties are multiplied still further by the presence of AIDS and increasing numbers of elderly and long-term prisoners. The contemporary corrections system is having to deal with a different type of inmate, one who is more prone to violence, and with a prison society where racial tensions are great. How well this correctional challenge is met will have an important impact on American society.

CHECKPOINT

14. What are the major characteristics of today's prisoners?

A Question of ETHICS

The policy directive was precise:

> All inmates will be tested for HIV. All inmates found to be positive will be placed in Wing A, regardless of their physical condition, conviction offense, or time remaining in their sentence.

Testing for the deadly virus began at Elmwood State Prison soon after Warden True's directive was posted. All of the 753 inmates were tested over a three-week period, and every new prisoner entering the institution first went to the medical unit to have blood drawn for laboratory examination.

Six weeks after the directive was posted, the test results were known. For most of the inmates there was relief in the knowledge that they had not contracted the virus. For a few, however, the notice to report to the prison doctor was followed shortly by what amounted to a medical death sentence. Hearing the news that they had tested positive was traumatic. Most responded with an expletive; others burst into tears; still others sat in stunned silence.

Word of the new policy at the prison was leaked to the press. The state chapter of the American Civil Liberties Union and the Howard Association for Prisoners' Rights reacted immediately, with the groups calling for a meeting with Warden True. In a press conference they protested the "state's invasion of privacy" and the "discriminatory act of segregating gays and drug users, most of the latter being African American and Hispanic." They emphasized that it would be years before most of the infected would come down with a "full" case of AIDS; compassion, not stigmatization, should be the response of corrections to the disease.

Warden True told reporters that he had a responsibility for the health of all inmates and that the policy had been developed to prevent transmission of the disease. He said that although the HIV inmates would be segregated, they would have access to all the facilities available to the general population, but at separate times. He denied that he intended to stigmatize the twenty prisoners who had thus far tested positive.

What do you suppose Warden True considered in developing this policy? Is his policy likely to cause harm or good? Is it ethical to segregate the prison population? Is it ethical to add conditions to parole for prisoners who test HIV positive?

Summary

- From colonial days to the present, methods of criminal sanctions that are considered appropriate have varied.
- The development of the penitentiary signaled a shift away from corporal punishment.
- The Pennsylvania and New York systems were competing approaches to implementing the ideas of the penitentiary.
- The Declaration of Principles of 1870 contained the key elements for the reformatory and rehabilitation models of corrections.
- The administration of corrections in the United States is fragmented in that various levels of government are involved.

- Jails, which are administered by local government, hold persons awaiting trial as well as sentenced offenders.
- Prison populations have more than doubled during the past decade; there has also been a great increase in facilities and staff to supervise them.

Questions for Review

1. What were the major differences between the New York and Pennsylvania systems in the nineteenth century?
2. What are some of the pressures on administrators of local jails?
3. What types of correctional programs exist in your state? What agencies of government run them?
4. Why are private prisons a corrections option that is attractive to some state legislators?
5. What explanations might be given for the increased use of incarceration during the past two decades?

ANSWERS TO CHECKPOINTS

1. A period in the late eighteenth century when philosophers rethought the nature of society and the place of the individual in the world. New ideas about criminality, methods of punishment, and government arose from the Enlightenment.
2. Four principles: secure and sanitary building, inspection to ensure that offenders followed the rules, abolition of fees, and a reformatory regime.
3. The Pennsylvania system of separate confinement held inmates in isolation from one another. The New York congregate system kept inmates in their cells at night, but they worked in shops during the day.
4. The Declaration of Principles advocated indeterminate sentences, rehabilitation programs, classifications based on improvements in character, and release on parole.
5. Separation of women prisoners from men, care in keeping with women's needs, women's prisons staffed by women.
6. Rehabilitation model: criminal behavior is the result of a biological, intellectual, or social deficiency; clinicians should diagnose the problem and prescribe treatment; when cured, the offender may be released. Community model: the goal of corrections is to reintegrate the offender into the community, so rehabilitation should be carried out in the community rather than in prison if possible; correctional workers should serve as advocates for offenders in their dealings with government agencies. Crime control model: criminal behavior can be controlled by greater use of incarceration and other forms of strict supervision.
7. The Federal Bureau of Prisons of the Department of Justice and the Administrative Office of the United States Courts, which handles probation.
8. Prisons: Department of corrections. Probation: judiciary or executive branch department. Intermediate sanctions: judiciary, probation department, department of corrections. Parole: executive agency.
9. In favor: costs are lower yet conditions are the same or better than prisons run by the government. Opposed: incarceration should be a function of government, not an enterprise for private profit. Private interests can skew public policy.
10. Holding of offenders before trial and incarceration of offenders sentenced to short terms.
11. High inmate turnover, lack of services, scarce resources.
12. Regional factors, better police and prosecution, tougher sentencing, prison construction, the war on drugs.
13. New prison beds will quickly become filled because judges will be less hesitant to sentence people to prison and because the corrections bureaucracy needs the space to be used.
14. Today's prisoners are largely males in their late twenties to early thirties with less than a high school education. They are disproportionately members of minority groups.

Chapter 12

Community Corrections: Probation and Intermediate Sanctions

Community Corrections: Assumptions

Probation: Correction without Incarceration

- *Origins and Evolution of Probation*
- *Organization of Probation*
- *Probation Services*
- *Revocation of Probation*
- *Assessing Probation*

Intermediate Sanctions in the Community

- *Intermediate Sanctions Administered Primarily by the Judiciary*
- *Intermediate Sanctions Administered in the Community*
- *Intermediate Sanctions Administered in Institutions and the Community*
- *Implementing Intermediate Sanctions*

Community Corrections: Approaching the Twenty-First Century

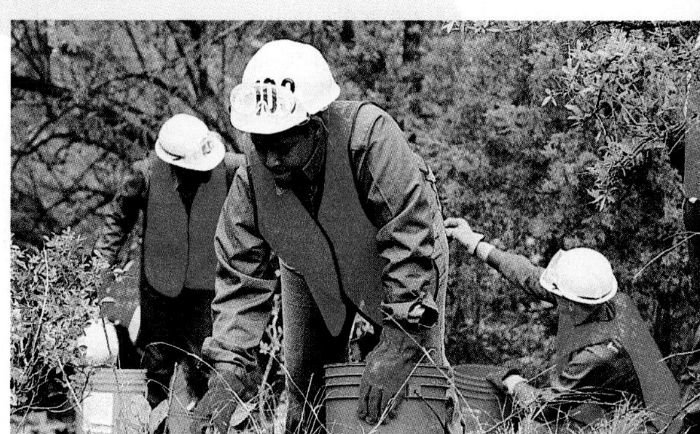

TODD HARRISON emptied the trash into the waiting truck as his co-workers moved from can to can in the Bayside, Florida, recreation area. He wore his usual uniform—a baseball cap turned backwards, sunglasses, and a T-shirt emblazoned "B.U.M." Harrison was one of ten probationers working under the watchful eye of Rich Clark, a community service supervisor employed by the nonprofit organization Upward Now, Inc. Two years before, Harrison had been sentenced to three years on probation and 100 hours of community service for a larceny conviction. Because Todd was 19 at the time and had no prior record, the judge had given him a community sentence instead of sending him to prison—the usual sentence for more experienced criminals convicted of the same offense. Harrison lives with his mother, works the late shift at a convenience store, reports to his probation officer monthly, and spends five hours every Saturday under Clark's supervision to complete his community service. Things are looking up for Todd Harrison as he moves toward completion of his punishment.

Since the early nineteenth century, supervision in the community has been recognized as an appropriate punishment for some offenders. Although probation was developed in the 1840s and widely used by the 1920s, incarceration remained the usual sentence for serious crimes until the 1960s. At that time, with a new emphasis on community corrections, judges sentenced increased numbers of offenders to sanctions carried out in the community. As a result, incarceration rates fell as probation was viewed as the "punishment of choice" for most first-time offenders.

But as Americans wearied of crime in the 1980s, legislatures passed tough sentencing laws and specified incarceration as the new priority punishment. The "war on drugs" further increased the numbers of offenders incarcerated as well as added to the numbers under probation supervision. By the late 1980s criminal justice scholars recognized that many imprisoned offenders, if properly supervised, could be punished more cheaply in the community. Yet probation was clearly inappropriate for offenders whose crimes were serious and who could not be effectively supervised by officers with large caseloads. What was needed was a set of intermediate sanctions, less restrictive of freedom than prison but more restrictive than probation. These sanctions came to include intensive probation supervision, home confinement, monetary sanctions, and boot camps (Morris and Tonry, 1990:3).

In years to come, community corrections can be expected to play a much greater role in the criminal justice system. Already three-quarters of offenders are under correctional supervision in the community (Figure 12.1). This portion is likely to increase as states try to deal with the high costs of incarceration. Probation and intermediate sanctions appear to many criminal justice experts to be less expensive and just as effective as imprisonment (Petersilia, 1995).

Questions for Inquiry

What are the philosophical assumptions underlying community corrections?

How did probation evolve, and in what ways are probation sentences implemented today?

What are the types of intermediate sanctions, and how are they administered?

What are the issues of community corrections as we move toward the twenty-first century?

COMMUNITY CORRECTIONS: ASSUMPTIONS

Community corrections seeks to keep offenders in the community by building ties to family, employment, and other normal sources of stability and success. This model of corrections assumes that the offender must change, but it recognizes that factors within the community that might encourage criminal behavior (unemployment, for example) must also change.

Four factors are usually cited in support of community corrections:

1. Many offenders' criminal records and current offenses are not serious enough to warrant incarceration.
2. Community supervision is cheaper than incarceration.
3. Rates of **recidivism**, or returning to crime, are no higher for those under community supervision than those who go to prison.
4. Incarceration is more destructive to both the offender and society. In addition to the harmful effects of prison life, incarceration adds to the suffering of family members, particularly children.

recidivism

A return to criminal behavior.

Community corrections is based on the goal of finding the "least-restrictive alternative"—punishing the offender only as severely as needed to protect the community and to satisfy the public. Advocates call for programs to assist offenders in the community so they will have opportunities to succeed in law-abiding activities and to reduce their contact with the criminal world.

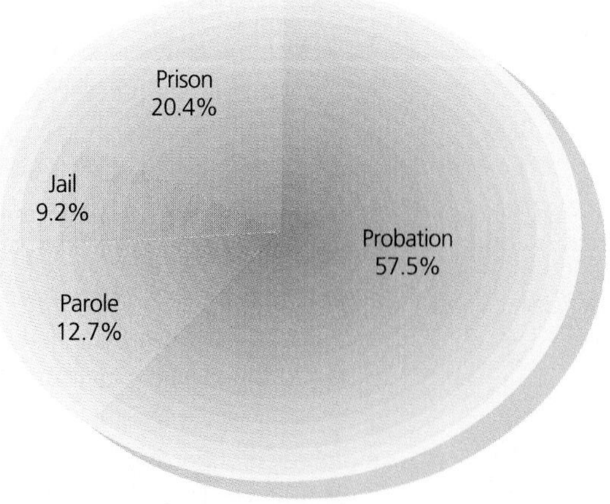

Figure 12.1
Percentage of persons in each category of correctional supervision

Although most people think of corrections as prisons and jails, in fact almost three-quarters of offenders are supervised within the community.

SOURCE: U.S. Department of Justice, Bureau of Justice Statistics, "Nation's Probation and Parole Population Reached Almost 3.9 Million Last Year," press release, August 14, 1997.

CHECKPOINT

1. What are the four main assumptions underlying community corrections?

(Answers are at the end of the chapter.)

PROBATION: CORRECTION WITHOUT INCARCERATION

Probation is the conditional release of the offender into the community under the supervision of correctional officials. Probationers live at home with their families and work at regular jobs, but they must report regularly to their probation officers. They must also abide by certain conditions, such as submitting to drug tests, obeying curfews, and staying away from certain people or parts of town. Although probation is mainly used for lesser offenses, states are increasingly using probation for more serious felonies, as shown in Figure 12.2.

probation

A sentence allowing the offender to serve the sanctions imposed by the court in the community under supervision.

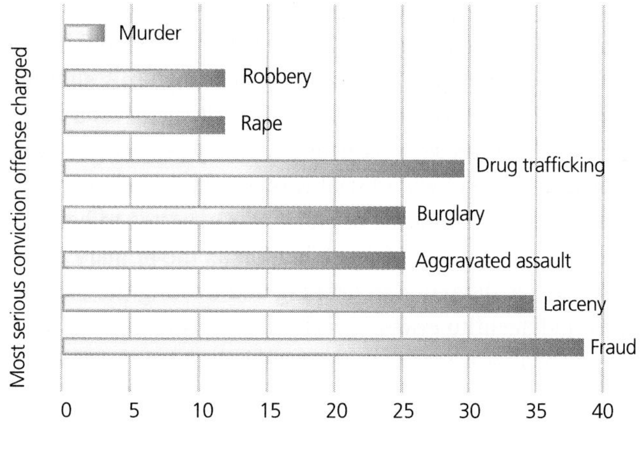

Figure 12.2
Felony sentences to probation in state courts

Although most people on probation have been convicted of misdemeanors, states have increasingly used this sanction for serious offenders. Shown here are the percentages of offenders sentenced to probation listed by the most serious charge for which they were convicted.

SOURCE: U.S. Department of Justice, Bureau of Justice Statistics, *Bulletin* (July 1997), 3.

Probation may be combined with other sanctions, such as fines, restitution, and community service. Fulfillment of these other sanctions may, in effect, become a condition for successful completion of probation. The sentencing court retains authority over the probationer, and if he or she violates the conditions or commits another crime, the judge may order the entire sentence to be served in prison.

The number of probationers now under supervision is at a record high and is still rising. Much has been written about overcrowded prisons, but the adult probation population has also been increasing—by more than 7 percent a year, up 176 percent since 1980. Today, more than 3 million offenders are on probation, yet probation budgets in many states have been cut and caseloads increased as greater resources are diverted to prisons (BJS, 1997. *Sourcebook*:503).

Although probation has many benefits that cause it to be chosen over incarceration, the public often sees it as merely a "slap on the wrist" for offenders. This view is so widespread that even a scholarly work on correctional policy has referred to probation as a kind of "standing joke" (Davis and Smith, 1994). With caseloads

WORK*Perspective*

As a freshman at Michigan State University, I enrolled in "Introduction to Criminal Justice." One of our guest speakers was a former felon. He had been in prison and was rehabilitated. His story so impressed me that I declared criminal justice with an emphasis on corrections as my major and psychology as a minor.

During my junior and senior years I did volunteer work to learn about jobs in corrections. I volunteered as a clerical worker at the county jail, helped with arts and crafts projects at the juvenile detention facility, and supervised recreation activities in a halfway house for young adult offenders. In my senior year I accepted an internship with a pretrial diversion program in the local prosecutor's office. I interviewed people charged with nonviolent crimes and recommended whether they should be accepted into the diversion program. Diversion consisted of payment of fees, community service, and minimal supervision in lieu of prosecution. My internship supervisor recommended me for a full-time position as a juvenile probation officer, but I declined the job offer because it required relocation to a different city.

Robin Osterhaven
Chief Probation Officer

State District Court
Lansing, Michigan

After graduation I worked in jobs outside of criminal justice for four years in my small hometown. When I decided to look for work elsewhere, a friend in the sheriff's office told me about an advertised position for a probation officer in another part of the state. I applied for the position and was hired. As a probation officer for more than a decade, I have learned much about the job and about myself, especially with the help of a mentor in the probation office.

Based on my experiences in getting started with my career, I recommend that students interested in criminal justice professions develop good communication skills; do volunteer work and internships to gain experience; and be outgoing, firm, and forthright in working with other people. Employment opportunities often arise from personal contacts, including those developed in student internships. I also believe that gaining knowledge about substance abuse is essential because it has such a big impact on criminal justice.

As a district court probation officer in Michigan, I work with adults, age 17 and over, convicted of misdemeanors. The majority of cases involve drinking and driving or assaultive behaviors. I conduct presentence interviews and background investigations to formulate sentence recommendations. I also talk to victims in the course of preparing my sentence recommendation reports for the judges. Each report is submitted to the judge and read by the defendant and the defense attorney. As a regular probation officer, I used to supervise a caseload of 200 people. As a supervisor of other probation officers, I now have a smaller caseload. I also conduct probation violation hearings to determine if probation should be revoked for offenders who violate their release conditions. I listen to probationers when they need to talk and I refer them to community resources for substance abuse, family, employment, and other problems. Much of my work involves people with substance abuse problems. As the chief probation officer, I have additional responsibilities: supervising employees and student interns, preparing the annual budget, and evaluating our policies and practices.

Probation work involves many difficult discretionary decisions. For example, I may have to recommend a sentence for two cases—both 22-year-old women, unemployed, and convicted of retail fraud second-degree (shoplifting). Both women have no prior arrest history, and the items taken were valued at less than $100. One stole baby clothes for her infant, and the other stole a pair of designer jeans for herself. What would you recommend? Probation or jail time?

I look at many factors in making my sentence recommendations. I examine the offender's prior arrest and conviction history to see if they have previously committed similar offenses that will weigh against them. I look at their driving record. Are they irresponsible drivers? Do they pay their traffic tickets and appear in court? Obviously, I also consider the seriousness of the offense and whether they injured a victim. I am interested in whether they show regret and remorse about their actions. I look for their expressed willingness to seek counseling, participate in Alcoholics Anonymous, and obey probation conditions. I check to see whether they followed through when given opportunities to be on probation and sought help in the past. I also evaluate the general circumstances of their lives to see the extent to which they need or will benefit from probation supervision. The judge ultimately determines the sentence, but my recommendation to the judge includes my consideration of these factors.

Nearly every day I see people struggling with many issues. One probationer needs a job, is alcoholic, and does not have a driver's license. Another struggles to support a family on minimum wage but must come up with money to pay court fees and the costs of anger-control counseling. These are some of the problems we address by referring probationers to community resources and reminding them of the possible consequences if they fail to follow the judge's orders.

WORK*Perspective*

probation officer is less important than the quality of the services and the supervision the probationers get.

During the past decade probation officials have developed methods of classifying clients according to their service needs, the element of risk they pose to the community, and the chance they will commit another offense. Through this process probationers may be supervised less as they continue to live within the conditions of their sentence. Classification of probationers according to their risk of committing another crime fits the deserved-punishment model of the criminal sanction in that the most serious cases receive the greatest restrictions and supervision (Clear and O'Leary, 1984:77-100).

Whether serious cases actually receive more supervision is influenced by a number of factors. Consider the war on drugs. It has significantly increased probation levels in urban areas because large numbers of drug dealers and people convicted of drug possession are placed on probation. Many of these offenders have committed violent acts and live in inner-city areas marked by drug dealing and turf battles to control drug markets. Under these conditions, direct supervision can be a dangerous task for the probation officer. In some urban areas, probationers are merely required to telephone or mail reports of their current residence and employment. In such cases, it is hard to see how any goal of the sanctions—deserved punishment, rehabilitation, deterrence, or incapacitation—is actually being realized. If none of these objectives is being met, the offender is getting off scot-free.

IDEAS IN PRACTICE

As a probation officer in Philadelphia, you are trying to manage a 300-person caseload. The probationers have committed a mixed range of offenses, many have been on probation before, and several have served jail or prison sentences. One-third of your clients have been on probation for less than six months, one third for six months to a year, and one third for more than one year.

What are some of the strategies that you will use to best meet the service and supervision needs of your clients?

CHECKPOINT

4. What are the major tasks of probation officers?

Revocation of Probation

Between one-fifth and one-third of probationers violate the provisions of their sentences and may have their probation revoked by the judge (Geerken and Hayes, 1993:549). Because probation is usually granted in conjunction with a suspended jail or prison sentence, incarceration may follow revocation. Revocation of probation can occur for either a technical violation or a new arrest. Technical violations occur when a probationer fails to meet the conditions of a sentence by, for instance, violating curfew, failing a drug test, or using alcohol. Officers have discretion as to whether or not they bring this fact to the judge's attention.

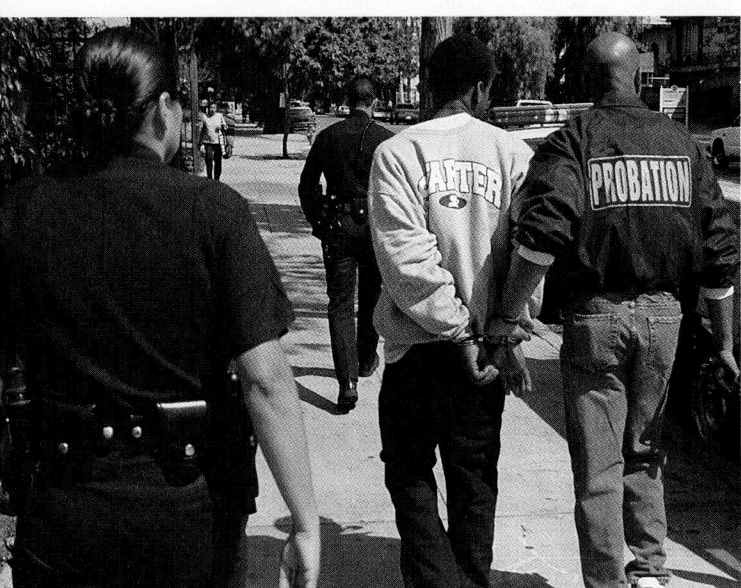

Providing direct supervision of drug offenders has become a dangerous task for probation officers. Here, the probation officer has police assistance in bringing a client to court for revocation.

Probation officers and judges have widely varying notions of what constitutes grounds for revoking probation. Once the officer has decided to call a violation to the attention of the court, the probationer may be arrested or summoned for a revocation hearing. Because the contemporary emphasis is on avoiding incarceration except for flagrant and continual violation of the conditions of probation, most revocations today occur because of a new arrest or conviction. Yet one study in California found that many of these "failures" stayed on probation after their convictions, even though the new offense was often serious. This study suggests that once a person is on probation, serious misbehavior will not necessarily result in removal from the community (Petersilia et al., 1985:39).

In 1967 the U.S. Supreme Court gave its first opinion concerning the due process rights of probationers at a revocation hearing. In ***Mempha v. Rhay*** (1967) the justices determined that a state probationer had a right to counsel at a revocation and sentencing hearing, but the Court did not refer to any requirement for a hearing. This issue was addressed in ***Gagnon v. Scarpelli*** (1973), in which the justices ruled that before probation or parole can be revoked, the offender is entitled to a preliminary and a final hearing and to specific elements of due process. When a probationer is taken into custody for violating the conditions of probation, a preliminary hearing must be held to determine whether probable cause exists to believe that the incident occurred. If there is a finding of probable cause, a final hearing, where the revocation decision is made, is mandatory. At these hearings the probationer has the right to cross-examine witnesses and to be given notice of the alleged violations and a written report of the proceedings. The Court ruled, though, that the probationer does not have an automatic right to counsel—this decision is to be made on a case-by-case basis. At the final hearing, the judge decides whether to continue probation or to impose tougher restrictions, such as incarceration.

***Mempha v. Rhay* (1967)**

Probationers have the right to counsel at a revocation and sentencing hearing.

CHECKPOINT

5. What are the grounds for probation revocation?
6. What rights does a probationer have while revocation is being considered?

***Gagnon v. Scarpelli* (1973)**

Before probation can be revoked, a two-stage hearing must be held and the offender provided with specific elements of due process.

Assessing Probation

Probation is at a crossroads. Some critics see probation as nothing more than a slap on the wrist, an absence of punishment. Because of officers' huge caseloads, probationers often receive very little guidance, supervision, or assistance. While the credibility of probation is low in the eyes of the public, caseloads are growing dramatically and, in view of the crowding in prisons and jails, will probably continue to do so.

How effective can probation be? We learned earlier that from one-fifth to one-third of probationers fail to fulfill the conditions of their sentences. Although this recidivism rate is lower than that of those who have been incarcerated, researchers question whether this is a direct result of supervision or an indirect result of the maturing of the probationers. Most offenders placed on probation do not become career criminals, their criminal activity is short-lived, and they become stable citizens as they obtain jobs and get married. Most of those who are arrested a second time do not repeat their mistakes again.

What rallies support for probation is its relatively low cost: keeping an offender on probation rather than behind bars costs roughly $1,000 a year, a savings of more than $20,000 a year (Abadinsky, 1997). However, these savings may not satisfy community members who hear of a sex offender on probation who repeats his crime.

In recent years as prisons have become overcrowded, increasing numbers of felony offenders have been placed on probation. Almost half (46 percent) of all convicted felons are given probation (Petersilia, 1995:18). More than 75 percent of probationers are addicted to drugs or alcohol. These factors present new challenges for probation because officers can no longer assume that their clients pose little threat to society and that they have the skills to live productive lives in the community.

To offer a viable alternative to incarceration, probation services need the resources to appropriately supervise and assist their clients. The new demands on probation have brought calls for increased electronic monitoring and for risk management systems that provide different levels of supervision for different kinds of offenders.

INTERMEDIATE SANCTIONS IN THE COMMUNITY

Dissatisfaction with the traditional means of probation supervision, coupled with prison crowding, has resulted in a call for new kinds of intermediate sanctions in the community. The call is for sanctions that restrict the offender more than simple probation does and that constitute actual punishment for more serious offenders. The case for intermediate sanctions can be made on several grounds, but Norval Morris and Michael Tonry said it this way: "Prison is used excessively; probation is used even more excessively; between the two is a near vacuum of purposive and enforced punishments" (Morris and Tonry, 1990:3). They urged the creation of punishments that are more restrictive than probation yet match the severity of the offense and the characteristics of the offender, and that can be carried out while still protecting the community.

Intermediate sanctions may be viewed as a continuum—a range of punishments that vary in levels of intrusiveness and control, as shown in Figure 12.3. Probation plus a fine or community service may be appropriate for minor offenses, while six weeks of boot camp followed by intensive probation supervision may be right for serious crimes. But will offenders be able to fulfill the conditions added to probation? Moreover, if prisons are overcrowded, is incarceration a believable threat if offenders fail to comply (Blomberg and Lucken, 1993:470)?

Many different types of intermediate sanctions are being used across the country. Let's divide them into (1) those administered primarily by the judiciary (fines, restitution, and forfeiture); (2) those primarily administered in the community and having a supervision component (home confinement, community service, day reporting centers, and intensive probation supervision); and (3) those administered inside institutions and followed by community supervision (boot camp). Remember that sanctions may be imposed in combination—for example, a fine and probation, or boot camp with community service and probation.

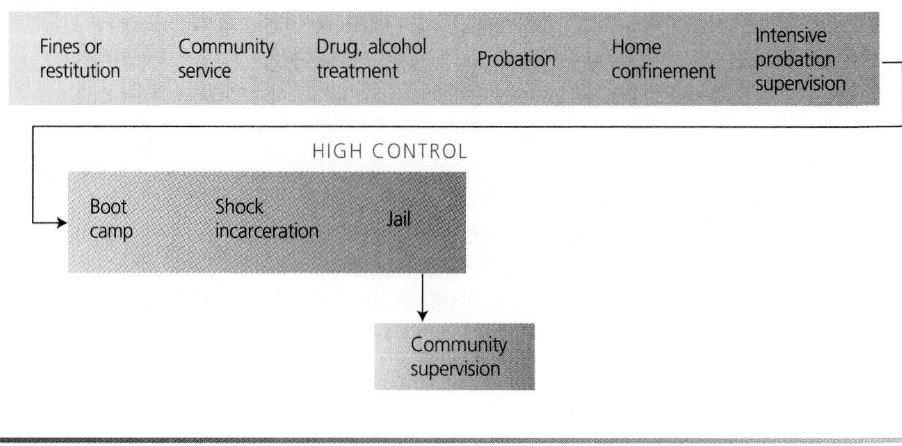

Figure 12.3
Continuum of intermediate sanctions

Judges may use a range of intermediate sanctions , from those in which the offender requires a low level of control to those in which the offender requires a high level of control.

CHECKPOINT

7. What is the main argument for intermediate sanctions?
8. What is meant by a "continuum of sanctions"?

Intermediate Sanctions Administered Primarily by the Judiciary

A number of intermediate sanctions are administered primarily by the judiciary. We discuss three below—fines, restitution, and forfeiture. Because all three involve the transfer of money or property from the offender to the government or crime victim, the judiciary is considered the proper branch not only to impose the sanction but also to collect what is due.

Fines

Fines are routinely imposed today for offenses ranging from traffic violations to felonies. Studies have shown that the fine is used widely as a criminal sanction and that well over $1 billion in fines is collected annually by courts across the country (Hillsman, Sichel, and Mahoney, 1983). Yet compared with other Western democracies, the United States makes little use of fines as the sole punishment for crimes more serious than motor vehicle violations. Instead, fines typically are used in the United States in conjunction with other sanctions, such as probation and incarceration—for example, two years of probation and a $500 fine.

fine

A sum of money to be paid to the state by a convicted person as punishment for an offense.

Many judges cite the difficulty of collecting fines as the reason that they do not impose this punishment more often. They report that enforcing payment of fines often takes a back seat to the demanding flow of criminal prosecutions, sentencing decisions, and probation revocations. Perhaps the judiciary sees little incentive to expend its own resources in administering the collection of fines because the proceeds are not earmarked for the courts.

In addition, judges point out that many offenders are poor, so it is difficult for them to pay fines, and they might even commit additional illegal acts to get the money. Furthermore, reliance on fines as an alternative to incarceration might enable affluent offenders to "buy" their way out of jail with little discomfort, while the poor would have to serve time. Finally, in cases in which a poor offender actually can pay, payment might be most burdensome to his or her family, who would suffer the loss of bare necessities.

Fines are used extensively in Europe and they are strongly enforced (Tonry and Hamilton, 1995:16). They are normally the only punishment for a wide range of crimes, with amounts geared to the severity of the offense and the resources of the offender. To deal with the concern that fines exact a heavier toll on the poor than on the wealthy, Sweden and Germany have developed the day fine. They achieve fairness by imposing different levels of fines on offenders who have committed the same offense but who have different levels of income. The day-fine concept has been adapted to the U.S. system and has been tested in Arizona, Connecticut, Iowa, and Oregon.

Restitution

In its simplest form, **restitution** is repayment by an offender to a victim who has suffered some form of financial loss from the crime. In the Middle Ages restitution was a common way to settle a criminal case (Karmen, 1996:297). The offender was ordered to pay the victim or do the victim's work. With the growth of the modern state the use of retribution, with the victim and the offender privately agreeing upon the nature and amount, declined. Instead, the state prosecuted offenders, and punishments focused on the wrong the offender had done to society.

Victim restitution has been a part of the U.S. criminal justice system throughout our history though it is still largely unpublicized. In many instances, restitution derives from informal agreements between law enforcement officials and offenders at the police station, during plea bargaining, or in the prosecutor's sentence recommendations. Only since the late 1970s has restitution been institutionalized in many jurisdictions, usually as one of the conditions of probation. One study has shown that most offenders ordered to pay restitution completed their probation successfully (Weitekamp, 1995:68).

As with fines, convicted offenders have differing abilities to pay restitution, and the conditions inevitably fall more harshly on less-affluent offenders.

IDEAS IN PRACTICE

In the day-fine system, offenders with differing economic circumstances who have committed the same crime are fined at levels according to their daily income. Consider the following:

An hourly-wage restaurant dishwasher making $50 per day and a business executive making $300 per day have been convicted of the same offense. According to sentencing guidelines the fine is ten days' pay. Compute the fine that each offender must pay.

Is the day-fine system just?

Someone who has the "good fortune" to be victimized by an affluent criminal may receive full compensation, while someone victimized by a poor offender may never receive a penny.

restitution

Repayment—in the form of money or service—by an offender to a victim who has suffered some financial loss from the offense.

Restitution is more easily imposed when the "damage" inflicted can be easily measured—medical costs or the value of property destroyed or stolen, for instance. But what should be the restitution for the terror of an attempted rape?

Forfeiture

With passage of two laws in 1970—the Racketeer Influenced and Corrupt Organizations Act (RICO) and the Continuing Criminal Enterprise Act (CCE), Congress resurrected forfeiture, a criminal sanction that had not been used in the United States since the American Revolution. Similar laws are now found in most states, particularly to deal with trafficking in controlled substances and organized crime.

forfeiture

Seizure by the government of property and other assets derived from or used in criminal activity.

Forfeiture is seizure by the government of property and other assets derived from or used in criminal activity. Assets seized by federal and state agencies through forfeiture can be quite considerable. For example, the Drug Enforcement Administration alone seizes assets (including cash, real estate, vehicles, vessels, and airplanes) valued at more than $1 billion annually (BJS, 1992. *Drugs, Crime, and the Justice System*:156). However, concern has been raised about the excessive use of this sanction, since forfeited assets often go into the budget of the law enforcement agency taking the action (Blumenson and Nilsen, 1998).

In a 1993 opinion, the Supreme Court ruled that the Eighth Amendment's ban on excessive fines requires that the seriousness of the offense be related to the property that is taken (*Austin v. U.S.*, 1993). The ruling places limits on the government's ability to seize property and invites the judiciary to monitor the government's forfeiture activities when convicted offenders challenge them.

Critics argue that ownership of the seized property is often unclear. For example, in Hartford, Connecticut, a woman's home was seized because her grandson, unbeknownst to her, was using it as a base for selling drugs.

CHECKPOINT

9. Distinguish between fines, restitution, and forfeiture.
10. What are some of the problems of implementing these sanctions?

Intermediate Sanctions Administered in the Community

One basic argument for intermediate sanctions is that probation, as traditionally practiced, is inadequate for the large numbers of offenders whom probation officers must supervise today. Probation leaders have responded to this criticism by developing new intermediate sanction programs and expanding old ones. Here we examine four: home confinement, community service, day reporting centers, and intensive supervision probation.

Home Confinement

With the increase in prison crowding and technological innovations that provide for electronic monitoring, **home confinement**, in which convicted offenders must remain at home during specific periods, has gained attention. Offenders under home confinement (often called "house arrest") may face other restrictions, such as strictly monitored curfews and check-in times as well as the usual probation rules on alcohol and drugs. Some offenders are allowed to go to a place of employment, education, or treatment during the day but must return to their homes by a specified hour.

home confinement

A sentence requiring the offender to remain inside his or her home during specified periods.

Home confinement has the advantage of flexibility because it can be used as a sole sanction or in combination with other penalties. It can be imposed at almost any point in the criminal justice process: during the pretrial period, after a short term in jail or prison, or as a condition of probation or parole (Renzema, 1992:41). In addition, home confinement relieves the government of the responsibility to provide the offender with food, clothing, and housing, as it must do in prisons. Home confinement programs have grown and proliferated. Florida, for example, has more than 13,000 offenders under this type of supervision (Blomberg, Bales, and Reed, 1993).

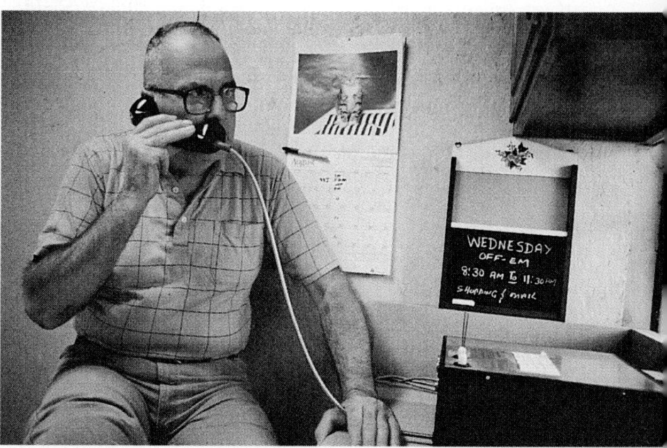

Larry Ingles, given a one-year sentence of home confinement for DWI, answers his electronic monitoring call. Failure to answer the telephone within three minutes may result in revocation of probation.

The development of electronic monitoring equipment to check on an offender's whereabouts has made home confinement an enforceable sentencing option (Baumer and Mendelsohn, 1992:54). Reliable estimates of the number of offenders currently being monitored are difficult to obtain because manufacturers of the equipment consider this confidential information. However, the best estimates are that about 70,000 people are being monitored at any given time (Vaughan, 1994:4).

Despite favorable publicity, certain legal, technical, and correctional issues must be addressed before home confinement with electronic monitoring can become a standard punishment. *First*, some criminal justice scholars question its constitutionality: monitoring may violate the Fourth Amendment's protection against unreasonable searches and seizures. The issue is a clash between the constitutionally protected reasonable expectation of privacy and the invasion of one's home by surveillance devices. *Second*, technical problems with the monitoring devices are still extensive, often giving erroneous reports that the offender is home. *Third*, failure rates may prove to be high. Being one's own warden is difficult, and visits by former criminal associates and other enticements may become problematic for many offenders (Renzema, 1992:41). Some observers believe that four months of full-time monitoring is about the limit before a violation will occur (Clear and Braga, 1995:435).

Community Service

A **community service** sentence requires the offender to perform a certain amount of unpaid labor in the community. Community service may take a variety of forms, including assisting in social service agencies, cleaning parks and roadsides, and assisting the poor. The sentence specifies the number of hours to be worked and usually requires supervision by a probation officer. Community service can be tailored to the skills and abilities of offenders. For example, less-educated offenders might pick up litter along the highway, while those with schooling may teach reading in evening literacy classes. Many judges order community service when an

community service

A sentence requiring the offender to perform a certain amount of unpaid labor in the community.

offender obviously cannot pay a fine. The offender's effort to make reparation to the community offended by the crime also has symbolic value.

Although community service has many supporters, some labor unions and workers criticize it for possibly taking jobs away from law-abiding citizens. In addition, some experts believe that if community service is the only sanction, it may be too mild a punishment, especially for upper-class and white-collar criminals (McDonald, 1986).

Day Reporting Centers

day reporting center

A community correctional center where an offender reports each day to comply with elements of a sentence.

Day reporting centers—community correctional centers to which the offender must report each day to carry out elements of the sentence—are another option in a number of states (Parent, 1990). Designed to ensure that probationers with employment and treatment stipulations attached to their sentences are followed, these centers also increase the likelihood that probation supervision will be considered credible by offenders and the general public.

Most day reporting centers incorporate multiple correctional methods. For example, in some centers offenders are required to be in the facility for eight hours or to report for drug urine checks before going to work. Centers that have a rehabilitation component carry out drug and alcohol treatment, literacy programs, and job searches. Others provide contact levels equal to or greater than intensive supervision programs (Diggs and Peiper, 1994:9-13).

Most of these programs have not yet been formally evaluated. In determining success with regard to recidivism, it is important to examine who is being treated. If such centers are used only for selected offenders with a low risk of returning to crime, it will be difficult to know whether the centers themselves are effective.

CHECKPOINT

11. What are some of the problems associated with home confinement?
12. What goes on at a day reporting center?

Intensive Supervision Probation

intensive supervision probation (ISP)

Probation granted under conditions of strict reporting to a probation officer with a limited caseload.

Intensive supervision probation (ISP) has been presented as a means of dealing in the community with offenders who need greater restrictions than traditional programs can provide. Jurisdictions in every state have programs to intensively supervise such offenders. Intensive supervision probation uses probation as an intermediate form of punishment by imposing conditions of strict and frequent reporting to a probation officer who has a limited caseload. ISP programs are of two general types: probation diversion and institutional diversion.

Probation diversion puts offenders thought to be too risky for routine supervision under intensive surveillance. Institutional diversion selects low-risk offenders sentenced to prison and provides supervision for them in the community (Clear and Braga, 1995:429). It is believed that daily contact between the probationer and the probation officer may cut rearrest rates and help the offender obtain treatment services in the community. Offenders have incentives to obey rules, knowing that they must meet with their probation officers daily and in some cases must speak with them even more frequently. Additional restrictions—curfews, electronic monitoring, drug and alcohol testing—are often imposed on offenders.

ISP programs have been called "old style" probation because each officer has only twenty clients and frequent face-to-face contacts are required. But questions have been raised about how much of a difference constant surveillance can make to probationers with numerous problems. Such offenders frequently need help to get a job, counseling to deal with emotional and family situations, and a variety of support systems to avoid drug or alcohol problems that may have contributed to their criminality. Yet ISP may be a way of getting the large number of felons who are drug addicted into treatment (Gendreau, Cullen, and Bonta, 1994).

ISP has become popular among probation administrators, judges, and prosecutors because it presents a "tough" image of community supervision and addresses the problem of prison crowding. Most programs require a specific number of monthly contacts with officers; performance of community service; curfews; drug and alcohol abuse testing; and referral to appropriate job training, education, or treatment programs.

Observers have warned that ISP is not a "cure" for the rising costs and other problems facing corrections systems. Ironically, ISP can also increase the number of probationers sent to prison. All evaluations of ISP find that, probably because of the closer contact with clients, probation officers uncover more violations of rules than they do in regular probation. Therefore, ISP programs often have higher failure rates than regular probation, even though their clients produce fewer arrests (Tonry and Lynch, 1996:116).

Another surprising finding is that when given the option of serving prison terms or participating in ISP, many offenders have chosen prison. In New Jersey, 15 percent of offenders withdrew their applications for ISP once they learned the conditions and requirements. Similarly, when offenders in Marion County, Oregon, were asked if they would participate in ISP, one-third chose prison instead (Petersilia, 1990b:24). Apparently some offenders would rather spend a short time in prison, where conditions differ little from their accustomed life, to a longer period under demanding conditions in the community. To these offenders ISP does not represent freedom because it is so intrusive and the risk of revocation is perceived as high.

Despite problems and continuing questions about its effectiveness, ISP has rejuvenated probation. Some of the most effective offender supervision is being carried out by these programs (Clear and Hardyman, 1990:42). As we noted in our discussion of regular probation, the size of a probation officer's caseload, within reasonable limits, is often less important in preventing recidivism than the quality of supervision and assistance provided to probationers. If ISP is properly implemented, it may improve the quality of supervision and services that foster success for more kinds of offenders.

CHECKPOINT

13. How does intensive supervision probation differ from traditional probation?

Intermediate Sanctions Administered in Institutions and the Community

Among the most publicized intermediate sanctions are the **boot camps** now operated by thirty states and the Federal Bureau of Prisons (MacKenzie, 1994). Often referred to as **shock incarceration**, these programs vary, but all are based on the

boot camp/shock incarceration

A short-term institutional sentence, usually followed by probation, that puts the offender through a physical regimen designed to develop discipline and respect for authority.

belief that young offenders can be "shocked" out of their criminal ways. Boot camps put offenders through a thirty- to ninety-day physical regimen designed to develop discipline and respect for authority. Like the Marine Corps, most programs emphasize a spit-and-polish environment and keep offenders in a disciplined and demanding routine that seeks ultimately to built self-esteem. Most camps also include education, job training programs, and other rehabilitation services. On successful completion of the program, offenders are released to the community. At this point probation officers take over, and the conditions of the sentence are imposed.

Military-type drilling is part of the regimen at most boot camps such as at this Federal Intensive Confinement Center for Women in Bryan, Texas. Evaluations of boot camps have faded the initial optimism about this approach.

Evaluations of boot camp programs have faded the initial optimism about the approach (Tonry, 1996:108-114). Critics suggest that the emphasis on physical training ignores young offenders' real problems. Some point out that, like the military, boot camp builds esprit de corps and solidarity, characteristics that have the potential for improving the leadership qualities of the young offender and therefore actually enhancing a criminal career. In addition, a study of offenders released from Louisiana boot camps revealed that 37 percent were arrested at least once during their first year of freedom, compared to 25.7 percent of parolees (*Newsweek*, February 21, 1994, p. 26). However, a multistate evaluation found lower rates of recidivism in states with a strong rehabilitative emphasis (MacKenzie, 1994:16). It has also been found that, like intensive supervision probation, boot camps do not automatically reduce prison crowding (MacKenzie, 1995; MacKenzie and Piquero, 1994).

Defenders of boot camps argue that the camps are accomplishing their goals, but that education and employment opportunities are lacking back in the participants' inner-city communities. Because boot camps are very popular with the public, which imagines that strict discipline and harsh conditions will instill positive attitudes in young offenders, such camps are likely to continue operating whether or not they are more effective than probation or prison.

CHECKPOINT

14. What are some typical activities at a boot camp?

Implementing Intermediate Sanctions

Although the use of intermediate sanctions has spread rapidly, three major questions have emerged about their implementation: (1) Which agencies should implement the sanctions? (2) Which offenders should be admitted to these programs? (3) Will the "community corrections net" widen as a result of these policies so that more people will come under correctional supervision?

Administrative politics is an ongoing factor in corrections, as in any public service organization. In many states, agencies compete for the additional funding needed to run the programs. The traditional agencies of community corrections, such as probation offices, could receive the funding, or the new programs could be contracted out to nonprofit organizations. Probation organizations argue that they know the field, have the experienced staff, and—given the additional

CLOSE-UP

After Boot Camp, a Harder Discipline

Nelson Colon misses waking up to the blast of reveille. He sometimes yearns for those sixteen-hour days filled with military drills and nine-mile runs. He even thinks fondly of the surly drill instructors who shouted in his face.

During his four months at New Jersey's boot camp, Mr. Colon adapted to the rigors of military life with little difficulty. He says it was a lot easier than what he faces now. He is back in his old neighborhood, trying to stay away from old friends and old ways.

So far, Mr. Colon, 18, has managed to stay out of trouble since he graduated with the camp's first class of twenty cadets in June. Yet each day, he said, he fears he will be pulled back onto the corner, only two blocks away, where he was first arrested for selling drugs at age 15.

New Jersey's program includes a "stabilization and reintegration" component that follows boot camp graduation. This includes intensive supervision for up to eighteen months and some help getting back into school and finding a job.

Even with that support, eleven of the fifty-one cadets who graduated from New Jersey's three boot camp classes in June are back in jail. Another two are missing.

A 10 P.M. curfew helps keep Mr. Colon off the streets. His parole officer checks in with him almost daily, sometimes stopping by at 11 to make sure he is inside. He is enrolling in night classes to help him earn his high school equivalency certificate, and he plans on attending Narcotics Anonymous meetings.

His biggest problems are the same ones that tens of thousands of Camden residents confront daily. Camden's unemployment rate exceeds 20 percent. There are few jobs in this troubled city, particularly for young men who have dropped out of high school. Mr. Colon has found work as a stock clerk in a sneaker store, but it is miles away at a shopping center on a busy highway, and he has no transportation there.

Selling drugs paid a lot more than stacking shoe boxes and did not require commuting. Mr. Colon says he pushes those thoughts of easy money out of his head and tries to remember what the boot camp's drill instructors told him over and over again.

"They used to tell us, 'It's up to you.' You have to have self-accountability. You have to be reliable for your own actions, not because some person wanted you to do it. They taught us not to follow, to lead. That was one of the most important things."

Mr. Colon said his immediate goal was to find a job that he could get to more easily and then save enough to get as far away from Camden as possible. "I want to get out of here," he said.

"The people's mentality here is real petty. Life isn't nothing to them. The other night, they killed one of the guys I grew up with. They shot him a couple of times. My old friends came around and knocked on my door at one o'clock in the morning to tell me." He said it was his eighth childhood friend to die.

SOURCE: Condensed from Jennifer Preston, *New York Times*, September 3, 1995, p. B1.

resources—could do an excellent job. They correctly point out that a great many offenders sentenced to intermediate sanctions are also on probation. Critics of giving this role to probation services argue that the established agencies are not receptive to innovation. They say that probation agencies place a high priority on the traditional supervision function and would not actively help clients solve their problems.

The different types of offenders who are given intermediate sanctions give rise to a second issue in the implementation debate. One school of thought focuses on the seriousness of the offense and the other on the problems of the offender. If offenders are categorized by the seriousness of their offenses, they may be given such close supervision that they will not be able to abide by the sentence. Sanctions for serious offenders may accumulate to include, for example, probation, drug testing, addiction treatment, and home confinement (Blomberg and Lucken, 1993). As the number of sentencing conditions is increased, even the most willing probationer finds it hard to fulfill every one of them.

Some agencies want to accept into their intermediate sanctions program only those offenders who *will* succeed. These agencies are concerned about their success ratio, especially because of threats to future funding if the program does not reduce recidivism. Critics point out that this strategy leads to "creaming," taking the most promising offenders and leaving those with worse problems to traditional sanctions.

net widening

Process in which the new sentencing options increase rather than reduce control over the offenders' lives.

The third issue concerns **net widening**, a process in which the sanction increases rather than reduces the control over the offender's life. This can occur when a judge imposes a *more* intrusive sentence than usual. For example, rather than merely giving an offender probation, the judge might also require that the offender perform community service. Critics argue that the intermediate sanction reforms have created

- Wider nets. Intermediate sanctions increase the proportion of individuals in society whose behavior is regulated or controlled by the state.
- Stronger nets. Intermediate sanctions augment the state's capacity to control individuals by intensifying the state's intervention powers.
- Different nets. Intermediate sanctions transfer or create jurisdictional authority from one agency or control system to another. (Austin and Krisberg, 1982)

The creation of intermediate sanctions has been a major development in corrections. These sanctions have been advocated as a less-costly alternative to incarceration and a more effective alternative to probation. But how have they been working? Michael Tonry and Mary Lynch have written the discouraging news that "few such programs have diverted large numbers of offenders from prison, saved public monies or prison beds, or reduced recidivism rates" (Tonry and Lynch, 1996:99). With incarceration rates still at record highs and probation caseloads increasing, intermediate sanctions will probably play a major role in corrections as we enter the new century. However, correctional reform has always had its limitations, and intermediate sanctions may not achieve the goals of their advocates (Cullen, Wright, and Applegate, 1996:69).

CHECKPOINT

15. What are three problems in the implementation of intermediate sanctions?

COMMUNITY CORRECTIONS: APPROACHING THE TWENTY-FIRST CENTURY

In January 1997 there were 3.9 million Americans under community supervision. Since 1990 the number of offenders has increased 3.3 percent each year, and the total is now 250 percent greater than in 1980 (BJS, 1997. Press release, June 30). Yet despite this tremendous growth, community corrections often lacks public support. Intermediate sanctions and other forms of community corrections suffer from the image of being "soft on crime." As a result, some localities provide resources for traditional criminal justice and human services agencies but not for community corrections.

Community corrections also faces the reality that offenders today require closer supervision than those formerly placed on probation. The crimes, criminal records, and drug problems of contemporary offenders are often worse than those of lawbreakers of earlier eras. In New York, for example, 77 percent of probationers are convicted felons, and about a third of these have been found guilty of violent crimes. Yet these people are supervised by probation officers whose caseloads number in the hundreds (Petersilia, 1993:61). Obviously, such officers cannot provide effective supervision and services to all their probationers.

Community corrections is burdened by even greater caseload pressures as we approach the twenty-first century. With responsibility for about three-fourths of all offenders under correctional supervision, community corrections needs an infusion of additional resources. The public support that is essential will be forthcoming only if citizens believe that offenders are being given appropriate punishments. Joan Petersilia has argued that too many crime control policies are focused solely on the short term. She believes that long-term investments in community corrections will pay off for both the offender and the community (Petersilia, 1995). But before new policies can be put in place, there must be a shift of public opinion in support of community corrections.

Summary

- Community supervision through probation and intermediate sanctions is a growing part of the criminal justice system.
- Probation is imposed on about two-thirds of offenders. Persons with this sentence live in the community according to conditions set by the judge and under the supervision of a probation officer.
- Intermediate sanctions are designed as punishments that are more restrictive than probation and less restrictive than prison.
- The range of intermediate sanctions available allows judges to design sentences that incorporate one or more of the punishments.
- Some intermediate sanctions are implemented by courts (fines, restitution, forfeiture), others in the community (home confinement, community service, day reporting centers, intensive supervision probation), and in institutions and the community (boot camps).
- Increasingly, electronic monitoring is being used along with many community sanctions.
- As we approach the twenty-first century, the use of community corrections is expected to grow, in spite of the problems of implementing these programs.

Questions for Review

1. What is the aim of community corrections?
2. What is the nature of probation, and how is it organized?
3. What is the purpose of intermediate sanctions?
4. What are the primary forms of intermediate sanctions?
5. Why is net widening a concern?

ANSWERS TO CHECKPOINTS

1. Many offenders' crimes and records do not warrant incarceration; community supervision is cheaper; recidivism rates for those supervised in the community are no higher than for those who serve prison time; incarceration is more destructive to the offender and society.
2. A Boston bootmaker who became the first probation officer by taking responsibility for a convicted offender before sentencing.
3. Risk control.
4. To assist judges by preparing presentence reports and to provide assistance and supervision to offenders in the community.
5. An arrest for a new offense and a technical violation of the conditions of probation that were set by the judge.
6. Right to a preliminary and final hearing, right to cross-examine witnesses, right to notice of the alleged violations, and right to a written report of the proceedings. Right to counsel is determined on a case-by-case basis.
7. Need for sentencing options that are more restrictive than simple probation, that match the severity of the offense and the characteristics of the offender, and that still protect the community; prison overcrowding; dissatisfaction with traditional probation.

8. A range of punishments that vary in levels of intrusiveness and control over the offender.
9. A fine is a sum of money paid to the government by the offender. Restitution is a sum of money paid to the victim by the offender. Forfeiture is the taking by the government of assets derived from or used in criminal activity.
10. Most offenders are poor and cannot pay, offenders may commit additional crimes to pay monetary sanctions, and resources are not allocated by the courts for collection and enforcement.
11. Home confinement may violate the Fourth Amendment's protections against unreasonable searches, monitoring devices have technical problems, and failure rates are high because offenders can't tolerate home confinement for very long.
12. Drug and alcohol treatment, job searches, educational programs, and sometimes just offenders reporting in.
13. In ISP the offender is required to make more strict and frequent reporting to an officer with a much smaller caseload.
14. Boot camp activities are maintaining a spit-and-polish environment and strict discipline; involvement in physical activity; and educational, vocational, and rehabilitative services.
15. Which agencies should implement the sanctions? Which offenders should be admitted to these programs? Will the "community corrections net" be widened?

Chapter 13

Incarceration and Prison Society

The Modern Prison: Legacy of the Past

Goals of Incarceration

Prison Organization
- *Three Lines of Command*
- *The Importance of Management*

Governing a Society of Captives
- *The Limits of Total Power*
- *Rewards and Punishments*
- *Gaining Cooperation: Exchange Relationships*
- *Inmate Leadership*
- *The Challenge of Governing Prisons*

Correctional Officers: The Linchpin of Management
- *The Officer's Role*
- *Recruitment of Officers*

The Convict World
- *Adaptive Roles*
- *The Prison Economy*

Women in Prison
- *Social Relationships*
- *Male and Female Subcultures Compared*
- *Programs and the Female Role*
- *Medical Services*
- *Mothers and Their Children*

Prison Programs
- *Classification of Prisoners*
- *Educational Programs*
- *Vocational Education*
- *Prison Industries*
- *Rehabilitative Programs*

Violence in Prison
- *Assaultive Behavior and Inmate Characteristics*
- *Prisoner-Prisoner Violence*
- *Prisoner-Officer Violence*
- *Officer-Prisoner Violence*
- *Decreasing Prison Violence*

Prisoners' Rights
- *First Amendment*
- *Fourth Amendment*
- *Eighth Amendment*
- *Fourteenth Amendment*
- *Impact of the Prisoners' Rights Movement*

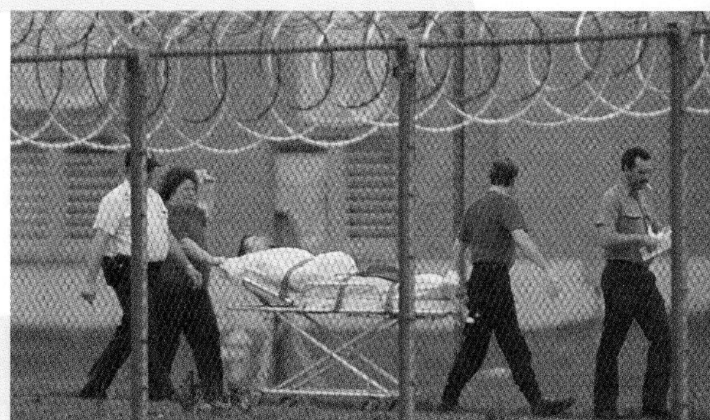

ON EASTER SUNDAY in 1993 a fight broke out in the recreation yard at the Southern Ohio Correction Facility in Lucasville, a "supermax" prison reserved for the most violent and incorrigible offenders. Within minutes the fight grew into a full-scale riot. Eight correctional officers were taken hostage by the 450 prisoners who barricaded themselves inside Cellblock L. The prisoners held their ground—and their hostages—for more than a week. During the uprising, prisoners murdered others whom they regarded as "snitches." The bodies of six inmates were dumped in the recreation yard.

When the prisoners threatened to kill one of the hostages, a spokesperson for the state said it was a "standard threat they've been issuing." Shortly thereafter, correctional officer Robert Vallandingham was murdered. According to another hostage, the prisoners killed the officer because they were angry that their threats were not being taken seriously. Eventually, the prisoners negotiated their surrender, the remaining hostages were released, and the state began prosecuting some prisoners on criminal charges stemming from the riot and murders.

These periodic eruptions of prison violence bring public attention to life behind bars. Maximum security prisons like Lucasville are not the only correctional institutions that simmer with trouble. Many others—even most—experience the racial conflict, gangs, allegations of brutality, and inmate violence that can bring tensions inside to the boiling point. Violence is relatively infrequent only because most institutions manage to keep the lid on the cauldron.

In this chapter we examine incarceration and prison society. We focus on such issues as the goals of incarceration, the challenges of management, and the inmate's experience while living in prison. We will also look at violence in prison and the policies and programs that may keep correctional institutions from boiling over.

THE MODERN PRISON: LEGACY OF THE PAST

Questions for Inquiry

How is a prison organized?

What are the assumptions of each model of incarceration?

How is a prison governed?

What is the role of correctional officers?

What is it like to be in prison?

What programs are available to prisoners?

What constitutional rights do prisoners have?

American correctional institutions have always been more varied than movies or novels portray them. Fictional depictions of prison life are typically set in a fortress, the "big house"—the maximum security prisons where the inmates are tough and the guards are just as tough or tougher. Although big houses predominated in much of the country during the first half of the twentieth century, many prisons were built on another model. In the South, for instance, prisoners worked outside at farm labor, and the massive walled structures were not so common.

The typical big house of the 1940s and 1950s was a walled prison with large, tiered cellblocks, a yard, shops, and industrial workshops. The prisoners, in an average population of about 2,500 per institution, came from both urban and rural areas, were usually poor, and outside the South they were predominantly white. Prison society was isolated; access to visitors, mail, and other communication was restricted. Prisoners' days were strictly structured, with rules enforced by the guards. There was a basic division between inmates and staff; rank was observed and discipline maintained. In the big house, few treatment programs existed; custody was the primary goal.

During the 1960s and early 1970s, when the rehabilitation model was dominant, many states built new prisons and converted others into "correctional institutions." Treatment programs administered by counselors and teachers became a major part of prison life, although the institutions actually continued to give priority to the custody goals of security, discipline, and order.

During the past thirty years, as the population of the United States has changed, so has the prison population. There has been a major increase in the number of African-American and Hispanic-American inmates. More inmates come from urban areas, and more have been convicted of drug-related and violent offenses. Former street gangs, often organized along racial lines, today regroup inside prisons, and in many institutions they have raised the level of violence.

As discussed in Chapter 11, the population of state and federal prisons has more than doubled in the last decade (BJS, 1998. *Bulletin*, January). This increase has led to greater tensions inside overcrowded institutions. Although today's correctional administrators seek to provide humane incarceration, they must struggle with limited resources and shortages of cell space. Thus, the modern prison faces many of the difficult problems that confront other parts of the criminal justice system: racial conflicts, legal issues, limited resources, and growing populations. Despite these challenges, can prisons still achieve their objectives? The answer to this question depends, in part, on how we define the goals of incarceration.

CHECKPOINT

1. How does today's prison differ from the "big house" of the past?

(Answers are at the end of the chapter.)

GOALS OF INCARCERATION

Security is what most people consider the dominant purpose of a prison, given the nature of the inmates and the need to protect the staff and the community. High walls, barbed-wire fences, searches, checkpoints, and regular counts of inmates serve the security function: few inmates escape. Prisons are expected to be impersonal, quasi-military institutions where strict discipline, minimal levels of amenities, and restrictions on freedom carry out the punishment of criminals.

Some legislators have argued that weight lifting, basketball, and other prison physical exercise activities are frills that should be restricted. Wardens, however, believe that these activities are important means of keeping prisoners busy and reducing tensions.

Three models of incarceration have been prominent since the early 1940s: custodial, rehabilitation, and reintegration. Each is associated with one style of institutional organization and emphasizes the goal of incarceration as dictated by public policies.

1. The **custodial model** is based on the assumption that prisoners have been incarcerated for the purpose of incapacitation, deterrence, or retribution. It emphasizes security, discipline, and order and subordinates the prisoner to the authority of the warden. Discipline is strict, and most aspects of behavior are regulated. This model was prevalent in corrections before World War II, and it dominates most maximum security institutions today.
2. The **rehabilitation model**, developed during the 1950s, emphasizes treatment programs designed to reform the offender. According to this model, security and housekeeping activities are viewed primarily as preconditions for rehabilitative efforts. As all aspects of the organization should be directed toward rehabilitation, professional treatment specialists have a higher status than other employees. Since the rethinking of the rehabilitation goal in the 1970s, treatment programs still exist in most institutions, but very few prisons conform to this model today.
3. The **reintegration model** is linked to the structures and goals of community corrections. This model emphasizes maintaining the offenders' ties to family and community as a method of reform, recognizing that they will be returning to society. Prisons that have adopted the reintegration model gradually give inmates greater freedom and responsibility during their confinement, moving them to halfway houses or work release programs before placing them under community supervision.

Correctional institutions that conform to each of these models can be found, but most prisons are mainly custodial. Nevertheless, treatment programs do exist, and because almost all inmates return to society at some point, even the most custodial institutions must prepare them for their reintegration.

We ask a lot of our prisons. As Charles Logan notes, "We ask them to correct the incorrigible, rehabilitate the wretched, deter the determined, restrain the dangerous, and punish the wicked" (Logan, 1993:5). Prisons are expected to pursue many different and often incompatible goals, so as institutions they are almost doomed to fail. Logan believes that the basic purpose of imprisonment is to punish offenders fairly and justly through lengths of confinement proportional to the seriousness of their crimes. If we accept this as the purpose, there are implications for the organization and management of prisons that must be addressed.

custodial model

A model of incarceration that emphasizes security, discipline, and order.

rehabilitation model

A model of corrections that emphasizes the provision of treatment programs designed to reform the offender.

reintegration model

A model of a correctional institution that emphasizes maintaining the offender's ties to family and community as a method of reform, recognizing that the offender will be returning to society.

CHECKPOINT

2. What three models of prison have been predominant since the 1940s?

But I continue to like the mayoral analogy, because prisons must provide almost all of the goods and services a small town must make available to those who live and work there. These include the basics like the structure itself and heat, water, light, food, and clothing. Also, given the population living there, a large "police force"—corrections officers and their supervisors—is needed.

The services in prisons that many people don't think about are education, religion, leisure activities, a general and law library, and programs for change—alcohol and drug counseling and cognitive programs that address criminal thinking. Prisoner organizations that offer the opportunity to engage in prosocial activities also need to be offered. If we don't give prisoners something constructive to do with their free time, they'll still find something to do, and given their past choices there is no reason to think that that "something" will be positive!

While discussions of prison operations tend to focus on the prisoners, the most difficult decisions I make have to do with staff. The selection and promotion of qualified and ethical staff is critical, of course, but we usually have an employment record to assist with those decisions. The much more difficult task is in dealing with staff members who are dishonest, who willfully violate the rules, or who simply prove to be unqualified. I've been a warden fifteen years as I write this, so I can speak from hard experience. Staff members have resigned in lieu of the discipline I would otherwise have had to impose. I have fired a few others for overfamiliarity with prisoners, excessive use of force, or involvement with drugs or alcohol. Prison staff function as a close-knit family, so it is very painful to remove personnel. You are not only letting that person go, but you're affecting the lives of co-workers and the employee's family. Worst of all, the offenders for whom we're supposed to be role models always discover the details of the dismissal and use that information to support their flawed belief that "everyone is dishonest; we just got caught." Nevertheless, the integrity of the system requires that we discharge major violators to demonstrate to staff and prisoners that irresponsible behavior has serious consequences. So it must be done, but doing it is a more difficult part of the job than the very long hours I seem to have to put in to stay on top of things. The hours matter little when the work is as interesting and exciting as that provided by this career.

WORK*Perspective*

The custodial employees are the most numerous. They are normally organized along military lines, from warden to captain to officer, with accompanying pay differentials down the chain of command. The professional personnel associated with other prison functions, such as industry supervisors, clinicians, and teachers, are not part of the custodial structure and have little in common with its staff. All employees are responsible to the warden, but the treatment personnel and the civilian supervisors of the workshops have their own salary scales and titles. In the Workperspective Warden Pamela K. Withrow describes her position as similar to being the mayor of a small town.

The multiple goals and separate employee lines of command often mean the administration of prisons is marked by ambiguity and conflict. There is ambiguity in the often-contradictory goals imposed on prisons, as noted by Logan. Conflict between different segments of staff (custodial versus treatment, for instance), as well as between staff and inmates, presents significant challenges for administrators.

So how do prisons really function? The U.S. prison may not conform to the ideal goals of corrections, and the formal organization of staff and inmates may bear little resemblance to the ongoing reality of the informal relations among them, but somehow order *is* kept and a routine is followed. Next, we discuss how that happens.

The Importance of Management

One of the amazing facts about prisons is that most of the time they work. Order is maintained and activities are carried out, despite the wide variation in administrative policies and practices at different prisons.

Although most prisons have similar organizational structures, management styles vary. John DiIulio studied the management of selected prisons in Texas, California, and Michigan (DiIulio, 1987), finding differences in leadership philosophy, political environment, and administrative style of individual wardens. He believes that prisons can be governed, violence can be minimized, and services can be provided to inmates if correctional managers provide proper leadership.

DiIulio suggests that prison systems perform well if managers work competently with the political and other pressures that make for administrative uncertainty and instability. In particular, he points to the success of wardens whose management style can be characterized as "management by walking around." This means that wardens must be "hands-on" and proactive, paying close attention to details, rather than waiting for problems to arise. They must know what is going on inside, yet also recognize the need for outside support. This means they are not strangers either in the cellblocks or in the aisles of state legislatures (DiIulio, 1987:242; 1993b:438). From this perspective, making prisons work is a function of leadership and the application of management principles. But how does one govern a society of captives?

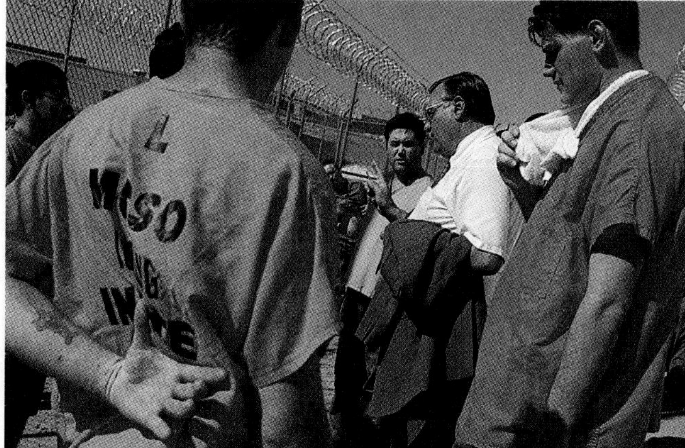

"Management by Walking Around" is a style that successful wardens have adopted. This means that they must be "hands-on" and proactive, paying close attention to details, rather than waiting for problems to arise.

CHECKPOINT

3. How are prisons different from other organizations in society?
4. What are the multiple goals pursued in today's prisons?
5. Which management style does DiIulio believe is most effective?

GOVERNING A SOCIETY OF CAPTIVES

Much of the public believes that prisons are operated in an authoritarian manner. In such a society, correctional officers *give* orders and inmates *follow* orders. Strictly enforced rules specify what the captives may and may not do. Staff members have the right to grant rewards and to inflict punishment. In theory, any inmate who does not follow the rules could be placed in solitary confinement. Because the officers have a monopoly on the legal means of enforcing rules and can be backed up by the state police and the National Guard if necessary, many people believe that there should be no ambiguity about how the prison is run.

If we accept the premise that well-run prisons are important for the inmates, staff, and society, what are the problems that must be faced and solved by correctional administrators? Four features distinguish the governing of prisons from the administration of other public institutions: (1) the limits of total power, (2) the limited rewards and punishments that officials can use, (3) the exchange relations between correctional officers and inmates, and (4) the strength of inmate leadership. As we review each of these, we should also consider what administrative and leadership styles can best be used by corrections managers to achieve the goal of a prison that is safe, humane, and able to serve the needs of the inmates.

The Limits of Total Power

Imagine a prison society populated by hostile and uncooperative captives ruled by force, one in which prisoners can be legally isolated from one another, physically abused until they cooperate, and put under continuous surveillance. Theoretically, such a prison society is possible. In reality, however, the power of correctional officers is limited, because many prisoners have little to lose by misbehaving, and officers are unarmed and have only limited ability to force compliance with rules. Perhaps more important, forcing people to do anything is basically inefficient and impractical as well, because the usual ratio of inmates to officers is 40 to 1 (Hepburn, 1985).

Rewards and Punishments

Because the use of physical coercion is permitted in few situations, corrections officials must gain compliance and maintain control through a limited system of rewards and punishments. For example, privileges such as allocations of good time, choice job assignments, and favorable parole reports may be offered in exchange for obedience. The reward system is defective, however, because most privileges are given to the inmate at the start of the sentence and are taken away only if rules are broken. Few additional rewards can be granted for progress or exceptional behavior, although a desired work assignment or transfer to the honor cellblock will induce some prisoners to maintain good behavior.

Punishments include denial of future good-time credits, loss of recreation or other privileges, and transfer to "administrative segregation" cells for major infractions or consistent misbehavior. One problem is that punishment for breaking the rules does not greatly change the prisoner's usual status. Because they are already deprived of many freedoms and valued goods—heterosexual relations, money, choice of clothing, and so on—inmates have little left to lose. Not allowing an inmate to attend a recreational period may not carry much weight. Moreover, there are legal limitations on the types of punishments that officials can impose.

Gaining Cooperation: Exchange Relationships

Correctional officers can obtain inmates' cooperation through the exchange relationships described in earlier chapters. The key officials in these exchanges are the housing-unit officers who work closely with the prisoners throughout the day in the cellblock, workshop, or recreation area. They count prisoners, sign passes, check groups of inmates as they come and go, and search for contraband. These are the minor details of an officer's eight-hour shift.

Although the formal rules require a social distance between officers and inmates, physical closeness makes them aware that each is dependent on the other. The officers need the cooperation of the prisoners so they will look good to their superiors, and the inmates depend on the guards to relax the rules or occasionally look the other way. For example, officers in a midwestern prison told Stan Stojkovic that flexibility in rule enforcement was especially important to the ability of prisoners to cope with their environment. As one officer said, "Phone calls are really important to guys in this place.... you cut off their calls and they get pissed. So what I do is give them a little extra and they are good to me." Yet the officers also told Stojkovic that they would be crazy to intervene to stop illicit sex or drug use (Stojkovic, 1990).

Correctional officers must be careful not to pay too high a price for the cooperation of their charges. Officers who establish sub-rosa, or secret, relationships can be manipulated by prisoners into smuggling contraband or committing other illegal acts. Officers are under pressure to work effectively with prisoners and may be blackmailed into doing illegitimate favors in return for cooperation. A dilemma that correctional officers frequently face is posed in A Question of Ethics.

Inmate Leadership

Some officials try to use inmate leaders to control other convicts. Inmate leaders have been "tested" over time so that they are neither pushed around by other inmates nor distrusted as stool pigeons. Because the staff can rely on them, they serve as the essential communications link between staff and inmates. Their ability to acquire inside information and gain access to higher officials brings inmate leaders the respect of other prisoners and special privileges from officials. In turn, they distribute these benefits to other prisoners, thus bolstering their own influence within the society. In practice, however, prison administrators of the big-house era were more successful at using inmate leaders to maintain order than today's administrators are. In most of today's institutions, prisoners are divided by race, ethnicity, age, and gang affiliation, so that no single leadership structure exists.

A Question of ETHICS

After three years of daily contact, correctional officer Bill MacLeod and Jack Douglas, who was serving a three- to five-year sentence, knew each other very well. They were both devoted to the Red Sox and the Celtics. Throughout the year they would chat about the fortunes of their teams and the outlook ahead. MacLeod got to know and like Douglas. They were about the same age and had come from similar backgrounds. Why they were now on opposite sides of the cell bars was something that MacLeod could not figure out.

One day Douglas called to MacLeod and said that he needed money because he had lost a bet gambling on the Red Sox. Douglas said that his wife would send him the money but that it couldn't come through the prison mail to him in cash. And a check or money order would show on his commissary account.

"The guy wants cash. If he doesn't get it, I'm dead." Douglas took a breath and then rushed on with his request. "Could you bring it in for me? She'll mail the money to you at home. You could just drop the envelope on my bed."

"You know the rules. No gambling and no money," said MacLeod.

"But I'm scared shitless. It will be no big deal for you and it will make all the difference for me. Come on, we've gotten along well all these years. I think of you as being different from those other officers."

What should MacLeod do? Is this kind of request likely to be a one-time occurrence with Douglas? What if MacLeod's sergeant finds out? What if other inmates learn about it?

The Challenge of Governing Prisons

The factors of total power, rewards and punishments, exchange relationships, and inmate leadership exist in every prison and must be managed. How they are managed greatly influences the quality of prison life. DiIulio's research challenges the common assumption of many correctional administrators that "the cons run the joint" (DiIulio, 1987). Instead, successful wardens have made their prisons "work" by applying management principles within the context of their own style of leadership. Prisons can be governed, violence can be minimized, and services can be provided to the inmates if correctional executives and wardens show leadership appropriate to the task. Governing prisons is an extraordinary challenge, but it can be and has been effectively accomplished.

CHECKPOINT

6. What four factors make the governing of prisons different from administering other public institutions?

CORRECTIONAL OFFICERS: THE LINCHPIN OF MANAGEMENT

A prison is supposed to simultaneously keep, use, and serve its inmates. The achievement of these goals depends heavily on the performance of its correctional officers. Their job isn't easy. Not only do they work long and difficult hours with a hostile client population, but their superiors expect them to do so with few resources or punishments at their disposal. Most of what they are expected to do must be accomplished by gaining and keeping the cooperation of the prisoners.

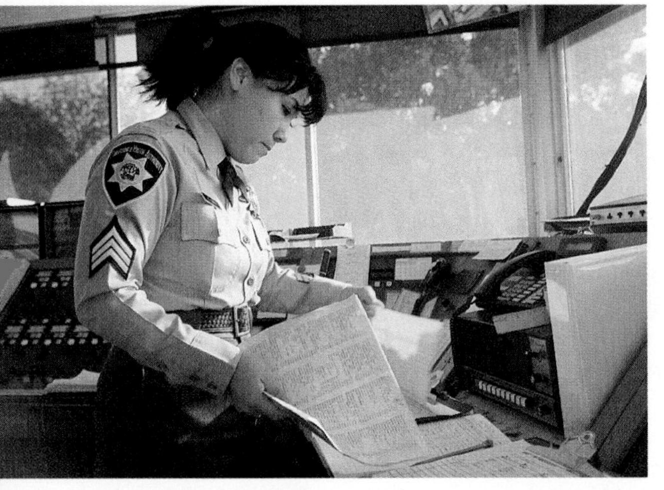

Increasing numbers of women have become correctional officers in prisons for males. What are the pluses and minuses of having women in these roles?

The Officer's Role

In the contemporary prison the officer is the crucial professional because he or she has the closest contact with the prisoners and is expected to perform a variety of tasks. Correctional officers are no longer responsible merely for "guarding." Instead, they are expected to counsel, supervise, protect, and process the inmates under their care. But the officer also works as a member of a complex bureaucratic organization and is expected to deal with clients impersonally and to follow formal procedures. Fulfilling these contradictory role expectations is difficult in itself, and the difficulty is exacerbated by the physical closeness of the officer and inmate over long periods. In the Workperspective Officer Karl Lewis uses his knowledge of prison society in making a difficult decision.

Recruitment of Officers

Employment as a correctional officer is not a glamorous, sought-after occupation. The work is thought to be boring, the pay is low, and career advancement is almost nonexistent. Studies have shown that one of the primary incentives for becoming involved in correctional work is the security that civil service status provides. In addition, prisons offer better employment options than other employers in the rural areas where most correctional facilities are located. Because correctional officers are recruited locally, most are rural and white, in contrast to the majority of prisoners, who come from urban areas and are often either African American or Hispanic American.

WORK*Perspective*

Karl G. Lewis
Classification Counselor

Connecticut Department of Correction

I was hired by the Department of Correction soon after completing my B.A. in English literature. I attended the academy and was assigned to the high-security unit at the Connecticut Correctional Institution–Cheshire as a classification officer. It was here that I began my criminal justice education, working with a wide variety of offenders, including those in the general population, punitive housing, and protective custody. After completing a year as a trainee, I was promoted to Correctional Rehabilitation Service Officer–I, which is a line classification officer with responsibility for determining the housing, programs, and work assignments of the inmates.

At the urging of the deputy warden I enrolled in the Master of Public Affairs program at the University of Connecticut. I was fortunate in that my graduate work, completed part-time, allowed me to study the position of criminal justice agencies in the web of government. This further enriched my professional experience. After a stint at a minimum-security prerelease facility, I was promoted to Classification Officer–Senior Grade. I was then transferred to the Connecticut Board of Parole as a case analyst, working directly with the board members in the hearing process. During an administrative reorganization I was reassigned to the high-security unit at Cheshire with expanded responsibilities commensurate with my experience.

Senior classification officers are part of a unit management team, often acting alternatively as a treatment or custody supervisor in the absence of the unit manager. I found the decisions I had to make as a custody supervisor to be the most difficult, and the most important, of my career.

When working with general-population, high-security inmates, custody supervisors commonly receive requests for transfer to the segregated housing unit known as "Protective Custody" (P.C.). One day in the summer of 1996, while I was monitoring a recreation period, an inmate asked to speak to me in private. I called him into the unit manager's office, and he told me that he wanted to "check in" to P.C. He said that he owed a debt to certain gang members over cigarettes. The inmate, who looked much younger than his 24 years, was unwilling to identify the parties who allegedly were threatening him, other than to give general details—for example, "the tall Spanish guy from the upper tier." This was understandable, because if he identified the perpetrators he risked being labeled a "snitch," which could lead to serious, even mortal consequences.

Although the inmate was agitated by the situation, I could not justify even temporary segregation given the lack of detail. However, if I sent him back to his own housing unit he might act in such a way as to be a danger to himself, staff, other inmates, or the orderly operation of the institution. As a precaution, I transferred the inmate to a different part of the facility where he would have no contact with his tormentors. This would give me time to investigate the situation.

It turned out that the inmate's story was a fabrication. In fact, he was in considerably more difficulty than he was willing to admit. Reviewing his criminal history I saw that he had been convicted of sexually assaulting a child in an adjoining state in the late 1980s. I also noted that he had had adjustment problems in other facilities, having twice requested, unsuccessfully, to be transferred to P.C. One of the department's intelligence officers learned that the sexual assault victim was the son of a high-ranking prison gang leader in the other state. It was therefore only a matter of time before an inmate at Cheshire found out who the young man was and he was marked as a target.

With this information I was able to justify a change of classification from general population to protective custody. Cheshire's 200-bed P.C. unit serves the entire correctional system and houses snitches, sexual offenders, and former Latin Kings and Aryan Brotherhood gang members. Divided into two units, inmates eat, recreate, and participate in programs only in Protective Custody—they have no contact with the general population. The inmate I placed in P.C. had eighteen to thirty-six months to go on a four-year definite sentence for a drug-related burglary. It is unlikely that he will leave P.C. until he is released.

WORK*Perspective*

The great increase in the prison population has brought a demand for more correctional officers. Salaries have been raised so that the yearly average entry-level pay runs between $16,000 in some southern and rural states to $29,000 in states such as Massachusetts and New Jersey (BJS, 1997. *Sourcebook*:94). Women officers are no longer restricted to working with female offenders, and the number of correctional officers from minority groups has increased dramatically.

Correctional officers are responsible for the smooth day-to-day functioning of prisons. As they deal with inmates, officers must understand the culture of the "convict world" and the ways prisoners adapt to their social and physical environment.

CHECKPOINT

7. Why are correctional officers called the "linchpin of management?"

THE CONVICT WORLD

In many ways, an American maximum security prison hosts a world and culture unto itself. As the Close-up reveals, entering prison is stressful because one does not know the traditions, norms, slang, and leadership structure of the convict society. Some members may choose to associate with only a few close friends; others form cliques along racial or "professional" lines. Still others may be the politicians of the convict society: they attempt to represent convict interests and distribute valued goods in return for support. Just as there is a social culture in the free world, there is a prisoner subculture on the "inside."

inmate code

The values and norms of the prison social system that define the inmate's idea of the model prisoner.

As in any society, the convict world has certain norms and values. Often described as the **inmate code**, these norms and values develop within the prison social system and help define the inmate's image of the model prisoner. For example, inmates should never inform on each other, pry into each other's affairs, run off at the mouth, or put another inmate on the spot. They must be tough and not trust the officers or the principles that the guards stand for. Further, guards are "hacks" or "screws"; the officials are wrong and the prisoners are right.

CLOSE-UP

One Man's Walk through Atlanta's Jungle

Michael G. Santos

I was not expecting to receive the southern hospitality for which Atlanta is famous when the bus turned into the penitentiary's large, circular drive, but neither did I expect to see a dozen uniformed prison guards—all carrying machine guns—surround the bus when it stopped. A month in transit already had passed by the time we made it to the U.S. Penitentiary (USP) in Atlanta, the institution that would hold me (along with over 2,000 other felons) until we were transferred to other prisons, we were released, or we were dead.

I left the jail in Tacoma, Washington, on the first of August, but I didn't see the huge gray walls that surround USP Atlanta until the first of September. That month was spent in a bus operated by the U.S. Marshal Service as it moved across the country, picking up federal prisoners in local jails and dropping them off at various Bureau of Prison facilities.

As I crossed the country, I listened to tales from numerous prisoners who sat beside me on the bus. There wasn't much to discuss except what was to come. Each of us was chained at the hands and feet. There were neither magazines to read nor music playing. Mostly people spoke about a riot that had taken place behind USP Atlanta's walls a few months earlier. A lot of the men had been to prison before, and Atlanta would be nothing new. Those prisoners only talked about reuniting with old friends, explaining prison routine, or sat like stone-cold statues waiting for what was to come. I'd never been confined before, so it was hard to tune out the stories that others were telling. While I was listening, though, I remember telling myself that I *would* survive this sentence. No matter what it took, I *would* survive.

I was in my early twenties, younger than perhaps every other prisoner on the bus. Pimples spotted my face as I began my term, but I was certain my black hair would be white by the time I finished. I had been sentenced to forty-five years by a U.S. District Court Judge in Tacoma on charges related to cocaine trafficking. I was expected to serve close to thirty years before release. It was hard then—just as it is hard now—to believe the sentence was real. The best thing I could do, I reasoned, was to stay to myself. I'd heard the same rumors that every suburban kid hears about prison. I was anxious about what was to come, but I was determined to make it out alive and with my mind intact. Now it was all to begin.

After the bus stopped, the guards began calling us off by last name and prison number. It is not easy to walk with a twelve-inch chain connected to each ankle and wrists bound to a chain that runs around the waist, but when my name was called, I managed to wobble through the bus's aisle, hop down the steps, and then begin the long march up the stairs leading to the fortress. As I was moving to the prison's doors, I remember glancing over my shoulder, knowing it would be the last time I'd see the world from the outside of prison walls for a long time.

Once inside the institution, the guards began unlocking my chains. About fifty other prisoners arrived with me that day, so the guards had plenty of chains to unlock, but their work didn't stop there. They also had to squeeze us through the dehumanizing admissions machine. The machine begins with photographs, fingerprints, and interrogations. Then comes the worst part, the strip search, where each prisoner stands before a prison official, naked, and responds to the scream "Lift up your arms in the air! Let me see the back of your hands! Run your fingers through your hair! Open your mouth! Stick your tongue out! Lift your balls! Turn around! Bend over! Spread your ass! Wider! Lift the bottom of your feet! Move on!" The strip search, I later learned, is a ritual Atlanta's officers inflict on prisoners every time they have contact with anyone from outside the walls and sometimes randomly as prisoners walk down the corridor.

There was a lot of hatred behind those walls. Walking through the prison must be something like walking through a jungle, I imagined, not knowing whether others perceive you as predator or prey, knowing that you must remain always alert, watching every step, knowing that the wrong step may be the one that sucks you into the quicksand. The tension is ever present; I felt it wrapped all over, under, and around me. I remember it bothering me that I didn't have enough hatred, because not hating in the jungle is a weakness. As the serpents slither, they spot that lack of hatred and salivate over a potential target.

Every prisoner despises confinement, but each must decide how he or she is going to do the time. Most of the men run in packs. They want the other prisoners either to run with them or run away from them. I wasn't interested in doing either. Instead of scheming on how I could become king of the jungle, I thought about ways that I could advance my release date. Earning academic credentials, keeping a clean record, and initiating projects that would benefit the communities both inside and outside of prison walls seemed the most promising goals for me to achieve. Yet working toward these goals was more dangerous than running with the pack; it didn't take me long to learn that prisoners running in herds will put forth more energy to cause others to lose than they will to win themselves. Prison is a twisted world, a menagerie.

I found that a highly structured schedule would not only move me closer to my goals, but also would limit potential conflicts inside the prison. There is a pecking order in every prison, and prisoners vying for attention don't want to see others cutting their own path. I saw that bullies generally look for weaker targets, so I began an exercise routine that would keep me physically strong. If I were strong, I figured, others would be more reluctant to try me. Through discipline, I found, I could develop physical strength. Yet I've never figured out how to develop the look of a killer, or the hatred off which that look feeds.

I don't know whether the strategies I have developed for doing time are right for everyone. But they are working for me. Still, I know that I may spend many more years in prison. The only fear I have—and as I'm working on my eighth year, it's still here—is that someone will try me and drag me into an altercation that may jeopardize my spotless disciplinary record. I've been successful in avoiding the ever-present quicksand on my walk through the jungle so far, but I know that on any given day something may throw me off balance or I may take a wrong step. And one wrong step in this jungle can drown me in quicksand, sucking me into the abysmal world of prison forever. That wrong step also could mean the loss of life, mine or someone else's.

In prison, more than anywhere else I know, understanding that some things are beyond an individual's sphere of control is vital. No matter how much preparation is made, the steel and concrete jungle is a dangerous place in which to live.

SOURCE: Written for this book by Michael G. Santos, currently finishing the eleventh year of a forty-five-year sentence for drug trafficking. He is now incarcerated at Federal Correctional Institution-Fort Dix, New Jersey. While in prison he has completed bachelor's and master's degrees. Friends have constructed a home page for Michael at www.halcyon.com//garyt/freedom/.

Some sociologists believe that the code emerges within the institution as a way to lessen the pain of imprisonment (Sykes, 1958); others believe that it is part of the criminal subculture that prisoners bring with them (Irwin and Cressey, 1962). The inmate who follows the code can be expected to enjoy a certain amount of admiration from other inmates as a "right guy" or a "real man." Those who break the code are labeled "rat" or "punk" and will probably spend their prison lives at the bottom of the convict social structure, alienated from the rest of the population and targeted for abuse (Sykes, 1958:84).

A single, overriding inmate code may not exist in the institutions of the 1990s (Benaquisto and Freed, 1996: 481). Instead, convict society has divided itself along racial lines (Carroll, 1974; Irwin, 1980). Apparently reflecting tensions in American society, many prisons now are marked by racially motivated violence, organizations based on race, and voluntary segregation by inmates by race whenever possible—for example, in recreation areas and dining halls.

In a society without a single code of behavior that is accepted by the entire population, the task of administrators becomes much more difficult. They must be aware of the different groups, recognize the norms and rules that members hold, and deal with the leaders of many cliques rather than with a few inmates who have risen to top positions in the inmate society (Carroll, 1974).

CHECKPOINT

8. What are the key elements of the inmate code?
9. Why is it unlikely that a single, overriding inmate code exists in today's prisons?

Adaptive Roles

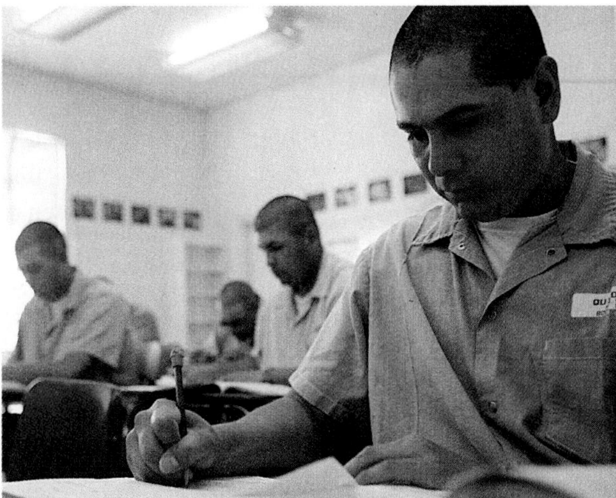

Every prisoner must answer the question, "How am I going to do my time?" Some will glean as much as they can from prison programs, while other will adopt the role of "jailing" by making the prison their "home."

On entering prison, a newcomer ("fish") is confronted by the question "How am I going to do my time?" Some may decide to withdraw into their own world and isolate themselves from their fellow prisoners. Others may decide to become full participants in the convict social system. That choice, which is influenced by prisoners' values and experiences, will, in turn, help to determine the strategies for survival and success that they will use while in prison.

Four terms describe the basic role orientations that most male inmates use to adapt to prison: "doing time," "gleaning," "jailing," and functioning as a "disorganized criminal" (Irwin, 1970).

Those who are "doing time" view their prison term as a brief, inevitable break in their criminal careers, a cost of doing business. They tend to avoid trouble, serve their time quietly, and work for release as soon as possible. Inmates who are "gleaning" try to take advantage of prison programs to better themselves and improve their prospects for success after release. "Jailing" is the choice of those who cut themselves off from the outside and try to construct a life within the prison. These are often "state-raised" youths who have spent much of their lives in institutional settings and who identify little with the values of free society.

A fourth role orientation—the "disorganized criminal"—describes inmates who are unable to develop any of the other three orientations. They may be of low intelligence or afflicted with psychological or physical disabilities and therefore are targets of exploitation by other prisoners.

As the number of roles suggests, prisoners are not part of an undifferentiated mass. Individual convicts choose to play specific roles in prison society. The roles they choose reflect the physical and social environment they have experienced and also influence the relationships and interactions they will develop in prison.

CHECKPOINT

10. What are the four role orientations of adult males in prisons?

The Prison Economy

In prison, as in the outside world, individuals desire goods and services that are not freely provided by the authorities. Although the state feeds, clothes, and houses all prisoners, amenities are sparse. In recent years the number of items that a prisoner may purchase or receive through legitimate channels has increased. In some state institutions, for example, inmates may own television sets, civilian clothing, and hot plates. However, these few luxuries are not enjoyed by all prisoners, nor do they satisfy lingering desires for a variety of other goods.

Recognizing that prisoners do have some needs that are not met, prisons have a commissary, a store from which inmates may, on a scheduled basis, purchase a limited number of items—toilet articles, tobacco, snacks, and other food products—in exchange for credits drawn on their "bank accounts." The size of a bank account depends on the amount of money deposited upon the inmate's entrance, gifts sent by relatives, and amounts earned in the low-paying prison industries.

But the peanut butter, soap, and cigarettes of the typical prison store in no way satisfy the consumer needs and desires of most prisoners. Consequently, an informal, underground economy is a major element in prison society. Many items taken for granted on the outside are inordinately valued on the inside. For example, talcum powder and deodorant become more important because of the limited bathing facilities. Goods and services that a prisoner would not have consumed at all outside prison can have exaggerated importance inside. Unable to enjoy their accustomed alcoholic beverages, some offenders will seek the same effect by sniffing glue. Or to distinguish themselves from others, offenders may pay laundry workers to iron a shirt in a particular way.

David Kalinich has documented the prison economy at the State Prison of Southern Michigan in Jackson (Kalinich, 1980). He learned that a market economy provides the goods and services not available or not allowed by prison authorities. As a principal feature of the prison culture, this informal economy reinforces the norms and roles of the social system and influences the nature of interpersonal relationships. The extent of the underground economy and its ability to produce desired goods and services—food, drugs, alcohol, sex, preferred living conditions—vary according to the extent of official surveillance, the demands of the consumers, and the opportunities for entrepreneurship. Inmates' success as "hustlers" determines the luxuries and power they can enjoy.

The standard currency in the prison economy is cigarettes. Because real money is prohibited and a barter system is somewhat restrictive, "cigarette money" is a useful substitute. Cigarettes are not contraband, are easily transferable, have a stable and well-known standard of value, and come in "denominations" of singles, packs, and cartons. And of course they are in demand by smokers. Even those who do not smoke keep cigarettes as prison currency.

Certain positions in the prison society enhance opportunities for entrepreneurs. For example, inmates assigned to work in the kitchen, warehouse, and administrative office steal food, clothing, building materials, and even information to sell or trade to other prisoners. The goods may then become part of other market transactions. Thus, the exchange of a dozen eggs for two packs of cigarettes may result in the reselling of the eggs in the form of egg sandwiches made on a hot plate for five cigarettes each. Meanwhile, the kitchen worker who stole the eggs may use the income to get a laundry worker to starch his shirts, to get drugs from a hospital orderly, or to pay a "punk" for sexual favors. The transactions wind on and on.

But economic transactions can cause problems when goods are stolen, debts are not paid, or agreements are broken. In the eyes of prison administrators, the subrosa economy not only is a gross violation of the rules against stolen contraband, but it also may lead to violence. Officials try to disrupt the economy by periodic "lockdowns" and inspections. Confiscation of contraband may result in temporary shortages and price readjustments, but gradually business returns. The prison economy, like that of the outside world, allocates goods and services, rewards and sanctions, and it is closely linked to the society it serves.

CHECKPOINT

11. Why does an underground economy exist in prison?
12. Why are prison administrators wary of the prison economy?

WOMEN IN PRISON

New arrivals are searched at the Central California Women's Facility. Almost half of male inmates are serving time for violent offenses; among women less than one third are, and they are also less violent once imprisoned.

Most studies of prisons have been based on institutions for males. How do prisons for women differ from prisons for men, and what are the special problems of female inmates?

Women constitute only 6.4 percent (78,000) of the entire U.S. prison population. This figure is up from 4 percent in 1980, in part because of an increase in drug convictions. More significantly, since 1980 the rate of growth in the number of incarcerated women has been greater than that of men. In fact, between 1986 and 1994 the male population in state and federal prisons increased 209 percent while that of women increased 289 percent (BJS, 1995. *Bulletin*, April).

Men's and women's prisons differ in a number of ways. Women's prisons are smaller and less security-conscious, and the relationships between inmates and staff are less structured. Women inmates are less committed to the inmate code, and physical aggression and violence seem to be less common. The hidden economy is not as well developed. And because women serve shorter sentences, there is perhaps more fluidity in the prison society as new members join and others leave (Rierden, 1997).

Although institutional facilities for women are generally smaller, better staffed, and less fortresslike than those for men, these advantages may pale when the problems of remoteness and heterogeneity are considered. Because few states operate more than one prison for women and some operate none, inmates are generally far removed from their families, friends, and attorneys. In addition, because the number of inmates is small, there is less pressure to design programs to meet an individual offender's security and treatment needs. Rehabilitation programs are few, and dangerous inmates are not segregated from those who have committed minor offenses.

Incarcerated women are young (their average age is 29) and poorly educated (fewer than half have finished high school). They were employed before conviction at unskilled jobs, and about 60 percent are African Americans or Hispanic Americans. Nearly half were caring for dependents when they were admitted, most without a male companion. Few had alcohol problems, but about half were drug abusers (Pollock-Byrne, 1990:57). Figure 13.2 presents some of the characteristics of female prisoners.

CHECKPOINT

13. What reasons are given for the smaller number of facilities and programs in women's prisons?

Social Relationships

Three terms in prison slang—"square," "cool," and "in the life"—correspond to the real-world identities of noncriminal, professional, and habitual offenders in women's correctional institutions (Heffernan, 1972:88). "Square" has the same

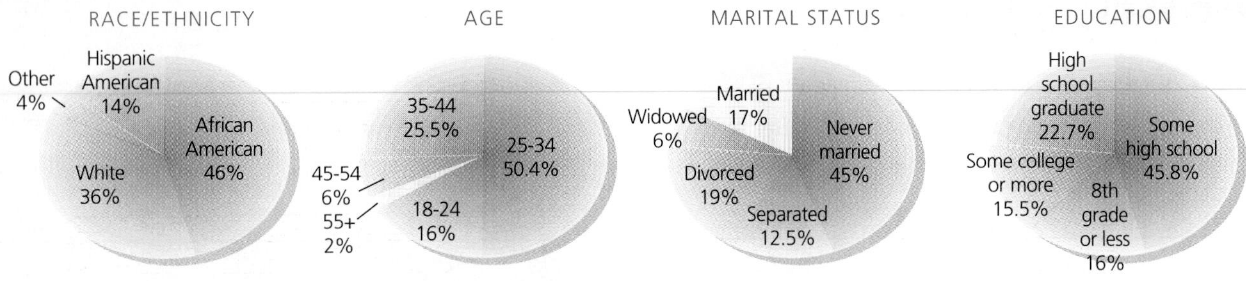

Figure 13.2
Characteristics of female prisoners

Like their male counterparts, female prisoners typically are young, have low education levels, are members of minority groups, and are incarcerated for a serious offense.

SOURCE: U.S. Department of Justice, Bureau of Justice Statistics, *Special Report* (Washington, D.C.: Government Printing Office, March 1994).

meaning it has in the outside world: the word describes a person who holds to conventional norms and values. For example, a woman who killed her husband in a moment of rage is likely to be "square." She attempts to maintain a conventional life while incarcerated, strives to gain the respect of officers and fellow inmates, and seeks to be a "good Christian woman." "Cool" prisoners are professional criminals who "keep busy, play around, stay out of trouble, and get out." They attempt to manipulate others and get through their incarceration on "easy time," seeking to gain as many amenities as they can without risking a longer stay.

By contrast, "in the life" is to be antisocial in prison, just as one was on the outside. Those who are "in the life"—about 50 percent of women in prison—are habitual offenders who have been involved in prostitution, drugs, and gambling. Because they have frequently served previous prison terms, they interact with others with similar experiences and find community within the prison. It is important to them to stand firm against authority (Heffernan, 1972).

What types of social relationships do women prisoners maintain? As in all types of penal institutions, homosexual relationships are found. Among women prisoners, these relationships are more likely to be voluntary than coerced. More important, female inmates tend to form pseudofamilies in which they adopt various roles—father, mother, daughter, sister—and interact as a unit (Propper, 1981; 1982). Heffernan views these "play" families as a "direct, conscious substitution for the family relationships broken by imprisonment, or . . . the development of roles that perhaps were not fulfilled in the actual home environment" (Heffernan, 1972:41-42). Such links help relieve the tensions of prison life, assist the socialization of the new inmate, and allow individuals to act according to clearly defined roles and rules.

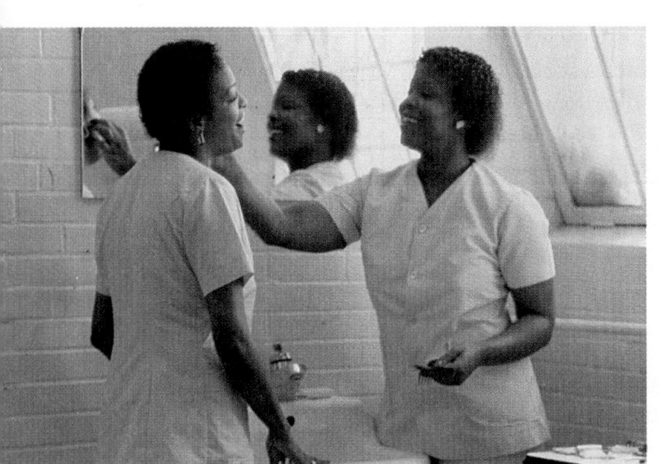

Compared with the convict society in prisons for males, many female prisoners form pseudofamilies, developing strong bonds with family members. Women participate more in programs than do men, yet the range of opportunities is more limited than in prisons for males.

Male and Female Subcultures Compared

The prison subculture of women has many parallels with that of men—and a number of major differences. A principal difference between men's and women's prisons lies in interpersonal relations. Male prisoners seem to have a greater sense that they act as individuals and that their behavior is evaluated by the yardstick of the prison culture. In a comparative study of four men's prisons and one women's prison, James Fox noted that male prisoners have their gangs or cliques but not the network of "family" relationships that has been found among female prisoners. Fox found little sharing in men's institutions.

Men are expected to do their own time. The norms stress autonomy, self-sufficiency, and the ability to cope with one's own problems (Fox, 1982).

In prisons for women, close ties seem to exist among small groups of inmates. These extended families, which may include homosexual couple relationships, provide emotional support and emphasize the sharing of resources.

The little data that exist indicate that women are less likely to engage in violent acts against fellow inmates than are men (Kruttschnitt and Krmopotich, 1990:371). Some researchers have attributed the distinctive female prison subculture to the nurturing, maternal qualities of women. Others have criticized this analysis as a stereotype of female behavior, imputing to women sex-specific personality characteristics.

Programs and the Female Role

The two major criticisms of programs in women's prisons are that they lack the variety of the vocational and educational programs available in male institutions, and that existing programs tend to conform to sexual stereotypes of "female" occupations—cosmetology, food service, housekeeping, sewing. Although such activities reflect the roles of women in past decades, they do not fit the employment opportunities and needs of women today, especially those who must support their households as single parents. Vocational and educational programs are crucial for passing time in prison and for improving life upon release, yet women prisoners often have few opportunities (Weisheit, 1985).

Merry Morash and her colleagues found that gender stereotypes shaped the content of vocational programs (Morash, Haarr, and Rucker, 1994). The American Correctional Association reported in 1990 that prisons have few work assignments for incarcerated women, and those that do exist do not teach marketable job skills (American Correctional Association, 1990). However, the range of offerings in many prisons for women has increased in recent years with the addition of business education, computer training, auto repair, and carpentry to the more traditional offerings.

Medical Services

Women's prisons generally do not have proper medical services. Yet women usually have more serious health problems than men because of their higher incidence of asthma, drug abuse, diabetes, and heart disorder; many women also have gynecological problems (Bershard, 1985; Yang, 1990). A higher proportion of women than men report receiving medical services in prison, yet women's institutions are less likely than men's to have full-time medical staff or hospital facilities.

Mothers and Their Children

Incarcerated mothers worry a great deal about their children. About 75 percent of women inmates are mothers, with an average of two dependent children each. An estimated 167,000 children in the United States—two-thirds of whom are under ten years of age—have mothers who are in jail or prison (BJS, 1994. *Special Report*,

Prison Industries

Prison industries, which trace their roots to the early workshops of New York's Auburn Penitentiary, are intended to teach work habits and skills that will assist prisoners' reentry into the outside workforce. In practice, institutions rely on prison labor to provide basic food, maintenance, clerical, and other institutional services. In addition, many prisons contain manufacturing facilities that produce goods, such as office furniture and clothing, to be used in correctional and other state institutions.

The prison industries system has had a checkered career. During the nineteenth century, factories were established in many prisons, and inmates manufactured items that were sold on the open market. With the rise of the labor movement, however, state legislatures and Congress passed laws restricting the sale of prison-made goods so that they would not compete with those made by free workers (Hawkins, 1983). The Federal Bureau of Prisons and some states have developed industries, but generally their products are not sold on the free market and the percentage of prisoners employed varies greatly. One survey revealed that the number of inmates employed in prison industries ranged from 1 percent in some states to a high of 30 percent, with the average at 9 percent (Butterfield, 1995a).

Although the idea of employing inmates sounds attractive, the economic value may be offset by the inefficiencies of prison work. Turnover is great because many inmates are transferred among several institutions or released over a two-year period. Many prisoners have low education levels and lack steady work habits, making it difficult for them to perform many of the tasks of modern production. An additional cost to efficiency is the need to periodically stop production to count heads and to check that tools and materials have not been stolen (Flanagan and Maguire, 1993).

Rehabilitative Programs

Rehabilitative programs seek to treat the personal defects thought to have brought about the inmate's criminality. Most people agree that rehabilitating offenders is a desirable goal, but the amount of emphasis that should be given to these programs is much debated.

In most correctional systems, a range of psychological, behavior, and social services programs is available. How much they are used seems to vary according to the goals of the institution and the attitudes of administrators. Nationally, very little money is spent for treatment services, and these programs reach only 5 percent of the inmate population. Rehabilitative programs remain a part of correctional institutions, but their emphasis has diminished. Indeed, incarceration's current goal of humane custody implies no effort to change inmates.

CHECKPOINT

18. Why have legislatures and the general public been so critical of educational and rehabilitative programs in prisons?
19. What problems are encountered in vocational training programs?
20. Why have legislatures restricted prison industries?

VIOLENCE IN PRISON

Prisons provide a perfect recipe for violence. They confine in cramped quarters a thousand men, some with histories of violent behavior. While incarcerated, they are not allowed contact with women, and they live under highly restrictive conditions. Sometimes these conditions spark collective violence, as in the riots at Attica, New York (1971), Santa Fe, New Mexico (1980), Atlanta, Georgia (1987), and Lucasville, Ohio (1993).

Although such events are widely reported in the news media, few people are aware of the level of everyday interpersonal violence in U.S. prisons. Each year about 150 prisoners commit suicide, about 70 perish in deaths "caused by another," and 400 die of unknown causes that were apparently not natural, self-inflicted, accidental, or resulting from homicide. In recent years there have been about 25,000 assaults by other inmates (*USA Today*, August 8, 1997, p. 1). Great numbers of prisoners live in a state of constant uneasiness, always on the lookout for persons who might subject them to homosexual demands, steal their few possessions, or otherwise make their lives more painful.

Assaults in correctional institutions raise serious questions for administrators, criminal justice specialists, and the general public. What are the causes of prison violence, and what can be done about it? We consider these questions as we examine the three main categories of prison violence: prisoner-prisoner, prisoner-officer, and officer-prisoner.

Assaultive Behavior and Inmate Characteristics

To begin to understand prison violence we must first know more about inmates, because violent behavior in prisons is related to the characteristics of the people who are incarcerated. Three characteristics stand out: age, attitudes, and race.

Age

Young males between the ages of 16 and 24, both inside and outside prison, are more prone to violence than their elders (Simon, 1993:263). Not surprisingly, 96 percent of adult prisoners are men, with an average age of 27 at the time of admission.

The young not only have greater physical strength, but they also lack the commitments to career and family that are thought to restrict antisocial behavior. In addition, many young men have difficulty defining their position in society, so many of their interactions with others are interpreted as challenges to their status.

Machismo, the concept of male honor and the sacredness of one's reputation as a man, has a direct bearing on violence among the young because it requires physical retaliation against those who insult one's honor. The potential for violence among such prisoners is clear.

Latin Kings gang members Terrence "King Bullet" Boyd, Giovanni "King G" Lara, and George "King Paradise" Sepulveda, convicted of murder, extortion, drug sales, and firearms offenses leave the Federal courthouse in Providence, R.I., for prison. They will undoubtedly assume leadership roles among their fellow Latin Kings who are already incarcerated.

Attitudes

One sociological theory of crime suggests that a subculture of violence exists among low-income groups, and in its value system it is "tolerable, expected, or required"

(Wolfgang and Ferracuti, 1967:263). Arguments are settled and decisions are made by the fist rather than by verbal persuasion. Many inmates bring these attitudes into prison with them.

Race

Race has become a major divisive factor in today's prisons, reflecting tensions in the larger society. Racist attitudes seem to be acceptable in most institutions and have become part of the convict code. The fact of forced association, having to live with persons with whom one would not be likely to associate on the outside, exaggerates and amplifies racial conflict. Violence against members of another race may be how some inmates deal with the frustrations of their lives both inside and outside prison. In addition, the presence of gangs organized along racial lines contributes to violence in prison.

Prisoner-Prisoner Violence

Although prison folklore may attribute violence to brutal guards, most violence in prison is inmate to inmate. These levels of violence are not necessarily related to the size of the prisoner population in a particular facility. The sad fact is that uncounted inmates are injured by assaults. The climate of violence in prisons has no free-world counterpart. Yet it might also be argued that most prisoners come from violent neighborhoods, and perhaps they are safer in prison than they would be on the outside. But *are* they safer?

Racial or ethnic gangs are now linked to acts of violence in the prison systems of forty states as well as in the federal system (see Figure 13.3). The gang wars of the streets are often continued inside (Trout, 1992:62). Gangs are organized primarily with the intention of controlling an institution's drug, gambling, loan sharking, prostitution, extortion, and debt-collection rackets. In addition, gangs protect their members from other gangs and instill a sense of macho camaraderie (Hunt et al., 1993:398).

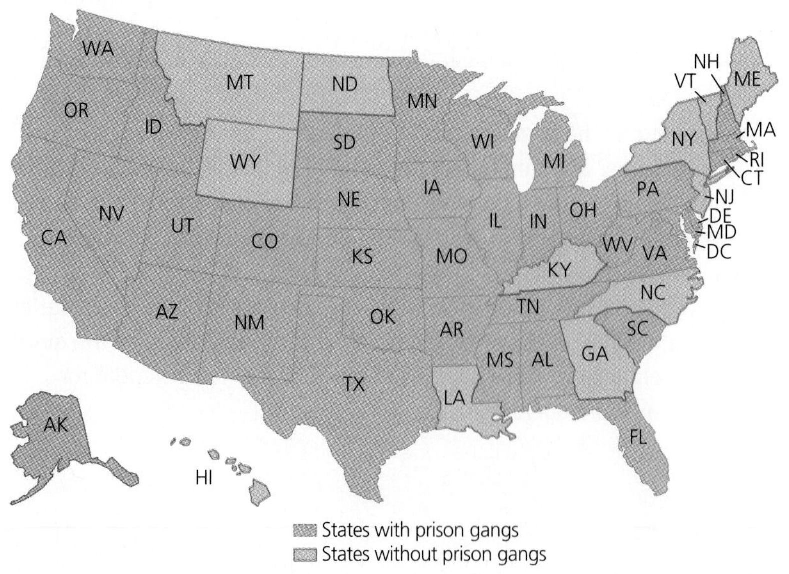

Figure 13.3
States with prison gangs

Racial and ethnic gangs are major causes of prison violence. What factors may account for the role of gangs in American prisons?

SOURCE: American Correctional Association, *Gangs in Correctional Institutions: A National Assessment* (Laurel, Md.: American Correctional Association, 1993).

For many victims of prisoner-prisoner violence, the only way to escape physical abuse, homosexual threats, or the fear of assault is to enter the protective custody unit found in most prisons. Life is not pleasant for these inmates. Usually they are let out of their cells only briefly to exercise and shower. Inmates who ask to "lock up" have little chance of returning to the general prison population without being viewed as a weakling—a snitch or a punk—to be preyed on.

CHECKPOINT

21. Which inmate characteristics are thought to be factors in prison violence?
22. Why are gangs such a threat to prison order?

Prisoner-Officer Violence

The mass media have focused on riots in which guards are taken hostage, injured, and killed. However, violence against officers typically occurs in specific situations and against certain individuals. The number of such incidents is surprising: in 1995, more than 14,000 prison staff members were assaulted by inmates (*USA Today*, August 8, 1997, p. 1). Correctional officers do not carry weapons because a prisoner may seize them. However, prisoners do manage to obtain lethal weapons and can use the element of surprise to injure an officer. Attacks may take the form of an object thrown from an upper tier, verbal threats and taunts, or an officer's "accidental" fall down a flight of stairs. The need for an officer to be constantly watchful against personal attacks adds to the level of stress and keeps many officers at a distance from inmates.

Officer-Prisoner Violence

A fact of life in many institutions is unauthorized physical violence by officers against inmates. Stories abound of guards giving individual prisoners "the treatment" when supervisors are not looking. Many guards view physical force as an everyday, legitimate procedure. In some institutions, authorized "goon squads" consisting of physically powerful officers use their muscle to maintain order and the status quo.

Correctional officers are expected to follow departmental rules in their dealings with prisoners, yet supervisors are generally unable to directly observe staff-prisoner confrontations. Further, prisoner complaints about officer brutality are often not believed until an individual officer gains a reputation for harshness. Still, wardens may feel they must uphold the actions of their officers in order to retain their support.

Decreasing Prison Violence

Five factors contribute to prison violence, as listed by Lee Bowker: (1) inadequate supervision by staff members, (2) architectural design that promotes rather than inhibits victimization, (3) the easy availability of deadly weapons, (4) the housing of violence-prone prisoners near relatively defenseless persons, and (5) a general high level of tension produced by close quarters (Bowker, 1982:64). The physical size and condition of the prison and the relations between inmates and staff also have a bearing on violence.

Effective prison management may decrease the level of assaultive behavior by limiting opportunities for attacks. To do so, wardens and correctional officers must recognize the types of people with whom they are dealing, the role of prison gangs, and the structure of institutions. John DiIulio argues that no group of inmates is "unmanageable [and] no combination of political, social, budgetary, architectural, or other factors makes good management impossible" (DiIulio, 1990b:12). He points to such varied institutions as the California Men's Colony, New York City's Tombs and Rikers Island, the Federal Bureau of Prisons, and the Texas Department of Corrections under the leadership of George Beto. At these institutions good management practices resulted in prisons and jails where inmates can "do time" without fearing for their personal safety. Wardens who exert leadership and effectively manage their prisons maintain an environment of governance so that problems do not fester and erupt into violent confrontations. In sum, prisons must be made safe places.

CHECKPOINT

23. List the five factors thought to contribute to prison violence.

PRISONERS' RIGHTS

Legal assistance attorneys are often able to "nip a problem in the bud" before it develops into litigation. By advising their clients as to the legal merits of the complaints, they are able to discourage frivolous suits.

Prior to the 1960s, most courts maintained a **hands-off policy** with respect to prisons. Only a few state courts had recognized rights for prisoners (Wallace, 1994). In general, judges felt that prisoners did not have protected rights and that courts should defer to the expertise of correctional administrators in deciding how to run prisons.

But since the 1960s prisoners have gained access to the courts to contest decisions made by officers and aspects of their incarceration that they believe violate basic rights. Judicial decisions have defined and recognized the constitutional rights of incarcerated offenders and the need for policies and procedures that respect those rights (Smith, C. E., 1993).

The greatest departure from the hands-off policy was in 1964, when the Supreme Court ruled in ***Cooper v. Pate*** that prisoners are entitled to the protections of the Civil Rights Act of 1871 and may challenge conditions of their confinement in the federal courts. This legislation (designated as Volume 42 of the United States Code, Section 1983, or 42 U.S.C. 1983) imposes civil liability on any person who deprives another of constitutional rights.

Because of the decision in Cooper *v.* Pate, the federal courts now recognize that prisoners may sue state officials over such things as brutality by guards, inadequate nutrition and medical care, theft of personal property, and the denial of basic rights.

The first successful prisoners' rights cases involved the most excessive of prison abuses: brutality and inhuman physical conditions. Gradually, however, prison litigation has focused more directly on the daily activities of the institution, especially on the administrative rules that regulate inmates' conduct. The result has been a series of court decisions concerning the First, Fourth, Eighth, and Fourteenth Amendments to the Constitution.

hands-off policy

Judges should not interfere with the administration of correctional institutions.

CHECKPOINT

24. What is meant by the hands-off policy?
25. Why is the case of *Cooper v. Pate* important to the expansion of prisoners' rights?

***Cooper v. Pate* (1964)**

Prisoners are entitled to the protection of the Civil Rights Act of 1871 and may challenge the conditions of their confinement in federal courts.

First Amendment

The First Amendment guarantees freedom of speech, press, assembly, petition, and religion. Prisoners have successfully challenged many of the restrictions of prison life—access to reading materials, censorship of mail, and rules affecting some religious practices—in the courts.

Since 1970 the federal and state courts have extended the rights of freedom of speech and expression to prisoners, requiring correctional administrators to show why restrictions on these rights must be imposed. For example, in 1974 the Supreme Court said that censorship of mail could be allowed only when officials could demonstrate a substantial governmental interest in maintaining security (*Procunier v. Martinez*). The result: markedly increased communication between inmates and the outside world. However, in ***Turner v. Safley*** (1987) the Court upheld a Missouri ban on correspondence between inmates, saying that such a regulation was reasonably related to legitimate penological interests.

***Turner v. Safley* (1987)**

Inmates do not have a right to receive mail from each other, and this mail can be banned if it is "reasonably related to legitimate penological interests."

The First Amendment also prevents Congress from making laws respecting the establishment of religion or prohibiting its free exercise. Although freedom of belief has not been challenged, cases concerning the free exercise of religion have caused the judiciary some problems, especially when the religious practice may interfere with prison routine.

The growth of the Black Muslim religion in prisons set the stage for suits demanding that this group be granted the same privileges as other faiths (special diets, access to clergy and religious publications, opportunities for group worship). Attorneys for the Muslims succeeded in winning several important cases that helped establish for prisoners the First Amendment right to free exercise of religion. These decisions also have helped Native Americans, Orthodox Jews, and other minority groups to practice their religions while incarcerated. Additional First Amendment cases by Muslims and others clarified the permissible scope of corrections officials' censorship of mail and reading materials.

Fourth Amendment

The Fourth Amendment prohibits "unreasonable" searches and seizures, but courts have not been active in extending these protections to prisoners. Thus regulations viewed as reasonable to maintain security and order in an institution may be justified. For example, the 1984 decision in ***Hudson v. Palmer*** upheld the right of officials to search cells and confiscate any materials found.

Hudson v. Palmer **(1984)**

Prison officials have a right to search cells and confiscate from inmates any materials found.

The Supreme Court's opinions with regard to the Fourth Amendment reveal the fine balance between institutional needs and inmates' right to privacy. Body searches have been harder for administrators to justify than cell searches, for example. But body searches have been upheld when they are part of a policy clearly related to an identifiable and legitimate institutional need and when they are not intended to humiliate or degrade prisoners.

Eighth Amendment

The Eighth Amendment prohibits cruel and unusual punishment. The courts have interpreted this to mean that prisons must maintain decent living conditions and minimum standards of health. The courts have applied three principal tests to determine whether or not conditions violate the protection of the Eighth Amendment: (1) whether the punishment shocks the conscience of a civilized society, (2) whether the punishment is unnecessarily cruel, and (3) whether the punishment goes beyond the legitimate aims of the correctional institution.

Federal courts have ruled that, although some aspects of prison life may be acceptable, the combination of various factors—the totality of conditions—may be such that life in the institution may constitute cruel and unusual punishment. When brutality, unsanitary facilities, overcrowding, and inadequate food have been found, judges have used the Eighth Amendment to order sweeping changes and, in some cases, even to take over administration of entire prisons or corrections systems. In these cases judges have ordered wardens to follow specific internal procedures and to spend money on certain improvements. In recent years, courts have looked for "deliberate indifference" on the part of corrections officials to find improper conditions (*Wilson v. Seiter*, 1991).

CHECKPOINT

26. Which amendment to the Bill of Rights has been most influential in expanding prisoners' rights?

Fourteenth Amendment

Two clauses of the Fourteenth Amendment are relevant to the question of prisoners' rights—those requiring procedural due process and equal protection. In the 1970s the Supreme Court began to insist on procedural fairness in the disciplining of prisoners. Two of the most sensitive of institutional decisions are the process that sends inmates to solitary confinement and the method by which inmates may lose good-time credit because of misconduct.

Wolff v. McDonnell **(1974)**

Basic elements of procedural due process must be present when decisions are made about the disciplining of inmates.

In the case of ***Wolff v. McDonnell*** (1974), the court ruled that basic elements of procedural due process must be present when decisions are made about the disciplining of inmates. Specifically, prisoners have a right to receive notice of the complaint, to have a fair hearing, to confront witnesses, to get help in preparing for the hearing, and to be given a written statement of the decision. Yet the Court has also said that there is no right to counsel at a disciplinary hearing.

As a result of the Supreme Court decisions, most prisons have established rules that provide elements of due process in disciplinary proceedings. In many institutions, a disciplinary committee receives the charges, conducts hearings, and decides guilt and punishment. Even with these protections, however, the fact remains that prisoners are powerless and may fear further punishment if they too strongly challenge the disciplinary decisions of the warden.

Institutional practices or conditions that discriminate against prisoners on the basis of race, gender, or religion have been held unconstitutional. In 1968 the Supreme Court firmly established that racial discrimination may not be official policy within prison walls (*Lee v. Washington*). Racial segregation is justified only temporarily during periods when violence between the races is on the verge of occurring.

CHECKPOINT

27. Which two clauses of the Fourteenth Amendment have been interpreted by the Supreme Court to apply to prisoners' rights?

Impact of the Prisoners' Rights Movement

Although the Supreme Court in recent years has been less supportive of the expansion of prisoners' rights, there have been some general changes in American corrections since the late 1970s (Feeley and Hanson, 1990). The most obvious are concrete improvements in institutional living conditions and administrative practices. Law libraries and legal assistance are now generally available; communication with the outside is easier; religious practices are protected; inmate complaint procedures have been developed; and due process requirements are emphasized. Prisoners in solitary confinement undoubtedly suffer less neglect than they did before. Although overcrowding is still a major problem in most institutions, many conditions are much improved and the more brutalizing elements of prison life have been diminished. These changes were not entirely the result of court orders, however. They also coincide with the growth in influence of college-educated corrections professionals who have sought on their own to improve prisons.

Summary

- Three models of incarceration have been prominent since the 1940s. The custodial model emphasizes the maintenance of security. The rehabilitation model views security and housekeeping activities as mainly a framework for treatment efforts. The reintegration model recognizes that prisoners must be prepared for their return to society.
- The public's belief that the warden and officers have total power over the inmates is outdated.
- Good management through effective leadership can maintain the quality of prison life as measured by levels of order, amenities, and service.
- Correctional officers, because they are constantly in close contact with the prisoners, are the real linchpins in the prison system. The effectiveness of the institution lies heavily on their shoulders.

- Inmates do not serve their time in isolation but are members of a subculture with its own traditions, norms, and leadership structure.
- Inmates deal with the pain of incarceration by assuming an adaptive role and lifestyle.
- An underground economy exists in prisons to meet the needs of prisoners for goods and services not provided by the state.
- Only a small portion of the inmate population is female. This is cited as the reason for the limited programs and services available to women prisoners.
- Social relationships among female inmates differ from those of their mail counterparts. Women tend to form pseudofamilies in prison. Many women experience the added stress of being responsible for their children on the outside.
- Educational, vocational, industrial, and treatment programs are available in prisons. Administrators believe these programs are important for maintaining order.
- Prison violence is a major problem confronting administrators. The characteristics of the inmates and the rise of gangs contribute to this problem.
- The prisoners' rights movement, through lawsuits in the federal courts, has brought many changes to the administration and conditions of American prisons.

Questions for Review

1. How do modern prisons differ from those in the past?
2. What are the characteristics of prisons that make them different from other institutions?
3. What must a prison administrator do to ensure successful management?
4. What Supreme Court decisions are most significant to corrections today? What effect has each had on correctional institutions?

ANSWERS TO CHECKPOINTS

1. The racial makeup of the inmate population has changed, more inmates are from urban areas and have been convicted for drug-related or violent offenses, the inmate population is fragmented along racial and ethnic lines.
2. The custodial, rehabilitation, and reintegration models.
3. It is a place where a group of employees manages a group of captives.
4. Keeping (custody), using (working), serving (treatment).
5. Management by walking around.
6. The defects of total power, the limited rewards and punishments that officials can use, exchange relations between correctional officers and inmates, and the strength of inmate leadership.
7. They have the closest contact with the inmates.
8. The norms and values of prison society that help define the inmate's image of the model prisoner.
9. Because prison society is fragmented by racial and ethnic divisions.
10. Doing time, gleaning, jailing, and functioning as a disorganized criminal.
11. To provide goods and services not available through regular channels.
12. The prison economy is responsible for the exploitation of other prisoners and has the potential for violence.
13. The small number of female inmates compared to the number of males.
14. The distance of prisons from homes, intermittent telephone privileges, and unnatural visiting environment.
15. Children are placed with relatives or in foster care.
16. Programs keep prisoners busy, resulting in fewer tensions.
17. Classification by a committee according to the needs of the inmate or of the institution.
18. They are thought to "coddle" prisoners and give them resources not available to free residents.
19. Many programs train inmates for trades for which there is already an adequate labor supply or in which the skills are outdated. They are inefficient because of the low education level and poor work habits of the prisoners. Production has to be stopped for periodic head counts and checks on tools and materials.
20. Pressures because free workers make competing products at higher wages.
21. Age, attitudes, and race.
22. Gang wars continue inside.

23. Inadequate supervision, architectural design, availability of weapons, housing of violence-prone inmates with the defenseless, and the high level of tension of people living in close quarters.
24. Judges' belief that prisoners do not have protected rights and that the courts should not become involved in the administration of prisons.
25. *Cooper v. Pate* allowed state prisoners to challenge the conditions of their confinement in the federal courts.
26. The First Amendment rights concerning free speech and free exercise of religion.
27. The due process and equal protection clauses.

Chapter 14

Release and Supervision in the Community

Parole: Reentry into Society

- *The Origins of Parole*
- *The Development of Parole in the United States*

Release Mechanisms

- *Discretionary Release*
- *Mandatory Release*
- *Unconditional Release*
- *The Organization of Releasing Authorities*
- *The Decision to Release*

Supervision in the Community

- *Community Programs Following Release*
- *Parole Officer: Cop or Social Worker?*
- *Adjustment to Life Outside Prison*
- *Revocation of Parole*
- *The Future of Parole*

AFTER THREE YEARS, three months, and four days in Stanhope Correctional Facility, Ben Brooks was ready to go before the Board of Parole. He woke with butterflies in his stomach, realizing that at nine o'clock he was to walk into the hearing room to confront a roomful of strangers. As he lay on his bunk he rehearsed the answers to the questions he thought the board members might ask: "How do you feel about the person you assaulted?" "What have you done with your time while incarcerated?" "What have you learned here that will convince the board that you will follow a crime-free life in the community?" "What are your plans for employment and housing?" According to prison scuttlebutt, these were the types of questions asked, and you had to be prepared to answer that you were sorry for your past mistakes, had taken advantage of the prison programs, had a job waiting for you, and planned to live with your family. You had to "ring bells" with the board.

At breakfast, friends dropped by Ben's table to reassure him that he had it made. As one said, "Ben, you've done everything they've said to do. What else can they expect?" That was the problem: *What did they expect*?

At eight-thirty Officer Kearney came by the cell. "Time to go, Ben." They walked out of the housing unit and down the long prison corridors to a group of chairs outside the hearing room. Other prisoners were already seated there. "Sit here, Ben. They'll call when they're ready. Good luck."

At ten minutes past nine the door opened and an officer called, "First case, Brooks." Ben got up and walked into the room. "Please take a seat, Mr. Brooks," said the African American seated at the center at the table. Ben knew he was Reverend Perry, a man with a reputation of being tough but fair. To his left was a white man, Mr. MacDonald, and to his right a Hispanic woman, Ms. Lopez. The white man led the questioning.

"Mr. Brooks. You were convicted of armed robbery and sentenced to a term of six to ten years. Please tell the board what you have learned during your incarceration."

Ben paused and then answered hesitantly, "Well, I learned that to commit such a stupid act was a mistake. I was under a lot of pressure when I pulled the robbery and now am sorry for what I did."

"You severely injured the woman you held up. What might you tell her if she were sitting in this room today?"

"I would just have to say I'm sorry, it will never happen again."

"But this is not the first time you have been convicted. What makes you think it will never happen again?"

"Well, this is the first time I was sent to prison. You see things a lot differently from here."

Ms. Lopez spoke up. "You have a good prison record—member of the Toastmaster's Club, passed your GED, kept your nose clean. Tell the board about your future plans should you be released."

"My brother says I can live with him until I get on my feet, and there is a letter in my file telling you that I have a job waiting at a meat-processing plant. I will be living in my hometown, but I don't intend to see my old buddies again. You can be sure that I am now on the straight and narrow."

"But you committed a heinous crime. That woman suffered a lot. Why should the board believe that you won't do it again?"

"All I can say is that I'm different now."

"Thank you, Mr. Brooks," said Reverend Perry. "You will hear from us by this evening."

Ben got up and walked out of the room. It had taken only eight minutes, yet it seemed like hours. Eight minutes in which his future was being decided. Would it be back to the cell or out on the street? It would be about ten hours before he would learn his fate.

Today, scenes like this one still occur, but fewer states maintain parole boards or allow boards the wide discretion they had in the past. In this chapter we examine the mechanisms of prison release and study the supervision of offenders in the community. We will look especially at the problems confronting offenders as they reenter society. Try to imagine yourself as Ben Brooks. Three weeks after his appearance before the board, he left Stanhope, having been given transportation back to his hometown, a list of rules to follow, and a date to report to his parole officer. What do you think was his first reaction to family, friends, and a community he had not seen in years?

Questions for Inquiry

What is parole, and how does it operate today?

What effects do mandatory and discretionary release have on the criminal justice system?

What programs ease the transition of the offender back to society, and how are ex-offenders supervised in the community?

What is the purpose of the pardon?

What restrictions does society place on ex-offenders?

PAROLE: REENTRY INTO SOCIETY

Parole is the *conditional* release of an offender from incarceration but not from the legal custody of the state. During most of the twentieth century the word parole referred to both a release mechanism and a method of community supervision. The word still has this general meaning, but because some states have adopted determinate sentencing and parole guidelines, we must now distinguish between parole as a release mechanism and as a method of supervision. Although the releasing mechanisms have changed, most former prisoners are still required to serve a period of time under parole supervision.

parole

The conditional release of an inmate from incarceration under supervision after part of the prison sentence has been served.

Only felons are released on parole; adults convicted of misdemeanors are usually released immediately after they have finished serving their sentences. Every year almost 400,000 felons are conditionally released from prison and allowed to live under parole supervision in the community. Today 700,000 people are under parole supervision, a rate of 359 for every 100,000 adult Americans (BJS, 1997. *Sourcebook*:502). With the doubling of the incarcerated population during the past twenty years, it is not surprising that the number of parolees has also doubled.

The Origins of Parole

Parole in the United States evolved during the nineteenth century from the English, Australian, and Irish practices of conditional pardon, apprenticeship by indenture, transportation of criminals from one country to another, and the issuance of "tickets of leave." These were all methods of moving criminals out of prison. Such practices generally did not develop as part of any coherent theory of punishment or to promote any particular goal of the criminal sanction. Instead, they were responses to problems of overcrowding, unemployment, and the cost of incarceration.

The practice of punishing offenders by keeping them under the authority of the government, but not confined to an institution, developed as Britain was establishing colonies. As early as 1587, England had passed the Act of Banishment, by which criminals and "rogues" could be sent to the colonies as laborers for the king in exchange for a pardon. The pardons initially were unconditional, but they eventually became conditional after the offender had completed a period of service. During the eighteenth century English convicts were released and indentured to private persons to work in the colonies until the end of a set term.

After the American colonies gained independence, Australia became the major colonial destination for offenders banished from England. The governor of Australia was given the power to pardon felons. Initially, unconditional pardons were given to offenders with good work records and good behavior. As problems arose with the behavior of some pardoned offenders, pardons became conditional. The essential condition was a requirement that prisoners support themselves and remain within a specific district. This method of parole, known as "ticket of leave," was similar to the modern concept of parole, except that the released prisoner was not under government supervision.

A key figure in developing the concept of parole in the nineteenth century was Captain Alexander Maconochie, an administrator of British penal colonies in Tasmania and elsewhere in the South Pacific. A critic of definite prison terms, Maconochie devised a system of rewards for good conduct, labor, and study. Under his classification procedure prisoners could pass through stages of increasing responsibility and freedom: (1) strict imprisonment, (2) labor on government chain gangs, (3) freedom within a limited area, (4) a ticket of leave or parole resulting in a conditional pardon, and (5) full restoration of liberty. Like modern correctional practices, this procedure assumed that prisoners should be prepared gradually for release. In the transition from imprisonment to conditional release to full freedom we can see the roots of the American system of parole.

Maconochie's idea of requiring prisoners to earn their early release caught on first in Ireland. There, Sir Walter Crofton built on Maconochie's idea that an offender's progress in prison and a ticket of leave were linked. Prisoners who graduated through Crofton's three successive levels of treatment were released on parole under a series of conditions. Most significant was the requirement that parolees submit monthly reports to the police. In Dublin, a special civilian inspector helped releasees find jobs, visited them periodically, and supervised their activities.

CHECKPOINT

1. In what countries did the concept of parole first develop?
2. What were the contributions of Alexander Maconochie and Sir Walter Crofton?

(Answers are at the end of the chapter.)

The Development of Parole in the United States

In the United States, parole developed during the prison reform movement of the latter half of the nineteenth century. Relying on the ideas of Maconochie and Crofton, American reformers such as Zebulon Brockway of the Elmira State Reformatory in New York began to experiment with the concept of parole. After New York adopted indeterminate sentences in 1876, Brockway started to release prisoners on parole. Under the new sentencing law, prisoners could be released when their conduct showed they were ready to return to society.

As originally implemented, the parole system in New York did not require supervision by the police. Instead, volunteers from citizens' reform groups assisted with the parolee's reintegration into society. As parole became more common and applied to larger numbers of offenders, states replaced the volunteer supervisors with correctional employees.

Many individuals and groups in the United States opposed the release of convicts before they had completed the entire sentence that they had earned by their crimes. However, the use of parole continued to spread. By 1900, twenty states had parole systems, and by 1932, forty-four states and the federal government had them (Friedman, 1993:304). Today every state has some procedure for the release of offenders before the end of their sentences.

Although it has been used in the United States for more than a century, parole remains controversial. To many people, parole allows convicted offenders to avoid serving the full sentence they deserve. Public pressure to be tougher on criminals has led half the states and the federal government to restructure their sentencing laws and release mechanisms.

RELEASE MECHANISMS

Except for the small number who die in prison, all inmates will eventually be released to live in the community. Until the mid-1970s all states and the federal government had systems that allowed parole boards to determine the exact date for an inmate to leave prison. With the move to determinate sentencing and more rigid parole guidelines, parole boards were abolished or their powers reduced in many states. There are now three basic mechanisms for persons to be released from prison: (l) discretionary release, (2) mandatory release, and (3) unconditional release. Figure 14.1 shows the percentage of felons released by each of these mechanisms.

Discretionary Release

In states that have retained indeterminate sentences, **discretionary release** by parole board continues to be the way most felons leave prison. The parole board's discretion operates within the boundaries set by the sentence and the penal law. This approach (illustrated by the case of Ben Brooks) allows the parole board to assess the prisoner's readiness for release within the minimum and maximum terms of the sentence. The process places great faith in the ability of parole board members to make accurate predictions about the future behavior of offenders.

discretionary release

The release of an inmate from prison to conditional supervision at the discretion of the parole board within the boundaries set by the sentence and the penal law.

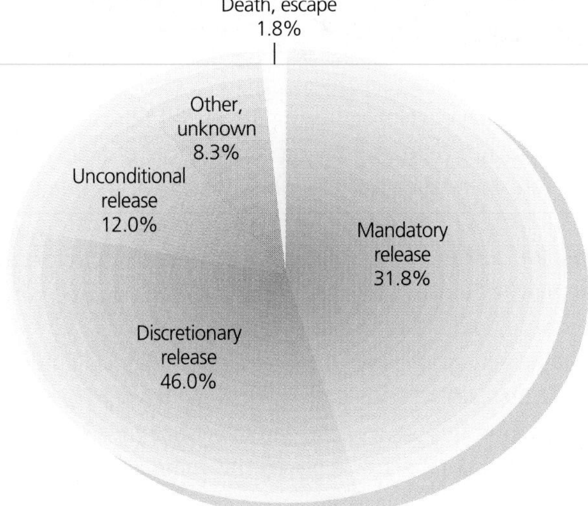

Figure 14.1
Methods of release from state prison

Felons are released from prison to the community, usually under parole supervision, through means that vary depending on the law.

SOURCE: U.S. Department of Justice, Bureau of Justice Statistics, *National Corrections Reporting Program*, 1992 (Washington, D.C.: Government Printing Office, 1994), 36.

Mandatory Release

mandatory release

The required release of an inmate from incarceration to community supervision upon the expiration of a certain time period, as specified by a determinate sentencing law or parole guidelines.

Mandatory release is so named because it occurs after an inmate has served time equal to the total sentence minus good time, if any, or to a certain percentage of the total sentence as specified by law. It is found in federal jurisdictions and states with determinate sentences and parole guidelines. Under mandatory release no parole board makes discretionary decisions about when inmates are released; the length of the time served is a matter of bookkeeping to ensure that the correct amount of good time and other credits has been allocated and checking that the sentence has been accurately interpreted. The prisoner is released to the supervision of a parole officer for the remainder of the sentence minus good time.

Unconditional Release

unconditional release

The release of an inmate from incarceration without any further correctional supervision; the inmate cannot be returned to prison for any remaining portion of the sentence for the current offense.

A small percentage of prisoners are given an **unconditional release**. These are inmates who are released from further correctional supervision and cannot be returned to prison for any remaining portion of the sentence for a current offense. Such offenders have been incarcerated until expiration of their sentences, have had their sentences commuted, or have been pardoned.

The Organization of Releasing Authorities

Parole boards tend to be organized either as a part of a department of corrections or as an independent agency of government. Some commentators have argued that an independent parole board is less likely to be influenced by staff considerations, such as the need to reduce the prison population and the desire to punish inmates who do not conform to institutional rules.

Whether a parole board is independent or a part of the corrections department, it cannot exist in a vacuum. Board members cannot ignore the public's attitudes. If a parolee commits a crime that arouses public indignation, the board members inevitably will make decisions more cautiously to avoid public condemnation and embarrassment.

Parole boards also are susceptible to influence from departments of corrections and must maintain good working relations with them. For example, if even an autonomous board develops a conflict with the department, the department may not cooperate in providing the board with information it needs. By contrast, a board that is closely tied to corrections officials may receive complete cooperation yet be viewed by prisoners and the general public as merely the rubber stamp of the department.

Most people assume that parole boards are made up of experts on human behavior who can accurately evaluate whether an inmate is ready for release. In some states that view is reasonably accurate. In other states, parole board members may be chosen because of political considerations. Governors may also seek to appoint citizens who fit specific racial, geographic, occupational, and other demographic criteria. Parole boards act much like a jury: they can apply the community's values in determining whether particular offenders deserve to be released.

CHECKPOINT

3. Distinguish among mandatory release, discretionary release, and unconditional release.
4. What are the two ways that parole boards are organized?

The Decision to Release

An inmate's eligibility for release to community supervision on parole depends on requirements set by law and on the sentence imposed by the court. As we have noted, in the states with determinate sentences or parole guidelines, release is mandatory once the offender has served the required amount of time. In nearly half the states, however, the release decision is discretionary, and the parole board has the authority to establish a release date. The board determines the date on the basis of the sufficiency of rehabilitation and the individual characteristics of each inmate.

Based on the rehabilitation model, which links indeterminate sentences with treatment programs, discretionary release is designed to allow the parole board to release inmates to conditional supervision in the community when they are judged "ready" to live as law-abiding citizens (Talarico, 1988).

Recall that eligibility for release is usually the minimum term of the sentence minus good time. As an example of the computation of parole eligibility, let's look at the case of Ben Brooks (see Figure 14.2). At the time of sentencing Brooks had been held in jail for six months awaiting trial and disposition of his case. He was given a sentence of a minimum of five years and a maximum of ten years for robbery with violence. Brooks did well at Stanhope, the maximum security prison to which he was sent. He did not get into trouble and was thus able to save up good-time credit at the rate of one day for every four that he spent on good behavior. In addition, he was given meritorious credit of thirty days when he completed his high school equivalency test after attending the prison school for two years. After serving three years, three months, and four days of his sentence, he appeared before the board of parole and was granted release into the community.

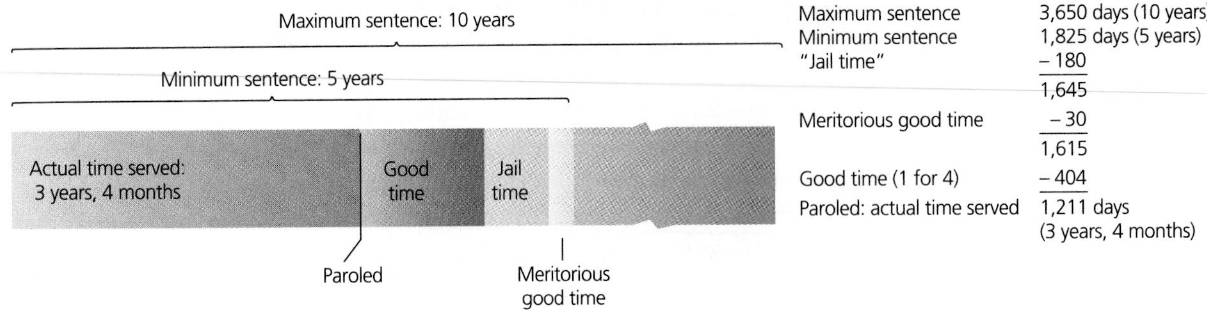

Figure 14.2
Computing parole eligibility for Ben Brooks

Various good-time reductions to the minimum sentence are allowed in most correctional systems to determine eligibility for parole. Note how a five- to ten-year sentence can be reduced to three years, four months actually served.

What criteria guide the parole board as it makes a decision? A formal statement of standards may list elements such as inmates' attitudes toward their families, their insights into the causes of their past conduct, and the adequacy of their housing and employment plan after release. Participation in educational or treatment programs also weighs heavily with board members, as illustrated by the case of Jim Allen in A Question of Ethics. Written statements from the victim, defense attorney, prosecutor, and offender's family may also be presented to the board (McLeod, 1989).

As noted earlier, parole board members are also concerned about public criticism. Because of the public's attitudes, notorious offenders such as Sirhan Sirhan, the man convicted of assassinating presidential candidate Robert Kennedy in 1968, and multiple murderer Charles Manson are unlikely ever to gain parole release even if they behave well in prison.

Structuring Parole Decisions

In response to criticism that the release decisions of parole boards are somewhat arbitrary, many states have adopted parole guidelines. As with sentencing guidelines, a "severity scale" ranks crimes according to their seriousness and a "salient factor" score measures the offender's criminal history (drug arrests, prior record, age at first conviction, and so on) and risk factors considered relevant to successful completion of parole (see Tables 14.1 and 14.2). By placing the offender's salient factor score next to his or her particular offense on the severity scale, the board, the inmate, and correctional officials may calculate the **presumptive parole date** soon after the offender enters prison. This is the date by which the inmate can expect to be released if he or she has no disciplinary or other problems during incarceration. The presumptive parole date may be modified on a scheduled basis. The date of release may be advanced because of good conduct and superior achievement, or

A Question of ETHICS

The five members of the parole board questioned Jim Allen, an offender with a long history of sex offenses involving teenage boys. Now approaching 45 and having met the eligibility requirement for a hearing, Allen respectfully answered the board members.

Toward the end of the hearing, Richard Edwards, a dentist who had recently been appointed to the board, spoke up: "Your institutional record is good, you have a parole plan, a job has been promised, and your sister says she will help you. All of that looks good, but I just can't vote for your parole. You haven't attended the behavior modification program for sex offenders. I think you're going to repeat your crime. I have a 13-year-old son, and I don't want him or other boys to run the risk of meeting your kind."

Allen looked shocked. The other members had seemed ready to grant his release.

"But I'm ready for parole. I won't do that stuff again. I didn't go to that program because electroshock to my private area is not going to help me. I've been here five years of the seven-year max and have stayed out of trouble. The judge didn't say I was to be further punished in prison by therapy."

After Jim Allen left the room, the board discussed his case. "You know, Rich, he has a point. He has been a model prisoner and has served a good portion of his sentence," remarked Brian Lynch, a long-term board member. "Besides, we don't know if Dr. Hankin's program works."

"I know, but can we really let someone like that out on the streets?"

Are the results of the behavior-modification program for sex offenders relevant to the parole board's decision? Is the purpose of the sentence to punish Allen for what he did or for what he might do in the future? Would you vote for his release on parole? Would your vote be the same if his case had received media attention?

it may be postponed if disciplinary infractions occur or a suitable community supervision plan is not developed.

presumptive parole date

The presumed release date stipulated by parole guidelines if the offender serves time without disciplinary or other incidents.

	Criminal History/Risk Factor	Points	Score
A	No prior felony convictions as an adult or juvenile:	3	
	One prior felony conviction:	2	
	Two or three prior felony convictions:	1	
	Four or more prior felony convictions:	0	———
B	No prior felony or misdemeanor incarcerations (that is, executed sentences of 90 days or more) as an adult or juvenile:	2	
	One or two prior incarcerations:	1	
	Three or more prior incarcerations:	0	———
C	Verified period of 3 years conviction-free in the community prior to the present commitment:	1	
	Otherwise:	0	———
D	Age at commencement of behavior leading to this incarceration was ———: Date of birth was ———/———/———.		
	26 or older and at least one point received in A, B, or C:	2	
	26 or older and no points received in A, B, or C:	1	
	21 to under 26 and at least one point received in A, B, or C:	0	
	21 to under 26 and no points received in A, B, or C:	0	
	Under 21:	0	———
E	Present commitment does not include parole, probation, failure to appear, release agreement, escape, or custody violation:	2	
	Present commitment involves probation, release, agreement, or failure to appear violation:	1	
	Present commitment involves parole, escape, or custody violation:	0	
F	Has no admitted or documented substance abuse problem within a 3-year period in the community immediately preceding the commission of the crime conviction:	1	
	Otherwise:	0	
	Total history/risk assessment score:		———

Table 14.1
Criminal history/risk assessment under the Oregon Guidelines for Adult Offenders

The amount of time to be served is related to the severity of the offense and to the criminal history/risk assessment of the inmate. The criminal history score is determined by adding the points assigned to each factor in the table.

SOURCE: Adapted from State of Oregon, Board of Parole, ORS Chapter 144, Rule 255-35-015.

CHECKPOINT

5. What major factors do parole boards consider when deciding on discretionary release?
6. What do prisoners believe improves their chances for release?

The Impact of Release Mechanisms

Parole release mechanisms do more than simply determine the date at which a particular prisoner will be sent back into the community. Parole release also has an enormous impact on other parts of the system, including sentencing, plea bargaining, and the size of prison populations (Walker, 1993b:141).

One important effect of discretionary release is that the parole board can shorten a sentence imposed by a judge. Even in states that have mandatory release, various potential reductions built into the sentence mean that the full sentence is rarely

Offense Severity	Criminal History/Risk Assessment Score 11–9 Excellent	8–6 Good	5–3 Fair	2–0 Poor
Category 1: Bigamy, criminal mischief I, dogfighting, incest, possession of stolen vehicle	6	6	6–10	12–18
Category 2: Abandonment of a child, bribing a witness, criminal homicide, perjury, possession of controlled substance	6	6–10	10–14	16–24
Category 3: Assault III, forgery I, sexual abuse, trafficking in stolen vehicles	6–10	10–14	14–20	22–32
Category 4: Aggravated theft, assault II, coercion, criminally negligent homicide, robbery II	10–16	16–22	22–30	32–44
Category 5: Burglary I, escape I, manslaughter II, racketeering, rape I	16–24	24–36	40–52	56–72
Category 6: Arson I, kidnapping I, rape II, sodomy I	30–40	44–56	60–80	90–130
Category 7: Aggravated murder, treason	96–120	120–156	156–192	192–240
Category 8: Aggravated murder (stranger–stranger, cruelty to victim, prior murder conviction)	20–168	168–228	228–288	288–life

Table 14.2
Number of months to be served before release under the Oregon guidelines

The presumptive release date is determined by finding the intersection of the criminal history score (Table 14.1) and the category of the offense. An offender with an assessment score between 6 and 8, convicted of a category 3 offense, could expect to serve between 10 and 14 months.

SOURCE: Adapted from State of Oregon, Board of Parole, ORS Chapter 144, Rules 255-75-026 and 255-75-035.

served. Good time, for example, can reduce punishment even if the offender is not eligible for parole.

To understand the impact of release mechanisms on criminal punishment, we need to compare the amount of time actually served in prison with the sentence specified by the judge. In some jurisdictions, up to 80 percent of felons sentenced to prison are released to the community after their first appearance before a parole board. As we have seen, eligibility for discretionary release is ordinarily determined by the minimum term of the sentence minus good time and jail time. Good time allows the minimum sentence to be reduced for good behavior during incarceration or for exceptional performance of assigned tasks or personal achievement.

Although there is considerable variation among the states, on a national basis felony inmates serve an estimated average of only two years before release. The amount of time served in prison varies with the nature of the offense. Figure 14.3 shows the estimated time served for selected offenses.

The probability of release well before the end of the formal sentence encourages plea bargaining by both prosecutors and defendants. Prosecutors can get the benefits of quick, cooperative plea bargains that look tough in the eyes of the public. Meanwhile, the defendant agrees to plead guilty and accept the sentence because of the high likelihood of early release through parole.

Besides the benefits of parole to prosecutors, supporters of discretion for the paroling authority argue that parole offers invaluable benefits for the overall system. Discretionary release makes the penal code less harsh. If the legislature must establish exceptionally strict punishments as a means of conveying a "tough-on-crime" image to frustrated and angry voters, parole can permit sentence adjustments that make the punishment fit the crime. For example, everyone convicted of larceny may not have caused the same amount of harm, yet some legislatively mandated sentencing schemes may impose equally strict sentences on everyone convicted of larceny. Early release on parole can be granted to an offender who is less deserving of strict punishment, such as someone who voluntarily makes restitution, cooperates with the police, or shows genuine regret.

A major criticism of parole is that it has shifted responsibility for many of the primary criminal justice decisions from a judge, who holds legal procedures uppermost, to an administrative board, where discretion rules. By their legal education, judges are knowledgeable about constitutional rights and the need to provide basic legal protections. By contrast, parole board members may not have knowledge

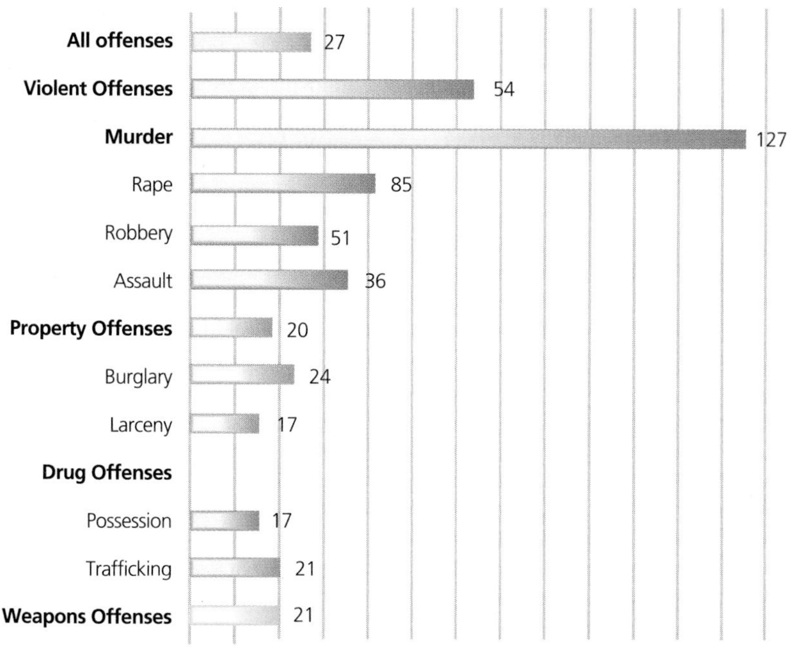

Figure 14.3
Estimated time served (in months) by state prisoners for selected offenses

The data indicate that the average felony offender going to prison for the first time spends two years in prison. How would you expect the public to react to that fact?

SOURCE: Patrick A. Langan and Jodi Brown, "Felony Sentences in State Courts," Bureau of Justice Statistics, *Bulletin* (January 1997),

about and sensitivity to constitutional values. In most states with discretionary release, parole decisions are made in secret hearings, with only board members, the inmate, and correctional officers present. Should we place such significant discretionary power in the hands of parole boards? With so little oversight over their decision making and so few constraints on their decisions, some parole board members will make arbitrary or discriminatory decisions that are inconsistent with the values underlying our constitutional system and civil rights.

CHECKPOINT

7. What are the influences of parole release on the rest of the criminal justice system?

SUPERVISION IN THE COMMUNITY

When a prisoner is released, family and community relations have to be reforged. Parole officers are essential helpers during this period of adjustment.

Parolees must abide by certain conditions when they are released from prison. If they violate these conditions, they may be returned to prison to serve out their complete sentence behind bars. They cannot commit additional crimes, and they must live according to rules designed both to help them adjust to society and to control their movements. These rules may require them to abstain from alcoholic beverages, keep away from former associates, maintain good work habits, and leave the state only with permission. The restrictions are justified on the ground that people who have been incarcerated must gradually readjust to the community. Presumably the rules will make them less susceptible to the negative temptations of a free society and less likely to fall back into their preconviction habits and associations. However, the strict enforcement of these rules may create problems for parolees who are unable to fulfill all of the demands placed upon them. For example, it may be impossible for a parolee to be tested for drugs, attend an AA meeting, and work full-time while also meeting family obligations. The heavy burden of the rules also raises questions about the appropriateness of imposing standards of conduct on parolees that are not imposed on law-abiding citizens.

The day they come out of prison, parolees face a staggering array of problems. In most states, they are given only clothes, a token amount of money, a list of rules governing their conditional release, and the name and address of the parole supervisor to whom they must report within twenty-four hours. Although having a job lined up is often a condition for release, actually becoming employed may be another matter. Most ex-convicts are unskilled or semiskilled, and the conditions of parole may restrict their movements and prevent them from relocating to areas where jobs are plentiful. If the parolee is African American, male, and under 30, he joins the largest group of unemployed people. Moreover, in most states, laws prevent former prisoners from working in certain types of establishments—where alcohol is sold, for example—thus ruling out many jobs. In many trades, union affiliation is a requirement for employment, and there are restrictions on the admission of new members. Finally, many parolees, as well as other ex-convicts, face a significant dilemma. If they are truthful about their backgrounds, many employers will not hire them. If they are not truthful, they can be fired for lying if the employer ever learns about their conviction. Some problems that parolees encounter when they reenter the community are illustrated in the Close-up. As you read about Jerome Washington's experience, ask yourself what problems you might encounter after a long term in "max."

CLOSE-UP

Returning to America

Returning to America after living in France, China, Swaziland, or the high Himalayas is one thing, but returning to America after serving sixteen years and three months in maximum security, mostly in Attica, is something altogether different.

In 1972 when I went to prison, Nixon was president and politicians were still thought to be ethical; Patti Hearst was involved in a self-kidnapping conspiracy with the SLA; the Supreme Court was reasonably balanced; the Vietnam war was winding down, but the weekly body count was still news. The HIV virus was unknown and free sex had more fans than the Super Bowl. Although everybody was not living the American Dream, and some people felt that life was hopeless, most were optimistic about the future and many had a strong commitment to social activism. People cared, and even the most disadvantaged could still dream without fear of having nightmares.

Soon after I got out I was with my brother, Freddy. We were standing at Columbus Circle, a major hub, a New York City crossroads. Freddy was my guide. He asked where I'd like to go; what I'd like to do; what I'd like to see. Did I want to meet new people, or just hang out, drift from place to place? Suddenly, life was a smorgasbord, a cornucopia of enticements and alluring temptations. I didn't know where to start, what to do first. Prison was my immediate reference point, and there, decisions related to physical movement were made by the guards, not by me. "We can't stand here all day," my brother said, over and over.

"Go slow," I told myself as I recalled a number of prisoners who shortly after release returned to prison with new convictions and new sentences. They tried to make everything happen at once, all at the same time. Like children, they wanted instant gratification. Played all their cards at the same time, swung before the ball got to the plate, struck out and found themselves back in a cell where their only landscape was the sun setting against the prison wall.

After my release from prison, the world presented me with a lot of maybes and possibilities. It takes time to sort things out, put them into workable categories. Sometimes while walking on the streets, I feel as though a spaceship has left me on the wrong planet. At other times everything seems natural and falls into place. Still, a bit of uncertainty lurks behind everything, everywhere.

I decided to do life the same way I did prison. Nothing fancy. One step at a time, one day at a time, and, most of all, don't forget to breathe.

"Let's just hang out," I told my brother, "go with the flow, move with the groove."

Freddy was supportive and sensitive. He understood that I needed to relearn the rhythm of the streets, tune in on the city, explore my new freedom, and tune out on prison. I had no preference about which direction we'd walk or which street we'd take. Freddy didn't seem to have any preference either. He just started off, leaving me to stay where I was or to catch up. I learned a quick but important lesson. It was this kind of small, ordinary decision—often taken for granted and overlooked—that I missed most in prison. Now, by just walking off and letting me decide what to do, Freddy was tuning me in again to this level of free choice.

The morning after my release from prison found me in Harlem. I was staying with Bert, a longtime family friend. I woke at dawn. There was no excitement. No stage fright or butterflies to signal the first day of the rest of my life. Looking up from sleep I could have dreamed my release from prison the day before. The sky was as gray as a prison sky—the same sky I had seen for the past sixteen years and three months.

Not long after I went to prison, I woke in the middle of the night and sat up on the side of the bed. The cell was so quiet I could hear cockroaches foraging in my garbage.

"When I get out of prison," I said to myself, "sex can wait." Thinking of what I would most like to do, I said, "I'm going to eat strawberries! Big! Fresh! Red strawberries!" And that became my mantra for the rest of the time I was in prison.

On the day I was released, Kathrin, a friend, a sister, my confidante, came to pick me up. She was there with her camera, taking photos of me as I walked through the last gate to freedom. She drove me to the house where she lived with her husband and son and fed me steamed shrimp, French champagne, and strawberries!

SOURCE: Jerome Washington, *Iron House: Stories From the Yard* (New York: Vintage, 1994), 155-163.

Jerome Washington, a writer, is now discharged from parole supervision and is living in California.

Other reentry problems may plague parolees. For many, the transition from the highly structured life in prison to the open society is too difficult to manage. Many just do not have the social, psychological, and material resources to cope with the temptations and complications of modern life. For these parolees, freedom may be short-lived as they fall back into forbidden activities such as drinking, using drugs, and stealing.

Community Programs Following Release

Various programs have been developed to assist parolees in reentering society. Some help prepare offenders for release while they are still in prison; others provide employment and housing assistance after release. Together the programs are intended to help the offender progress steadily toward reintegration into the community.

Programs of partial confinement prior to parole are used to test the offender's readiness for full release. Community-based corrections assumes that the goal is to choose, from the several alternatives to incarceration, the least-restrictive one that will lead to eventual reintegration.

Among the many programs developed to assist offenders in their return to the community, three are especially important: work and educational release, furloughs, and residential programs. Although similar in many ways, each offers a specific approach to helping formerly incarcerated individuals reenter the community.

Work and Educational Release

Programs of **work and educational release**, in which inmates are released from correctional institutions during the day to work or attend school, were first established

work and educational release

The daytime release of inmates from correctional institutions so they can work or attend school.

in Vermont in 1906. However, the Huber Act, passed by the Wisconsin legislature in 1913, is usually cited as the model on which such programs are based. By 1972 most states and the federal government had instituted these programs.

Although most work and educational release programs are justifiable as rehabilitation, many correctional administrators and legislators also like them because they cost relatively little. In some states, a portion of the inmate's earnings from work outside may be deducted for room and board. One problem is that in some states, organized labor complains that these programs take jobs from free citizens. Furthermore, the releasee's contact with the community increases the chances that contraband may be brought into the institution. To deal with such bootlegging and to assist in the reintegration process, some states and counties have built special work and educational release units in urban areas where offenders live away from the prison.

Furloughs

Isolation from loved ones is one of the pains of imprisonment. Although conjugal visits have been a part of correctional programs in many countries, they have been used in only a few U.S. correctional systems. Many penologists view the **furlough**—the temporary release of an inmate from a correctional institution for a visit home—as a meaningful approach to inmate reintegration.

furlough

The temporary release of an inmate from a correctional institution for a brief period, usually one to three days, for a visit home. Such programs help maintain family ties and prepare inmates for release on parole.

Furloughs are thought to offer an excellent means of testing an inmate's ability to cope with the larger society. Through home visits the inmate can renew family ties and relieve the tensions of confinement. Most administrators also feel that furloughs are good for prisoners' morale. The general public, however, does not always support the concept. Public outrage is inevitable if an offender on furlough commits another crime or fails to return. Correctional authorities are often nervous about using furloughs because they fear being blamed for such incidents.

Residential Programs

The **community correctional center** is an institution that houses soon-to-be-released inmates and connects them to community services, resources, and support. It may take a number of forms, such as halfway houses, prerelease centers, and correctional service centers, and serve a variety of offender clients. Most programs require offenders to reside at the facility while they work in the community or visit with their families. Other facilities are designed primarily to provide services and programs for parolees. Often these facilities are established in former private homes or small hotels, creating a homey, less institutional environment. Individual rooms, group dining rooms, and other homelike features are maintained whenever possible.

community correctional center

An institution, usually in an urban area, that houses inmates soon to be released. Such centers are designed to help inmates establish community ties and thus promote their reintegration with society.

The term ***halfway house*** has been applied to a variety of community correctional facilities and programs in which felons work in the community but reside in the halfway house during nonworking hours. Most halfway houses are operated under contract by private, nonprofit organizations. Halfway houses range from secure institutions in the community with programs designed to assist inmates who are preparing for release on parole to group homes where parolees, probationers, or persons diverted from the system are able to live with minimal supervision and direction. Some halfway houses are organized to deliver special treatment services, such as programs designed to deal with alcohol, drug, or mental problems. In the Workperspective Lisa Zimmer describes the residential treatment program with which she is associated.

halfway house

A correctional facility housing convicted felons who spend a portion of their day at work in the community but reside in the halfway house during nonworking hours.

WORK*Perspective*

Lisa A. Zimmer
Chemical Dependency Counselor

Residential Treatment Program for Convicted Offenders
Cincinnati, Ohio

I hold a bachelor's degree in journalism from Northwestern University. After eleven years in the field of public relations, I knew I wanted to find a career that made a greater contribution to people and society, even if it meant accepting a smaller salary. I went back to school to earn a master's degree in social work at the University of Kentucky. During the field experience of my graduate program I worked for two semesters at a hospital providing psychiatric emergency services. There I observed that most of my patients had substance abuse problems that contributed to their mental problems. To learn more about substance abuse I served additional field placements in treatment programs for offenders with this problem.

I now work for an agency that has a contract with the county to provide substance abuse treatment in a residential facility for people serving misdemeanor jail sentences. The clients live in two large dormitory rooms that can house a total of fifty males. Security is maintained by county correctional officers. Judges may ask that specific offenders with chemical dependency problems be considered for our program. If they are selected and successfully complete the 90- to 120-day treatment program, they are usually released by the judge to two years of probation. While on probation they must continue treatment. I recognize that the prospect of early release rather than a genuine desire to address substance abuse problems serves as the primary motivation for many of my clients.

Chemical dependency treatment is sorely needed in the corrections environment. Our treatment involves individual and group counseling. In group sessions, counselors encourage clients to share thoughts and experiences, analyze their problems together, and confront one another about avoiding important personal issues. Special group meetings deal with certain problems, such as alcohol, drugs, or assaultive behavior.

I am a social worker by training and by philosophy. As such, I am an advocate for my clients. However, I am not opposed to penalties for the crimes they have committed. I bear a responsibility to the public, too. However, we don't have a crystal ball to tell us how our clients will behave in the future. The possibility always exists that someone released from the program will commit additional crimes with tragic consequences, so I do not take my responsibilities lightly.

I make decisions on a daily basis about how to counsel clients and facilitate their group discussions. I also must make more difficult decisions, such as recommending that a client return to jail if he is not making genuine efforts to participate in the program or is violating rules. This is a particularly difficult decision when I am told that one client has threatened another client, grounds for a return to jail to serve out the sentence. If I have conflicting versions of events, whom should I believe? I always look for additional evidence, such as witnesses or others who have been threatened by the same person. The last thing I would want is to send someone back if he has done nothing wrong. On the other hand, I bear responsibility for the safety of clients and staff and for success of the program. Thus a decision may have to be made—one that will cause someone to serve months in jail—based on our best judgment, even if we cannot know with absolute certainty exactly what happened.

WORK*Perspective*

Community resistance has been a significant impediment to the development of community-based corrections facilities and even has forced some successful facilities to close. Few neighborhoods want to host halfway houses or treatment centers for convicts. Many communities, often wealthier ones, have blocked placement of halfway houses or treatment centers within their boundaries. One result of this "not in my backyard" attitude is that centers are usually established in deteriorating neighborhoods inhabited by poor people, who lack the political power and resources to block unpopular programs.

Today, the future of residential programs is unclear. Originally advocated for both rehabilitative and financial reasons, they do not seem to be saving as much money for the correctional system as officials had hoped. Medical care, education, vocational rehabilitation, and therapy are expensive. Thus, the costs of quality community programs are likely to be about the same as the costs of incarceration. Effective programs require the services of teachers, counselors, and other professional personnel. Moreover, in order to be truly effective, these officials must work with small numbers of offenders. The savings realized from the use of fewer custodial personnel may be offset by the costs of counseling and other professional services.

If recidivism rates of offenders who have been involved in community treatment were proven to be lower, these costs might more readily be justified. However, the available data are discouraging. The excitement and optimism that greeted the community correctional movement may have been unwarranted.

CHECKPOINT

8. What are three programs designed to ease the reentry of offenders into the community?

Parole Officer Corey Burke drops by unannounced to visit a paroled sex offender in the man's apartment. Burke sees his job as neither to exact retribution nor to offer compassion, but to keep parolees from committing another crime.

Parole Officer: Cop or Social Worker?

After release, a parolee's principal contact with the criminal justice system is through the parole officer, who has the dual responsibility of providing surveillance and assistance. The parole officer is responsible for seeing that the parolee follows the conditions imposed by the parole board.

The conditions imposed by Connecticut's Board of Parole are quite substantial and not atypical. Consider how difficult it must be for a parole officer to monitor the following twelve conditions, especially when the officer is responsible for many parolees at once:

1. Upon release from the institution, you must follow the instructions of the institutional parole officer (or other designated authority of the Division of

Parole) with regard to reporting to your supervising parole officer and/or fulfilling any other obligations.

2. You must report to your parole officer when instructed to do so and must permit your parole officer or any parole officer to visit you at your home and place of employment at any time.
3. You must work steadily, and you must secure the permission of your parole officer before changing your residence or your employment, and you must report any change of residence or employment to your parole officer within twenty-four hours of such change.
4. You must submit written reports as instructed by your parole officer.
5. You must not leave the state of Connecticut without first obtaining permission from your parole officer.
6. You must not apply for a motor vehicle operator's license, or own, purchase, or operate any motor vehicle without first obtaining permission from your parole officer.
7. You must not marry without first obtaining written permission from your parole officer.
8. You must not own, possess, use, sell, or have under your control at any time any deadly weapons or firearms.
9. You must not possess, use, or traffic in any narcotic, hallucinatory, or other harmful drugs in violation of the law.
10. You must support your dependents, if any, and assume toward them all moral and legal obligations.
11. (a) You shall not consume alcoholic beverages to excess. (b) You shall totally abstain from the use of alcoholic beverages or liquors. (Strike out either a or b, leaving whichever clause is applicable.)
12. You must comply with all laws and conduct yourself as a good citizen. You must show by your attitude, cooperation, choice of associates, and places of amusement and recreation that you are a proper person to remain on parole.

Huge caseloads—typically fifty to seventy parolees—make effective supervision practically impossible in some states. Although parole officers have smaller caseloads than probation officers, offenders who have just been released from prison require more extensive services. One reason is that parolees, by the very fact of their incarceration, have generally committed much more serious crimes. Another reason is that probationers continue their lives in the community while living under a set of restrictive conditions, whereas parolees are making a very difficult transition from the highly structured prison environment back to a society in which they have previously failed to live as law-abiding citizens. It is exceptionally difficult for a parole officer to monitor, control, and assist clients who may have little knowledge of or experience with living successfully within society's rules.

Parole officers are asked to play two different roles: cop and social worker. In their role as police officer they are given the power to restrict many aspects of the parolee's life, to enforce the conditions of release, and to initiate revocation proceedings if parole conditions are violated. Like other officials in the criminal justice system, the parole officer has extensive discretion in low-visibility situations. In many states parole officers have the authority to search the parolee's house without warning, to arrest him or her without the possibility of bail for suspected violations, and to suspend parole pending a hearing before the board. This authoritarian component of the parole officer's role can give the ex-offender a sense of insecurity and hamper the development of mutual trust. The law enforcement powers are granted to parole officers so that the community can be protected from offenders who are coming out of prison. However, because these powers diminish the possibility that the officer will develop a close relationship with the client, they may weaken the officer's other role of assisting the parolee's readjustment to the community (Clear and Latessa, 1993:441).

Parole officers must also act as social workers by helping the parolee find a job and restore family ties. Officers must be prepared to serve as agent-mediators between parolees and the organizations with which they deal and to channel them to social agencies, such as psychiatric clinics, where they can obtain help. As caseworkers, officers work to develop a relationship that allows parolees to confide their frustrations and concerns. Because parolees are not likely to do this if they are constantly aware of the parole officer's ability to send them back to prison, some researchers have suggested that parole officers' conflicting responsibilities of cop and social worker should be separated. Parole officers could maintain the supervisory aspects of the position, and other personnel—perhaps a separate parole counselor—could perform the casework functions. Another option would be for parole officers to be charged solely with social work duties, while local police check for violations.

The parole officer works within a bureaucratic environment. The difficulties faced by many parolees are so complex that the officer's job is almost impossible. At the same time, like most other human services organizations, parole agencies are short on resources and expertise. As a result, they frequently must classify parolees and give priority to those most in need. To serve those with the greatest need, most parole officers spend more time with the newly released. As the officer gains greater confidence in the parolee, the level of supervision can be adjusted to "active" or "reduced" surveillance. Depending on how the parolee has functioned in the community, he or she eventually may be allowed to check in with the officer periodically rather than submit to regular home visits, searches, and other intrusive monitoring.

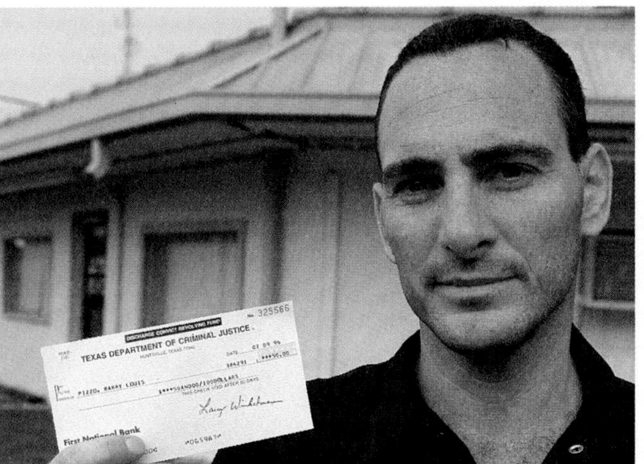

Most inmates leave prison with their clothes, a limited amount of money, and the address of their parole officer. Often there is no family member or friend at the gate, and the prospects for housing and a job are limited. Adjustment to the realities of life in the community are just as great as adjustment to prison life on the way in.

CHECKPOINT

9. What are some of the rules most parolees must follow while they are supervised in the community?
10. What are the major tasks of parole officers?

Adjustment to Life Outside Prison

With little preparation the ex-offender moves from the highly structured, authoritarian life of the institution into a world filled with temptations and complicated problems. Suddenly, ex-convicts who are unaccustomed to undertaking even simple tasks like going to the store for groceries are expected to assume pressing, complex responsibilities. Finding a job and a place to live aren't the only problems the newly released person faces. The parolee must also make significant social and psychological role adjustments. A male ex-convict, for example, is suddenly required to become not only a parolee but also an employee, a neighbor, a father, a husband,

and a son. The expectations, norms, and social relations in the free world are quite different from those learned in prison. The relatively predictable inmate code is replaced by society's often unclear rules of behavior—rules that the offender had failed to cope with during his or her previous life in free society.

The "Dangerous" Parolee

The public's assumptions about ex-offenders are shaped by news reports of brutal crimes committed by parolees. The murder of 12-year-old Polly Klaas by parolee Richard Davis and the rape and murder of 7-year-old Megan Kanka by a paroled sex offender motivated legislators in thirty-five states to enact "offender notification" laws. These laws require that the public be notified of the whereabouts of "potentially dangerous" sex offenders. In some states paroled sex offenders must register with the police, while in others, immediate neighbors must be informed. In these "Megan's Law" states, parolees have been "hounded" from communities, the media have televised the parolee's homecoming, and neighbors have assaulted parolees they erroneously thought were sex offenders.

Jesse Timmendequas, the repeat sex offender who raped and murdered 7-year-old Megan Kanka, was sentenced to death in a Trenton, New Jersey, courtroom. Like the public uproar following the murder of Polly Klaas in California, the New Jersey legislature passed "Megan's Law," requiring that neighbors of paroled sex offenders be notified. President Clinton signed a national version of the legislation in 1996.

Kansas and five other states—Arizona, California, Minnesota, Washington, and Wisconsin—have passed laws allowing confinement of certain sex offenders past the expiration of their prison terms. In 1997 the Supreme Court upheld the Kansas Sexually Violent Offender Act, which allows commitment to a mental hospital of those found to have a "mental abnormality" and are likely to commit other sexual offenses. The case, *Kansas v. Hendricks*, involved an offender who, over a forty-year period, had been repeatedly convicted of child molesting (1997).

The fact of repeat violence fuels a public perception that parolees represent a continuing threat to the public welfare. The result of this preoccupation with potential parolee criminality may mean even a harder line against parolees. Although the laws that have been enacted are directed primarily at people who have committed sex offenses against children, there is concern that the community will target all parolees, making it even more difficult for ex-offenders to successfully reenter society.

Parole and Recidivism

The reentry problems of parolees are reflected in their rearrest rates. As shown in Figure 14.4, about 25 percent are arrested during the first six months, almost 40 percent within the first year, and 62 percent within three years. About 40 percent of those rearrested will be reincarcerated within three years.

It is not surprising that the recidivism rate is so high when we consider that today's average ex-convict has been convicted of serious crimes (83 percent for violent or property offenses), has a criminal record of multiple arrests (8.4 prior arrests), and has been incarcerated before (67 percent) (BJS, 1989. *Special Report*, April). These are not the people who have run afoul of the law only once, when they made a bad decision or acted impulsively. Instead, most prisoners have committed serious crimes and have a long history of difficulties with the criminal justice system. The numbers indicate that a large percentage of today's inmates are career criminals who will resort to their old habits upon release. Moreover, the experience of spending time in prison is essentially designed to punish people for their harmful acts. By itself, the experience of incarceration is unlikely to teach anyone how to succeed in the

IDEAS IN PRACTICE

Carl DeFlumer has spent 42 of his 62 years in prison for killing a boy when he was 14 and sodomizing another 29 years later. In September 1994, the New York State Board of Parole granted his release to live with his sister. Word of DeFlumer's impending release caused a howl of protest in Bethlehem, the rural community where his sister lives. Residents expressed fear for the safety of their children. As one said, "You need a building permit to put a fence in your yard. But they can put one of these guys next door and not even tell you."

Should residents be allowed to determine if parolees can live in their community? What should happen to offenders who complete their sentences and have no place to reside?

community. In fact, the artificial environment of prisons moves people farther away from the atmosphere, attitudes, habits, and responsibilities that make for success in American society.

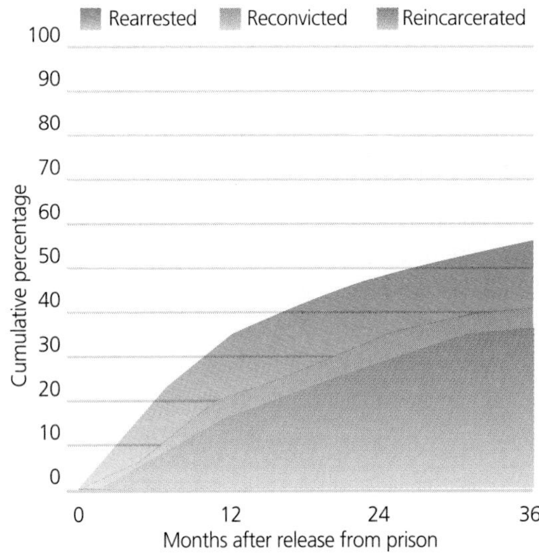

Figure 14.4
Cumulative percentage of state prisoners rearrested, reconvicted, and reincarcerated 36 months after release

The first year after release is the period of greatest probability for recidivism.

SOURCE: U.S. Department of Justice, Bureau of Justice Statistics, *Special Report* (April 1989).

CHECKPOINT

11. What are some of the major problems faced by parolees?
12. What are "offender notification laws"?

Revocation of Parole

Always hanging over the ex-inmate's head is the potential revocation of parole for committing a new crime or failing to adhere to the parole contract. Because parolees still have the status of inmate, some corrections experts believe that parole should be easily revoked without formal procedures, hearings, or rules of evidence. In some states, liberal parole policies have been justified to the public on the grounds that revocation is swift and can be imposed before a crime is committed. For example, state statutes may provide that a parole officer who has reasonable cause to believe that the parolee has lapsed or is about to lapse into criminal ways or has otherwise violated the conditions of parole should report these suspicions to the parole board so the parolee can be apprehended. Statutes may also permit parole officers to take the parolee into custody and call for a revocation hearing. The parolee who leaves the state or has been charged with a new offense is usually arrested and detained until a revocation hearing or a criminal trial is held.

***Morrissey v. Brewer* (1972)**

Due process rights require a prompt, informal inquiry by an impartial hearing officer before parole may be revoked. The parolee may present relevant information and confront witnesses.

If the parole officer alleges that a technical (noncriminal) violation of the parole contract has occurred, a revocation proceeding will be held before the parolee is sent back to prison. In the case of ***Morrissey v. Brewer*** (1972), the U.S. Supreme Court held that a parolee who faces parole revocation must be accorded due process rights and a prompt, informal inquiry before an impartial hearing officer. However, the Court distinguished the requirements of such a proceeding from the normal requirements of the criminal trial. In the case of parole revocation, the Court requires a two-step hearing process through which the parole board determines whether the contract has been violated. Parolees have the right to be notified of the charges against them, to know the evidence against them, to be allowed to speak on their own behalf, to present witnesses, and to confront the witnesses against them.

The number of parole revocations is difficult to determine because most published data do not distinguish between parolees returned to prison for technical violations and those sent back for new criminal offenses. One recent study found that 22 percent of state inmates were on parole at the time of their recommitment to prison. Eighty percent were returned following conviction on a new offense, while the remainder were in prison for a technical violation (BJS, 1995. *Special Report*, August:2).

Because prisons are so overcrowded, most revocations occur only when the parolee has been arrested on a serious charge or cannot be located by the parole officer. Given the size of the normal caseload, most parole officers are unable to monitor parolees closely and thus may be unaware of technical violations. Under the new requirements for prompt and fair hearings, some parole boards discourage officers from issuing violation warrants following infractions of parole rules unless there is evidence of new crimes.

CHECKPOINT

13. What two conditions may result in the revocation of parole?
14. What due process requirements must be followed in the parole revocation process?

The Future of Parole

The effectiveness of corrections is usually measured by the recidivism rate. Despite the modest success of parole and various release methods, as measured by recidivism rates, these programs are likely to expand. As prison populations rise, demands that felons be allowed to serve part of their time in the community will undoubtedly mount. These demands will not come from the public, which typically believes that all offenders should serve their full sentences. Instead, they will come from legislators and corrections officials who recognize that we lack the money and facilities to incarcerate all offenders for the complete terms of their sentences. In states with discretionary release, parole provides one of the few ways for correctional officials to relieve institutional pressures. In many states where mandatory release is the way out of prison, offenders nearing expiration of their terms are being moved to community facilities so they can begin the reintegration process. Although many offenders are not successfully integrated into the community, we must recognize that most offenders will end up back in free society whether or not they serve their full sentences. Parole and community programs represent an effort to address the inevitability of their return. Even if such programs do not prevent all offenders from leaving the life of crime, they do help some to turn their lives around.

Summary

- Conditional release from prison on parole is the primary method by which inmates return to society. While on parole they remain under correctional supervision.
- There are three types of release: mandatory, discretionary, and unconditional.
- Parole boards exercise the discretion to consider various factors in making the decision to release.
- Parolees are released from prison on the condition that they do not again violate the law and that they live according to rules designed both to help them adjust to society and to control their movements.
- Parole officers are assigned to assist ex-inmates in making the transition to society and to ensure that they follow the conditions of their release.
- Upon release, offenders face a number of problems: they must find housing and employment and renew relationships with family and friends.
- Community corrections assumes that reentry should be a gradual process through which parolees should be assisted. Halfway houses, work and educational release, furloughs, and community correctional centers are geared to ease the transition.

Questions for Review

1. What are the basic assumptions of parole?
2. How do mandatory release, discretionary release, and unconditional release differ?
3. What is the role of the parole officer?
4. What problems confront parolees upon their release?

ANSWERS TO CHECKPOINTS

1. England, Australia, Ireland.
2. Maconochie developed a classification procedure through which prisoners could earn increasing responsibility and freedom. Crofton linked Maconochie's idea of an offender's progress in prison to the ticket of leave and supervision in the community.
3. Discretionary release is the release of an inmate from incarceration to supervision at the discretion of the parole board within the boundaries set by the sentence and the penal law. Mandatory release is the required release of an inmate from incarceration to community supervision upon the expiration of a certain time period, as specified by a determinate sentencing law or parole guidelines. Unconditional release is the release of an inmate from incarceration without any further correctional supervision; the inmate cannot be returned to prison for any remaining portion of the sentence for the current offense.
4. As part of the department of corrections or an independent agency of the government.
5. The severity of the offense, characteristics of the offender, readiness for parole, good-time credit, participation in education and treatment programs, attitudes, plan after release, written statements from victim, offender's family, and so forth.
6. Participation in prison educational and treatment programs.
7. Parole release affects sentencing, encourages plea bargaining, relieves prison crowding, makes the sentence less harsh, and encourages good behavior in prison.
8. Work and educational release programs, furlough programs, residential programs.
9. Make required reports to parole officer, do not leave the state without permission, do not use alcohol or drugs, maintain employment, attend required treatment programs.
10. Surveillance and assistance.
11. Finding housing and employment, having a shortage of money, and reestablishing relationships with family and friends.
12. Laws requiring sex offenders to notify the police or residents that they are living in the community.
13. Arrest for a new crime, or a technical violation of one or more of the conditions of parole.
14. In a two-step hearing process, the parolee has the right to be notified of the charges, to know the evidence against him or her, to be heard, to present witnesses, and to confront witnesses.

INSIDE THE CRIMINAL JUSTICE SYSTEM AND BEYOND: ONE MAN'S JOURNEY

Prison

The trip from the county jail to prison, a bus ride known among prisoners as "the chain," can be an unsettling experience. On this particular trip I was accompanied by about thirty other inmates. The scenery we saw outside the grilled windows changed as we headed southeast out of Los Angeles. Freeways, business districts, and suburban neighborhoods were left behind and replaced by small towns, farms, and livestock. During the ride I thought about all I would be missing out there, all the things I wouldn't be able to do wherever I was going, and wondered what my future would bring. For first-termers "the chain" can be as scary as hell. For others it may be routine. Most probably wonder if they'll get out alive. I always did.

Once again, my destination was the Regional Guidance Center at Chino. Only this time, rather than coming for a ninety-day evaluation, I would be classified as a "new commitment." Instead of being "evaluated," I would be processed and sent to another facility somewhere within the state. As we approached the institution I saw the familiar-looking guard towers, chainlink fences covered with barbed razor wire, and the outside windows of the cellblocks. Once we arrived, the bus passed through an electronically operated gate. Our entrance was monitored by armed guards. It was here that I experienced that fleeting sense of impending doom, the feeling that I might never get out of prison again. After the bus stopped we sat for several minutes, chained together and relatively quiet, until the guards came and escorted us inside.

After entering the guidance center I was again booked—fingerprinted, photographed, searched—and told where to live. Given that I had just come from here, being new wasn't that big a deal. Besides, I was getting used to these places. Yet the time I spent inside in the years to come unquestionably affected my sense of identity and ideas about life. After two months of processing, including psychological and physical examinations, I was sent to the California Correctional Center at Lassen, a facility more commonly known as "Susanville," the town in which it is located.

In prison I learned to hate and to do whatever I could to use drugs without compromising my integrity. All myths aside, drugs are hard to get in prison. I learned what it's like to be a minority. Mostly, I learned to see myself and the world from the perspective of a convict.

Life inside is extremely monotonous, although life-threatening situations can arise in a heartbeat. Prison is a world in which you can never show weakness, where you adapt to survive, and where race and "fitting in" are very important. In prison it's not so much what crime you did (except for heinous crimes such as sex offenses or crimes against children—those offenders get no respect), but who you are within that world that determines how you are seen and treated both by fellow inmates and prison workers. And who you are is gauged by the people you run with, how you carry yourself, and your character. And it all takes place within a structure of nearly total control and oppression.

People often ask me what it is really like in prison. The answer depends on historical context, where you are doing time, and who you are. It is different now than it was twenty years ago. It will vary and depend on political ideology, level of custody (maximum or minimum), what color you are (and how that matches with the racial composition of the prison), how old you are, how much experience you have within the system, and, of course, the perspectives you bring with you into the institution. But the degrading, dehumanizing effects of prison are usually similar because they stem from the same structural roots.

Prisoners are, by definition, a threat to society and in need of control. Therefore, we (I include myself here because I am writing from the perspective of a convict) must be confined, observed, and kept in our place.

ONE MAN'S JOURNEY (CONTINUED)

To achieve these goals our keepers tell us where and when to eat, sleep, go to the bathroom, exercise, and work. What we see, hear, smell, touch, and do on a daily basis depends on them. We are deprived of privacy, heterosexual relationships, education, employment (except at the most menial levels), and the ability to attain material things. Adding to these effects is the contempt with which we are often treated by prison officials.

Sadly, most of the hate and anger generated from the structure of prisons are directed toward other inmates. We seldom focus our attention on changing the conditions and people who bind us. For the most part, we accept our situation as being "the way it is." Perhaps we do this because we believe we deserve it. After all, we are in prison and the guards are just doing their jobs. But sometimes the veils we hide behind are ripped apart as the harsh realities of life become impossible to deny, often as a result of institutionalized violence.

One day, during my months at Susanville, a friend told me that everyone was getting together to have a work strike. Once in the yard I saw something that I never saw before or since: all the races (brown, white, black) were participating in a single act of defiance against the conditions of the prison. Leaders from each race acted as representatives, spoke openly about our needs, and emphasized that this was to be a nonviolent strike. We would simply not go to work until our demands were met.

Within fifteen minutes of this gathering, we heard "Yard recall, yard recall, all men return to your dorms" over the loudspeakers. To establish more control than was possible from the gun towers, extra guards armed with rifles appeared at strategic locations on the roofs of our housing units. We were herded inside our dorms, placed on lockdown status, and fed sack lunches (two baloney sandwiches and an apple) twice a day.

On the afternoon of the fourth day we heard bullets ricocheting against the bricks that made up the lower part of the dorm walls. Above the bricks were windows, out of which we could see the yard, the gun towers, and the guards on the roofs. The bullets made a loud pinging sound like you hear in movies. A friend of mine, five feet away, turned toward me and said, "They're poppin' caps out there [shooting bullets]!" Someone else said, "Those ain't real bullets," as if it weren't possible for such a thing to happen. Next thing I know, my friend fell to the ground and said, "I'm hit." Thinking he was joking, I told him, "Quit bullshitting, get up." But I quickly saw blood coming from his groin area. He really had been shot.

With reality becoming obvious and the bullets still pinging, we all dropped to the floor. I grabbed my friend (who was moaning in agony), dragged him under my bunk for safety, put a tourniquet on his wound, and tried to calm him until the guards came and took him out of there.

That evening, after things had settled down, we saw the "goon squad," a row of twelve guards, three in each row, dressed in full battle gear with helmets and clubs, coming across the yard toward our end of the prison. For a few minutes we lost sight of the "gooners," but before long we saw all the men from an upstairs dorm running across the yard, the goon squad right behind them.

Over the course of that long night every man in the prison was "guided" to what is called a "classification hearing," a legal procedure that must take place before a body can be transferred to another institution. Until the early hours of the following day, many inmates were openly beaten during their journeys to the hearing. It was like watching a live version of the Rodney King beating, right in front of our eyes. At classification we were asked, "Are you ready to work?" Those who said no were shipped to another prison.

Of the more than one thousand inmates housed in that prison, over 120 were transferred that night. Three were shot and many more seriously hurt. Interestingly, television newscasters reported that "inmates were violently rioting" (a lie) in the local prison but were now "back under control."

After the strike was "resolved," I went back to my clerk job in "Receiving and Release" (the place where inmates enter and leave the prison). After seeing my friend shot and all the beatings that had taken place, I had to ask my boss (a sergeant) why the guards had to hurt so many people that night. He answered, "They just want you guys to know who is running this joint."

Over the next several months the story about what happened got out.

ONE MAN'S JOURNEY (CONTINUED)

People from the state capital came to investigate. About 200 inmates took lie detector tests to validate their stories. Not one guard would agree to do the same. And nobody forced the issue. To my knowledge, nothing was ever done to rectify the damage that had been done that day. It is as if it never happened.

Similarly, the harsh reality of living in prison is seldom acknowledged. Does anyone deserve to live in such an environment? Does it matter if one is convicted for murder or possession of drugs? Apparently not. Why you are sentenced to prison makes little difference once you're on the inside.

After being in prison for twelve months I appeared before a parole board that consisted of two men who talked to me as if I were some kind of dog. Their comments were based on my "history," which they had in front of them in a file: rap sheet, prior presentence investigations, police reports, and the results from the ninety-day evaluation. For the most part they harassed and belittled me with questions about my past. The only thing I said was yes when they asked me if I understood them. After they'd had their say, I was asked to step outside the room while they made a decision. They told me they decided to give me a total of twenty-six months (from the time of arrest until release), which was about what I'd expected. They also told me that if I didn't start acting right, the next time they saw me would be at Folsom Prison and they would bury me so deep I'd never see daylight again. As I left the room I felt great. Many people I knew didn't get a "date" at all and had to wait another year just to appear.

In my final years in prison, the perception I had about myself and the world took a dramatic shift, largely as the result of attending two years of college classes. Learning was exciting. It opened my eyes to things I never knew and helped me see that there were other, more important things to do besides using heroin. In 1992 I was discharged from parole. And I'm still in school.

Coming Home

Getting released from prison is like coming home from a war. The more time you do the greater the shock. From a world where great meaning comes from the color of your skin, whom you hang out with, which bench you sit on in the yard, and where you eat in the chow hall, you find yourself out here. Choices. Kids. Shopping. Women. Asshole car drivers. Pets. Around people who define themselves based on their jobs, how many "things" they have, or their political affiliation. Life inside was structured. You clearly knew your place—count time, chow line, yard line, sick line. Out here it's really different.

I was assigned to a parole officer known as "Lock-'em-up Tom." Like my old probation officer, Tom told me he didn't think I had a chance of making it. He said I would have to regularly test for drugs and attend Twelve-Step meetings at least three times a week. When I informed him that I no longer had a drug problem, he smiled and said, "Well, Chuck, that might be true. But you also don't know how to live out here. Its kinda like the first time you went to jail—it was something new. You had to learn about it and adapt in order to survive. As I see it, that's what you need to do now—only in reverse. By getting involved with other clean addicts you might just learn how." Tom never did lock me up. He spied on me, tested me, and always talked down to me. Yet his ideas about what I'd have to do to make it were definitely grounded in reality. In many ways I am still learning how to live out here.

Part 5

The Juvenile Justice System

CRIMES committed by juveniles are a serious national problem. The *Uniform Crime Reports* show that just over one-third of the people arrested for an index crime are under 18 years of age. Children who are charged with crimes, who have been neglected by their parents, or whose behavior is judged to require official action enter the juvenile justice system, an independent process that is interrelated with the adult system.

Many of the procedures used in handling juvenile problems are similar to those used with adults, but the overriding philosophy of juvenile justice is somewhat different, and the state may intrude into the lives of children to a much greater extent. In recent years there have been political and legal moves to reduce the differences in the two systems.

The Crime Control Period (1980–Present)

Policies on juvenile crime have shifted since 1980 to an emphasis on crime control. With the public demanding a "crackdown on crime," legislators have responded by changing the juvenile system. Greater attention is now being focused on repeat offenders, with policy makers calling for harsher punishment of juveniles who commit crimes (Forst and Blomquist, 1992:1).

Schall v. Martin (1984)

Juveniles can be held in preventive detention if there is concern that they may commit additional crimes while awaiting court action.

In ***Schall v. Martin*** (1984), the Supreme Court significantly departed from the trend toward increased juvenile rights when it upheld New York's law allowing the preventive detention of juveniles. The Court confirmed that the general notion of *parens patriae* was a primary basis for the juvenile court, equal in importance to the Court's desire to protect the community from crime. Thus, juveniles may be held in preventive detention before trial if they are deemed a "risk" to the community.

The *Schall* decision reflects the ambivalence permeating the juvenile justice system. On one side are the liberal reformers, who call for increased procedural and substantive legal protections for juveniles accused of crime. On the other side are conservatives devoted to crime control policies and alarmed by the rise in juvenile crime.

The present crime control policy has brought many more juveniles to be tried in adult courts. As noted by Alex Kotlowitz, "the crackdown on children has gone well beyond those accused of violent crimes" (Kotlowitz, 1994:4). Today, a much higher percentage of cases involving juveniles are being adjudicated in the adult criminal courts (OJJDP, 1996. *Juvenile Justice Bulletin*, July).

In spite of the increasingly tough policies directed at juvenile offenders, changes that occurred during the juvenile rights period continue to have a profound impact. Lawyers are now routinely present at court hearings and other stages of the process, adding a note of formality that was not present twenty years ago. Status offenders seldom end up in secure, punitive environments such as training schools. The juvenile justice system looks more like the adult justice system than it did, but it still is less formal. Its stated intention is also less harsh: to keep juveniles in the community whenever possible.

Public support for a get-tough stance toward older juveniles seems to be growing. The juvenile court, where the use of discretion and the desire to rehabilitate were uppermost, has become a system of rules and procedures similar to adult courts. With deserved punishment more prominent as a correctional goal, more severe sentences are being given to juveniles who are repeat offenders.

CHECKPOINT

5. What was the function of a House of Refuge?
6. What were the major elements of the Illinois Juvenile Court Act of 1899?
7. What was the main point of the decision in *In re Gault*?

THE JUVENILE JUSTICE SYSTEM

Juvenile justice operates through a variety of procedures in different states; even different counties within the same states will follow different procedures. The offenses committed by juveniles are mostly violations of state laws, so the federal government has little involvement in the juvenile justice system.

Even though differences exist among and within states, the juvenile justice system is characterized by two key factors: (1) the age of clients and (2) the categories of cases under juvenile rather than adult court jurisdiction.

Age of Clients

Age normally determines whether a person is processed through the juvenile or adult justice system. The upper age limit for a juvenile varies from 16 to 18: in thirty-eight states and the District of Columbia it is the eighteenth birthday; in eight states, the seventeenth; and in the remainder, the sixteenth. In all states, judges have the discretion to transfer juveniles to adult courts through a waiver hearing—that is, a hearing in which the juvenile court judge waives, or gives up, jurisdiction of the case. Figure 15.2 shows the ages at which juveniles can be transferred to adult court.

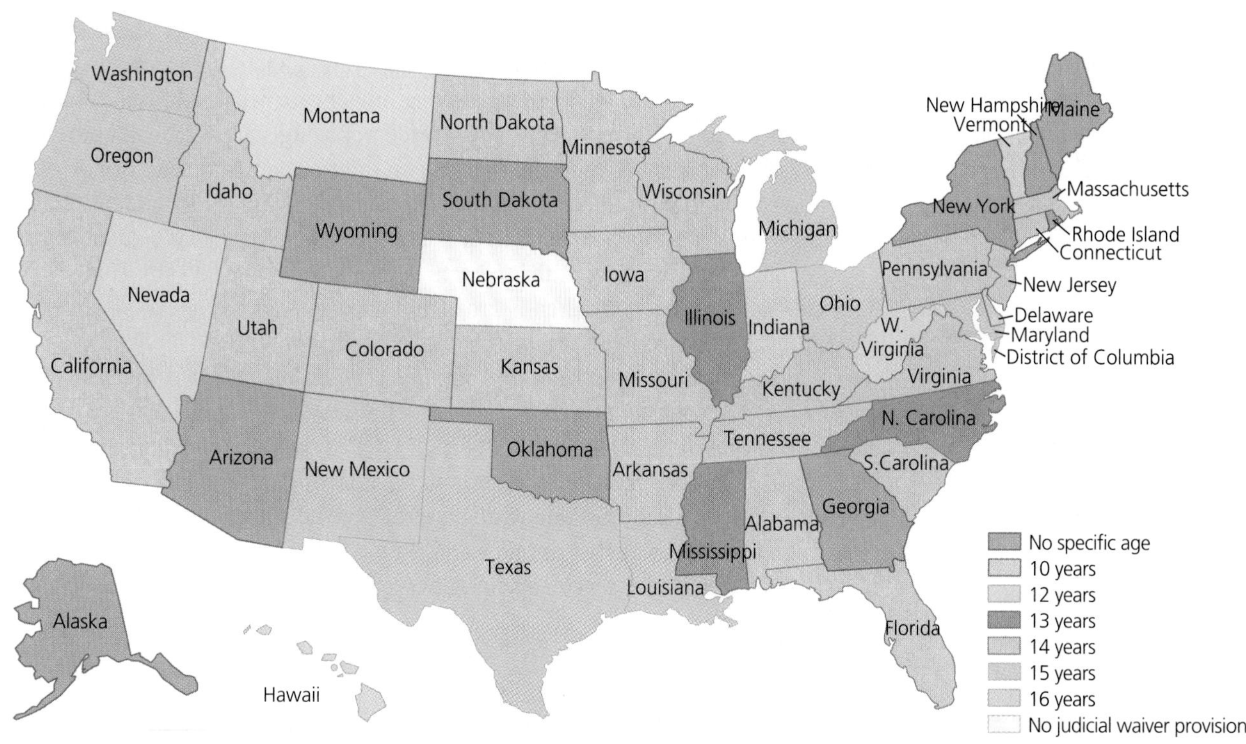

Figure 15.2
The youngest age at which juveniles may be transferred to adult criminal court by waiver of juvenile jurisdiction

The waiver provisions of states vary greatly, and no clear regional or other factors explain the differences.

SOURCE: U.S. Department of Justice, Office of Juvenile Justice and Delinquency Prevention, *Juvenile Offenders and Victims: A National Report* (Washington, D.C.: Government Printing Office, 1995), 88.

Categories of Cases under Juvenile Court Jurisdiction

Four types of cases are under the jurisdiction of the juvenile justice system: delinquency, status offenses, neglect, and dependency. Mixing together within the same system young criminals and children who suffer from their parents' inadequacies is a practice that dates from the early history of juvenile justice.

Delinquent children have committed acts that if committed by an adult would be criminal—for example, auto theft, robbery, or assault. Juvenile courts handle about

Chicago police discovered nineteen children living in this squalid, rodent-infested apartment. The kitchen stove did not work, and the children were sharing food with dogs. Six adults were charged with contributing to neglect of children.

1.5 million delinquency cases each year, 80 percent involving males and 31 percent involving African Americans. Among the criminal charges brought before the juvenile court, approximately 20 percent are for crimes against the person, 57 for property offenses, 5 percent for drug law violations, and 17 percent for public order offenses. The Close-up tells the story of Fernando, whose behavior has led to frequent contact with the juvenile justice system.

Recall that status offenses are acts that are illegal only if they are committed by juveniles. Status offenders have not violated a penal code; instead they are charged with being ungovernable or incorrigible: as runaways, truants, or persons in need of supervision (**PINS**). Status offenders make up about 10 percent of the juvenile court caseload.

Juvenile justice also deals with problems of neglect and dependency—situations in which children are viewed as being hurt through no fault of their own because their parents have failed to provide a proper environment for them. Such situations have been the concern of most juvenile justice systems since the turn of the century. The state's proper role was seen as acting as a parent to a child whose own parents are unable or unwilling to provide proper care. Illinois, for example, defines a **neglected child** as one who is not receiving proper care because of some action or inaction of his or her parents. This may include not being sent to school, not receiving medical care, being abandoned, living in an injurious environment, or not receiving some other care necessary for the child's well-being. A **dependent child** either is without a parent or guardian or is not receiving proper care because of the physical or mental disability of that person. As we can see, the law governing neglected and dependent children is broad and encompasses a range of situations in which the child is viewed as a victim of adult behavior.

Nationally about 75 percent of the cases referred to the juvenile courts are delinquency cases, 20 percent of which are status offenses. About 20 percent are dependency and neglect cases, and about 5 percent involve special proceedings, such as adoption. The system, then, deals with both criminal and noncriminal cases. Often juveniles who have done nothing wrong are categorized, either officially or in the public mind, as delinquents. In some states little effort is made in prejudicial detention facilities or in social service agencies to separate the classes of juveniles.

delinquent

A child who has committed an act that if committed by an adult would be criminal.

PINS

Acronym for "person in need of supervision," a term that designates juveniles who are either status offenders or thought to be on the verge of trouble.

neglected child

A child who is not receiving proper care because of some action or inaction of his or her parents.

dependent child

A child who has no parent or guardian or whose parents are unable to give proper care.

CHECKPOINT

8. What are the jurisdictional criteria for the juvenile court?

JUVENILE JUSTICE OPERATIONS

Underlying the juvenile justice system is the philosophy that the police, judges, and correctional officials should be primarily concerned with the interests of the child. Prevention of delinquency is the system's justification for intervening in the lives of juveniles who are involved in either status or criminal offenses.

In theory at least, juvenile system proceedings are to be conducted in a nonadversarial environment, and juvenile court is a place where the judge, social workers,

CLOSE-UP

Fernando, 16, Finds a Sanctuary in Crime

Fernando Morales was glad to discuss his life as a 16-year-old drug dealer, but he had one stipulation owing to his status as a fugitive. He explained that he had recently escaped from Long Lane School, a state correctional institution that became his home after he was caught with $1,100 worth of heroin known as P.

"The Five-O caught me right here with the bundles of P," he said, referring to a police officer, as he stood in front of a boarded-up house on Bridgeport's East Side. "They sentenced me to eighteen months, but I jetted after four. Three of us got out a bathroom window. We ran through the woods and stole a car. Then we got back here and the Five-O's came to my apartment, and I had to jump out the side window on the second floor."

What Future?

Since his escape in December, Fernando had been on the run for weeks. He still went to the weekly meetings of his gang, but he was afraid to go back to his apartment, afraid even to go to a friend's place to pick up the three guns he had stashed away. "I would love to get my baby, Uzi, but it's too hot now."

"Could you bring a photographer here?" he asked. "I want my picture in the newspaper. I'd love to have me holding a bundle right there on the front page so the cops can see it. They're going to bug out."

The other dealers on the corner looked on with a certain admiration. They realized that a publicity campaign might not be the smartest long-term career move for a fugitive drug dealer—"Man, you be the one bugging out," another dealer told him—but they also recognized the logic in Fernando's attitude. He was living his life according to a common assumption on these streets: There is no future.

When you ask the Hispanic teenagers selling drugs here what they expect to be doing in five years, you tend to get a lot of bored shrugs. Occasionally they'll talk about being back in school or being a retired drug dealer in a Porsche. But the most common answer is the one that Fernando gave without hesitation or emotion: "Dead or in jail."

The story of how Fernando got that way is a particularly sad one, but the basic elements are fairly typical in the lives of drug dealers and gang members in any urban ghetto. He has grown up amid tenements, housing projects, torched buildings, and abandoned factories. His role models have been adults who use "the city" and "the state" primarily as terms for the different types of welfare checks. His neighborhood is a place where 13-year-olds know by heart the visiting hours at local prisons.

The Family: A Mother Leaves, a Father Drinks

Fernando Morales was born in Bridgeport, Connecticut, on September 16, 1976, and his mother moved out a few months later. Since then he has occasionally run into her on the street. Neither he nor his relatives can say exactly why she left—or why she didn't take Fernando and her other son with her—but the general assumption is that she was tired of being hit by their father.

The father, Bernabe Morales, who was 24 years old and had emigrated from Puerto Rico as a teenager, moved the two boys in with his mother at the P. T. Barnum public housing project. Fernando lived there until the age of 8, when his grandmother died....

After that Fernando and his brother Bernard lived sometimes with their father and his current girlfriend, sometimes with relatives in Bridgeport or Puerto Rico. They eventually settled with their father's cousin, Monserrate Bruno, who already had ten children living in her two-bedroom apartment....

His father, by all accounts, was a charming, generous man when sober but something else altogether when drinking or doing drugs. He was arrested more than two dozen times, usually for fighting or drugs, and spent five years in jail while Fernando was growing up. He lived on welfare, odd jobs, and money from selling drugs, a trade that was taken up by both his sons.

The "Industry": Moving Up in the Drug Trade

Fernando's school days ended two years ago, when he dropped out of ninth grade. "School was corny," he explained. "I was smart, I learned quick, but I got bored. I was just learning things when I could be out making money."

Fernando might have found other opportunities—he had relatives working in fast-food restaurants and repair shops, and one cousin tried to interest him in a job distributing bread that might pay $700 a week—but nothing with such quick rewards as the drug business flourishing on the East Side.

He had friends and relatives in the business, and he started as one of the runners on the street corner making sales or directing buyers to another runner holding the marijuana, cocaine, crack, or heroin. The runners on each block buy their drugs—paying, for instance, $200 for fifty bags of crack that sell for $250—from the block's lieutenant, who supervises them and takes the money to the absentee dealer called the owner of the block.

By this winter Fernando had moved up slightly on the corporate ladder. "I'm not the block lieutenant yet, but I have some runners selling for me," he explained as he sat in a bar near the block. Another teenager came in with money for him, which he proudly added to a thick wad in his pocket. "You see? I make money while they work for me."

Fernando still worked the block himself, too, standing on the corner watching for cars slowing down, shouting "You want

P?" or responding to veteran customers for crack who asked, "Got any slab, man?" Fernando said he usually made between $100 and $300 a day, and that the money usually went as quickly as it came.

He had recently bought a car for $500 and wrecked it making a fast turn into a telephone pole. He spent money on gold chains with crucifixes, rings, Nike sneakers, Timberland boots, an assortment of Russell hooded sweatshirts called hoodies, gang dues, trips to New York City, and his 23-year-old girlfriend.

His dream was to get out of Bridgeport. "I'd be living fat somewhere. I'd go to somewhere hot, Florida or Puerto Rico or somewhere, buy me a house, get six blazing girls with dope bodies." In the meantime, he tried not to think about what his product was doing to his customers.

"Sometimes it bothers me. But see, I'm a hustler. I got to look out for myself. I got to be making money. Forget them. If you put that in your head, you're going to be caught out. You going to be a sucker. You going to be like them." He said he had used marijuana, cocaine, and angel dust himself, but made a point of never using crack or heroin, the drugs that plagued the last years of his father's life. . . .

The Gangs: "Like a Family" of Drug Dealers

"I cried a little, that's it," was all that Fernando would say about his father's death. But he did allow that it had something to do with his subsequent decision to join a Hispanic gang named Neta. He went with friends to a meeting, answered questions during an initiation ceremony, and began wearing its colors, a necklace of red, white, and blue beads.

"It's like a family, and you need that if you've lost your own family," he said. "At the meetings we talk about having heart, trust, and all that. We don't disrespect nobody. If we need money, we get it. If I need anything they're right there to help me."

Neta is allied with Bridgeport's most notorious gang, the Latin Kings, and both claim to be peaceful Hispanic cultural organizations opposed to drug use. But they are financed at least indirectly by the drug trade, because many members like Fernando work independently in drug operations, and the drug dealers' disputes can turn into gang wars. . . .

"I like guns, I like stealing cars, I like selling drugs, and I like money," he said. "I got to go to the block. That's where I get my spirit at. When I die, my spirit's going to be at the block, still making money. Booming.". . .

"I'll be selling till I get my act together. I'm just a little kid. Nothing runs through my head. All I think about is doing crazy things. But when I be big, I know I need education. If I get caught and do a couple of years, I'll come out and go back to school. But I don't have that in my head yet. I'll have my little fun while I'm out."

SOURCE: John Tierney, *New York Times*, April 13, 1993, pp. Al, B6.

clinicians, and probation officers work together to diagnose the child's problem and select a rehabilitative program to combat it. Juvenile justice is a bureaucracy based on an ideology of social work and staffed primarily by persons who think of themselves as members of the helping professions. Even the recent emphasis on crime control and punishment has not removed the philosophy of rehabilitation from most juvenile justice systems. In order to rehabilitate offenders, officials need to apply substantial powers of discretion, but this is hard to do when resources are scarce.

Like the adult criminal justice system, juvenile justice functions within a context of exchange relationships between officials of various agencies that influence decisions. The juvenile court must deal not only with children and their parents, but also with patrol officers, probation officers, welfare officials, social workers, psychologists, and the heads of treatment institutions—all of whom have their own goals, perceptions of delinquency, and concepts of treatment.

Police Interface

Many police departments, especially in cities, have special juvenile units. The juvenile officer often is carefully selected and trained to relate to youths, is knowledgeable about relevant legal issues, and is sensitive to the special needs of young offenders. The juvenile officer is also an important link between the police and other community institutions, such as schools, recreation facilities, and organizations serving young people.

Most complaints against juveniles are brought by the police, although they may be initiated by an injured party, school officials, or even the parents. The police must make three major decisions with regard to the processing of juveniles:

1. Whether to take the child into custody
2. Whether to request that the child be detained following apprehension
3. Whether to refer the child to court

The police exercise enormous discretion in these decisions. They do extensive screening and make informal adjustments in the street and at the station house. In communities where law enforcement officials have developed close relationships with residents or where law enforcement policy dictates, the police may deal with violations by giving warnings to the juveniles and notifying their parents. Figure 15.3 shows the disposition of juveniles taken into police custody.

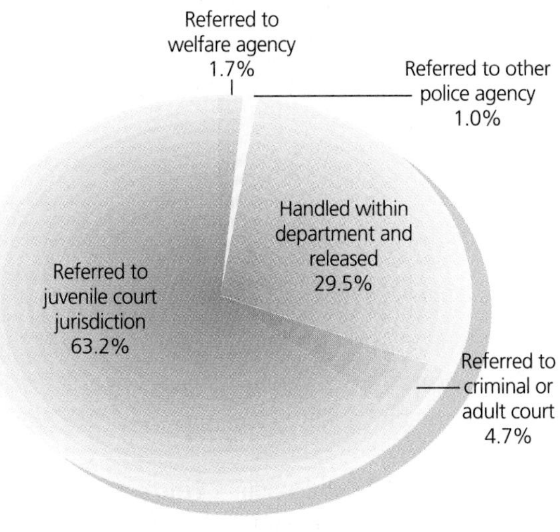

Figure 15.3
Disposition of juveniles taken into police custody

The police have discretion in the disposition of juvenile arrest cases. What factors may influence how a case is disposed?

SOURCE: U.S. Department of Justice, Bureau of Justice Statistics, *Sourcebook of Criminal Justice Statistics, 1995* (Washington, D.C.: Government Printing Office, 1996), 430.

Initial decisions about what to do with each suspected offender are influenced by such factors as the officer's attitude toward the juvenile, the juvenile's family, the offense, and the court; the predominant attitude of the community; and the officer's conception of his or her own role. Also viewed as important in determining the disposition of juvenile cases at the arrest stage is the child's prior record and demeanor.

Although young people commit many serious crimes, the juvenile function of police work is concerned largely with order maintenance. In most incidents of this sort the law is ambiguous, and blame cannot easily be assigned. Many offenses committed by juveniles that involve physical or monetary damage are minor infractions: breaking windows, hanging around the business district, disturbing the peace, adolescent sexual behavior, and shoplifting. Here the function of the investigating officer is not so much to solve crimes as to handle the often legally uncertain complaints involving juveniles. The officer seeks both to satisfy the complainant and to keep the youth from future trouble. Given this emphasis on settling cases within the community—rather than on strictly enforcing the law—the police power to arrest is a weapon that can be used to deter juveniles from criminal activity and to encourage them to conform to the law.

Intake

When the police or an aggrieved party believes that the juvenile justice system should take formal action, a complaint is filed with a special division of the juvenile probation department for preliminary screening and evaluation. During this intake stage, an officer reviews the case to determine whether the alleged facts are sufficient for the juvenile court to take jurisdiction or whether some other action would be in the child's interest. The intake officer thus has considerable discretion and power. Nationally, between 40 and 50 percent of all referrals from the police are disposed of at this stage, without formal processing by a judge.

In most juvenile justice systems, the probation officer plays a crucial role during the intake phase. Because intake is essentially a screening process to determine whether a case should be referred to the court or to a social agency, often a judge does not supervise it. Informal discussions among the probation officer, the parents, and the child help the authorities learn about the child's social situation, diagnose behavioral problems, and recommend treatment possibilities. As you read the Workperspective of Juvenile Court Probation Officer Paul Meyer, imagine the difficult decisions that such officials must make.

Diversion

diversion

The process of screening children out of the juvenile justice system without a decision by the court.

Diversion is the process of screening children out of the juvenile justice system without a decision by the court. Although informal ways of diverting alleged delinquents away from the courts and toward community agencies have always existed, the number and types of diversion programs have greatly expanded during the past three decades. In keeping with the philosophy of the juvenile court, many juvenile justice professionals believe that diversion should be promoted as much as possible. When behavioral problems can be identified early, the child should be given access to the necessary remedial education, drug or alcohol treatment, and counseling programs without being taken before a judge and labeled delinquent. However, the increased availability of diversion programs has apparently widened the reach of juvenile courts by drawing into the system children who formerly would have been dealt with through informal means.

Transfer to Adult Court

A juvenile's delinquency case may be transferred to the adult criminal court through judicial waiver, legislative exclusion, and prosecutorial discretion.

judicial waiver

Procedure by which the juvenile court waives its jurisdiction and transfers a juvenile case to the adult criminal court.

Judicial waiver is the procedure by which the juvenile court gives up its jurisdiction and transfers the case to the adult criminal court. Although the laws of most states specify that juvenile court jurisdiction should be waived when the child is "no longer amenable to treatment," in fact the controlling factors are usually the juvenile's age, his or her offense history, and the seriousness of the offense. Many

WORK*Perspective*

Paul Meyer
Juvenile Probation Officer–Case Manager
Lorain, Ohio

I was unsure of my interests during my first years of college. As a junior at Ohio University I finally chose a major: sociology/criminology. I found myself increasingly interested in the criminal justice system, especially investigation and other aspects related to policing. However, my career ultimately took a slightly different path within criminal justice when I was offered opportunities to work with juvenile offenders.

When I graduated from college, I headed back to my hometown and worked at various jobs while applying for criminal justice positions. After job hunting for a number of months, I accepted a job as a youth leader working in a residential facility for juvenile offenders. I supervised daily activities in a cottage housing twenty teenage offenders. Six months later I was offered a juvenile probation officer position for which I had previously applied.

The county's Domestic Relations Court administers the juvenile probation department. Probation officers are supervised by a chief probation officer who is under the court administrator and the two domestic relations judges responsible for juvenile cases. When I was a regular juvenile probation officer, my caseload reached as high as ninety probationers—although the department wants to keep the number closer to fifty per officer. When I became a probation officer–case manager in the special program for juveniles with substance abuse or mental health problems, my caseload dropped below twenty. Now my caseload is small enough that I can really get to know each juvenile assigned to my supervision. I talk to my kids about their problems, their schoolwork, and their family situations. I will be told immediately if any of my probationers miss substance abuse counseling sessions. Thus I can investigate right away the reasons for the kid's failure to appear as required. I also become well acquainted with the kids' families. I try to work with the families so they will be better able to guide and assist their troubled kids.

Juvenile probation officers face especially difficult decisions when recommending whether to keep juvenile suspects in custody or to release them to their parents. When a juvenile is arrested and held in custody, he or she must be given a hearing within twenty-four hours. The only people in attendance at a typical hearing will be a magistrate, who is a lawyer working as a part-time judicial officer, the probation officer called in to handle the case, the juvenile suspect, and the suspect's parents. The hearing will determine whether there is enough evidence to continue the case and whether the juvenile should be held in custody. The only information available to the probation officer is the preliminary police report about the crime, statements made by the juvenile at the hearing in response to the magistrate's questions, and statements made by the parents during the hearing. After the magistrate informs the suspect of his or her rights, asks questions, and permits the suspect and the parents to speak, the probation officer—who has often stood by silently listening to the others at the hearing—will be asked for a recommendation about detention. In the vast majority of cases the magistrate will follow the probation officer's recommendation about detention. Thus the probation officer's quick judgment, based on limited information, has great influence over the suspect's immediate freedom.

Several factors can influence the probation officer's recommendation. In addition to information about the seriousness of the offense and the suspect's behavior, the recommendation may rest on the parents' statements during the hearing. Do they seem concerned and demonstrate a willingness to take action to control and guide the juvenile? If so, there is a very good chance that the juvenile will be released while the case proceeds. Other factors may also encourage release, such as a lack of available space in juvenile detention facilities.

My most difficult decisions often arose when a youth was arrested as a result of family violence. For example, the police may arrest a juvenile if they are called to intervene in a fistfight between a parent and a teenage child. If a parent is physically abusing or assaulting a teenager, I want to protect the youth from being sent back into a violent family situation. But how can I tell who is at fault in family violence? I do not want to detain a juvenile suspect needlessly, but I don't want to place the child in a situation where he or she will be victimized. Knowing what to do is very difficult, especially because a probation officer must quickly make a judgment based on limited information.

WORK*Perspective*

legislative exclusion

The legislature excludes from juvenile court jurisdiction certain offenses such as murder, armed robbery, or rape.

prosecutorial discretion

The power of the prosecutor to decide that a youth should be referred from the juvenile system to the adult criminal justice system.

states now place on the youth the burden of proving that he or she is amenable to treatment (Zimring, 1991).

As a "tougher" approach to juvenile crime took hold in the 1970s, some legislatures passed laws excluding murder and certain other offenses from the juvenile court—a process called **legislative exclusion**. However, other legislatures have extended the range of offenses that can be automatically transferred to adult court to include forcible rape, armed robbery, and other violent crimes (Feld, 1993a:239).

A few states allow **prosecutorial discretion** as to whether to charge certain juveniles in the juvenile or adult court. Laws typically limit the discretion of prosecutors to criteria based on the age of the offender and the nature of the offense. For example, Arkansas gives prosecutors this power over those aged 14 and above if they are charged with capital crimes, murder, or other personal offenses. However, in that state 16 is the minimum age for the exercise of prosecutorial discretion for other felony offenses.

Detention

detention

A period of temporary custody of a juvenile before disposition of his or her case.

After it has been decided that some formal action should be taken against a juvenile, the juvenile court must take up the question of whether to place the youth in **detention**, or temporary custody, until disposition of the case. An intake officer of the juvenile court usually makes this decision.

One of the early reforms of the juvenile justice system was to ensure that children were not held in jails in the company of adults who were also awaiting trial or sentencing. To mix juveniles—some of whom are status offenders or under the protection of the court because they are neglected—in the same public facility with adults accused of crimes has long been thought unjust, but in many areas, separate detention facilities for juveniles do not exist.

Normally, within twenty-four hours after the juvenile is taken into custody, a detention hearing is held to determine if the youth can be released in the care of a parent, guardian, or group home until adjudication. Many states do not provide the right to bail for children. Some children will be detained to keep them from committing other crimes while awaiting trial. Others are held to protect them from the possibility of harm from gang members or parents. Still others may not appear in court as required if they are released.

The conditions in many detention facilities are poor; abuse is often reported. Although much attention is focused on the adjudication processes of the juvenile court and the sanctions imposed by judges, many more children are punished through confinement in detention centers and jails before any court action has taken place than are punished by the courts. An estimated half-million juveniles are detained each year, sometimes for several months. On any day, two-thirds of those in detention are awaiting adjudication; the remaining third have already been to court and are awaiting disposition or placement in another facility (OJJDP, 1995. *Juvenile Officers and Victims* 143).

Adjudication

New York City Judge Michael Corriero presides over a special courtroom of the adult system for juveniles aged 13–15 accused of violent crimes. Although he can hand out life terms to youths guilty of murder and up to 10 years for first-degree robbery, he sentences many to counseling and probation. The laws of most states now send violent youths to the adult criminal court.

The primary questions before the court are whether to attach the label "delinquent" to a juvenile and what sanctions to apply. The Supreme Court's decision in *Gault* (1967) and other due process rulings mandated changes in criminal proceedings that have changed the philosophy and actions of the juvenile court. Contemporary proceedings are more formal than those of the past, although juvenile courts are still more informal than adult courts. Copies of petitions with specific charges must be given to the parents and child; counsel may be present and free counsel may be appointed if the juvenile cannot pay; witnesses may be cross-examined; and a transcript of the proceedings must be kept.

As with other Supreme Court decisions, local practice may differ sharply from the procedures spelled out in the high court's rulings. Juveniles and their parents often waive their rights in response to suggestions from the judge or probation officer. The lower social status of the offender's parents, the intimidating atmosphere of the court, and judicial hints that the outcome will be more favorable if a lawyer is not present are reasons the procedures outlined in *Gault* may not be followed. The litany of "getting treatment," "doing what's right for the child," and "working out a just solution" may sound enticing, especially to people who are unfamiliar with the intricacies of formal legal procedures. In actual practice, then, juveniles still lack many of the protections given to adult offenders. Some of the differences between the juvenile and adult criminal justice systems are listed in Table 15.2.

The Adjudicatory Process

In some jurisdictions, the adjudication process is more adversarial than it was before the *Gault* decision. Like adult cases, however, juvenile cases tend to be adjudicated in a style that conforms to the crime control model of criminal justice administration. This means that most cases are settled in preliminary hearings by a plea agreement, and few go on to formal trial.

At the preliminary hearing, the youth is notified of the charges and his or her rights, and counsel may be present. Because the juvenile has usually admitted guilt

Alternative Dispositions

Although probation and commitment to an institution are the major dispositional options, judges have wide discretion to warn, to fine, to arrange for restitution, to refer a juvenile for treatment at either a public or a private community agency, or to withhold judgment.

Judges sometimes suspend judgment, or continue cases without a finding, when they wish to put a youth under supervision but are reluctant to apply the label "delinquent." Judgment may be suspended for a definite or indefinite period of time. The judge holds off on giving a definitive judgment for possible use should a youth misbehave while under the informal supervision of a probation officer or parents.

Probation

The most common method of handling juvenile offenders is to place them on probation. Juvenile probation operates in much the same way as adult probation, and it is sometimes carried out by the same agency. In two respects, however, juvenile probation can differ markedly from adult probation. First, juvenile probation has traditionally been better funded, so that officers have had smaller caseloads. Second, the juvenile probation officer is often infused with the sense that the offender is worthwhile and can change, and that the job is valuable and enjoyable. Such attitudes make for greater creativity than is possible with adult probation. For example, a young offender can be paired with a "big brother" or "big sister" from the community.

Community Treatment

In the past decade, treatment in community-based facilities has become much more common. Today there are more private, nonprofit agencies that contract with states to provide services for troubled youths. Community-based options include foster homes in which juvenile offenders live with families, usually for a short period of time, and group homes, often privately run facilities for groups of twelve to twenty juvenile offenders. Each group home has several staff personnel who work as counselors or houseparents on eight- or twenty-four-hour shifts. Group home placements can allow juveniles to attend local schools, provide individual and group counseling, and offer a more structured life than most of the residents received in their own homes. However, critics suggest that group homes often are mismanaged and may do little more than "warehouse" youths.

Institutional Care

Incarceration of juveniles has traditionally meant commitment to a state institution, often called a "training school," "reform school," or "industrial school." Large custodial training schools located in outlying areas remain the typical institutions to which juveniles are committed, although in the past decade an increasing number of privately maintained facilities have accepted residents sent by the courts. Experiments with boot camps for juveniles have been tried in a number of states. A recent census revealed that nearly 98,000 juveniles were admitted during the year to 3,200 public and private centers, with 62 percent of these youths in public facilities (OJJDP, 1995. *Juvenile Officers and Victims*: 164). The average length of time juveniles spend in long-term facilities is six months. Approximately 32,000 juveniles per year are placed in noncorrectional private facilities such as schools for the emotionally disturbed, training schools, halfway houses, and even military academies.

One result of the increased adjudication of juveniles in criminal court is an increase of young people in state prisons. Nationally almost 5,000 people under age 18 are incarcerated in adult correctional institutions (NIJ, 1997. *Research in Action*: 5).

Institutional Programs

Because of the emphasis on rehabilitation that has dominated juvenile justice for much of the past fifty years, a wide variety of treatment programs has been used. Counseling, education, vocational training, and an assortment of psychotherapy methods have been incorporated into the juvenile correctional programs of most states. Unfortunately, incarceration in a juvenile training institution primarily seems to prepare many offenders for entry into adult corrections. John Irwin's concept of the state-raised youth is a useful way of looking at children who come in contact with institutional life at an early age, lack family relationships and structure, become accustomed to living in a correctional facility, and are unable to function in other environments (Irwin, 1970).

CHECKPOINT

9. What three discretionary decisions are made by the police with regard to processing of juveniles?
10. What five factors influence the police in deciding the disposition of a case?
11. What is the purpose of diversion?
12. What are five sentencing dispositions available to the judge?

A Question of ETHICS

Residents of the Lovelock Home had been committed by the juvenile court because they were either delinquent or neglected. All twenty-five boys, aged 7 to 15, were streetwise, tough, and interested only in getting out. The institution had a staff of social services professionals who tried to deal with the educational and psychological needs of the residents. Because state funding was short, these services looked better in the annual report than to an observer visiting Lovelock. Most of the time the residents watched television, played basketball in the backyard, or just hung out in one another's rooms.

Joe Klegg, the night supervisor, was tired from the eight-hour shift that he had just completed on his "second job" as a daytime convenience-store manager. The boys were watching television when he arrived at seven. Everything seemed calm. It should have been, because Joe had placed a tough 15-year-old, Randy Marshall, in charge. Joe had told Randy to keep the younger boys in line. Randy used his muscle and physical presence to intimidate the other residents. He knew that if the home was quiet and there was no trouble, he would be rewarded with special privileges such as a "pass" to go see his girlfriend. Joe wanted no hassles and a quiet house so that he could doze off when the boys went to sleep.

Does the situation at Lovelock Home raise ethical questions, or does it merely raise questions of poor management practices? What are the potential consequences for the residents? For Joe Klegg? What is the state's responsibility?

Results from a national survey of public custodial institutions showed that 40.7 percent of juveniles were incarcerated for violent offenses, 60 percent used drugs regularly, and 50 percent said that a family member had been in prison at some time in the past. Also, 88 percent of the residents were male, only 30 percent had grown up in a household with both parents, and the percentages of African Americans (42.8 percent) and Hispanic Americans (15.5 percent) were greater than the percentage of those groups in the general population (OJJDP, 1991. *OJJDP Update*, January:1). Figure 15.4 shows the types of offenses and nondelinquent reasons for the placement of juveniles in correctional facilities.

PROBLEMS AND PERSPECTIVES

Much criticism of juvenile justice has emphasized the disparity between the treatment ideal and the institutionalized practices of an ongoing bureaucratic system. Commentators have focused on how the language of social reformers has disguised the day-to-day operations in which elements of due process are lacking and custodial incarceration is all too frequent. Other criticisms have emphasized that the juvenile justice system is apparently unable to control juvenile crime.

The juvenile court, in both theory and practice, is a remarkably complex institution that must perform a wide variety of functions, so many that it is inevitable that goals and values will collide. In many states the same judges, probation officers, and social workers are asked to deal with both neglected children and young criminals.

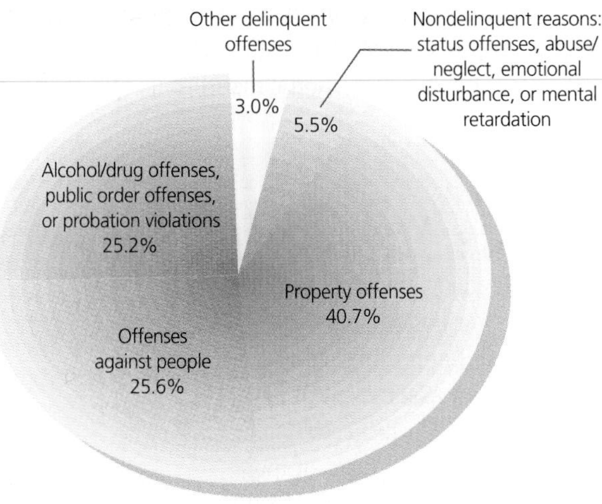

Figure 15.4
Juveniles in public facilities: types of offenses and nondelinquent reasons for placement

SOURCE: U.S. Department of Justice, Office of Juvenile Justice and Delinquency Prevention, *OJJDP Update on Statistics* (January 1991), 4.

Although departments of social services may deal primarily with cases of neglect, the distinction between the criminal and the neglected child is often not maintained.

In addition to recognizing that the juvenile system has organizational problems, we must acknowledge that we still have only limited understanding of the causes of delinquency and its prevention or treatment. Over the years, various social and behavioral theories have been advanced to explain delinquency. One generation looked to slum conditions as the cause of juvenile crime, and another points to the affluence of the suburbs. Psychologists may stress masculine insecurity in a matriarchal family structure, and some sociologists note the peer group pressures of the gang. The array of theories has led to an array of proposed—and often contradictory—treatments. In such confusion, those interested in the problems of youth may despair. What is clear is that additional research is needed to give insights into the causes of delinquency and the treatment of juvenile offenders.

What trends may foretell the future of juvenile justice? It appears that the conservative crime control policies that have hit the adult criminal justice system—with their emphasis on deterrence, retribution, and getting tough—have influenced juvenile justice. One can point to growing levels of overcrowding in juvenile institutions, increased litigation challenging the abuse of children in training schools and detention centers, and higher rates of incarceration for minority youth. All of these problems have emerged during a period of declining youth populations and fewer arrests of juveniles. With the demographic trend now reversing and increased concern about drugs, one can expect a surge of adolescents going through their criminally high-risk years in a system and community unable to cope with them.

Summary

- Crimes committed by juveniles have increased since 1980.
- The history of juvenile justice comprises five periods: Puritan, House of Refuge, juvenile court, juvenile rights, and crime control.
- Creation of the juvenile court in 1899 established a separate juvenile justice system dealing with delinquency, neglected children, and dependent children.
- The *In re Gault* decision by the U.S. Supreme Court in 1967 brought due process to the juvenile justice system.

- Decisions by police officers and juvenile intake officers dispose of a large portion of cases that are never referred to the court.
- In juvenile court most cases are settled through a plea agreement.
- After conviction or plea, a disposition hearing is held. The judge reviews the offense and the juvenile's social history before passing sentence.
- Possible dispositions of a juvenile case include suspended judgment, probation, community treatment, or institutional care.
- Juvenile court jurisdiction is increasingly being waived so that youths may be tried in the adult criminal justice system.

ANSWERS TO CHECKPOINTS

1. There will be a greater number of youths in the crime-prone youth population.
2. Age 7.
3. Chancery courts had protective jurisdiction over children, especially those involved in issues of dependency, neglect, and property.
4. The state acting as parent.
5. To provide an environment where neglected children could learn good work and study habits, live in a disciplined and healthy environment, and develop character.
6. A separate court for delinquent, dependent, and neglected children; special legal procedures that were less adversarial than in the adult system; emphasis on diagnosis and treatment.
7. Procedural rights for juveniles, including notice of charges, right to counsel, right to confront and cross-examine witnesses, and protection against self-incrimination.
8. The age of the juvenile, usually under 16 or 18; and the category of case: delinquency, status offense, neglect, or dependency.
9. (1) Whether to take the child into custody, (2) whether to request that the child be detained, (3) whether to refer the child to court.
10. The seriousness of the offense, the officer's attitude toward the juvenile and toward his or her role, the child's behavioral history and demeanor, the juvenile's family, the court, attitude of the community.
11. To avoid formal proceedings when the child's best interests can be served by treatment in the community.
12. Alternative dispositions, probation, community treatment, institutional care, and dismissal.

Questions for Review

1. What are the major historical periods of juvenile justice in the United States?
2. What is the jurisdiction of the juvenile court system?
3. What are the major processes in the juvenile justice system?
4. What are the sentencing and institutional alternatives for juveniles who are judged delinquent?
5. What due process rights do juveniles have?

INSIDE THE CRIMINAL JUSTICE SYSTEM AND BEYOND: ONE MAN'S JOURNEY

Reflections

The other day, while stopped at a red light, I suddenly thought about all the years I spent in "those places." Cells, segregated chow halls, racial tension, monotony, overcrowded conditions. All the years spent being ordered around by judges, guards, and parole officers. And then I thought about *all the people who are there right now*. Not only are there many more people doing it than before, *but they are doing it for extensively longer periods of time*. The thought chilled me to the bone. It hasn't always been like this.

People used to consider rehabilitation as a valid justification for imprisonment. Those who broke the law were seen as less fortunate and in need of help. This was when societal goals included using the law to even up the socioeconomic playing field for women and minorities, when social programs designed to fight poverty were being implemented rather than cut, and when popular enemies included communists and crooked politicians. Now many dwell on the harm created by "single-parent families," "illegal immigrants," "welfare dependency," and the evils of affirmative action. And now we have the perfect scapegoat, someone everyone can hate—the criminal.

Today "criminals" are depicted as inherently "bad" people. They are blamed for, among other things, our economic problems, fear of going out at night, dilapidated schools, rundown neighborhoods, and our children's unhappiness. Prisons and all the things that go along with "protecting" the public (alarm systems, more prisons, gated communities, increased budgets for policing, new laws) are "sold" and "bought" as essential mechanisms of control. By keeping "these people" in their place "we" can live "normal," safe lives.

Our aim now is to punish instead of rehabilitate. Increasing levels of formal social control are the means by which crime is "fought." We seldom address crime-generating factors like our market mentality, which revolves around the need to have, to get, and to have yet more; the increasing economic gap between the "haves" and "have-nots"; capital flight; racism; child abuse; homophobia; chronic unemployment; rampant inequality; economic insecurity; and the desperation that leads to drug addiction and other social ills. Instead, our attention is diverted toward individuals. We seem to blindly accept the sanity of draconian sentencing policies such as mandatory minimum laws that require prison time for selling crack cocaine, even for first-time offenders. Or the "Three Strikes and You're Out Law" in California that, though designed to imprison violent offenders, has been twisted and reshaped so that today roughly 70 percent of those going to prison under this law do so for a nonviolent crime. After spending so many years in "those places," I find what I see today difficult to accept.

Today I find myself around academics and "experts" in the field of criminal justice. I hope that we can learn from each other. I am given the opportunity to write papers like this and speak in front of hundreds of students in undergraduate classes. I feel fortunate to be doing all this, and more than grateful to be free from the grips of addiction and the criminal justice system.

Yet the story is far from over. The nightmare continues. "Those places" are being jammed with bodies faster than they can be built. Prisons and jails become home to the unemployable, addicts, the underprivileged, and outcasts of society. And rather than help, or even punish, doing time on such a massive scale will likely have disastrous effects on individuals, families, and communities that will last lifetimes and beyond. Can it be that we are crippling or incapacitating "those people"? After being oppressed, controlled, and degraded (especially for long periods of time), inmates turn into angry, fearful human beings who are unable to cope with things that people out here deal with all the time. The difficulty of participating in interpersonal relationships, finding and retaining employment, controlling anger, and "fitting

ONE MAN'S JOURNEY (CONTINUED)

in," to name a few, can become insurmountable obstacles. Yet most of our efforts to do anything about the situation only worsens it.

Efforts to improve sophisticated techniques of identifying, labeling, and monitoring parolees, "gang" members, and other "miscreants" are continually being developed. The school I attended inside no longer offers college classes—funding was pulled. Lifting weights—a positive, healthy way to release energy—is no longer allowed in many prisons: can't let "them" get too strong.

Today I have a friend in the county jail facing sixty years to life under California's three-strikes law for possession of less than a gram of cocaine. He is an addict, 48 years old, and if convicted will probably never get out. His first two strikes were for burglaries in the 1970s. Over the last few years he has battled with his addiction and, at one time, made it nearly two years without using. If the laws would have been the way they are today before I got clean, I would have been "striked out" myself. *Is there anything wrong with all this?*

My hope is that we are entering a new era, one in which we work on replacing blame and increasing levels of social control with understanding and compassion. An era in which we acknowledge the reality of contemporary life, its horrors, and its injustices as well as its joys. And I hope we can begin to alter the way we view those we perceive as being different from ourselves. All of us have fears. All of us need to belong and fit in somewhere. Oppression, hatred, and blame do not build better lives for anyone. We all need hope.

Reducing violence and crime requires lessening the harm we do to one another—including criminals. I know that, for me, the way I lived for so many years in "those places" affected my self-image, outlook, and actions in such a way that I had become almost completely alienated from everything in the outside world. Luckily, education and my motivation to learn gave me a new perspective and some hope. It helped me *see more clearly*. I was lucky to make it. Maybe it's time that people out here begin to imagine what it's like to be locked up. What it's like to be pushed into a life of crime, addiction, desperation, and hopelessness. Maybe by taking a closer look at the real factors associated with crime, and by changing the way we "see" those who get caught up in the criminal justice system, we can begin to end the nightmare.

Appendix A

Constitution of the United States: Criminal Justice Amendments

The first ten amendments to the Constitution, known as the Bill of Rights, became effective on December 15, 1791.

IV The right of the people to be secure in their persons, houses, papers, and effects, against unreasonable searches and seizures, shall not be violated, and no warrants shall issue but upon probable cause, supported by oath or affirmation, and particularly describing the place to be searched, and the persons or things to be seized.

V No person shall be held to answer for a capital or otherwise infamous crime, unless on a presentment or indictment of a grand jury, except in cases arising in the land or naval forces or in the militia when in actual service in time of war or public danger; nor shall any person be subject for the same offense to be twice put in jeopardy of life or limb; nor shall be compelled in any criminal case to be a witness against himself, nor be deprived of life, liberty, or property, without due process of law; nor shall private property be taken for public use without just compensation.

VI In all criminal prosecutions the accused shall enjoy the right to a speedy and public trial, by an impartial jury of the State and district wherein the crime shall have been committed, which district shall have been previously ascertained by law, and to be informed of the nature and cause of the accusation; to be confronted with the witnesses against him; to have compulsory process for obtaining witnesses in his favor, and to have the assistance of counsel for his defense.

VII Excessive bail shall not be required, nor excessive fines imposed, nor cruel and unusual punishments inflicted.

The Fourteenth Amendment became effective on July 28, 1868.

XIV Section 1. All persons born or naturalized in the United States, and subject to the jurisdiction thereof, are citizens of the United States and of the State wherein they reside. No State shall make or enforce any law which shall abridge the privileges or immunities of citizens of the United States; nor shall any State deprive any person of life, liberty, or property, without due process of law; nor deny to any person within its jurisdiction the equal protection of the laws.

B. *Defense Attorney*

Mission: Provide defense services for persons accused of crimes from the point of initial investigation to arraignment, dismissal, plea, trial, and appeal. Defense attorneys are engaged either in private practice or as public defenders.

Agencies: Defense attorneys are employed by private law firms, are engaged as individual (solo) practitioners, or are members of public defender agencies. See Chapter 8 for more information on the work of defense attorneys.

Entry: Defense attorneys must hold bachelor's and law degrees and be members of the state bar association. Admission to law schools is very competitive. New members of the bar often seek criminal defense work to gain trial experience before moving to a more lucrative civil practice. Other attorneys enjoy defense work and continue this type of practice for their entire careers. Entry-level salaries may be quite low for inexperienced solo practitioners. Most new public defenders are paid salaries comparable to beginning assistant prosecutors ($35,000).

More Information: College and university pre-law advisors, law school placement officers, local law firms, public defender offices.

C. *Paralegal, Legal Assistant, and Court Reporter*

Mission: Assist judicial administrators, prosecuting attorneys, defense attorneys. Paralegals and legal assistants may be assigned to a wide range of duties, including case preparation, legal research, client counseling, case scheduling, and record maintenance. Because they are not members of the bar, paralegals must work under a supervising attorney. The highly specialized position of court reporter involves the accurate recording of oral communications in the courtroom and legal offices.

Agencies: Paralegals and legal assistants may be found in all types of criminal justice offices, including such nonjudicial agencies as the police and corrections. Court reporters either work for judges or provide their services to attorneys through private firms.

Entry: Some postsecondary education such as an associate or bachelor's degree is expected. Specialized training for a career as a paralegal is available in most states. Excellent oral, written, and computer skills are important. Entry-level salaries are in the $15,000 to $20,000 range. Court reporters must receive training in order to pass qualifying examinations and become licensed in most states. Salaries are high in this demanding career.

More Information: High school, college, and university counselors. Additional information can be obtained from the technical schools that offer paralegal training, many of which have sites on the Internet. A Web page about court reporting as a career can be found at http://www.depo.com/abtcrng.htm

D. *Court Administrator*

Mission: To provide administrative services for the effective operation of courts. The work of court administrators runs the gamut from case scheduling to records management to program planning. See Chapter 7 for information about court administration.

Agencies: Court administrators may be found at all levels of courts—federal, state, and municipal.

Entry: The position of court administrator requires a bachelor's degree and advanced study. A background in public administration, business, computer science, or personnel is desirable. The Institute for Court Management of the National Center for State Courts provides short training courses and the Court Executive Development Program. Information can be found at their Web site: http://www.NCSC.dni.us/ncsc.htm. American University and the University of Southern California also offer programs in court management. Given the educational requirements, court administration salaries are quite high, often beginning at $35,000 and rising to the six figures in some states.

PART III CORRECTIONS

A. *Probation Officer*

Mission: Supervises offenders who are sentenced to community supervision by the federal, state, and county courts. This involves counseling and the provision of services to assist rehabilitation as well as surveillance to ensure that the probationer does not recidivate. Probation officers assist judges through the development of presentence reports. See Chapter 12 for more on the work of probation officers.

Agencies: Probation officers of the federal government work for the Administrative Office of the U.S. Courts. The organizational affiliations of state and county probation officers vary. In some regions they are part of statewide offices of adult probation or corrections of the executive branch; in others they are part of either the state or county judicial branch.

Entry: A bachelor's degree and experience are required in most states. Many probation officers come to the field after gaining experience in social work or an organization administering intermediate sanctions in the community. Criminal justice students often find that an internship with a probation office is an effective way of learning about the career and gaining entry. Salaries at the entry level range from $20,000 to $30,000.

More Information: College and university placement officers, criminal justice faculty, persons in the field. The American Probation and Parole Association Web site at http://www.csg.org/appa/appa.html provides job information.

B. *Community Correctional Counselor*

Mission: Provide supervision and services to offenders given intermediate sanctions in the community. The development of intermediate sanctions has greatly increased the number and range of positions in community corrections. Counselors and administrators are found working in community service, drug and alcohol treatment, electronic-monitoring, and job-training programs. See Chapter 12 for more information on community corrections.

Agencies: Community programs are run by public probation, parole, and corrections agencies as well as nonprofit organizations.

Entry: Because of the range of positions found in community corrections, some entry-level positions require an associate degree while others require a bachelor's and experience. Internships are a good way of learning about and gaining a full-time position. Salaries tend to be low, often below $20,000.

More Information: College and university placement offices, criminal justice faculty, and local community corrections agencies.

C. *Correctional Officer*

Mission: Supervises the treatment and custody of offenders in correctional institutions. Chapter 13 describes the mission and work environment of the corrections officer. Teachers, psychologists, medical technicians, administrators, and other professionals are also employed in correctional institutions.

Agencies: Federal, state, and county departments of corrections; private corporations operating correctional facilities.

Entry: Requirements differ by state, but all expect a high school diploma, some an associate's or a bachelor's degree. Good physical condition is required. Entry-level salaries start at about $20,000.

More Information: College and university placement offices, criminal justice faculty, state corrections departments, or county sheriff's departments. Information about employment in the Federal Bureau of Prisons can be found at http://www.bop.gov

D. *Parole Officer*

Mission: Supervise offenders in the community after their release from a correctional institution. Like probation officers, parole officers provide counseling and assistance to offenders. Parole officers are expected to place a high priority on surveillance to ensure that their clients live up to the terms of their release. See Chapter 14 for more on the work of parole officers.

Agencies: Parole supervision of federal offenders is provided by probation officers employed by the Administrative Office of the U.S. Courts. The organizational affiliation of state parole officers vary. In some states they work directly for the parole board, while in others they are assigned to units within either the department of corrections or the probation authority.

Entry: A bachelor's degree and experience are required in most states. Many parole officers come to their positions after gaining experience in law enforcement, social work, or a nonprofit organization administering community programs. Internships are an excellent way to learn about the work of parole officers and gain a permanent position. Written and oral examinations are required in some states.

More Information: College and university placement officers, criminal justice faculty, parole offices. The American Probation and Parole Association Web site at http://www.csg.org/appa/appa.html provides job information.

References

Abadinsky, H. 1997. *Probation and Parole*, 6th ed. Upper Saddle, N.J.: Prentice-Hall.

Acker, J. R., and C. S. Lanier. 1994. "In Fairness and Mercy: Statutory Mitigating Factors in Capital Punishment Cases." *Criminal Law Bulletin* 30:299–345.

_____. 1995. "Matters of Life or Death: The Sentencing Provisions in Capital Punishment Statutes." *Criminal Law Bulletin* 31:3–18.

Adler, F. 1975. *Sisters in Crime: The Rise of the New Female Criminal*. New York: McGraw-Hill.

Adler, S. J. 1994. *The Jury: Disorder in the Court*. New York: Doubleday.

Administrative Office of the U.S. Courts. 1994. *Judicial Business of the U.S. Courts*. Washington, D.C.: Administrative Office of the U.S. Courts.

Akhil, R.A. 1997. *The Constitution and Criminal Punishment: First Principles*. New Haven, Conn.: Yale University Press.

Akron Beacon Journal, December 3, 1991.

Alderman, J. D. 1994. "Leading the Public: The Media's Focus on Crime Shaped Sentiment." *The Public Perspective* (March/April):26–28.

Alexander, R., Jr. 1993. "The Demise of State Prisoners' Access to Federal Habeas Corpus." *Criminal Justice Policy Review* 6:55–70.

Amar, A. 1997. *The Constitution and Criminal Procedure: First Principles*. New Haven: Yale University Press.

American Correctional Association. 1996. *The Female Offender: What Does the Future Hold?* Alexandria, Va.: American Correctional Association.

Andrews, D. A., and J. Bonta. 1994. *The Psychology of Criminal Behavior.* Cincinnati: Anderson.

Austin, J., and B. Krisberg. 1982. "The Unmet Promise of Alternatives to Incarceration." *Crime and Delinquency* 28:374–409.

Baldus, D. C., G. Woodworth, and C. A. Pulaski. 1994. *Equal Justice and the Death Penalty: A Legal and Empirical Analysis*. Boston: Northeastern University Press.

Barnes, C. W., and R. Kingsnorth. 1996. "Race, Drug, and Criminal Sentencing: Hidden Effects of the Criminal Law." *Journal of Criminal Justice* 24:39–55.

Baumer, T. L., and R. I. Mendelsohn. 1992. "Electronic Monitoring Home Confinement: Does It Work," *Smart Sentencing: The Emergence of Intermediate Sanctions*, ed. J. M. Byrne, A. J. Lurigio, and J. Petersilia. Newbury Park, Calif.: Sage.

Baunach, P. J. 1985. *Mothers in Prison*. New Brunswick, N.J.: Transaction Books.

Bauza, M. 1997a. "Jurors Convict Sams in Killing." *Lansing State Journal*, October 9: 1B.

_____. 1997b. "Woman Sentenced in Drowning Death." *Lansing State Journal*, October 9:1B.

Bayley, D. H. 1986. "The Tactical Choice of Police Patrol Officers." *Journal of Criminal Justice* 14:329–348.

_____. 1992. "Comparative Organization of the Police in English-Speaking Countries," *Modern Policing*, ed. M. Tonry and N. Morris. Chicago: University of Chicago Press, 509–545.

_____. 1994. *Police for the Future*. New York: Oxford University Press.

Beck, A. J. 1997. "Growth, Change, and Stability in the U.S. Prison Population, 1980–1995." *Corrections Management Quarterly* 1:1.

Benaquisto, L., and P. J. Freed. 1996. "The Myth of Inmate Lawlessness: The Perceived Contradition between Self and Others in Inmates' Support for Criminal Justice Sanctioning Norms." *Law and Society Review* 30:481-511.

Bershard, L. 1985. "Discriminatory Treatment of the Female Offender in the Criminal Justice System." *Boston College Law Review* 26:389–438.

Biderman, A. D., and J. P. Lynch. 1991. *Understanding Crime Incidence Statistics*. New York: Springer-Verlag.

Bloch, P., and D. Anderson, 1974. *Policewomen on Patrol: First Report*. Washington, D.C.: Police Foundation.

Blomberg, T. G., W. Bales, and K. Reed. 1993. "Intermediate Punishment: Redistributing or Extending Social Control?" *Crime, Law and Social Change* 19:187–201.

Blomberg, T. G., and K. Lucken. 1993. "Intermediate Punishments and the Piling Up of Sanctions," *Criminal Justice: Law and Politics*, 6th ed., ed. G. F. Cole. Belmont, Calif.: Wadsworth, 470–482.

Blumberg, A. 1967. "The Practice of Law as a Confidence Game." *Law and Society Review* 1:11–39.

Blumberg, M. 1989. "Controlling Police Use of Deadly Force: Assessing Two Decades of Progress," *Critical Issues in Policing*, ed. G. Dunham and G. Alpert. Prospect Heights, Ill.: Waveland Press.

Blumenson, E., and E. Nilsen. 1998. "The Drug War's Hidden Economic Agenda." *The Nation* (March 9), p. 11.

Blumstein, A. 1993. "Making Rationality Relevant: The American Society of Criminology 1992 Presidential Address." *Criminology* 31 (January):1.

_____. 1995. "Youth Violence, Guns, and Illicit Drug Markets," *NIJ Research Preview*. Washington, D.C.: National Institute of Justice.

Boland, B., E. Brady, H. Tyson, and J. Bassler. 1983. *The Prosecution of Felony Arrests*. Washington, D.C.: Bureau of Justice Statistics.

Bowker, L. H. 1982. "Victimizers and Victims in American Correctional Institutions," *Pains of Imprisonment*, ed. R. Johnson and H. Toch. Beverly Hills, Calif.: Sage.

Bradley, C. 1992. "Reforming the Criminal Trial." *Indiana Law Journal* 68:659–664.

Brady, T. 1996. "Measuring What Matters," *Research in Brief*. Washington, D.C.: National Institute of Justice.

Brandl, S. 1993. "The Impact of Case Characteristics on Detectives' Decision Making." *Justice Quarterly* 10 (September):395–415.

Bray, K. 1992. "Reaching the Final Chapter in the Story of Peremptory Challenges." *U.C.L.A. Law Review* 40:517–555.

Bright, S. B. 1994. "Counsel for the Poor: The Death Sentence Not for the Worst Crime but for the Worst Lawyer." *Yale Law Journal* 103:1850.

Broeder, D. W. 1959. "The University of Chicago Jury Project." *Nebraska Law Review* 38:774–803.

Brown, M. K. 1981. *Working the Street*. New York: Russell Sage Foundation.

Buchanan, J. 1989. "Police/Prosecutor Teams: Innovations in Several Jurisdictions." *NIJ Reports* (May/June).

Bureau of the Census. 1991. *1990 Census*. Washington, D.C.: Government Printing Office.

Bureau of Justice Statistics (BJS). 1988. *Bulletin* (September).

_____. 1993. *Bulletin* (July).

_____. 1993. *Bulletin* (October).

_____. 1994. *Bulletin* (November).

_____. 1995. *Bulletin* (April).

_____. 1996. *Bulletin* (February).

_____. 1996. *Bulletin* (June).

_____. 1996. *Bulletin* (October).

_____. 1997. *Bulletin* (June).

_____. 1997. *Bulletin* (July).

_____. 1997. *Bulletin* (August).

_____. 1998. *Bulletin* (January).

_____. 1992. *Drugs, Crime and the Justice System*. Washington, D.C.: Government Printing Office.

_____. 1994. *National Crime Victimization Survey* (October).

_____. 1997. *National Crime Victimization Survey* (April).

_____. 1997. Press release (August 14).

_____. 1988. *Report to the Nation on Crime and Justice*, 2d ed. Washington, D.C.: Government Printing Office.

_____. 1996. *Selected Findings* (February).

_____. 1996. *Sourcebook of Criminal Justice Statistics—1995*. Washington, D.C.: Government Printing Office.

_____. 1997. *Sourcebook of Criminal Justice*

Statistics—1996. Washington, D.C.: Government Printing Office.

_____. 1994. *Special Report* (March).

_____. 1995. *Special Report* (August).

_____. 1993. *Survey of State Prison Inmates*. Washington, D.C.: Government Printing Office.

Butterfield, F. 1995a. "Idle Hands within the Devil's Own Playground." *New York Times*, July 16, p. E3.

_____. 1995b. "More Blacks in Their 20's Have Trouble with the Law." *New York Times*, October 5, p. A18.

_____. 1996. *All God's Children: The Bosket Family and the American Tradition of Violence*. New York: Avon Books.

_____. 1998. "Behind the Death Row Bottleneck." *New York Times*, January 25, p. WK1.

Buzawa, E. S., and C. G. Buzawa. 1990. *Domestic Violence: The Criminal Justice Response*. Newbury Park, Calif.: Sage.

Calhoun, F. 1990. *The Lawmen*. Washington, D.C.: Smithsonian Institution.

California, Attorney General, 1986. *Annual Report to the Legislature: Organized Crime in California*. Sacramento: Department of Justice.

Callahan, L. A., M. A. McGreevy, C. Cirincione, and H. J. Steadman. 1992. "Measuring the Effects of the Guilty but Mentally Ill (GBMI) Verdict." *Law and Human Behavior* 16:447–462.

Camp, C. G., and G. M. Camp. 1994. *Corrections Yearbook*. South Salem, N.Y.: Criminal Justice Institute.

Camp, D. D. 1993. "Out of the Quagmire: After *Jacobson v. United States*: Toward a More Balanced Entrapment Standard." *Journal of Criminal Law and Criminology* 83:1055–1097.

Cao, L., A. Adams, and V. Jensen. 1997. "A Test of the Black Subculture of Violence Thesis: A Research Note." *Criminology* 35:367-379.

Carns, T. W., and J. Kruse. 1991. *Alaska's Plea Bargaining Ban: Re-evaluated*. Anchorage: Alaska Judicial Council.

Carr, J. G. 1993. "Bail Bondsmen and the Federal Courts." *Federal Probation* 57 (March):9–14.

Carroll, L. 1974. *Hacks, Blacks, and Cons: Race Relations in a Maximum Security Prison*. Lexington, Mass.: Lexington Books.

Casper, J. D. 1971. "Did You Have a Lawyer When You Went to Court? No, I Had a Public Defender." *Yale Review of Law and Social Change* 1:4–9.

Caulfield, S. L. 1994. "Life or Death Decision: Prosecutorial Power vs. Equality of Justice." *Journal of Contemporary Criminal Justice* 5:233–247.

Champion, D. J. 1989. "Private Counsels and Public Defenders: A Look at Weak Cases, Prior Records, and Leniency in Plea Bargaining." *Journal of Criminal Justice* 17:253–263.

Chapper, J. A., and R. A. Hanson. 1989. *Understanding Reversible Error in Criminal Appeals*. Williamsburg, Va.: National Center for State Courts.

Chermak, S. M. 1995. *Victims in the News: Crime and the American News Media*. Boulder, Colo.: Westview Press.

Chin, K. 1990. *Chinese Subculture and Criminality: Non-Traditional Crime Groups in America*. New York: Greenwood Press.

Chiricos, T. G., and W. D. Bales. 1991. "Unemployment and Punishment: An Empirical Assessment." *Criminology* 29:701–724.

Chiricos, T. G., and C. Crawford. 1995. "Race and Imprisonment: A Contextual Assessment of the Evidence," *Ethnicity, Race, and Crime: Perspectives Across Time and Place*, ed. D. F. Hawkins. Albany: State University of New York Press.

Christopher, R. L. 1994. "Mistake of Fact in the Objective Theory of Justification." *Journal of Criminal Law and Criminology* 85:295–332.

Church, T. W. 1985. "Examining Local Legal Culture." *American Bar Foundation Research Journal* (Summer):449.

Clark, J. , and D. A. Henry. 1997. "The Pretrial Release Decision." *Judicature* 81:76-81.

Clear, T. R. 1994. *Harm in American Penology*. Albany: State University of New York Press.

Clear, T. R., and A. A. Braga. 1995. "Community Corrections," *Crime*, ed. J. Q. Wilson and J. Petersilia. San Francisco: ICS Press, 421–444.

Clear, T. R., and G. F. Cole. 1997. *American Corrections*, 4th ed. Belmont, Calif.: Wadsworth.

Clear, T. R., and P. L. Hardyman. 1990. "The New Intensive Supervision Movement." *Crime and Delinquency* 36:42.

Clear, T. R., and E. J. Latessa. 1993. "Surveillance vs. Control: Probation Officers' Roles in Intensive Supervision." *Justice Quarterly* 10:441.

Clear, T. R., and V. O'Leary. 1984. *Controlling the Offender in the Community*. Lexington, Mass.: Lexington Books.

Cohen, L. E., and M. Felson. 1979. "Social Change and Crime Rates: A Routine Activity Approach." *American Sociological Review* 44:588–608.

Cohen, M., T. R. Miller, and S. B. Rossman. 1990. "The Costs and Consequences of Violent Behavior in the United States." Paper prepared for the Panel on the Understanding and Control of Violent Behavior, National Research Council, National Academy of Sciences, Washington, D.C.

Commission on Accreditation for Law Enforcement Agencies. 1989. *Standards for Law Enforcement Accreditation*. Fairfax, Va.: Commission on Accreditation for Law Enforcement Agencies.

Connors, E., T. Lundregan, N. Miller, and T. McEwen. 1996. *Convicted by Juries, Exonerated by Science: Case Studies in the Use of DNA Evidence to Establish Innocence after Trial*. Washington, D.C.: National Institute of Justice.

Cooney, M. 1994. "Evidence as Partisanship." *Law and Society Review* 28:833–858.

Cowan, C. C., W. C. Thompson, and P. C. Ellsworth. 1984. "The Effects of Death Qualification on Jurors' Predisposition to Convict and on the Quality of Deliberation." *Law and Human Behavior* 8:60.

Crew, B. K. 1991. "Race Differences in Felony Charging Sentencing: Toward an Integration of Decision-Making and Negotiation Models." *Journal of Crime and Justice* 14:99–122.

Cullen, F. T., E. J. Latessa, V. S. Burton, Jr., and L. X. Lombardo. 1993. "The Correctional Orientation of Prison Wardens: Is the Rehabilitative Ideal Supported?" *Criminology* 31 (February):69–92.

Cullen, F. T., T. Leming, B. Link, and J. Wozniak. 1985. "The Impact of Social Supports in Police Stress," *Criminology* 23:503–522.

Cullen, F. T., J. P. Wright, and B. K. Applegate. 1996. "Control in the Community: The Limits of Reform?" *Choosing Correctional Options That Work: Defining the Demand and Evaluating the Supply*, ed. A. T. Harland. Thousand Oaks, Calif.: Sage, 69–116.

Cuniff, M. 1987. *Sentencing Outcomes in Twenty-Eight Felony Courts*. Washington, D.C.: National Institute of Justice.

Cunningham, W. C., J. J. Strauchs, and C. W. Van Meter. 1990. *Private Security Trends*, 1970 to the Year 2000. Boston: Butterworth-Heinemann.

_____. 1991. *Private Security: Patterns and Trends*. Washington, D.C.: National Institute of Justice.

Daly, K., and R. L. Bordt. 1995. "Sex Effects and Sentencing: An Analysis of the Statistical Literature." *Justice Quarterly* 12 (March):141–175.

Daly, K., and M. Chesney-Lind. 1988. "Feminism and Criminology." *Justice Quarterly* 5 (1988):497.

Davis, M., R. Lundman, and R. Martinez, Jr. 1991. "Private Corporate Justice: Store Police, Shoplifters, and Civil Recovery." *Social Problems* 38:395–408.

Davis, R. C., and B. E. Smith. 1994. "The Effects of Victim Impact Statements on Sentencing Decisions: A Test in an Urban Setting." *Justice Quarterly* 11 (September):3.

Decker, S. H., R. Wright, A. Redfern, and D. Smith. 1993. "A Woman's Place Is in the Home: Females and Residential Burglary." *Justice Quarterly* 10 (March):142.

del Carmen, R. 1991. *Civil Liabilities in American Policing*. Englewood Cliffs, N.J.: Brady.

Diamond, S. S. 1990. "Scientific Jury Selection: What Social Scientists Know and Do Not Know." *Judicature* 73:178.

Diggs, D. W., and S. L. Peiper. 1994. "Using Day Reporting Centers as an Alternative to Jail." *Federal Probation* 58 (March):9–13.

DiIulio, J. J., Jr. 1987. *Governing Prisons*. New York: Free Press.

_____. 1990. *No Escape: The Future of American Corrections*. New York: Basic Books.

_____. 1993a. "Rethinking the Criminal Justice System: Toward a New Paradigm," *Performance Measures for the Criminal Justice System*. Washington, D.C.: Bureau of Justice Statistics.

_____. 1993b. "Well-Governed Prisons Are Possible," *Criminal Justice: Law and Politics*, 6th ed., ed. G. F. Cole. Belmont, Calif.: Wadsworth.

_____. 1995. "Why Violent Crime Rates Have Dropped." *Wall Street Journal*, September 6, p. A19.

Dillehay, R. C., and M. R. Sandys. 1996. "Life under *Wainwright v. Witt*: Juror Dispositions and Death Qualification." *Law and Human Behavior* 20:147–165.

Donziger, S. R., ed. 1996. *The Real War on Crime: The Report of the National Criminal Justice Commission*. New York: Harper Collins.

DuBois, P. L. 1980. *From Ballot to Bench: Judicial Elections and the Quest for Accountability*. Austin: University of Texas Press.

Edna McConnell Clark Foundation. 1997. *Seeking Justice: Crime and Punishment in America*. New York: Edna McConnell Clark Foundation.

Eisenstein, J., R. B. Flemming, and P. F. Nardulli. 1988. *The Contours of Justice: Communities and Their Courts*. Boston: Little, Brown.

Eisenstein, J., and H. Jacob. 1977. *Felony Justice: An Organizational Analysis of Criminal Courts*. Boston: Little, Brown.

Elliott, D. S. 1989. "Criminal Justice Procedures in Family Violence Crimes," *Crime and Justice*, vol. 11, ed. M. Tonry and N. Morris. Chicago: University of Chicago Press, 427–480.

Emmelman, D. S. 1996. "Trial by Plea Bargain: Case Settlement as a Product of Recursive Decisionmaking." *Law and Society Review* 30:335–360.

Eskridge, C. W. 1986. *Pretrial Release Programming*. New York: Clark Boardman.

Federal Bureau of Investigation. 1996. *Crime in the United States—1995*. Washington, D.C.: Government Printing Office.

_____. 1997. *Crime in the United States—1996*. Washington, D.C.: Government Printing Office.

Feeley, M. M. 1979. *The Process Is the Punishment*. New York: Russell Sage Foundation.

Feeley, M. M., and R. A. Hanson. 1990. "The Impact of Judicial Intervention on Prisons and Jails: A Framework of Analysis and a Review of the Literature," *Courts, Corrections, and the Constitution*, ed. J. J. DiIulio, Jr. New York: Oxford University Press.

Feld, B. C. 1993a. "Criminalizing the American Juvenile Court," *Crime and Justice: A Review of Research*, vol. 17, ed. M. Tonry. Chicago: University of Chicago Press, 197–280.

_____. 1993b. "Juvenile (In)Justice and the Criminal Court Alternative." *Crime and Delinquency* 39:403–424.

Felice, J. D., and J. C. Kilwein. 1992. "Strike One, Strike Two . . . : The History and Prospect for Judicial Reform in Ohio." *Judicature* 75:193–200.

Ferdinand, P. 1997. "Judge Reduces Verdict, Frees Au Pair: Murder Conviction Cut to Manslaughter." *Washington Post*, November 11, p. A1.

Fetzer, P. L. 1989. "Execution of the Mentally Retarded: A Punishment without Justification." *South Carolina Law Review* 40:419.

Fisher, B. 1993. "What Works: Block Watch Meetings or Crime Prevention Seminars?" *Journal of Crime and Justice* 16:1.

Flanagan, T. J. 1991. "Adaptation and Adjustment among Long-Term Prisoners." *Federal Prison Journal* 2 (Spring):41–51.

_____. ed. 1995. *Long-Term Imprisonment*. Thousand Oaks, Calif.: Sage.

Flanagan, T. J., and K. Maguire. 1993. "A Full Employment Policy for Prisons in the United States: Some Arguments, Estimates, and Implications." *Journal of Criminal Justice* 21:117–130.

Flemming, R. B. , P. F. Nardulli, and J. Eisenstein. 1992. *The Craft of Justice: Politics and Work in Criminal Court Communities*. Philadelphia: University of Pennsylvania Press.

Florida, Department of Corrections. 1991. *Mandatory Minimum Sentences in Florida: Past Trends and Future Implications*. Tallahassee: Department of Corrections.

Flowers, R. B. 1988. *Minorities and Criminality*. Westport, Conn.: Greenwood Press.

Forst, B. 1995. "Prosecution and Sentencing," *Crime*, ed. J. Q. Wilson and J. Petersilia. San Francisco: ICS Press.

Forst, M. L., and M. Blomquist. 1992. "Punishment, Accountability, and the New Juvenile Justice." *Justice and Family Court Journal* 43:1.

Foucault, M. 1977. *Discipline and Punish*, trans. A. Sheridan. New York: Pantheon.

Fox, J. G. 1982. *Organizational and Racial Conflict in Maximum Security Prisons*. Lexington, Mass.: Lexington Books.

_____. 1996. *Trends in Juvenile Violence: A Report to the United States Attorney General on Current and Future Rates of Juvenile Offending*. Boston: Northeastern University.

Frank, J., S. G. Brandl, F. T. Cullen, and A. Stichman. 1996. "Reassessing the Impact of Race on Citizens' Attitudes toward the Police: A Research Note." *Justice Quarterly* 13 (June):320–334.

Frase, R. S. 1995. "State Sentencing Guidelines: Still Going Strong." *Judicature* 78 (January/February):173.

Free, M. D. 1996. *African Americans and the Criminal Justice System*. New York: Garland.

Friday, P. C., S. Metzger, and D. Walters. 1991. "Policing Domestic Violence: Perceptions, Experience, and Reality." *Criminal Justice Review* 16:198–213.

Fridell, L. 1990. "Decision Making of the District Attorney: Diverting or Prosecuting Intrafamilial Child Sexual Abuse Offenders." *Criminal Justice Policy Review* 4:249–267.

Friedman, L. M. 1993. *Crime and Punishment in American History*. New York: Basic Books.

Friedman, L. M., and R. V. Percival. 1981. *The Roots of Justice: Crime and Punishment in Alameda County, California, 1870–1910*. Chapel Hill, N.C.: University of North Carolina Press.

Frohmann, L. 1997. "Convictability and Discordant Locales: Reproducing Race, Class, and Gender Ideologies in Prosecutorial Decisionmaking." *Law and Society Review* 31:531-556.

Fukurai, H. 1996. "Race, Social Class, and Jury Participation: New Dimensions for Evaluating Discrimination in Jury Service and Jury Selection." *Journal of Criminal Justice* 24:71–88.

Fyfe, J. 1993. "Police Use of Deadly Force: Research and Reform," *Criminal Justice: Law and Politics*, 6th ed, ed. G. F. Cole. Belmont, Calif.: Wadsworth.

Gardner, M. A. 1993. "Section 1983 Actions under *Miranda*: A Critical View of the Right to Avoid Interrogation." *American Criminal Law Review* 30:1277–1328.

Garner, J., and E. Clemmer. 1986. *Danger to Police in Domestic Disturbances—A New Look*. Washington, D.C.: Bureau of Justice Statistics.

Garner J., T. Schade, J. Hepburn, and J. Buchanan. 1995. "Measuring the Continuum of Force Used by and against the Police." *Criminal Justice Review* 20 (Autumn):146–168.

Geerken, M., and H. D. Hayes. 1993. "Probation and Parole: Public Risks and the Future of Incarceration Alternatives." *Criminology* 31 (November):549–564.

Geller, W. A., and M. S. Scott. 1992. *Deadly Force: What We Know*. Washington, D.C.: Police Executive Research Foundation.

Gendreau, P., F. T. Cullen, and J. Bonta. 1994. "Intensive Rehabilitation Supervision: The Next Generation in Community Corrections?" *Federal Probation* 58:72–78.

Gershman, B. L. 1993. "Themes of Injustice: Wrongful Convictions, Racial Prejudice, and Lawyer Incompetence." *Criminal Law Bulletin* 29:502–515.

Goldstein, H. 1979. "Improving Policing: A Problem-Oriented Approach." *Crime and Delinquency* 25:236–257.

_____. 1990. *Problem-Oriented Policing*. New York: McGraw-Hill.

Goodpaster, G. 1986. "The Adversary System, Advocacy, and Effective Assistance of Counsel in Criminal Cases." *New York University Review of Law and Social Change* 14:90.

Goolkasian, G. A., R. W. Geddes, and W. DeJong. 1989. "Coping with Police Stress," *Critical Issues in Policing*, ed. R. G. Dunham and G. P. Alpert. Prospect Heights, Ill.: Waveland Press, 498–507.

Graber, D. A. 1980. *Crime News and the Public*. New York: Praeger.

Graham, B. L. 1995. "Judicial Recruitment and Racial Diversity on State Courts," *Courts and Justice*, ed. G. L. Mays and P. R. Gregware. Prospect Heights, Ill.: Waveland Press.

Greenwood, P., J. M. Chaiken, and J. Petersilia. 1977. *Criminal Investigation Process*. Lexington, Mass.: Lexington Books.

Griset, P. L. 1993. "Determinate Sentencing and the High Cost of Overblown Rhetoric: The New York Experience." *Crime and Delinquency* 39 (April):552.

Hagan, F. E. 1997. *Political Crime: Ideology and Criminality*. Needham Heights, Mass.: Allyn & Bacon.

Hagan, J., and R. D. Peterson. 1995. "Criminal Inequality in America: Patterns and Consequences," *Crime and Inequality*, ed. J. Hagan and R. D. Peterson. Stanford, Calif.: Stanford University Press, 14–36.

Hall, J. 1947. *General Principles of Criminal Law*, 2d ed. Indianapolis: Bobbs-Merrill.

Hall, W. K., and L. T. Aspin. 1987. "What Twenty Years of Judicial Retention Elections Have Told Us." *Judicature* 70:340.

Hans, V., and N. Vidmar. 1986. *Judging the Jury*. New York: Plenum Press.

Hanson, R. A., and J. Chapper. 1991. *Indigent Defense Systems*. Williamsburg, Va.: National Center for State Courts.

Hastie, R., S. Penrod, and N. Pennington. 1983. *Inside the Jury*. Cambridge, Mass.: Harvard University Press.

Hawkins, G. 1983. "Prison Labor and Prison Industries," *Crime and Justice*, ed. M. Tonry and N. Morris. Chicago: University of Chicago Press.

Heffernan, E. 1972. *Making It In Prison*. New York: Wiley.

Henning, P. J. 1993. "Precedents in a Vacuum: The Supreme Court Continues to Tinker with Double Jeopardy." *American Criminal Law Review* 31:1–72.

Hensley, T. R., C. E. Smith, and J. A. Baugh. 1997. *The Changing Supreme Court: Constitutional Rights and Liberties*. St. Paul, Minn.: West Publishing.

Hepburn, J. R. 1985. "The Exercise of Power in Coercive Organizations: A Study of Prison Guards." *Criminology* 23:145–164.

Heumann, M. 1978. *Plea Bargaining*. Chicago: University of Chicago Press.

Hickey, T. J. 1995. "A Double Jeopardy Analysis of the Medgar Evers Murder Case." *Journal of Criminal Justice* 23:41–51.

Hillsman, S. T., J. L. Sichel, and B. Mahoney. 1983. *Fines in Sentencing*. New York: Vera Institute of Justice.

Hirschel, J. D., I. W. Hutchinson, C. W. Dean, and A. M. Mills. 1992. "Review Essay on the Law Enforcement Response to Spouse Abuse: Past, Present, and Future." *Justice Quarterly* 9:247–283.

Holmes, M. D., H. M. Hosch, H. C. Daudistel, D. A. Perez, and J. B. Graves. 1996. "Ethnicity, Legal Resources, and Felony Dispositions in Two Southwestern Jurisdictions." *Justice Quarterly* 13:11–29.

Houlden, P., and S. Balkin. 1985. "Costs and Quality Indigent Defense: Ad Hoc vs. Coordinated Assignment of the Private Bar within a Mixed System." *Justice System Journal* 10:159.

Howard, J. 1929. *The State of Prisons in England and Wales*. London: J. M. Dent [originally published in 1777].

Huff, C. R., and A. Rattner. 1988. "Convicted but Innocent: False Positives and the Criminal Justice Process," *Controversial Issues in Crime and Justice*, ed. J. E. Scott and T. Hirschi. Newbury Park, Calif.: Sage.

Hunt, G., S. Riegel, T. Morales, and D. Waldorf. 1993. "Changes in Prison Culture: Prison Gangs and the Case of the Pepsi Generation." *Social Problems* 40:398–409.

Ianni, F.A.J. 1973. *Ethnic Succession in Organized Crime*. Washington, D.C.: Government Printing Office.

Institute for Law and Social Research. 1980. *Pretrial Release and Misconduct in the District of Columbia*.

Irwin, J. 1970. *The Felon*. Englewood Cliffs, N.J.: Prentice-Hall.

_____. 1980. *Prisons in Turmoil*. Boston: Little, Brown.

Irwin, J., and D. Cressey. 1962. "Thieves, Convicts, and the Inmate Culture." *Social Problems* 10:142–155.

Jacob, H. 1973. *Urban Justice*. Boston: Little, Brown.

Jacobs, J. B. 1994. *Busting the Mob: United States v. Cosa Nostra*. New York: New York University Press.

Jacoby, J. 1979. "The Charging Policies of Prosecutors," *The Prosecutor*, ed. W. F. McDonald. Beverly Hills, Calif.: Sage.

_____. 1995. "Pushing the Envelope: Leadership in Prosecution." *Justice System Journal* 17:291–307.

Janikowski, W. R., and D. Giacopassi. 1993. "Pyrrhic Images, Dancing Shadows, and Flights of Fancy: The Drug Courier Profile as Legal Fiction." *Journal of Contemporary Criminal Justice* 9:60–69.

Johnson, D. R. 1981. *American Law Enforcement: A History*. St. Louis: Forum Press.

Kairys, D., J. B. Kadane, and J. P. Lehoczky. 1977. "Jury Representativeness: A Mandate for Multiple Source Lists." *California Law Review* 65:776–827.

Kalinich, D. B. 1980. *Power, Stability, and Contraband*. Prospect Heights, Ill.: Waveland Press.

Kalven, H., and H. Zeisel. 1966. *The American Jury*. Boston: Little, Brown.

Kappeler, V. E., M. Blumberg, and G. W. Potter. 1996. *The Mythology of Crime and Criminal Justice*, 2d ed. Prospect Heights, Ill.: Waveland Press.

Karmen, A. 1996. *Crime Victims*, 3d ed. Belmont, Calif.: Wadsworth.

Kauffman, K. 1988. *Prison Officers and Their World*. Cambridge, Mass.: Harvard University Press.

Keil, T. J., and G. F. Vito. 1991. "Fear of Crime and Attitudes toward Capital Punishment: A Structural Equations Model." *Justice Quarterly* 8 (December):447.

_____. 1992. "The Effects of the *Furman* and *Gregg* Decisions on Black-White Execution Ratios in the South." *Journal of Criminal Justice* 20:217–226.

Kelling, G. L. 1992. "Measuring What Matters: A New Way of Thinking about Crime and Public Order." *City Journal* (Spring).

Kelling, G. L., and W. J. Bratton. 1993. "Implementing Community Policing: The Administrative Problem," *Perspectives on Policing*, no. 17. Washington, D.C.: National Institute of Justice.

Kelling, G. L., and C. M. Coles. 1996. *Fixing Broken Windows: Restoring and Reducing Crime in Our Communities*. New York: Free Press.

Kelling, G. L., and M. Moore. 1988. "The Evolving Strategy of Policing," *Perspectives on Policing*, no. 13. Washington, D.C.: National Institute of Justice.

Kelling, G. L., T. Pate, D. Dieckman, and C. E. Brown. 1974. *The Kansas City Preventive Patrol Experiments: A Summary Report*. Washington, D.C.: Police Foundation.

Kerstetter, W. A. 1985. "Who Disciplines the Police? Who Should?" *Police Leadership in America*, ed. W. A. Geller. New York: Praeger, 141–181.

King, N. J. 1994. "The Effects of Race-Conscious Jury Selection on Public Confidence in the Fairness of Jury Proceedings: An Empirical Puzzle." *American Criminal Law Review* 31:1177–1202.

Kleinknecht, W. 1996. *The New Ethnic Mobs: The Changing Face of Organized Crime in America*. New York: Free Press.

Klofas, J., and J. Yandrasits. 1989. "'Guilty but Mentally Ill' and the Jury Trial: A Case Study." *Criminal Law Bulletin* 24:424.

Kopstein, A. J., and P. T. Roth. 1990. *Drug Abuse among Race/Ethnic Minorities*. Washington, D.C.: National Institute on Drug Abuse.

Kotlowitz, A. 1994. "Their Crimes Don't Make Them Adults." *New York Times Magazine*, February 13, p. 40.

Kramer, G. P., and D. M. Koenig. 1990. "Do Jurors Understand Criminal Justice Instructions? Analyzing the Results of the Michigan Juror Comprehension Project." *University of Michigan Journal of Law Reform* 23:401–437.

Kramer, J. H., and J. T. Ulmer. 1996. "Sentencing Disparity and Departures from Guidelines." *Justice Quarterly* 13 (March):81.

Kruttschnitt, C., and S. Krmopotich. 1990. "Aggressive Behavior among Female Inmates: An Exploratory Study." *Justice Quarterly* 7 (June):371.

Kurtz, H. 1997. "The Crime Spree on Network News." *Washington Post*, August 12, p. 1.

Langbein, J. H. 1992. "On the Myth of Written Constitutions: The Disappearance of the Criminal Jury Trial." *Harvard Journal of Law and Public Policy* 15:119–127.

Lansing (Mich.) *State Journal*, October 3, 1997.

Lear, E. T. 1995. "Contemplating the Successive Prosecution Phenomenon in the Federal System." *Journal of Criminal Law and Criminology* 85:625–675.

Leo, R. A. 1996. "Miranda's Revenge: Police Interrogation as a Confidence Game." *Law and Society Review* 30:259-288.

Levin, M. 1994. "Urban Politics and Policy Outcomes: The Criminal Courts," *Criminal Justice: Law and Politics*, 6th ed., ed. G. F. Cole. Belmont, Calif.: Wadsworth.

Levine, J. P. 1992. *Juries and Politics*. Belmont, Calif.: Wadsworth.

_____. 1996. "The Case Study as a Jury Research Methodology." *Journal of Criminal Justice* 24:351–360.

Lilly, J. R. 1993. "The Corrections-Commercial Complex." *Crime and Delinquency* 39 (April):150.

Logan, C. 1993. "Criminal Justice Performance Measures in Prison," *Criminal Justice Performance Measures*. Washington, D.C.: Government Printing Office.

Logan, C., and J. J. DiIulio, Jr. 1993. "Ten Deadly Myths about Crime and Punishment in the United States," *Criminal Justice: Law and Politics*, ed. G. F. Cole. Belmont, Calif.: Wadsworth, 486–502.

Lovrich, N. P., and C. H. Sheldon. 1994. "Is Voting for State Judges a Flight of Fancy or a Reflection of Policy and Value Preferences?" *Justice System Journal* 16:57–71.

Lynch, J. 1995. "Crime in International Perspective," *Crime*, ed. J. Q. Wilson and J. Petersilia. San Francisco: ICS Press, 11–38.

MacKenzie, D. L. 1994. "Boot Camps: A National Assessment." *Overcrowded Times* 5:1.

_____. 1995. "Boot Camp Prisons and Recidivism in Eight States." *Criminology* 33:327–358.

MacKenzie, D. L., and A. Piquero. 1994. "The Impact of Shock Incarceration Programs on Prison Crowding." *Crime and Delinquency* 40 (April):222–249.

Mann, C. R. 1993. *Unequal Justice: A Question of Color*. Bloomington: Indiana University Press.

Manning, P. K. 1977. *Police Work*. Cambridge, Mass.: MIT Press.

Marsh, J. R. 1994. "Performing Pretrial Services: A Challenge in the Federal Criminal Justice System." *Federal Probation* 58 (December):3–10.

Martin, S. E. 1989. "Women in Policing: The Eighties and Beyond," *Police and Society*, ed. D. Kenney. New York: Praeger.

_____. 1991. "The Effectiveness of Affirmative Action." *Justice Quarterly* 8:489–504.

Martinson, R. 1974. "What Works? Questions and Answers about Prison Reform." *The Public Interest* (Spring):25.

Maschke, K. J. 1995. "Prosecutors as Crime Creators: The Case of Prenatal Drug Use." *Criminal Justice Review* 20:21–33.

McCorkle, R. C. 1993. "Research Note: Punish and Rehabilitate? Public Attitudes toward Six Common Crimes." *Crime and Delinquency* 39 (April):240.

McCoy, C. 1986. "Policing the Homeless." *Criminal Law Bulletin* 22 (May/June):263.

_____. 1993. *Politics and Plea Bargaining: Victims' Rights in California*. Philadelphia: University of Pennsylvania Press.

_____. 1995. "Is the Trial Penalty Inevitable?" Paper presented at the annual meeting of the Law and Society Association, Phoenix, Arizona (June).

McDonald, D. 1986. *Punishment without Walls*. New Brunswick, N.J.: Rutgers University Press.

McGabey, R. 1986. "Economic Conditions: Neighborhod Organization and Urban Crime," *Crime and Justice*, vol. 8, ed. A. J. Reiss and M. Tonry. Chicago: University of Chicago Press.

McGarrell, E. F. 1993. "Institutional Theory and the Stability of a Conflict Model of the Incarceration Rate." *Justice Quarterly* 10 (March):23.

McLeod, M. 1989. "Getting Free: Victim Participation in Parole Board Decisions." *Criminal Justice* 4.

Meier, R. F., and T. D. Miethe. 1993. "Understanding Theories of Criminal Victimization," *Crime and Justice: A Review of the Research*, ed. M. Tonry. Chicago: University of Chicago Press.

Melekian, B. 1990. "Police and the Homeless." *FBI Law Enforcement Bulletin* 59:1–7.

Miethe, T. D. 1995. "Fear and Withdrawal from Urban Life." *Annals of the American Academy of Political and Social Science*, 539 (May):14–27.

Miethe, T. D., and C. A. Moore. 1989. "Sentencing Guidelines: Their Effects in Minnesota," *Research in Brief*. Washington, D.C.: National Institute of Justice.

Miller, J. L., and J. J. Sloan. 1994. "A Study of Criminal Justice Discretion." *Journal of Criminal Justice* 22:107–123.

Miller, M., and M. Guggenheim. 1990. "Pretrial Detention and Punishment." *Minnesota Law Review* 75:335–426.

Monkkonen, E. H. 1981. *Police in Urban America, 1869–1920*. Cambridge, England: Cambridge University Press.

_____. 1992. "History of the Urban Police," *Modern Policing*, ed. M. Tonry and N. Morris. Chicago: University of Chicago Press.

Moore, J. W. 1994. "Locked In." *National Journal*, July 30, p. 1785.

Moore, M. 1992. "Problem-Solving and Community Policing," *Modern Policing*, ed. M. Tonry and N. Morris. Chicago: University of Chicago Press, 99–158.

Moore, M., and G. L. Kelling. 1983. "To Serve and to Protect: Learning from Police History." *The Public Interest* (Winter):55.

Morash, M., R. N. Haarr, and L. Rucker. 1994. "A Comparison of Programming for Women and Men in the U.S. Prisons in the 1980s." *Crime and Delinquency* 40 (April):197.

Morris, N. 1995. "The Contemporary Prison 1965–Present," *The Oxford History of the Prison*, ed. N. Morris and D. J. Rothman. New York: Oxford University Press.

Morris, N., and M. Tonry. 1990. *Between Prison and Probation: Intermediate Punishments in a Rational Sentencing System*. New York: Oxford University Press.

Murphy, P. V. 1992. "Organizing for Community Policing," *Issues in Policing: New Perspectives*, ed. J. W. Bizzack. Lexington, Ky.: Autumn Press, 113–128.

NAACP Legal Defense and Education Fund. 1997. *Death Row*, USA (Summer).

Nagel, R. F. 1990. "The Myth of the General Right to Bail." *The Public Interest* (Winter):84–97.

Nardulli, P. F. 1983. "The Societal Costs of the Exclusionary Rule: An Empirical Assessment." *American Bar Foundation Journal*, 585–690.

_____. 1986. "Insider Justice: Defense Attorneys and the Handling of Felony Cases." *Journal of Criminal Law and Criminology* 79:416.

National Institute of Justice, n.d. *Crime File* "Insanity Defense" (film prepared by Norval Morris). Washington, D.C.: Government Printing Office.

_____. 1988. *Research in Action*. Washington, D.C.: Government Printing Office. (January).

_____. 1997. *Research in Action*. Washington, D.C.: Government Printing Office.

_____. 1984. *Research in Brief*. Washington D.C.: Government Printing Office.

_____. 1996. *Victim Costs and Consequences: A New Look*. Washington, D.C.: Government Printing Office.

Neufeld, P. J., and N. Colman. 1990. "When Science Takes the Witness Stand." *Scientific American* 262 (May):46.

New York, Office of Justice Systems Analysis. 1991. *The Incarceration of Minority Defendants: An Identification of Disparity in New York State, 1985-1986*. Albany: New York State Division of Criminal Justice Services.

Newman, T. C. 1996. "Fair Cross-Section and Good Intention: Representation in Federal Juries." *Justice System Journal* 18:211–232.

Newsweek, April 25,1988.

_____, February 24, 1994.

_____, May 6, 1996.

New York Times, July 15, 1989.

_____, April 7, 1992.

_____, December 27, 1992.

_____, August 8, 1994.

_____, September 1, 1994.

_____, November 13, 1994.

_____, April 17,1995.

_____, November 1, 1995.

_____, July 3, 1996.

_____, December 2, 1996.

_____, January 1, 1997.

_____, January 5, 1997.

_____, September 28, 1997.

_____, October 5, 1997.

_____, October 9, 1997.

_____, October 10, 1997.

_____, October 12, 1997.

_____, October 14, 1997.

O'Brien, R. M. 1996. "Police Productivity and Crime Rates: 1973–1992," *Criminology* 34:183–207.

Office of Juvenile Justice and Delinquency Prevention. 1996. *Juvenile Justice Bulletin*, July.

____. 1997. *Juvenile Justice Bulletin*, February.

____.1995. *Juvenile Officers and Victims: A National Report*. Washington, D.C.: Government Printing Office.

____. 1991. *OJJDP Update on Statistics*, January.

Packer, H. L. 1968. *The Limits of the Criminal Sanction*. Stanford, Calif.: Stanford University Press.

Parent, D. G. 1990. *Day Reporting Centers for Criminal Offenders: A Descriptive Analysis of Existing Programs*. Washington, D.C.: National Institute of Justice.

Pate, A. M., and L. A. Fridell. 1993. *Police Use of Force: Official Reports, Citizen Complaints, and Legal Consequences*. Washington, D.C.: Police Foundation.

Peoples, J. M. 1995. "Helping Pretrial Services Clients Find Jobs." *Federal Probation* 59 (March):14–18.

Perkins, C. A., J. J. Stephan, and A. J. Beck. 1995. "Jails and Jail Inmates 1993–94." Bureau of Justice Statistics, *Bulletin* (April).

Perkins, D. B., and J. D. Jamieson. 1995. "Judicial Probable Cause Determinations after *County of Riverside v. McLaughlin*." *Criminal Law Bulletin* 31:534–546.

Petersilia, J. 1990. "When Probation Becomes More Dreaded Than Prison." *Federal Probation* (March):24.

____. 1993. "Measuring the Performance of Community Corrections," *Performance Measures for the Criminal Justice System*. Washington, D.C.: Bureau of Justice Statistics.

____. 1995. "A Crime Control Rationale for Reinvesting in Community Corrections." *Prison Journal* 75 (December):479–496.

Petersilia, J., and S. Turner. 1987. "Guideline-Based Justice Prediction and Racial Minorities," *Crime and Justice*, vol. 15, ed. N. Morris and M. Tonry. Chicago: University of Chicago Press.

____. 1989. "The Potential of Intermediate Sanctions." *State Government* (March/April):65.

Pisciotta, A. W. 1994. *Benevolent Repression: Social Control and the American Reformatory-Prison Movement*. New York: New York University Press.

Platt, A. 1977. *The Child Savers*, 2d ed. Chicago: University of Chicago Press.

Pollock-Byrne, J. 1990. *Women, Prisons and Crime*. Pacific Grove, Calif.: Brooks/Cole.

President's Commission on Law Enforcement and the Administration of Justice, 1967. *The Challenge of Crime in a Free Society*. Washington, D.C.: Government Printing Office.

Propper, A. 1981. *Prison Homosexuality*. Lexington, Mass.: Lexington Books.

____. 1982. "Make Believe Families and Homosexuality among Imprisoned Girls." *Criminology* 20:127–139.

Pursley, R. D. 1995. "The Federal Habeas Corpus Process: Unraveling the Issues." *Criminal Justice Policy Review* 7 (June):115.

Radelet, M. L., H. A. Bedeau, and C. E. Putnam. 1992. *In Spite of Innocence*. Boston: Northeastern University Press.

Rafter, N. H. 1983. "Prisons for Women, 1790–1980," *Crime and Justice*, 5th ed., ed. M. Tonry and N. Morris. Chicago: University of Chicago Press.

Reaves, B. A. 1992. *State and Local Police Departments*, 1990. Washington, D.C.: Bureau of Justice Statistics.

Regoli, R. M., J. P. Crank, and R. G. Culbertson. 1987. "Rejoinder—Police Cynicism: Theory Development and Reconstruction." *Justice Quarterly* 4:281–286.

Reiss, A. J., Jr. 1988. *Private Employment of Public Police*. Washington, D.C.: National Institute of Justice.

____. 1992. "Police Organization in the Twentieth Century," *Crime and Justice: A Review of Research*, vol. 15, ed. M. Tonry and N. Morris. Chicago: University of Chicago Press, 51–97.

Renzema, M. 1992. "Home Confinement Programs: Development, Implementation, and Impact," *Smart Sentencing: The Emergence of Intermediate Sanctions*, ed. J. M. Byrne, A. J. Lurigio, and J. Petersilia. Newbury Park, Calif.: Sage, 41–53.

Richardson, J. E. 1993. "It's Not Easy Being Green: The Scope of the Fifth Amendment Right to Counsel." *American Criminal Law Review* 31:145–167.

Rierden, A. 1997. *The Farm: Life Inside a Women's Prison*. Amherst, Mass.: University of Massachusetts Press.

Robin, G. D. 1993. "Inquisitive Cops, Investigative Stops, and Drug Courier Hops: Returning to the Scene of the Crime." *Journal of Contemporary Criminal Justice* 9:41–59.

Robinson, P. H. 1993. "Foreword: The Criminal-Civil Distinction and Dangerous Blameless Offenders." *Journal of Criminal Law and Criminology* 83:693–717.

Roper, R., and V. Flango. 1983. "Trials before Judges and Juries." *Justice System Journal* 8:186–198.

Rosen, L. 1995. "The Creation of the Uniform Crime Report: The Role of Social Science." *Social Science History* 19 (Summer): 215–238.

Rosenbaum, J. L. 1989. "Family Dysfunction and Female Delinquency." *Crime and Delinquency* 35:31.

Rosenbaum, R. 1989. "Too Young to Die?" *New York Times Magazine*, March 12, p. 60.

Rothman, D. J. 1971. *The Discovery of the Asylum: Social Order and Disorder in the New Republic*. Boston: Little, Brown.

____. 1980. *Conscience and Convenience*. Boston: Little, Brown.

Rousey, D. C. 1984. "Cops and Guns: Police Use of Deadly Force in Nineteenth-Century New Orleans." *American Journal of Legal History* 28:41–66.

Rubenstein, M. L., and T. J. White. 1979. "Alaska's Ban on Plea Bargaining." *Law and Society* 13:367–390.

Ryan, J. P., A. Ashman, B. D. Sales, and S. Shane-DuBow. 1980. *American Trial Judges*. New York: Free Press.

Schmidt, J., and E. H. Steury. 1989. "Prosecutorial Discretion in Filing Charges in Domestic Violence Cases." *Criminology* 27:487.

Scott, E. J. 1981. *Calls for Service: Citizen Demand and Initial Police Response*. Washington, D.C.: Government Printing Office.

Scott, T. 1985. "Pretrial Detention under the Bail Reform Act of 1984." *American Criminal Law Review* 21:21–34.

Sellin, T. 1970. "The Origin of the Pennsylvania System of Prison Discipline." *Prison Journal* 50 (Spring–Summer):15.

Sherman, A. 1994. *Wasting America's Future*. Boston: Beacon Press.

Sherman, L. W. 1983. "Patrol Strategies for Police," *Crime and Public Policy*, ed. J. Q. Wilson. San Francisco: ICS Press, 149–154.

____. 1990. "Police Crackdowns: Initial and Residual Deterrence," *Crime and Justice*, ed. M. Tonry and N. Morris. Chicago: University of Chicago Press, 1–48.

____. 1992. *Policing Domestic Violence: Experiments and Dilemmas*. New York: Free Press.

____. 1995. "The Police," *Crime*, ed. J. Q. Wilson and J. Petersilia. San Francisco: ICS Press, 327–348.

Sherman, L. W., and R. A. Berk. 1984. "The Specific Effects of Arrest for Domestic Assault." *American Sociological Review* 49:261–272.

Sherman, L. W., and E. G. Cohn. 1986. "Citizens Killed by Big City Police: 1970–84." Unpublished manuscript, Crime Control Institute, Washington, D.C., October.

Sherman, L. W., P. R. Gartin, and M. E. Buerger. 1989. "Hot Spots of Predatory Crime: Routine Activities and the Criminology of Place." *Criminology* 27:27–55.

Sherman, L. W., and D. P. Rogan. 1995a. "Effects of Gun Seizures on Gun Violence: 'Hot Spots' Patrol in Kansas City." *Justice Quarterly* 12 (December):673–693.

____. 1995b. "Deterrent Effects of Police Raids on Crack Houses: A Randomized Controlled Experiment." *Justice Quarterly* 12 (December):755–781.

Sherman, L. W., J. D. Schmidt, D. P. Rogan, P. R. Gartin, E. G. Cohn, D. J. Collins, and A. R. Bacich. 1991. "From Initial Deterrence to Long-Term Escalation: Short Custody Arrest for Poverty Ghetto Domestic Violence." *Criminology* 29:821–850.

Sherman, L. W., and D. A. Weisburd. 1995. "General Deterrent Effects of Police Patrol in Crime 'Hot Spots': A Randomized Controlled Trial." *Justice Quarterly* 12 (December): 625–648.

Shichor, D. 1995. *Punishment for Profit: Private Prisons/Public Concerns*. Thousand Oaks, Calif.: Sage.

Sichel, J. 1978. *Women on Patrol.* Washington, D.C.: Government Printing Office.

Simon, L. M. S. 1993. "Prison Behavior and the Victim-Offender Relationships among Violent Offenders." *Justice Quarterly* 10 (September):263.

Simon, R. 1975. *Women and Crime*. Lexington, Mass.: D.C. Heath.

Simpson, S. S. 1989. "Feminist Theory, Crime, and Justice." *Criminology* 27 (November): 605–632.

Skogan, W. G. 1990. *Disorder and Decline: Crime and the Spiral of Decay in America.* New York: Free Press.

_____. 1995. "Crime and Racial Fears of White Americans." *Annals of the American Academy of Political and Social Science*, 539 (May):59–71.

Skogan, W. G., and S. M. Hartnett. 1997. *Community Policing, Chicago Style*. New York: Oxford University Press.

Skogan, W. G., and M. G. Maxfield. 1981. *Coping with Crime*. Newbury Park, Calif.: Sage.

Skolnick, J. H. 1966. *Justice without Trial: Law Enforcement in a Democratic Society*. New York: Wiley.

Skolnick, J. H., and J. J. Fyfe. 1993. *Above the Law: Police and Excessive Use of Force*. New York: Free Press.

Smith, C. E. 1990. *United States Magistrates in the Federal Courts: Subordinate Judges*. New York: Praeger.

_____. 1993. "Black Muslims and the Development of Prisoners' Rights." *Journal of Black Studies* 24:131–146.

_____. 1994. "Imagery, Politics, and Jury Reform," *Akron Law Review* 28:77–95.

_____. 1995a. "The Constitution and Criminal Punishment: The Emerging Visions of Justices Scalia and Thomas." *Drake Law Review* 43:593–613.

_____. 1995b. "Federal Habeas Corpus Reform: The State's Perspective." *Justice System Journal* 18:1–11.

_____. 1995c. "Judicial Policy Making and Habeas Corpus Reform." *Criminal Justice Policy Review* 7:91–114.

_____. 1996. "Criminal Justice and the 1995–96 U.S. Supreme Court Term." *University of Detroit-Mercy Law Review* 74:1-25.

Smith, C. E., and J. R. Hurst. 1996. "Law and Police Agencies' Policies: Perceptions of the Relative Impact of Constitutional Law Decisions and Civil Liability Decisions." Paper given at the annual meeting of the American Society of Criminology, Chicago.

Smith, C. E., and A. A. Jones. 1993. "The Rehnquist Court's Activism and the Risk of Injustice." *Connecticut Law Review* 26:53–77.

Smith, C. E., and R. Ochoa. 1996. "The Peremptory Challenge in the Eyes of the Trial Judge." *Judicature* 79:185–189.

Sorensen, J. R., J. M. Marquart, and D. E. Brock. 1993. "Factors Related to Killings of Felons by Police Officers: A Test of the Community Violence and Conflict Hypotheses." *Justice Quarterly* 10:417–440.

Spangenberg, R. L., and M. L. Beeman. 1995. "Indigent Defense Systems in the United States." *Law and Contemporary Problems* 58:31–49.

Spears, L. 1991. "Contract Counsel: A Different Way to Defend the Poor—How It's Working in North Dakota." *American Bar Association Journal on Criminal Justice* 6:24–31.

Spelman, W. G., and D. K. Brown. 1984. *Calling the Police: Citizen Reporting of Serious Crime*. Washington, D.C.: Police Executive Research Forum.

Spelman, W. G., and J. Eck. 1987. "Problem-Oriented Policing," U.S. Department of Justice, National Institute of Justice, *Research in Brief.* Washington, D.C.: Government Printing Office.

Sperlich, P. W. 1980. "And Then There Were Six: The Decline of the American Jury." *Judicature* 63:262–279.

Spohn, C. 1992. "An Analysis of the 'Jury Trial Penalty' and Its Effect on Black and White Offenders." *The Justice Professional* 7:93–97.

Spohn, C., J. Gruhl, and S. Welch. 1987. "The Impact of the Ethnicity and Gender of Defendants on the Decision to Reject or Dismiss Felony Charges." *Criminology* 25:175–191.

Stafford, M. C., and M. Warr. 1993. "A Reconceptualization of General and Specific Deterrence." *Journal of Research in Crime and Delinquency* 30 (May):123.

Stanford, M. R., and B. L. Mowry. 1990. "Domestic Disturbance Danger Rate." *Journal of Police Science and Administration* 17:244–249.

Stanko, E. 1988. "The Impact of Victim Assessment on Prosecutors' Screening Decisions: The Case of the New York District Attorney's Office," *Criminal Justice: Law and Politics*, 5th ed., ed. G. F. Cole. Pacific Grove, Calif.: Brooks/Cole.

Stark, R. 1987. "Decent Places: A Theory of the Ecology of Crime." *Criminology* 25:893–909.

Steffensmeier, D. 1983. "Organization Properties and Sex Segregation in the Underworld: Building a Sociological Theory of Sex Differences in Crime." *Social Forces* 61:1010.

Steffensmeier, D., J. Kramer, and C. Streifel. 1993. "Gender and Imprisonment Decisions." *Criminology* 31:411–446.

Steinman, M. 1988. "Anticipating Rank and File Police Reactions to Arrest Policies Regarding Spouse Abuse." *Criminal Justice Research Bulletin* 4:1–5.

Steury, E., and N. Frank. 1990. "Gender Bias and Pretrial Release: More Pieces of the Puzzle." *Journal of Criminal Justice* 18:417–432.

Stoddard, E. R. 1968. "The Informal 'Code' of Police Deviancy: A Group Approach to Blue-Coat Crime." *Journal of Criminal Law, Criminology, and Police Science* 59:204–211.

Stojkovic, S. 1990. "Accounts of Prison Work: Corrections Officers' Portrayals of Their Work Worlds." *Perspectives on Social Problems* 2:211–230.

Strodtbeck, F., R. James, and G. Hawkins. 1957. "Social Status in Jury Deliberations." *American Sociological Review* 22:713–719.

Surette, R. 1992. *Media, Crime, and Criminal Justice*. Pacific Grove, Calif.: Brooks/Cole.

Sutton, J. 1988. *Stubborn Children: Controlling Delinquency in the United States*. Berkeley: University of California Press.

Sykes, G. M. 1958. *The Society of Captives*. Princeton, N.J.: Princeton University Press.

Szasz, A. 1986. "Corporations, Organized Crime, and the Disposal of Hazardous Waste: An Examination of the Making of a Criminogenic Regulatory Structure." *Criminology* 24:1–28.

Talarico, S. M. 1988. "The Dilemmas of Parole Decision Making." *Criminal Justice: Law and Politics*, 5th ed., ed. G. F. Cole. Pacific Grove, Calif.: Brooks/Cole, 442–451.

Thomas, C. W. 1995. *Private Adult Correctional Facility Census*, 8th ed. Gainesville: Center for Studies in Criminology and Law, University of Florida.

Tonry, M. 1992. "Mandatory Penalties," *Crime and Justice: A Review of Research*, ed. M. Tonry. Chicago: University of Chicago Press.

_____. 1993. "Sentencing Commissions and Their Guidelines," *Crime and Justice*, vol. 17, ed. M. Tonry. Chicago: University of Chicago Press.

_____. 1995. *Malign Neglect: Race, Crime, and Punishment in America*. New York: Oxford University Press.

_____. 1996. *Sentencing Matters*. New York: Oxford University Press.

Tonry, M., and K. Hamilton, eds. 1995. *Intermediate Sanctions in Overcrowded Times*. Boston: Northeastern University Press.

Tonry, M., and M. Lynch. 1996. "Intermediate Sanctions," *Crime and Justice*, vol. 20, ed. M. Tonry. Chicago: University of Chicago Press, 99–144.

Traub, J. 1996. "The Criminals of Tomorrow." *New Yorker*, November 4, pp. 50–65.

Trout, C. 1992. "Taking a New Look at an Old Problem." *Corrections Today* (July):62–67.

Turner, M. G., J. L. Sundt, B. K. Applegate, and F. T. Cullen. 1995. "Three Strikes and You're Out Legislation: A National Assessment." *Federal Probation* (September):16–18.

Uchida, C., and T. Bynum. 1991. "Search Warrants, Motions to Suppress, and 'Lost Cases': The Effects of the Exclusionary Rule in Seven Jurisdictions." *Journal of Criminal Law and Criminology* 81:1034–1066.

Uphoff, R. J. 1992. "The Criminal Defense Lawyer: Zealous Advocate, Double Agent, or Beleaguered Dealer?" *Criminal Law Bulletin* 28:419–456.

USA Today, February 26, 1997.

_____, August 8, 1997.

_____, October 3, 1997.

Utz, P. 1978. *Settling the Facts*. Lexington, Mass.: Lexington Books.

Uviller, H. R. 1996. *Virtual Justice: The Flawed Prosecution of Crime in America*. New Haven, Conn.: Yale University Press.

Vaughan, J. B. 1994. "1994 Electronic Monitoring Survey." *Journal of Offender Monitoring* 7:1–8.

von Hirsch, A. 1976. *Doing Justice*. New York: Hill and Wang.

Walker, S. 1993a. "Putting Justice Back into Criminal Justice: Notes for a Liberal Criminal Justice Policy," *Criminal Justice: Law and Politics*, 6th ed, ed. G. F. Cole. Belmont, Calif.: Wadsworth, 503–516.

_____. 1993b. *Taming the System: The Control of Discretion in Criminal Justice 1950–1990*. New York: Oxford University Press.

_____. 1994. *Sense and Nonsense about Crime and Drugs*, 3d ed. Belmont, Calif.: Wadsworth.

Walker, S., and V. W. Bumphus. 1991. "Civilian Review of the Police, 1991: A National Survey of the Fifty Largest Cities," *Criminal Justice Policy Focus*, Criminal Justice Policy Research Group, Department of Criminal Justice, University of Nebraska at Omaha.

Walker, S., C. Spohn, and M. DeLone. 1996. *The Color of Justice*. Belmont, Calif.: Wadsworth.

Walker, S., and K. B. Turner. 1992. "A Decade of Modest Progress: Employment of Black and Hispanic Police Officers, 1983–1992." Department of Criminal Justice, University of Nebraska at Omaha.

Walker, S., and B. Wright. 1995. "Citizen Review of the Police, 1994: A National Survey," *Fresh Perspectives*. Washington, D.C.: Police Executive Research Forum.

Wallace, D. H. 1994. "The Eighth Amendment and Prison Deprivations: Historical Revisions." *Criminal Law Bulletin* 30:5–29.

Walsh, W. 1989. "Private/Public Police Stereotypes: A Different Perspective." *Security Journal* 1:21–27.

Wall Street Journal, December 10, 1992.

Warr, M. 1993. "Fear of Victimization." *The Public Perspective* (November/December): 25–28.

_____. 1994. "Public Perceptions and Reactions to Violent Offending and Victimization," *Understanding and Preventing Violence, Vol. IV: Dimensions and Consequences of Violence*, ed. A. J. Reiss and J. A. Roth. Washington, D.C.: National Academy Press.

Washington Post, September 17, 1997.

_____, November 11, 1997.

Wasserman, D. T. 1990. *A Sword for the Convicted: Representing Indigent Defendants on Appeal*. New York: Greenwood Press.

Watson, R. A., and R. G. Downing. 1969. *The Politics of the Bench and Bar: Judicial Selection under the Missouri Nonpartisan Court Plan*. New York: John Wiley & Sons.

Weinstein, J. B. 1992. "A Trial Judge's Second Impression of the Federal Sentencing Guidelines." *Southern California Law Review* 66:357.

Weis, J. 1976. "Liberation and Crime: The Invention of the New Female Criminal." *Crime and Social Justice* 1:17.

Weisburd, D. A., and L. Green. 1995. "Measuring Immediate Spatial Displacement: Methodological Issues and Problems," *Crime and Place: Crime Prevention Studies*, vol. 4, ed. D. A. Weisburd and J. E. Eck. Monsey, N.Y.: Criminal Justice Press.

Weisheit, R. 1985. "Trends in Programs for Female Offenders: The Use of Private Agencies as Service Providers." *International Journal of Offender Therapy and Comparative Criminology* 29:35–42.

Weitekamp, E. 1995. "Restitution," *Intermediate Sanctions in Overcrowded Times*, ed. M. Tonry and K. Hamilton. Boston: Northeastern University Press, 65–68.

Welch, M. 1994. "Jail Overcrowding: Social Sanitation and the Warehousing of the Urban Underclass," *Critical Issues in Crime and Justice*, ed. A. Roberts. Thousand Oaks, Calif.: Sage, 249–274.

White, M. S. 1995. "The Nonverbal Behaviors in Jury Selection." *Criminal Law Bulletin* 31:414–445.

Wice, P. B. 1978. *Criminal Lawyers: An Endangered Species*. Beverly Hills, Calif.: Sage.

_____. 1995. "Court Reform and Judicial Leadership: A Theoretical Discussion." *Justice System Journal* 17:309–321.

Wilbanks, William. 1987. *The Myth of a Racist Criminal Justice System*. Pacific Grove, Calif.: Brooks/Cole.

Williams, H., and P. V. Murphy. 1990. "The Evolving Strategy of Police: A Minority View," *Perspectives on Policing*, no. 13. Washington, D.C.: National Institute of Justice.

Williams, H., and A. M. Pate. 1987. "Returning to First Principles: Reducing the Fear of Crime in Newark." *Crime and Delinquency* 33 (January):53–59.

Wilson, J. Q. 1968. *Varieties of Police Behavior*. Cambridge, Mass.: Harvard University Press.

_____. 1983. *Thinking about Crime*, 2d. rev. ed. New York: Basic Books.

Wilson, J. Q., and G. L. Kelling. 1982. "Broken Windows: The Police and Neighborhood Safety." *Atlantic Monthly*, March, pp. 29–38.

Wolfgang, M. E., and F. Ferracuti. 1967. *The Subculture of Violence*. London: Tavistock.

Worden, A. P. 1991. "Privatizing Due Process: Issues in the Comparison of Assigned Counsel, Public Defenders, and Contracted Indigent Defense Counsel." *Justice System Journal* 15:390–418.

_____. 1993. "The Attitudes of Women and Men in Policing: Testing Conventional and Contemporary Wisdom." *Criminology* 31 (May):203–241.

_____. 1994. "Counsel for the Poor: An Evaluation of Contracting for Indigent Criminal Defense." *Justice Quarterly* 10:613–637.

_____. 1995. "The Judge's Role in Plea Bargaining: An Analysis of Judges' Agreement with Prosecutors' Sentencing Recommendations." *Justice Quarterly* 12:257–278.

Wright, J. D., J. F. Sheley, and M. Dwayne Smith. 1992. "Kids, Guns, and Killing Fields." *Society* 30 (November/December):84.

Yang, S. S. 1990. "The Unique Treatment Needs of Female Substance Abusers: The Obligation of the Criminal Justice System to Provide Parity Services." *Medicine and Law* 9:1018–1027.

Zedner, L. 1995. "Wayward Sisters," *The Oxford History of Prisons*, ed. N. Morris and D. J. Rothman. New York: Oxford University Press, 329–361.

Zimbardo, P. G. 1994. *Transforming California's Prisons into Expensive Old Age Homes for Felons: Enormous Hidden Costs and Consequences for Taxpayers*. San Francisco: Center on Juvenile and Criminal Justice.

Zimmer, L. 1987. "Operation Pressure Point: The Disruption of Street-Level Trade on New York's Lower East Side." Occasional papers from the Center for Research in Crime and Justice, New York University School of Law.

Zimring, F. 1991. "The Treatment of Hard Cases in American Juvenile Justice: In Defense of Discretionary Waiver." *Notre Dame Journal of Law, Ethics, and Public Policy* 5:267.

Cases Cited

Apodaca v. Oregon, 406 U.S. 404(1972)
Arizona v. Hicks, 480 U.S. 321 (1987)
Austin v. U.S. , 509 U.S. 602 (1993)
Barron v. Baltimore, 32 U.S. 243 (1833)
Batson v. Kentucky, 476 U.S. 79 (1986)
Blackledge v. Allison, 431 U.S. 71 (1976)
Bordenkircher v. Hayes, 343 U.S. 357 (1978)
Boykin v. Alabama, 395 U.S. 238 (1969)
Burch v. Louisiana, 441 U.S. 130 (1979)
California v. Acevedo, 111 S.Ct. 1982 (1991)
Chimel v. California, 395 U.S. 752 (1969)
Coleman v. Alabama, 399 U.S. 1 (1970)
Cooper v. Pate, 378 U.S. 546 (1964)
Delaware v. Prouse, 440 U.S. 648 (1979)
Douglas v. California, 372 U.S. 353 (1963)
Durham v. United States, 214 F.2d 862 (D.C. Cir. 1954)
Escobedo v. Illinois, 378 U.S. 347 (1964)
Felker v. Turpin, 116 S.Ct. 2333 (1996)
Furman v. Georgia, 408 U.S. 238 (1972)
Gagnon v. Scarpelli, 411 U.S. 778 (1973)
Gardner v. Florida, 430 U.S. 349 (1977)
Georgia v. McCollum, 505 U.S. 42 (1992)
Gideon v. Wainwright, 372 U.S. 335 (1963)
Graham v. Connor, 490 U.S. 386 (1989)
Gregg v. Georgia, 428 U.S. 153 (1976)
Hudson v. Palmer, 468 U.S. 517 (1984)
Illinois v. Rodriguez, 110 S.Ct. 2793 (1990)
In re Gault, 387 U.S. 9 (1967)
Jacobson v. United States, 112 S.Ct. 1535 (1992)
J.E.B. v. Alabama ex rel. T. B., 511 U.S. 114 (1994)
Kansas v. Hendricks, 117 S.Ct. 2072 (1997)
Kent v. United States, 383 U.S. 541 (1966)
Lee v. Washington, 390 U.S. 333 (1968)
Lewis v. United States, 116 S.Ct. 2163 (1996)
M'Naughten's Case, 8 Eng. Rep. 718 (1843)
Mapp v. Ohio, 367 U.S. 643 (1961)
Maryland v. Wilson, 117 S.Ct. 882 (1997)

McCleskey v. Kemp, 478 U.S. 1019 (1987)
Mempha v. Rhay, 389 U.S. 128 (1967)
Michigan Department of State Police v. *Sitz*, 496 U.S. 440 (1990)
Miranda v. Arizona, 384 U.S. 436 (1966)
Monell v. Department of Social Services for the City of New York, 436 U.S. 658 (1978)
Montana v. Egelhoff, 116 S.Ct. 2013 (1996)
Morrissey v. Brewer, 408 U.S. 471 (1972)
New York v. Class, 475 U.S. 321 (1986)
New York v. Quarles, 467 U.S. 649 (1984)
Nix v. Williams, 467 U.S. 431 (1984)
North Carolina v. Alford, 400 U.S. 25 (1970)
Penry v. Lynaugh, 492 U.S. 302 (1989)
Powell v. Alabama, 287 U.S. 45 (1932)
Procunier v. Martinez, 416 U.S. 396 (1974)
Purkett v. Elem, 115 S.Ct. 1769 (1995)
Queen v. Dudley and Stephens, 14 Q. B. D. 273 (1884)
Ricketts v. Adamson, 481 U.S. 1 (1987)
Robinson v. California, 370 U.S. 660 (1962)
Ross v. Moffitt, 417 U.S. 660 (1974)
Santobello v. New York, 404 U.S. 260 (1971)
Schall v. Martin, 467 U.S. 253 (1984)
Scott v. Illinois, 440 U.S. 367 (1979)
Stanford v. Kentucky, 492 U.S. 361 (1989)
Strickland v. Washington, 466 U.S. 686 (1984)
Tennessee v. Garner, 471 U.S. 1 (1985)
Terry v. Ohio, 392 U.S. 1 (1968)
Thompson v. Oklahoma, 108 S.Ct. 1687 (1988)
Trop v. Dulles, 356 U.S. 86 (1958)
Turner v. Safley, 482 U.S. 78 (1984)
United States v. Cronic, 444 U.S. 654 (1984)
United States v. Leon, 468 U.S. 897 (1984)
United States v. Ross, 102 S.Ct. 2157 (1982)
United States v. Salerno and Cafero, 481 U.S. 739 (1987)
United States v. Wade, 388 U.S. 218 (1967)
Weeks v. United States, 232 U.S. 383 (1914)
Wilkins v. Missouri, 492 U.S. 361 (1989)
Williams v. Florida, 399 U.S. 78 (1970)
Williams v. New York, 337 U.S. 241 (1949)
Wilson v. Seiter, 111 S.Ct. 232 (1991)
Wolff v. McDonnell, 418 U.S. 539 (1974)

Glossary

A

accusatory process The series of events from the arrest of a suspect to the filing of a formal charge (through an indictment or information) with the court.

adjudication The process of determining the guilt or innocence of a defendant.

admissible evidence Evidence that has been gathered by the police according to the law as specified in the Constitution, court decisions, and statutes.

aggressive patrol A patrol strategy designed to maximize the number of police interventions and observations in the community.

appeal A request to a higher court that it review actions taken in a completed trial.

appellate courts Courts that do not try criminal cases but hear appeals of decisions of lower courts.

arraignment The court appearance of an accused person in which the charges are read and the accused person, advised by a lawyer, pleads guilty or not guilty.

arrest The physical taking of a person into custody on the ground that there is reason to believe that he or she has committed a criminal offense. Police may use only reasonable physical force in making an arrest. The purpose of the arrest is to hold the accused for a court proceeding.

assigned counsel An attorney in private practice assigned by a court to represent an indigent. The attorney's fee is paid by the government with jurisdiction over the case.

B

bail An amount of money specified by a judge to be paid as a condition of pretrial release to ensure that the accused will appear in court as required.

***Barron v. Baltimore* (1833)** The protections of the Bill of Rights apply only to actions of the federal government.

bench trial Trial conducted by a judge who acts as finder of fact and determines issues of law. No jury participates.

Bill of Rights The first ten amendments added to the U.S. Constitution to protect individuals' rights against infringement by government.

boot camp/shock incarceration A short-term institutional sentence, usually followed by probation, that puts the offender through a physical regimen designed to develop discipline and respect for authority.

***Bordenkircher v. Hayes* (1978)** A defendant's rights were not violated by a prosecutor who warned that not to accept a guilty plea would result in a harsher sentence.

***Boykin v. Alabama* (1969)** Defendants must state that they are voluntarily making a plea of guilty.

C

challenge for cause Removal of a prospective juror by showing that he or she has some bias or some other legal disability. The number of such challenges permitted to attorneys is unlimited.

circumstantial evidence Evidence provided by a witness from which a jury must infer a fact.

citation A written order or summons issued by a law enforcement officer directing an alleged offender to appear in court at a specified time to answer a criminal charge.

civil law Law regulating the relationships between or among individuals, usually involving property, contract, or business disputes.

classification The process of assigning an inmate to a category specifying his or her needs for security, treatment, education, work assignment, and readiness for release.

clearance rate The percentage of crimes known to the police that they believe they have solved through an arrest; a statistic used to measure a police department's productivity.

community correctional center An institution, usually in an urban area, that houses inmates soon to be released. Such centers are designed to help inmates establish community ties and thus promote their reintegration with society.

community corrections A model of corrections based on the goal of reintegrating the offender into the community.

community service A sentence requiring the offender to perform a certain amount of unpaid labor in the community.

congregate system A penitentiary system, developed in Auburn, New York, in which each inmate was held in isolation during the night but worked and ate with fellow prisoners during the day under a rule of silence.

continuance An adjournment of a scheduled case until a later date.

contract counsel An attorney in private practice who contracts with the government to represent all indigent defendants in a county during a set period of time and for a specified dollar amount.

***Cooper v. Pate* (1964)** Prisoners are entitled to the protection of the Civil Rights Act of 1871 and may challenge the conditions of their confinement in federal courts.

corrections The variety of programs, services, facilities, and organizations responsible for the management of people who have been accused or convicted of criminal offenses.

count Each separate offense of which a person is accused in an indictment or an information.

crime A specific act of commission or omission in violation of the law for which a punishment is prescribed.

crime control model A model of the criminal justice system that assumes freedom is so important that every effort must be made to repress crime; it emphasizes efficiency, speed, finality, and the capacity to apprehend, try, convict, and dispose of a high proportion of offenders.

crime control model of corrections A model of corrections based on the assumption that criminal behavior can be controlled by more use of incarceration and other forms of strict supervision.

crimes without victims Offenses involving a willing and private exchange of illegal goods or services that are in strong demand. Participants do not feel they are being harmed, but these crimes are prosecuted on the ground that society as a whole is being injured.

custodial model A model of incarceration that emphasizes security, discipline, and order.

D

dark figure of crime A metaphor that emphasizes the dangerous dimension of crime that is never reported to the police.

day reporting center A community correctional center where an offender reports each day to comply with elements of a sentence.

defense attorney The lawyer who represents the accused and the convicted offender in their dealings with criminal justice officials.

delinquent A child who has committed an act that if committed by an adult would be criminal.

demonstrative evidence Evidence that is not based on witness testimony but that demonstrates information relevant to the crime, such as maps, X-rays, and photographs; includes real evidence involved in the crime.

dependent child A child who has no parent or guardian or whose parents are unable to give proper care.

detention A period of temporary custody of a juvenile before disposition of his or her case.

determinate sentence A sentence that fixes the term of imprisonment to a specific period of time.

differential response A patrol strategy that assigns priorities to calls for service and chooses the appropriate response.

direct evidence Eyewitness accounts.

directed patrol A proactive form of patrolling that directs resources to known high-crime areas.

discovery A prosecutor's pretrial disclosure to the defense of facts and evidence to be introduced at trial.

discretion The authority to make decisions without reference to specific rules or facts, using instead one's own judgment; allows for individualization and informality in the administration of justice.

discretionary release The release of an inmate from prison to conditional supervision at the discretion of the parole board within the boundaries set by the sentence and the penal law.

disparities The inequality of treatment of one group by the criminal justice system, compared to the treatment accorded other groups.

diversion The process of screening children out of the juvenile justice system without a decision by the court.

double jeopardy The subjecting of a person to prosecution more than once in the same jurisdiction for the same offense; prohibited by the Fifth Amendment.

dual court system A system consisting of a separate judicial structure for each state in addition to a national structure. Each case is tried in a court of the same jurisdiction as that of the law or laws broken.

due process model A model of the criminal justice system that assumes freedom is so important that every effort must be made to ensure that criminal justice decisions are based on reliable information; it emphasizes the adversarial process, the rights of defendants, and formal decision-making procedures.

E

Enlightenment A movement during the eighteenth century in England and France, in which concepts of liberalism, rationalism, equality, and individualism dominated social and political thinking.

entrapment The defense that the individual was induced by the police to commit the criminal act.

Escobedo v. Illinois **(1964)** An attorney must be provided to suspects when they are taken into police custody.

exchange A mutual transfer of resources; a balance of benefits and deficits that flow from behavior based on decisions about the values and costs of alternatives.

exclusionary rule The principle that illegally obtained evidence must be excluded from a trial.

F

federalism A system of government in which power is divided between a central (national) government and regional (state) governments.

felonies Serious crimes usually carrying a penalty of death or incarceration for more than one year.

filtering process A screening operation; a process by which criminal justice officials screen out some cases while advancing others to the next level of decision making.

fine A sum of money to be paid to the state by a convicted person as punishment for an offense.

forfeiture Seizure by the government of property and other assets derived from or used in criminal activity.

frankpledge A system in old English law in which members of a tithing, a group of ten families, pledged to be responsible for keeping order and bringing violators of the law to court.

fundamental fairness A legal doctrine supporting the idea that so long as a state's conduct maintains basic standards of fairness, the Constitution has not been violated.

furlough The temporary release of an inmate from a correctional institution for a brief period, usually one to three days, for a visit home. Such programs help maintain family ties and prepare inmates for release on parole.

Furman v. Georgia **(1972)** The death penalty, as administered, constituted cruel and unusual treatment.

G

Gagnon v. Scarpelli **(1973)** Before probation can be revoked, a two-stage hearing must be held and the offender provided with specific elements of due process.

general deterrence Punishment of criminals that is intended to be an example to the general public and to discourage the commission of offenses by others.

Gideon v. Wainwright **(1963)** Defendants have a right to counsel in felony cases. States must provide defense counsel in felony cases for those who cannot pay for it themselves.

going rate Local view of the appropriate sentence for the offense, the defendant's prior record, and other characteristics.

Gregg v. Georgia **(1976)** Death penalty laws are constitutional if they require judge and jury to consider certain mitigating and aggravating circumstances in deciding which convicted murderers should be sentenced to death.

H

habeas corpus A writ or judicial order requesting the release of a person being detained in a jail, prison, or mental hospital. If a judge finds the person is being held improperly, the writ may be granted and the person released.

halfway house A correctional facility housing convicted felons who spend a portion of their day at work in the community but reside in the halfway house during nonworking hours.

hands-off policy Judges should not interfere with the administration of correctional institutions.

home confinement A sentence requiring the offender to remain inside his or her home during specified periods.

Hudson v. Palmer **(1984)** Prison officials have a right to search cells and confiscate from inmates any materials found.

I

In re Gault (1967) Juveniles have the right to counsel, to confront and examine accusers, and to have adequate notice of charges when there is the possibility of confinement as a punishment.

incapacitation Depriving an offender of the ability to commit crimes against society, usually by detaining the offender in prison.

inchoate offense Conduct that is criminal even though the harm that the law seeks to prevent has not been done but merely planned or attempted.

incorporation The extension of the due process clause of the Fourteenth Amendment to make binding on state governments the rights guaranteed in the first ten amendments to the U.S. Constitution (the Bill of Rights).

indeterminate sentence An indefinite period set by a judge that specifies a minimum and a maximum time served in prison. Sometime after serving the minimum sentence, the offender may be eligible for parole. Because it is based on the idea that the time necessary for treatment cannot be set, the indeterminate sentence is closely associated with rehabilitation.

indictment A document returned by a grand jury as a "true bill" charging an individual with a specific crime on the basis of a determination of probable cause as presented by a prosecuting attorney.

information A document charging an individual with a specific crime. It is prepared by a prosecuting attorney and presented to a court at a preliminary hearing.

inmate code The values and norms of the prison social system that define the inmate's idea of the model prisoner.

intensive supervision probation (ISP) Probation granted under conditions of strict reporting to a probation officer with a limited caseload.

intermediate sanctions A variety of punishments that are more restrictive than traditional probation but less severe and less costly than incarceration.

internal affairs unit A branch of a police department that receives and investigates complaints against officers alleging violation of rules and policies.

J

judicial waiver Procedure by which the juvenile court waives its jurisdiction and transfers a juvenile case to the adult criminal court.

jurisdiction The geographic territory or legal boundaries within which control may be exercised; the range of a court's authority.

jury A panel of citizens selected according to law and sworn to determine matters of fact in a criminal case and to deliver a verdict of guilty or not guilty.

L

law enforcement The police function of controlling crime by intervening in situations in which the law has clearly been violated and the police need to identify and apprehend the guilty person.

legal sufficiency The presence of the minimum legal elements necessary for prosecution of a case. When a prosecutor's decision to prosecute a case is customarily based on legal sufficiency, a great many cases are accepted for prosecution, but the majority of them are disposed of by plea bargaining or dismissal.

legislative exclusion The legislature excludes from juvenile court jurisdiction certain offenses such as murder, armed robbery, or rape.

line functions Police components that directly perform field operations and carry out the basic functions of patrol, investigation, traffic, vice, juvenile, and so on.

local legal culture Norms shared by members of a court community as to how cases should be handled and how a participant should behave in the judicial process.

M

mandatory release The required release of an inmate from incarceration to community supervision upon the expiration of a certain time period, as specified by a determinate sentencing law or parole guidelines.

mandatory sentence A sentence determined by statutes and requiring that a certain penalty be imposed and carried out for convicted offenders who meet certain criteria.

***Mapp v. Ohio* (1961)** The Fourth Amendment protects citizens from unreasonable searches and seizures by state officials.

***McCleskey v. Kemp* (1987)** Rejected a challenge of Georgia's death penalty on grounds of racial discrimination.

medical model A model of corrections based on the assumption that criminal behavior is caused by biological or psychological conditions that require treatment.

***Mempha v. Rhay* (1967)** Probationers have the right to counsel at a revocation and sentencing hearing.

***mens rea* "Guilty mind"** or blameworthy state of mind, necessary for legal responsibility for a criminal offense; criminal intent, as distinguished from innocent intent.

merit selection A reform plan by which judges are nominated by a commission and appointed by the governor for a given period. When the term expires, the voters are asked to approve or disapprove the judge for a succeeding term. If the judge is disapproved, the committee nominates a successor for the governor's appointment.

***Miranda v. Arizona* (1966)** Confessions made by suspects who were not notified of their due process rights cannot be admitted as evidence.

misdemeanors Offenses less serious than felonies and usually punishable by incarceration of no more than a year, probation, or intermediate sanction.

***Morrissey v. Brewer* (1972)** Due process rights require a prompt, informal inquiry by an impartial hearing officer before parole may be revoked. The parolee may present relevant information and confront witnesses.

motion An application to a court requesting that an order be issued to bring about a specified action.

N

National Crime Victimization Surveys (NCVS) Interviews of samples of the U.S. population conducted by the Bureau of Justice Statistics to determine the number and types of criminal victimizations and thus the extent of unreported as well as reported crime.

National Incident-Based Reporting System (NIBRS) A reporting system in which the police describe each offense in a crime incident, together with data describing the offender, victim, and property.

neglected child A child who is not receiving proper care because of some action or inaction of his or her parents.

net widening Process in which the new sentencing options increase rather than reduce control over the offenders' lives.

nolle prosequi An entry made by a prosecutor on the record of a case and announced in court to indicate that the charges specified will not be prosecuted. In effect, the charges are thereby dismissed.

nonpartisan election An election in which candidates who are not endorsed by political parties are presented to voters for selection.

***North Carolina v. Alford* (1970)** A plea of guilty may be accepted for the purpose of a lesser sentence by a defendant who maintains his or her innocence.

O

occupational crime Criminal offenses committed through opportunities created in a legal business or occupation.

order maintenance The police function of preventing behavior that disturbs or threatens to disturb the public peace or that involves face-to-face conflict among two or more persons. In such situations the police exercise discretion in deciding whether a law has been broken.

organized crime A framework for the perpetration of criminal acts—usually in fields such as gambling, drugs, and prostitution—providing illegal services that are in great demand.

P

parens patriae The state as parent; the state as guardian and protector of all citizens (such as juveniles) who are unable to protect themselves.

parole The conditional release of an inmate from incarceration under supervision after part of the prison sentence has been served.

partisan election An election in which candidates endorsed by political parties are presented to voters for selection.

penitentiary An institution intended to punish criminals by isolating them from society and from one another so they can reflect on their past misdeeds, repent, and reform.

penology A branch of criminology dealing with the management of prisons and the treatment of offenders.

peremptory challenge Removal of a prospective juror without giving a reason. Attorneys are allowed a limited number of such challenges.

PINS Acronym for "person in need of supervision," a term that designates juveniles who are either status offenders or thought to be on the verge of trouble.

plea bargain A defendant's plea of guilty to a criminal charge with the reasonable expectation of receiving some consideration from the state for doing so, usually a reduction of the charge. The defendant's ultimate goal is a penalty lighter than the one formally warranted by the charged offense.

plea bargaining Entering a plea of guilty to a criminal charge with the expectation of receiving a penalty lighter than the one carried by the original offense.

political crimes Acts that constitute a threat against the state (such as treason, sedition, or espionage).

***Powell v. Alabama* (1932)** An attorney must be provided to a defendant facing the death penalty.

presentence report Report prepared by a probation officer, who investigates a convicted offender's background to help the judge select an appropriate sentence.

presumptive parole date The presumed release date stipulated by parole guidelines if the offender serves time without disciplinary or other incidents.

presumptive sentence A sentence for which the legislature or a commission sets a minimum and maximum range of months or years. Judges are to fix the length of the sentence within that range, allowing for special circumstances.

preventive detention Holding a defendant for trial based on a judge's finding that, if the defendant were released on bail, he or she would endanger the safety of any other person and the community or would flee.

preventive patrol A form of patrolling that makes the police presence known in order to deter crime and to make officers available for quick response to calls.

proactive Acting in anticipation, such as an active search for offenders initiated by the police without waiting for a crime to be reported. Arrests for crimes without victims are usually proactive.

probable cause The criterion for deciding whether evidence is strong enough to uphold an arrest or to support issuing an arrest or search warrant. Also, the facts upholding the belief that a crime has been committed and that the accused committed the offense.

probation A sentence allowing the offender to serve the sanctions imposed by the court in the community under supervision.

problem-oriented policing An approach to policing in which officers routinely seek to identify, analyze, and respond to the circumstances underlying the incidents that prompt citizens to call the police.

procedural criminal law Law defining the procedures that criminal justice officials must follow in enforcement, adjudication, and correction.

procedural due process The constitutional requirement that all persons be treated fairly and justly by government officials. An accused person can be arrested, prosecuted, tried, and punished only in accordance with procedures prescribed by law.

prosecuting attorney A legal representative of the state with sole responsibility for bringing criminal charges. In some states referred to as district attorney, state's attorney, commonwealth attorney, or county attorney.

prosecutorial discretion The power of the prosecutor to decide that a youth should be referred from the juvenile system to the adult criminal justice system.

public defender An attorney employed on a full-time, salaried basis by the government to represent indigents.

R

reactive Occurring in response, such as police activity in response to notification that a crime has been committed.

real evidence Physical evidence such as a weapon, records, fingerprints, stolen property—objects actually involved in the crime.

reasonable doubt The standard used by a juror to decide if the prosecution has provided enough evidence for conviction. Jurors should vote for acquittal if they think there is a reasonable doubt.

recidivism A return to criminal behavior.

rehabilitation The goal of restoring a convicted offender to a constructive place in society through some form of vocational or educational training or therapy.

rehabilitation model A model of corrections that emphasizes the need to restore a convicted offender to a constructive place in society through some form of vocational or educational training or therapy.

reintegration model A model of a correctional institution that emphasizes maintaining the offender's ties to family and community as a method of reform, recognizing that the offender will be returning to society.

release on recognizance (ROR) Pretrial release granted on the defendant's promise to appear in court because the judge believes that the defendant's ties in the community guarantee that he or she will appear.

restitution Repayment—in the form of money or service—by an offender to a victim who has suffered some financial loss from the offense.

retribution Punishment inflicted on a person who has infringed on the rights of others and so deserves to be penalized. The severity of the sanction should fit the seriousness of the crime.

Ricketts v. Adamson **(1987)** Defendants must uphold the plea agreement or suffer the consequences.

S

Santobello v. New York **(1971)** When a guilty plea rests on a promise of a prosecutor, it must be fulfilled.

Schall v. Martin **(1984)** Juveniles can be held in preventive detention if there is concern that they may commit additional crimes while awaiting court action.

search warrant An order of a judge that allows a police officer to search a designated place for specific persons or items to be seized.

selective incapacitation Making the best use of expensive and limited prison space by targeting for incarceration those individuals whose incapacity will do the most to reduce crime in society.

self-incrimination The act of exposing oneself to prosecution by being forced to respond to questions whose answers may reveal that one has committed a crime. The Fifth Amendment protects defendants against self-incrimination. In any criminal proceeding the prosecution must prove the charges by means of evidence other than the testimony of the accused.

sentencing guidelines A mechanism to indicate to judges the expected sanction for certain offenses, in order to reduce disparities in sentencing.

separate confinement A penitentiary system, developed in Pennsylvania, in which each inmate was held in isolation from other inmates. All activities, including craft work, took place in the cells.

service The police function of providing assistance to the public, usually in matters unrelated to crime.

shock probation A sentence in which the offender is released after a short incarceration and resentenced to probation.

socialization The process by which the rules, symbols, and values of a group or subculture are learned by its members.

special deterrence Punishment that is inflicted on criminals to discourage them from committing future crimes.

state attorney general Chief legal officer of a state responsible for both civil and criminal matters.

status offense Any act committed by a juvenile that is considered unacceptable for a child, such as truancy or running away from home, but that would not be a crime if it were committed by an adult.

strict liability An obligation or duty that when broken is an offense that can be judged criminal without a showing of mens rea, or criminal intent; usually applied to regulatory offenses involving health and safety.

subculture The symbols, beliefs, and values shared by members of a subgroup within the larger society.

substantive criminal law Law defining the acts that are subject to punishment, and specifying the punishments for such offenses.

sworn officers Police employees who have taken an oath and been given powers by the state to make arrests and use necessary force, in accordance with their duties.

system A complex whole consisting of interdependent parts whose operations are directed toward goals and are influenced by the environment within which it functions.

system efficiency Policy of the prosecutor's office that encourages speedy and early disposition of cases in response to caseload pressures. Weak cases are screened out at intake, and other nontrial alternatives are used as the primary means of disposition.

T

Tennessee v. Garner **(1985)** Deadly force may not be used against an unarmed and fleeing suspect unless it is necessary to prevent the escape and unless the officer has probable cause to believe that the suspect poses a significant threat of death or serious injury to the officers or others.

Terry v. Ohio **(1968)** A police officer may stop and frisk an individual if it is reasonable to suspect that a crime has been committed.

testimony Oral evidence provided by a legally competent witness.

trial courts of general jurisdiction Criminal courts with jurisdiction over all offenses, including felonies. In some states these courts may also hear appeals.

trial courts of limited jurisdiction Criminal courts with trial jurisdiction over misdemeanor cases and preliminary matters in felony cases. Sometimes these courts hold felony trials that may result in penalties below a specified limit.

trial sufficiency The presence of sufficient legal elements to ensure successful prosecution of a case. When a prosecutor's decision to prosecute a case is customarily based on trial sufficiency, only cases that seem certain to result in conviction at trial are accepted for prosecution. Use of plea bargaining is minimal; good police work and court capacity to go to trial are required.

***Turner v. Safley* (1987)** Inmates do not have a right to receive mail from each other, and this mail can be banned if it is "reasonably related to legitimate penological interests."

U

unconditional release The release of an inmate from incarceration without any further correctional supervision; the inmate cannot be returned to prison for any remaining portion of the sentence for the current offense.

Uniform Crime Reports (UCR) An annually published statistical summary of crimes reported to the police, based on voluntary reports to the FBI by local, state, and federal law enforcement agencies.

United States attorney Officials responsible for the prosecution of crimes that violate the laws of the United States. Appointed by the president and assigned to a U.S. district court jurisdiction.

***United States v. Leon* (1984)** Evidence seized using a warrant that is later found to be defective is valid if the officer was acting in good faith.

***United States v. Salerno* (1987)** Preventive detention provisions of the Bail Reform Act of 1984 are upheld as a legitimate use of governmental power designed to prevent people from committing crimes while on bail.

V

victimology A field of criminology that examines the role the victim plays in precipitating a criminal incident.

visible crimes Offenses against persons and property committed primarily by members of the lower class. Often referred to as "street crimes" or "ordinary crimes," these are the offenses most upsetting to the public.

voir dire A questioning of prospective jurors in order to screen out persons the attorneys think may be biased or incapable of delivering a fair verdict.

W

warrant A court order authorizing police officials to take certain actions, for example, to arrest suspects or to search premises.

***Williams v. Florida* (1970)** Juries of fewer than twelve members are constitutional.

***Wolff v. McDonnell* (1974)** Basic elements of procedural due process must be present when decisions are made about the disciplining of inmates.

work and educational release The daytime release of inmates from correctional institutions so they can work or attend school.

workgroup A collection of individuals who interact in the workplace on a continuing basis, share goals, develop norms regarding how activities should be carried out, and eventually establish a network of roles that differentiates the group from others.

working personality A set of emotional and behavioral characteristics developed by a member of an occupational group in response to the work situation and environmental influences.

Name Index

A

Abadinsky, H., 283
Acker, J. R., 66
Adams, A., 19
Adams, Randall Dale, 248
Adler, F., 17, 18
Adler, S. J., 219
Albert, Marv, 150–151
Alderman, J. D., 15
Alexander, R., Jr., 221
Amar, A., 61
Anderson, D., 126
Andrews, D. A., 315
Applegate, B. K., 231, 292
Armentano, Phillip N., 199
Armstrong, Ricardo, 168
Ashman, A., 154
Aspin, L. T., 159
Augustus, John, 278
Austin, J., 292

B

Bacich, A. R., 90
Bailey, F. Lee, 192
Baldus, D. C., 66, 237
Bales, W., 287
Balkin, S., 194
Barnes, C. W., 159
Basqurell, Barry, 107
Bassler, J., 181
Batzer, James, 243
Baugh, J. A., 67
Baumer, T. L., 287
Baunach, P. J., 314
Bauza, M., 203
Bayley, D. H., 73, 88, 108, 109, 111, 114
Beck, A. J., 169, 269
Bedeau, H. A., 200
Beeman, M. L., 196, 197
Benaquisto, L., 308
Bentham, Jeremy, 226
Berk, R. A., 90
Bershard, L., 313
Beto, George, 320
Biderman, A. D., 8
Black, Roy, 150
Blackmun, Harry, 65
Bloch, P., 126
Blocker, David G., 110
Blomberg, T. G., 284, 287, 291
Blomquist, M., 358
Blumberg, A., 198
Blumberg, M., 15
Blumenson, E., 286
Blumstein, A., 20, 270
Boland, B., 181
Bonta, J., 315
Bordt, R. L., 244
Bowker, L. H., 320
Boyd, Terrence "King Bullet", 317
Bradley, C., 217
Brady, E., 181
Brady, T., 98
Braga, A. A., 287, 288
Brandl, S. G., 112, 126
Bratton, W. J., 108
Bray, K., 214
Brennan, William, 65
Bright, S. B., 196, 199
Brock, D. E., 135
Brockway, Zebulon, 259, 329
Broeder, D. W., 218
Brooks, Ben, 326 327
Brown, C. E., 102
Brown, D. K., 103, 104
Brown, M. K., 129
Bruck, David, 177
Buchanan, J., 134, 181
Buchanan, John L., 83
Buerger, M. E., 103
Bumphus, V. W., 138
Burger, Warren, 60, 61
Burke, Corey, 340
Burrows, Joe and Shari, 248
Burton, V. S., Jr., 229
Bush, George, 6
Butterfield, F., 20, 66, 315, 316
Buzawa, C. G., 90
Buzawa, E. S., 90
Byrd, Kevin, 248

C

Calhoun, F., 76
Callahan, L. A., 57
Camp, C. G., 272
Camp, D. D., 53
Camp, G. M., 272
Cao, L., 19
Carns, T. W., 208
Carone, Shirley, 314
Carr, J. G., 163
Carroll, L., 308
Casper, J. D., 194
Caulfield, S. L., 178
Chaiken, J. M., 113
Champion, D. J., 205
Chapper, J. A., 197, 220
Chermak, S. M., 15
Chesney-Lind, M., 17
Chin, K., 6
Chiricos, T. G., 20
Christopher, R. L., 54
Church, T. W., 170
Cirincione, C., 57
Clark, J., 165
Clark, Rich, 275
Clear, T. R., 169, 228, 281, 287, 288, 289, 342
Clemmer, E., 90
Clinton, Bill, 22, 239, 343
Cochran, Johnnie, 192
Cohen, L. E., 103
Cohen, M., 105
Cohn, E. G., 90, 135
Cole, G. F., 169
Coleman, Claude, 21
Coles, C. M., 6, 16, 79, 133
Collins, D. J., 90
Colman, N., 113
Colon, Nelson, 291
Connors, E., 113
Cooney, M., 204
Corriero, Michael, 367
Cosby, Ennis, 2
Cowan, C. C., 213
Crank, J. P., 129
Crawford, C., 20
Cressey, D., 308
Crew, B. K., 160
Crofton, Sir Walter, 328
Culbertson, R. G., 129
Cullen, F. T., 126, 130, 229, 231, 289, 292
Cunanan, Andrew, 12
Cuniff, M., 208
Cunningham, W. C., 141

D

Dahmer, Jeffrey, 55
Daley, Richard M., 168
Daly, K., 17, 244
Daudistel, H. C., 163
Davis, M., 145
Davis, R. C., 277
Davis, Richard Allen, 225
Dean, C. W., 90
Decker, S. H., 18
Degan, William, 25
Dejong, W., 130
del Carmen, R., 140
DeLone, M., 19, 132, 135, 248
Dershowitz, Alan, 192
Diamond, S. S., 214
Dieckman, D., 102
Diggs, D. W., 288
Dillehay, R. C., 214
Dilulio, J. J., Jr., 11, 22, 26, 301, 320, 353
Donziger, S. R., 2, 3, 20, 254, 268
Dowd, Michael, 122
Downing, R. G., 159
DuBois, P. L., 157
duPont, John, 57

E

Eappens, Matthew, 202, 212
Earp, Wyatt, 76
Eck, J., 107
Eisenstein, J., 170, 171, 172, 205
Elliott, D. S., 90
Ellsworth, P. C., 213
Elmore, Clark, 193
Emmelman, D. S., 204

Eriksson, Anna, 225
Eskridge, C. W., 167

F

Farnham, Elizabeth, 259
Feeley, M. M., 241, 323
Feld, B. C., 357, 366
Felice, J. D., 157
Felson, M., 103
Ferdinand, P., 202
Ferracuti, F., 318
Fetzer, P. L., 238
Fielding, Henry, 74
Fielding, Sir John, 74
Fisher, B., 11
Fisher, Larry Lee, 231–232
Flanagan, T. J., 273, 316
Flango, V., 219
Flemming, R. B., 170, 171, 205
Flowers, R. B., 19
Forst, B., 209, 358
Fosdic, Raymond, 77
Foucault, M., 255
Fox, J. G., 11, 313, 353
Frank, J., 126
Frank, N., 169
Frase, R. S., 246
Free, M. D., 19
Freed, P. J., 308
Friday, P. C., 91
Fridell, L. A., 135, 185
Friedman, L. M., 3, 41, 323, 356
Frohmann, L., 182
Fry, Elizabeth Gurney, 259
Fuhrman, Mark, 132
Fukurai, H., 213
Fuld, Leonhard, 77
Fyfe, J. J., 134, 136, 139

G

Gardner, M. A., 63
Garner, J., 90, 134
Gartin, P. R., 90, 103
Geddes, R. W., 130
Geerken, M., 282
Geller, W. A., 135
Gendreau, P., 289
Gershman, B. L., 199
Giacopassi, D., 62
Gilbert, Terry, 31
Goldstein, H.., 78, 79, 107
Goldstone, Linda, 168
Goodpaster, G., 199
Goolkasian, G. A., 130
Graber, D. A., 15
Graham, B. L., 154
Graves, J. B., 163
Green, L., 103
Greenwood, P., 113
Griset, P. L., 231
Gruhl, J., 185
Guggenheim, M., 168
Guthrie, Adrian, 254

H

Haarr, R. N., 313
Hagan, F. E., 6
Hagan, J., 18
Hall, J., 49, 50
Hall, W. K., 159
Hamilton, K., 285
Hans, V., 64, 210
Hanson, R. A., 197, 220, 323
Hardyman, P. L., 289
Harnett, S. M., 106
Harper, Chris, 107
Harris, Kevin, 25, 185
Harris, Mary Belle, 260
Harrison, Todd, 275
Hastie, R., 218
Hawkins, G., 218, 316
Hayes, H. D., 282
Hearst, Patricia, 192
Heffernan, E., 311, 312
Hendricks, Leroy, 46
Henning, P. J., 63
Henry, D. A., 165
Hensley, T. R., 67
Hepburn, J. R., 134, 302
Heumann, M., 207
Hickey, T. J., 63
Hickok, Wild Bill, 76
Hillsman, S. T., 285
Hinckley, John, 57
Hirschel, J. D., 90
Hitt, Tim, 141
Holmes, M. D., 163
Hoover, J. Edgar, 81
Horiuchi, Lon, 25, 185
Hosch, H. M., 163
Houlden, P., 194
Howard, J., 256
Huff, C. R., 248
Hunt, G., 318
Hurst, J. R., 140
Hutchinson, I. W., 90
Hutt, Abraham V., 190

I

Ianni, F. A. J., 6
Ingles, Larry, 284
Irwin, J., 308, 309, 371

J

Jackson, Thomas, 4
Jacob, H., 89, 172
Jacobs, J. B., 6
Jacoby, J., 178, 183
James, R., 218
James, Rudy, 254
Jamieson, J. D., 60
Janikowski, W. R., 62
Jensen, V., 19
Johnson, D. R., 75
Jones, A. A., 199
Jones, Radford W., 142

K

Kaczynski, Theodore, 56
Kadane, J. B., 213
Kairys, D., 213
Kalinich, D. B., 310
Kalven, H., 219
Kanka, Megan, 343
Kappeler, V. E., 15
Karmen, A., 12, 285
Keil, T. J., 66, 235
Kelling, G. L., 6, 15, 16, 75, 78, 79, 98, 102, 108, 133
Kelly, Alex, 161
Kendrick, Benjamin, 150–151
Kennedy, John F., 29
Kennedy, Michael, 38
Kennedy, Robert, 332
Kerstetter, W. A., 139
Kevorkian, Jack, 4
Kilwein, J. C., 157
King, N. J., 64
King, Rodney, 64, 134
Kingsnorth, R., 159
Klaas, Polly, 225, 343
Kleinknecht, W., 6
Klofas, J., 57
Kmororowski, Jon, 193
Koenig, D. M., 217
Kopstein, A. J., 19
Kotlowitz, A., 358
Kramer, G. P., 217
Kramer, J. H., 244, 247
Krisberg, B., 292
Krmopotich, S., 313
Kruse, J., 208
Kruttschnitt, C., 313
Kurtz, H., 15

L

LaCourse, Dave, 232
Langbein, J. H., 209
Lanier, C. S., 66
Lara, Giovanni "King G", 317
Latessa, E. J., 229, 342
Laun, Tim, 117
Lear, E. T., 63
Lehoczky, J. P., 213
Leming, T., 130
Leo, R. A., 63
Levin, M., 242
Levine, J. P., 64, 218
Lewis, Karl G., 305
Lilly, J. R., 265
Link, B., 130
Logan, C., 22, 297
Lombado, L. X., 229
Louima, Abner, 134
Lovrich, N. P., 157
Lucken, K., 284, 291
Lundman, R., 145
Lundregan, T., 113
Lynch, J. P., 3, 8
Lynch, M., 289, 292

M

MacKenzie, D. L., 289, 290
Maconochie, Alexander, 328
Maguire, K., 316
Mahoney, B., 285
Mann, C. R., 19, 21
Manning, P. K., 74
Manson, Charles, 332
Marino, Carmen, 31
Marquart, J. M., 135
Marsh, J. R., 163
Marshall, Thurgood, 65
Martin, S. E., 126

Martinez, Michael, 129
Martinez, R., Jr., 145
Martinson, R., 229
Maschke, K. J., 180
Masterson, Bat, 76
Maxfield, M. G., 15
McCall, Brent, 93
McCorkle, R. C., 229
McCoy, C., 108, 204, 208
McDonald, D., 288
McDougald, Charles E., 129
McEwen, T., 113
McGabey, R., 133
McGarrell, E. F., 269
McGreevy, M. A., 57
McLeod, M., 332
McVeigh, Timothy, 41, 72
Meier, R. F., 12, 13
Melekian, B., 108
Mendelsohn, R. I, 287
Menendez, Erik and Lyle, 224–225
Metzger, S., 91
Meyer, Paul, 365
Miethe, T. D., 12, 13, 15, 247
Miller, J. L., 160
Miller, M., 168
Miller, N., 113
Miller, T. R., 105
Monkkonen, E. H., 76, 78
Moore, C. A., 247
Moore, J. W., 270 78
Moore, M., 75, 78, 79, 105, 106
Morales, Fernando, 361 362
Morales, T., 318
Morash, M., 313
Morgan, Virginia M., 164
Morris, Gregory, 352
Morris, N., 234, 272, 275, 283
Mower, Gordon, 159
Mowry, B. L., 90
Murphy, Cristina, 127
Murphy, P. V., 75, 106

N

Nagel, R. F., 161
Nardulli, P. F., 119, 170, 171, 197, 205
Neufeld, P. J., 113
Newman, T. C., 213
Nichols, Terry, 41
Nilsen, E., 286
Nisbett, Jerome, 352

O

O'Brien, R. M., 11
O'Leary, V., 281
Ochoa, R., 64, 214
Osterhaven, Robin, 280
Oswald, Lee Harvey, 29

P

Packer, H. L., 43, 44
Paetzold, William, 198–199
Parent, D. G., 288
Parks, Anthony, 315
Pate, A. M., 109, 135
Pate, T., 102
Paul II, Pope, 235
Peel, Sir Robert, 74
Peiper, S. L., 288
Pennington, N., 218
Penrod, S., 218
Penry, Johnny Paul, 238
Peoples, J. M., 163
Percival, R. V., 41
Perez, D. A., 163
Perkins, C. A., 169
Perkins, D. B., 60
Petersilia, J., 113, 234, 247, 276, 279, 282, 283, 289, 292, 293
Peterson, R. D., 18
Piquero, A., 290
Pisciotta, A. W., 259
Platt, A., 356
Pollock-Byrne, J., 311
Pope, Thomas, 176–177
Potter, G. W., 15
Prejean, Dalton, 238
Propper, A., 312
Pulaski, C. A., 66, 237
Pursley, R. D., 239
Putnam, C. E., 200

R

Radelet, M. L., 200
Rafter, N. H., 260
Ramsey, JonBenet, 109
Rattner, A., 248
Reagan, Ronald, 57, 270
Reaves, B. A., 105, 163, 167, 169
Redfern, A., 18
Reed, K., 287
Regoli, R. M., 129
Rehnquist, William, 61, 239
Reilly, John, 93, 101
Reiss, A. J., Jr., 78, 143
Renzema, M., 287
Richardson, J. E., 63
Riegel, S., 318
Rierden, A., 311
Roberts, Brian, 21
Roberts, Simon, 254
Robertson, Pat, 235
Robin, G. D., 62
Robinson, P. H., 58
Rogan, D. P., 90, 103
Roper, R., 219
Rosen, L., 7
Rosenbaum, J. L., 18
Rosenbaum, R., 238
Rossman, S. B., 105
Roth, P. T., 19
Rothman, D. J., 255, 258, 356
Rousey, D. C., 76
Rubenstein, M. L., 208
Ruby, Jack, 29
Rucker, L., 313
Ryan, J. P., 154

S

Sales, B. D., 154
Salvi, John, 160
Sandys, M. R., 214
Santos, Michael G., 307–308
Schade, T., 134
Schmidt, J. D., 90, 91
Schultz, David, 57
Scott, E. J., 87
Scott, M. S., 135
Scott, T., 167
Sears, Tyrone, 315
Sellin, T., 257
Sepulveda, George "King Paradise", 317
Shane-Dubow, S., 154
Shapiro, Robert, 192
Sheck, Barry, 212
Sheldon, C. H., 157
Sheley, J. F., 353
Sheppard, Sam, 31
Sherman, A., 19
Sherman, L. W., 90, 102, 103, 104, 105, 106, 135
Shichor, D., 265
Sichel, J. L., 126, 285
Simon, L. M. S., 317
Simon, R., 17, 18
Simpson, O. J., 41, 132, 192
Sirhan, Sirhan, 332
Skogan, W. G., 13, 15, 106, 133
Skolnick, J. H., 107, 127, 134, 139
Sloan, J. J., 160
Smith, B. E., 277
Smith, Bruce, 77
Smith, C. E., 64, 67, 140, 167, 199, 211, 214, 221, 320
Smith, Charles Z., 158
Smith, D., 18
Smith, David, 314
Smith, M. Dwayne, 353
Smith, Susan, 176–177
Sorenson, J. R., 135
Spangenberg, R. L., 196, 197
Sparks, Michael, 193
Spears, L., 195
Spelman, W. G., 103, 104, 107
Spence, Gerry, 188
Sperlich, P. W., 211
Spohn, C., 19, 132, 135, 185, 208, 248
Sprungl, Greg, 185
Stafford, M. C., 226, 227
Stanford, M. R., 90
Stanko, E., 182
Stark, R., 14
Steffensmeier, D., 18, 244
Steinman, M., 91
Stephan, J. J., 169
Steury, E. H., 91, 169
Stichman, A., 126
Stoddard, E., 137
Stojkovic, S., 303
Strauchs, J. J., 141
Streifel, C., 244
Strodtbeck, F., 218
Sundt, J. L., 231
Surette, R., 15
Suster, Ronald, 31
Sutton, J., 356
Sykes, G. M., 308
Symington, Fife, 5
Szasz, A., 5

T

Talarico, S. M., 331
Terry, Chuck, 69–70, 147148, 250–252, 347–349

Thill, Nathan, 6
Thomas, C. W., 265
Thompson, W. C., 213
Timmendequas, Jesse, 343
Tonry, M., 19, 21, 232, 234, 246, 275, 283, 285, 289, 290, 292
Townes, Sandra, 154
Traub, J., 353
Trout, C., 318
Tucker, Karla Faye, 235
Turner, K. B., 125, 126
Turner, M. G., 231
Turner, S., 234, 247
Tyson, H., 181
Tyson, Mike, 192

U

Ulmer, J. T., 247
Uphoff, R. J., 198
Utz, P., 205
Uviller, H. R., 61

V

Van Meter, C. W., 141
Vaughan, J. B., 287
Versace, Gianni, 12
Vidmar, N., 64, 210
Vito, G. F., 66, 235
Vollmer, August, 77
von Hirsch, A., 226

W

Waldorf, D., 318
Walker, S., 19, 22, 125, 126, 132, 135, 138, 139, 248, 333
Wallace, D. H., 320
Walsh, W., 145
Walters, D., 91
Warr, M., 15, 226, 227
Warren, Earl, 59, 60, 65
Wasserman, D. T., 219
Watson, R. A., 159
Weaver, Randy, 25, 188
Weinstein, J. B., 247
Weisberg, Stanley, 224
Weisburd, D. A., 103
Weisheit, R., 313
Weitekamp, E., 286
Welch, M., 169
Welch, S., 185
West, Cornel, 21
White, M. S., 214
White, T. J., 208
Wice, P. B., 154, 191
Wilbanks, William, 19
Williams, Charles, 257
Williams, H., 75, 109
Williams, Hernando, 168
Wilson, J. Q., 15, 79, 84, 106
Wilson, O. W., 77, 78
Winslow, Allyn, 352
Withrow, Pamela K., 299
Wolfgang, M. E., 318
Wood, Kimba, 122
Woodbury, Denise, 25, 185
Woodward, Louise, 202, 212
Woodworth, G., 66, 237
Worden, A. P., 126, 172, 194, 195, 206
Wozniak, J., 130
Wright, B., 139
Wright, J. D., 353
Wright, J. P., 292
Wright, R., 18

Y

Yandrasits, J., 57
Yang, S. S., 313

Z

Zedner, L, 259
Zeisel, H., 219
Zimbardo, P. G., 272
Zimmer, L., 115
Zimmer, Lisa A., 339
Zimring, F., 366
Zobel, Hiller, 202
Zoglin, Kathryn, 186

Subject Index

***Note:* Page numbers in boldface type indicate pages on which terms are defined.**

A

Accusatory process, 185, **188**
Actual time served, 232–233
Actus res, 49
Adequacy of counsel, 199–200
Adjudication, **36**
Adjustment to life outside prison, 342–344
Admissible evidence, **116**
African Americans
  bail, 163
  judges, 154
  police officers, 125–126
  prisoners, 248
  racial disparities, and, 18–21, 131–133
Aggravated assault, 52
Aggressive patrol, 105–106
AIDS, 272
Ambiguity delays, 103
Antifencing efforts, 106
Antiterrorism and Effective Death Penalty Act, 221
Apodaca v. Oregon, 65
Appeals, 40, **219**–221
  basis for, 219–220
  death penalty, 238–239
  evaluation of, process, 221
  habeas corpus, 220–221
Appellate courts, **151**
Apprehension, 111–112
Argersinger v. Hamlin, 193
Arizona v. Hicks, 118
Arraignment, 40, 159, **161**
Arrest, **38, 118**
Arson, 52
Assigned counsel, **194**
Attorney competence, 199–200
Attorney general, 178
Austin v. U.S., 286
Automobile searches, 117

B

Bail, 39, **161**
  amount of, 163
  bail bondsmen, 162
  reform, 165–168
Bail Reform Act, 167
Barron v. Baltimore, **59**
Batson v. Kennedy, 214
Battering, 89–91
Bench trial, **209**
Bill of Rights, **58**–59, 377
Blackledge v. Allison, 204
Bobbies, 74
Bondsmen, 162
Booking, 39
Boot camps, **289**–290
Bordenkircher v. Hayes, 207
Bow Street Runners, 74
Boykin v. Alabama, 206
Breaking or entering, 52
"Broken Windows: The Police and Neighbourhood Safety" (Wilson/Kelling), 79
Burch v. Louisiana, 211
Burglary, 51–52

C

CALEA, 139
California v. Acevedo, 62
Capital punishment, 235–239
Careers
  community correctional counselor, 381
  correctional officer, 382
  court administrator, 380–381
  defense attorney, 379–380
  federal law enforcement officer, 378–379
  municipal police officer, 378
  paralegal/legal assistant/court reporter, 380
  parole officer, 382
  private security, 379
  probation officer, 381
  prosecuting attorney, 379
Celebrated cases, 41
Challenge for cause, **214**
Charging, 39
Children, 54
Chimel v. California, 116
Cigarette money, 310
Cincinnati Declaration of Principles, 258
Circuit courts of appeals, 152
Circumstantial evidence, **215**
Citation, **166**
Citizen watch groups, 133
Citizen's arrest, 143
City police forces, 82
Civil law, **48**
Civilian review boards, 138–139
Clearance rate, **98**
Closing arguments, 216–217
Coercion, 54
Coleman v. Alabama, 64, 193
Commission on Accreditation for Law Enforcement Agencies (CALEA), 139
Community correctional center, **338**
Community correctional counselor, 381
Community corrections, **261**, 264, 275–294
  assumptions, 276
  future of, 292–293
  intermediate sanctions. *See* Intermediate sanction probation, 277–283
Community crime prevention, 133
Community policing, 78–80, 106–108
Community programs following release, 337–340
Community service, 234, **287**–288
Comprehensive Crime Control Act, 57
Conditional release, 165
Confessions, 63, 119
Conflict delays, 104
Congregate system, **258**
Conjugal visits, 338
Constitutional rights, 66. *See also* specific constitutional amendments
Continuance, **205**
Contract counsel, **194**–195
Cooper v. Pate, 320–**321**
Coping delays, 104
Correctional officers, 304–306, 382
Corrections, 36, 40, 254–274, **255**, *See also* Prisons
  careers, 381–382
  Cincinnati Declaration of Principles, 258
  community model, 261
  composition of prisons, 271–273
  crime control model, 262
  elderly prisoners, 272
  Elmira Reformatory, 259
  federal corrections system, 262–263
  historical development, 255–262
  HIV/AIDS, 272
  incarceration trends, 267–270
  jails, 266–267
  juvenile justice, and, 369–371
  long-term inmates, 272–273
  medical model, 261
  New York system, 258
  Pennsylvania system, 257
  prison construction, 270
  private prisons, 265–266
  rehabilitation model, 260
  state corrections system, 263–266
  women, and, 259–260, 264–265
Corrections Corporation of America, 265
Corruption, 136–137
Count, 180–**181**
County police forces, 81–82
Court administrator, 380–381
Courtroom workgroups, 171–173
Courts, 35–36
  careers, 379–381
  courtroom procedure, 170
  felony, 241–242
  lower, 241
  misdemeanor, 241
  state, 153
  structure/hierarchy, 151–153
Crime, **3**
  costs of, 15
  defined, 4
  elements of, 51
  fear of, 15–16
  how much, 7–9
  statutory definition, 51–52
  trends, 9–12
  types, 4–7
Crime control model, **43**
Crime control model of corrections, **262**
Crimes without victims, 6–7

Criminal homicide, 52
Criminal justice system, 25–45
 characteristics, 31–34
 crime control model, 43
 decision making, 37–41
 due process model, 43–44
 federal involvement, 28–30
 goals, 26–28
 system perspective, 31
 wedding cake model, 41–42
Criminal justice wedding cake, 42
Criminal sanctions. *See also* Sentencing
 actual time served, 232–233
 death penalty, 235–239
 determinate sentences, 230–231
 goals, 225–229
 incarceration, 230–233
 indeterminate sentences, 230
 intermediate sanctions, 234
 mandatory sentence, 231–232
 probation, 234–235
Cruel and unusual punishment, 65–66
Custodial model, **297**

D

Dangerous parolee, 343
Dark figure of crime, 7
Day reporting centers, **288**
Death penalty, 66, 235–239
Decision making, 37–41
Defendant, **38**
Defense attorneys, 187–200, **188**
 agent-mediators, as, 198
 attorney competence, 199–200
 beleaguered dealers, as, 198
 career profile, 379–380
 indigent defendants, and, 193–197
 private counsel, 191–192
 private vs. public defense, 197–200
 realities of the job, 188–189, 192
 role, 188
Defenses, 52–58
Delaware v. Prouse, 117
Delinquent, 359–**360**
Demonstrative evidence, **215**
Dependent child, **360**
Detention, **366**–367
Determinate sentences, **230**–231
Deterrence, 226–227
Differential response, **97**
Direct evidence, **215**
Directed patrol, **103**
Discovery, **181**
Discretion, **32**
Discretionary release, **329**
Disorganized criminal, 309
Disparities, 18–21, **19**
Diversion, **364**
DNA fingerprinting, 113
Doing time, 309
Domestic violence, 89–91
Double jeopardy, **59**, 63–64
Douglas v. California, 64
Drug enforcement, 115, 270
Drunkenness, 55
Dual court system, **35**
Due process, 59–60
Due process model, **43**
Duress, 54
Durham Rule, 57
Durham v. United States, 57

E

Eastern Penitentiary, 256–257
Eighth Amendment, 65, 322
Elderly prisoners, 272
Elmira Reformatory, 259
Enlightenment, 255–**256**
Entrapment, **53**
Equal Employment Opportunity Act, 124
Escobedo v. Illinois, **63**, 193
Ethics
 assigned counsel, 196
 bail, 162
 correctional officer–inmate relationships, 303
 HIV/AIDS testing of prisoners, 273
 interrogation based on physical
  characteristics, 62
 judges, 156
 jury duty, 211
 parole board, 332
 plea bargaining, 205
 police corruption, 137
 presentence report, 246
 search and seizure, 119
 taking matters into own hands, 27
 training school (juveniles), 371
Evidence, 215–216
Ex post facto laws, 49
Exchange, **31**
Exclusionary rule, 61
Execution of minors, 238
External stress, 130

F

Federal Bureau of Investigation (FBI), 80–81
Federal Bureau of Prisons, 263
Federal corrections system, 262–263
Federal law enforcement agencies, 80–81
Federal Probation and Pretrial
 Services System, 263
Federalism, **28**
Felker v. Turpin, 221
Felonies, **4**, 41–**42**
Felony courts, 241–242
Felony sentences, 242
Field interrogations, 117
Fifth Amendment, 62, 377
Filtering process, **33**–34
Fines, 285
First Amendment, 321
Fixing Broken Windows (Wilson/Coles), 79
Foot patrol, 105
Forcible rape, 52
Forensic techniques, 112–113
Forfeiture, **286**
Fourteenth Amendment, 59, 322–323, 377
Fourth Amendment, 60–62, 321–322, 377
Frankpledge, **73**
Frisking, 117
Fully secured bail, 165
Fundamental fairness, **59**
Furlough, **338**
Furman v. Georgia, 65, **235**

G

Gagnon v. Scarpelli, 282–**283**
Gardner v. Florida, 246
General deterrence, **226**
Genotypic features, 113
Georgia v. McCollum, 214
Gideon v. Wainwright, **64**, 193
Gilbert v. California, 193
Gleaning, 309
Going rate, **170**
Good-faith exception to exclusionary rule, 120
Good time, 232, 240
Graham v. Connor, **135**
Grand jury, 39
Grass eaters, 136
Gregg v. Georgia, **65**, **236**
Gubernatorial appointment, 157
Guilty pleas, 205. *See also* Plea bargaining
Guns, 106

H

Habeas corpus, **220**–221
Halfway house, **338**
Handguns, 106
Hands-off policy, 320–**321**
Hendricks v. Kansas, 343
Hispanic Americans
 bail, 163
 police officers, 125–126
 prisoners, 248
 racial disparities, 18–21, 131–133
HIV/AIDS, 272
Home confinement, 287
Homicide offenses, 52
Hot spots, 103
House arrest, **287**
House of Refuge of New York, 356
Huber Act, 338
Hudson v. Palmer, 322

I

Illinois v. Rodriguez, 118
Illinois Juvenile Court Act, 356
Immaturity, 54
Implicit plea bargaining, 206
Imprisonment, 230–233. *See also* Prisons
In re Gault, 64, **357**
Incapacitation, 227–**228**
Incarceration, 230–233, 297. *See also* Prisons
Incarceration trends, 267–270
Inchoate offenses, 50
Incident-driven policing, 96
Incorporation, 60
Indeterminate sentences, 228, 230
Indictment, **39**
Indigent defendants, 193–197
Individual deterrence, 227
Industrial school, 370
Inevitable discovery exception, 120
Information, **39**
Inmate code, **306**
Innocent yet convicted persons, 248
Insanity, 56–58
Intensive supervision probation (ISP), **288**–289
Intermediate sanctions, **234**, 283–292
 boot camps, 289–290
 community service, 287–288
 day reporting centers, 288

fines, 285
forfeiture, 286
home confinement, 287
implementation, 290–292
intensive supervision probation, 288–289
restitution, 285–286
Internal affairs unit, **138**
Interrogation, 118–120
Intoxication, 55
Investigation, 38, 109–113
Irresistible impulse test, 56
ISP programs, 288–289

J

J.E.B. v. Alabama ex rel. T.B., 214
Jacobson v. United States, 53
Jailing, 309
Jails, 266–267
Jobs. *See* Careers, Workperspectives
Judges, 153–154
functions, 154–156
instructions to jury, 217
methods of selection, 156–159
who are they, 154
Judicial waiver, **364**
Jurisdiction, **73, 151**
Jury, **209**
deliberation, 218
selection of, 212–215
Jury duty, 211
Jury trial, 210–211. *See also* Trial process
Juvenile Justice and Delinquency Prevention Act, 357
Juvenile justice system, 352–373
adjudicatory process, 367–368
age of clients, 359
alternative dispositions, 370
categories of cases, 359–360
community treatment, 370
corrections, 369–371
crime control period (1980-present), 358
detention/temporary custody, 366–367
disposition, 368–369
diversion, 364
historical development, 354–358
institutional care, 370–371
institutional programs, 371
intake, 364
juvenile court period (1899–1960), 356–357
juvenile rights period (1960–1980), 357
police interface, 362–364
probation, 370
problems/perspectives, 371–372
refuge period (1824–1899), 355–356
statistics, 353
transfer to adult court, 364, 366

K

Kansas v. Hendricks, 47
Kent v. United States, 357

L

Larceny-theft, 52
Large police departments, 94
Law enforcement, **87**–88
Lee v. Washington, 323
Legal sufficiency, 184–**185**
Legalistic style of policing, 85
Legislative exclusion, **366**
Lewis v. United States, 65
Life imprisonment, 229
Lifestyle-exposure model of victimization, 13
Line functions, **98**
Local legal culture, **170**
Long-term inmates, 272–273
Low-income city dwellers, 13
Lower courts, 241
Lyman School for Boys, 356

M

M'Naghten Rule, 56
Malice aforethought, 52
Management by walking around, 301
Mandatory release, **330**
Mandatory sentence, **231**–232
Map v. Ohio, **61**, 116
Maryland v. Wilson, 117
Massachusetts Stubborn Child Law, 354
Maximum security prison, 264
McCleskey v. Kemp, 66, **237**
Meat eaters, 136
Medical model, 260–**261**
Medium security prison, 264
Megan's Law, 343
Mempha v. Rhay, **282**
Mens rea, **50**
Mental illness, 56–58
Merit selection, **157**
Metropolitan Police Act, 74
Michigan Department of State Police v. Sitz, 117
Minimum security prison, 264
Miranda v. Arizona, 63, 193
Miranda warnings, 63, 119
Misdemeanor courts, 241
Misdemeanors, 4, **6**, **42**
Missouri Plan, 157
Mistake, 54–55
Monell v. Department of Social Services for the City of New York, 140
Montana v. Egelhoff, 55
Moore v. Illinois, 193
Morrissey v. Brewer, **344**
Motion, **161**
Motor vehicle theft, 52
Motorized patrol, 105
Municipal police forces, 82
Murder, 52

N

National Crime Victimization Surveys (NCVS), **9**
National Incident-Based Reporting System (NIBRS), **8**
NCVS, 9
Necessity, 54
Neglected child, 360
Net widening, 291
New York v. Class, 118
New York v. Quarles, **63**, 119
NIBRS, **8**
911 system, 97
Nix v. Williams, 120
Nolle prosequi, **181**
Nonpartisan election, **157**
North Carolina v. Alford, **206**

O

Occupational crime, 5–**6**
Offender notification laws, 343
One-person vs. two-person patrol units, 105
Opening statements, 215
Operational stress, 130
Order maintenance, **86**–87
Ordinary crime, 6
Organizational response, 96–98
Organizational stress, 130
Organized crime, 5–**6**

P

Parens patriae, 354
Parole, **327**
decision to release, 331–334
future of, 345
historical development, 328
origins of, 328
parole boards, 330–331
pros/cons, 334
recidivism, and, 343–344
revocation of, 344–345
Parole boards, 330–331
Parole officers, 340–342, 382
Partisan election, **157**
Patrol function, 99–109
Penal code, 48
Penitentiary, **256**
Penology, **258**
Percentage bail, 165
Peremptory cause, **214**
Personal stress, 130
PINS, **360**
Plain-view doctrine, 117–118
Plea bargain, **31**
Plea bargaining, 40, 182, **203**–209
criticisms, 207–208
exchange relationships, and, 204–206
implicit, 206
justifications, 207
legal issues, 206–207
reform, 208–209
tactics, 205
Police
abuse of power, and, 134–137
arrest, 118
authority, 128
careers, 378–379
citizens, and, 88–89
civic accountability, 138–140
civil liability suits, 140
composition of force, 124–126
corruption, 136–137
dangerous situations, 128
discretion, 89
domestic violence, and, 89–91
drug enforcement, 115
duties, 35
force, use of, 134–136
functions, 85–88
historical development, 73–80
interrogation, 118–120
investigation, 109–113
isolation, 128–129
juvenile justice, and, 362–364
large departments, 94
line vs. staff functions, 98

minority officers, 125–126
multicultural communities, and, 131–133
organization, 80–82, 94–95
organizational response, 96–98
patrol function, 99–109
private employment, 143–144
productivity, 98
recruitment, 12
relationship between private/public law enforcement, 144–145
response time, 103–104
search and seizure, 60–62, 116–118
standards/accreditation, 139–140
stress, 129–130
styles of policing, 85
subculture, 126–130
traffic regulation, 114
training, 123–124
urban departments, 94
use of limited resources, 83
vice laws, 114–115
women officers, 126
working personality, 127–128
Police brutality, 134–136
Political crime, 6–7
Political era, 75–77
Posse, 76
Powell v. Alabama, **59**
Preliminary hearing, 39
Presentence report, **218, 244**–246
Presumptive parole date, 332–334, **333**
Presumptive sentence, **231**
Pretrial detention, 169
Pretrial release. *See* Bail
Pretrial withdrawal of cases, 160
Preventive detention, **167**–168
Preventive patrol, 99–**100**, 102
Prison construction, 270
Prisons, 295–325. *See also* Corrections
classification, 315
correctional officers, 304–306
economic system, 309–310
educational programs, 315
Eighth Amendment, 322
First Amendment, 321
Fourteenth Amendment, 322–323
Fourth Amendment, 321–322
goals of incarceration, 297
governing, 301–304
incarcerated mothers, 313–314
increase in prison population, 296
inmate code, 306–308
lines of command, 298–300
management, 301
prison industries, 316
prisoners' rights, 320–323
prisoners' rights' movement, 323
programs, 314–316
race, 318
rehabilitative programs, 316
rewards/punishments, 302
role orientation, 309
underground economy, 310
violence, 317–320
vocational education, 315
wardens, 299–301
women, and, 311–314
Private policing, 141–145
Private prisons, 265–266
Privately secured bail, 165
Proactive, **96**
Probable cause, **159**
Probation, **234**–235, **277**
evaluation of, 283
juveniles, 370
nature of job, 279–281
organization of, 279
origins/evaluation, 278
revocation of, 282
Probation officer, 381
Problem-oriented policing, **107**
Procedural criminal law, **48**
Procedural due process, 58
Procunier v. Martinez, 321
Professional policing, 77–78
Profiles. *See* Workperspectives
Progressives, 77, 260
Prosecuting attorney, **177**
Prosecutorial discretion, **366**
Prosecutors, 177–187
career profile, 379
case evaluation, 185, 187
decision-making policies, 182–187
discretion, 180–181
election of, 178
influence, 178–179
policy models, 183–185
relationships, 181–182
role, 179–180
Public defender, **194**, 196
Public policy issues, 21–23
Public safety exception to *Miranda* warnings, 119–120
Punishment. *See* Criminal sanctions
Purkett v. Elem, 214

Q

Queen v. M'Naughten, 56

R

Racial disparities, 18–21
Reactive, **96**
Real evidence, **215**
Reasonable doubt, **217**
Rebuttal witnesses, 216
Recidivism, **276**, 343–344
Reform school, 370
Rehabilitation model, **260, 297**
Rehabilitation, **228**–229
Reintegration model, **297**
Release, 41
Release mechanisms, 329–335
Release on recognizance (ROR), 167
Residential treatment programs, 338
Response time, 103
Restitution, 285–**286**
Retribution, 225–**226**
Ricketts v. Adamson, 207
Right to counsel, 64–65, 193
Right to jury, 64–65
Robbery, 52
Robinson v. California, 49
ROR, 167
Ross v. Moffitt, 64, 193
Ruby Ridge incident, 25
Rules of evidence, 216

S

Santobello v. New York, **203**, 206
Schall v. Martin, **358**
Scott v. Illinois, 64
Search warrant, **116**
Searches incident to lawful arrest, 116
Selective incapacitation, **228**
Self-defense, 53–54
Self-incrimination, 59, 62–63
Sentencing, 40, 239–248. *See also* Criminal sanctions
administrative context of courts, and, 240–242
attitudes/values of judges, and, 242–244
guidelines, 246–247
presentence report, 244–246
who gets the harshest punishment, 248
Sentencing guidelines, **246**–247
Separate confinement, **257**
Service, **87**
Service style of policing, 85
Seven principles of criminal law, 49
Seventh Amendment, 377
Sheriffs, 81–82
Shock incarceration, **289**
Shock probation, **234**
Sisters in Crime: The Rise of the New Female Criminal (Adler), 17
Sixth Amendment, 64, 377
Slow plea process, 206
Socialization, 124–**125**
Special deterrence, **227**
Special populations, 108
Split probation, 234
Spousal abuse, 89–91
Staff functions, 98
Stanford v. Kentucky, 238
State attorney general, **178**
State corrections systems, 263–266
State courts, 153
State courts of appeals, 152
State of Prisons in England and Wales, The (Howard), 256
State police forces, 81
State prison systems, 264
State supreme courts, 152
Status offense, **357**
Statute of Winchester, 74
Stings, 106
Street crime, 6
Stress, 129–130
Strickland v. Washington, 193, 199
Strict liability, **50**
Subculture, **126**–127
Substantial capacity test, 57
Substantive criminal law, **48**
Supervision in the community, 335–345
adjustment to life outside prison, 342–344
community programs following release, 337–340
parole officers, 340–342
revocation of parole, 344–345
Supreme Court of the United States, 152
Sworn officers, **99**
System efficiency, 184–**185**

T

Take-back-the-streets tactics, 96
Ten percent cash bail, 167

Tennessee v. Garner, **135**
Terry v. Ohio, **117**
Testimony, **215**
The Queen v. Dudley and Stephens, 54
Thin Blue Line, The, 248
Third-party custody, 165
Thompson v. Oklahoma, 238
311 system, 97
Three-strikes law, 231
Threshold inquiries, 117
Traffic regulation, 114
Training school, 370
Trial courts of general jurisdiction, **151**
Trial courts of limited jurisdiction, 151
Trial process, 212–218
  closing arguments, 216–217
  decision by jury, 217–218
  instructions to jury, 217
  jury selection, 212–215
  opening statements, 215
  presentation of defense evidence, 216
  presentation of prosecution's evidence, 215–216
  presentation of rebuttal witnesses, 216
  sentencing, 218
Trial sufficiency, 185, **188**
Trop v. Dulles, 65
True bill, 39
Truth-in-sentencing laws, 233
Turner v. Safley, **321**

U

U.S. v. Ross, 117
UCR, 7
Unconditional release, **330**
Uniform Crime Reports (UCR), **7**
United States attorney, **178**
United States v. Cronic, 199
United States v. Henry, 193
United States v. Leon, 61, **120**
United States v. Salerno and Cafero, 65, **168**
United States v. Wade, 64, 193
Unsecured bail, 165
Urban police departments, 94

V

Verdict, 218
Vice laws, 114-115
Victimology, **12**
Victims
  criminal justice system, and, 16
  role of, in crime, 17
  who is victimized, 12-14
Violent Crime Control and Law Enforcement Act, 108
Visible crime, 6-7
Voir dire, **214**

W

Wackenhut Corrections Corporation, 265
Walnut Street Jail, 257
War on drugs, 270
Warrant, 38-**39**
Warrantless searches, 116-118
Watchman style of policing, 85
Wedding cake model, 42
Weeks v. United States, 61
Wilkins v. Missouri, 238
Williams v. Florida, 64, 211
Williams v. New York, 246
Wilson v. Seiter, 322
Wolff v. McDonnell, **322**
Women
  boot camps, 290
  crime, and, 17-18
  police officers, 126
  prisons, and, 259-260, 264-265, 311-314
Women and Crime (Simon), 17
Work and educational release, **337**-338
Workperspectives
  chemical dependency counselor, 339-340
  child abuse and neglect investigator, 110-111
  correctional officer, 305-306
  defense attorney, 190-191
  justice, 158-159
  juvenile probation officer, 365-366
  magistrate judge, 164-165
  patrol officer, 101-102
  police commander, 83-84
  private security, 142-143
  probation officer, 280-281
  prosecutor, 186-187
  state trial judge, 243-244
  warden, 299-300
Workgroup, **171**
Working personality, 127-**128**

Y

Youth crime. *See* Juvenile justice system

Photo Credits

p. 1 © Sandra Baker/The Gamma Liaison Network; p. 2 (top) © Nick Ut/AP/Wide World Photos, Inc.; p. 2 (bottom) © David Karp/AP/Wide World Photos, Inc.; p. 4 © Richard Sheinwald/AP/Wide World Photos, Inc.; p. 5 © Ken Levine/AP/Wide World Photos, Inc.; p. 6 © Karl Gehring/The Denver Post; p. 12 © Susan Greenwood/The Gamma Liaison Network; p. 17 © Phyllis Picardi/The Picture Cube; p. 18 © Fritz Hoffmann/The Image Works; p. 22 © Stephen Jaffe/Reuters/Archive Photos; p. 25 © Spokesman Review/The Gamma Liaison Network; p. 26 © Carolina Kroon/Impact Visuals; p. 31 © Tony Dejak/AP/Wide World Photos, Inc.; p. 35 © Steven Rubin/The Image Works; p. 36 © Zigy Kaluzny/The Gamma Liaison Network; p. 41 © Orlin Wagner/AP/Wide World Photos, Inc.; p. 46 © AP/Wide World Photos, Inc.; p. 48 © Archive Photos; p. 51 © Jennie Zeiner/AP/Wide World Photos, Inc.; p. 56 © Bruce Ely/The Gamma Liaison Network; p. 60 © Chris Brown/Stock, Boston; p. 71 © Ralf-Finn Hestoft/SABA Press; p. 72 © Rick Bowmer/AP/Wide World Photos, Inc.; p. 75 Culver Pictures, Inc.; p. 81 © Bob Daemmrick/The Image Works; p. 86 (left to right) © Misha Erwitt/Magnum; © Rene Burri/Magnum; © Christopher Brown/Stock, Boston; p. 88 © Gary Wagner/Stock, Boston; p. 90 © Michael Newman/PhotoEdit; p. 93 © William Wilson Lewis III/AP/Wide World Photos, Inc.; p. 96 © Todd Yates/Black Star; p. 100 © Steve Liss/Time Magazine; p. 109 © Dave Sartin/The Gamma Liaison Network; p. 117 © Li-Hua Lan/The Image Works; p. 122 © Paul Hurschmann/AP/Wide World Photos, Inc.; p. 126 © Stephen Agricola/Stock, Boston; p. 127 © Nubar Alexanian/Stock, Boston; p. 129 © AP/Wide World Photos, Inc.; p. 131 © Richard Perry/Sygma; p. 134 © Pool/Reuters/Archive Photos; p. 141 © Jack Kurtz/Impact Visuals; p. 149 © Terry Wild Studio; p. 150 © Dennis Cook/AP/Wide World Photos, Inc.; p. 154 © Dick Blume/The Image Works; p. 159 © Suzanne Dunn/The Image Works; p. 160 © AP/Wide World Photos, Inc.; p. 161 © Ron Frehm/AP/Wide World Photos, Inc.; p. 169 © Bob Daemmrich/Stock, Boston; p. 171 © Owen/Black Star; p. 176 © Charlotte Observer/SABA Press; p 179 © Sygma; p. 181 © John Neubauer/PhotoEdit; p. 185 © AP/Wide World Photos, Inc.; p. 188 © Mike Theiler/Reuters/Archive Photos; p. 193 © AP/Wide World Photos, Inc.; p. 202 © AP/Wide World Photos, Inc.; p. 204 © Dawson Jones/Stock, Boston; p. 209 © James Pickerell/The Image Works; p. 212 © The Gamma Liaison Network; p. 224 © Lee Celano/Reuters/Archive Photos; p. 225 © Pool/Reuters/Archive Photos; p. 227 © Steve Lehman/SABA Press; p. 234 © Andrew Lichtenstein/Impact Visuals; p. 235 © Bob Daemmrich/The Image Works; p. 238 © Adrees A. Latif/Reuters/Archive Photos; p. 243 © Ron Manistee; p. 248 © Mark Cowan/AP/Wide World Photos, Inc.; p. 253 © Mark Richards/PhotoEdit; p. 254 © Hall Anderson/Ketchikan Daily News; p. 255 © American Stock/Archive Photos; p. 256 © Archive Photos; p. 259 © Jack Spratt/The Image Works; p. 264 © AP/Wide World Photos, Inc.; p. 272 © Ed Kashi; p. 275 © Bob Daemmrich/The Image Works; p. 282 © A. Ramey/Woodfin Camp & Associates; p. 287 © Jack Kurtz/Impact Visuals; p. 290 © Joseph Rodriquez/Black Star; p. 295 © Ralf-Finn Hestoft/SABA Press; p. 297 © Steve Lehman/SABA Press; p. 301 © Jeffry D. Scott/Impact Visuals; p. 304 © A. Ramey/PhotoEdit; p. 309 © Steve Lehman/SABA Press; p. 311 © Jane Evelyn Atwood/Contact Press Images; p. 312 © A. Ramey/PhotoEdit; p. 314 © Jane Evelyn Atwood/Contact Press Images; p. 315 © AP/Wide World Photos, Inc.; p. 317 © Matt York/AP/Wide World Photos, Inc.; p. 320 © Mark Sultz/AP/Wide World Photos, Inc.; p. 326 © John Curtis; p. 335 © David Woo/Stock, Boston; p. 340 Chang W. Lee/NYT Pictures; p. 342 © Andrew Lichtenstein/Sygma; p. 343 © AP/Wide World Photos, Inc.; p. 351 © Andrew Lichtenstein/The Image Works; p. 352 © Billy Barnes/Stock, Boston; p. 353 © Shmuel Thaler/Jeroboam; p. 360 © Mark Elias/AP/Wide World Photos, Inc.; p. 367 © Rafael Fuchs/Outline Press; p. 369 © Jeffrey Lowe.